Microeconomics

Microeconomics:
A Contemporary Approach

Charles L. Cole
California State University
Long Beach

Under the Editorship of
William J. Baumol
Princeton University

HARCOURT BRACE JOVANOVICH, INC.

NEW YORK CHICAGO SAN FRANCISCO ATLANTA

ISBN: 0-15-558620-3

Library of Congress Catalog Card Number: 72-94219

Printed in the United States of America

Illustrations by ECL Art Associates, Inc.

To my mother and father

Foreword

The knack of simple exposition without sacrifice of fundamentals is a gift that is rather rare. Professor Cole has demonstrated this ability before and in this volume he shows it once again.

The book covers the conventional microeconomic materials and does not try to do so in a particularly unconventional way. However, the author succeeds in bringing a feeling of pertinence to an area that so often appears to be a set of distant abstractions. Happily, the demand for "instant relevance" that pervaded the campuses a few years ago seems to be fading. But this does not mean that the desire for materials that do cast light on substantive and pressing issues was unjustified. Rather, the point is that the comparative advantage of the college and university lies in bringing to such issues careful and systematic analysis that can be helpful in understanding them and in the formulation of effective policy.

Professor Cole's book undertakes to meet the need for such materials in the area in which he writes. It guides the student through the body of formal micro theory, explaining to him the methods of analysis that it provides and the uses to which the tools can be put. The reader is led to feel neither that he has been subjected to a set of arrid formalities, nor that he has been denied the rigorous materials that economic theory has to offer him. The need for such a book is clear enough.

WILLIAM J. BAUMOL

Princeton, New Jersey

Preface

When I was a student in what was then called "price and allocation theory," long before anyone ever used the word "relevant," much less understood what it meant, our professor told us that the first rule of getting along in the course was never to try to find out what the stuff was good for. "If you have to ask," he warned us, "you don't belong in this class." In those innocent days, such professorial pomposity did not affront us; indeed, we thought we were being complimented, and we certainly were never going to ask. Eventually, our professor did give us his vision of the nature of the subject. It was, he revealed, a game—a game that, like football, is complicated, and dangerous, and can be played for college credit.

After surviving several more years of courses in price (now microeconomic) theory, as both student and teacher, I have come to feel sorry for my erstwhile mentor, for I suspect he was suffering from one of the most tragic of all afflictions; he did not believe in what he was doing. But he taught better than he knew. I did learn what microeconomic theory is good for. It is a powerful ignorance remover.

Ironically, in today's setting, economic theory is especially good for just those people most likely to flee from it in a well-meant, but poorly mapped, search for benevolence. Today, so many people want to do good but know so little how to do it. It is a delusion to think that one can save the world without knowing the world. It is an even greater delusion to believe that one can know the world

from some combination of experience, common sense, and good will. Experience comes too late; common sense is all too likely to be a consensus of widely held ignorance; and good will is too often blind.

In a sense, of course, those who search for understanding outside the sciences are right; the world *is* too big to know. But much about it is knowable and susceptible to change, and that is where theory comes in. Theory helps to make the otherwise incomprehensible world manageable. *That* is the message which teachers of economics must impart. *That* is the spirit of this book.

Anyone who has taught economic theory has, I am sure, no false impressions about the popularity of the subject. Appraisals are plentiful: "It doesn't help people." "I can understand the words but not the graphs." "It tries to reduce human behavior to quantitative terms." "I'll never remember how to derive a demand curve." "How will it help me get a job?" And, of course, "It's boring."

There is some truth here, but there is also, perhaps, a certain lack of candor. This country puts up with an inexcusable amount of inefficiency, waste, chicanery, and inhumanity because decent human beings frequently find it easier to be guided by sentiment and opinion than by understanding. This is possibly the key to the lack of enthusiasm of many well-intentioned people for economics. When we look for the causes of the low incomes of minority groups, of the high incomes of sports and entertainment personalities and certain professionals, of smog, of inflation, and of all the other cases of too much or too little, we find that *we* are the cause, either directly or by default. Economic theory may be only a mirror of reality, but it is a cold, clear mirror. How many people like what they see? As Pogo says, "We have met the enemy, and he is us." If we want to do good, we must face up to reality.

The hardest, but the most rewarding task of teachers of economic theory, it seems to me, is to keep continually before their students, even when they are enmeshed in the intricacies of the long-run average total cost curve, the idea that the rather laborious study of economic theory leads on through adversity to the good end of explaining the economic world. And, having learned something of that world, students will be better equipped to improve it.

This book is the end product of numerous drafts and revisions, expertly typed by Susan Gabbard and Linda Waller from a bulky manuscript. I am deeply appreciative of the great service rendered me by the economists who read and criticized the manuscript in its various stages. For their considerable help, I must mention especially Professor Joseph M. Perry of the University of Florida and Professor Thomas Palm of Portland State University. Many times, they were very encouraging, and when they were not, they were most helpful. My deepest thanks are due Professor William Baumol of Princeton University. Professor Baumol read the manuscript in its entirety (much of it more than once) and made many comments and suggestions of inestimable worth to me. But the book is mine, and so there is only one source of such undetected errors as remain, and that is

CHARLES L. COLE

Contents

Microeconomics

1

What Is Practice?

"That's all right in theory but not in practice." Is this venerable maxim the epitome of common sense, or is it just plain nonsense? Why is it usually assumed that there is some kind of antipathy between theory and practice?

Most texts on the theories of any intellectual discipline—economics, chemistry, biology—commence with a discussion of the generally worthwhile but unfortunately dull answer to their self-posed question: "What is theory?" This formidable and profound question doesn't really put the matter in proper perspective. More to the point is the query, "What is practice?"

By common stereotype, practical people are supposed to have considerable respect for money and those who can make it, while theoretical types are uninterested in pecuniary gain and are down-right hostile to the "money grubbers" of the world (although one quietly suspects that this is just a pose intellectuals affect for the purpose of concealing their incompetence in monetary matters).

A book on microeconomics obviously must be theoretical, but it seems reasonable to expect that it also should contain something about economic activity. Despite the pious protestations of economists, most people see economic activity as related to the *practice* of making money. Is it possible that untutored opinion might be correct? Is it even possible that a microeconomics book might be about practice? How can we know for sure unless we know what practice is?

The preceding question may seem to forewarn of considerable foolishness to come. Doesn't everybody know what practice is? We may think so, but let us see if we really do. For example, a good part of this book is about the business firm. One of the commonly accepted ideas about the firm is that it exists to make a monetary profit for its owners and that the bigger the profit, the better (for the owners at least). Assuming that this is what a business firm does, *how* does it do it? What is the practice of making a profit?

IN QUEST OF PRACTICE

As sound, practical people, we are determined to avoid theoretical explanations and to "stick to the facts" as we search to understand the practice of the profit-maximizing firm. One of the simplest and most accessible statements of fact about an enterprise is the firm's annual report. We turn first to the income statement—that set of figures showing income and outgo for the year. Boiling down the information we find here, we discover that the subject firm had total sales of $4 million, but that the cost of the things it sold, plus the expenses of operating the firm, amounted to $3 million. The net profit (total sales less total costs) is $1 million. These are the coldest facts that we will ever get about this business.

But these facts, attested to as they are by a highly reputable and very expensive firm of certified public accountants, provide us with no insight into *how* the firm managed to make a net profit of $1 million. From the quantitative facts of the firm's income statement, we have learned absolutely nothing about the *practice* of the firm.

We decide, then, to turn to some very practical "how-to-do-it" books on the art (or is it science?) of business management. Among these books we find one that reveals twenty-five sure-fire hints for writing snappy advertising copy that *sells* and another esoteric and inspirational treatise showing how positive thinking can lead from failure to success in selling ladies' shoes in just one week. After reviewing these and kindred volumes, we begin to suspect we are being put on. About all we can glean from these practical books is the very common-sense (certainly not theoretical) idea that to make money in business one must buy cheap and sell dear. Although this seems to bring us a bit closer to practice, we are still left with the big question: How?

Giving up on "practical" books, we decide to do what we should have done all along—go straightway to the most practical, informed, and reliable source of all—the businessman himself. We resolve to try first a businessman we believe to be the epitome of the free-enterprise entrepreneur, a nonsubsidized farmer. After explaining our mission to him and winning him over by telling him of our distaste for theory, we go straight to the point and ask him how he makes his profit. Happily, he does not throw us right out. After a few words about how he does *not* make a profit, owing to the stupidity of government bureaucrats, the depravity of Congress, the red hue of farm labor leaders,

the rapacity of food processors, and the callousness of the American people generally, he tells us that he just does the best he can.

Listening to him we begin to see a man buffeted about by economic and natural forces over which he has no control. He seems to have no say at all in determining the selling price of his output. It is "they," he says, who control his prices and costs, and "they" invariably set the former too low and the latter too high. "They" practice the how-to-do-it books' principles, but "they" force the farmer to do the reverse—to buy dear and sell cheap. And, of course, this dreary economic picture is made even more dismal by the perversity of Mother Nature.

Unfortunately, it is not clear who "they" are and how "they" come by such economic power, and we are left with more questions than we had before. We take leave of the farmer and decide to interview another, hopefully less helpless, businessman.

The farmer was convinced that the conditions of his economic life were dictated by outside forces. Suspecting that one of these forces might be the man who sells the farmer his supplies, we decide to visit a merchant who operates a farm supply store. We put our practical question to the merchant: "How do you go about making a profit in your business?" Like the farmer, the merchant also feels himself to be in the grip of pincers. However, from the merchant's point of view, the farmer is one claw of the pincers, and the manufacturers of his inventory are the other. Is practice just blame and counterblame?

Stripping away the numerous injustices done to the merchant, we see a man who does appear to have some measure of control over his economic destiny. Within limits at least, he is able to determine the prices of the goods he sells, usually by tacking on some percentage of the cost of the item as a markup. For example, if the cost (wholesale price) of five gallons of insecticide is $5, the retailer adds $2 to the price he paid the wholesaler and sells the product to his customers for $7.

Progress at last! Now we have an example of practice. To make a profit, all one has to do is price the goods in one's inventory at a figure equal to cost plus a percentage of that cost. But as we reflect on this practice, we wonder what the best possible markup is under any and all circumstances. Does the markup vary with the product? Is the merchant maximizing his profit? Further inquiry provides some answers. Not every item in his stock is marked up by the same percentage; some goods carry larger markups than others, and there are some items that are for sale at a price below the merchant's cost of acquisition. Moreover, the markup on a particular item varies rather widely over the year. For example, the markup on insecticide, which is now 40 percent, dwindles to 10 percent in January. Explaining the variation, the dealer tells us what our sharp minds had already figured out—namely, that the markup is high when the bugs are at their destructive worst and lowest when there are neither bugs nor crops for them to eat.

We feel it is time to close our notebooks and ponder some refinements of our basic questions. Why at slow seasons of the year is the markup on in-

secticide reduced from 40 to 10 percent? Why isn't it reduced to 15 percent or to 12 3/4 percent? Does the merchant really know what he is doing, or are his business practices just hit-and-miss? We realize that the answers will come only through further investigation.

We now make bold to broach a powerful force in the economic lives of both the farmer and his supplier. If a great part of the farmer's costs are determined by what the store owner charges for insecticide, seed, and equipment, and the merchant's prices, in turn, are heavily influenced by the prices he pays for his inventory items, it seems likely that the key to the practice of profit-making lies somewhere within the firms that produce chemicals, seeds, and implements. So, we make an appointment to see the president of a chemical company.

Unexpectedly, the executive disarms us; the story he tells is not at all what we thought we would hear from a great business mogul. He declares that he is not an economic Zeus hurling down prices like thunderbolts from the forty-sixth floor of his Wall Street Olympus. If anything, he says, he is more severely buffeted about than either the farmer or the merchant. He must contend with forces more severe and unpredictable than those faced by the farmer and the retailer. Contrary to the impression the farmer has of the impersonality of the free market, the executive sees it as more comfortable than his own situation in which he is under the continual scrutiny of a few keenly rivalrous competitors.

Although the public may believe that there is some fraternal bond uniting top executives in an exclusive gentlemen's club, the fact is that each executive must behave as if the destruction of rival firms was a principal goal. Not that any executive really expects to destroy his rivals; none of them is defenseless enough for that to happen. What the president means is that the competitive situation is so intense that any successful executive must press constantly for every advantage and leave no chinks in his own defenses.

The "destruction" he speaks of is the by-product of an unceasing search for new products, cost reduction, expanded markets, and improved marketing techniques. It is not enough, say, merely to introduce a new product. The would-be innovator must consider carefully the effects of its own actions on other firms. The firms in the industry are so interrelated that if there is any "key" to business success it is being able to anticipate your rivals' reactions to your own moves.

The president argues that he has less control over his affairs than do far smaller entrepreneurs. He is inclined to agree with the farmers that the prices they pay for their capital goods are excessive. He would like to reduce the prices of his agricultural chemicals, but the most elemental knowledge of strategy leads to the inescapable conclusion that his alert rivals would match his every price reduction, so his sales would not expand enough to allow him to maintain his present modest profit level. As if to anticipate our next thrust, he adds that the situation entails more than merely the reduction of his profits. The rival firms are so sensitive to price changes that if he were to lower his

firm's prices, he might commence a price war that would culminate in the demise of all the firms.

The severity of competitive reality induces in us a feeling of compassion for the businessman and his colleagues. We suggest it might be an improvement if the firms could agree on a reasonable level of prices and maintain them. Unfortunately, says our host, not only would some firms find it tempting to bolt the agreement, but the government is ready to prosecute businessmen who attempt to mitigate the harsh forces of competition through consultation and agreement.

Sympathetic, but still hoping for an answer to our query on pricing and profits, we press the question: Isn't he, within some range *above* the presumably fairer and lower prices, able to do pretty much as he pleases? The president fixes us with a baleful stare; we infer that we are not close to the truth after all. No, he doesn't set his prices. How could he? The market does it—a market that includes farmers, each of whom fondly believes himself to be economically powerless, but who collectively wield such enormous economic clout that no so-called captain of industry could prevail against them.

Our minds are becoming confused. How can these several entrepreneurs, practical men all, have such widely varying assessments of their places and power in the economy? We are roused from our reflection, however, as the president commences a denunciation of the hitherto blameless farmer for his total ignorance of the problems of the manufacturer of agricultural chemicals. Then our host suddenly shifts his attack to the American consumer, that inconstant ninny who can't decide whether he wants to have lots of sprayed but bugless food at a low price, or less but unsprayed food at a high price.

All of a sudden, the truth dawns on us. We have been wrong all along. The producer is not the key to the practice of moneymaking; the consumer is. On the pretext of not wasting more of his time, we courteously thank our host and leave, impatient to find some representatives of the class of powerful consumers whom we can interview.

As we begin looking, it occurs to us that *we* are consumers. And goodness knows, we don't have any power, and even worse, we don't really know how we would use it if we did. Moreover, we are pretty sure that most of our fellow consumers are as powerless and as innocent of the practice of moneymaking as we. Someday, we say to ourselves, we must *think* about the information that we have gathered. An uncomfortable thought drifts across our tired minds; could we possibly have to *theorize* in order to find out what practice is?

THEORIZING TO DISCOVER PRACTICE

Who would expect to find any roots of philosophy in statistics? They are there. Data-gathering—the pursuit of the facts of practice in their most rudi-

mentary form—is a very humane exercise; for it teaches, as does no other activity, an essential point about man; he is not omniscient. The human condition is finite. Taken by itself, this conclusion is depressing, but it should not be taken by itself. Man has been compensated for his finite nature; he can *abstract*.

Far from being impractical, abstractionists—the makers of theories—are the most down to earth of all people; for they realize that *it is impossible to know anything for a fact!* The universe as it stands—even a small segment of it—cannot be comprehended at all. It is largely for this reason (although there are others) that the various intellectual disciplines exist. Abstraction is not speculation; abstraction is simplification. All of us abstract whenever we don't understand very much. Abstraction is not the antithesis of practice; it is not intellectual snobbery; it is practice simplified, so that people can understand what is going on. Abstraction is the beginning of understanding.

Let us now consider some of the evidence of practice that we gathered in our visits with the three businessmen. All of them declared that, to varying degrees, they were at the mercy of external forces. The farmer felt that he had no control over the prices of either the goods he sold or the things he bought. The merchant appeared to have some control over his selling prices; he was free to vary his markups, but his markups were based on the prices he was charged for his inventory. The chemical manufacturer seemed to have the most control over his affairs, but he was clearly constrained by the anticipated reactions of his rivals, government policy, his dealer organization, and, finally, consumers—not just the immediate buyers of his insecticide, but the consumers of the foods made from crops treated with his chemicals.

How can any sense be made of these observations? The farmer's situation seems to be the least complicated, so why not start with him? Perhaps the best way to begin is to construct a *model* farmer, not a Disneyland automaton that spouts conventional wisdom, but *an abstract economic model farmer*. We started with a real farmer, and we didn't get very far. Perhaps our model farmer will be more helpful.

Let us attribute to the model enterpriser the goal we assumed at the outset of our investigation: to make as much money as possible for the enterprise (more accurately, for its owners). This assumption now becomes a *postulate* of our model. (A postulate is a given condition; once made it is not open to question.)

We shall also incorporate into our model the condition described by the farmer—that the firm has no control over the price at which its output is sold or the prices of the goods (inputs) it buys to help to produce its output. What would the firm do if either one, or both, of these exogenous (here, beyond the control of the firm) variables were to change?

It occurs to us that one of the problems we encountered with our "real world" observations was that too many things were happening at once. Our perceptive and analytical abilities are, alas, too limited to take everything into account at the same time. In our model firm we do not have to put up with this

difficult situation because we can control the variables. Let us assume that just one variable is allowed to change at a time, all other variables remaining constant. This assumption, widely used in science, is called *ceteris paribus.* *Ceteris paribus* is Latin for "other things being equal." (If you have studied calculus, you have encountered it under the name of partial differentiation.) For our first trial, we will allow the firm to respond to a change in the price of its output, so we specify that input prices ("other things") shall remain constant ("equal") while the price of the output rises.

But, before we go on, let us consider the nature of the assumption we have just made. What about *ceteris paribus?* Is it too unrealistic to be useful? Suppose a physics student wants to study the gravitational relationship between a freely falling object and the earth. He must make sure he does not confuse other forces with the gravitational attraction between the earth and the object. Thus, he may isolate the object in a vacuum chamber. No one supposes that most objects fall to earth in a vacuum, but it seems entirely reasonable that if one wants to study how the mass of the earth acts on another mass, one should not brook interference from the wind. Thus, if economists desire to study the relationship between the price of good X and the quantity of good X demanded, they should not allow a simultaneous change in the price of good Y or in the prices of the inputs used in making good X to interfere with such economic analysis. *Ceteris paribus* is used to bring sharply into focus that which might otherwise be obscure or confused with other forces. By isolating each of the determinants of demand and studying its effects on consumer behavior, we will make much greater progress toward the development of a complete theory of consumer demand than if we attempt to interpret the effects of a great number of variables simultaneously changing in different ways.

We shall now make a prediction about what the firm will do. Our prediction takes the form of a *hypothesis*. A hypothesis is an "if-then" proposition. Ours says, "If the selling price rises, then the firm will attempt to produce a greater quantity of output." The tentative basis for our hypothesis is that if the firm were maximizing profit before the price rose, it would have to make some adjustment in the face cf a price change. Now if the selling price rises and input prices remain unchanged, it seems reasonable to assert that it would be more profitable to sell a larger output at the new and higher price than the same volume of output that maximized profit at the former, lower price.

Remembering that our hypothesis is only a bare first approximation, we nevertheless decide to test it. An essential requirement of a meaningful hypothetical statement is that it must be propounded in a testable form; that is, it must be capable of being falsified. That may sound as if we are intentionally trying to frame a partially true statement instead of a wholly true one. Viewed in a certain light, that is indeed the case. The income statement with which we began our investigation is absolutely true *as a statement*. (Its facts may be hokum, but its arithmetic is not.) Where did that accounting report get us? It showed net income to be $1 million when $3 million is subtracted from $4 million. Is there any way of testing it? Can you imagine any other result?

Of course, one plus three cannot equal anything but four in common arithmetic since 1 + 3 is simply an alternative way of writing 4. The accounting statement and the identity (not equation) 1 + 3 = 4 are *tautologies* or *truisms*; no one disputes their usefulness, but they tell us nothing that is not implicit in the statements themselves; their conclusions are merely rearrangements of already known data.

To test our hypothesis, we must search for supporting empirical evidence. Before we undertake this testing procedure, we should prepare ourselves to interpret any possible findings. If we find overwhelming evidence that our hypothesis is correct, will this prove it and cause it to be made into a "law"? No. Hypothetical statements cannot be proved; they can only be noncontradicted. At any time, we may discover information that is contrary to our hypothesis. If we discover such information, should we conclude that our hypothesis has been disproved? Not necessarily. It may be that our evidence is incorrect or that our interpretation of it is faulty. On the other hand, if repeated tests by ourselves and other investigators uncover information that simply will not conform to the predictions of our hypothesis, we have a substantial indication that our hypothesis should be modified or abandoned.

Suppose our search shows no observable correlation between prices and the quantities offered by firms. Everything appears to be random. Are we washed up as theorists? It would be premature to judge. Maybe the data are at variance with our assumptions. For example, it is possible that other things have not remained equal; perhaps input prices have not remained constant. It is not yet time to despair. There are statistical procedures to eliminate the effects of extraneous forces on business behavior. We should try these before concluding that our hypothesis is faulty.

We might as well make our imaginary testing situation easy for us, so let us assume that we have found a set of data covering a period in which there were no changes in input prices paid by farmers. In fact, the only variable that changes is the price of the output. To our dismay, we find no correlation between the prices paid on one day and the quantity sold on the same day. There isn't even any observable relationship between the prices paid on one day and the quantity sold several days later.

It is still not time to be discouraged. Facts by themselves don't mean very much, but their interpretation may open some interesting new paths. There is a reason for the lack of correlation between the prices on one day and the quantities offered on the same day or within a few days. Farmers cannot very easily adjust this season's output to this season's prices—you can't very easily turn off a cow or a plum tree. The prices that would bear most heavily on farmers' plans seem likely to be those of the *previous* season. Our hypothesis is not really wrong after all; it just needed a little fine tuning.

Our original (crude) hypothesis can be expressed symbolically in *functional notation* as

$$X_s = f(P_x), \text{ ceteris paribus}$$

This expression is *read* literally as: "The quantity of good *X* supplied is a function of its price, other things remaining equal." It *means* that, other things being equal, the quantity of *X* supplied to the market is in some way dependent on the price of the good itself. Our refined hypothesis stated in functional notation would appear as

$$(X_s)_t = f(P_X)_{t-1}, \text{ ceteris paribus}$$

This statement is merely a more restricted form of the original hypothesis. It says: "Other things being equal, the quantity of good *X* supplied to the market in the present time period or season, *t*, is determined by the price of the good in the preceding season ($t - 1$).

We now subject our refined hypothesis to testing and are gratified to discover that we have what appears to be a noncontradicted hypothesis. Our hypothesis is not trivial, but we should be careful not to claim too much for it. It merely asserts the direct relationship between the price of the good and the quantity supplied, subject to the time lag, but it does not state the exact nature of that relationship. We might be able to discover that relationship with further work.

We have made a start, but we are far from a complete theory of the firm. Our hypothesis is as yet noncontradicted, but it doesn't really explain enough. It doesn't, for example, tell us how much more will be produced in response to a given price rise. Observation indicates that farmers do not expand their production and productive capacities without limit every time the price of their output rises. Some force must operate to choke off production despite the possibility of each farmer selling all that he can produce at any given price. We will not have a complete theory of the firm until we have identified and explained that force.

Another basic matter remaining to be explained is the determination of the price of the good itself. Our hypothesis assumes a *given* price. But theorists do not simply accept price as a given. Somehow, a price is determined, and our devotion to science demands that there be a rational explanation that can be demonstrated objectively. By formulating hypotheses, testing them, then rejecting, accepting, or modifying them as necessary, we may be able to find out what the facts conceal: Just what is practice?

THE RELATIONSHIP
BETWEEN THEORY AND PRACTICE

Because they make no distinction between theorizing and speculation—between what is unknown and what is unknowable—some people hold theories in contempt. One way to distinguish a theory from a non-theory is that a theory always states a proposition about the nature of *knowable* (i.e., intellectually transmissible) reality and states it in a form that can be tested.

By now it is clear that the old saw of an antipathy between theory and practice is just so much anti-intellectual nonsense. Good theorizing is always about practice; its sole reason for being is to explain reality. Indeed, we may go further and assert that theory *defines* reality. As Albert Einstein once remarked to Werner Heisenberg, "It is theory which decides what we can observe."

No responsible scientist contends that the best of theories are statements of "The Truth." By their very nature, theories cannot be the truth because they are incomplete reflections of reality. However, their abstract nature does not make them any less valid than, say, the *Mona Lisa*, which, for all its mysterious elegance, is only an incomplete reflection of a woman.

POSITIVE AND NORMATIVE THEORIES

Some persons of goodwill have little use for theories, theorizing, and theorists because they believe that intellectual activity should be devoted to bettering the human condition. For example, some humanitarians become rather irked with economists who always seem to be concerned with explaining what makes the quantity supplied equal to the quantity demanded, when presumably they could better spend their time showing how whatever quantity is supplied could be distributed on a more equitable basis. The latter task very probably sounds more interesting, but it is not the proper role of economists as such. Nor, indeed, could it be realistically attempted without the groundwork of the former task having been done.

To the possible disappointment of social reformers, the sciences are concerned with explaining what *is*, not what *ought* to be. The sciences are *positive* disciplines; that is, again, they are involved with explaining things as they are. A positive theory is a totally unadorned explanation of an event—past, present, or future.

This attitude is not at variance with the notion that scientists should use their sciences to help mankind. Indeed, positive theories can be formidable aids in the achievement of moral (i.e., normative) goals. But positive theory cannot *determine* such goals. *Given* a normatively determined end, the positive theorist can help to explain how to achieve the goal, maintain it, and determine the costs involved. In doing so, he might be said to be developing a normative theory.

Here is a brief example. Positive economic theory helps to explain how income is in fact distributed to the members of the economy. A normative theory of income distribution might seek to explain how income could be distributed so as to achieve an apportionment that society considers more just. It is necessary to know the positive theory in order to make the necessary economic changes demanded by the interests of justice and also to ensure that the benefits of the desired end will not be eaten up by too great a cost.

ECONOMIC THEORY IN GENERAL
AND MICROECONOMIC THEORY IN PARTICULAR

Much of our discussion has been relevant to the theoretical aspects of any discipline, but our examples have been developed in terms of economic phenomena. What makes them economic? The fact that behind every one of them lies the necessity of explaining an economic situation; that is, a situation in which *choice* is an inescapable necessity.

Economizing is the act of compulsory choice. A choice must be made whenever several ends exist that cannot all be attained simultaneously. This state is the economic problem, and it is the common lot of mankind. The economic situation arises, not only whenever we must try to stretch our limited incomes over our vast desires for material goods, but whenever we do not have enough time to enjoy all the supposedly free goods of this world or to do those things necessary to become the person we know is somewhere within us.

The prescriptions drawn from positive economic theory are generally intended to reduce to a minimum the costs of achieving a *desired* end. Conversely, they also indicate how to maximize the returns from a given expenditure.

Since the mid-1930's, economics has been a bifurcated discipline; its two major segments are macroeconomics and microeconomics. Macroeconomics, the younger of the two fields, is concerned with the functioning of the entire economy. Its province is, so to speak, the forest as a whole rather than the individual trees. It is concerned with *aggregate* demand and supply, the generalized demand and supply of all goods and services, rather than with the demands and the supplies of particular goods and services. Instead of attempting to explain the determination of the prices of individual goods and services, macroeconomics investigates the *general* price level. It deals with governmental policies—fiscal, monetary, and income—that have generalized, economy-wide repercussions, instead of with the effects of direct government intervention in the market and within particular firms.

Microeconomics—the subject of this book—is devoted to the study of individual economic units functioning within an economy. It looks at the trees rather than at the forest. It is the branch of economic theory that attempts to explain the economic behavior of people as consumers, as resource supplies, and as the operators of business enterprises.

In economics, it is impossible to understand any kind of economic phenomena properly without a full understanding of both microeconomic and macroeconomic theory. For example, the study of the interrelationships among wage rates, unemployment, and inflation requires detailed knowledge of both major segments of economic theory. In some ways, it is unfortunate that the growth of knowledge has been such that micro- and macroeconomics must be separated early in one's economic education. In any case, one has to get started some time, and that is what we shall do right now.

2

Consumer and Market Demand

Adam Smith said, in one of his more notable comments: "Consumption is the sole end and purpose of all production; and the interest of the producer ought to be attended to, only so far as it may be necessary for promoting that of the consumer."[1] Accordingly, we shall begin our study of microeconomic theory with demands of consumers for goods.

CONSUMERS' DEMAND FOR GOODS

As the passage from Adam Smith indicates, demand is one of the most fundamental concepts in economics. It is the fusion of two conditions. A consumer demands a good whenever he wants some *thing*—tangible or intangible—and has the means at his disposal to acquire that thing.

The theory of consumer demand seeks to identify the economic reasons behind the demand of an individual consumer for a specific good. Although no economist would deny that the physical, biological, and psychological reasons underlying individual wants are important, the investigation of these determinants of demand is left to other disciplines; economists do not inquire into such matters as why some people like coffee and others like tea and still

[1] Adam Smith, *The Wealth of Nations* (New York: The Modern Library, 1937), p. 625. Originally published in 1776.

others intensely dislike both. For economists, the old Latin maxim *de gustibus non est disputandum* applies.[2] We may regard any thing that any person wants as a good insofar as that person is concerned. A good is a want-satisfier. A particular thing might not satisfy any of your wants or my wants; indeed, both of us might view the item as a nuisance, but if some person wants it, to that person the item is a good.

A want-satisfier—a good—may be tangible or intangible. It may be as substantial as the Hoover Dam or as ephemeral as the opening sounds of Beethoven's *Fifth Symphony*. Often, intangible goods are called services, but in this book we shall simply call all want-satisfiers goods, whether they are cement or symphonies.

To facilitate our discussion, let us assign the symbol X to a particular good. We know that X is a good if a consumer has a taste for it. To have a *demand* for X, the consumer must have some means (such as income) of translating his taste into a purchase. Suppose an individual has no income at all; would it still be possible for him to have a demand for good X? The answer is yes if the consumer has a stock of purchasing power called wealth, often held as money balances but sometimes held in less liquid form.[3] Taste and purchasing power together establish the potential for demand. But why does the consumer demand a specific quantity of the good X (where quantity demanded is defined to include zero)? Taste and income alone do not determine how much of a good a consumer will buy. We all know that we consider the price of a good extremely important in our purchase decision. We know also that most goods have substitutes and that the prices of those substitute goods enter into our decision of how much of the subject good we will buy. Thus, if goods Y and Z are in some sense substitutes for good X, their prices, as well as the price of good X itself, are determinants of the demand for good X. Another reasonable determinant of how much of a good a consumer demands is his expectations. If, for example, he believes that inflationary price increases are threatened, he may increase his present purchases of the good.

Now we have identified the variables that economists regard as the most important determinants of consumer demand. To facilitate the manipulation of these variables, we shall assign them symbols as follows:

The consumer's taste for good X T_X
The consumer's income I

---

[2] Roughly translated, "There is no accounting for tastes."

[3] *Wealth* is a stock, or store, of valuable things and is measured at a point in time; for example, a person has $1,000 in his savings account on April 20. *Claims* on valuable things, such as money and securities, would be considered as much a part of an individual's wealth as his house and car. An individual can purchase new goods by liquidating his presently held wealth or claims on wealth— that is, by converting them into money. *Income* is a *flow* of goods and services or claims (usually in the form of money) on goods and services. The goods and services are called *real* income, and claims on goods and services are called *monetary* income. The same distinction applies to wealth. The valuable things are called real wealth, and claims on valuable things are monetary wealth. Since income is a flow, it is measured over a period of time and is expressed as a rate, for example, $500 per month or $6,000 per year.

The price of good X	P_X
The price of good Y (a substitute for X)	P_Y
The price of good Z (also a substitute for X)	P_Z
The consumer's stock of purchasing power or wealth	W
The consumer's expectations	F

These items are the independent variables in what we shall call the consumer's demand function. By *independent* we mean that these variables are taken as given; we do not examine their origins or causes. For example, given the consumer's taste for filet mignon, his income, the price of filet mignon, the price of hamburger, the price of sirloin, the state of his bank account, and his prediction of what is going to happen in the economy, *how much* filet mignon will he buy? The quantity of filet mignon he buys is also a variable; but unlike the others in the list, it is a *dependent* variable, for the quantity demanded of a particular good is determined by the independent variables of the consumer's demand function.

For analytical convenience, economists succinctly state the relationships between the independent and dependent variables involved in the consumer's demand for a particular good in functional notation. Thus, the expression $X_D = f(T_X, I, P_X, P_Y, P_Z, W, F)$ says that the quantity of good X demanded (the dependent variable) is a *function of*, or is *determined by*, the independent variables contained within the parentheses. The *functional* form of the consumer's demand equation does not tell us the precise nature of the relationship between the dependent and independent variables; it merely asserts that some relationship exists between them.

CETERIS PARIBUS

To examine the relationships among one dependent variable and even as few as five independent variables is a difficult task, and its complexity would more likely confuse than further our understanding of economics. We shall therefore employ one of the most useful techniques in science—abstraction. To abstract is to simplify, and simplification should not be thought of as cowardice if our acquisition of knowledge is accelerated by its use.

Utilizing the *ceteris paribus* technique, explained in Chapter 1, we shall assume that all the independent variables except the price of the good itself (P_X) remain constant.[4] This form permits us to study the consumer's reaction to a change in the price of the subject good. Let us now write the demand function as

$$Q_X = f(P_X, \overline{P}_Y, \overline{P}_Z, \overline{T}_X, \overline{I}, \overline{W}, \overline{F})$$

[4] The relationship between the quantity demanded of a good and its price is chosen for analysis, not because the price of a good is necessarily the most powerful determinant of the quantity demanded, but because a great part of the work of theoretical economics is the explanation of price.

where Q_x is the quantity of X demanded. Alternatively, the function can be written more simply as $Q_x = f(P_x)$, understanding that the *ceteris paribus* assumption is implied. (The bars over every variable except P_x indicate their *assumed* constancy.)

THE LAW OF DEMAND

Figure 2-1 depicts a demand curve for good X. The curve has a negative slope (it slopes downward to the right) showing that, under the assumption of *ceteris paribus*, there is an inverse relationship between the quantity demanded of the subject good and its price. In other words: *ceteris paribus*, the lower the price of good X, the greater the quantity the consumer will demand. In the next chapter we shall develop a theory to explain *why* the demand curve has a negative slope; for now, we shall take its slope as given.

The graphical conventions of economics assign the independent variable to the vertical axis (ordinate) and the dependent variable to the horizontal axis (abscissa). Since a consumer's demand for a good can be expressed as a schedule of the various quantities of the good that he will buy at different prices, the price of the particular good (the independent variable) is shown on the vertical axis, and the quantity of the good (the dependent variable) is plotted on the horizontal axis.

The quantity of the good is expressed as a *flow* over time. There is no meaning to the statement "If the price of X is $3, I shall buy 4 units of X." The demand curve, or schedule, must specify how much of a good the consumer will buy over a definite time period. If the time period applicable to Figure 2-1 is one week, then the information the graph conveys is that at a price of $3 per unit, the consumer will buy 4 units of X per week, spending a total of $12 for

FIGURE 2-1

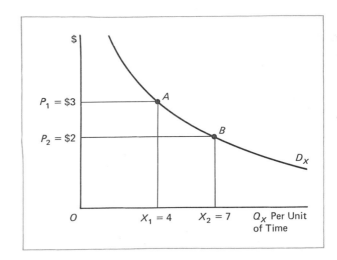

Consumer and Market Demand

all 4 units. Should the price be $2 apiece, he will buy 7 units of the good per week and pay a total of $14 for all 7 units.

A demand curve depicts an "if-then" situation. Suppose we make a graphical record of a consumer's behavior, noting his response to changes in the price of good X. Invoking the *ceteris paribus* assumption, if the price of X is $3 per unit, the individual demands 4 units of X per week. If we project a perpendicular from the $3 intercept on the vertical (price) axis and another perpendicular from the 4X intercept on the horizontal (quantity) axis, they will have a common point of intersection at A. A is one point on the individual consumer's demand curve. If this process is repeated a number of times for different prices (and quantities), a series of points will be located. A curve drawn through these points is the consumer's demand curve.

From the standpoint of consumer spending on a specific good, the demand curve is the boundary of a set of points; it represents a maximum. For example, the demand curve in Figure 2-1 says that the consumer will pay up to $3 apiece for 4 units of X if 4 units are available. If he could find only 3 units, he would still be willing to pay $3 per unit for them. He would not, however, agree to pay $3 per unit for more than 4 units per week. *Ceteris paribus*, the consumer will buy no more than 4 units per week unless the price falls.

By similar reasoning, $3 is the maximum price per unit the consumer will pay if he is to buy 4 units, *ceteris paribus*. Obviously, he would be willing to pay $2 per unit for 4 units of X. In other words, if 4 units of X per week are available to the consumer, he is willing to pay any amount up to and including $12 for the total quantity. Thus, we may regard the consumer's demand curve as the boundary of a feasible set of price and quantity combinations. This feasible set lies along and to the left of the demand curve. *Given price*, the demand curve is the boundary of a set of possible purchases. *Given quantity*, the demand curve is the boundary of a set of acceptable prices.

MARKET DEMAND CURVES

A market is made up of all the buyers and sellers of a particular good. It is the context in which they bargain with each other and in which the conditions of exchange are determined. The market demand curve for a good is simply the horizontal summation of the individual demand curves of all buyers of that particular good.

Suppose Charlie and Linus comprise the demand side of the market for good X (they are used here as a convenient abstraction for the very great number of individuals who normally constitute the demand side of the market for a concrete good). In Figure 2-2, Charlie's demand curve for X is D_C; Linus's curve is D_L. At a price of P_1, Charlie is at point C_1 on his demand curve, and Linus is at point L_1 on his curve. Charlie demands quantity $(OX_1)_C$ of X, and Linus demands $(OX_1)_L$. If we now construct a grid for the market demand

FIGURE 2-2

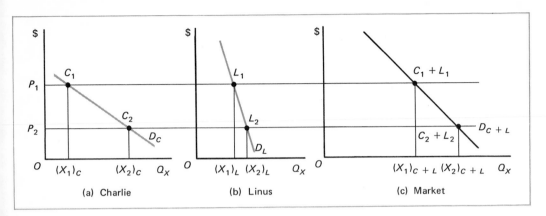

(a) Charlie   (b) Linus   (c) Market

curve and horizontally sum points C_1 and L_1 we obtain point $C_1 + L_1$ on the market demand curve. This shows us that the market demand for good X is $(OX_1)_C + (OX_1)_L = (OX_1)_{C+L}$, which is, of course, nothing more than the sum of the individual quantities of X demanded when its price is P_1. By allowing the price of X to change and repeating this process, we can obtain a series of points on the market demand curve for the good.

PRICE AND NONPRICE PHENOMENA

Consider Figure 2-3. Suppose the consumer ordinarily purchases OX_1 units of X per week. Then this pattern changes; his consumption of X increases by X_1X_2 units. Now his total weekly purchases of the good are OX_2 units. What has happened? The graph shows two possible explanations. One depicts a movement from A to B, and the other involves a movement from A to C.

To determine which movement is involved, we must bear in mind that forces other than the price of the good determine the individual's demand. These are the variables in the demand function over which we placed bars to indicate their assumed constancy. If there is no change in the price of the good, and the consumer buys a different quantity, it must be that one, some, or all of the remaining determinants of the demand for X have changed. Suppose, for example, that advertising has persuaded the consumer to buy more X. His taste for X will have been increased, and as a result, he will buy more X at any given price. Suppose, on the other hand, that the price of good Y, a substitute for good X, falls. The consumer may decide to substitute some Y for X and, consequently, will buy less X at any given price. If a consumer alters his purchases of a good in the absence of any change in the price of the good itself, the explanation cannot involve a movement along a given demand curve. Rather, the demand curve itself must shift. Depending on whether the con-

sumer buys more or less of the good, the resultant movement of the demand curve is called, respectively, an *upward shift in demand* or a *downward shift in demand*. Thus in Figure 2-3, if the consumer originally purchases OX_1 units of X at price OP_1 and subsequently buys OX_2 units at the same price, there has been an increase in his demand for X as shown by the upward shift of his demand curve (from D_1 to D_2). Conversely, if the consumer had been initially at point C on D_2 and had reduced his purchases by X_1X_2 units, his demand for good X would be said to have decreased as evidenced by a downward shift in the demand curve from D_2 to D_1.

Whereas the situation just described is called a *change in demand,* an adjustment in purchase plans caused by a change in the price of the good itself is called a *change in quantity demanded.* Thus, if the same increase in the purchase of X had been induced by a reduction in price, all other determinants of demand remaining constant, the phenomenon would be called an increase in quantity demanded. Conversely, if the consumer had been initially intending to buy OX_2 units of X and subsequently decided to reduce his purchases of X to OX_1 units in consequence of a rise in the price of the good, he would have manifested a decrease in the quantity demanded of good X. Determining whether a change in the purchase of a good occurs in response to a shift in the demand curve or a movement along a given demand curve is necessary to avoid drawing erroneous conclusions. Suppose, for example, we are examining the behavior of coffee prices over a period of years, and we notice that despite an increase in retail prices, coffee consumption has increased. It might be tempting to draw a smooth curve through the price-quantity combinations and to conclude that the demand curve for coffee is upward sloping. This procedure would lead us to the erroneous conclusion that people buy more coffee in response to an increase in its price. If we could isolate sta-

FIGURE 2-3

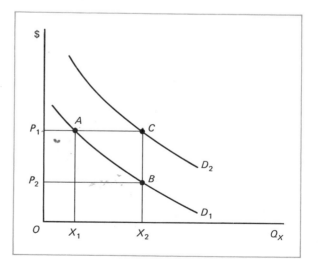

tistically the price changes in the coffee market from changes in consumers' incomes, their tastes, and the prices of coffee substitutes, we would find that the law of demand holds. The increase in the sales of coffee is actually attributable to upward shifts of the coffee demand curve, not to movements upward along a positively sloped demand curve.

ELASTICITIES OF DEMAND

The dollars that consumers spend for goods are the dollars that business firms receive. We shall now examine what happens to consumer expenditures, or, alternatively, business firm revenues, in response to isolated changes in three different variables: the price of the good itself, consumer income, and the prices of other goods. The measures that tell us how consumer expenditures (business revenues) are affected by changes in the previously specified variables are called *elasticities of demand*.

PRICE ELASTICITY OF DEMAND

If we know the price elasticity of demand for a good, we can predict what will happen to consumer expenditures on that good in response to a change in its price.

Several times in recent years the economy of the United States has been subjected to severe inflationary pressure. With mounting public opposition to inflationary wage increases, it is surprising to find the head of a large auto workers' union insisting that automobile manufacturers could afford to give their employees a wage increase that would be noninflationary if it were accompanied by a reduction in the price of automobiles. But how could the auto firms pay higher wages if they reduced the prices of their products? The answer, the union official contends, lies in the price elasticity of demand for new cars. He argues that the numerical value of the coefficient of price elasticity is such as to indicate that the increased sales of automobiles would more than offset the decrease in price, with the result that the auto firms' total revenues would rise, permitting a wage increase for those who build automobiles.

The price elasticity of demand also explains economic behavior that some persons find repugnant in a world in which some people go hungry. Every so often, farmers destroy their crops. Obviously, then they have less to sell. Even so, their incomes rise. Once again, the answer to this strange phenomenon lies in the price elasticity of demand. In this case, the rise in prices more than offsets the decrease in quantity sold, and the total receipts of farmers increases.

We shall now investigate in more detail the price elasticity of demand, the indicator of the response of consumer expenditure to a given change in the price of a good.

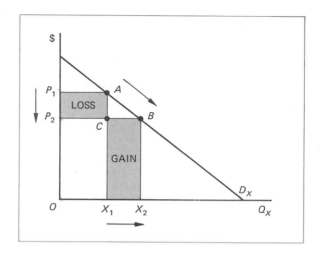

FIGURE 2-4

Elastic demand. In Figure 2-4, the market demand curve for good *X* is shown as a straight line for analytical convenience.[5] The total expenditures, *E*, of consumers for a good is equal to the price of the good multiplied by the quantity sold, or $E = PQ$. Suppose initially that when the price is OP_1, consumers buy quantity OX_1. Graphically, the product of this price times the accompanying quantity is the area of the rectangle $OX_1AP_1 = E_1$. Assume that price is lowered to OP_2. Total expenditures are now equal to the area of the rectangle $OX_2BP_2 = E_2$. How do E_1 and E_2 compare in size? Rectangles OX_1AP_1 and OX_2BP_2 have area OX_1CP_2 in common. Lowering the price from OP_1 to OP_2, brings about a gross loss in consumer expenditures equal to the area of rectangle P_2CAP_1. But owing to the increase in the quantity sold at OP_2, there is a gross gain in consumer expenditures equal to the area of rectangle X_1X_2BC. Since the gross gain exceeds the gross loss, there is a net gain in consumer expenditures of $X_1X_2BC - P_2CAP_1$ as a result of the price reduction.

If the movement on the demand curve were reversed from *B* to *A*, the price increase would result in a reduction in total consumer expenditures on good *X*; for the area of the gross gain (now the rectangle P_2CAP_1) would be less than the area of gross loss (now the rectangle X_1X_2BC). When total consumer expenditures increase in response to a fall in price, or decrease in response to a rise, the demand for the product is said to be *elastic*.

Inelastic demand. The demand curve in Figure 2-5 is the same curve shown in Figure 2-4. Suppose price is OP_3; consumer expenditures, E_3, are equal to the rectangle OX_3FP_3. If price is reduced to OP_4, consumer expenditures, E_4, will now be equal to the area of OX_4GP_4. The gross loss, P_4HFP_3, involved in the price reduction exceeds the gross gain, X_3X_4GH, with the result

[5] For convenience, a straight-line (linear) demand curve is generally used in this book.

Elasticities of Demand | **21**

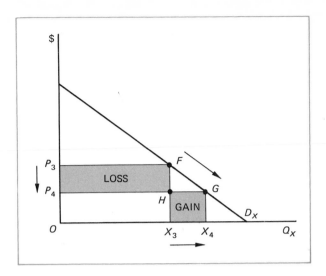

FIGURE 2-5

that there is a net decrease in total consumer spending. If the movement on the demand curve were reversed (from G to F), the gross gain (now P_4HFP_3) would exceed the gross loss (now X_3X_4GH), and there would be an increase in consumer spending as a result of a price increase. When total consumer expenditures decrease in response to a fall in price, or increase in response to a rise, the demand for the product is said to be *inelastic*.

Unitarily elastic demand. Since these price changes have occurred on the same demand curve, it is meaningless to speak of the demand for good X as being elastic or inelastic. We have seen that it can be either, depending on the price of the good. In the region AB (Figure 2-4), at relatively high prices, the demand for good X is elastic. In the region FG (Figure 2-5), at relatively low prices, the demand for good X is inelastic. Suppose we now attempt to esti-mate the price elasticity of demand for good X in the middle of its price range.

The demand curve in Figure 2-6 is again the same curve. Points I and J are equidistant from point M, the midpoint of the demand curve. The areas of P_6KIP_5 and X_5X_6JK are approximately equal (the closer I and J are to M, the more nearly will the areas representing gross loss and gross gain be equal); there-fore, we can conclude that price changes clustered around the midpoint of a linear demand curve result in very small changes in total consumer expendi-tures. In the limiting case, when total consumer expenditures do not change in response to a fall or a rise in price, the demand for the product is said to be *unitarily elastic*.

What does elasticity indicate? The price elasticity of demand shows how strongly consumers react to price changes with changes in the quantity they demand. If demand is elastic, consumers respond strongly, with the

Consumer and Market Demand

result that the total amount they spend on the good rises when price falls and falls when price is raised. If demand is inelastic, consumers respond rather weakly to changes in price, the relative stability of quantity demanded producing a rise in total expenditures when price increases and a reduction in expenditures when price falls. If demand is unitarily elastic, a rise or a fall in price is met by an offsetting change in the quantity demanded, so there is no change in total consumer spending.

TABLE 2-1	*Demand*	$\downarrow P$	$\uparrow P$
	Elastic	$\uparrow E$	$\downarrow E$
	Inelastic	$\downarrow E$	$\uparrow E$
	Unitarily elastic	$\overline{E}$	$\overline{E}$

We can summarize these associated phenomena in tabular form. The left-hand column shows the response of expenditure to a fall in price; the right-hand column shows how expenditure behaves when price rises. The table shows that changes in price and expenditure are inversely related when demand is elastic, directly related when demand is inelastic. There is no change in expenditure whatever the direction of the change in price when demand is unitarily elastic.

The coefficient of the price elasticity of demand. If we could specify just *how* elastic or inelastic the demand for a good is, then we could predict with greater accuracy consumer response to a projected price change. Is it possible to compare the change in the quantity demanded with the change in

FIGURE 2-6

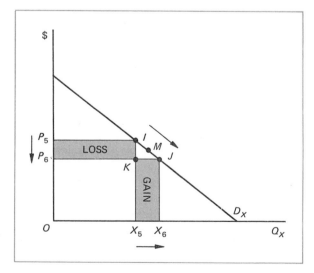

price to obtain a numerical value of elasticity? If we tentatively define the *coefficient of price elasticity* (ϵ_p) as the ratio of the change in quantity (ΔQ) demanded to the change in price (ΔP),[6] then for the price change indicated in Figure 2-7

$$\epsilon_p = \frac{\Delta Q}{\Delta P} = \frac{3-2}{-(6-5)} = -\frac{1}{1} = -1$$

According to our tentative formulation, the value of the elasticity coefficient is −1. Suppose that we have been expressing Q_x in dozens per week, and we now want to use the number of individual units of good X, then

$$\epsilon_p = \frac{\Delta Q}{\Delta P} = \frac{36-24}{-(6-5)} = -\frac{12}{1} = -12$$

Changing the units in which the quantity of the good is expressed results in a rather consequential change in the value of the elasticity coefficient, although none of the conditions of consumer demand has changed. If we were to express price in cents, instead of dollars, we would obtain another value for the elasticity coefficient, and if quantity were expressed in gross, instead of individual units or dozens, we would obtain still another value, and so on. Obviously, a measuring device that varies so much in response to a variation in the units in which the price and quantity variables are expressed is almost without meaning.

Arc elasticity of demand. Instead of using absolute changes in price and quantity, let us attempt to develop an elasticity coefficient based on *relative* changes in price and quantity. Our formula[7]

$$\epsilon_p = -\frac{\text{percentage change in } Q}{\text{percentage change in } P}$$

or

$$\epsilon_p = -\frac{\dfrac{\Delta Q}{Q}}{\dfrac{\Delta P}{P}} = -\frac{\Delta Q}{Q} \cdot \frac{P}{\Delta P} = -\frac{\Delta Q}{\Delta P} \cdot \frac{P}{Q}$$

We shall now add a minus sign to the ratio, so that the elasticity coefficient will have a positive value. The negative value of the coefficient merely reflects the slope of the demand curve, and for the sake of convenience, we shall eliminate

---

[6] The Greek capital letter Δ (delta) is read "the change in." The minus sign has been added to the denominator of the above fraction to reflect the one dollar *decrease* in price. Thus, the value of ϵ_p is expressed here as a negative number.

[7] Note that we are now multiplying our original tentative formula by the ratio of price to quantity.

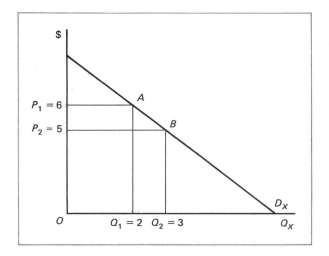

FIGURE 2-7

it. Now, whether we express the quantity in dozens or in individual units of good X, the value of the coefficient is the same.

$$\epsilon_p = -\frac{3 - 2}{-(6 - 5)} \cdot \frac{6}{2} = \frac{1}{1} \cdot 3 = 3$$

$$\epsilon_p = -\frac{36 - 24}{-(6 - 5)} \cdot \frac{6}{24} = \frac{12}{1} \cdot \frac{1}{4} = 3$$

By using relative, instead of absolute, changes, we have made the value of the elasticity coefficient independent of the units in which the price and quantity variables are expressed.

The type of elasticity obtained from this formula is called *arc elasticity* because it is measured over an arc, or distance, on a demand curve, for example, *AB* on the demand curve in Figure 2-7. Since we proceeded from *A* to *B*, the base price and quantity are those associated with point *A*. Suppose we now reverse the direction of the preceding example and move from *B* to *A* (the case of a price rise). Now the base figures for price and quantity are those associated with point *B*. Using these base figures, we obtain

$$\epsilon_p = -\frac{-(3 - 2)}{6 - 5} \cdot \frac{5}{3} = \frac{1}{1} \cdot \frac{5}{3} = 1\frac{2}{3}$$

This value varies rather markedly from that previously obtained. It seems that once again we have a formula that yields inconsistent results. What is the problem and, more important, what is its solution? To an extent, the problem is in our method. We are attempting to evaluate the elasticity coefficient at a point on the demand curve (for a specific price and quantity combination), but we are measuring the coefficient over a finite (i.e., measurable) distance on the

demand curve. This inconsistency leads to the ambiguity (is the value of ϵ_P 3 or 1 2/3?) in our results.

We shall dispose of our problem by employing an arbitrary convention. Instead of solving our formula for point A or B, we shall solve for a point, M, midway between them. In other words, we shall compromise between the two results and take the average of the two values at points A and B. The averaging formula is

$$\epsilon_P = -\frac{Q_1 - Q_2}{Q_1 + Q_2} \cdot \frac{P_1 + P_2}{P_1 - P_2}$$

Substituting the values from Figure 2-7 into the above formula, we obtain

$$\epsilon_P = -\frac{2 - 3}{2 + 3} \cdot \frac{6 + 5}{6 - 5} = \frac{1}{5} \cdot \frac{11}{1} = \frac{11}{5} = 2\frac{1}{5}$$

Now it makes no difference whether we measure elasticity for a decrease or an increase in price.

When the value of the elasticity coefficient exceeds 1, demand is said to be elastic. When the value of the elasticity coefficient is less than 1, demand is said to be inelastic. And when the value of the coefficient is 1, demand is unitarily elastic. These relationships are summarized in Table 2-2.

TABLE 2-2	ϵ_P	Demand
	> 1	Elastic
	= 1	Unitarily elastic
	< 1	Inelastic

Limiting cases. The numerical coefficient of elasticity allows us to compare degrees of elasticity and inelasticity. Although the value of the coefficient can assume any number, three limiting cases are illustrated here.

The first case, perfectly inelastic demand, is shown in Figure 2-8(a). The value of the elasticity coefficient is zero throughout the length of the demand curve D_a because the value of the numerator in the formula is zero (there is no quantity change accompanying any change in price).

The second case, infinitely elastic demand, is shown in Figure 2-8(b). Here, price is uniformly P_0 regardless of the quantity demanded. As there is no possibility of a price change, the denominator of the elasticity coefficient is zero. In mathematics, the result of an operation in which the divisor is zero is undefined, but the quotient is often said (somewhat carelessly) to be "infinite." This may be made clearer if you think of dividing a given number by a progressively smaller number. For example, $1/.01 = 100$, and $1/.001 = 1,000$. You can put any number of zeros you wish between the decimal point and the num-

FIGURE 2-8

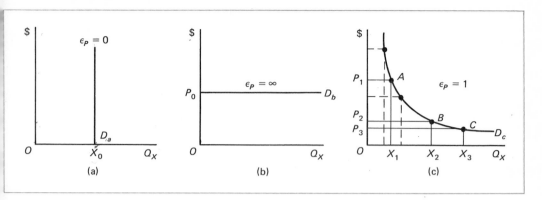

ber 1 in the denominator. The more zeros there are, the larger will be the quotient. As the fixed dividend is divided by an ever increasing divisor, the quotient is said to be approaching infinity as a limit.

Suppose that for any change in price, the total expenditures of consumers are always the same. The demand curve, D_c, shown in Figure 2-8(c) must be such that all rectangles inscribed beneath it are equal in area. The price elasticity of demand is uniformly 1 for any price change. A demand curve with this peculiar property traces out a special curve known in mathematics as a rectangular hyperbola.

Geometric determination of elasticity—point elasticity. If we could make the distance between two points on a demand curve small enough, any differences in the values of the elasticity coefficient computed going up or down the demand curve would become so small as to be negligible.

Using Figure 2-9, suppose we are interested in determining the elasticity of demand in the vicinity of point G on the demand curve AB; that is, we wish to determine the elasticity of demand for X when the price is OP. Now suppose the price of X is allowed to fall to OP'. This price decrease is accompanied by a change in quantity demanded, from X to X', and therefore a movement along the demand curve from G to G'. Using the arc elasticity formula, we know that the greater the distance between G and G', the greater will be the error in the approximation of the elasticity of demand in the vicinity of price OP. But we do not need to restrict ourselves to a distance as great as GG'. Conceptually, let us collapse that distance until the separation between the two points approaches zero. By moving the points closer together, we can cause the fall in price to become negligible, so negligible in fact that there is no ambiguity at all in selecting a base price, since for all practical purposes OP = OP'.[8]

---

[8] We may represent what we have done symbolically by writing that $\Delta P > 0$, but that $\Delta P \rightarrow 0$. This statement asserts that since the change in price exceeds zero, there is in fact a true change in price, but that in *approaching* zero this change has become infinitesimal.

FIGURE 2-9

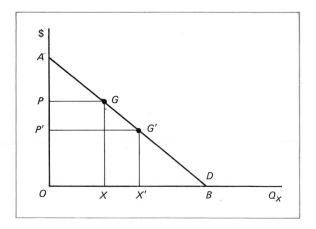

Using this process, we have allowed ΔP to come as close to zero as we like without actually letting it become zero.

If ΔP has been so reduced that the distance PP' is infinitesimal, then how can we use an elasticity formula (that is, $\epsilon_p = \Delta Q/\Delta P \cdot P/Q$) that involves *changes* in price and quantity? Consider the ratio $\Delta Q/\Delta P$. It is the reciprocal of the slope of the demand curve. The slope of the demand curve AB is OA/OB. The reciprocal of this ratio is OB/OA.

In Figure 2-9, we can identify at least three similar triangles: OBA, XBG, and PGA.[9] Since the triangles are similar, the reciprocal of the slope of $AB = OB/OA = XB/XG = PG/PA$.

We may now determine the elasticity of demand at point G (at price OP) by inspection. For example, $\Delta Q/\Delta P = PG/PA$ and $P/Q = OP/OX = OP/PG$. Since $OP > PA$, we know that the demand for X is elastic in the vicinity of price OP. We can also prove that $\epsilon_p = XB/OX$, since $OP/PA = XB/PG$ and $PG = OX$. Finally, since $XB/PG = BG/GA$, the latter ratio gives us the value of ϵ_p. In summary, we have established that at price OP, $\epsilon_p = OP/PA = XB/OX = BG/GA$.

The geometric determination of elasticity proves that the varying slopes of demand curves do not affect the elasticity of demand at any given price if all the demand curves under consideration have a common intercept on the vertical axis. Demand curve DD_1 in Figure 2-10(a) is much steeper than DD_2 with which it has a common intercept on the price axis at point D, yet for any given price both curves have the same elasticity of demand. For example, at price OP, $\epsilon_p = OP/PD$.

---

[9] These triangles are similar in that they all have three equal angles. They are right triangles by construction. Therefore, the angles at points, O, X, and P are equal. Triangles OBA and PGA have the angle at A in common. Thus, the angles at G (angle PGA) and B must be equal. Triangles XBG and OBA have the angle at B in common. Therefore, the angles at A and G (angle XGB) are equal. Since triangle PGA is similar to triangle OBA, which is, in turn, similar to triangle XBG, triangles PGA and XBG must also be similar.

Similarly, the price elasticity of demand is the same at any given quantity for all demand curves having a common intercept on the horizontal axis. In Figure 2-10(b), the elasticity of demand for curves D_1D and D_2D is the same at quantity OX, namely $\epsilon_p = XD/OX$.

An extension of this analysis makes it possible to locate points of equal elasticity on demand curves that do not have common intercepts. In Figure 2-10(c), our problem is to find points of equal elasticity on the demand curves D_1D_1 and D_2D_2. At point N_1 on D_1D_1, $\epsilon_p = OP_1/P_1D_1$. Although D_1D_1 and D_2D_2 do not have common intercepts, we can construct an imaginary demand curve D_1D_2 having a common intercept with each real curve. Since D_1D_1 and the imaginary demand curve D_1D_2 have a common intercept on the vertical axis, the elasticity of demand is equal at points N_1 and N_i. The real demand curve D_2D_2 has a common intercept on the horizontal axis with the imaginary demand curve. Since all demand curves having a common intercept on the horizontal axis have the same price elasticity at any given quantity, the point on D_2D_2 having the same elasticity as N_i on D_1D_2 must be located vertically above N_i, and is, therefore, N_2.

FIGURE 2-10

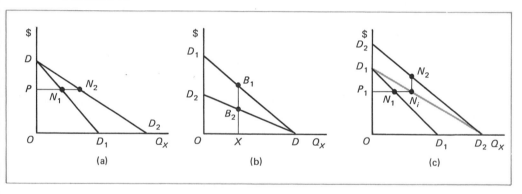

(a)   (b)   (c)

Elasticity on a nonlinear demand curve. How can the elasticity of demand be determined if the demand curve is nonlinear, like DD' in Figure 2-11? Suppose we wish to determine the elasticity of demand at price OP. If we draw line TT' tangent to DD' at point M, we know that the slope of TT' is equal to the slope of DD' at the given price. We may now treat TT' as if it were the demand curve and determine the elasticity geometrically. Thus, at price OP,

$$\epsilon_p = \frac{OP}{PT} = \frac{T'M}{MT} = \frac{M'T'}{OM'}$$

Determinants of the price elasticity of demand. What forces determine the price elasticity of demand? Suppose a consumer regards a particular good

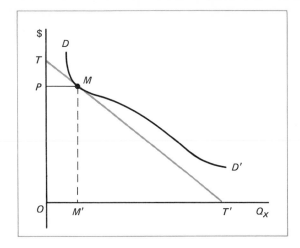

FIGURE 2-11

as an indispensable item—a life-sustaining drug, for example, for which there is no substitute. If the quantity the individual consumes is totally independent of the price of the good, the coefficient of price elasticity is zero. Therefore, the more necessary the good is to its consumer, the more inelastic the consumer's demand for it will be. If the consumer is easily able to substitute one good for another, the demand for each of the two goods will be highly elastic.

The demand for a good is likely to be inelastic also if its price is low and the quantity that the consumer buys over a period of time is small, so that expenditures for it constitute a slight part of a consumer's budget. It is reasonable to assume that the demand for table salt is highly inelastic (which it is) because it is somewhat of a necessity; there are few substitutes for it; its price is low; and a consumer does not buy much in a year's time. At the other extreme, it would be reasonable to expect that the elasticity of demand for new stereophonic tape decks would be high. They are widely regarded as a luxury; turntable units are a good substitute for them; and they have a fairly high unit price.

Income Elasticity

How do consumers react to changes in their incomes? If an individual receives a pay increase, does he buy more or less of a given good? From our previous discussion of the demand function, we know that income is an important determinant of demand. Under the *ceteris paribus* assumption, when the price of the good is varied, the consumer moves *along* a given demand curve. When income is varied, the entire demand curve almost always shifts. Thus, income is a variable that enters into the determination of the location and configuration of a particular demand curve. The measure of consumer response to a change in income is *income elasticity*, ϵ_I, and is defined as the ratio of the percentage change in the quantity of the good purchased to the

percentage change in the consumer's income. The formula for ϵ_I is written

$$\epsilon_I = \frac{\frac{\Delta Q}{Q}}{\frac{\Delta I}{I}} = \frac{\Delta Q}{\Delta I} \cdot \frac{I}{Q}$$

Note that no minus sign is inserted before the ratio. Here the sign of the fraction is itself important. What if the sign of the coefficient were positive? We would know that ΔI and ΔQ were moving in the same direction—for example, an increase in income would be accompanied by an increase in the sale of good X. If the sign of the income elasticity coefficient is positive, the good in question is said to be a *superior* good, which is defined as a good for which there is a direct relation between consumption and income. When the sign of the coefficient is negative, and, therefore, ΔI and ΔQ are moving in opposite directions, the good in question is said to be *inferior*. Finally, if the value of the coefficient is zero, the quantity purchased does not respond to a change in the consumer's income. In this book, we shall define such a good as *neutral*.

Measures of income elasticity are helpful in determining which goods consumers consider to be necessities and which they feel are luxuries. It is likely that the greater the value of the income elasticity coefficient, the more luxurious the good is. Such a good might be considered a more legitimate object for an excise or sales tax than a good having a low income elasticity. Goods having high income elasticities of demand would include fur coats, jewelry, vacation travel, champagne, and prestige automobiles. Among goods having extremely low or negative income elasticities of demand are bread, macaroni, potatoes, tortillas, bus transportation to work and back, and women's dress material. We can conclude, then, that a sales tax placed on items having negative income elasticities (inferior goods) are likely to bear heavily on lower income groups, since a great part of their incomes are likely to be for such goods.

CROSS–ELASTICITY OF DEMAND

What if the price of one good changes? Will this have any effect on the demand for *another* good? The demand function shows that the prices of all other goods are determinants of the demand for the subject good. Thus, a determinant of the demand for good X is the price of good Y as shown in the demand function

$$X_D = f(P_Y), \textit{ ceteris paribus}$$

The extent of the effect a price change in one good has on the quantity demanded for another good is shown by the *coefficient of cross-elasticity*. This measure is defined as the ratio of the percentage change in the quantity de-

manded for one good to the percentage change in the price of the other good. The formula for this coefficient is

$$\epsilon_{XY} = \frac{\dfrac{\Delta Q_X}{Q_X}}{\dfrac{\Delta P_Y}{P_Y}} = \frac{\Delta Q_X}{\Delta P_Y} \cdot \frac{P_Y}{Q_X}$$

Cross-elasticity of demand indicates the relationship goods bear to one another in the minds of consumers. Suppose the sign of the coefficient is negative, as it would be if, say, the price of Y were to fall and in consequence of this the quantity demanded of X were to increase. This would indicate that the relationship between goods X and Y is one of *complementarity.* Two goods are complementary if a fall (rise) in the price of one good causes the consumer to buy more (less) of the other. Suppose X is gin. If the price of gin falls, the consumer, in accord with the law of demand, will buy more of it. If he likes to use the gin to make martinis, it is likely that he will also buy more vermouth and more olives. For many drinkers, gin, vermouth, and olives are complementary goods.

On the other hand, it would seem reasonable that if the price of gin were to rise, a number of imbibing consumers would increase their purchases of vodka. To many minds, gin and vodka are substitute goods. When the coefficient of cross-elasticity is positive, as it would be in this example, the relation between the goods is one of *substitutability.*

Suppose the value of the coefficient is zero, as would be likely if we were comparing a fall in the price of typewriter ribbons with the sale of Rolls-Royces. When the cross-elasticity of demand is zero, the relationship between the goods is one of *independence.* For all practical purposes, most goods may be considered to be independent of all other goods. In a precise sense, however, most goods do bear some relationship to one another, since, under the ubiquitous presence of scarcity, few goods are free, and the purchase of one good means doing without another.

SUMMARY

A consumer demands a certain quantity of a particular good when he has a want for the good and the purchasing power to acquire some units of it. The demand function summarizes the relationship between the independent variables that determine how much of a good a consumer will buy and the dependent variable, which is the amount he does buy. Using the technique of *ceteris paribus,* it is possible to derive a demand curve that will show how much of a good a consumer will demand once the price of the good is specified. According to the law of demand, the theory of which will be developed in the two following chapters, the relationship between price and quantity is inverse.

Ceteris paribus, when there is a change in any determinant of demand, other than the price of the good itself, the result is a shift in the entire demand curve, or schedule. A change in any one of these determinants will *not* induce the consumer to move along a given demand curve. It is possible that a number of determinants other than the price of the good itself may change simultaneously. If the forces making for an increase in demand predominate, the demand curve will shift upward. The consumer will buy more of the good at any given price. If, on the other hand, the forces making for a decrease in demand predominate, the demand curve will shift downward. The consumer will buy less of the good at any given price. To avoid ambiguity, we must distinguish between changes in quantity demanded and changes in demand. The former are caused solely by changes in the price of the good itself and are shown as movements along a given demand curve. The latter are caused by any of the other determinants of demand and are depicted as shifts in the entire demand curve.

The market demand curve for a good is simply the horizontal summation of the individual demand curves of all consumers of the particular good.

When the price of a good changes, the total expenditures of consumers for that good may increase, decrease, or remain constant. Knowing the price elasticity of demand for a particular good permits one to predict the direction of change in consumer expenditures in response to a given change in price. The price elasticity of demand is thus a measure of the sensitivity of consumers to changes in price. Its principal determinant is the extent to which consumers can substitute one good for another. If the demand for a good is elastic (if the numerical value of the coefficient of elasticity is greater than one), changes in price and changes in total expenditure will move in opposite directions. If the demand for a good is inelastic (the numerical value of the elasticity coefficient is less than one), changes in price and changes in total expenditure will move in the same direction. If the demand for the good is unitarily elastic (the numerical value of the elasticity coefficient is one), there will be no change in total expenditures in response to a change in price.

The numerical value of the price elasticity coefficient is computed by dividing the percentage change in quantity by the percentage change in the price inducing the change in quantity demanded. To avoid ambiguity, an averaging formula is used that yields uniform results whether elasticity is computed for a decrease or an increase in price.

The price elasticity of demand at a point on the demand curve may be determined geometrically. This allows a quick appraisal of whether the elasticity of demand for the good is greater than, less than, or equal to, one.

The income elasticity of demand indicates how sensitive consumer spending for a particular good is to changes in income. The coefficient of income elasticity is computed by dividing the percentage change in the quantity purchased by the percentage change in the consumer's income. In the case of income elasticity, the *sign* of the coefficient is important. If it is positive, consumers buy more of the good with an increase in income, and the good in ques-

tion is then said to be superior. If the sign of the coefficient is negative, consumers buy less of the good in response to an increase in their incomes, and the good is said to be inferior. If there is no change in the quantity purchased in response to a change in income, the value of the coefficient will be zero, and the good in question is said to be neutral.

The cross-elasticity of demand indicates whether goods are complements or substitutes—or are independent of one another. The coefficient of cross-elasticity is computed by dividing the percentage change in quantity purchased by the percentage change in the price of another good. Here also the sign of the coefficient is important. If the sign is positive, an increase in the price of one good causes the quantity purchased of another good to increase. The relationship between the goods is then defined as one of substitutability. Goods are said to be in a complementary relation when the sign of the coefficient is negative, for, in this case, an increase in the price of one good will cause a decrease in the quantity purchased of another good. If the value of the cross-elasticity coefficient is zero, then a change in the price of one good has no effect on the quantity purchased of the other. In this case, there is no relationship between the goods, and they are classified as independent.

An Introduction to the Basic Theory of Consumer Behavior

The demand curves of the preceding chapter were simply taken as given. In this chapter, we begin a search for their origins. A single point on a consumer's demand curve may represent a complex pattern of decision-making. The consumer himself may not know how complicated his decision process is. For example, suppose that if the price of Coca-Cola were 25¢ a bottle, you would buy six bottles per week. The demand curve indicates that if the price were to fall you would buy more. Why? Is it simply because Coke is now relatively cheaper than the other goods you have been accustomed to buying, or is it because the fall in price has, in effect, made you richer? If the latter, then won't you also buy more of other goods? Both reasons may apply. If so, which is the more important reason for buying more Coke? If you buy more goods to go along with your increased consumption of Coca-Cola, which goods do you buy—ice, glasses, popcorn, phonograph records, magazines? And if you buy more of these goods, do you buy more or less of other things?

It appears that a change in the price of Coca-Cola could effect changes in the consumption of other items, some of them apparently having little to do with an increase in Coke drinking. Might it be true that a point on an individual's demand curve for Coca-

Cola is determined simultaneously with points on his demand curves for Shell gasoline, Bic pens, Heinz ketchup, and, yes, Pepsi-Cola?

On what principles do you arrange your purchases of the things you buy? What goal are you trying, perhaps unconsciously, to attain? On what basis, for example, do you cut off your purchases of Coca-Cola at a certain level and allocate some of your income to the purchase of Bic pens? These are the types of questions we examine in this and the next two chapters. Keep in mind, however, that we are attempting to explain the economic influences on consumers' demand curves for goods and services; we are not concerned with individual preferences—for example, why one individual might like a blouse of the finest crepe de Chine, while another might want a hair shirt. As we observed in the preceding chapter, there is no accounting for tastes.

As we begin our search for the economic determinants and consequences of consumer demand, we shall make two very plausible assumptions: (1) that each consumer has virtually limitless wants for innumerable goods and services and (2) that he experiences a definite limitation in his ability to acquire everything he desires.

CARDINAL UTILITY THEORY

It seems reasonable to assert that every normal individual desires to make himself better off, and so we shall postulate that the model consumers of this book are determined to make themselves as well off as possible, *in their own subjective estimation*, and that *in the economic sphere* there is accomplished by the consumption of goods and services. We shall regard such consumers as *rational.*

The ability of a good or a service to make an individual feel he is better off is called *utility.* We shall resolutely refuse to define utility as "happiness," "pleasure," "satisfaction," or, most certainly, as "usefulness." Utility is simply an index that increases whenever an individual feels his sense of well-being has increased as a result of making some thing, or collection of things, his own.

The consumer's apparently infinite capacity for an increase in total utility does not mean that he cannot become sated with one or several goods. It is even possible for him to get so much of choice-object X that his total utility would decline if he got more of it. At that point, X would confer disutility, and to that individual it would be a "bad," or a "discommodity." His utility index would rise if he could get rid of some of it. But the rational consumer will not allow himself to become sated with one good. Before he gets so much X that it becomes a nuisance, he will stop buying it and use the dollars he has left to acquire the utility-increasing goods Y and Z and so on. By allocating his expenditures to all the goods that interest him, the rational consumer attempts to make his personal utility index, U, as large as his budget will allow.

THE UTILITY FUNCTION

It is convenient to summarize the relation between a consumer and the objects of his choice in a utility function,

$$U = f(X, Y, Z, \ldots, N)$$

which asserts that the total utility of the consumer, as he himself judges it, is dependent on his consumption of goods X, Y, and Z, as well as other unspecified goods.

The axiom of consumer behavior asserts that each individual strives to maximize his total utility index. The utility function asserts that *in the economic sphere,* the individual's index of total utility rises with the consumption of goods, since human wants are insatiable.

THE CONSTRAINED MAXIMUM

The essence of economics is scarcity. To the consumer, scarcity means that he cannot have all of the utility-conferring objects and events that he wants at the same time. The limitations of his income and his time preclude his attainment of an unconstrained maximum of utility. Finite man is forced to settle for a *constrained* maximum.

In explaining how the consumer allocates his scarce dollars over the virtually limitless objects he might choose, it is convenient to assume that the amount of utility a consumer derives from a particular good, or collection of goods, can be expressed in cardinal numbers—that is, numbers such as 1, 2, 3, . . . , 45, . . . , 726, and so on.[1]

UTILITY FUNCTION FOR A SINGLE GOOD

Let us consider how a consumer's utility behaves when, for purposes of analysis, his consumption of all goods other than X is held constant. We may now write his utility function as

$$U = f(X), \text{ ceteris paribus}$$

This form of the utility function is interpreted as asserting that the consumer's total utility is changed solely by variations in his stock of good X when there are no changes in his stocks of all other goods. The hypothetical data in Table 3-1 illustrate the nature of this function. The column headed Q_x shows

[1] The possibility of measuring utility in cardinal numbers has been a subject of prolonged controversy in economics. Indeed, the type of utility analysis developed in the next section is derived from the work of theorists who deny not only the possibility of measuring subjective utility but even that the individual thinks cardinally.

TABLE 3-1

Q_x	U_x	MU_x
0	0	
		200
1	200	
		100
2	300	
		30
3	330	
		10
4	340	
		0
5	340	
		−4
6	336	

the number of units of the good in the possession of the consumer over some period of time—for example, a week. The column headed U_x shows the amount of utility, expressed in "utils," that the consumer derives from *good X alone*. When the consumer has no X, he receives zero utility from it. When he has one unit of X, the good contributes 200 utils to his aggregate of utility.

The consumer's utility is expressed in cardinal numbers. These numbers tell us a great deal about the consumer's preferences. For example, they show us not only that he prefers 2 units of X to 1 unit of X but that 2 units of X are preferred 1 1/2 times as much as 1 unit. Thus, cardinal numbers show not only the direction of the consumer's preferences but also their intensity.

DIMINISHING MARGINAL UTILITY

The information contained in Table 3-1 is plotted as a bar graph in Figure 3-1. Each bar shows the utility the consumer derives from X at a particular level of consumption.

The consumer continues to gain utility up to and including the fourth unit of X. Once he has 4 units of X, one more unit neither adds to nor detracts from his level of well-being. He is indifferent to enlarging his collection from 4 to 5. And if he were to increase his stock of X to 6 units, his total utility would actually decline. It seems reasonable to assume that he will not give up his scarce dollars to buy more than 4 units of X.

The "risers" on the steps formed by the bar graph grow smaller as the stock of X increases. The difference between the heights of any two adjacent bar graphs is called marginal utility. *Marginal utility* is the change in total utility produced by a 1-unit change in the subject good (the consumption of all other goods remaining constant). The marginal utility associated with this illustrative utility function is presented graphically in Figure 3-2 and is tabulated in Table 3-1 under the column headed MU_x. The data show us that if, for example, the consumer were to increase his consumption of X from 3 to 4

FIGURE 3-1

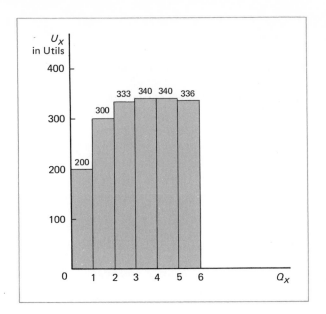

units, his total utility index (U_x) would rise from 330 to 340 utils; therefore, his marginal utility (MU_x) is 10 utils.

In sum, then, the consumer's utility continues to rise up to and including the fourth unit of X, but it rises at a decreasing rate; each increase in utility—marginal utility—is smaller than any previous increase. At some point, the increase in utility stops, and marginal utility becomes zero. Beyond this point, the consumer is sated with the good, and his utility at the margin (marginal utility) becomes negative—that is, his total utility falls.

The decreasing rate of increase in total utility is known as the principle of *diminishing marginal utility*. This "law" of diminishing marginal utility holds

FIGURE 3-2

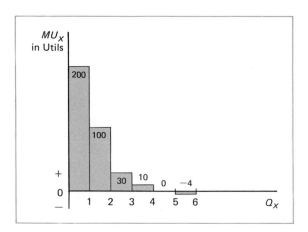

that, all other things being equal (*ceteris paribus*), as the consumer increases his consumption of a given good, a point will be reached at which the rate of increase in the consumer's total utility will fall. This law does not rule out the possibility of *increasing* marginal utility—that is, an increase of total utility at an increasing rate. For example, the law would not be violated if Table 3-1 showed the consumer's total utility to be 500 utils at 2 units and 900 utils at 3 units. In this case, marginal utility would be 300 and 400 utils, respectively. The law insists only that at some point marginal utility must diminish.

Diminishing marginal utility reflects the well-known human propensity to attach successively less importance to any unit of a thing the more one has of it. For example, if a person has only one glass of water a day, that amount of water will be quite important to him. If he has two glasses a day, then neither glass will be as important to him as either one would be if it constituted his entire daily water supply. Similarly, if he has enough water each day to fill a swimming pool, the addition or loss of one glass of water would be a matter of negligible importance to him.

Whenever a consumer considers adding to or subtracting from his stock of a particular good, he is said to be *at the margin*. Thus, marginal utility is often referred to as *utility at the margin*.

Sometimes marginal utility is spoken of as the utility contributed by the "last" unit of a good. The example commonly given to illustrate this conception is that of an individual eating homogeneous items of food. Assume that *X* in Table 3-1 is soda crackers. The first cracker gives the individual 200 units of utility, the second 100 units, the third 30 units, and so on. If the individual eats only three soda crackers, his total utility is 330 units, and his utility at the margin is 30. Presumably, this is the amount of utility contributed by the third, or last, soda cracker eaten.

Suppose, however, the items in question are not consumed immediately but are stored or consumed very gradually. Say that *X* in Table 3-1 is the symbol for homogeneous chairs. The individual has acquired four of them. Which is the "last" chair? How can a different amount of utility be attributed to any one chair, regardless of the order purchased? They are all identical, so each of them should contribute the same marginal utility to the consumer. Pick any chair at random; take it away from the consumer; his total utility will decrease by 10 utils. With only three chairs left, his total utility will be 330 utils, and the marginal utility of *any* chair to him is 30 utils. *The marginal utility of each item in a stock of goods is equal to that of any other item in the collection.* Thus, when the hypothetical consumer of Table 3-1 has, say, 4 units of good *X*, it is incorrect to conclude that the marginal utility of the fourth unit is 10 utils, the marginal utility of the third unit is 30 utils, and so on. The marginal utility of each of the 4 units is the same, that is, 10 utils. The correct way of expressing this situation is to say that if the individual has 4 units of *X*, the marginal utility of good *X* to him is 10 utils. Should the individual's stock of good *X* decrease to 3 units, the marginal utility of each of the 3 units would be 30 utils. Should the individual's stock of good *X* increase to 5 units, not only would the marginal utility of the fifth unit be zero, but the marginal utility of

each of the units previously in his collection would fall to zero. The addition of a unit of a particular good to an individual's stock reduces the importance of each unit in that stock.

What, then, is marginal utility? It is exactly what its name implies: it is the change in total utility at the margin; that is, it shows what happens to total utility when the consumer alters his stock of a particular good. Strictly speaking, marginal utility is the rate of change in total utility.

POINT MARGINAL UTILITY

Table 3-1 shows the figures for marginal utility entered *between* the quantity figures. For example, it is apparent that the tables do not state that marginal utility is 30 utils *when* the consumer has 3 units of X. This follows from the definition of marginal utility expressed in the formula

$$MU_x = \frac{\Delta U_x}{\Delta X}$$

where ΔX represents a 1-unit change in quantity. Since marginal utility involves a change, we say that the individual's total utility changes by 30 utils as he increases his holdings of good X from 2 to 3 units and that his total utility changes by 10 utils when he increases his collection of X from 3 to 4 units.

Our inability to express marginal utility *at* a particular level stems from the relatively large 1-unit changes used in the table. It is considerably more convenient to talk about a consumer's marginal utility at a particular number of units. Suppose that a good is susceptible to continuous variation—that is, it can be limitlessly subdivided, like water, sand, salt, electricity. For such goods, we can draw up a smooth, rather than a stepped, curve to show the change in the consumer's utility as his consumption of the good changes.

The smooth curve OU_x in Figure 3-3 shows the utility of the consumer

FIGURE 3-3

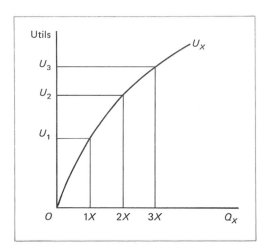

increasing at a decreasing rate throughout its entire length. Diminishing marginal utility has set in at the outset of consumption. The curve is, therefore, uniformly concave with respect to the horizontal axis.[2] The horizontal axis is marked off in uniform 1-unit increments of X. One unit of X yields the consumer OU_1 utils. If the individual acquires another unit of X, so that $\Delta X = 1$ and $Q_X = 2$, his total utility is OU_2, and his marginal utility is U_1U_2; and since $U_1U_2 < OU_1$, we see that marginal utility is diminishing. Similarly, if he acquires still another unit, so that $\Delta X = 1$ and $Q_X = 3$, his marginal utility is U_2U_3. In accordance with the law of diminishing marginal utility, $U_2U_3 < U_1U_2$.

Now consider the total utility curve in Figure 3-4. On curve OU_X, utility increases at an increasing rate from the outset of consumption. Up to point I, the point of inflection, the curve is *convex* with respect to the horizontal axis.[3] Utility is increasing at an increasing rate. (This situation of increasing marginal utility can occur if more of the good increases the consumer's enjoyment of the units of the good he already has—as, for example, in the case of a fourth

FIGURE 3-4

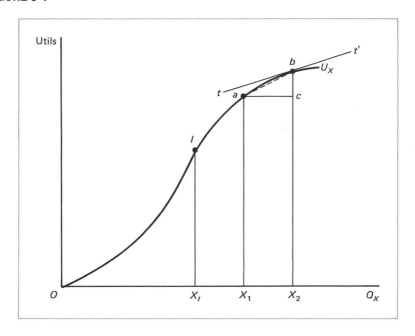

---

[2] *Concave* and *convex* are terms frequently used throughout this book to describe certain curves. With respect to the horizontal axis of the graph of Figure 3-3, a concave curve is like an inverted bowl. It is often said that it would "spill water." A convex curve would be like an upright bowl in relation to the horizontal axis. It would, therefore, "hold water."

[3] At its *point of inflection*, a curve changes the direction of its curvature. From the origin to point I, the curve is convex with respect to the horizontal axis. It becomes increasingly steep over the segment from O to I. At point I it reaches its maximum slope. To the right of point I, the curve becomes less steep and, therefore, is concave with respect to the horizontal axis.

Introduction to Consumer Behavior Theory

tire that allows the consumer to take the three he already has out of storage and run his automobile.) At point *I* on the curve, the law of diminishing marginal utility becomes evident, and beyond that point, additions to the consumer's stock of *X* cause his utility to increase at a decreasing rate.

Now let us consider the section of the utility curve between points *a* and *b*, that region in which the individual increases his consumption of the good from OX_1 to OX_2 units. Assuming that the change in *X* is 1 unit,

$$MU_X = \frac{OU_1 - OU_2}{OX_2 - OX_1} = \frac{U_1 U_2}{X_1 X_2} = \frac{cb}{ac} = \frac{\Delta U}{\Delta X}$$

The ratio of a change in a vertical distance to an accompanying horizontal distance is the formula for the slope of a straight line. Therefore, on curve OU_X, the ratio $\Delta U/\Delta X$ is the slope of the line segment connecting points *a* and *b* on the utility curve. Being a straight line, segment *ab* has a constant slope. The line OU_X is, however, curvilinear, and its slope is therefore inconstant. Yet from inspection it appears that the slope of the straight line *ab* is probably a fairly good approximation of the slope of OU_X between points *a* and *b*. When we are dealing geometrically with a smooth curve, there is no reason to insist that $\Delta Q = 1$ unit. We can make ΔQ as small as we wish so long as we do not let it actually become zero; so, conceptually, let us reduce the distance between X_1 and X_2 so that $\Delta X \to 0$. We have made the distance between X_1 and X_2 approximate zero, even though our process holds that $\Delta X > 0$. As the distance on the horizontal axis is collapsed, the distance *ab* $\to 0$, and a straight line joining points *a* and *b* becomes an even better approximation of the slope of curve OU_X between these points. In the limit, the straight line segment no longer joins two points on the curve; it becomes *tangent* to the curve.[4] The slope of the tangent is an excellent approximation of the slope of the curve in the vicinity of the point of tangency. Now we can speak of the marginal utility of a good to a consumer when he has a certain quantity of the good. This is called *point* marginal utility.

Using Figure 3-4, let us determine the marginal utility of *X* to the consumer when he has OX_2 units of the good. Since marginal utility involves a change in the consumer's stock of the good, we shall increase his holdings of *X*, so that $OX_2 = OX_1 + \Delta X$, where ΔX approaches zero (mentally collapse the distance $X_1 X_2$ until it is infinitesimal). We shall determine the slope of curve OU_X in the vicinity of point *b* by drawing a straight line *tt'* tangent to the curve

---

[4] The concept of a *limit* is fundamental to calculus and is frequently used in economic theory. Suppose *ab* represents a positive distance on a straight line. We may reduce progressively the distance between points *a* and *b* by one-half of the original distance, and then by one-half of the new distance, and then by one-half of that distance, and so on. Doing this, the distance can always be made smaller and yet remain positive. Even though it is positive, in becoming progressively smaller, *b* is moving closer to *a*. Consider the ratio $n/(n + 1)$. As *n* grows larger, the value of the ratio approximates 1 ever more closely. It will never equal 1 no matter how large *n* is made, but since the discrepancy between its value and 1 becomes progressively smaller with the increase in the value of *n*, 1 is said to be the limit of the ratio as *n* grows larger.

at *b*. The slope of the tangent is the numerical value of the marginal utility of X to the consumer when he has OX_2 units of the good. The numerical value of the marginal utility obtained by this process is called point marginal utility because it involves infinitesimal changes in X.[5]

THE MARGINAL UTILITY CURVE

The use of a smooth, continuous total utility curve permits us to derive a continuous marginal utility curve. The marginal utility curve in Figure 3-5 is negatively sloped throughout the length shown, reflecting the law of diminishing marginal utility. The graph permits us to read directly the consumer's marginal utility associated with a particular quantity of the good.

THE CONSUMER'S GRAND TOTAL OF UTILITY

No consumer restricts his consumption to one particular good. When an individual consumes a number of different goods, what is his aggregate (total) utility? Early cardinal theorists, such as Carl Menger, Leon Walras, and Alfred Marshall, assumed that it was simply the arithmetic grand total of the total utilities the consumer derived from each of the goods he consumed. Thus, if $U_X = 45$, $U_Y = 100$, and $U_Z = 20$, the consumer's grand total of utility would be 165 utils.

Later cardinal theorists, among them Francis Y. Edgeworth and Irving Fisher, doubted that the consumer's grand total of utility could be determined so simply. They contended that the utility received from any one good cannot be considered separately from other goods consumed by the individual. Sup-

FIGURE 3-5

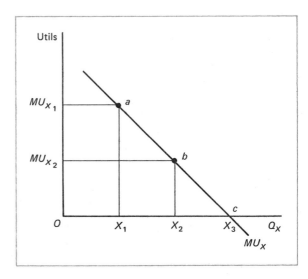

Introduction to Consumer Behavior Theory

pose X is a hamburger, Y is a Coke, and Z is French fries. Even if it is possible to determine that the total utility the consumer derives from ingesting this combination is, say, 165 utils, these more recent cardinalists would insist that the amount of utility contributed by any one good depends on the utility furnished by each of the other two items. For example, substituting a glass of buttermilk for the Coca-Cola may change not only the grand total of utility but the utility provided by each of the remaining goods. In other words, the later cardinalist view holds that utility is a function of the entire group of goods that the individual consumes—that is, that $U = f(X, Y, Z)$, where U is the grand total of utility. It rejects the idea that the grand total of utility is the sum of utilities from separate functions for each good—that is, that $U = U_x(X) + U_y(Y) + U_z(Z)$.

CONSUMER EQUILIBRIUM

A consumer is in equilibrium when he has allocated his limited income among a number of goods so that no reallocation of money income will increase the total utility he derives from all the goods he consumes. In determining consumer equilibrium, we require that the consumer dispose of all of his income (saving is a disposition of income).

We shall now determine the equilibrium condition for a consumer whose budget and choice situation is established by the equation

$$M = Q_x P_x + Q_y P_y$$

where M is his money income over a certain time period, Q_x and Q_y are the quantities of the goods on which he spends all of his income during the time period, and P_x and P_y are the prices of X and Y.

Suppose that when the consumer has X_1 units of X and Y_1 units of Y, he derives 18 utils at the margin from each of the two goods; that is, $MU_x = MU_y = 18$ utils. Is the consumer in equilibrium—has he maximized his total utility? Suppose $P_x = \$2$ and $P_y = \$3$. This additional information shows clearly that the simple equalization of the marginal utilities derived from all the goods one consumes does not, in itself, indicate an equilibrium solution. The consumer is not interested in the absolute amount of marginal utility he receives from the goods he consumes. What is of interest to him is the marginal utility *per dollar*. In the situation posed here, the consumer realizes 9 utils per dollar from X and 6 utils per dollar from Y. Since 1 unit of good X gives him more utility per dollar than 1 unit of good Y, it is reasonable to expect that the consumer will cut back on dollars spent for Y and increase the amount he spends for X.

Suppose the consumer makes a tentative experiment: he transfers $1 from Y to X. The results of this transfer can be tabulated as follows:

$-6U$ from the loss of $1 worth of Y
$+9U$ from the gain of $1 worth of X
$+3U$ net gain in total utility

The consumer has a net gain of 3 utils from this transfer of $1 from Y to X. As long as he can make a net gain by reallocating his dollars, he will continue to move from Y to X. But his reallocational activities are subject to the law of diminishing marginal utility. As he accumulates more X, he lowers its marginal utility to him; conversely, as he reduces his Y consumption, he raises its marginal utility. As long as the reallocation continues, the marginal utilities of each good per dollar must be approaching each other in value. The consumer will cease to reallocate his income when each good provides him with the same amount of marginal utility per dollar. Thus, the equilibrium condition of the consumer may be expressed

$$\frac{MU_X}{P_X} = \frac{MU_Y}{P_Y}$$

Given our hypothetical prices for goods X and Y, a possible equilibrium solution for the consumer is

$$\frac{MU_X}{P_X} = \frac{16U}{\$2} = \frac{MU_Y}{P_Y} = \frac{24U}{\$3} = \frac{8U}{\$1}$$

For any number of goods, the consumer is in equilibrium when

$$\frac{MU_X}{P_X} = \frac{MU_Y}{P_Y} = \frac{MU_Z}{P_Z} = \cdots = \frac{MU_N}{P_N} = MU_M$$

In equilibrium—when he has maximized his utility—the consumer arranges his expenditures so that he receives equal marginal utility per dollar spent on every good he buys, which in turn equals the marginal utility of $1 of money income (MU_M) to him.[6]
    The expression

$$\frac{MU_X}{P_X} = \frac{MU_Y}{P_Y}$$

can be rewritten

$$\frac{MU_X}{MU_Y} = \frac{P_X}{P_Y}$$

This shows us the equilibrium condition in a different light. The ratio MU_X/MU_Y shows the rate at which the consumer is *willing* to substitute one good for another. For example, if $MU_X = 24$ and $MU_Y = 16$, then

---

[6] The marginal utility of money income per dollar is MU_M/P_M, but it may be written MU_M, since, of course, the price of a dollar is $1.

    Introduction to Consumer Behavior Theory

$$\frac{MU_X}{MU_Y} = \frac{24}{16} = \frac{3}{2}$$

The consumer is willing to substitute 2 units of X for 3 units of Y. To put it another way, 24 = 1 1/2(16). Therefore, we know that the consumer subjectively values 1 unit of X 1 1/2 times as much as he values 1 unit of Y. He is *indifferent* to whether he has 1 unit of X or 1 1/2 units of Y. If 1 unit of X were taken from him and replaced with 1 1/2 units of Y, he would experience no change in his total utility.

The ratio P_X/P_Y shows the rate at which the consumer *can* substitute one good for another. This ratio of prices is the market, or objective, rate of substitution. Suppose $P_X = \$15$, and $P_Y = \$10$, then

$$\frac{P_X}{P_Y} = \frac{\$15}{\$10} = 1\frac{1}{2}$$

Since $\$15 = 1\,1/2(\$10)$, the market values 1 unit of X at 1 1/2 times the value of 1 unit of Y. If the consumer gives up 1 unit of X, he can have 1 1/2 more units of Y. If we recombine the two ratios—subjective and objective—we see that

$$\frac{MU_X}{MU_Y} = \frac{24U}{16U} = \frac{P_X}{P_Y} = \frac{\$15}{\$10}$$

The rate at which the consumer is *willing* to substitute one good for the other is equal to the rate at which he *can* substitute the goods. When the *willing* (subjective) *ratio* is equal to the *can* (objective) *ratio*, the consumer has maximized his total utility.

Let us assume a contrary situation. Suppose

$$\frac{MU_X}{MU_Y} = \frac{6U}{20U} \quad \text{and} \quad \frac{P_X}{P_Y} = \frac{\$2}{\$10}$$

To the consumer, 1 unit of X has the subjective value (utility) three-tenths the value of 1 unit of Y. But in the market, 1 unit of X has the objective value (price) of only two-tenths the value of a unit of Y. The consumer's subjective valuation of X is 10 percent greater than the market's objective valuation. While he is prepared to give up three-tenths of a unit of Y to gain 1 more unit of X, the market holds that he need give up only two-tenths of a unit of Y in exchange for 1 more unit of X. Therefore he should buy more X and less Y. As he reallocates his expenditures to accomplish this, he will lower MU_X and raise MU_Y, bringing the "willing" ratio closer to the "can" ratio. When the two ratios are equal, the consumer will have achieved equilibrium. No further reallocation of his dollars can improve his position. The logic behind the consumer's efforts to bring the subjective ratio into equivalence with the objective ratio is the essence of the cardinal utility theory of consumer choice.

THE THEORY OF ORDINAL UTILITY

By the 1930's, a number of economists had become disenchanted with cardinal utility theory for various reasons. Some objected to the assumption of measurable utility, doubting that consumers think cardinally. Others, less concerned with the problems of measurable utility, simply asserted that the assumption of cardinality was superfluous. These noncardinalists attempted to develop a new theory of consumer behavior based on assumptions less restrictive than those of the cardinal theorists. Whether or not they produced a superior theory has been the subject of intense and prolonged debate among the methodologists of the discipline, but their work does meet the test of good theorizing.

THE RATIONAL CONSUMER

Cardinal utility theory assumes that a consumer's utility index can be expressed in cardinal numbers. This suggests that utility can be measured and that consumers are able to think of and express the intensity of their preferences with extreme accuracy. Ordinal theorists question these assumptions. According to the ordinalist all a consumer can do is to rank, or order, his preferences—hence the name *ordinal* utility.

The complete weak ordering. Ordinal utility theory begins with two extremely plausible assumptions about the consumer. The first asserts that the consumer is able to rank his preferences over an entire field of choice. That is, confronted by any number of choice-objects, he is able to assign a rank to every single item—a *complete* ordering. For example, suppose the consumer is faced with the alternatives A_1, A_2, and A_3. He must be able to name the order of his preference—that is, A_3 **P** A_2 **P** A_1, where **P** is read "is preferred to." The consumer is allowed some leeway in the sense that the ranking of a tie is permitted. Thus, a perfectly acceptable ranking is A_3 **I** A_2 **I** A_1, where **I** is read "is indifferent to." The ranking of indifference means that the consumer considers A_1, A_2, and A_3 to be perfect substitutes for one another. He could not make a choice among them. Forced to take *one* of them, he would have to resort to some random decision process (such as flipping a coin) to make his selection. However, as we shall discover, once prices enter into the consumer's calculations, he will rarely have difficulty making a choice.

Indifference and preference may be combined in one ranking as is the case with A_1 **I** A_2 **P** A_3. Here the consumer says that he cannot choose between alternatives 1 and 2, but that he prefers both of them to alternative 3. This is an example of a *complete weak ordering* (since it contains an indifference ranking), while the ordering A_3 **P** A_2 **P** A_1 is called *strong*. Under the assumptions of ordinal utility theory, a rational consumer must be able to give at least a complete weak ordering over his entire field of choice. Note that

"rational" as used here has to do, not with the qualitative nature of the consumer's desires, but with his ability to order his preferences.

Requiring the consumer to supply a complete weak ordering is much less than what cardinal utility theory expects of him. For example, consider the ranking A_1 **P** A_2 **P** A_3 **I** A_4. The possibilities of rankings in both types of theory are shown in Table 3-2. The ordinal rankings follow directly from the cardinal

TABLE 3-2	Ordinal	Cardinal I	Cardinal II
	A_1	1,000,000	10,000,000
	A_2	250,000	10
	A_3 or A_4	1	2

rankings; no matter which column is used, the place-ranking is the same, but the cardinal rankings supply much more detailed information about the consumer's subjective attitude toward the alternatives. A cardinal ranking shows not only the *direction* of the consumer's preference (as does ordinal theory) but also his *intensity* of preference. For example, in the table, alternative A_1 is the consumer's top choice. In both cardinal rankings he prefers A_1 considerably more than A_2, but in Cardinal I, A_1 is preferred only four times as much as A_2, whereas in Cardinal II, the consumer prefers A_1 1 million times over A_2. Similarly, although A_2 is preferred to A_3 or A_4 (between which the ranking is indifference in both the ordinal and cardinal systems), the distance between A_2 and A_3 or A_4 is much greater in Cardinal I than it is in Cardinal II.

Transitivity. The second fundamental axiom of ordinal utility is that the consumer must be consistent in the ordering of his choice-objects. For example, let us suppose that the consumer confronted with the alternatives A_1, A_2, and A_3, says, A_2 **P** A_3 and A_3 **P** A_1. These two pairings, involving three alternatives, are the only orderings the consumer is required to make. From this information, we axiomatize the final ranking, A_2 **P** A_1.

An internally consistent ordering is said to be *transitive*. Although intransitive relations may exist—for example, A_2 **P** A_3 **P** A_1 **P** A_2—in economic theory a rational consumer does not produce such orderings. According to the theory, a person cannot say, for example, "I prefer coffee to tea and tea to milk, but I prefer milk to coffee."

Nonsatiability. Another axiom that we may add to the previous two is that of *nonsatiation*. Although microeconomic theory can deal with instances of total satiation, we shall specify here that none of the consumers in our models ever have enough of *all* things including such goods as leisure time, hours of contemplation, time to help others. (Review Chapter 1 if the basic idea of this axiom and its relation to the concept of scarcity is unclear.)

The abstract goods X and Y used in our analysis are surrogates for all the possible objects of consumer choice. We restrict our model of the economic world to two goods purely for the convenience of our (somewhat limited) minds. As is the case with all abstraction, our intention is to generalize

this two-good model for the better understanding of a multi-good world. If *X* and *Y* stand for all the possible objects of individual choice, then our model will not permit the consumer to become satiated with both of them. Indeed, as we observed in the previous chapter, the rational consumer will not permit himself to become sated with even *one* good; before this happens, he will switch his expenditures to another good.

THE UTILITY SURFACE

Assuming for the moment that we can employ cardinal utility, let us consider the total utility curves of an individual whose field of choice consists of the goods *X* and *Y*. If we look at each of the two curves of Figure 3-6 in isolation from each other, we can conclude that if the individual has OX_0 units of *X*, he derives OU_{X_0} utils from the good, and if he has OY_0 units of *Y*, he receives OU_{Y_0} units of utility from *Y*. It might then seem reasonable to conclude that

$$TU_0 = OU_{X_0} + OU_{Y_0}$$

Should his consumption of *X* increase to OX_1 units, similar reasoning would lead us to say

$$TU_1 = OU_{X_1} + OU_{Y_0}$$

and that necessarily, $TU_1 > TU_0$. Strictly speaking, this follows only if the utilities derived from different goods are additive and if the goods are independent.[7]

Let us now drop both of these assumptions but for the present retain the underlying premise of the preceding chapter that utility can be expressed in cardinal numbers. Many of the goods we consume have the relationship of dependency. The amount of *X* consumed has a bearing on the amount of utility derived from the amount of *Y* consumed. Suppose an individual is eating a lunch consisting of a hamburger and French fries. His total utility from ingesting this combination is 100 utils. If we take the French fries away from him, suppose his total utility drops to 50 utils. Can we conclude that the French fries are responsible for 50 of the 100 utils he gains from his lunch? Not necessarily, since for most people, French fries alone are not much of a lunch. Take the hamburger away, leaving only the potatoes, and the consumer's level of utility might fall to 10 utils. It is the *combination* of 1 hamburger and a given

---

[7] *Additive* means that the quantities under consideration may legitimately be added together, as in the case of a person who has 3 pencils, is given 3 more, and then has 6. Three oranges and 3 volts of electricity could not be added together to produce 6 units of anything meaningful. In other words, to be additive, utilities must be homogeneous. Is the utility derived from eating a fine dinner homogeneous with the utility derived from reading a fine economics book? If not, the two utilities cannot be added together.

Goods are *independent* when consumption of one good has no effect upon the utility that a consumer derives from the consumption of another good. In this sense, paper clips and automobiles are almost surely independent of each other, while the utilities one derives from steak and potatoes are very likely dependent.

FIGURE 3-6

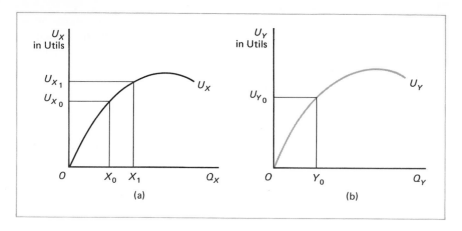

(a)

(b)

amount of French fries that yields the consumer 100 utils. In this example, the utility that the consumer derives from any item is *dependent*, not only on the quantity he consumes of this particular good, but on the quantity he consumes of another good. This interrelationship of the utilities derived from different goods is called the *dependency effect.*

We now assume that the total utility experienced from the consumption of X and Y can be expressed cardinally, although the amount derived from each separately cannot. For example, suppose the consumer has a basket of goods $4X + 6Y$ that yields him 100 utils. Having dropped the assumption of additivity we cannot assert, say, that $40U_x + 60U_y = 100U$. All we know is that as a unit the basket of goods $4X + 6Y \rightarrow 100U$. (The arrow, as used here, is read "yields.")

The dependency relation requires that the subject good have a different total utility curve for every amount of all *other* goods consumed. In Figure 3-7, the total utility curves show how the utility of the consumer changes when he has a constant amount of Y, and X is varied.

FIGURE 3-7

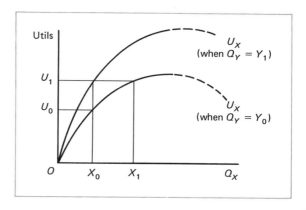

Suppose the amount of Y in the consumer's possession is Y_0. As the consumer changes his consumption of X, his utility follows the path described by the curve $Q_Y = Y_0$. If the amount of X he consumes along with Y_0 units of Y is OX_0, his total utility is OU_0. Suppose, with Y held constant at Y_0, the consumer increases his consumption of X by X_0X_1 units. The consumer's total utility increases by U_0U_1 utils.

The same increase in total utility could be obtained if the consumer held his consumption of X constant at OX_0 units but increased his consumption of Y to Y_1 units. A new utility curve, $Q_Y = Y_1$, must be drawn to show that with an increase in the amount of Y in the consumer's possession, any given amount of X will combine with the new Y to yield a higher utility index than with the original amount of Y.

Note that the subscript X has been dropped from the utility indices. They are labeled U_0 and U_1, rather than U_{X_0} and U_{X_1} because the amount of utility cannot be attributed to X alone. Thus, the amount of utility shown as OU_0 is not the contribution of X alone but is rather the *joint* contribution of OX_0 units of X and Y_0 units of Y. Therefore, we should write, as we have previously in this section, $X_0 + Y_0 \rightarrow U_0$.

Constructing a utility surface. Dependency relations between goods are handled more easily by use of a three-dimensional utility surface. Such a surface can be constructed from utility curves of the type discussed in the previous section. Because the rational consumer does not permit himself to become sated with any one good, the diminishing-utility portions of these curves (the dashed portions in Figure 3-7) will be eliminated henceforth as irrelevant.

The three-dimensional utility surface of Figure 3-8 has been "built up" from sets of total utility curves for specific goods under the assumption of dependency. For example, curve Y_1M' shows how the consumer's total utility changes as his consumption of X changes, *given* that the consumer has OY_1 units of Y to consume along with X. The curve Y_2N' is interpreted in the same way, except that the consumer has the larger amount of Y—OY_2. Curve X_1G' shows how the consumer's total utility changes in response to variations in his consumption of Y when the amount of X he consumes is OX_1. Curve X_2H' shows the same information when the consumer's holdings of X have been increased by X_1X_2 units.

The utility curves are planes within our three-dimensional model, and they are infinite in number. Hence, the utility surface should be thought of as a smooth-surfaced solid. One may think of it as looking something like one-quarter of a beehive. The planes are formed by cutting down through the surface perpendicular to the base plane.

The base plane itself is called a *commodity space*. Any point on the base plane denotes a particular commodity basket composed of the goods X and Y. The quantities of X and Y making up a particular basket are read from the edges of the base plane nearest the reader. Thus, if the consumer is at point B on the commodity space (the base plane of the surface), he has a basket contain-

FIGURE 3-8

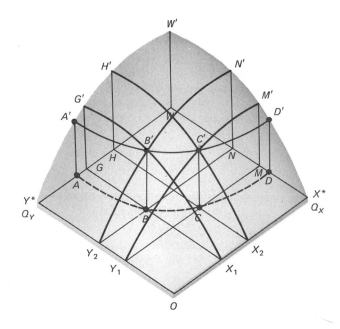

ing OX_1 units of X and OY_2 units of Y. If he is at point C, his basket consists of OX_2 units of X and OY_1 units of Y.

The height of the surface represents the total utility of the consumer. To find the total utility yielded the consumer by a particular basket, we erect a perpendicular from the appropriate point on the commodity space to the surface. For example, suppose the individual has the basket denoted by point B on the commodity space (OX_1 units of X and OY_2 units of Y); then his total utility is the vertical distance from the floor at B to the surface at B'. Should the individual have the basket denoted by point W (OX^* units of X and OY^* units of Y), his total utility would be represented by the vertical distance WW'.

Assume now that the individual is at point B' on his utility surface. His total utility is BB'. If the individual is at C' on the surface, his total utility is CC'. The height of point C' above the base plane happens to be the same as that of point B'; thus, BB' = CC'. Since these heights indicate total utility, the consumer is equally well off at either point. At point B', he has basket $OX_1 + OY_2$; at C', he has basket $OX_2 + OY_1$. The second basket has X_1X_2 more X in it than does basket B', but it has Y_1Y_2 less Y. Since the consumer's utility is the same at C' as it is at B', it must be that X_1X_2 *more* units of X can substitute for the loss of Y_1Y_2 units of Y.

A contour line has been drawn through points A', B', C', and D'. All these points are of equal height above the base plane. It follows that *all* points on this contour line show combinations of X and Y that yield the consumer equal utility. The contour line A'B'C'D' follows the face of the utility surface and hence is rounded. The dashed line on the base plane is obtained by draw-

ing a smooth curve through the points at the ends of perpendiculars dropped from points of equal height on the utility surface. It follows that the dashed line ABCD must be an exact image, or map, of the contour A'B'C'D'.

The higher any contour lies on the utility surface, the greater is the consumer's total utility. Figure 3-9 shows contours on a utility surface at the 100, 200, and 300 util levels. Assume that the consumer's stock of X is held constant at X_0. As we move left from the origin along the Y edge of the surface, the consumer's holdings of Y increase, and his utility index rises. Contour lines have been drawn through points A', B', and C'. As was noted before, all points on a given contour line, although they denote *different baskets* of X and Y, denote baskets giving the *same utility* to the consumer. Thus, the consumer receives 300 utils whether he is at C' or R'. As before, curves drawn through the end points of perpendiculars dropped from the surface to the base plane would trace out the image of the associated contour. Drawing a sufficient number of these curves on the base plane would yield a contour map of the utility surface much like the contour map of a geological mountain.

FIGURE 3-9

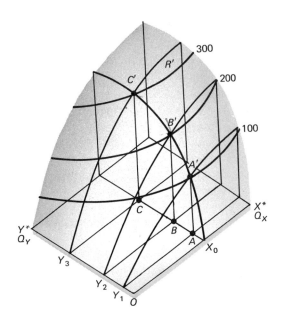

Figure 3-10 shows such a map. The utility surface has been removed from the base plane, and the base plane has been rotated so as to square the figure on the page. Henceforth, we will dispense with the utility surface and use a map of the surface produced in this way.

The smooth convex-to-the-origin curves in Figure 3-10, taken together, form a partial map of the utility surface of Figure 3-9. Each capital letter corresponds to its primed counterpart on the surface. A particular curve shows

Introduction to Consumer Behavior Theory

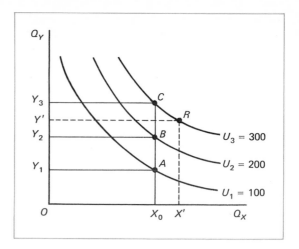

FIGURE 3-10

a *specific level* of utility. Thus, *any* point on $U_3 = 300$ utils—that is, any point on U_3 shows a basket of goods giving the consumer 300 utils. Thus, for instance, either basket X_0Y_3 or basket $X'Y'$ provides the consumer with 300 units of utility.

INDIFFERENCE CURVES

Most of what we have done so far is compatible with cardinal utility analysis. Essentially, the major change up to this point has been to drop partial equilibrium analysis in favor of a multivariate equilibrium technique.[8] Now, following the ordinalists mentioned earlier, we shall require of the consumers in our models only that they be able to fulfill the two axiomatic conditions set at the beginning of this section. That is, they must be able to make a complete weak ordering of the items they consume, and the relationships thus described must be transitive. Henceforth, consumers will be regarded as having no knowledge of the number of utils they receive from consumption.

With respect to the utility surface, we are now like surveyors attempting to fix the heights of various points on a mountain without any form of altimeter. We cannot fix *absolute* heights, but we can establish *relative* heights; that is, we can tell only whether one level is higher or lower than another. This means, for example, that in Figures 3-9 and 3-10 we are no longer able to label either the contours of the surface or the map of those contours with specific amounts of utility. Now, what do we know? First, we know that when the individual is at any point on the contour passing through C' in Figure 3-9, his utility is greater than if he is on either of the two contours passing through B' or A'. Similarly, we know if he is at any point on the contour passing through B', his utility is less than it would be at C' or R' but greater than it would be if he were at A' or

---

[8] "Multivariate" signifies that the number of variables in a particular analytical situation exceeds one.

at any point on the contour passing through A'. We also know, as we did before, that if an individual is on a specific contour, his utility is the same regardless of his position at that level. Thus, although we no longer have the slightest idea of the consumer's utility index at point C', we know that its value is the same at R'. Finally, we know that the same type of relative information that the utility surface conveys to us may be gathered from the map of the surface.

If any points at a given level provide the consumer with equal utility, then, regardless of the numerical value of that utility, it must be that the consumer is *indifferent* among the various points. The same conclusion follows using a map of the surface. The consumer would just as soon be at R on U_3 as he would be at C. He would prefer C and R over B, and he would prefer B over A. Henceforth, we shall call curves of the type appearing in Figure 3-10 *indifference curves,* since the consumer is indifferent to being at any point on the particular curve.

The nature and properties of indifference curves. All the properties of indifference curves follow naturally from the utility surface from which they are derived.

1. *The consumer prefers indifference curves farther to the right.* The farther an indifference curve lies from the origin—that is, the larger the holdings of commodities to which it corresponds—the more any point on it is preferred by the consumer. Thus, we know that U_3 **P** U_2 **P** U_1. This follows from the fact that when one contour of the surface is higher than another, it maps as an indifference curve to the right of any curve mapping as a lower contour.

2. *Indifference curves never intersect.* Since each indifference curve represents a specific level of utility, or height, on the utility surface, it is impossible for them to intersect.

A proof of this proposition can be derived from logic. Assume that two purported indifference curves intersecting at M lie on the commodity space (see Figure 3-11). The point V lies on curve I_1. If curve I_1 is an indifference curve, then V **I** M, since M also lies on curve I_1. Point T lies on curve I_2. Again, if curve I_2 is an indifference curve, T **I** M, since both points are common to the curve. By the rule of transitivity, it follows that V **I** T. But this is an absurdity, since the baskets denoted by T and V have equal amounts of good X in them, but the basket established by V has more Y in it. The rational consumer prefers a larger basket. Thus, V **P** T, and it cannot be that points V and T are both indifferent to point M. We are involved in a logical contradiction that is resolved by concluding that curves I_1 and I_2 cannot be indifference curves.

3. *Indifference curves have a negative slope.* Since X and Y are goods, an increase in any one of them will cause the consumer's utility to increase. Suppose the amount of Y a consumer has is held constant while he acquires more X. In Figure 3-12, assume the consumer has the basket $X_0 Y_0$. This puts him at point J on indifference curve I_0. If his basket is enlarged to $X_1 Y_0$, he must

FIGURE 3-11

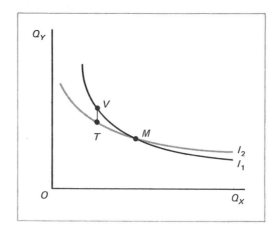

prefer it to the previous basket, since $X_1Y_0 > X_0Y_0$ implies X_1Y_0 **P** X_0Y_0 or K **P** J. It follows that K lies on a "higher" (farther to the right) indifference curve.

Since an indifference curve requires that $\Delta U = 0$ for any change occurring along it, and since both X and Y are capable of conferring utility on the consumer, it follows that if the individual is to remain on a given indifference curve when his consumption of one good is increased, his consumption of other goods must be decreased. Only a negatively sloped curve can show the required inverse relationship.

4. *Indifference curves are convex with respect to the origin.* Commencing at A on indifference curve I_0 in Figure 3-13, as the consumer moves downward along the curve substituting increases of X for given decrements of Y, the amount of X required to keep him on I_0 grows ever larger. The path traced by the consumer as he moves from A to G is convex with respect to the origin. Why? It must be that as he adds to his stock of X and decreases his stock of Y,

FIGURE 3-12

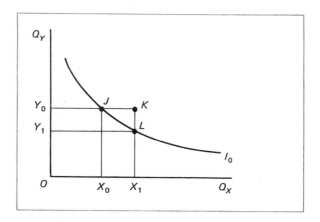

FIGURE 3-13

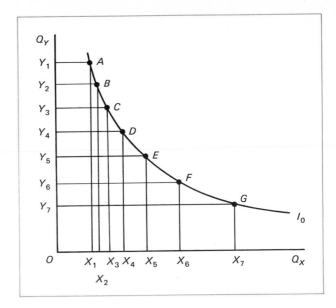

he regards X as a successively poorer substitute for Y. Let's examine this important proposition more closely.

The diminishing marginal rate of substitution. The rate at which one good can be substituted for another while leaving the consumer's utility index unchanged is called the marginal rate of substitution. The marginal rate of substitution of X for Y is expressed by the formula

$$MRS_{XY} = \frac{\Delta Y}{\Delta X}$$

Thus, if $MRS_{XY} = \Delta Y/\Delta X = 3/1$, we know that in the consumer's estimation his level of utility will not change if the loss of 3 units of Y is compensated by the gain of 1 unit of X.

In Figure 3-14, $\Delta X_1 = \Delta X_2$, but $\Delta Y_1 > \Delta Y_2$. Thus, we see that as the consumer moves from A to B

$$(MRS_{XY})_{A, B} = \frac{-(OY_1 - OY_2)}{OX_2 - OX_1} = -\frac{Y_1 Y_2}{X_1 X_2} = -\frac{\Delta Y_1}{\Delta X_1}$$

Then, if the consumer moves from B to C, continuing to acquire more X (and losing more Y)

$$(MRS_{XY})_{B, C} = \frac{-(OY_2 - OY_3)}{OX_3 - OX_2} = -\frac{Y_2 Y_3}{X_2 X_3} = -\frac{\Delta Y_2}{\Delta X_2}$$

FIGURE 3-14

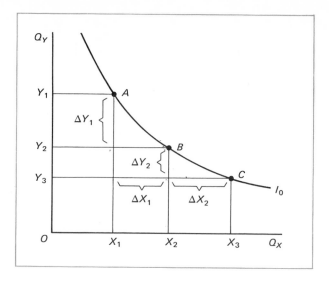

and, neglecting the minus signs (they merely show the negative slope of the indifference curve),

$$\frac{\Delta Y_1}{\Delta X_1} > \frac{\Delta Y_2}{\Delta X_2} \quad \text{or} \quad (MRS_{XY})_{A,\,B} > (MRS_{XY})_{B,\,C}$$

The marginal rate of substitution of X for Y *diminishes* as the consumer acquires a larger stock of X (and a smaller stock of Y).

Since the ratio $\Delta Y/\Delta X$ expresses the change in the vertical distance (loss of Y) along an indifference curve accompanying the compensatory change in horizontal distance (gain of X), the marginal rate of substitution is the formula for the slope of the indifference curve. In the limit—that is, when $\Delta X \to 0$— the slope of a tangent drawn to the indifference curve gives the value of the marginal rate of substitution of X for Y at the point of tangency. In Figure 3-15, the point marginal rate of substitution of X for Y when the consumer has the basket $X_a Y_a$ is the slope of the indifference curve in the vicinity of A, that slope being very nearly approximated by the slope of the tangent *TT*. If the consumer's basket is $X_b Y_b$, the marginal rate of substitution of X for Y is the slope of I_0 in the vicinity of B, in this case very closely approximated by the slope of the tangent *tt*. Tangent *TT* is steeper than *tt*, which shows that

$$\left(\frac{\Delta Y}{\Delta X}\right)_A > \left(\frac{\Delta Y}{\Delta X}\right)_B$$

The ability of X to substitute for Y is less at B than at A. Since the slopes of tangents drawn to I_0 grow consecutively less steep as we move from A to B, we

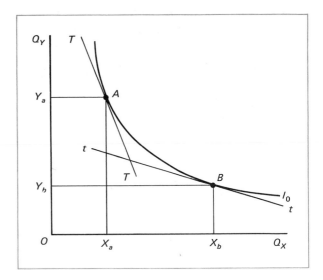

FIGURE 3-15

can conclude that the marginal rate of substitution of *X* for *Y* diminishes as the consumer's stock of *X* becomes larger.

Diminishing marginal utility and the diminishing marginal rate of sub-stitution. The principle of the diminishing marginal rate of substitution may sound like the law of diminishing marginal utility, but the two ideas are different. Marginal utility shows by how much a consumer's total (cardinal) utility index changes as his consumption of a particular good is changed, *ceteris paribus*. His marginal utility for the given good diminishes as his stock of it grows, be-cause any addition to that stock reduces the importance of any single unit in it.

On the other hand, the diminishing marginal rate of substitution excludes any changes in the consumer's total utility. It is defined only for movements along a specific indifference curve. As the consumer substitutes *X* for *Y*, the composition of his basket changes, but the utility to him of *any* basket is the same as that of any other basket. As the consumer moves downward along a given indifference curve, the ability of *X* to substitute for *Y* falls. This is so because as the consumer increases his holdings of *X* and decreases his hold-ings of *Y*, *X* becomes less important to him *in relation to Y*.

A major distinction, then, between the diminishing marginal utility *of a good* and the diminishing marginal rate of substitution *between two goods*, is the reference base. Marginal utility is concerned with the consumer's sub-jective estimate of the importance of a unit of a good to him in terms of the size of his stock of *that same* good. The marginal rate of substitution deals with the consumer's subjective estimate of the importance of a unit of *one* good to him in terms of what must happen to the number of units in his stock of *an-other* good if he gains or loses a unit of the first good.

Introduction to Consumer Behavior Theory

SUMMARY

The basic proposition of the theory of consumer behavior is that the consumer attempts to maximize his total utility. Cardinal utility theory assumes measurable utility indexes expressed in cardinal numbers. A consumer's utility index rises with his increasing consumption of goods and services. The law of diminishing marginal utility holds that once the consumer's holdings of a particular good reach a certain level, additional units of that good will increase his utility at a decreasing rate. The law of diminishing marginal utility is not incompatible with increasing or constant marginal utility up to a particular point. A consumer has maximized his total utility (in a two-good world) whenever $MU_X/P_X = MU_Y/P_Y$.

Ordinal utility theory asserts that the assumption of cardinality is unnecessary to a fully developed theory of consumer behavior. All that is required is that the consumer be able to order his preferences and that his preference pattern be transitive. Weak orderings (indifference) are acceptable.

The ability of units of one good to substitute for units of another without the consumer experiencing any change in his total utility is called the marginal rate of substitution. If X is replacing Y, the marginal rate of substitution of X for Y will fall as the consumer's stock of X increases. This principle is called the diminishing marginal rate of substitution. It is not the same concept as diminishing marginal utility.

A locus of points among which the consumer is indifferent may be plotted in a commodity space as an indifference curve. Owing to the principle of the diminishing marginal rate of substitution, an indifference curve is convex with respect to the origin of the commodity space. A family of indifference curves comprises the consumer's indifference map. These negatively sloped, convex curves never intersect. The farther an indifference curve lies from the origin, the more a point on it is desired by the consumer. In Chapter 4, we will see how a consumer can achieve only a constrained maximum of total utility when he is in equilibrium.

The Basic Theory
of Consumer Behavior

Here we continue the development of the theory of ordinal utility begun in Chapter 3. Most of the chapter will be devoted to an economic study of an individual who is attempting to maximize his total utility under the constraints imposed on him by his limited income. Later we shall derive the consumer's demand curve from a knowledge of his budget and his ordinally ranked preferences. Then we shall attempt to isolate the two basic reasons a consumer changes the quantity he demands of a good when its price is changed. We shall also be able to classify goods by changes in a consumer's pattern of purchases when his income changes.

THE ACT OF CONSUMER CHOICE

THE CONSUMER'S BUDGET

The consumer's limited budget is the stern reality that forces his choice of a unique basket of goods. Suppose the consumer has a budget of N dollars per month to spend on X and Y; we may write his budget equation as

$$N = P_X Q_X + P_Y Q_Y$$

where $P_X Q_X$ (the price of X multiplied by the quantity of X purchased) is the amount out of N dollars per month that he spends on X, and $P_Y Q_Y$ is the total amount out of his budget that he spends on Y.

If the consumer were to spend his entire budget on good Y, then

$$N = P_Y Q_Y \quad \text{or, solving for } Q_Y, \quad Q_Y = \frac{N}{P_Y} = Y^*$$

where Y^* is the largest amount of Y he can buy. On the other hand, if the consumer were to spend his total income on X, the budget equation would read $N = P_X Q_X$. Solving for Q_X,

$$Q_X = \frac{N}{P_X} = X^*$$

which is the maximum amount of X that the consumer can buy with his N dollars.

What if, as is likely to be the case, the consumer wants his basket to be composed of some X and some Y? If we assume, for the moment, that the consumer buys a given quantity of X, we can solve the budget equation for Q_Y

$$Q_Y = \frac{N}{P_Y} - \frac{P_X}{P_Y} \cdot Q_X$$

Suppose that the consumer's budget is $500 a month and that the prices of X and Y are $1 and $5, respectively. If the consumer buys 10 units of X per month,

$$Q_Y = \frac{\$500}{\$5} - \frac{\$1}{\$5} \cdot 10$$

$$Q_Y = 100 - 2$$

$$Q_Y = 98$$

Now we know that if the consumer buys 10 units of X per month, he can buy 98 units of Y. Joining the coordinates from 10X and 98Y, we obtain a point on the consumer's budget line. Now, let us double his monthly consumption of X. The budget equation (solved for Q_Y) now reads

$$Q_Y = \frac{\$500}{\$5} - \frac{\$1}{\$5} \cdot 20$$

$$Q_Y = 100 - 4$$

$$Q_Y = 96$$

Again, plotting a point at the intersection of the two coordinates ($Q_X = 20$, $Q_Y = 96$), we obtain another point on the consumer's budget line.

Without even plotting other points on the budget line, we know from the pattern of the solutions we have so far obtained what the general appearance

of the budget line must be. We have seen that for every 10-unit increase in the purchase of X, the consumer must cut his consumption of Y by two units—or by 1 unit for every 5-unit increase in the consumption of X. The ratio of 1 to 5 is the ratio of P_x/P_y. Since the prices of X and Y are given to the consumer (and the market transactions of one consumer cannot affect the prices of the goods he buys), the ratio P_x/P_y is a constant in the equation. A graph of this constant relationship necessarily must be a straight line and have a negative slope, in this case, of 1/5. Now that we know that the slope of the budget line is constant, we see that there is no need to determine any points on it other that those at its ends. Once we have determined the maximum amounts of X and Y that the consumer can buy with his N dollars (i.e., X^* or Y^*), we may simply plot those points on the graph and join them with a straight line; this line is the graphical representation of the consumer's budget equation. Since, $N/P_Y = OY^*$ and $N/P_X = OX^*$ and

$$\frac{P_X}{P_Y} = \frac{\dfrac{N}{P_Y}}{\dfrac{N}{P_X}}$$

we know that the slope of the budget line may also be expressed by the ratio

$$\frac{OY^*}{OX^*}$$

THE ATTAINMENT OF CONSUMER EQUILIBRIUM

We are now ready to develop the theory of the optimal basket. The consumer's indifference map shows us what the individual would like to do and what he is willing to do. We assume that he would like to reach the peak of his utility surface, but, as we have seen, the budget limitation prevents this. For a particular basket on a given indifference curve, we can tell from the slope of the curve (the marginal rate of substitution), what the consumer would be willing to do. For example, suppose the consumer's $MRS_{XY} = 3/1$. This means that given the basket he now has, he would experience no change in his subjective estimate of his well-being if 3 units of Y in his basket were replaced with 1 unit of X. Should this exchange occur, we would expect that in conformity with the principle of the diminishing marginal rate of substitution, his MRS_{XY} would fall. His MRS_{XY} might now be 2/1, indicating that since his stock of Y has been decreased and his collection of X has been increased by the exchange, in order to remain at his current level of well-being, he would now be willing to give up only 2 units of Y in exchange for 1 unit of X.

The budget line defines what the consumer can do with his limited income. He is able to buy any basket of goods lying under or on the line. Under the requirement that his total income be exhausted on the goods comprising

his basket, the consumer in our model chooses his basket from among those points in the commodity space lying *on* his budget line.

Now that we know what the consumer *wants, is willing,* and *is able* to do, let us see what he *will* do. Figure 4-1 superimposes the budget line of the consumer on his indifference map. It is intuitively obvious that the consumer will choose the basket denoted by point *E*—the basket composed of $O\bar{X}$ units of X and $O\bar{Y}$ units of Y ($O\bar{X} + O\bar{Y}$). Point *E* is located on indifference curve I_4, the highest indifference curve the consumer can reach. Curve I_5 represents a higher level of utility, but no point on I_5 can be reached given the consumer's present budget. The consumer's budget permits him to buy any basket lying on Y^*X^*, such as *F*, for example, but possible baskets other than *E* will yield the consumer a level of utility lower than that which he need accept. Clearly, point *E* on indifference curve I_4 is his optimal basket.

Points *H* and *J* also lie on I_4, and, therefore, the consumer must be indifferent between the baskets they represent and the basket denoted by *E*. However, the baskets associated with points *H* and *J* are beyond the consumer's means, so even though the consumer's ranking is *E* I *J* I *H*, he has no difficulty in selecting *E* as his optimal basket. When the budget limitation is introduced into the consumer's calculations, indifference does not lead to inaction.

We may describe the consumer's *optimal* basket as his *equilibrium* basket. A system is in equilibrium when, in the absence of external forces, it tends to remain in its current state. A system is in disequilibrium when, in the absence of external forces, it moves to attain a state different from the one in which it is currently situated. A self-equilibrating system tends to move away from any disequilibrium position to a position of equilibrium.

FIGURE 4-1

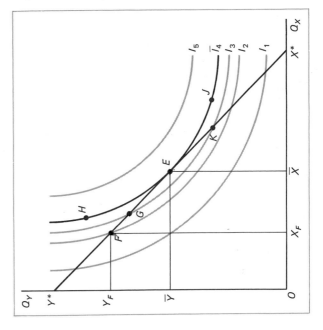

The equilibrium state itself may be characterized as stable or unstable. A system in stable equilibrium will, if disturbed by external forces, tend to return to its initial equilibrium solution once the external forces are removed—assuming, of course, that the conditions of equilibrium have not been changed. In a case of unstable equilibrium, external forces may cause the system to move into disequilibrium or into another position of (stable or unstable) equilibrium.

Figure 4-1 clearly shows a system with a stable equilibrium solution (point E). If the consumer initially contemplates the purchase of some other basket, such as that at G, he will understand that he can do better for himself with his limited income. He will move in the direction of point E, since a movement toward point F would make him worse off. Once he has attained point E, any movement away from it would be corrected since the consumer would discover he was worse off. Thus, we conclude that, given the consumer's indifference map and his budget line, point E—the point denoting the consumer's optimal basket—is a point of stable equilibrium.

Now that we have deduced the equilibrium solution of the consumer through the use of elementary logic, let us proceed to a more rigorous demonstration. Suppose the consumer is initially at point F; at that point, the slope of the indifference curve, I_2, is steeper than the slope of the budget line. This means

$$MRS_{XY} > \frac{P_X}{P_Y} \quad \text{or} \quad \frac{\Delta Y}{\Delta X} > \frac{P_X}{P_Y}$$

The rate at which the consumer is willing to substitute X for Y is greater than the rate at which the market allows him to substitute X for Y. For example, suppose that at point F, $MRS_{XY} = 4/1$ and $P_X/P_Y = 2/1$. The consumer is willing to give up 4 units of Y in order to gain 1 more unit of X, but the market says he need give up only 2 units of Y to get another unit of X. The consumer's subjective valuation of another unit of X is greater than the market's objective valuation of X. Obviously, at given prices, X is a "bargain" to the consumer, and he will acquire more of it.

As the consumer buys more X (and necessarily less Y), he moves downward along his budget curve in the direction of point E. Moving down the budget line, he encounters successively higher indifference curves; thus he is constantly increasing his utility level. For purposes of analysis, let us momentarily stop him in his journey at point G, which lies on the intersection of the budget curve and indifference curve I_3. Here, as at F, $MRS_{XY} > P_X/P_Y$. Suppose at G, $MRX_{XY} = 3/1$. Because the consumer is acquiring more of X, and is simultaneously reducing his consumption of Y, he now values an extra unit of X less than he did before. But he still values it more highly than does the market, so he will continue to expand his X purchases and curtail his Y purchases.

Let us stop him once again on his downward journey along the budget line, this time at point E, where the indifference curve I_4 is tangent to the budget

constraint line. The condition of tangency establishes the equal slope of both curves at this point; therefore, $MRS_{XY} = P_X/P_Y$. Since $P_X/P_Y = 2/1$ in our example, then at E, $MRS_{XY} = 2/1$ also. The rate at which the consumer is willing to substitute X for Y is equal to the objective rate of substitution the market forces on him. The consumer, therefore, ceases to substitute X for Y once he has reached E, and unless his tastes change or the prices of X or Y change, he will continue to consume the basket $\overline{XY}$ per specified time period.

For the sake of making the reasons for his state of equilibrium clearer, let us suppose that the consumer was overenthusiastic in substituting X for Y and overshot E, landing at K on I_3. The objective market rate of substitution, P_X/P_Y, remains the assumed 2/1. But at K, the slope of I_3 is less than the slope of the budget line. Assume that at K, $MRS_{XY} = .5/1$. The consumer is willing to give up only half a unit of Y in order to gain 1 more unit of X. His subjective valuation of the worth of another unit of X is less than the market's objective valuation of X. *In this sense,* the consumer has "too much X" and "not enough Y."[1] At K, the consumer is willing to give up 1 unit of X for half a unit of Y, but the market offers him a better bargain. The market will give him 2 units of Y for 1 unit of X. This being so, the consumer travels on his budget line from K toward E. As he does so, he crosses increasingly higher indifference curves, and his utility rises. As he acquires more Y at the sacrifice of X, his MRS_{XY} rises. Finally, as we saw before, when he arrives at E he will have brought his subjective marginal evaluation of X and Y into conformity with the market's judgment of their worth, and he will be in equilibrium. His utility will be maximized subject to the constraint of his budget, and having done the best for himself that he can, he will not stray from his optimal basket. Point E, therefore, is correctly described as denoting a condition of stable equilibrium.

A comparison of statements of consumer equilibrium. Is it possible to show that the cardinal and ordinal utility statements of consumer equilibrium are compatible? As they both purport to show the same thing, they should be identical. In the discussion of cardinal utility theory, we concluded that a consumer is in equilibrium when $MU_X/MU_Y = P_X/P_Y$. We know that $MU_X = \Delta U/\Delta X$ and $MU_Y = \Delta U/\Delta Y$. Thus, in the equilibrium of the consumer

$$\frac{\Delta U}{\Delta X} \div \frac{\Delta U}{\Delta Y} = \frac{P_X}{P_Y}$$

but

$$\frac{\Delta U}{\Delta X} \div \frac{\Delta U}{\Delta Y} = \frac{\Delta U}{\Delta X} \cdot \frac{\Delta Y}{\Delta U} = \frac{\Delta Y}{\Delta X} = MRS_{XY}$$

Thus, either approach leads to the same end result—namely, the consumer

[1] Note that this observation has nothing to do with the concepts of satiation and scarcity.

is in equilibrium when

$$MRS_{XY} = \frac{P_X}{P_Y} = \frac{MU_X}{MU_Y}$$

CORNER SOLUTIONS

In Figure 4-2 the individual specializes in the exclusive consumption of Y, spending his entire budget for OY* units. Indifference curve I_3 represents the highest utility level he can reach; therefore, his equilibrium point is at Y*. Economists call a solution occurring at one of the endpoints of the budget constraint line a *corner maximum*. If the budget line were flatter—for example, if the price of X were to fall—the individual might include some X in his basket. Thus, the fact that he is shown here to buy only Y does not permit us to infer that he has an implacable hatred of X.

What is the significance of corner solutions? Suppose we were to construct a 2,000-good model instead of a 2-good model, could we encounter the equivalent of the graphical corner solution? Do you buy some quantity of every good produced? If the subject consumer of a 2,000-good model did not buy some quantity of each of the 2,000 different goods, our more "realistic" model would yield a corner solution just as is the case with the simple 2-good model of Figure 4-2. Corner solutions, then, are highly realistic; they result whenever an individual does not buy all of the goods in a described universe.

The difficulty with corner solutions is that they severely cripple a geometric analysis. Fortunately, they present no obstacle to analysis when mathematical programming is employed. But that is beyond the scope of this book, so we will analyze only those two-dimensional graphical situations that have the interior solutions preferred by economists.

FIGURE 4-2

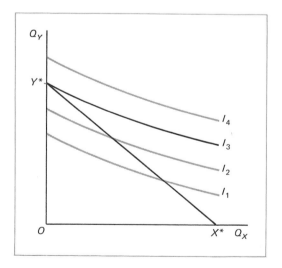

Concavity. Might consumers want to exclude the consumption of one good as they consume more of another? Some of us may like pizza *or* chocolate ice cream, while the thought of pizza *and* chocolate ice cream may leave us queasy.

Let us now consider the system of *concave* indifference curves in Figure 4-3. Suppose the consumer's budget line is Y^*X^* and that initially he is at point E on I_1. Although his $MRS_{XY} = P_x/P_y$, E cannot be a point of equilibrium; for, given his budget, it is possible for him to reach the higher indifference curve I_4 at Y^*. Once again, we have a corner solution; the consumer specializes completely in the consumption of Y.

FIGURE 4-3

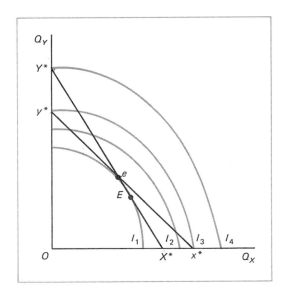

With the budget represented by y^*x^*, the consumer, if he begins at e, can reach a higher indifference curve in two ways. But which way will he go? He can reach I_3 by specializing entirely in X or entirely in Y. However, unlike the preceding case, we cannot tell what the consumer will do except to say that he will totally exclude X or totally exclude Y. The solution is, thus, in part indeterminate. This does not mean that the consumer is unable to decide what he will do; it means only that in this type of situation, with a two-good model, economic analysis is unable to predict the precise outcome. If Y is chocolate ice cream and X is pizza, a consumer who likes one *or* the other but not both together, may, on deciding to consume one of the goods, eliminate the other from his basket.

Concave indifference curves do not imply consumer irrationality. They do not show monomania in consumption. The peculiar situation of apparent total specialization is attributable to the use of a two-good model. The consumer excludes one good from his basket merely because he does not want

to consume it along with another good that he has decided to include in his basket. In a two-good world, the result of this is necessarily specialization in the consumption of one commodity. But in a model with more than two goods, exclusion of one good clearly produces no such specialization. Since most of our models are limited by their two-dimensional geometric nature to a two-good world, we shall terminate our discussion of concave indifference curves with the observation that we must keep in mind not only the powers but also the limitations of our model.

Straight-line indifference curves. What if a consumer cannot tell the difference between two goods—for example, the proverbial colorblind consumer who is trying to distinguish between a red shirt and a green shirt of the same style? Or what if a consumer is simply indifferent between 1 unit of one good and 1 unit of another good? (This is not the same as saying that he is indifferent to various *baskets* of goods.) In such a case, the marginal rate of substitution between the two goods is constant, and therefore the consumer's indifference curves must be straight lines.

A family of indifference curves for goods the consumer regards as *perfect substitutes* for one another is shown in Figure 4-4. As long as the consumer's budget line is not coincident with one of the indifference curves, the solution is determinate. In Figure 4-4, the consumer has reached the highest attainable indifference curve, I_3, by purchasing a basket containing only X.

FIGURE 4-4

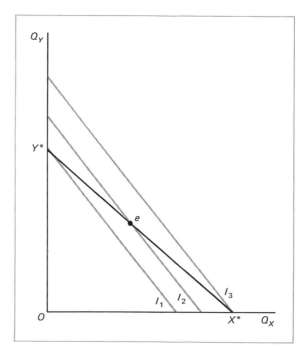

THE INFLUENCE OF EXTERNAL FORCES ON CONSUMER BEHAVIOR

INCOME CHANGES

If the consumer's income changes, his set of maximal baskets changes, and he must locate his optimal basket in the new maximal set. In Figure 4-5, the Y^*X^* curves show the behavior of a consumer under successively larger budgets. The parallel budget lines indicate that relative prices are held constant, so that we may isolate the consumer's behavior when his income changes. The optimal baskets arranged in the order of ascending budgets are A, A', and A'', respectively. The curve drawn through the points of tangency between indifference and budget curves is the *income-consumption* curve (*I-C*). It is the locus of all optimal baskets at various income levels, the prices of all goods remaining constant, and it allows us to locate the optimal basket for any given level of the consumer's income.

The income-consumption curve makes it possible to classify goods on the basis of what action the consumer takes in respect to them when his income changes. For example, in Figure 4-5, the income-consumption curve is positively sloped, showing that as the consumer's income increases, he takes more of both X and Y. Such goods, whose purchase correlates positively with changes in income, are classified as *superior* goods.

Consider the negatively sloped income-consumption curve of Figure 4-6. As in the preceding figure, X is a superior good; the consumer buys more of it with an increase in income. But his consumption of Y falls, and therefore Y is classified as an *inferior* good. The consumer's purchases of an inferior good change inversely with changes in his income.

As we have seen, it is possible for all goods to be superior. Is it also pos-

FIGURE 4-5

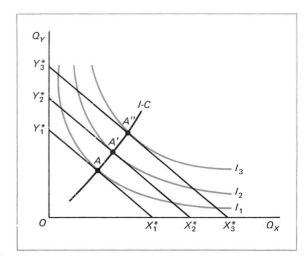

FIGURE 4-6

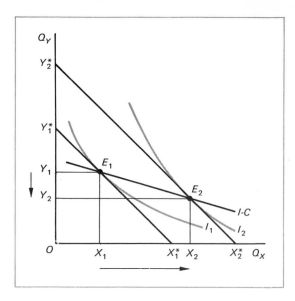

sible for all goods to be inferior? Suppose the consumer receives an income increment of ΔN dollars. If both X and Y are inferior, the consumer will not buy as many units of each as he did before he received his raise. If prior to his raise

$$N = Q_X P_X + Q_Y P_Y$$

it must be that after his increase in income that

$$N + \Delta N > (Q_X - \Delta Q_X)P_X + (Q_Y - \Delta Q_Y)P_Y$$

If the consumer's behavior is explained by assuming that he now *saves* some of his income, we must hold either that a third good, saving, has been added to our model—this third good being superior—or that we have a logical impossibility, since X or Y must include saving, and, hence, be superior after all.

In Figure 4-7, Y is shown as a superior good, and X is inferior. As in Figure 4-6, the income-consumption curve is negatively sloped. For Y to be the superior good and X to be inferior, the equilibrium point at the higher level of income must lie above and to the left of the initial equilibrium point, showing that with an increase in income, the consumer buys more Y and less X. If X is superior and Y inferior, the equilibrium point at the higher income level will lie to the right and below the initial point, showing that the consumer buys more X and less Y at a higher income level.

In Figure 4-8, the Y-content of the consumer's optimal basket remains OY_1 regardless of the size of his income and the amount of X in the basket. This produces an income-consumption curve parallel to the X axis. Since good Y does not respond to changes in the consumer's income, it is classified as a

FIGURE 4-7

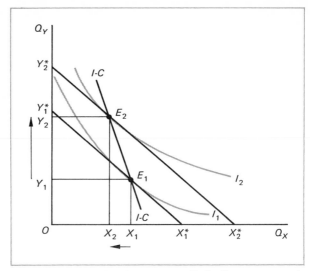

neutral good. (Such a good could be an absolute necessity in the consumer's life that is taken only in a definite quantity, irrespective of economic considerations—for example, insulin. Or it might be something that is consumed conventionally by rich and poor alike and that takes a small part of the consumer's budget, such as table salt.)

Goods as necessities and luxuries. Suppose that from a diagram incorporating an income-consumption curve, we plot as points on another curve the quantity of the good taken at given amounts of income. Suppose the points fall into the pattern of the curve in Figure 4-9(a). This type of curve is called an Engel curve, after Christian Lorenz Ernst Engel, who employed such curves in a study of economic welfare. In Figure 4-9(a), the curve shows that the *rate* of consumption of good X decreases as the consumer's income increases.

FIGURE 4-8

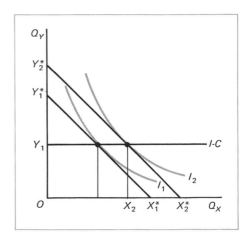

FIGURE 4-9

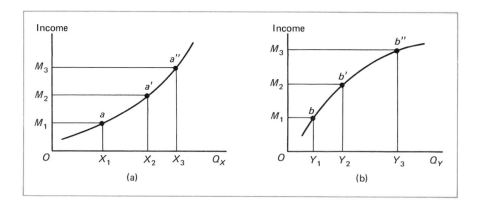

(a)

(b)

Since the curve has a positive slope, more of the good is purchased at higher income levels, so the good is superior, but the rate of increase is a declining function of income. In other words, as the consumer's income increases, he devotes successively smaller amounts of each increase to the purchase of good X. Food, clothing, and housing are goods that usually bear such a relationship to increasing income. The type of goods producing a curve such as that in Figure 4-9(a) would seem to be those commonly regarded as necessities.

The Engel curve in Figure 4-9(b) shows that the consumer spends ever greater amounts of an increasing income on good Y. Examples of such a good might be vacations, books, club memberships, diamonds, savings, and investments—goods commonly classified as luxuries.

Engel curves derived from a sample of households may help policy-makers to determine which goods are suitable objects for a sales tax. For example, if the aim of taxing policy is to avoid regressivity, a good whose purchase is very slightly expanded as income increases would not be a desirable object for a sales tax.

It must be observed, however, that Engel curves provide only guides, not scientifically derived rules of moral conduct. Analytical techniques must be applied to policy questions with discretion. If they yield information, they nevertheless cannot define objectives; these are the responsibility of the policy-maker. It may be that another loaf of bread is not more socially desirable than a Beethoven recording.

PRICE CHANGES

Suppose now that *ceteris paribus,* we vary the price of one good and trace the consumer's path to various points of equilibrium.

In Figure 4-10(a), with the prices of X and Y, the consumer's indifference map, and his income given, the individual is initially in equilibrium at G. If the

FIGURE 4-10

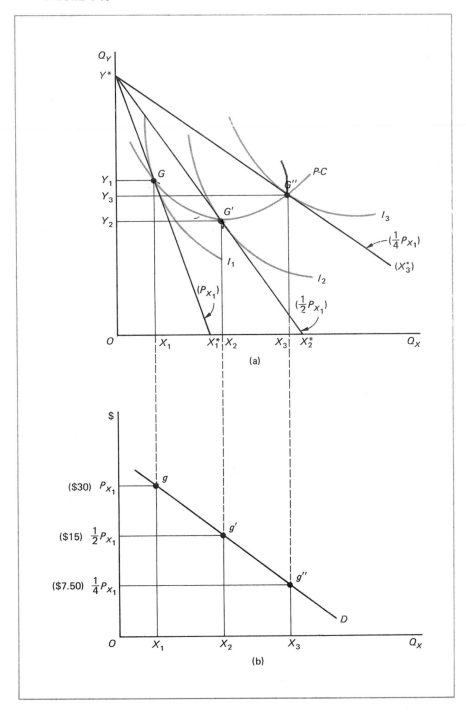

(a)

(b)

price of good X is lowered and everything else is held constant, the budget line will pivot counterclockwise around point Y^*. Suppose now from the initial equilibrium position, we reduce the price of X to one-half of its former amount, *ceteris paribus;* the consumer can buy twice as much X as before. The price reduction will cause the budget line to rotate counterclockwise around point Y^* until it reaches the intercept denoted by point X_2^*, such that $OX_2^* = 2(OX_1^*)$. If the consumer were specializing entirely in the purchase of X, he could buy twice as much X as before the price fall. With the price fall, the consumer achieves a new equilibrium at G'. Suppose now the price of X is cut to one-fourth its initial level. The budget line rotates counterclockwise until its point of intersection on the horizontal axis (not shown on the figure) becomes X_3^*, where $OX_3^* = 4(OX_1^*) = 2(OX_2^*)$. The consumer now establishes a new equilibrium at G''.

If we draw a smooth curve through points G, G', and G'', we obtain a *price-consumption* curve. It traces out the path of consumer adjustment as the price of X is varied, everything else remaining constant. Given the price of X, we can determine how much X (and Y) the consumer will buy.

Derivation of the consumer's demand curve. The price consumption curve gives us the information we need to derive the consumer's demand curve. Indeed, the price-consumption curve is a form of demand curve itself. It shows the amount of good Y the consumer is willing to give up in order to have good X. Similarly, the consumer's total money expenditures on good X show how much Y (all other goods) the consumer is foregoing in order to have a given amount of X.

To derive the customary consumer demand curve, we must use a graph that shows the money price of X on the vertical axis. The horizontal axis of the graph in Figure 4-10(b) is identical with that of the graph in Figure 4-10(a).

The price of X may be obtained directly from the commodity space diagram since it is implicit in the slope of the budget line; that is, $P_X = N/OX_1^*$. Let us assume that P_{X_1}, the initial price, is $30. If we subsequently halve the price, and then quarter it, $1/2\, P_{X_1}$ and $1/4\, P_{X_1}$ are $15 and $7.50, respectively. Once we have the price ordinates, we obtain the quantities bought at those prices from the indifference diagram. Drawing a smooth curve through the points obtained in Figure 4-10(b) produces the standard demand curve of the individual consumer for good X.[2]

A glance at the price-consumption curve of Figure 4-10(a) shows it to be U-shaped. Is there any particular significance to this? To find out, let us re-define good Y as the consumer's money income for the specified time period. This is equivalent to defining Y as all of the non-X goods the consumer can have in conjunction with a specific amount of X. Be redefining Y as his money income, we can observe directly the consumer's total expenditure for X at any

---

[2] We draw a smooth curve because we assume that there are no sharp breaks or discontinuities in the consumer's demand for good X and that if we had plotted points for many different prices, they would tend to lie in the pattern indicated by the demand curve of Figure 4-10.

given price. If the consumer buys nothing, he retains the quantity of his entire money income, OY^*. If he buys OX_1 units of X, he spends Y^*Y_1 dollars, and has OY_1 dollars left. When the price of X is lowered to $1/2\ P_{X_1} = \$15$, he spends more money on the good (Y_1Y_2 more); therefore, in the region GG', his demand for X is elastic with respect to price. In this region, the price-consumption curve has a negative slope. A negatively sloped price-consumption curve must always show increased expenditures for the subject good in response to price cuts. It is a sign of elastic demand in the associated region. The elastic demand for X in this region also can be noted on the demand curve in Figure 4-10(b). A reduction in price to one-half the initial level produces a more than compensating increase in the quantity sold.

If the price is now reduced from $1/2\ P_{X_1}$ to $1/4\ P_{X_1} = \$7.50$, the total amount the consumer spends on the good decreases. In the region $G'G''$ of the price-consumption curve, the demand for X must be inelastic. To show a reduction in expenditures, the price-consumption curve must be positively sloped. Inelastic demand for X is shown on the demand curve in Figure 4-10(b) in the region $g'g''$. Here, a reduction in price to one-fourth the initial amount produces a proportionately smaller increase in the quantity sold.

By elimination, we may conclude that the lowest point on a price-consumption curve shows unitary elasticity of demand. The region of zero slope of a price-consumption curve is indicative of unitary price elasticity of demand.

ISOLATION OF THE INCOME AND SUBSTITUTION EFFECTS

THE NORMAL, SUPERIOR GOOD

What motivations underlie the demand curve? We have derived the consumer's demand curve from his indifference map, observing him react to changes in the price of a particular good. But now let us attempt to discover the purely economic (not psychological) motivations behind the consumer's responses to changes in price.

What happens to a consumer when the price of a good is reduced? The demand curve of Figure 4-10 shows that he demands a larger quantity of good X. As the price of the good is reduced from P_{X_1} to $1/2\ P_{X_1}$, the consumer buys X_1X_2 more units of the good. Why does he do this?

Suppose the consumer is a confirmed meat eater; he likes many different meats, among them steak and ham. Suppose his butcher runs a special on ham. The law of demand leads us to predict that the consumer will buy more ham. Why? For one thing, ham has now become cheap in relation to steak. The meat-loving consumer will be led to substitute ham for steak in his menus because ham has become a bargain. Thus, with a reduction in the price of a good, the consumer becomes involved in the so-called *substitution effect*, whereby he tends to substitute the now cheaper good for the other now relatively more expensive goods in his basket.

Is there any other reason for the consumer to buy more *X*? The fall in the price of *X* means that he need give up less of his income to buy any given quantity of *X*; he has experienced an increase in his purchasing power. An increase in purchasing power can also be gained by a rise in one's income. Here, although the consumer's increased purchasing power has originated in the fall in the price of one of the goods he buys, we can conclude that some of the increase in his purchase of *X* must be due to an *income effect* occasioned by the price drop.

If our conjectures are correct, we may assert that the increase in the quantity demanded of *X* (X_1X_2 in Figure 4-10) is made up of two components: a substitution effect and an income effect. We may regard the increased quantity demanded (X_1X_2) as the *total effect*. Our next task will be to see if it is possible to decompose the total effect in order to discover just how much of the change in the quantity demanded of *X* is due to each effect.

Assume the consumer is initially in equilibrium at point E_0 in Figure 4-11. The price of *X* falls, the budget line rotates counterclockwise, and the consumer establishes a new equilibrium at point E_1. Since the fall in price has induced the consumer to increase his purchases of *X* from $O\bar{X}_0$ to $O\bar{X}_1$, we know that *X* is a normal good—that is, a good whose demand curve is negatively sloped. We know also that in the depicted price range, the demand for the good is elastic, since a price-consumption curve passing through the two equilibrium points would have a negative slope.

We now wish to decompose the movement from E_0 to E_1 into its constituent parts. In so doing, we shall isolate the substitution and income effects and be able to determine the classification of the good according to the income effect.

To isolate the substitution effect, we must eliminate the income-increasing effects of a price fall; we want to see what the consumer will do purely in

FIGURE 4-11

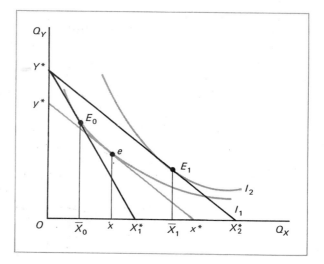

respect to an alteration in the relative values of the goods he buys. We shall return the consumer to his initial utility level by drawing a *fictitious* budget line, y^*x^*, parallel to the new actual budget line $Y^*X_2^*$, such that the fictitious constraint line is tangent to the initial indifference curve, I_1. By doing this, we utilize the *new* price ratio, shown by the slope of $Y^*Y_2^*$, but make the consumer no better off than he was before the fall in price. The leftward movement of the imaginary constraint line theoretically decompensates the consumer for the apparent gain in real income accruing to him in consequence of the price fall. Thus, without being made better off by the price fall, but being put in the position of having to adjust his subjective evaluation of the worth of X and Y in light of the market's new objective evaluation of the goods, we see that the consumer moves from E_0 on I_1 to e on the same indifference curve. Since the consumer is now reacting solely to the change in the relative values of the goods, we know he buys $\bar{X}_0 x$ more units of X as a substitute for the now relatively more expensive Y. Hence, the quantity $\bar{X}_0 x$ of the increase in quantity demanded produced by the fall in the price of X is accounted for by the substitution effect.

The remaining amount purchased, $x\bar{X}_1$ is taken because of the income effect. The fictitious "shift" of the budget line from $Y^*X_1^*$ to y^*x^* is not, of course, due to a change in the consumer's money income but merely represents the consumer's gain in purchasing power owing to a fall in the price of one of the goods he buys. The fall in the price of X gives him greater purchasing power; this is equivalent to an increase in money income, *ceteris paribus*. The income effect brings the consumer from point e on indifference curve I_1 to E_1 on indifference curve I_2, and is thus responsible for $x\bar{X}_1$ units of the increase in quantity demanded.

Since the income *effect* alone induces the consumer to purchase more of the good, as would an increase in income alone, X is a superior good.

By decomposing the increase in quantity demanded, we see that there are two forces producing the negative slope of a demand curve that could be derived from Figure 4-11. Both the income and substitution effects lead the consumer to buy more of the good in consequence of a fall in its price, so, in this case at least, one effect reinforces the other.

There is an erroneous belief that the demand for a superior good cannot be inelastic. This is not so, as is shown in Figure 4-12. Here, for practice, we shall reverse the preceding example and trace the substitution and income effects for a price increase. The inelastic nature of the demand for good X can be seen by drawing a price-consumption curve through the two points of equilibrium, E_0 and E_1. The curve is positively sloped and shows that the consumer will spend more on X if its price rises.

The consumer is initially in equilibrium at point E_0. Subsequently, the price of X is raised, and the budget line rotates clockwise around point Y^* to become $Y^*X_1^*$. The increase in price reduces the utility level of the consumer, and it falls to the lower indifference curve I_2, establishing a new equilibrium at E_1. The *total* effect of the price increase is the reduction of the consumer's purchase of X in the amount X_1X_2. To isolate the substitution and income ef-

FIGURE 4-12

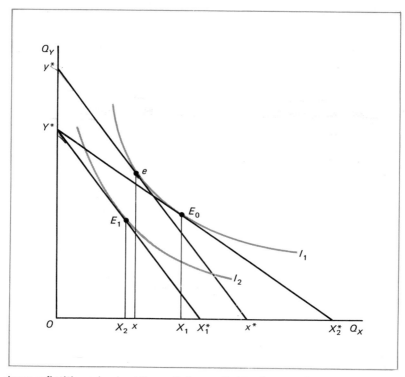

fects, we draw a fictitious budget line, y^*x^*, parallel to the new budget line and tangent to I_1 at e. We have returned the consumer to his old level of utility, and now we can see what he does in response to a pure price change. He moves from E_0 to e on the same indifference curve (I_1), substituting Y for the now more expensive X. The substitution effect, therefore, induces him to reduce his purchases of X in the amount X_1x. Figure 4-12 shows that this is not the entire reduction; there remains the amount xX_2. This is, of course, accounted for by the income effect. The consumer has been made poorer by the rise in the price of X, so he reduces his X consumption for that reason also.

We see that, as before, we are dealing with a superior good. The income effect causes the consumer to behave as if he had experienced a reduction in money income; he cuts his purchases of X just as he would have if his paycheck had been reduced. If purchases of the good correlate directly with changes in income, the good is superior.

SUBSTITUTION AND INCOME EFFECTS COMPARED

Good X in the preceding discussion is a normal good, since an increase in its price causes the quantity demanded to fall. Thus, in the case of the two examples illustrated in Figures 4-11 and 4-12, there are two reasons for the

negative slopes of the associated demand curves—the substitution and income effects, both of them working in the same direction.

In all cases, the substitution effect always involves a movement along the *initial* indifference curve. This is so because the technique of decomposition requires restoring the consumer to the ordinal utility index he held before the price change. The fictitious budget line, therefore, is always drawn tangent to the initial curve. Thus, decomposing the total effect to reveal the substitution effect involves a movement from the initial point of actual equilibrium to a second point of imaginary equilibrium on the same curve. In consequence of this, the substitution effect must *always* contribute to the negative slope of the demand curve. Since the substitution effect always involves an inverse relationship between changes in *price* and quantity demanded, it is always negative. That is,

$$\downarrow P \rightarrow \uparrow Q$$
$$\uparrow P \rightarrow \downarrow Q$$

What about the income effect? It measures the response of the consumer to a change in purchasing power. In Figure 4-11, the income effect involves a purchase by the consumer of an amount of X over and above the increase in quantity demanded that is motivated by the substitution effect. In Figure 4-12, the income effect reinforced the negative substitution effect. Because X became more expensive, the consumer cut his purchases of X by $X_1 x$ units. Because he was made poorer by the increase in price, he cut his purchases further by the amount $x X_2$. In both cases, the income effect works in the *same* direction as the negative substitution effect, yet the income effect is *positive*. For a superior good, in which changes in either real or money income are correlated positively with changes in the consumer's purchases of the subject good:

$$\uparrow N_r \rightarrow \uparrow Q$$
$$\downarrow N_r \rightarrow \downarrow Q$$

Real income and the amount of the good purchased move in the same direction.

THE NORMAL, INFERIOR GOOD

As we have seen, the substitution effect is always negative. But the income effect may be either positive or negative (or even absent), depending on whether the subject good is superior or inferior. If the good is inferior, the income effect must be negative, and, as one might infer from a reading of the preceding section, a negative substitution effect and a negative income effect work in *opposite* directions. Possibly, the two negative effects could cancel each other out, leading to no change in the consumer's purchases of the subject good.

Consumer Theory

The case of the normal, inferior good is shown in Figure 4-13. Good Z is a normal good; when the price of Z is reduced, the consumer moves from his initial equilibrium point at E_0 to a new optimal basket at E_1. Accordingly, he has increased his purchases in the amount Z_0Z_1. However, here the substitution and income effects work against each other. The substitution effect alone would induce the consumer to take more of the good than he actually does. If the substitution effect were the sole force behind the demand curve, the price fall would lead to an increase in quantity demanded equal to Z_0z and to an equilibrium at e. But in this case, the income effect works against the always negative substitution effect, pulling the consumer back from e to E_1, reducing the initial expansion by zZ_1 units. Here, the income effect is negative. An increase in the consumer's real income leads him to decrease his purchases of the good. The reason that he actually purchases more of it is that the negative substitution effect overpowers the negative income effect. (Remember, when the substitution and income effects have the same sign, they work against each other.) Good Z is a normal, but inferior, good. If the income effect moderates, rather than enhances, the direction of the substitution effect, the good is inferior.

Although an inferior good has a negatively sloped demand curve, there is only one reason for that negative slope, the substitution effect. The income effect, considered in isolation, works in the direction of producing a positively sloped demand curve.

FIGURE 4-13

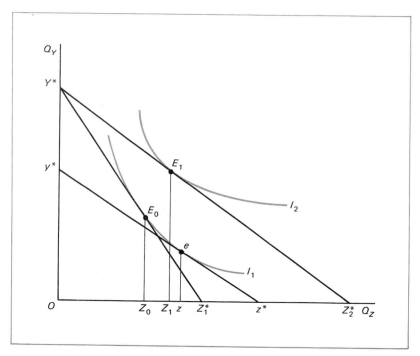

THE GIFFEN GOOD

In the case of an inferior good, the negative income effect tends to restrain the always negative, although relatively greater, substitution effect. Is it possible that the negative income effect might be so great as to more than offset the negative substitution effect, thus producing a *positively* sloped demand curve? It is possible, but it is highly improbable, because in the case of the vast majority of goods, the income effect, whether positive or negative, is minuscule compared to the substitution effect. The figures showing the decomposition of the total effect overstate the strength of the income effect merely to make the graphs easier to read. In actuality, the greater part of a consumer's response to a price change can be traced to the substitution effect—largely because of the very slight effect a small reduction in the price of most goods has on the consumer's total budget. If, for example, the price of a can of pork and beans is reduced, the consumer is made better off, but the degree of increase in his real income is so slight that it is unlikely he will be greatly motivated by it.

Figure 4-14 shows a curious situation. Initially, the consumer is purchasing OX_0 units of X, but after the price fall, represented by the rotation of the budget line from $Y^*X_1^*$ to $Y^*X_2^*$, the consumer *reduces* his purchases of X by X_0X_1 units. Decomposing the total effect—the reduction in quantity demanded,

FIGURE 4-14

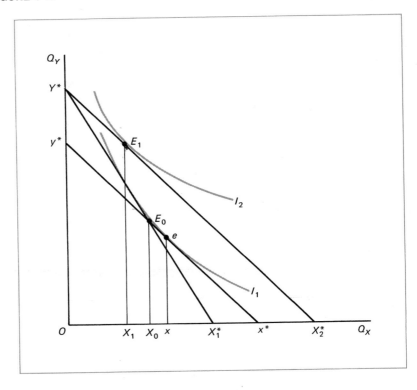

X_0X_1—we see that the negative substitution effect does induce the consumer to take more of the good. If there were no income effect, the consumer would substitute the now less expensive X for Y and increase the quantity he demands by X_0x units. But a negative income effect is present, which, in moving the consumer from e (the imaginary equilibrium point) to E_1 (the final equilibrium point), overcomes the negative substitution effect. This good conforms to the definition of an inferior good; if the consumer's income increases, he buys less of it. However, it cannot be a normal good; here quantity demanded is directly related to price; therefore, the demand curve for good X must have a positive slope. The law of demand is violated!

Can good X possibly be a "snob" good? A snob good is usually defined as a thing some people buy because they believe its consumption (or ownership) contributes to their social position. Since the ability to pay a high price for something may be evidence of an exalted economic and social position, snobs may buy more of a good, the *higher* its price. But such a description hardly seems applicable to the present good, which is, to the contrary, an inferior good—that is, a good one buys less of if his income increases. It would be a curious snob good that is purchased in greater quantity at lower income levels than at high levels. Indeed, this particular commodity could be characterized as an ultra-inferior good. When its price falls (as is shown in the figure), the income effect shows the consumer decreasing his purchase of X (as is the case with the ordinary inferior, but normal, good). But in this case, because the income effect is so large relative to the substitution effect, the subject consumer actually does reduce his consumption of X. Even though price changes and the quantities demanded of snob goods may seem to be directly related, as is the case with the present good, one would expect the income effect of goods having snob appeal to be positive.[3]

What kind of a good can this be? It may seem that we are merely drawing a diagram with such a large negative income effect that graphically the hypothetical consumer buys less of the good when its price falls. Suppose, however, that the good in question is a major staple in the diet of persons who expend a very large part of their incomes on it. In such circumstances, any change in the price of the good is a momentous economic event to its consumers. In a number of Asiatic countries, rice may be such a good. When the price of such an item falls, it will have a great effect on the lives of its habitual consumers. The negative income effect allows them to turn to alternative sources of food energy. The difference between this good and the ordinary inferior good is that here the good requires such a great part of the income of its buyers that the income effect is enormous. The good is inferior; it has a negative income effect; and the negative income effect is so large it more than offsets the negative substitution effect. Conversely, if price rises, people buy more of the good. If a great part of one's income is expended on the good, a rise in its price will profoundly affect real income, and the income effect will be

---

[3] An analysis of the demand for snob goods, showing that the law of demand is not violated by the apparent direct relationship of price and quantity changes, is included in Chapter 5.

large. Consumers will feel so much poorer as a result of the price increase that they will decrease their consumption of alternative sources of carbohydrates and buy more rice.

A good that is so strongly inferior as to have a positively sloped demand curve is called a "Giffen good" in honor of Sir Robert Giffen, who, many years ago, reportedly noticed that Irish peasants bought more potatoes (bread in the case of the English poor) when the price of this entrenched staple rose. Giffen goods are rarely encountered, if at all, in a modern industrial economy. Even when they do occur, the majority of consumers do not react to price changes in a way that produces a positively sloped *market* demand curve. Thus, although it is possible for rice to be an ultra-inferior good in certain parts of the world and under certain conditions, the worldwide market demand curve would steadfastly continue to slope downward, and the behavior of the quantity of rice sold on organized commodity exchanges would conform to the law of demand. It is probably safe to assert that in real markets, taken as a whole, there are no exceptions to the law of demand.

SUMMARY

The consumer's goal is to reach the highest attainable indifference curve. His ability to reach his goal is limited by his purchasing power. His budget line depicts graphically the limits of his ability to maximize his utility. Its slope is determined by the relative prices of the items that he buys. The consumer is said to be in equilibrium (he has maximized his total utility) when his total budget is allocated among the various objects of consumer choice in such a way that the marginal rate of substitution of one good for the other is equal to the ratio of their prices. This is depicted graphically by the tangency of the budget line and an indifference curve.

Goods may be classified as superior or inferior. If the consumer purchases more of a good when his income increases, the good is said to be superior. If he purchases less of it under the same conditions, it is said to be inferior. Regardless of whether goods are superior or inferior, they are normal if greater quantities are purchased when their prices fall. If a smaller quantity of a good is purchased when its price falls, the behavior of its consumers violates the law of demand. Such a commodity is classified as a Giffen, or ultra-inferior, good. The phenomenon of Giffen goods is considered to be virtually nonexistent.

Isolation of the so-called substitution and income effects helps to explain the states of superiority, inferiority, and ultra-inferiority. The substitution and income effects also help to explain the underlying *economic* reasons for consumer demand for a specific good.

The body of the theory of consumer behavior has undergone, and is undergoing, repeated modifications. A few of the more recent developments are examined in the next chapter.

5

Further Topics in the Theory of Consumer Behavior

Here, we will refine and expand the basic models of consumer behavior developed in the two preceding chapters. In general, the material contained in this chapter is more difficult than that presented in the rest of the book, but it will be worth the reader's efforts because it explains some rather interesting phenomena.

AN EXAMPLE OF INDIFFERENCE CURVE ANALYSIS

A community's attempts to ameliorate economic inequities often go awry. One reason for this may be the general lack of rigorous methods of analysis in the social sciences, the very disciplines concerned with such problems. Economists, however, have had somewhat greater success than other social scientists in creating rigorous techniques for analyzing those social problems commonly classified as "economic." Thus, they may be able to offer informed guidance to the community's policymakers whenever these leaders are confronted by those (usually difficult) social problems.

The exercise that follows has a threefold purpose. First, it shows the application of the indifference curve technique to a well-defined social problem. Second, it clarifies the nature and extent of the benefits and costs of alternative social programs. Finally, and probably most important, it shows the limitations of analytic technique; recognition of these limitations is particularly important in

the solution of problems involving human beings. It is essential to remember that the purpose of the rigorous analysis of social problems is to provide informed guidance for the policy-maker, whose final decision ideally must be an adroit combination of science and art. Uninformed art and untempered science are both likely to be inhumane.

One major social problem is the plight of those unable to earn sufficient income to maintain a decent standard of living. Common solutions are to allow them price concessions on essential items or to grant them an income supplement. The first method usually consists of some kind of food-stamp program. Needy persons receive an allotment of food stamps that permit them to buy community-approved goods at prices below those charged to all other customers. When the merchant turns these stamps in to the supervising governmental agency, he is reimbursed by the public treasury for the difference between the amount the general public would pay and the amount actually paid by aided persons. The income supplement method takes the form of outright relief payments or a negative income tax. Figure 5-1 compares both methods.

Assume initially that the consumer's budget line is AB; he achieves equilibrium at point 1 on indifference curve I_0. If the prices of selected goods including X are reduced, the consumer's budget line will rotate counterclockwise around A, becoming AB'. With a lower price for X, the consumer's utility index rises, and he attains a new equilibrium at 2 on indifference curve I_1. In doing so, he expands his purchases of X in the amount X_1X_2. Since the price has been made lower, through food stamps or a similar device, only to selected consumers, the general public faces prices given by the slope of AB. The merchant must be reimbursed for the difference between what the food-stamp user pays and what he would pay for the same amount of the good if he were buying it at the regular market price.

Let the vertical axis measure the money income of the consumer; his income is, thus, OA. Before he receives the food stamps, he was buying OX_1 quantity of X, for which he would pay a total of CA dollars. When he can buy X at the lower price, he consumes OX_2 units of the good and pays a total of DA dollars for it. The fall in price has induced him to increase his own expenditures for the good in the amount of DC dollars. The amount DA, however, does not fully pay for OX_2 units of X. How much is this quantity of the good worth at its prevailing market price? If the same consumer, unsubsidized, were to purchase OX_2 units of the good, he would follow along the budget curve AB until he reached point F. His total expenditures for OX_2 units at the market price would be GA dollars. The subsidized consumer, then, pays only DA dollars for a quantity of the good worth GA dollars. This leaves the amount $GA - DA = GD$ dollars that must be refunded to the seller by the government.

Suppose, now, that the income supplement method is used to improve the needy consumer's position. The object of the program is to advance the consumer to the same utility index that could be attained by the price reduction. Since the needy consumer will face the same market prices as everybody

FIGURE 5-1

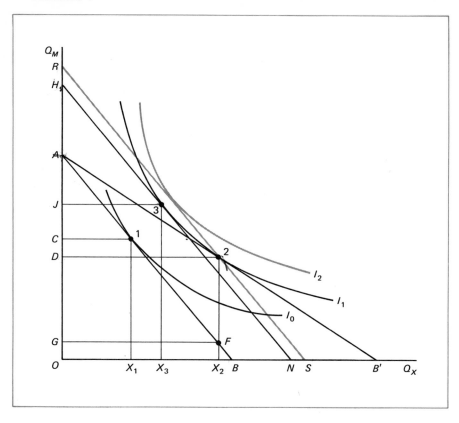

else, his new budget line, *HN*, must be parallel to *AB*. The amount of the income supplement necessary to place him on the desired indifference curve, *I'*, is *AH*.

A comparison of the two methods of aiding a needy consumer reveals several important differences. The most obvious distinction is the difference in the cost to the government. A subsidized price policy costs the public treasury *GD* dollars; the income supplement requires *AH* dollars. Since *AH* < *GD*,[1] the income supplement program is less costly to the taxpayer. Another possible advantage of the supplemental income policy from the taxpayer's point of view is that the selective price reduction policy appears to involve spillover benefits in the form of subsidy to the producers of good *X*.[2] The income grant

[1] We know that *AH* < *GD*, since *GD* = *F2* and *F2* exceeds the vertical distance *AH* between the parallel lines *AB* and *HN*.

[2] A benefit is said to "spill over" if it confers utility on some party other than the anticipated primary beneficiary. Thus, when a home owner plants a tree in his front yard, he probably does so primarily to please himself, but it is likely that numerous passers-by will also enjoy the tree.

is paid directly to the person for whom the aid is specifically intended, and he disposes of the supplement as he sees fit. The price-reduction program forces the government to pick out specific goods for the consumer's augmented consumption, which inevitably benefits the sellers of those goods. Their total receipts under the two-price policy are GA, while under the income supplement program, their total revenues would fall to HJ. Whether this is of consequence to the general public is, of course, a public policy question.

How does the needy consumer feel about the two programs? The diagram suggests that he would be neutral, since the ultimate result of either program is to put him on the same indifference curve. The loss of $X_2 X_3$ units of X involved in moving from point 2 to point 3 is compensated by the extra purchasing power, in the amount DJ, that he retains for non-X goods. However, we observe that he can be made just as well off at point 3 as he is at 2 for less money. This suggests that the consumer puts a tangible value on being allowed a freer choice in the determination of the composition of his basket of goods. To further illustrate this, we will suppose the government decides to use an income supplement program, but instead of maintaining the consumer at a specific utility index, it gives him the total amount paid to producers under the two-price program; in other words, the consumer is provided with an income supplement sufficient to buy the basket of goods indicated by point 2. The results of this approach are shown in Figure 5-1.

Initially, the consumer is in equilibrium at point 1, at which I_0 and AB are tangent. A lowering of price would permit the consumer to purchase the basket indicated by point 2. Suppose that instead of distorting the price structure by granting price reductions to selected individuals, the government grants an income supplement that would enable the grantees to purchase the same baskets they would buy under a price reduction program. The budget line of such a consumer, then, moves to the right, parallel to the initial budget line, until it passes *through* point 2. The new budget line is RS, and the amount of the income supplement is AR.

It is obvious that an income supplement paid directly to the individual makes him better off than allowing him to pay a lower price for selected items. Although the individual *can* buy the basket at 2, he will not do so, since the income supplement allows him to buy a basket of goods lying on a higher indifference curve, I_2.

Apparently, it may be argued that if a society has in mind a definite benefit, expressed in terms of dollars, that it wishes to confer on specific individuals—say, poor people—dollar-for-dollar, a direct income supplement will make the aided individual better off than a program of selective price reductions. Why is this?

The answer is very simple if the question is stated, "Which would you prefer, a reduction in the prices of *some* of the things you buy or a reduction in the prices of *all* of them?" An increase in one's income, in effect, lowers the prices of all goods.

As we have seen, a reduction in the price of a specific good produces

two phenomena, the income and substitution effects. A reduction in the price of any one good makes the consumer better off in the sense that his income now goes further; he can buy more of all goods. At the same time, the usually more powerful substitution effect leads the consumer to purchase more of the subject good in place of all other goods, which, in relation to the subject good, have become more expensive. A price reduction "biases" the consumer's choice in favor of the good whose price has fallen. Thus, when food stamps are given to a needy consumer, unquestionably the individual is made better off, but the composition of his basket is now weighted in favor of those goods for which the stamps have been provided. It is true that there is an income effect; the individual will be able to buy more of all goods, but the more powerful substitution effect will outweigh the income effect of a selective price reduction, and the individual will be led to purchase relatively more of those goods for which he has stamps.

An income supplement allows the aided consumer an unfettered choice within the limits of his augmented income. He is free to dispose of his income in the way that pleases him most. No substitution effect is involved in a direct income benefit. There is no distortion of the price structure inducing the individual to alter the composition of his basket in a particular direction. Since an income supplement increases the consumer's *general* purchasing power, it will make him better off than the selective price reductions of a food-stamp program.

There are, of course, arguments for selective price reductions. For example, a common fear is that persons given income supplements will utilize their additional purchasing power unwisely, spending too little on the things they "should" have and too much on things they don't need. The merits of this contention are not within the scope of microeconomic theory. *If* the argument is taken as valid for the purposes of analytic comment, it is true, as we have seen, that selective price reductions can be used to bias the composition of a consumer's basket in the direction of those items the community defines as "good." Say there is a general conviction that needy people will spend an income supplement on some more milk but a great deal more beer, and the public feels this is undesirable. It can induce greater milk consumption by issuing food stamps for milk instead of the income supplement.

A text on economic theory should not disregard the practical politics of a situation. Often, appalling as it may seem to some people, the decision on what goods should have their prices reduced is made in the light of which producers, rather than which consumers, need help. As a result, a basic guide to the selection of what items should be included in a food-stamp program is often simply a matter of identifying those products of which there is a surplus.

Moreover, selective price reductions are likely to be *less inflationary* than the large-scale granting of substantial income supplements, especially if there is a surplus of the price-reduced items. Granting income supplements to households with high marginal propensities to consume (that is, households that tend to spend for consumption a high proportion of any increase in their

income) may help to raise the prices of items widely consumed by self-sufficient households.

The purpose of this section has been, not to discuss alternative issues in social policy, but to show what light economic analysis can cast on fundamental economic problems and also to show how, in most cases, the application of analysis requires tempering with judgment and experience.

AN UPWARD–SLOPING MARKET "DEMAND CURVE" FOR A NORMAL GOOD

Thorstein Veblen, a leading figure of the American institutionalist school of economics, coined the well-known phrase "conspicuous consumption" in his celebrated work, *The Theory of the Leisure Class.*[3] Goods that are supposed to arouse others to envy or admire their possessors are the prizes sought by conspicuous consumers. Harvey Leibenstein has subjected Veblen's colorful writing to an interesting analytical study,[4] in which he calls such phenomena "the Veblen effect." This section is based on his work, with the modification that consumers use the *price* of a good as an indicator of its quality. For example, an individual shopping for a wedding present may choose a higher priced but possibly otherwise less desirable good in order to show the recipients that money is no object. Similarly, buyers unable to use any criteria other than the respective prices of two goods of the same general type may buy the more expensive one on the assumption that if one brand costs more than the other, it must be a better product. If the good is to be shown to or shared with others who also use price as an indicator of intrinsic worth (of either the good or its purchaser), a large part of the utility of the good is imparted by its price. An example of this phenomenon can be found in the liquor industry. Vodka is made with virtually pharmaceutical homogeneity. Yet, there is considerable variation in the prices of different brands bearing identical proofs. Moreover, a number of distillers produce vodkas of the same proof under several different brand names, promoting them in different markets at different prices for each brand. The president of one distillery, when asked the difference between two very differently priced brands of his firm's products, replied, "It's largely a matter of labels." We can assume, then, that the insecure or unsure consumer, seeking to please his similarly insecure guests, will purchase the higher priced vodka in an (often successful) effort to persuade them of his good taste, knowledgeability, and magnanimity.

In effect, for such buyers the price of the good is itself one of the major qualities they are buying. Such behavior cannot be described as irrational. A major reason for buying the good is for its buyer to be admired or envied. If

[3] Thorstein Veblen, *The Theory of the Leisure Class* (New York: The New American Library, undated). Originally published in 1899.

[4] Harvey Leibenstein, "Bandwagon, Snob, and Veblen Effects in the Theory of Consumer Demand," *The Quarterly Journal of Economics* (May 1950), pp. 183–207.

the price produces this effect, the consumer may have received his money's worth.

A demand function for a good of the Veblen type must incorporate the price of the good as if it were two different variables. In one sense, it performs its usual function; once the demand curve is located, it determines the quantity of the good demanded. In its other role, price is one of the determinants of the position and shape of the demand curve, being used by the customer to give him an insight into an intrinsic quality of the good that he cannot see or is afraid others cannot see. Thus, abstracting from the nonprice determinants of demand, we may define the demand function for a Veblen-type good as

$$(Q_v)_D = f(P_v, P_r)$$

Where P_v represents price as used in the conventional demand function and P_r represents the price as one of the determinants of the shape and position of the demand curve. The expression holds that the quantity demanded of the Veblen good is a function of its price, but that price has two different roles. In the consumer's decision-making process, the price of the good itself helps to determine the consumer's attitude toward it. Once this attitude is set, the price may fluctuate without affecting the consumer's basic assessment of quality. Then the price of the good operates as in the conventional case, the quantity demanded varying inversely with changes in price.

To explore this idea further, consider Figure 5-2, in which good V is a Veblen good. Assume that D_1 is the demand curve for the Veblen good when

FIGURE 5-2

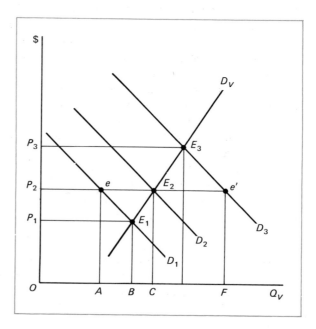

the price of the good is P_1—more precisely when $P_r = P_1$. Suppose this is the price that sets the consumer's attitude toward the good. At price P_1, consumers will buy quantity OB of the good.

What happens if the price rises to OP_2? Do consumers ride up the demand curve and cut their purchases to OA, or does the whole demand curve shift rightward so that they buy OC units? What they do depends on the psychological effect of the price change. If the price OP_1 sets consumers' tastes for the good, and if they believe, despite an actual market price of OP_2, that the good basically is "an OP_1 good," they will ride up demand curve D_1 to point e, cutting their purchases of the good by AB units. On the other hand, if each consumer believes that other consumers, and the people who are watching him, judge the good to be more desirable because of its increase in price to OP_2, the demand curve will shift to D_2. Then, if the good can be had for OP_2 dollars in the market, the quantity demanded will be OC. Once the price P_2 has established the character of the good in consumers' minds, should there be any change in price, consumers will move along demand curve D_2. For example, a rise in price to OP_3 will not cause the demand curve to shift to D_3 unless consumers once again subjectively reassess the character of the good. If they do—that is, if the good becomes intrinsically more desirable because of an increase in its price—the demand curve will again shift to the right.

The curve D_v may be thought of as the market demand curve for a Veblen-type good. It appears to violate the law of demand, since its positive slope indicates a direct relationship between changes in price and quantity. Actually, it is probably sounder analytically to regard it as a *quasi-demand curve* (and thus not strictly within the purview of the law of demand), since it is simply the path of equilibrium points on separate and well-defined market demand curves, for example, D_1, D_2, D_3. The equilibrium solution on each market demand curve is the point at which the actual price is equal to the representational price. Curve D_v merely identifies the locus of these points. Thus, owing to the twofold nature of price, the law of demand is not violated.

The derivation of the D_v curve (the Veblenesque demand curve, if you wish) makes possible the isolation of what Leibenstein calls the Veblen effect. We shall use Leibenstein's method here, although as pointed out previously, in this section the Veblen good is defined differently from the usage in the original Leibenstein analysis.

Let us start from the equilibrium solution at E_1. Suppose the price is increased to OP_2. Those consumers whose tastes are not influenced by the change in price (i.e., those who consider good V to still be basically a "P_1 good") will ride up the demand curve D_1 from E_1 to e, reducing the quantity they demand by AB units. Leibenstein calls this action the "price effect." On the other hand, consumers who interpret the increase in the price of the good as an increase in its desirability will move the demand curve rightward to D_2. Then, at price OP_2, the quantity demanded will be OC, the increase over the previous amount being AC. This distance ($AC = eE_2$) shows the magnitude of

what Leibenstein calls the "Veblen effect." Combining the price and Veblen effects, which work in opposite directions, the "net effect" is $OC - OA = BC$ units. The overall increase in quantity demanded shows that consumers rely heavily on the price of good V in forming their judgments about it.

The differences between Veblen and Giffen goods are quite marked. A Giffen good (see Chapter 4) in no way qualifies as a "snob good." It is an ultra-inferior good, a commonplace in the lives of its consumers, and they do not use its price to judge its quality. The Veblen good does, however, fulfill the requirements for an item of conspicuous consumption. Concerned that they do not know much about the good, or that their acquaintances may question their tastes, the insecure consumers of a Veblen good hope its price will speak to, and for, them.

THE MEASUREMENT OF UTILITY

Is it, or is it not, possible to measure utility? In 1953, in a monumental work called *The Theory of Games and Economic Behavior,* mathematician John von Neumann and economist Oskar Morgenstern proposed a method for stating *intra*personal degrees of utility in cardinal numbers.[5] This kind of cardinal utility is different from that of the classical and neoclassical cardinalists and for that reason is often called "von Neumann-Morgenstern (or simply N-M) cardinal utility."[6]

Up to now our discussion of consumer choice has omitted any considerations of uncertainty. We have assumed that when, for example, the consumer chooses between X and Y, he acts on the belief that the goods are what they are purported to be. In fact, the consumer may be taking a chance when he buys goods, and it is possible that he has some idea of the chance he is taking and that this probabalistic knowledge affects his decision. For example, say a consumer prefers cantaloupe to a bottle of cola. But he knows it is almost certain that the bottle of cola will conform to his idea of what such a soft drink should be like while melons can be disappointing. Suppose he estimates that there is a 99.9 percent chance that the bottle of soft drink will turn out as expected but that there is only a 30 percent chance that the melon will be good. Taking these probabilities into consideration, the consumer may well buy a bottle of cola rather than the melon, despite the fact that he prefers melon. If the probability of the melon being good could be increased—say, to 60 percent—perhaps he would choose the melon.

If probabilities can be assigned to the goodness of melons, records, and

---

[5] John von Neumann and Oskar Morgenstern, *The Theory of Games and Economic Behavior* (Princeton, N.J., Princeton University Press, 1953). Originally published in 1944. This section is based on material contained in Chapter 1, section 3, pp. 15–31.

[6] The cardinal utility theory of Chapter 3 is essentially neoclassical. For a brief presentation of the work of classical and neoclassical economists see Charles L. Cole, *The Economic Fabric of Society* (New York: Harcourt Brace Jovanovich, 1969), especially Chapters 3, 4, and 6.

light bulbs, uncertainty changes to risk. Uncertainty implies a total absence of information of how things will turn out; risk, on the other hand, involves knowing something about the probability of an event occurring.

There is no question that the existence of risk changes a choice-making situation. If a consumer is informed of the probability of his attaining a desired end, his choice-behavior is modified significantly from what it would be in the presence of absolute certainty or total uncertainty. For example, if it were absolutely certain that a particular number would turn up on every spin of a roulette wheel, a casino would attract no customers. Individuals will not bet against each other on a "sure thing." At the other extreme, suppose one were playing roulette with a wheel on which *the numbers themselves* were constantly changing in a random fashion so that the numbers were not limited to those on the board, or wheel; then no probability could be assigned to the likelihood of any number turning up. Obviously, a game based on a roulette wheel of infinite probabilities would be preposterous! No one would wager on the outcome of such a procedure. It is when the probabilities of a particular event happening are known that people are willing to declare with an objective numeraire—money—their expectancy of that given event happening.[7] If expectational states are objectified in a numerical form, they can be arranged to form an index, and perhaps that index might partake of some of the characteristics of a utility scale.

Suppose that a consumer is confronted with several prizes, as one might be on a television game show—a trip to Europe (t), a luxurious automobile (a), a mink coat (m), and a lifetime supply of soap (s). She will have a definite idea of her preferences; say they are

$$t \; \mathbf{P} \; m \; \mathbf{P} \; a \; \mathbf{P} \; s$$

The trip to Europe is the highest ranked alternative, the lifetime supply of soap the lowest. Suppose we now assign numerical values—utility indexes—to the two choices representing the extreme points on her utility scale, the highest- and lowest-ranked alternatives. Assume

$$U_t = 1{,}000$$

$$U_s = 1$$

As pointed out in the section on comparative orderings in the previous chapter, the values assigned to U_t and U_s could be any numbers, as long as the consumer's ranking is preserved. We could just as well have decided that $U_t = 10{,}432$ and $U_s = -17$. What we are doing here is much like the calibration of a

---

[7] A *numeraire* is a counter. Pounds, dollars, quarts, degrees of temperature, and so on, are all numeraires. The most common numeraire in economics is obviously money and, when referred to a specific economy, is the basic monetary unit of that economy. Thus, the dollar is the monetary numeraire in the United States and Canada, while in Japan it is the yen.

centigrade thermometer. The boiling point of water is assigned the value 100° C., and the freezing point is assigned the value of 0° C. The same phenomena are represented on the Fahrenheit scale as 212° F. and 32° F., respectively. Whichever values we choose for the end points, we can make equal divisions in the interval between them to produce a utility scale. The scale is an empty invention, however, unless we can place the consumer's other alternatives—m and a—on it in proper relation to the end points and to each other. This determination is our next task.

Suppose now, somewhat in the fashion of daytime television, we play a game with the consumer. We bring out a bowl filled with 100 colored balls. The consumer is blindfolded and told that if she draws a red ball she may have her highest ranked choice, the trip to Europe, but if she draws a green ball she will receive the lowest ranked alternative, the lifetime supply of soap. At all times, she is informed accurately of the number of balls of each color in the bowl so that she knows precisely the probability of achieving her most desired goal. At the same time, she offered the option of *not* drawing a ball from the bowl and taking her second-ranked choice, the mink coat, home with her.

We begin with the bowl filled with 100 red balls. It is absolutely certain that the consumer will win the trip to Europe; nevertheless we go through the formality of asking her if she would prefer the absolute certainty of a trip to Europe to the absolute certainty of a mink coat. And, of course, she chooses the trip to Europe. Now we remove 1 red ball from the bowl and replace it with a green ball. The balls are thoroughly stirred to make sure that any drawing will be perfectly random. The certainty of a trip to Europe is gone. There is now a 99 percent chance that she can still go to Europe but, at the same time, 1 chance in 100 that a draw from the bowl will give her the lifetime supply of soap. Under these circumstances, we again ask her, "Which do you prefer, a 99 percent chance of going to Europe or the absolute certainty of having a mink coat?" Let us say that she still opts for Europe. Now we make the odds more adverse by removing another red ball, replacing it with a second green ball. On the next draw from the bowl, she is 98 percent certain of going to Europe, but there is a 2 percent chance she will win the soap. Even so, she says she would rather try for Europe than win a mink coat. Suppose now, to hurry things along, we take 28 more red balls out of the bowl, replacing them with 28 green balls. The probability of a trip to Europe has dropped to 70 percent, while chances are now 30 out of 100 that she will get a lifetime supply of soap. By now, the odds favoring a trip to Europe may have become too adverse; the consumer says she prefers the certainty of the second-ranked mink coat to a 7 out of 10 chance of going to Europe.

We have gone too far. We are looking for that particular probability of going to Europe which will make the consumer indifferent between that opportunity and the certainty of winning the mink coat. Suppose it turns out that when 89 of the 100 balls in the bowl are red, the consumer declares herself indifferent to winning the mink coat or participating in a drawing that gives her an 89 percent chance of going to Europe and an 11 percent chance of a

lifetime supply of soap. In other words, at this point, the consumer would have to flip a coin to choose between the mink coat and the *drawing*. (Note that the choice is *not* between the mink and the trip.)

If the consumer is indifferent between the mink coat and the drawing, the utility index of the mink coat must be the sum of the probabilistically weighted utilities assigned to the end point items. The weighted indexes are obtained by multiplying the utility index assigned to each event by the probability of the occurrence of the event. The desired utility index must be given by the formula

$$U_m = P(U_t) + (1 - P)(U_s)$$

Where P is the probability of going to Europe and $(1 - P)$ is necessarily the probability of winning a lifetime supply of soap. Substituting in the above formula, we have

$$U_m = 0.89(1,000) + 0.11(1)$$

$$= 890 + 0.11$$

$$U_m = 890.11 \text{ utils}$$

To obtain the utility index of the automobile, we simply repeat the process. The same procedure can be used for any number of alternatives, so we can build up a whole scale of cardinal numbers showing the utility a consumer assigns to a risky prospect.

Has the von Neumann-Morgenstern procedure vindicated the cardinalist school and made possible a wholly introspective theory of consumer behavior? The numbers *are* cardinal. To say that $U_t = 1,000$ utils and $U_m = 890.11$ utils seems to be saying something more than t **P** m. But even if the numbers are cardinal, do they form the indexes hypothesized by the members of the cardinalist school? In the traditional sense, cardinal utility numbers accurately express the intensity of an individual's desire for particular goods. If a cardinal index can be expressed, an ordinal ranking must be a corollary—that is, if we know how strongly a consumer wants each of a variety of goods, we can rank those goods in order of preference. In the ordinary sense, the reverse ordering procedure cannot be the case, but this seems to be what has happened here. The consumer first gave an ordinal ranking of the goods; *then* we derived a cardinal index. The *sequence* of these acts is important. For the moment, assume the numbers we have obtained are indexes in the traditional cardinalist sense. In that case, the individual will rank the trip to Europe first and the mink coat second *because* she attaches the indexes 1,000 and 890.11, respectively, to them. In the von Neumann-Morgenstern procedure, this is not the case; the indexes 1,000 and 890.11 have been attached to the European trip and the mink because the consumer ordinally ranked them first and second, respectively. There is a great deal of difference between the two cases, and

that difference is one of causation. The traditional cardinalist school would say that the trip to Europe is the most highly (subjectively) valued alternative because it confers 1,000 units of utility on the consumer. The von Neumann-Morgenstern index says the trip to Europe has the index 1,000 assigned to it because it was the highest number in a set of numbers and was placed at the top of the consumer's preferences. It appears, then, that insofar as the consumer's relative preferences for various goods are concerned, von Neumann-Morgenstern cardinal utility provides no greater information than the rankings of the ordinalist school.

In fact, it does not provide even that information. In von Neumann-Morgenstern utility theory, *risky* choice is introduced as an element. Thus, the choice situation is different from that in the ordinary ordinalist case, and, accordingly, the information we obtain is different. In our example, the consumer was forced to gamble under conditions of known risk. She was offered the certainty of a mink coat as against the possibility of a trip to Europe. Suppose another consumer is brought in to play the game. Assume that her ordering reverses the first two rankings of the first player: she prefers the mink coat to the trip to Europe. Following our usual procedure, we assign an index of 1,000 utils to the mink coat. We know that the desired utility index of the trip to Europe must be less than 1,000, yet when given the alternative between the certainty of a trip to Europe and the known probability of a mink coat, the second player always chooses the second-ranked trip to Europe. Is she irrational? No, she simply dislikes risk, and given the choice between the certainty of having a less desired outcome, she prefers it to the risk of not having a more desired outcome. This is what von Neumann-Morgenstern cardinal utility measures, the degree of risk aversion of an individual.

Consider once again the first consumer. Suppose her index for the coat were 750 utils, rather than 890.11. Would this show that she likes the mink coat any less? We cannot tell. All we know for certain is that she is more willing to take a chance. That may be because there is a greater gap between the utility to her of the trip and that of the coat (i.e., she likes the coat relatively less); but it is just as likely, perhaps more so, that she simply has a greater preference for gambling—for taking a chance. Measuring a person's assessment of risky outcomes is an achievement, but it seems, unfortunately, to have slight bearing on the theory of consumer choice.

THE ELIMINATION OF THE SUBJECTIVE ELEMENT IN THE THEORY OF CONSUMER BEHAVIOR— REVEALED PREFERENCE THEORY

Is there any possibility of making an empirical investigation of the nature of indifference curves? If they do exist, is it reasonable to suppose that they are convex with respect to the origin? Does it really make any difference to economic theory whether consumers think of their utility in cardinal or ordinal

terms or, indeed, whether they think of it at all? Some interesting insights into these questions have been provided by the economist Paul A. Samuelson in a classic article describing a theory of consumer behavior that requires no evaluation of consumers' subjective preferences.[8] Samuelson's method succeeds in eliminating all traces of the concept of utility from the theory of consumer demand. The fundamental assumption is that the consumer reveals his preferences by buying whatever market basket he prefers among those he can afford, so there is no need to inquire into his preference orderings, much less to express these subjective evaluations in cardinal numbers. From this objective theory it is possible to derive a number of the theorems of consumer demand obtained in systems relying on the assumptions of cardinal or ordinal utility.

To propound a theory of revealed preference, it is necessary to impose some rules on the procedure so that what is observed is the reaction of the consumer to a price change and nothing else. First, we must assume that the consumer's tastes remain constant; when he switches from one basket of goods to another, the new choice must not be due, even in part, to a change in his tastes. Second, we assume that the consumer is logical, that the choices he makes fall in a transitive ordering.[9] The final and crucial requirement is that we assume the consumer can be induced to purchase a particular good if its price is made sufficiently low.

Suppose the consumer has the income and faces the commodity prices shown by the budget line ab in Figure 5-3(a). Under these circumstances, he is observed to choose the basket denoted by point W on ab, consisting of OX_W units of X and OY_W units of Y. This basket is said to be "revealed preferred" to any other basket he *could* buy for the same or a smaller amount of money. He has the purchasing power to acquire *any* basket lying on or under ab, since any combination costs no more than W, but he chooses the basket at W. Clearly, he must consider $X_W Y_W$ an optimal basket. As is already implicit in the preceding argument, it follows that any other basket on or under ab is inferior to the basket at point W.

Also, it is clear that any basket denoted by a point lying on either of the two perpendicular lines radiating from point W or lying within the field demarcated by those lines is revealed as preferred to W. This is so, since any point on the boundaries of or within this defined area contains at least as much of one good as W and more of the other good.

Without more information supplied by the consumer himself, we have no way of knowing whether points lying between ab and the lines radiating from W are superior or inferior to that point. Shortly, we shall obtain such information, but let us pause to note that we are obtaining some empirical verification for the assumed convex slope of the indifference curve. Point W must lie at the point where the consumer's currently attained indifference curve is

[8] Paul A. Samuelson, "Consumption Theory in Terms of Revealed Preference," *Economica*, XV, New Series (November 1948), pp. 243–53.
[9] *Transitive* orderings are discussed in Chapter 3.

FIGURE 5-3

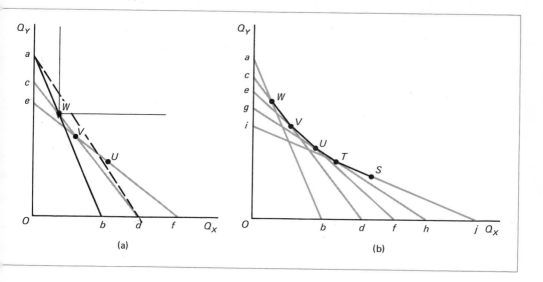

(a)   (b)

tangent to his present budget line *ab*. Wherever the indifference curve is, it cannot enter the area demarcated by the perpendicular lines radiating from *W* since every point on or within those lines is preferred to *W*. Neither can the indifference curve lie beneath the area demarcated by the budget line *ab* or on the budget line itself, since any such point has been revealed as inferior to *W*.[10] It must be, then, that the indifference curve passing through point *W* is convex to the origin, since this is the only curvature that permits it to pass through the revealed optimal point without entering zones of inferiority or superiority. Thus, some very simple assumptions, noted at the beginning of this section, plus one observation of consumer behavior in response to a given income and given set of prices have permitted us to verify deductively the principle of the diminishing marginal rate of substitution. Of course, at the present time, except for point *W*, we know only the *general shape* of the as yet unlocated indifference curve.

To proceed with the theory of revealed preference, let us disequilibrate the consumer. Suppose that the price of *X* falls so that the consumer could, if he chose to, buy *Od* units of it. This time, however, his budget line is not allowed to become the dashed line *ad*; instead, he is decompensated so that any basket he is now able to buy is no more expensive than the one indicated by point *W*. Accordingly, we shall draw the new compensated budget line from

[10] Note that (as was explained in the preceding chapter) the remote and trivial possibility exists that the indifference curve is coincident with *ab*. This would be so if *X* and *Y* were perfect substitutes, in which case the consumer's choice of basket ($X_w Y_w$) would have been made by some random selection process. Strictly speaking, such a choice is ruled out under the assumptions of the revealed preference theory.

d through point *W*. The consumer can now, if he wishes, continue to purchase basket *W*, or any other basket lying on or under *cd*. We know that he will not choose any basket lying on or under the *cW* segment of *cd*, since all such points have been determined previously to be inferior to *W*. The consumer's choice must, therefore, fall on the *Wd* segment of *cd*. Suppose the consumer chooses the basket at *V*. Point *V* is revealed preferred to any other point on *Wd*. The consumer's preference is as clear as it was when, at the initial budget and set of prices, he chose basket *W*. Following disequilibration, the consumer is still able to buy basket *W*, but he chooses the combination of goods in basket *V*.

By continuing to change the price of good *X* and compensating (decompensating) the consumer so that the previous basket remains in his maximal set, we can determine as many points of revealed preference as we like. The budget line *ef* shows another reduction in the price of *X*; now the consumer could buy *Of* units if he used up all his income on the good. Once again, however, he is decompensated so that basket *V* remains in his maximal set. Note that basket *W* is no longer in the maximal set, since the consumer no longer possesses sufficient income to buy it; but the superiority of basket *V* over basket *W* has been determined, so our interest now is directed to what the consumer does in relation to basket *V*. We know the consumer will choose no basket lying along the *eV* segment of *ef*. These points have been revealed as inferior to *V*, and the consumer is still able to purchase *V*.

Suppose the consumer chooses basket *U*. The basket at *U* is revealed as preferred over *V*, just as *V* was revealed as preferred over *W*. Therefore, under the assumption of transitivity, the consumer has produced the ordering *U P V P W*. Two more baskets are observed in Figure 5-3(b). Baskets *T* and *S* have been determined in the manner of baskets *U* and *V*.

What have we accomplished so far? In the first place, we are obtaining an ordinal ranking of alternative baskets from observations of empirical data alone; that is, budgets, prices, and acts of consumer choice. But we are also moving closer to determining the actual shape and location of one of the consumer's indifference curves.

The series of line segments connecting the points we have obtained are shown as heavy lines in Figure 5-3(b). The figure *WVUTS* produced by these line segments approaches a smooth convex curve. Its appearance *suggests* an indifference curve. If we follow our assumptions strictly, it cannot be an indifference curve, but we can convert it into one if we temporarily amend our assumptions. Return to the initial point *W*, which we *know* lies on the indifference curve that we are seeking. Suppose the price of *X* is changed, and the consumer's new (decompensated) budget line becomes *ef*. This is all as before. But at this point, we depart from our initial assumptions and allow for a weak ordering.[11] The consumer is instructed to find a basket on *ef* that is a perfect substitute for *W*. He names the basket at *V*; therefore, he has produced the ranking *W I V*. The points *W* and *V* now are points on his indifference curve.

---

[11] Weak orderings are discussed in Chapter 3.

If the same procedure is carried out for all the other points, then all the points we have obtained—W, V, U, T, and S—are points on the desired indifference curve, and the line segments joining them do yield a figure approaching the desired indifference curve as a limit. This indifference curve must be convex to the origin as is hypothesized in ordinal utility theory.

This treatment has been a shortcut to the derivation of an indifference curve. Having shown the convexity of the curve, we shall return to our initial set of assumptions, which precludes WVUTS from being the desired indifference curve (because V, U, T, and S were revealed as preferred to W). Point W, of course, does lie on the curve, and we do have the figure aWVUTSj that forms the extreme right boundary of the indifference curve. Since W has been revealed as preferred to any other point on ab, and the remaining points on aWVUTSj have been revealed as preferred to W, the indifference curve must approach W from above and from left of ab, become tangent to ab at W, and then lie to the left of the figure comprised of the line segments joining a, W, V, U, T, S, and j.

Figure 5-4 shows the right-hand boundary of the indifference curve, with the original compensated budget lines removed for the sake of clarity. To locate a left-hand boundary of the desired indifference curve, we pick a basket

FIGURE 5-4

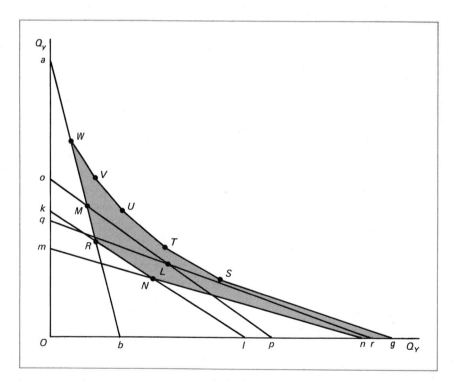

known to be inferior to *W*. Any other point on *ab* is such a basket. Assume the inferior basket is *R*. Under the basic assumption of revealed preference, there is a price at which a consumer can be induced to purchase any basket. Therefore, the price of *X* and the consumer's income, as shown by the budget line *kl*, are adjusted until he buys the basket at *R*. We know that *R* is inferior to *W* because the consumer chose *W* when it was possible for him to have *R*. Now we have "forced" *R* on him by lowering the price of *X* from what it was when his budget line was *ab* and then decompensating him until *R* became the most attractive basket he could buy. Now, when *R* is the optimal basket, we know that *N* must indicate an inferior basket. Once again, we employ the fundamental assumption to induce the consumer to purchase that collection of goods.

We have now located the zone in which the desired indifference curve must lie. This is shown in Figure 5-4 as the shaded area, bounded by *WVUTSg* on the right and *WRNn* on the left. This must be so since *W* lies on the desired indifference curve, and the remainder of the points on the right boundary were all revealed as preferred to any other point on *ab*, including *R*. Thus the desired indifference curve, after it passes through *W*, must lie to the right of *R*. Point *N* has been revealed inferior to *R* and therefore must be inferior to *W*. All other points on the line segment *Nn* have been identified as inferior to *N* and are, hence, inferior to *W*. Thus, we now know that the desired indifference curve must lie somewhere in the shaded area between *WVUTSg* on the right and *WRNn* on the left. Although this area allows room for indifference curves other than the one we seek, what we have now is a great advance on our previous information, which was simply that the desired indifference curve passed through point *W*. We now know a very large area *not* occupied by the indifference curve. Moreover, we can continue the process to narrow down the shaded area, thus coming ever closer to the desired curve itself. For example, the next step is to locate a point within the shaded area superior to points *R* and *N*, but not superior to *W*. Referring again to Figure 5-4, we begin this process by locating another basket, *M*, on *ab* that must be inferior to *W*. The consumer is induced to purchase *M* by our causing his budget line to become *op*. Point *M*, of course, lies on the previously determined left-hand boundary of the indifference curve, so we have not yet advanced our knowledge. But now let us locate a point on *op* lying within the shaded area. Such a point must be superior to *R* and *N*, since any point within the shaded area has been determined to be superior to all points lying on the left-hand boundary of the area. Let us choose point *L*. Point *L* has been revealed as inferior to *M*, since when the consumer's budget line was *op*, he chose *M*. Point *M* was previously revealed inferior to *W*. Thus, *L* is inferior to *W* but superior to *R* and *N*. The desired indifference curve through *W* must, therefore, pass to the left of the line segment *TS* but to the right of *L*. At this point, we are approaching more nearly the precise location of the desired indifference curve.

Although the derivation of an indifference curve under the theory of revealed preference is obviously a tedious process, such an empirical determina-

Consumer Behavior Theory — Further Topics

tion is clearly possible. We can see, by means of revealed preference theory, whether indifference curves do exist, that if they do exist they are convex with respect to the origin, and that economists need not be concerned with whether the consumer thinks in cardinal or ordinal terms. All we need do is watch what he does under the very simple assumption that his preference pattern is transitive.

CONSUMER'S SURPLUS

"You get what you pay for." Like most old saws, this one should be regarded skeptically. Probably most people, in attacking the idea, would argue that buyers frequently get less than they expect from goods purchased with both money and high hopes. But this argument really misses the point of the slogan, since it is likely to be based on the buyer's unrealistic expectations or on the seller's chicanery. Entirely apart from emotional or moral states, is it possible for one's purchases to yield a totality of utility unequal to the disutility incurred in acquiring the wherewithal to make them?

Suppose an individual buys five cups of coffee per day. Let us assume that his marginal utility at this level of consumption is 10 utils. If the consumer buys five cups of coffee per day, he must require that each cup furnish him with at least 10 utils. If each cup does this, the total utility that he derives from consuming five cups of coffee would be 50 utils. But we know that his total utility must be greater than 50 utils. Since the consumption of coffee is subject to the law of diminishing marginal utility, we know that if he were to stop his daily coffee consumption with four cups, the marginal utility of a cup of coffee would be greater than 10 utils. Consuming goods under conditions of diminishing marginal utility causes the total utility that the consumer derives from a particular good to exceed the product of the marginal utility of the good multiplied by the number of units consumed. Suppose that the coffee drinker's total utility is 200 utils. Under our assumed data, this amount is 150 more utils than he requires as a minimum of utility from a total of five cups of coffee daily. Thus, the consumer may be said to have acquired a *surplus* of 150 utils over and above the utils he requires as a minimum from the consumption of five cups of coffee.

MARSHALLIAN CONSUMER'S SURPLUS

Alfred Marshall contended in his *Principles* that it is possible to determine the monetary equivalent of the consumer's surplus, since the individual's demand curve is derived from his marginal utility schedule for a particular good.[12]

Figure 5-5 shows a linear demand curve for coffee. Since the consumer

[12] Alfred Marshall, *Principles of Economics*, 8th edition (New York: Macmillan, 1948), pp. 124–34.

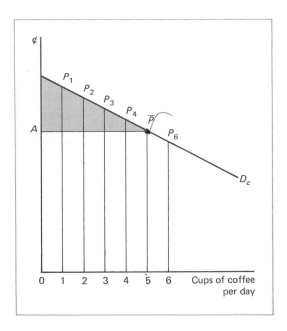

FIGURE 5-5

buys coffee under conditions of diminishing marginal utility, the greater the amount he has, the lower the price must be to induce him to buy an additional cup. If the price is P_1, he will buy one cup of coffee per day, but he will not pay P_1 for two cups. However, if the price is P_2, the quantity he demands is two cups. In the absence of price discrimination, the consumer will not be charged the highest price he would be willing to pay for one cup and a lower price for the next cup and a still lower price for another cup, and so on. He, as well as all other consumers of the good, will be charged a uniform price for all cups, and the quantity he demands will reflect the influence of this price.[13]

Nevertheless, the price the consumer would be willing to pay to have *a particular unit* of the good is unaffected by the price he does pay. Say the price is P_2 cents. He will buy two cups of coffee, but he would have been willing to have paid P_1 cents for one of those cups. If the consumer can buy both units for P_2 cents when he is willing to pay P_1 for one of the units, he must incur a "surplus" having a money equivalent of $P_1 - P_2$ cents in the course of the transaction. This money equivalent is measured by the difference between what he would be willing to pay for the two cups of coffee rather than do without them—$P_1 + P_2$ cents—and what he actually pays for both units—$2(P_2)$.

Figure 5-5 shows that the market price is $\bar{P}$ and that at this price the consumer demands five cups of coffee. When it comes to the fifth unit, his marginal evaluation of monetary worth of a cup of coffee is equivalent to the market price. But the marginal worth of any of the four other units of coffee in his

[13] The relationship between price discrimination and consumer's surplus is discussed in Chapter 10, pp. 266–70.

Consumer Behavior Theory—Further Topics

daily consumption is greater to him than the price he must pay for each of them. Therefore, he must acquire a surplus of utility on the whole basket. The extent of the monetary equivalent of this surplus is shown as the shaded area in Figure 5-5.[14]

In other words, at a price of $\bar{P}$, the consumer buys five cups of coffee per day and pays the total amount shown in Figure 5-5 as rectangle $OA\bar{P}5$. But he would have been willing to pay P_1 for 1 unit, $P_1 + P_2$ for 2 units, $P_1 + P_2 + P_3$ for 3 units, and so on, rather than do without the goods. Thus, he would have been willing to pay the amount shown by the shaded triangle in addition to the amount he actually paid—the unshaded rectangle $OA\bar{P}5$. Therefore, the shaded area is the monetary measure of his consumer's surplus. Buying coffee under conditions of diminishing marginal utility, he gets more than he pays for.

INDIFFERENCE CURVE ANALYSIS
OF THE MARSHALLIAN CONSUMER'S SURPLUS

In Figure 5-6, the good on the vertical axis is the consumer's money income. Since his income is general purchasing power, the vertical axis can be used to measure all of the non-X goods the consumer can have in combination with any given quantity of good X. The consumer's total income for the period in question is $OM = X_1M'$ dollars. If he chooses to consume no X, he

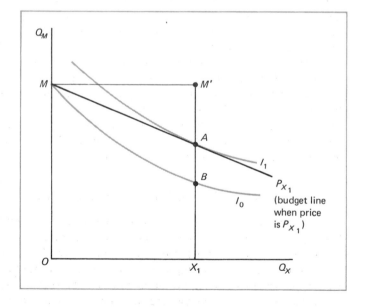

FIGURE 5-6

[14] Strictly speaking, the width of the strips representing 1-unit changes in quantity demanded must be reduced to minute increments to make this statement accurate, but the concept is better illustrated with relatively wide strips.

can buy another collection of goods worth OM dollars. The diagram reveals, however, that if the price of X is P_{X_1}, as is represented by the budget line radiating from point M, he will buy OX_1 quantity of X (determined by the point of tangency between the indifference curve and the budget line). This expenditure for X leaves him with X_1A dollars (the ability to purchase that dollar amount of other goods) and, thus, he must spend for OX_1 units of X, $X_1M' - X_1A = AM'$ dollars.

Indifference curve I_1 shows the various combinations of X and money (X and other goods) between which the consumer is indifferent at a particular utility index. All combinations of X and M, except the one at A, are beyond the reach of the consumer. There must be an indifference curve lying below I_1 showing combinations of X and M that are indifferent to a basket containing only M (that is, containing quantities of other goods the consumer could buy if he decided to take no X). Such a curve would pass through point M, the point at which the budget line intersects the vertical axis. This indifference curve is I_0, and it shows, for example, that the consumer is indifferent between a basket containing no X and $OM = X_1M'$ dollars' worth of non-X goods (the basket at M) and a basket containing OX_1 units of X and X_1B dollars' worth of non-X goods (the basket at B).

If the price of X is P_{X_1}, the consumer will, as we have noted, buy OX_1 units and pay AM' dollars for them. He would, however, be willing to pay up to BM' dollars to get the same amount. How do we know this? The consumer is indifferent between (1) not having any X and OM dollars' worth of other things and (2) OX_1 units of X and X_1B dollars' worth of other goods. The prevailing price of X enables him to have OX_1 units of X and BA *more* dollars' worth of other goods. The consumer is willing to give up BM' units of M to acquire OX_1 units of X. If each unit of X could be priced for him at its marginal worth, BM' units of M is what he would pay for the total amount of X. In fact, the price of every unit of X is less than what he is willing to pay for every unit of X except the marginal unit. Since he would be willing to pay BM' dollars for OX_1 units rather than do without, while the market requires only AM' dollars of him, *his consumer's surplus has the value of BA dollars.* The distance BA corresponds to the shaded area under the demand curve of Figure 5-5.

A REVISION OF CONSUMER'S SURPLUS

In the original theory of consumer's surplus, Alfred Marshall assumed that changes in prices would be so small in relation to the individual's money expenditures that the consumer's marginal utility of money income would remain constant. This assumption is incorporated in both Figures 5-5 and 5-6. Figure 5-6 shows the assumption explicitly. The vertical separation of the two indifference curves is everywhere the same; they are vertically parallel. If indifference curves are vertically parallel, then, for any given quantity of X, the slopes of all curves must be equal. Thus, at points A and B on curves I_1 and I_0, respectively, the marginal rate of substitution of X for M must be equal. We

Consumer Behavior Theory — Further Topics

know that $MRS_{XM} = MU_X/MU_M$.[15] A movement from A to B does not require the marginal utility of money income to rise, but if it is assumed to do so, then the marginal utility of good X must rise in the same proportion. If the marginal utilities of goods move in the same direction, the goods are substitutes.

In the analysis of the preceding section, no matter how large the consumer's income, his MRS_{XM} is the same for any given quantity of X. The sole reason MRS_{XM} will change is in response to a change in the quantity of X consumed. Therefore, MRS_{XM} is dependent only on the individual's consumption of X and not on the size of his money income or the amounts that he spends on other goods.

If we now assume that the marginal utility of money income varies inversely with changes in the size of that income, the indifference curves of Figure 5-6 must be redrawn. This has been done in Figure 5-7.

The indifference curves I_0 and I_1 are vertically parallel as in Figure 5-6, reflecting the assumed constancy of the marginal utility of money income. Under this assumption, the consumer's surplus is BA, as in the previous figure. If now the assumption of the constancy of the marginal utility of money income is dropped, even though the value of MU_X is the same at points A and B, the value of MU_M must be lower at A than at B, since the consumer has a greater amount of money left at A than he does at B (and the same amount of X). If the ratio of MU_X/MU_M is greater at A than at B (because MU_M is lower, and MU_X is the same), it follows that $(MRS_{XM})_A > (MRS_{XM})_B$. But if this is so, we can no longer be considering indifference curve I_1. If MU_M varies inversely with the consumer's money income (or money expenditures on all goods), any higher indifference curve must have a steeper slope than a lower one. Therefore,

FIGURE 5-7

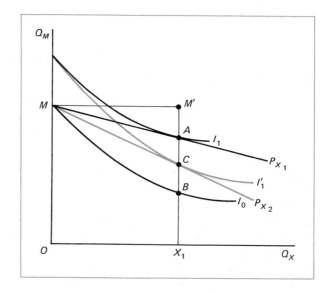

[15] This equality is explained in Chapter 4.

curve I_1 should approach I_0 as the quantity of X is increased. To reflect this behavior, curve I_1 has been redrawn as curve I_1'. Its steeper slope causes it to fall "below" I_1 at an increasing rate as the quantity of X is increased. Be careful to note, however, that I_1' is not really a lower indifference curve than I_1. Both curves represent *the same level of utility*. The consumer is indifferent between points A and C. Curve I_1' is simply curve I_1 drawn on a new assumption, namely that the marginal utility of money income is not constant. (Having redrawn I_1 as I_1' on the basis of this assumption, we must note that the curves are situated on an unusual indifference map. All indifference curves in an orthodox indifference map must be drawn under the same assumptions, but here we have juxtaposed two inconsistent curves for analytical purposes.)

If the relevant indifference curve is I_1, the consumer will buy OX_1 units of X if the price is P_{X_1}. If the indifference curve is I_1', he will buy the same quantity, but at the higher price of P_{X_2}.

According to the reconstructed indifference map, when the price of X is P_{X_2}, the consumer will pay a total of CM' dollars for OX_1 units of X. He would, however, be willing to pay as much as BM' dollars for the same quantity; this is BC dollars more than the market requires of him, and BC is, therefore, the dollar value of his consumer's surplus.

A comparison of the graphical representation of the two consumer's surpluses shows that the Marshallian surplus BA is larger than the redefined surplus BC. From this we may conclude that in the case of a superior good, the Marshallian surplus is an overstatement. Why is this so? If the individual is to consume the quantity indicated by the Marshallian analysis, but under the added assumption of the diminishing marginal utility of money income, he must be charged a higher price to compensate for the consumption-expanding income effect. This required increase in price reduces the surplus the consumer derives from a given quantity of good X.

COMPLEMENTARY GOODS

The use of a two-good, two-input, two-person economic model, while highly abstract, is sufficient to explain most economic phenomena. In some cases, however, such a model cannot comprehend all the possible relationships between economic variables. Complementarity among goods is such a case. A move along a convex indifference curve shows that in a two-good world, X is always a substitute for Y. The loss of utility occasioned by giving up some units of Y is always exactly compensated by the gain in utility accruing from the increase in the consumer's stock of X. We have noted that the substitution effect is always negative. Whenever the price of good X falls, the consumer substitutes more of the now cheaper X for Y. One thing may be confusing: we have encountered examples in which the price of X has fallen and more of both X and Y were taken. But this was not due to the relationship of complementarity. The substitution effect was still negative as it must be in a

two-good situation. Whenever more Y was taken, it was necessary that Y be a superior good and that the demand for X be inelastic. The price of X fell; the consumer bought more of it; but because he spent a smaller total amount for the good, he had more income to devote to buying everything else. In the two-good model, Y is "everything else" and is, necessarily, a superior good.

But, unlike the relationship in a two-good model, goods that exhibit a complementary relation must produce a *positive* substitution effect when the price of one item in the pair is reduced; that is, in consequence of a reduction in the price of X, not only must more X be bought, but more Y must be bought *solely* because X has become cheaper, not because the consumer feels himself to be better off. In other words, the income effect has nothing to do with complementarity.

But how can the substitution effect be positive? If we say that the relation of complementarity exists whenever the price of X falls and more Y is bought, what do we mean? Good X can become cheaper only in relation to some *other* good. If it becomes cheaper in relation to good Y must not the consumer buy more X and less Y? Not if there is also *another good* in relation to which X can become less expensive. Then *both* X and Y, in consequence of a fall in the price of X alone, can be substituted for the third good. An important lesson of the two-good model always holds true: a negative substitution effect must exist between at least one good in the consumer's universe and any or all other goods. All goods in the consumer's world may be substitutes, but not all may be complements.

In order to analyze the nature of complementarity, we must construct a three-good model. To facilitate the development of such a model, we shall specify that the third good is money income, M. With the introduction of the third good, we will be able to express the substitutability relationships between any pair of the goods. This can be done graphically, as in Figure 5-8, by drawing indifference curves at specific levels of the consumer's utility index for each of the three pairs of goods.

FIGURE 5-8

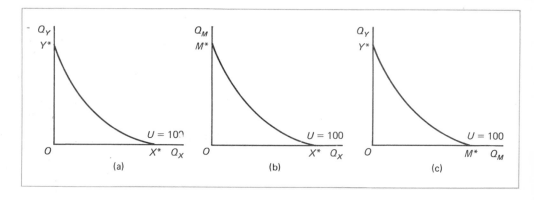

Each of the curves in Figure 5–8 shows a particular combination of the indicated pair of goods between which the consumer is indifferent. A (cardinal) numerical utility index ($U = 100$) has been added merely to emphasize that each of the three curves forms the maximum boundary of a set of the indicated goods capable of yielding a certain level of utility to the consumer; other than this, the utility index has no significance. At any point on each of the three curves, we can determine the marginal rate of substitution between the paired goods. Thus, in Figure 5-8, (a) shows MRS_{XY}, (b) shows MRS_{XM}, and (c) shows MRS_{MY}.

Since we are now dealing with a three-good model, the consumer can derive, say, 100 units of utility from a basket containing X, Y, and M without being *on* any of the depicted indifference curves. This may seem counter to the theory developed so far, unless one sees that a three-good model calls for an indifference *surface,* not a curve. Then, for a constant level of utility (e.g., 100 utils), the individual's basket must be located by a point on the surface. Strictly speaking, then, the curves in (a), (b), and (c) are the floor plan and side elevations of the three-dimensional indifference surface shown in Figure 5-9. Diagram (a) has been turned so that any movement on the X-axis is perpendicular to the reader; diagram (b) forms the floor of the model, and diagram (c) is in the same position as shown in Figure 5-8. Now, imagine that *all* points on each of the three boundary curves—Y^*X^*, M^*X^*, and Y^*M^*—are connected to each other by a continuous surface. You might imagine that a sheet of clear flexible plastic is being stretched between the boundary curves. This sheet, or surface, will be everywhere convex to the vertical Y-axis (not just the origin). A plane put between the surface and the Y-axis (e.g., a budget plane) would touch the surface at only one point. The surface would *bend away* from the plane at all other points. *If that plane* represents the consumer's budget constraint, the point of tangency would establish the consumer's optimal basket of X, Y, and M, since the point of tangency will occur with the highest attainable indifference surface just as is the case with the budget *line* and the highest attainable indifference *curve.* All points on the surface represent the same level of utility—here, 100 utils. As in the case of indifference curves, any indifference surface lying behind the given surface (farther from the reader) represents a lower level of utility ($U < 100$), and any indifference surface in front of the given surface (nearer the reader) represents a higher (but unattainable) level of utility ($U > 100$).

Be sure to distinguish this three-dimensional *indifference* surface from a three-dimensional *utility* surface. The construction of Figure 5-9 is the analogue of the two-good indifference curve. The utility surface proper to the three-dimensional indifference surface of Figure 5-9 requires *four* dimensions. The Y-designated contours in the figure (Y_1, Y_2, Y_3, etc.) do *not* represent higher levels of utility, since they all lie on the surface; they represent only what is visually apparent, greater levels of Y consumption at higher contours on the surface.

Point *A,* lying on the surface, represents a basket yielding 100 utils to

FIGURE 5-9

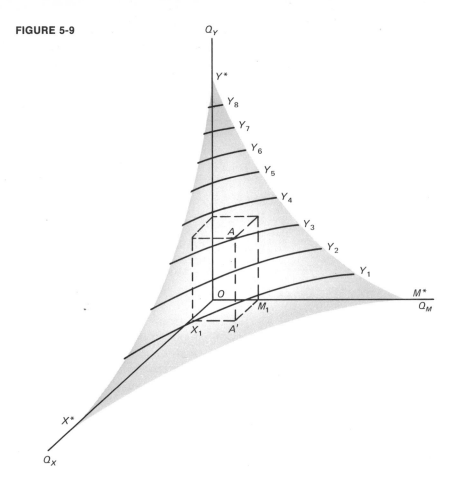

the consumer. This basket contains Y_3 units of Y. To find the amounts of the other goods in the basket, we drop a perpendicular from A to A' on the floor of the model. Then, running perpendiculars from A' to the M and X axes, we can determine the amounts of M and X that complete the consumer's basket. Our task is to find under what conditions a fall in the price of X will induce the consumer to take not only more X but also more Y without respect to the income effect.

Since it is more convenient to work with a two-dimensional graph than with a drawing of a three-dimensional model, we have drawn a map of an indifference surface in Figure 5-10. The convex Y contours are not the conventional indifference curves of the two-dimensional model, since *any* point lying in the space between the X and M axes represents a basket of goods (X, Y, and M) yielding the consumer the *same* amount of utility (i.e., here, 100 utils). Each convex contour line represents a specific amount of good Y. Note that in contrast to the map of the usual indifference curves, in this figure curves

FIGURE 5-10

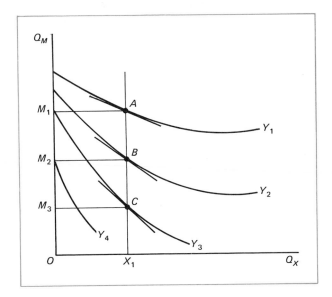

showing greater amounts of Y lie *closer* to the origin. Thus, a point on a specific contour—say, Y_2—shows the various combinations of X and M that, combined with the given amount of Y, yield the consumer 100 units of utility. As the amount of Y increases (as the consumer moves to a curve lying nearer the origin), the quantities of X and M can be reduced without the consumer experiencing any change in his utility index. The contours do show the marginal rate of substitution between X and M for a given amount of Y (and, of course, at a given utility index).

Assume that the quantity of X is held constant at OX_1 units. Initially, the consumer is at point A; his basket consists of Y_1 units of Y, X_1 units of X, and M_1 units of M. Now let the price of Y fall so that the consumer buys Y_2 units of Y. If he holds his consumption of X constant, he will have to give up M_1M_2 units of M, and he will move from A on Y_1 to B on Y_2. The consumer's utility index remains constant, but the slope of Y_2 at B is greater than the slope of Y_1 at A. This indicates that the marginal rate of substitution of X for M rose as the consumer increased his consumption of Y. At C, the slope of Y_3 is greater than the slope of Y_2 at B. Accordingly, $(MRS_{XM})_C > (MRS_{XM})_B > (MRS_{XM})_A$. If the marginal rate of substitution of X for M increases as the consumer increases his consumption of Y, it must mean that the ability of X to substitute for M becomes greater as the consumer buys more Y. The consumer becomes willing to part with increasing amounts of Y to gain another unit of X. For example, suppose $(MRS_{XM})_A = 2/1$ and $(MRS_{XM})_B = 3/1$. With Y_1 units of Y in his basket, the consumer is willing to give up 2 units of M to acquire another unit of X. But should the price of Y fall, so that the consumer can acquire a greater amount of Y—that is, Y_2—he becomes less willing to give up 3 units of M to get another unit of X. Goods X and Y must be complementary, because

each addition of Y to the consumer's basket causes him to become more willing to give up money income in order to acquire another unit of X. The value of money, in terms of a unit of X, falls as the price of Y falls. This is what the increasing marginal rate of substitution of good X for money means, and this is the precise nature of the complementary relationship between goods X and Y.

The negative substitution effect is present in the relation between money and the goods X and Y. When the price of Y falls, the consumer substitutes *both* X and Y for money. This is why a third good is needed for a complementary relationship to exist between any two goods.

It is now easy to see what must happen to the marginal utility of money income when two goods are complementary. As the consumer moves from point A on Y_1 to B on Y_2, the marginal utility of Y falls since more Y is consumed. If Y and X are complementary, the marginal utility of X must increase with a fall in the price of Y (shown by a rightward shift in the marginal utility curve for good X). Since $MRS_{XM} = MU_X/MU_M$, this increase in the marginal utility of X alone is sufficient to increase the marginal rate of substitution of X for M. It is also quite possible that the marginal utility of money income decreases. There are, then, two forces acting to increase MRS_{XM}. The decreasing marginal utility of money income in the case of complementary goods is explained by their relationship. Because it takes more X to go along with the increase in Y consumption, the acquisition of more X becomes more important to the consumer, and he will part with more money to enjoy the combination of X and Y. For example, a camera is not of much use without film. If the price of cameras falls, a new camera will be of no use until the consumer spends an additional amount of money for film (and processing). Complementarity is of extreme importance to film, record, and razor blade manufacturers, and it accounts for the low prices (sometimes zero) of cameras, record players, and razors.

Whatever happens to MU_X and MU_M in consequence of a fall in the price of Y, if MU_X/MU_M falls, the relationship between X and Y is one of complementarity. Thus, a map of an indifference surface will show contours of increasing steepness as the horizontal axis is approached. Accordingly, the indifference surface of Figure 5-11 does not have a symmetrical curvature; it must bend ever more sharply as it turns toward the reader.

The Theory of Production:
A Physical Analysis

With this chapter we make a transition from the sector of the economy that *consumes* goods and services to the sector that *produces* them.

THE PLACE OF PRODUCTION IN ECONOMICS

To economists, *production* is the *transformation of inputs into outputs.* The output of one productive process may be the input of another. Thus, to U.S. Steel, sheet steel is an output, but to General Motors it is an input. The *ultimate* object of production is to transform inputs into outputs that yield utility directly to consumers. The transforming agent is the business firm.[1]

It may be surprising to learn that economists' production theories are not specifications about how to combine resources to produce a desired output. Devising the techniques of production is the role of technologists; economists treat those techniques as parameters.[2] Yet economists must take cognizance of the physical realities of production, so they have developed what they call "production theory." Production theory consists of those

---

[1] Many earlier economics texts define production as the creation of utilities. This definition has the advantages of making it clear that activities such as transportation and storage are productive. For example, transportation may be said to give goods *place* utility and storage (of grain or furniture, for example) gives goods *time* utility.

[2] For our purposes, a *parameter* is information that is given.

methods and concepts economists use to restructure the technological conditions of production into forms that can be subjected to *economic* analysis.

THE PRODUCTION FUNCTION

What Is a Production Function?

Production functions are the cornerstone of production theory. It is a truism that output is dependent on inputs. In its most basic form, a production function merely states that truism, telling us that the output of a certain good (or service) bears some (unspecified) relation to the quantities of the inputs, or factors of production, that are combined to produce that output. Such an elemental production function can be written:

$$X = f(A, B, C, D, E)$$

This statement may be read, "The quantity produced of good X is a function of (dependent on) the quantities of the inputs A, B, C, D, and E, which are undefined." Depending on the classificatory scheme used for defining production factors, a production function might contain *any* number of separable inputs. In this case, the *general* form of such a production function could be written:

$$X = f(A, B, \ldots, N)$$

This functional equation tells us that there are N separable resources (inputs) that could be employed to produce good X, some of them being unspecified.

For our purposes, it is convenient to simplify the general form of the production function. Since the many forms a basic input may take have little, if any, significance for us, we shall subsume all forms of production factor under the headings "labor" and "capital." Labor includes all forms of human effort, mental and physical. Capital consists of all property resources, including appropriated natural resources as well as capital goods (i.e., the produced means of production). Allowing L to stand for labor and K to represent capital, we can write the two-input general production function for good X:

$$X = f(L, K)$$

Specific Form of the Production Function

A production function is stated in *specific* form if it tells us exactly *how* the quantity of an output is related to the amount of inputs. Experience indicates that even rather simple production functions can be difficult to summarize mathematically and often take the form of complex equations. The

simple function that we are about to meet is purely hypothetical and has been devised solely to show the general nature of specific production functions.

Suppose that as the result of an actual investigation, we have obtained the exact relationship among men (labor) and saws (capital) and blocks of ice (output) cut from a frozen lake. Let I represent the amount of ice in fifty-pound blocks cut from the lake per eight-hour day. Having defined the components of our function, suppose we find that the relationship among ice, labor, and capital can be expressed by the following equation:

$$I = 50\sqrt{L \cdot K}$$

This *specific* production function tells us that the number of fifty-pound blocks of ice cut from the lake each day is equal to the numerical value of the square root of the arithmetical product of the number of inputs of L and K multiplied by the constant factor 50.

To find I, the quantity of fifty-pound blocks of ice that can be cut from the lake in one day, substitute numerical data for the symbols. Suppose 8 men (labor) using 2 saws (capital) work on the lake: then

$$I = 50\sqrt{8 \cdot 2} = 50\sqrt{16}$$
$$= 50 \cdot 4$$
$$= 200$$

The output of ice, I, is 200 fifty-pound blocks per day. The same output can be produced if the input units are interchanged (i.e., $L = 2$ and $K = 8$). Then,

$$I = 50\sqrt{2 \cdot 8} = 200$$

since capital is able, up to a point at least, to substitute for labor. Here, 6 additional units of capital have replaced 6 units of labor, and production has remained at a constant level of 200 fifty-pound blocks of ice per day. The ability of inputs to substitute for each other is a major concern of this chapter.

How can the arithmetical product of labor multiplied by capital yield a result expressed as so many fifty-pound blocks of ice? The answer is that economists view production as the *transformation* of inputs into output. The numerical solution of a specific production function is the amount of a particular good yielded by a given resource combination.

THE PRODUCTION FUNCTION AND EFFICIENCY

Our example of the production function in specific form shows an output of 200 fifty-pound blocks of ice per day. Does this mean that the indicated

input combinations must yield this output? No, they may yield 200 blocks or any lesser quantity. The solution of a production function reports the *maximum* quantity of output obtainable from a given input combination or, alternatively, the *minimum* amount of inputs required to produce a desired output. In other words, a specific production function assumes technical efficiency. Suppose the target of our hypothetical ice-cutting firm is 200 blocks of ice per day and that the firm has only 2 saws. Its production staff knows, then, that the absolute minimum number of laborers the firm must use to achieve its goal is 8. The specific form of the production function states that fewer men— say, 7—using 2 saws cannot reach the output goal.

On the grounds of technical efficiency, then, combinations of inputs such as $8L + 2K$, $2K + 8L$, $4L + 4K$, $16L + 1K$, or $1L + 16K$ all can yield 200 fifty-pound blocks of ice per day.[3] Since any of these combinations is feasible, does this mean that each of the combinations would be equally useful to the firm? No, the choice of a particular combination is of profound importance. It is possible that in the firm's area, labor is more difficult to obtain than capital. In such a circumstance, the firm will choose an input combination that uses capital more intensively than labor. For example, in a labor-scarce area, the cost-minimizing firm would choose the input combination $2L + 8K$ over, say, $8L + 2K$. We see, therefore, that there are two criteria used by a firm in choosing the input combination to produce a desired level of output. The first criterion we have discussed is that of *technical* efficiency. For purposes of illustration, suppose that there is no difference in the relative scarcities of labor and capital in the region of our hypothetical firm. Under such conditions, the cost-minimizing firm could achieve its objectives (the desired quantity of output produced at the lowest cost) by choosing any technically efficient combination of labor and capital.

The second criterion is that of *economic* efficiency. Since there generally is a difference in the relative scarcities of inputs, the cost-minimizing firm will choose—from an array of technically efficient input combinations—the combination that will cost it the least. It will economize on the use of the relatively scarce resource.

Resource endowment explains why some geographic areas tend to use labor intensively, while other regions use capital intensively. For example, a few years ago a computer sciences specialist in an American university was invited to go to an underdeveloped nation to confer with the executives of an electric utility company about the type of computer the firm ought to acquire for use in billing its customers. The American found the billing department to be like a scene from a Charles Dickens novel. Clerks equipped with green eye-shades and black sleeve protectors sat on high stools at slant-topped desks writing out monthly statements in longhand. To the surprise of the firm's executives (and possibly to their chagrin), the consultant recommended that the

---

[3] These figures are input *combinations,* not production functions. These combinations substituted into the specific production function given in the text would produce 200 fifty-pound blocks of ice per day.

firm continue its current billing practices and forego the prestige of owning a computer. He had found that given the country's resource endowment, nineteenth-century billing methods were *economically* more efficient than those utilizing computers.

We assume, then, that a firm makes the selection of a particular process on the basis of input prices (economic efficiency) and that once a specific process is chosen, it operates it so as to produce a maximum output (technical efficiency).

PRODUCTION—THE SIMPLEST CASE: ONE VARIABLE INPUT

We shall now begin our search for the underlying "laws" of production. To make our task as simple as possible, we shall employ the *ceteris paribus* assumption and observe the response of output to a variation in only a single input.

THE TOTAL PRODUCT CURVE

Figure 6-1 shows two total product curves labeled TP_1 and TP_2. Each curve shows how the total output of X changes as a variable amount of L is combined with a given quantity of K. Curve TP_1 is drawn to reflect the firm's use of K_1 units of capital with different amounts of labor. For example, OL_1 units of labor combined with K_1 units of capital can produce a maximum of OX_1 units of output. If the labor input is increased to OL_2 units, K remaining fixed at K_1, the firm will increase its output by X_1X_2 units. Curve TP_2 shows how output changes when a larger amount of capital, K_2 units, is used with different amounts of labor.

The curves show the availability of two options to the firm if it wishes to produce OX_2 units of X. It may use OL_2 units of labor with K_1 units of capital or OL_1 units of L with K_2 units of K. If the firm uses OL_2 units of labor with K_2 units of capital, total output will rise to OX_3 units of X. Curve TP_2 lies above TP_1 since on TP_2 any given amount of labor has a greater amount of capital with which to work than any given amount of labor on TP_1 has.

THE LAWS OF DIMINISHING RETURNS

Anyone thinking casually about the relation between inputs and an output would probably accept readily the idea that the more inputs the firm uses, the greater will be its output. The total product curves of Figure 6-1 appear to confirm this common-sense notion. But let us look more closely. What if one input is increased against a fixed amount of all other inputs? How does output behave? Both curves show that for a given amount of capital, total output does increase with additional inputs of labor, but only up to a point. For

FIGURE 6-1

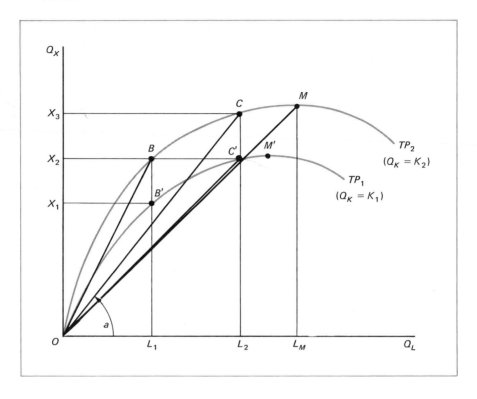

example, along curve TP_2, total output increases up to point M. To the right of point M, total output begins to decline. Apparently, using inputs of labor greater than OL_M units with K_2 units of capital exerts a negative influence on the production of X.

Another peculiarity of the total product curves is that they are concave with respect to the horizontal axis. What does this show? The labor input OL_2 is twice OL_1. Now consider curve TP_1: OX_2 is obviously less than twice OX_1. Apparently using twice as many units of L with a fixed amount of capital results in less than double the total output. Our next task is to determine why output behaves this way.

Diminishing total returns. In Figure 6-1, as we have said, total output increases up to point M on TP_2 and then falls. We will therefore call M the point at which the law of "diminishing total returns" takes effect. If total output falls beyond point M, inputs of L greater than OL_M must contribute negatively to production. The reason for this is implicit in the old adage, "Too many cooks spoil the broth." Diminishing total returns are encountered when so many units of the variable input are combined with fixed inputs that the former get in each other's way enough to make total output fall.

In some underdeveloped, mainly agricultural, countries, diminishing total returns are often assumed to be a problem. They are manifested in the phenomenon of disguised unemployment, or underemployment. In such economies, ordinary unemployment is not apparent to the casual observer. The population seems to be quite busy in, say, the rice paddies. Everybody works. Actually, there are too many people in the fields in the sense that if some laborers were withdrawn, total output at the least would not fall.

Diminishing average returns. The *average product* of a variable input is the amount of total output per unit of the variable factor. It is determined from the formula

$$AP_V = \frac{Q}{V}$$

where Q is total output and V is the number of units of the variable input required to produce that output. Thus, if 3 units of L are being combined with 7 units of K to yield 21 units of X, the average product of labor is

$$AP_L = \frac{X}{L} = \frac{21}{3} = 7 \text{ units of } X \text{ per unit of } L$$

If we assume that K is the variable input, the average product of K is

$$AP_K = \frac{X}{K} = \frac{21}{7} = 3 \text{ units of } X \text{ per unit of } K$$

Note that fixed inputs play no role in the *computation* of average product, since in short-run analysis, we are concerned only with the productivity of the variable input; but obviously, the fixed factors *do* enter into the determination of the average product of the variable input, since the fixed factors *and* the variable factor together determine the amount of total output.

Uses of average product. Average product is a convenient and familiar measure of productivity. It has been used since the time of the classical economists, especially in the Malthusian principle of population, to express the relation between numbers of human beings and the means of subsistence. If F represents the total output of food and N represents population (man being both the producer and consumer of food), with land being the fixed resource, the output of food per capita is given by the ratio F/N. Classical economists (Thomas Malthus, David Ricardo, John Stuart Mill) expressed their concept of an "optimum population" with this formula. Obviously, a maximum *total* output is not the same as a maximum *average* output. A case can be made that the most favorable relation between man and the means of subsistence is attained when the national product (Y) per person is at a maximum—when the ratio of Y to N is as large as possible.

The simplest form of the Malthusian principle of population holds that with technology and land held constant, the ratio of F to N will decrease over time. Man will expand his numbers to that the population will exceed an optimal size. The output of food (F) may grow (at least until the point of diminishing *total* returns is reached) as the number of laborers (N) to work in the fields increases, but F will not grow as fast as N; therefore, per capita output must fall. The reason for this is that there are diminishing *average* returns to labor on a fixed amount of land. Classical economists regarded this formula as portending ill. The prediction of the Malthusian population principle is well known: if population is not checked voluntarily, the standard of living must fall to the subsistence level. The "population explosion" is a grim reminder of the conclusions of Thomas Malthus' *Essay*.

As the total product curves of Figure 6-1 show, the falling ratio of total output to the variable input can be offset by using a greater amount of the fixed inputs. If more capital were used, the same amount of labor could produce more food. The per capita output of food is defined only for a *given* amount of capital.

Technology can alter the *shape* and location of the total product curves. An improvement in technology could *raise* TP_1 in Figure 6-1 to TP_2, and the same *amount* of all inputs (not necessarily the identical inputs) would then result in greater total output.

The classical economists are often charged with having ignored technology and the augmentation of capital. At the time in which most of them were working (the early 1800's), they apparently saw little evidence of the tremendous stimulus that changes in agricultural technology eventually would give to the output of food. Nevertheless, the basic logic of their proposition remains unimpaired. *Given* technology and the quantity of nonlabor inputs, the total product curve must be followed, and as population (the labor force) expands, output per capita will eventually fall. Only to the extent that technological improvements can offset continual increases in population will it be possible to avoid diminishing average returns. In those economies that have been unable to make use of the tools and techniques of a constantly improving agricultural technology, the phenomenon of a static or falling output per capita is an actual and unfortunate experience.

Today, the average product is commonly used to measure economic performance. A convenient time series to use in appraising the productive performance of a given economy is the *output per man hour* figures for a number of years. In comparative economics, output per capita figures may be used to help in making an assessment of economies as diverse as those of the U.S. and the U.S.S.R.

As a measuring device, the average product has two advantages. First, as a concept, it is easy to understand. Second, it provides a rough measure of the level of personal well-being in an economy. A report of total output without qualification says nothing about how much product is even theoretically available to each member of society. But data expressed in terms of output

per man must be interpreted cautiously. To some individuals, an increase in output per worker may suggest that the *personal* productivity of workers is rising and that wages therefore should be increased. But another possibility is that greater inputs of capital are responsible for the increase in per capita output and that the owners of capital have a claim to at least part of the increase in output. Whatever the case, the measure we call the average product *does not* attribute the creation of the entire output, or any specific portion of it, to the one particular input used as a base figure.

Law of diminishing average product. The tendency of output per unit of input to fall, *ceteris paribus,* is referred to as in the law of diminishing average product. This "law," or empirical hypothesis, holds that as the amount of a variable input is increased, other things remaining equal, a point will be reached at which the product per unit of the variable input (average product) will begin to decrease.

Consider Table 6-1. L is the variable input. The expression $(K = K_1)$ indicates that this example is predicated on the assumption that K is fixed in amount at K_1 units. The middle column shows the response of output (X) to changes in the variable input (L); and the third column shows average product—output at a specific input level, divided by that amount of the variable input. The subscript L appended to the expression AP specifies that the column refers to a situation in which L is the variable input.

TABLE 6-1

Labor $(K = K_1)$	Output (X)	AP_L $\left(\dfrac{X}{L}\right)$
0	0	0
1	100	100
2	150	75
3	180	60
4	200	50
5	225	45
6	186	31

In this tabular example, the average productivity of L falls from the outset of production. The total product curves depicted in Figure 6-1 show diminishing *average* returns to the variable input from the outset of production and so are compatible with the pattern of the average productivity figures in the third column of Table 6-1.

Graphical analysis of diminishing average returns. We shall now analyze diminishing average returns graphically. Once again, consider Figure 6-1.

Average product is total output divided by the variable input. When OL_2

units of L are used with K_2 units of K, $OX_3 = L_2C$ units of X are produced. There-fore, the average product of labor must be

$$AP_L = \frac{L_2C}{OL_2}$$

Graphically, the average product of the variable input is the vertical distance from the input (horizontal) axis to the given total product curve divided by the accompanying horizontal distance. But the ratio of a vertical distance to a corresponding horizontal distance is the formula for the slope of a straight line. Therefore, the average product of labor when OL_2 units of labor are being used with K_2 units of capital is the slope of line OC.[4]

In Figure 6-1, the average productivity of labor is falling from the outset of production. The greater the input of L, the less steep will be a line drawn from the origin to the corresponding point on a given total product curve. Comparing the slopes of lines OC and OM, we see that OC has a steeper slope than OM, indicating that the average product of L is falling as more L is used with K_2 units of capital. Thus, for the L inputs given,

$$\frac{L_1B}{OL_1} > \frac{L_2C}{OL_2} > \frac{L_MM}{OL_M}$$

Although *total* product is at a maximum at point M, the *average* product of L is less at OL_M units of input than at any lesser amount of the variable input.

As we have seen, the law of diminishing average returns merely reflects the common-sense proposition that as the number of units of the variable factor is increased against a fixed amount of other inputs, each unit of the variable input has, on the average, less of the fixed factor with which to work. For example, two men with one shovel between them may be able to excavate more earth in one day than one man with one shovel (total product increases), but because they must share the capital input between them, their average output may be less than double the output of one man with one shovel. The law of diminishing average returns, then, is based on relative factor scarcity and holds

[4] If you are familiar with trigonometry, you will have observed that the average product of a variable input is the tangent of the angle formed by the straight line drawn from the origin to a point on the total product curve. In Figure 6-1, line OC forms the hypotenuse of the right triangle OL_2C. With respect to angle a, the line L_2C depicting the output of X at OL_2 units of L is the *opposite* side. Line OL_2, depicting the amount of L units being used, is the *adjacent* side of the angle. In trigonometry, the ratio of the opposite side to the adjacent side is defined as the tangent of the given acute angle of a right triangle. The numerical value of the tangent of angle a, therefore, is the average product of L when OL_2 units are employed. (AP_L, employing OL_2 units = tangent of angle a = slope of line OC.) The tangent of an acute angle of a right triangle varies directly with the size of the angle. Since the average product of a variable input is the tangent of the angle formed by the input (horizontal) axis with a line drawn from the origin to a given point on the total product curve, the magnitude of the average product of the variable input is shown by the size of the particular angle.

that even if there is an increase in total output attributable to an increase in labor (the variable input), the ratio of output to labor falls.

Increasing and constant returns. Although the law of diminishing average returns holds that the ratio of output to input must eventually fall as the variable input is increased, *ceteris paribus,* is it possible that the ratio may *rise* or remain *constant* under similar conditions? Consider the information in Table 6-2. Here, the average product of L does not commence to fall until 5 units of the input are used. Up to the third unit of the variable input, the average product of L is *increasing.* From the third to the fourth units of the variable input, the average product of L is *constant.*

TABLE 6-2	Labor (L) $(K = K_1)$	Output (X)	AP_L $\left(\dfrac{X}{L}\right)$
	0	0	0
	1	0	0
	2	300	150
	3	600	200
	4	800	200
	5	900	180
	6	960	160

Increasing and constant returns to a variable input do not violate the law of diminishing average product. The law holds only that *beyond some point,* average productivity must fall. In Table 6-2, that does not occur until 5 units of L are used. The reason for increasing average productivity is that below some ratio of L to K, L is so scarce relative to K that the units of the variable input cannot make effective use of the fixed inputs. For example, think of a restaurant filled with fifty hungry people. They are likely to stay hungry if all the personnel except the manager go on strike. One man cannot very well take orders, cook, serve, make change, and wash dishes. The output of one man and a normal complement of restaurant equipment is likely to be almost nothing. But if one person will join the severely taxed manager, perhaps some positive output will result. If even more people will return to work—a waitress, a cook, a dishwasher, and a cashier—average product doubtless will rise. If too many cooks can spoil the broth, it is also possible that too few cooks cannot get the broth to the diners in time for them to enjoy it.

Another possible cause of increased average productivity is the likelihood of specialization as more workers are added to the fixed complement of restaurant equipment. Simply adding more multipurpose employees may increase average product up to a point, but the output per employee is likely to be further enhanced if cooks stick to cooking and the cashier stays at the cash

register. Time is lost if a chef has to wash his hands and come out of the kitchen every time a customer pays his bill. Not only does this simple division of labor engender greater average productivity, but the gaining of expertise inherent in specialization also contributes to greater output per person.

But, according to the law of diminishing average productivity, there comes a point when the increase in the ratio of output to variable input must halt and then decrease. In all productive processes, beyond some level of variable input usage, average product must decrease, although total output is still rising.

The total product curve of Figure 6-2 is compatible with Table 6-2. This curve does not begin at the origin. There is no output until the input of L is something greater than OL_2 units. Any smaller input of L—say, OL_1 units—does not yield an output. A certain minimum amount of L must be used with a given amount of K before any quantity of good X is produced. The curve is highly plausible; as noted before, there are many plants from which no output can be expected until the labor input has reached a certain minimum.

Diminishing marginal product. We have observed how total and average products change as the amount of one input is varied, *ceteris paribus*. Now let us observe another type of change: the *change* in total output in response to a change in input under the conditions of *ceteris paribus*. The change in total output produced by a change in input is called the *marginal*

FIGURE 6-2

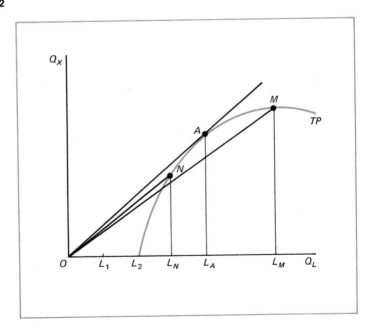

product of the variable factor. The formula for the marginal product of a variable input is

$$MP_V = \frac{\Delta Q}{\Delta V}$$

For our immediate purposes, it is convenient to compute the marginal product with 1-unit changes in the variable input. Thus, if 600 units of X initially were produced with a fixed amount of capital and 3 units of labor and a subsequent increase in the labor input to 4 units has caused total output to rise to 800 units of X, the marginal product of labor is 200X.

In Table 6-3, data for the marginal product of L have been entered in the fourth column. Note that the marginal product figures are entered *between* the various levels of L input, whereas total product and average product are associated with a specific amount of L. This is done because marginal product is the *change* in total output produced by a 1-unit change in the variable input.

In Table 6-3, marginal product increases until 3 units of L are used.

TABLE 6-3	Labor (L) (K = K₁)	Output (X)	AP_L $\left(\frac{X}{L}\right)$	MP_L $\left(\frac{\Delta X}{\Delta L}\right)$
	0	0	0	
				100
	1	100	100	
				200
	2	300	150	
				300
	3	600	200	
				200
	4	800	200	
				100
	5	900	180	
				60
	6	960	160	
				20
	7	980	140	
				4
	8	984	123	
				2
	9	990	110	
				0
	10	990	99	
				−11
	11	979	89	
				−19
	12	960	80	

Thereafter, the marginal productivity of labor falls. Increasing marginal productivity is the result of the increasingly efficient use of the fixed input by each unit of the variable factor for every increase in that variable factor. In the range of increasing marginal productivity, there are "too many" units of the fixed factor relative to the variable input. For example, assume a logger is trying to fell a large tree with a saw designed for use by two men—one pushing while the other pulls. Possibly one man could bring the tree down, but he would be a long time in doing so. In effect, the saw (the fixed input) is "too much" for one logger (the variable input). Adding a second man to the opposite end of the saw so that it can be used properly would cause the total output of trees felled to increase at an increasing rate. The addition of a second man would involve a more-than-twofold increase in output.

The law of diminishing marginal product holds that at some level of variable input usage, the change in total output occasioned by an increase in the variable factor must fall. In other words, although total output will continue to increase, it will do so at a decreasing rate. Again, consider our two-man saw example. If we add a third man, it is obvious that one sawyer must stand idle while two men work the saw. Yet, the total output of trees felled may still increase. The additional man can provide relief. One sawyer can rest while the other two work. Perhaps the saw can be kept in use for longer periods. But because no more than two men can work the saw at once, the addition of a third lumberman probably will not cause total output to increase by as much as it did when the labor force was increased from one to two men.

Table 6-3 shows that when marginal productivity is falling, average and total product may continue to rise. Indeed, even though marginal product is falling, as long as it exceeds average product, the average product will rise.

A simple analogy will easily clarify the relationships among the productivity measures. Suppose the combined weight of ten individuals in an elevator is 1,500 pounds. The average weight of these passengers is 150 pounds. What their average weight will be after the elevator makes its next stop depends on the weight of the (marginal) person who enters or leaves the conveyance. Suppose, at the next stop, a 183-pound individual gets on. The combined weight of the passengers now rises to 1,683 pounds, and their average weight increases to 153 pounds. The 3-pound increase in their average weight is the result of the weight of the additional (marginal) passenger being greater than the previous average weight. When the elevator stops again, a 165-pound passenger steps aboard. The total weight of the twelve passengers is now 1,848 pounds. Now, even though the marginal weight has fallen (from 183 to 165 pounds), the average weight continues to rise; it is 154 pounds. At a third stop, a 154-pound passenger boards the elevator. The total weight has risen to 2,002 pounds, but because the weight of the marginal passenger is equal to the average weight, average weight remains constant at 154 pounds. Finally, suppose a fourteenth passenger weighing 98 pounds enters. The total weight will now rise to 2,100 pounds, but in consequence of the weight of the marginal passenger being less than the average weight, the average weight falls to 150

pounds. In short, it is the *relationship* of the marginal weight to the average weight (greater than, equal to, or less than) that controls the behavior of the average and not the direction of change (up, constant, or down) in the marginal magnitude.

Graphical analysis of marginal product. Marginal product is defined as the change in total output produced by a change in one (the variable) input, all other inputs remaining constant. In Figure 6-3, total output rises from OX_1 to OX_2 units as a result of increasing the input of labor from OL_1 to OL_2 units. The change in total output (ΔX), X_1X_2, is equal to BS, and the change in the variable input (ΔL), L_1L_2, is equal to RB. Since the distance RS (on the total product curve) is traversed for the given increase in the variable input, the marginal product of L is the slope of the total product curve.

But there is a difficulty: over the distance RS, the slope of the total product curve is continuously changing (because it is a nonlinear curve), so we cannot properly speak of the slope of the total product curve between points R and S. The formula for marginal product would give us the *true* value of the

FIGURE 6-3

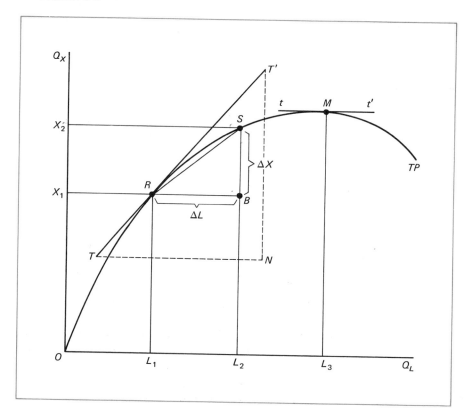

slope of the straight line connecting points R and S. The smaller the distance between R and S, the more nearly the slope of a straight line connecting them will approximate the slope of the portion of the curve lying between them. We shall make use of this fact to simplify our task of analyzing marginal product graphically.

It is unnecessary that the change in labor be represented by a distance as great as L_1L_2. Let us conceptually contract that distance by successively halving it. Since we can halve the distance between L_1 and L_2 an infinite number of times, we can, while keeping $\Delta L > 0$, make it *approach zero as a limit*. More simply, we are letting the distance between L_1 and L_2 get as close to zero as we like without actually becoming zero. By doing this, we are making the distance between R and S so small that the straight line connecting them must be very nearly tangent to the curve. Indeed, for all practical purposes, it can be considered tangent to the curve *at a specific point*.

In Figure 6-3, suppose we have ''collapsed'' the distance between L_1 and L_2 so that points R and S coalesce at point R. Let us draw the straight line TT' tangent to the total product curve at R. The slope of TT' will very nearly approximate the slope of the total product curve in the vicinity of point R. The slope of TT' is the ratio of NT' to TN.

Having adopted this graphical method of determining marginal product, we may now speak of the marginal productivity of labor when a *certain amount* of labor is employed (as contrasted with what it is *between* two different inputs of labor). This is the *point* marginal product rather than the average change in product occurring in response to a finite change in input. If we were to compile a table from our graph showing the responses of total and marginal product to changes in the variable input, we could now place the marginal product figures at *specific* levels of input.

We do not say that the marginal product of labor is the product of the ''last'' L unit used. We cannot identify a ''last'' unit of L. Perhaps all the L units were hired at once. If all the L units are of equal productivity, presumably each would contribute the same amount to production. The concept of marginal product is independent of the time sequence in which specific input units are used. The graphical analysis shows only that the marginal product of L is a specified amount when a given number of L units are employed.

What, then, does marginal product mean? The slope of a curve is its rate of change. Since the marginal product of labor *is* the slope of the total product curve, marginal product tells us at what *rate* total product will change for a very small increase or decrease in the variable input. For example, if the marginal productivity of L is one-half unit of X, we can expect a one-half-unit change in the output of X in response to a very small change in the input of L.

A tangent to point S on the total product curve in Figure 6-3 would be less steep than the tangent to point R, which illustrates the law of diminishing marginal productivity. The tangent to point M has no slope since it is a horizontal line; therefore, at the point of maximum *total* product, the *marginal* product of L is zero. If the input of L is changed so that a move away from M is made,

total output must fall; thus, *at M*, *L* makes no contribution at the margin to total output.

Increasing marginal product. Suppose a production function yields a range of increasing returns to the variable factor. Figure 6-4 shows a total product curve typical of such a function. The marginal productivity of *L* increases up to point *I* on the product curve. Any tangent drawn to points on the curve lying between the origin and point *I* will lie on the underside of the curve and become progressively steeper up to *I*. At point *I*, it is possible to draw a line only *through* the point and not tangent to it. Tangents drawn to any points lying between *I* and *M* will lie above the curve and will be successively less steep as the amount of the variable input is increased. This process reveals that point *I* is the point of maximum steepness on the total product curve; here the *rate of change* in total product is at its maximum. Geometrically, point *I* is the point of *inflection*. That is, the total product curve is *convex* with respect to the horizontal axis to the left of point *I* and *concave* with respect to the horizontal axis to the right of point *I*. In production theory, point *I* is the point of diminishing marginal returns.

Diminishing returns—summary. We have defined three different points of diminishing returns. These points are indicated in Figure 6-4. Point *I* is the point of diminishing *marginal* returns (DMR); point *A* is the point of dimin-

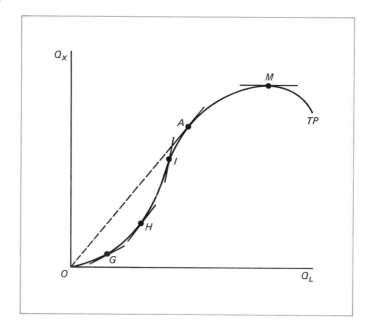

ishing *average* returns (DAR); and point *M* is the point of diminishing *total* returns (DTR).

Note how the several productivity measures are related. Up to point *I*, *all* the productivity measures are increasing. Beyond point *I*, the *marginal productivity* of the variable input is falling, while the average and total productivities of labor continue to rise. Beyond point *A*, the productivity of labor at the margin and *on the average* is falling, while total output continues to increase up to point *M*. Beyond *M*, *all* the productivity measures are decreasing.

DERIVATION OF AVERAGE
AND MARGINAL PRODUCT CURVES

A graph of the *average* product of a variable input can be obtained from the total product curve by plotting the ratios of total output to total variable input as points on a graph. Figures 6-5(a) and 6-6(a) show two total product curves. Figures 6-5(b) and 6-6(b) show their corresponding average product curves. In Figure 6-5(b), the average product curve falls continuously toward the horizontal axis. Since diminishing average productivity commences at the outset of production, there is no rising segment in this average product curve. Contrast this curve with the curve in Figure 6-6(b), which corresponds to a production function that yields no output until a certain minimum amount of the variable input is used—as shown in the total product curve of Figure 6-6(a).

From our previous discussion, we know that here the average product of *L* is at a maximum when OL_A units of the variable input are used. Point *A* in Figure 6-6(a) is the point of maximum average product. It corresponds to point *A′* in Figure 6-6(b). It is the highest point on the average product curve; therefore, average product increases up to point *A′* (as it does up to *A* on the total product curve) and falls thereafter.

The input axes of the total and average product curves of Figure 6-6 are identical; they both measure the same magnitude—the amount of the variable input. The vertical axes, however, are different. The vertical axis Figure 6-6(a) measures *total* output. Thus, the amount of output produced when the average productivity of *L* is at its maximum is OX_A units. The average product of *L* when OL_A units of labor are used is OX_A/OL_A, designated as X_A/L_A in Figure 6-6(b). (The scale of the vertical axes of the graphs of Figures 6-5(b) and 6-6(b) has been expanded to facilitate viewing.)

By plotting the slopes of tangents drawn to various points on a total product curve, we can obtain a graph of the *marginal* product of the variable input. The total product curve of graph (a) in Figure 6-5 would yield a marginal product curve such as that depicted in graph (b) of the same figure. Marginal product declines continuously from the outset of production, so that the marginal product curve is negatively sloped throughout its entire length. The same is true for the marginal product curve of Figure 6-6(b) even though there is a range of increasing *average* productivity. Point *M′* corresponds to point *M* on the

FIGURE 6-5

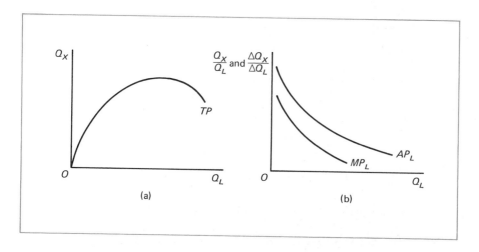

(a)

(b)

FIGURE 6-6

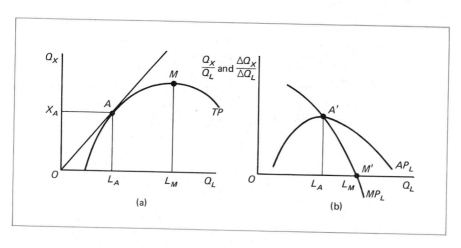

(a)

(b)

total product curve, for when OL_M units of L are employed, the marginal product of L is zero. If more than OL_M units of labor are used, the total output of X will fall, indicating that the marginal productivity of the variable input has become negative. Thus, the marginal product curves of Figures 6-5 and 6-6 extend below the horizontal axes (into the graphical quadrant of negative marginal productivity) beyond point M'.

Figure 6-7(b) shows a graph of the marginal product of labor that would be obtained from a production function yielding a range of increasing marginal returns to the variable factor. The marginal product of labor increases up to point I'; therefore, I' corresponds to point I in graph (a); it is the point

FIGURE 6-7

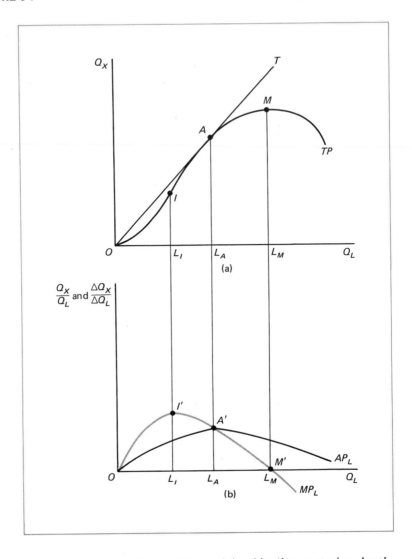

(a)

(b)

of diminishing *marginal* returns. Point *M'* is explained by the reasoning developed previously.

Productivity measure relationships. Up to OL_I units of labor, marginal productivity is rising; thus, *I'* is the highest point on the marginal productivity curve. Up to OL_A units of labor, the average productivity of the variable input continues to rise, as it does from the outset of production; but beyond OL_A labor units, average product falls. Therefore, *A'* is the highest point on the average product curve. Note that the marginal product curve intersects the

average product curve at point A'. Obviously, the marginal and average products of labor are equal when OL_A units of labor are used. This is not merely by chance. It is necessarily the case that when average product is at its maximum value it is equal to marginal product. The reason for this relationship is apparent in Figure 6-7. The maximum value for the average product of the variable input is determined by extending a ray from the origin that is tangent to the total product curve. The ray radiating from the origin in Figure 6-7(a) is tangent to the total product curve at A, so we know that A reveals the input at which the average productivity of labor is at its maximum. We determine the marginal product of the variable input by drawing a line tangent to the curve at a particular point. Line OT (identical to the ray discussed above) is tangent to the total product curve at A. Therefore, the ratio that expresses the average product—L_A/OL_A—also expresses the slope of the total product curve at A and, hence, is also the marginal product of labor. The only point on a total product curve at which average product and marginal product are equal is a point that can be fixed by a ray drawn from the origin tangent to the curve. At such a point, average product is necessarily at a maximum. We conclude from this graphical analysis that average product will always rise as long as it is less than marginal product. Average product will fall whenever it exceeds marginal product. When marginal product is neither rising nor falling, average product must be constant and at its maximum.

At input levels greater than OL_A units of labor, both the marginal and average product curves are falling, while the total product curve continues to rise. At OL_M units of labor, *total* product is at a maximum, and *marginal* product is zero. If labor is increased beyond OL_M units, total product will fall, and the marginal product curve will dip below the horizontal axis, indicating that marginal product is negative. Although the average product curve is falling, it does not become negative. Average product will equal zero only when total product is zero.

Production and cost theories. The productivity curves are important, not only in production theory, but in the theory of cost and in theories of business behavior. In Chapter 7, we will meet these curves again as cost curves. Cost curves are only modified product curves (taking account of input prices). Understanding this not only facilitates understanding the theory of cost but helps to make clear the sometimes not too obvious fact that basic physical relationships underlie the costs of production.

THE PRODUCTION SURFACE

Suppose we now drop the *ceteris paribus* assumption and attempt to discover how output is affected by concurrent changes in both (all) inputs. We already have described the components of the model necessary for this purpose; all we need to do now is assemble them properly. We will begin

with the familiar total product curves of the preceding sections. Two such curves are shown in Figure 6-8. Graph (a) shows a total product curve for labor drawn on the assumption that the amount of capital is fixed at K^* units. The total product curve for capital in graph (b) is drawn on the assumption that the amount of labor is fixed at L^* units. Each total product curve is drawn only for the range of positive marginal productivity of the associated variable input. For example, any additional input of labor beyond OL^* would cause the total product curve of graph (a) to turn downward. Both total product curves, in other words, are cut off at their maximum points.

The total product curves of Figure 6-8 are only two of an infinite number of such curves. Each input has a total product curve for every specific quantity of the other input. If we could combine these total product curves in a single graph, we could determine the output of X associated with any given quantities of the two inputs.

What would such a graph be like? It would require one axis to measure the input of labor, another axis to measure the input of capital, and a third axis to measure the output of good X; in short, it would be three-dimensional.

Figure 6-9 shows a three-dimensional *production surface*. Only seven of an infinite number of planes in the surface have been made visible. The planes are our familiar total product curves. The base plane on which the total product curves rest is called the *input space*. The inputs of labor and capital are measured along the right and left edges, respectively, of the input space. The origin of the figure is at O; the farther any point on an input edge lies from the origin, the greater is the quantity of input. The vertical distance above the input space measures the output of X; the higher any point is above the floor, the greater is the output of X.

The total product curves of Figure 6-8 have been placed on the input space at points L^* and K^*. Point X at the far corner of the input space (diagon-

FIGURE 6-8

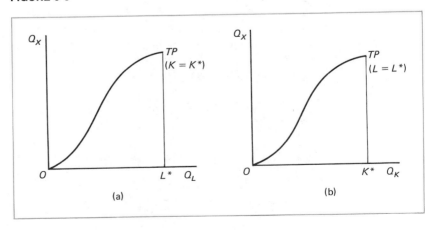

The Theory of Production

FIGURE 6-9

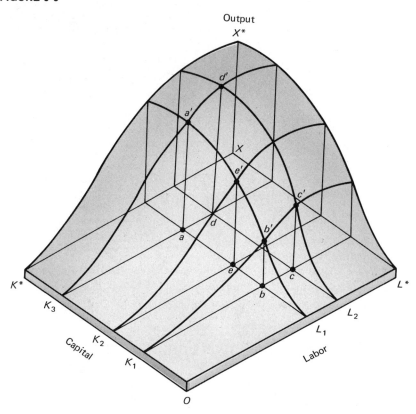

ally opposite the origin) represents the input combination $OL^* + OK^*$. The output produced is XX^*.

Now let us consider some of the other planes in the model. The plane at OK_3 shows how the total output of X changes when capital is held constant at OK_3 units and labor is varied from zero to OL^* units. The plane at OL_1 shows how the output of X changes when the input of labor is held constant at OL_1 units and capital is varied from zero to OK^* units. Suppose we wish to find the output of X yielded by the input combination $OL_1 + OK_3$. The two planes intersect at point a on the input space. The output of X is indicated by the distance from a on the floor to a point on the surface lying vertically above a. That point is a'. Therefore, the output of the input combination $OL_1 + OK_3$ is aa' units of X.

Suppose the input of L is held constant at OL_1 units, while the input of capital is reduced to OK_1 units. What will be the output of X resulting from this input combination? The two associated total product curves intersect at point b on the input space. The output yielded by this input combination,

$OL_1 + OK_1$, is the vertical distance from b to b' on the production surface; therefore, the associated output of X is bb' units. Similarly, the output of X yielded by the input combination $OL_2 + OK_1$ is cc' units of X. If the input combination is $OL_2 + OK_3$, the total output of X is dd' units.

Since there is an infinite number of planes (total product curves) in the graph, the surface is solid. Its face is smooth and continuous. It closely resembles one-quarter of a Christmas bell. Any point on the surface shows the amount of X produced by the technically efficient use of particular quantities of inputs. Be reversing the procedure we have been following, we can determine a technically efficient input combination for producing any given quantity of X. Suppose point e' on the surface is at the desired output level—indicated by its height above the input space. We drop a perpendicular from e' to the base plane (input space). The perpendicular strikes the input space at point e. Point e denotes a technically efficient combination of inputs that will yield ee' units of X. To find that combination, we draw perpendiculars from e along the surface of the base plane (input space) to the labor and capital edges. We find that the input combination is $OL_1 + OK_2$. So far, we can locate only *technically* efficient combinations. We must develop further analytical techniques before we can identify an *economically* efficient (least-cost) input combination for producing a desired quantity of X.

DISSECTION OF THE PRODUCTION SURFACE —TOTAL PRODUCT CURVES

Since the production surface is solid, it is possible to find any desired total product curve by taking a slice of that surface. For example, suppose we wish to find the total product curve for labor as defined for OK_2 units of capital. We must make a cut with a plane through the surface perpendicular to the base plane and parallel to the labor edge at OK_2 units of capital. The upper edge of the resulting plane is the desired total product curve.

We have now made our first dissection of the production surface. Note that any dissection made by passing a plane through the surface perpendicular to the input space and parallel to either the capital or the labor edge of the model yields a total product curve. As we continue our discussion of production theory, we shall make two other types of cut through the surface.

DISSECTION OF THE PRODUCTION SURFACE —SCALE PRODUCT CURVES

Suppose we now make a slice through the production surface perpendicular to the input space (base plane) and through the origin. In Figure 6-10(a), such a plane, $OVSN$, has been thrust through a production surface. The "floor plan" of the cutting plane is shown in Figure 6-10(b).

What is the purpose of making this cut? The bottom edge (the straight line OV) of plane $OVSN$ joins together combinations of L and K. At point V, L_1 units of L are combined with OK_1 units of K. To find out how many units of X are produced by this combination of L and K we need only project a line perpendicular to the input space from V to the production surface. The perpendicular intersects the production surface at Q. Since Q lies vertically above V, the amount of X produced by OL_1 units of L and OK_1 units of K is VQ units. Similarly, if OL' units of L are combined with OK' units of K, the amount of X produced will be given by a point on the production surface lying vertically above point V', shown in Figure 6-10(b).

The bottom edge (OV) of cutting plane $OVSN$ is a straight line. This means that an increase in *any one* input must be matched by a *proportionate* increase in *all other* inputs. If, in Figure 6-10(b), $OL_1 = 2(OL')$, then $OK_1 = 2(OK')$. We are interested in observing what happens to output when *all* inputs are increased proportionately. Thus, with this dissection, we are dropping the assumption of fixed inputs. The change occurring in output when all inputs are changed proportionately is known as a *return to scale*.

If the changes in all inputs are not proportionate, then some inputs are *relatively* fixed (that is, relative to other inputs), and the laws of diminishing returns will operate. For example, suppose that from an initial input combination of $2L + 2K$, labor is tripled and capital doubled, changing the input combination to $6L + 4K$. Now, although there is more of both labor and capital, there is less labor in relation to capital. Each unit of labor has less capital with

FIGURE 6-10

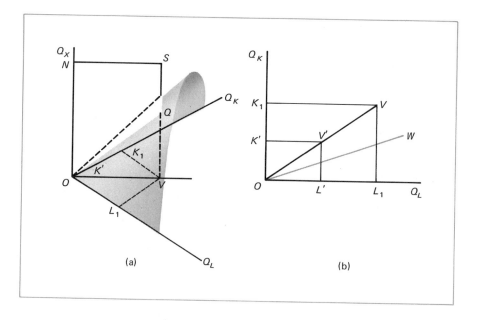

(a)

(b)

which to work. This is essentially the same situation as the one input variable case in which, say, labor is increased while capital is held constant.

How output responds to proportionate changes in all inputs can be determined by an inspection of the "top edge" (line OQ) of the cut in the production surface made by the intersecting plane. We shall call the top edge of the cut a *scale product curve*. It shows how output changes in response to changes in the scale of production—that is, to proportionate changes in all inputs. The scale product curve must occupy three dimensions. In Figure 6-10(a) it is obvious that OQ is a straight line. The slice of the production surface formed by the intersecting plane ($OVSN$) is the triangle OVQ. The top edge (the hypotenuse) of this triangle, line OQ, is important to us. If it is a straight line, as it is in this example, returns to scale are *constant*. As all inputs are increased proportionately along the straight line OV, output moves along OQ. Thus, proportionate increases in all inputs are matched by proportionate increases in output. From the construction of the production surface, we know that it doesn't matter whether the path of the increase in inputs lies along OV or along some other straight line out of the origin of the input space (say, OW); the path of the increase in output is also a straight line lying on the production surface. If, for example, OW in Figure 6-10(b) represents the path described by the proportionate increases in all inputs, we know that for every point on OW there is a point lying vertically above on the production surface and that these points on the production surface form a straight line. Any straight edge laid on the scale product curve will be tangent to all points on the production surface on which the curve lies.

A production function yielding increasing returns to a variable factor, all other factors held constant, can show constant returns to scale. Consider the production surface in Figure 6-11. This surface at first rises at an

FIGURE 6-11

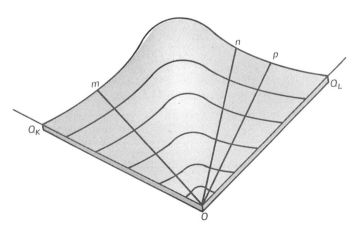

increasing rate from each edge, and then rises at a decreasing rate, after which it reaches its crest. A slice through this surface perpendicular to the base plane and parallel to one of the input edges would yield a total product curve similar to that in Figure 6-7. Nevertheless, this function gives constant returns to scale since a straight edge pivoted at the origin can be laid along the surface as is shown by the straight lines Om, On, and Op.

Consider now the production surface in Figure 6-12(a). As the surface radiates from the origin, it flares out like the top half of an old-fashioned phonograph horn. Cutting this surface with a plane perpendicular to the input space and through the origin, which is done in Figure 6-12(b), yields a plane the top edge of which is convex with respect to the input space. In Figure 6-12(b), line OV traces out a path of proportionate increases in L and K, and OQ, the scale product curve, shows the response of X to the input changes. Since OQ shows X increasing at an increasing rate, this production function must yield *increasing* returns to scale. Proportionate changes in all inputs yield a greater than proportionate change in output. Thus, if OL' units of L and OK' units of K are used, the output of X is equal to $V'Q'$ units. If L and K are increased proportionately, as is necessarily the case when path OV is followed, then, when OL_1 units of labor are used with OK_1 units of capital, the output of X is equal to VQ units, and $VQ/V'V > V'Q'/OV'$.

FIGURE 6-12

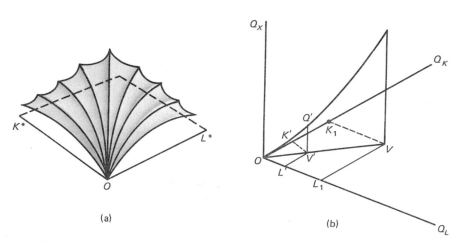

(a) (b)

The third and final case to be analyzed is that of *decreasing* returns to scale. Suppose that making a slice through the production surface perpendicular to the input space and through the origin, we obtain a plane like OVQ in Figure 6-13. The top edge of the plane, the scale product curve, is concave with respect to the input space, showing that as all inputs are increased pro-

FIGURE 6-13

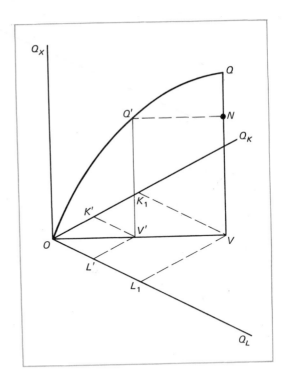

portionately, total output increases less than proportionately—i.e., increases at a decreasing rate. If OL_1 units of L are combined with OK_1 units of K, the result is VQ units of total output. Similarly, if OL' units of L are used with OK' units of K, the output of X is equal to $V'Q'$ units. Since the path traced out by the increase in the inputs is the straight line OV, we know that $OL'/OK' = L'L_1/K'K = OV'/V'V$. The vertical distance NQ shows the change in the output of X resulting from the proportionate increase in all the inputs. Since OQ rises at a decreasing rate, it must be the case that $V'Q'/OV' > VQ/OV$ or $NQ/V'V < L'L_1/K'K$. A proportionate increase in all inputs has produced a less than proportionate increase in output. Thus, curve OQ displays the phenomenon of decreasing returns to scale.

CAUSES OF RETURNS TO SCALE

What causes the phenomena of returns to scale? Returns to scale reflect only changes *internal* to the firm. They are not caused by changes in the nature of inputs or changes in input prices. If returns to scale are increasing, it must be that increasing the number of all inputs causes the firm to be more efficient. Decreasing returns to scale show the presence of increasing *inefficiencies* as the firm increases its inputs proportionately. Constant returns

to scale mean that neither efficiency nor inefficiency is encountered as a result of proportionate increases in all inputs.

Increasing returns to scale. The concept of returns to scale can be troublesome. It should not be confused with *historically* decreasing costs.[5] For example, in the early days of the automobile industry, engine blocks were drilled by workmen using conventional drill presses. The press operator had to position the block for every hole. Holes of different bore were drilled on different presses or the bits had to be changed on the same press. Obviously, a great deal of time, with its consequent cost, was spent in adjusting multi-purpose drill presses to the flow of product through the plant. Today, computer-operated, highly specialized drill assemblies drill a great number of holes of different size and position in an engine block at one time, the blocks themselves moving through the drill assemblies in a continuous flow. Technical progress, then, has reduced costs by changing the techniques of engine production. But this kind of cost decrease is not, strictly speaking, an instance of increasing returns to scale. Returns to scale, if they do exist, simply show how output changes if a firm were to alter the *scale* of its plant—that is, if it were to change the amounts of *all* inputs proportionately.

Recognizing this essential definition, some economists have argued that the only reasonable response of output to proportionate increases in all inputs in *any* productive process is constant returns to scale. They insist that if a process is exactly duplicated or triplicated, the increase in output should match exactly the increase in inputs. After all, every plant is just the *same* plant all over again, management included. This argument is unrealistic in its assumptions of how a firm would deploy increased inputs.

If we insist that production functions are predicated on the firm's *efficient* use of all inputs, then we may assume that the firm rearranges its techniques of production to avail itself of any benefits inherent in the use of a greater number of all inputs. For example, equal increases in all inputs may allow for the increasing specialization of each of the inputs, the specialization resulting in a proportionately greater increase in output. In such a case, the increase in all inputs allows each unit of an input to be used in a more effective way.

Suppose a typist (labor) with one typewriter (capital) can turn out thirty pages during a workday in which she must answer the phone, file papers, and so on. Now suppose that in an effort to increase the output of typing, labor and capital are doubled: a second typist is hired to operate a second typewriter. If the second girl *exactly duplicates* the work patterns of the first, we would expect constant returns to scale to result—in response to a doubling of all inputs, output would double to sixty pages per day. But this is not likely to

---

[5] The analysis of this book is static and does not consider changes occurring over time. We are concerned here with what can happen at a given moment in time.

happen. It is entirely possible that since there are now two typists, they will be able to divide their duties so that each can have some uninterrupted time at her typewriter. Then, even though she spends no *more* time typing, the first girl may be able to increase her output to forty pages. Even if the second girl can do no better than the first did—turn out thirty pages—the total output of two typists and two typewriters will be seventy pages a day, and output will have more than doubled, a case of increasing returns to scale.

Decreasing returns to scale. Many economists assert that returns to scale will decrease when changes in the scale of production cause inefficiency. Bureaucratic entanglements, increases in paperwork, and the inability of management to supervise a more complicated and more widely dispersed firm may result in output failing to match increases in inputs. Some economists hold that *decentralization* is a sign that a firm has begun to encounter decreasing returns to scale in its plants. In an effort to combat the tangle in communications and the impersonality of an enormous factory, the firm may decide to produce its outputs in a number of separate plants, each of which having what is hoped to be an optimal degree of autonomy. This works well in a multi-output firm whose products bear little or no relationship to one another—as, for example, in the electrical manufacturing industry, in which there is little in common between the fabrication of power generation equipment and the manufacture of fractional horsepower motors. (This is not to say that decentralization has no advantages in other situations.)

It is important to note that the forces leading to decentralization have nothing to do with a particular economic system. As the Soviet Union has expanded its productive capabilities, it has been troubled by increasing inefficiencies, particularly bureaucratic. The new winds of economic thought blowing through the U.S.S.R. are concerned largely with prescribing and implementing decentralization schemes within the framework of a planned economy.

The proper identification of decreasing returns to scale requires sharp scrutiny to be certain that scale changes are involved. Do decreasing returns to scale occur when a firm becomes so large that its management can no longer function effectively or that its paperwork multiplies so enormously as to be a hindrance to output? Very likely, these phenomena are not returns to scale, since the fact that management has to be spread over a greater volume of operations or that paperwork must be disproportionately expanded to maintain managerial surveillance is a clear statement that inputs have *not* been increased proportionately; management is a *relatively* fixed input. Thus, what is involved here is merely the law of diminishing returns.

Economists do not suppose a firm necessarily changes its inputs proportionately; they merely ask what *would* happen if such a change were to be made. The answer reveals whether there are inherent efficiencies or inefficiencies or the absence of both in a particular production function. To some extent, this question and its answer are like a physicist asking what would happen to certain substances at absolute zero. Even though absolute zero is un-

likely to be encountered, the answer may have great theoretical, and quite possibly practical, significance.

DISSECTION OF THE PRODUCTION SURFACE—ISOQUANTS

As the final dissection, we shall make a slice through the production surface parallel to the input space. This means that we are making a slice at a particular level of output. Since the production surface is based on objective technical information, the amount of output is a known magnitude.

Consider the production surface $OL^*X^*K^*$ in Figure 6-14. Only five of an infinite number of total product curves (planes) are made visible (the planes having intercepts in the input space at K^*, K_2, K_1, L_1, and L^*). The planes ap-

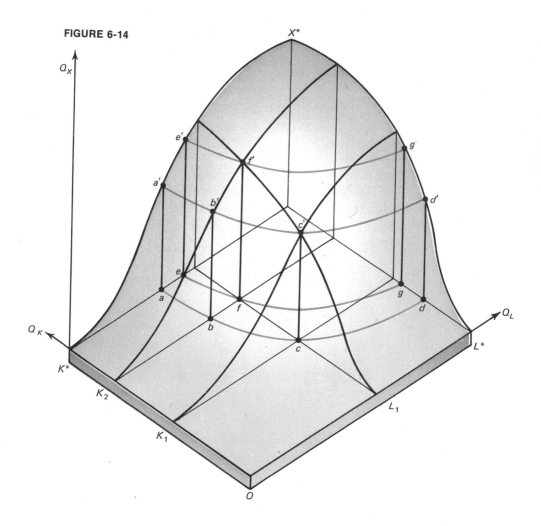

FIGURE 6-14

propriate to OL_1 units of L and OK_1 units of K intersect at the line segment cc'. Suppose we insert a cutting plane parallel to the input space at a height equal to cc'. Since the height of the production surface measures the quantity of good X, cc' shows the quantity of X produced by OL_1 units of L and OK_1 units of K. The cutting plane intersects the surface at points a', b', c', and d', and since the cutting plane is parallel to the input space, line segments aa', bb', and dd' are equal in height to cc'; that is, they all represent the same quantity of X. A line drawn along the surface through points a', b', c', and d' would pass through an infinite number of points, all lying at the same height above the input space. Such a line would follow the curvature of the surface and would be convex with respect to the reader.

Suppose that we drop perpendiculars from these indicated points on the production surface to the input space. On the input space we would locate points a, b, c, and d, each of which is vertically beneath its primed counterpart on the surface. If we join the new points with a curved line, the curve we obtain—$abcd$—will be an exact image (a map) of the level $a'b'c'd'$ on the production surface.

Repeating this procedure at different levels on the surface (different outputs of X), we can obtain a contour map of the surface. For example, curve efg traces out on the input space the level of the production surface $e'f'g'$. Generally, it is easier to study the phenomena of production using the contour map instead of the surface because the map requires only two dimensions.

In Figure 6-15, we have two curves, X_1 and X_2, convex to the origin, representing a map of the surface at two particular levels of output. If points a', b', c', and d' in Figure 6-14 indicate an output of, say, 100 tons of X, then points a, b, c, and d in Figures 6-14 and 6-15 (and, indeed, all points on the curves drawn through them) may be taken to represent 100 tons $= X_1$ units of output.

FIGURE 6-15

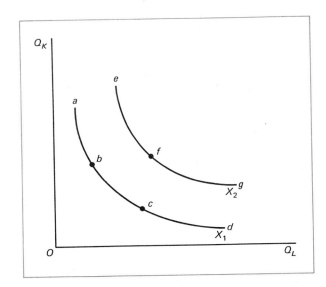

The Theory of Production

The same is true for all points on X_2 in Figure 6-15, except that they must represent an output greater than 100 tons, since X_2 was derived from points lying higher on the production surface. The exact amount of output that X_2 represents can be learned from the production surface. For example, assuming that the vertical distance $ee' = 125$ tons, then $X_2 = 125$ tons.

Curves such as X_1 and X_2 are called "isoquants" (from "iso" meaning equal and "quant" meaning quantity) because *any* point on a *particular* curve represents the same specific amount of total output as any other point on the same curve.

PROPERTIES OF ISOQUANT CURVES

Since isoquants are derived directly from the production surface (they form a contour map of the surface), their properties must reflect accurately the attributes of the surface.

Distance from the origin. The farther an isoquant lies from the origin, the greater the amount of output it represents. This is easy to see simply by looking at a drawing of the production surface. Drawing perpendiculars to the input space from points on increasingly higher levels of the production surface must trace out isoquant curves lying increasingly farther from the origin.

Nonintersection. Although the property of nonintersection of isoquants may seem self-evident, let us examine it as an exercise in logic. In Figure 6-16, consider the two isoquants X_1 and X_2 intersecting at point p. Point p lies on X_1, as does r. By the definition of an isoquant, the output of X at r must be the same as at p—namely, X_1 units. But p is also a point on X_2, and so is s. Again, by the definition of an isoquant, production must be the same at p and at s—namely, X_2. If the output at p is the same as at r, then it must be the same at s by the well-known logical axiom that magnitudes equal to one other thing must be equal to each other. But, *in fact*, the output at s is greater than the output

FIGURE 6-16

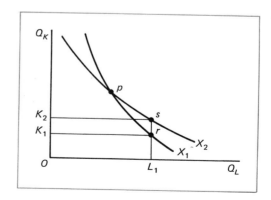

at r. Let us consider these two points. At r, OL_1 units of labor are being used with OK_1 units of K to produce X_1 units of X. At point s, the same amount of L is used with K_1K_2 *more* units of K. Production must be greater at s than at r because if capital is contributing positively to production, as it does in the relevant range of the isoquant, a greater amount of any input used with a fixed amount of all other inputs must yield a greater output. Therefore, Figure 6-16 shows a logical impossibility. Intersecting isoquants result in a paradox for which there is no resolution, so we conclude that isoquants never intersect.

Negative slope. The negative slope of an isoquant derives directly from the production surface. As we know, the output of X is the same at *any* point on a given isoquant. In the relevant range of an isoquant (the range in which a rational, profit-maximizing firm would operate), all inputs contribute positively to production.[6] Suppose, we start at point a on X_1 in Figure 6-17. If we add L_1L_2 units of L to the productive process *without reducing* the input of K, total output must rise. The amount of that total output is given by point a', which must lie on an isoquant situated to the right of X_1. The only way to hold the production of X constant when an input is increased is to withdraw some of the other inputs. The isoquant shows us that if we add L_1L_2 units of L to the productive process, K_1K_2 units of K must be withdrawn if production is to remain unchanged at X_1 units of X. As long as all inputs are able to contribute positively to production (as long as the inputs are substitutes for each other), a curve describing a locus of points of equal output, for changes in all inputs, must have a negative slope.

FIGURE 6-17

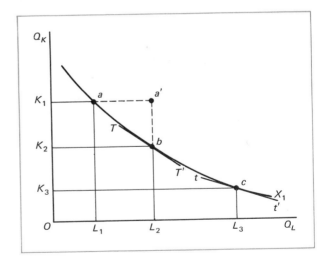

---

[6] A rational profit-maximizing firm would not willingly hire an input having negative marginal productivity. To do so would be to pay for a productive contribution of less than nothing!

Convexity. Figure 6-17 shows that X_1 is convex with respect to the origin. Although this property, too, follows naturally from the shape of the production surface, we should consider the meaning of convexity.

In the chart, K_1K_2 and K_2K_3 are equal decreases in the input of K. Suppose we start from a point on X_1. If the firm finds it expedient to replace K_1K_2 units of K with L while holding output constant at X_1, it will move along the isoquant from a to b. The amount of L needed to replace K_1K_2 units of K is L_1L_2 units. This means that L_1L_2 units of L can do the work formerly done by K_1K_2 units of K. Now suppose that the firm decides to dispose of an additional quantity of K equal in amount to the first reduction. This will cause the firm to move from b to c on X_1. This time, although $K_2K_3 = K_1K_2$, $L_2L_3 > L_1L_2$—that is, now more L is required to replace a diminution in K equal to the first reduction. Why is this? Although L is a substitute for K, it is not a *perfect* substitute. To an extent, L can perform the same functions as K, but it is not the same as K. There are limitations on the ability of any input to substitute for any other input. For example, up to a certain point, the same amount of a crop could be grown on successively smaller parcels of land as the land is cultivated more intensively—as more labor is applied to successively reduced acreages—but labor is not the same as land. The acreage cannot be reduced to zero if output is to be maintained at some given positive level.

The ability of labor to substitute for capital does not expire at once; it may be assumed to diminish gradually. This is why a path of constant output (an isoquant) is convex to the origin. As greater amounts of labor and smaller amounts of capital are used in the production of a given quantity of output, labor becomes successively less able to substitute for reductions in capital. Therefore, if production is to remain constant, labor must increase *at an increasing rate*.

What we have said of labor is also true of capital. Let us reverse the direction of travel on isoquant X_1. If the firm starts at point C and decides to add K_3K_2 units of K, it can dispense with L_3L_2 units of L. This brings it to point b. On a subsequent substitution of an equal amount of K (K_2K_1 units) for L, the firm will find it cannot reduce the input of L by an amount equal to L_3L_2 and maintain the same rate of output. Now, if the firm is to hold output constant at X_1 it can give only L_1L_2 units of L. As more K is substituted for L, K becomes successively less able to substitute for L. Therefore, as equal amounts of capital are successively introduced to replace labor, the amounts of labor that can be given up become successively smaller.

THE DECREASING MARGINAL RATE OF TECHNICAL SUBSTITUTION

The ability of one input to substitute for another while output remains invariant is called its *marginal rate of technical substitution*. Because the ability of one input to substitute for another in such circumstances gradually ap-

proaches a limit, the marginal rate of substitution of one input for another is said to *diminish*. In production theory, this phenomenon is known, understandably, as the *diminishing marginal rate of technical substitution.*

The formula for the marginal rate of technical substitution of labor for capital is

$$MRTS_{LK} = \frac{\Delta K}{\Delta L}$$

For example, in Figure 6-17, as the firm moves along X_1 from a to b, K_1K_2 units of capital are replaced by L_1L_2 units of labor. Thus, the marginal rate of technical substitution of L for K in the range a,b of isoquant X_1 is

$$(MRTS_{lk})_{a,b} = \frac{\Delta K}{\Delta L} = \frac{-(OK_1 - OK_2)}{OL_2 - OL_1} = -\frac{K_1K_2}{L_1L_2}$$

A minus sign is placed in the numerator since K_1K_2 represents a *decrease* in capital usage. Because any movement *along* an isoquant (in the relevant range of production) must involve a decrease in one output for an increase in another input, the marginal rate of technical substitution of one input for another is negative. Since a negative *MRTS* merely reflects the negative slope of the isoquant, from now on we will omit the minus sign. If the firm continues to move along X_1 from b to c

$$(MRTS_{LK})_{b,c} = \frac{\Delta K}{\Delta L} = \frac{K_2K_3}{L_2L_3}$$

Since $K_1K_2 = K_2K_3$ and $L_2L_3 > L_1L_2$, it follows that

$$\frac{K_1K_2}{L_1L_2} > \frac{K_2K_3}{L_2L_3} \qquad \text{or} \qquad (MRTS_{LK})_{a,b} > (MRTS_{LK})_{b,c}$$

The marginal rate of technical substitution of labor for capital over the range from b to c on X_1 is less than that rate over the range from a to b. This is a graphical illustration of the empirical hypothesis that the rate of technical substitution of labor for capital diminishes as more labor is substituted for capital, the output of X remaining constant.

The formula for the marginal rate of technical substitution is the formula for the slope of a line, since it is the ratio of the change in a vertical distance to an accompanying horizontal distance. We can make use of this fortunate fact to avoid the cumbersome task of dealing with the marginal rate of technical substitution over a range on an isoquant. Obviously, with the method we have used up to now, we cannot properly speak of the marginal rate of technical substitution of L for K at any particular *level* of input use. Since the slope of a convex isoquant is constantly changing, so does the marginal rate of tech-

nical substitution of one input for another as the firm moves along a given isoquant.

For our purposes, there is no reason why ΔL or ΔK need be finite changes. Therefore, let us allow ΔL to approach zero. If the increase in the input of labor is negligible, so will be the accompanying decrease in capital, and the resulting movement along the given isoquant will approach zero.

If the movement from point b on X_1 in Figure 6-17 is very small, the slope of TT', a straight line tangent to X_1 at b will closely approximate the slope of X_1 in the vicinity of b. Let us assume that the slope of TT' is 3/1; so we can state that the *point* marginal rate of technical substitution of L for K is also 3/1. Now consider point c. The slope of the straight line tt' tangent to X_1 at c closely approximates the slope of X_1 in the vicinity of point c. The slope of tt' is assumed to be 1/2; therefore, the $MRTS_{LK}$ at c is 1/2. The decreasing slopes of straight-line tangents to points occurring on an isoquant as the labor input is increased (and as the capital input is necessarily decreased) is another illustration of the diminishing marginal rate of technical substitution of labor for capital.

SCALE AND THE SPACING OF ISOQUANTS

In Figures 6-18(a), (b), and (c), we shall assume that the firm starts from an output of 10X and then expands its output, first to 20X and then to 30X. In graph (a), *constant* returns to scale are assumed. An output of 20X may be achieved by doubling the original inputs; that is, $L_1L_2 = OL_1$ and $K_1K_2 = OK_1$. Similarly, output may be tripled by a threefold increase in all inputs; that is, $L_2L_3 = L_1L_2 = OL_1$ and $K_2K_3 = K_1K_2 = OK_1$. If the changes in *each* input are proportionate, the points on the scale line OG must be equally spaced; that is, $OA = AB = BC$.[7] The 10-, 20-, and 30-unit isoquants are separated from

FIGURE 6-18

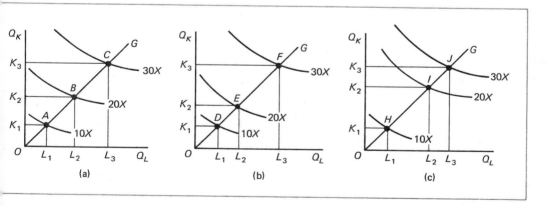

(a)   (b)   (c)

[7] The scale line is the map of the scale product curve.

each other by equal distances. This is what we would expect in an isoquant map depicting a production function that yields constant returns to scale.

Graph (b) depicts *decreasing* returns to scale. If, initially, the firm is producing an output of 10X, it must more than double both inputs to double output. To triple output, more than three times the amount of L and K used to produce 10X must be used. This is shown in Figure 6-18(b) where $OL_1 < L_1L_2 < L_2L_3$, and $OK_1 < K_1K_2 < K_2K_3$. In turn, on the scale line OG, $OD < DE < EF$. Isoquants showing output doubling, tripling, quadrupling, and so on, lie successively farther from each other.

Graph (c) shows the case of *increasing* returns to scale. Output can be doubled and tripled by less than twofold and threefold increases, respectively, in all inputs. In the figure, $OL_1 > L_1L_2 > L_2L_3$, and $OK_1 > K_1K_2 > K_2K_3$. Consequently, on the scale line OG, $OH > OI > OJ$. Isoquants showing output doubling, tripling, quadrupling, and so on, lie successively closer to each other.

RETURNS TO SCALE AND DIMINISHING RETURNS

In Figure 6-19, the phenomenon of (constant) returns to scale and the law of diminishing returns are compared. On the scale line OG, the distances OB, BB', B'B" are equal, showing proportionate increases in output in response to proportionate changes in all inputs. The line K_0H, parallel to the L axis, is drawn to show the response in output when K is held constant at OK_0 units and the input of L is varied. In this situation, ever greater quantities of L are required to yield equal increments in output. Although there are constant re-

FIGURE 6-19

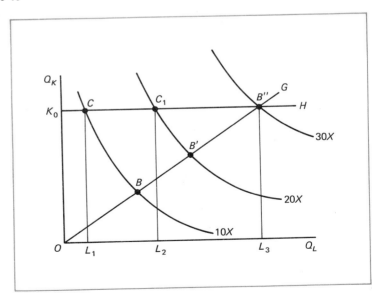

turns to scale when all inputs are increased proportionately, there are diminishing returns (here, from the outset of production) to labor when all other inputs (capital) are held constant. Since the marginal productivity of labor is falling, successively greater increases in labor are required to achieve given increases in output.

A UNIQUE PRODUCTION FUNCTION

Figures 6-18(a) and 6-19 both show a production function exhibiting constant returns to scale over the entire range of production. Such a production function has several unique properties, some of which we shall now consider.

In production theory, when an entire production function yields constant returns to scale, it is said to be *linearly homogeneous*—a description derived from the mathematical nature of the function. For example, given the production function

$$X = f(L, K)$$

suppose both L and K are increased z times. Constant returns to scale require that

$$z^n X = z^n f(L, K) = f(zL, zK) \text{ and that } n = 1$$

If, when each of the variables in a function is multiplied by a constant, the total function increases by some power of that constant, the function is said to be *homogeneous.* If the power of that constant is 1 (as it is in the case of constant returns to scale), the function is *linearly* homogeneous, or homogeneous in the first degree. If n is equal to 2, the increase in output would be given by $z^2 X$, and the function would be homogeneous in the second degree. When the value of n is greater than 1, the production function yields increasing returns to scale, since the amount of the increase of X necessarily will be greater than the proportionate increase, z, in L and K. On the other hand, when n is a positive number but less than 1—for example, if the increase in output is given by $z^{1/2} X$—the production function yields decreasing returns to scale, since the amount of the increase of X necessarily will be less than the proportionate increase in L and K.

Special properties of the linearly homogeneous production function. Suppose the input combination $3L + 4K$ yields $10X$. If the production function is linearly homogeneous then $2(3L + 4K)$, or $6L + 8K$, must yield $20X$, and $300L + 400K$ will yield $100X$. If $3L + 4K$ yields $10X$, another combination—say, $4L + 4K$—might yield $12X$ or $5L + 4K$ might produce $14X$. Whatever the case, a proportional change in all inputs will produce a proportional change in output, so if $4L + 4K \rightarrow 12X$, then $3(4L + 4K) \rightarrow 36X$. Regardless of the *absolute* amount of inputs used, the relationship between the input ratio and

output is constant. In our example, each 3 units of labor and 4 units of capital produces 10 units of output. It makes no difference whether the actual input combination is $3L + 4K$, $30L + 40K$, or $75L + 100K$; when 3 units of labor work with 4 units of capital, the result is 10 units of X. And, if there are 4 units of labor for every 4 units of capital, the result will always be 12 units of X for each such combination. This always being the case, the marginal productivities of the inputs must be unrelated to the *amounts* of the inputs in use but dependent on the *proportions* in which they are used.[8] Therefore, the relationships among the marginal productivities of all the inputs must vary only with input proportions.

Since $MRTS_{LK} = MP_L/MP_K$, it too depends only on input proportions.[9] Therefore, for any *given* input proportion, the marginal rate of substitution between the inputs is constant regardless of the amount of inputs being used, and, consequently, it is also independent of the volume of output.

The mathematical proof of this fact is rather complex; instead, let us try a logical and geometric analysis. In Figure 6-20, each total product curve for a variable input (labor) is drawn for a specific amount of the fixed input (capital). Thus, TP_1 shows how total output responds to changes in labor when the input of capital is K_1 units. For example, the input combination $L_1 + K_1$ yields OX_1 units of X. The input combination $L_2 + K_1$ produces OX_2 units of X.

Let us increase the input combination $L_1 + K_1$ by z times—that is, $z(L_1 + K_1) = zL_1 + zK_1$. The amount of X produced must now be shown on TP_2, which is drawn for zK_1 units of capital. The graph shows that the input combination $zL_1 + zK_1$ yields OX_3 units of X. If the production function is linearly homogeneous, $OX_3 = z(OX_1)$. Similarly, the input combination $L_2 + K_1$ yields OX_2 units of X. Under the assumption of linear homogeneity, the input combination $zL_2 + zK_1$ produces OX_4 units of X, where $OX_4 = z(OX_2)$.

It follows then that the average and marginal products for each input are equal for proportional changes in all inputs. With respect to the average product of labor

$$\frac{OX_1}{OL_1} = \frac{z(OX_1)}{z(OL_1)} = \frac{OX_3}{Oz(L_1)}$$

Similarly,

$$\frac{OX_2}{OL_2} = \frac{z(OX_2)}{z(OL_2)} = \frac{OX_4}{Oz(L_2)}$$

The line OT is the locus of all points of *average product maxima* when capital and labor are changed in constant proportion. Since the ratio of any

8 The mathematical proof of this proposition can be found in most first-year calculus texts in the section on linearly homogeneous functions.

9 $MP_L = \frac{\Delta X}{\Delta L}$, $MP_K = \frac{\Delta X}{\Delta K}$. $\frac{MP_L}{MP_K} = \frac{\Delta X}{\Delta L} \div \frac{\Delta X}{\Delta K} = \frac{\Delta X}{\Delta L} \cdot \frac{\Delta K}{\Delta X} = \frac{\Delta K}{\Delta L} = MRTS_{LK}$

The Theory of Production

FIGURE 6-20

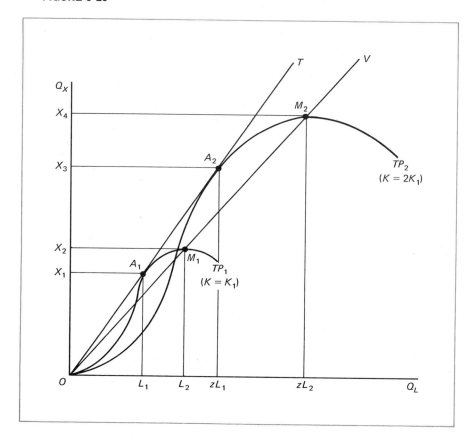

vertical distance to the corresponding horizontal distance is the same for any point on a straight line radiating out of the origin, each point on OT establishes the same average product for labor; and, for the same reason, at every point on OV, the average product of labor is the same.

If inputs are increased proportionately, we know also that OT is the locus of all points of the marginal productivity of labor when the average productivity of labor is at its maximum, since $MP_L = AP_L$ for AP_L maximum. Since OV traces a path of total product maxima for proportionate changes in all inputs, it must be simultaneously the locus of all points of $MP_L = 0$.

What is true of the total product curve of one input employed under conditions of linear homogeneity is true for the total product curves of all the other inputs. Therefore, this demonstration could be applied to a family of total product curves of capital, each of which is drawn for a specific amount of labor.

In this demonstration, we have shown that at two corresponding points (maximum AP and maximum TP) on every total product curve depicting the behavior of output under conditions of constant returns to scale, the marginal

Isoquants | **157**

products of the variable input are equal. In a linearly homogeneous production function, it is evident, then, that the marginal productivities of an input depend only on the proportions in which the inputs are combined, not on the absolute amounts of the inputs themselves. What is true of this readily identifiable pair of points (AP_{max} and TP_{max}) is also true of *any* corresponding points on the total product curves of linear homogeneous production functions. This is so because the total product curve of any input in a homogeneous production function is a *scale image* of any other total product curve for the same function. Thus, TP_2 in Figure 6-20 is TP_1 increased, or expanded, to twice the scale. For any increase—say, z—in all inputs, the scale of the total product curve must be expanded in the same (z) proportion. Thus, the marginal product of labor at any given level of input use will be the same when all inputs are expanded z times, since the total product curve of labor is expanded in every direction to z scale.

SUMMARY

Production theory attempts to explain phenomena occurring in the transformation of inputs into output—and explain them in a way that is useful in economic analysis.

In the simplest analysis of production, one input is varied while the others are held constant. As the variable input is increased, the three laws of diminishing returns are encountered. Diminishing *marginal* returns are observed first (perhaps from the outset of production or after a range of increasing marginal returns) and occur when successive equal increments in the variable input produce increasingly smaller increments in total output. As output is expanded further, diminishing *average* returns are incurred (they too may occur at the outset of production or after a range of increasing average returns). In the stage of diminishing average returns, the ratio of total output to the total number of units of the variable input falls as the variable input is increased. The third and final form of diminishing returns is diminishing *total* returns. In this case, increases in the variable input cause total output to decrease.

When the *ceteris paribus* assumption is dropped, we can see the behavior of output as all inputs are varied. The graphical depiction of a two-input production function is a three-dimensional *production surface,* which resembles one-quarter of a steeple bell. Its base plane is called an input space. The amounts of the inputs, labor and capital, are measured along the edges of the input space. The vertical height from any point in the input space to a point on the production surface measures the units of output produced by the indicated combination of labor and capital.

Dissecting the production surface reveals useful information about the productive process. There are three basic dissections. First, the production surface is sliced vertically with the cutting plane perpendicular to the input

space (the base plane of the surface) and parallel to one of its edges. The top edges of the planes thus obtained are *total product curves* and show how output behaves when one input is changed and the other remains constant. Thus, these planes show the three laws of diminishing returns: marginal, average, and total.

The second dissection is made with the cutting plane again perpendicular to the input space but this time passing through the origin of the base plane. The top edges of the planes obtained in this dissection are *scale product curves* and show how output behaves when both inputs are changed. Since the cutting plane makes a straight-line cut through the origin, the input changes are proportionate—that is, if labor is doubled, capital must also be doubled.

Increasing inputs proportionately reveals the phenomena of returns to scale. If output increases more than proportionately, returns to scale are said to increase. If output increases proportionately, the particular production function yields constant returns to scale. Finally, if output increases less than proportionately, the production function yields decreasing returns to scale. It is possible for all three types of returns to scale to be found in a single production function.

The third, and final, dissection of the production surface is achieved by inserting into the surface a cutting plane that is parallel to the input space. The section of the surface thus obtained is at a uniform height above the input space and so represents a given quantity of total output. Repeating this dissection several times and mapping the resulting sections on the input space will yield a diagram of a family of curves convex to the origin of the input space, and together these curves will form a contour map of the surface. Each curve is called an isoquant because any point on the curve represents the same quantity of total output. By referring particular points on a given isoquant to the input axes of the input space, it is possible to determine the various input combinations that will yield a given quantity of total output.

The convexity of the isoquants shows the principle of the diminishing marginal rate of technical substitution of inputs. To the degree that inputs are substitutes for each other, they can replace one another in a productive process without affecting the level of total output. However, because in nearly all cases they are *imperfect* substitutes for one another, as given amounts of one input are successively withdrawn, the maintenance of a specific level of output will require ever greater increments in the substitute input. Thus, the ability of the replacement input to substitute for the input being withdrawn diminishes at the margin.

The principle of the diminishing marginal rate of technical substitution should not be confused with the law of diminishing returns. In the former, *both* inputs are varied—one being withdrawn and the other increased. Diminishing returns applies when only *one* input is increased and the other remains constant.

A linearly homogeneous production function will yield constant returns to scale throughout the entire range of production. This means that there are

neither efficiencies nor inefficiencies in the production function itself. In a linearly homogeneous production function, returns to scale always involve a constant relationship between the inputs and output regardless of the absolute amounts of inputs used. Because of this unique situation, the marginal productivities of the inputs are unaffected by the amounts of inputs used and are determined solely by the proportions in which they are combined. This, in turn, means that the marginal rate of technical substitution of inputs is also determined solely by the proportions in which the inputs are used.

7

The Theory of Production: A Value Analysis

This chapter recasts the theory of Chapter 6 in value, or monetary, terms, expressing the physical realities of production as the costs of production. Much of the information about the effect of using alternative forms of technology comes to a firm's decision-makers as cost data.

THE COSTS OF PRODUCTION

OPPORTUNITY COSTS

Suppose upon graduating from college you can choose between two highly rated courses of action: you can go to work for a leading corporation at a yearly salary of $12,000, or you can work for yourself for the same apparent annual compensation. Being rather independent, you decide to work for yourself. Assuming that the financial reward of self-employment is as expected, is it true that being your own boss offers the same return as working for the corporation? What if you must invest $10,000 in inventory in order to operate your business? Suppose the going rate on a savings account is 5 percent. If you had gone to work for the corporation, you would have made the $12,000 you now make plus $500 interest on the $10,000, which you could have left in a savings account. Thus, in order to operate your own business, you are undergoing an *opportunity cost* of $500 per year. This opportunity cost is part of the

true cost of your business, whether it shows on your books or not. It is the $500 annual return you could, but do not, realize in an alternative employment of your resources.

An *opportunity,* or *alternative,* cost is the value of a resource in a forgone employment. The real value of your services, whether you know it or not, is $12,500, and not just $12,000 per year. It would seem to be desirable for each individual to know his opportunity cost, so that he can make rational economic decisions.

Suppose now that you know you are forgoing $500 per year, but you feel it is worth at least that amount to be your own boss. No one can quarrel with you on that point. But your decision has a social dimension as well as an economic one. The $500 differential is the economy's way of saying to you that it has higher-valued uses for your inputs. It is willing to pay $12,000 a year for your labor *and* $500 a year for your capital, rather than $12,000 for the services of both. Since you are, in effect, losing $500 a year, economists insist that this amount be included in your total cost of operation.

The opportunity cost concept is at the heart of the definition of cost because it shows that costs basically are *sacrifices,* or *alternatives forgone.* The value of any good that the economy produces is the value of another good that could have been produced with the same resources. For example, the value of a tree left standing in a forest is the value of the lumber it might have become. Since economists must be concerned with all costs, whether they are recorded in accounting records or not, they will include as costs to an economic system, the $500 differential in the salary example and the value of a standing tree as lumber.

Costs must be borne in any economic system. They are the monetary expression of the ultimate economic fact of scarcity. The efficient economy will reduce its costs, or sacrifices, to the least possible amount consistent with the production of those goods and services it values most.

EXPLICIT AND IMPLICIT COSTS

Economic activity cannot be appraised correctly unless all costs of production are taken into account. The most visible costs are those that involve direct money outlays. Economists call costs of this type *explicit costs.* When an employer meets his payroll by issuing checks to his employees, he is meeting an explicit cost of doing business. This expense will be reported in his accounts. But the employer must also take into consideration the physical deterioration and obsolescence of his capital assets. The gradual using up of their productive powers is a true cost to him—and to the economy—whether or not the fact is noted by a money amount. Even if the entrepreneur puts in his books some arbitrary charge for depreciation, this cost still does not involve a direct money outlay. But it is a cost nonetheless. Economists define this type of cost as an *implicit cost.* To economists, the total of explicit and

implicit costs constitutes the total, or combined, costs of a business enterprise. Unless both types of cost are fully recognized, the costs of the firm will be understated.

FIXED COST

In the preceding chapter, we observed that every total product curve of a variable input is drawn for a fixed amount of all other inputs. Since the total variable cost curve is the value analogue of the total product curve, it shows the costs of production attributable solely to the variable input. What about the other input(s)? If the amounts of other inputs are fixed, so must be their costs. For example, under the *ceteris paribus* assumption, if labor is variable, capital is held constant while the labor input and the output of the good are varied. If any inputs are fixed in amount while the output of the firm is varied, the costs of these fixed inputs cannot change with the change in output. We can therefore define the sum of the costs of all fixed inputs as *total fixed cost*.

When plotted against output, a curve depicting fixed cost appears as a horizontal straight line. Total fixed cost is shown as OF in Figure 7–1. No matter what the level of output may be, total fixed cost is always the same; for example, at zero output it is OF, and at the output OX_3, it is $X_3D = OF$.

Some texts define total fixed cost as the cost that does not change in the *short run*. This implies that fixed cost is variable in the *long run*. The short and long runs vary from firm to firm. Generally, the long run is defined as that period of time which is long enough for the firm to vary all its inputs. Given a long enough time period, the firm can change its entire physical plant. In the short run, the firm can change only the *rate* at which it operates its fixed input component—for example, by changing the number of hours worked by the labor input. Typical costs that are fixed in the short run include salaries

FIGURE 7-1

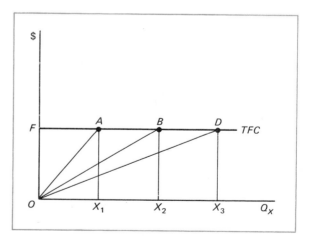

of employees under contract, depreciation, rent, interest, and taxes. Remember that these long-run costs are *paid* in the short run, but they do not vary with output in that period.

Firms for which a large proportion of total cost is fixed cost often are interested in "spreading the overhead"; that is, they strive for high-volume operations to spread their fixed cost over a large number of units of output. Railroads, airlines, and telephone companies are good examples of such firms. Since a great part of their assets is in the form of fixed plant and equipment, they are interested in operating at high volumes of output because expanding output may add relatively little to their total costs. The spreading of costs over output is best expressed in terms of *average fixed cost*. An average fixed cost is a fixed cost per unit of output; it is found by dividing total fixed cost by output:

$$AFC = \frac{TFC}{Q_X}$$

Table 7–1 shows how average fixed cost declines as output is increased. Total fixed cost is assumed to be $1,000,000. If the output is automobiles and the $1,000,000 is the total fixed cost of a stamping press and its die, it is easy to see why automobile manufacturers must produce at high output levels in order to justify the expenses of their heavy capital investments.

In Figure 7–1, average fixed cost when the output is OX_1 is X_1A/OX_1. Similarly, when output is OX_2, average fixed cost is X_2B/OX_2, and at OX_3, average fixed cost is X_3D/OX_3. Each of these ratios expresses the slope of a straight line joining the origin to a point on the total fixed cost curve corresponding to a particular output. Thus, for output OX_1, the slope of $OA = X_1A/OX_1$ is the average fixed cost of producing output OX_1. Similarly, the slope of $OB = X_2B/OX_2$ is the average fixed cost of producing output OX_2. The successively less steep slopes of OA, OB, and OD show that average fixed cost declines as output is expanded. This fact is shown also in the continuously declining average fixed cost curve of Figure 7-2. The average fixed cost of producing any output can be read directly on the vertical axis of the graph. The vertical distance $OC_1 = X_1A'$ in this chart gives the same information as the slope of line OA in Figure 7-1. If the average fixed cost of producing any output is expressed by the formula

TABLE 7-1	Units of Output	Average Fixed Cost
	1	$1,000,000
	2	500,000
	20	50,000
	200	5,000
	2,000	500
	20,000	50
	200,000	5

FIGURE 7-2

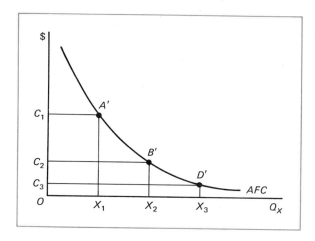

$AFC = TFC/Q_X$ then,

$$TFC = Q_X(AFC)$$

This is represented by the area of a rectangle such as $OX_2B'C_2$ under the curve, since that area equals $OX_2 \cdot X_2B' = Q(AFC)$. Any curve depicting average fixed cost is, then, necessarily a rectangular hyperbola, for a rectangular hyperbola is defined as a curve such that all rectangles inscribed beneath it are of equal area.

VARIABLE COST

Consider any total product curve of the preceding chapter. Suppose we interchange the axes of such a graph, as is done in Figure 7-3. (The reason for this will be explained shortly.) What would the total product curve look like? It would now be *concave* with respect to the horizontal axis up to point *I*, the point of inflection. This curve shows the same thing, but from a different point of view, as the conventional total product curve—namely, that total output increases at an increasing rate up to the point of diminishing marginal returns. But now let us look at the curve in Figure 7-3 from the standpoint of the variable input, labor. Up to point *I*, the amount of labor used to produce equal increments in output increases at a decreasing rate. Beyond point *I*, successively greater increments of labor must be used to produce equal increments in output.

Point *A* in Figure 7-3 is fixed by drawing a ray, *OG*, tangent to the curve so that it makes the *smallest* possible angle with the horizontal axis. This procedure tells us that the *ratio* of input (labor) to output (good *X*) is falling up to point *A*. Beyond point *A*, the ratio of the quantity of labor to the quantity of

FIGURE 7-3

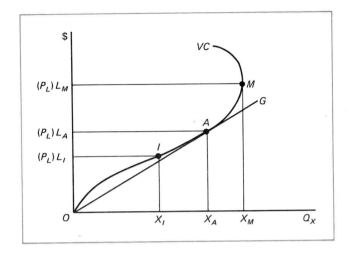

good X falls as the output of X is increased. Since the ratio used here, L/Q_X, is the reciprocal of the average product of labor, Q_X/L, the average product of labor increases up to point A and falls thereafter.

Point M is the same as the point of maximum output on a conventional total product curve.

The shape of the cost curve, including the points of the three types of diminishing returns, is determined by the physical nature of the productive process. As we said earlier, almost all cost theory is merely production theory restated in monetary terms (hence the title of this chapter).

Now let us multiply the number of labor units used to produce a given amount of output by the price of labor (P_L). This has been done in Figure 7-3. The vertical axis of the figure now describes the *cost* of the labor units required to produce a given amount of output. Thus, we have converted our total product curve into a *total variable cost curve*. It is a *variable* cost curve because it shows how cost changes as one input is varied, *ceteris paribus*, to effect a change in output.

We can now explain why we have inverted the axes. The reason is that it is conventional in economics to place data expressed in monetary units on the vertical axis of a graph. Therefore, as we come from the productivity graphs of the preceding chapter to the cost figures of this chapter, we now measure output along the horizontal axis and inputs (multiplied by price) on the vertical axis.

The vertical axis in Figure 7-3 now shows not only units of labor service but also the dollar cost of those services, since every physical unit on the axis has been multiplied by the constant P_L, the unit price of labor (the wage rate). This has merely raised the entire curve by a vertical distance equal to the value of the constant.[1] The configuration of the curve has not changed. If we as-

---

[1] It is possible, of course, for the price of a variable input to change. This situation will be discussed later.

The Theory of Production: A Value Analysis

sume, for the sake of convenience, that $P_L = \$1$, then not even the position of the curve is affected.

Viewing the total product curve as a total variable cost curve, then, calls for only a slight change in thinking. The new curve shows how *variable cost* changes as output changes. Total variable cost rises continuously as output is expanded, increasing at a decreasing rate up to point I, the point of diminishing marginal returns, after which it increases at an increasing rate. Up to point A, the point of diminishing average returns, cost *per unit* falls. Between A and M, output continues to rise but average cost also begins to rise. At point M, the expansion of output has reached its limit; adding more units of labor causes cost to continue its rise but forces output to lower levels.

TOTAL COST

Total cost is equal to the sum of variable cost and fixed cost. A graph of total cost may be obtained simply by vertically summing the two cost curves. In Figure 7-4, the fixed cost of producing output OX_1 is $X_1B_1 = OF$; the variable cost of production is B_1A_1; and the total cost of production is X_1A_1. For OX_2, fixed cost is $OF = X_2B_2$; variable cost is B_2A_2; and total cost is X_2A_2.

FIGURE 7-4

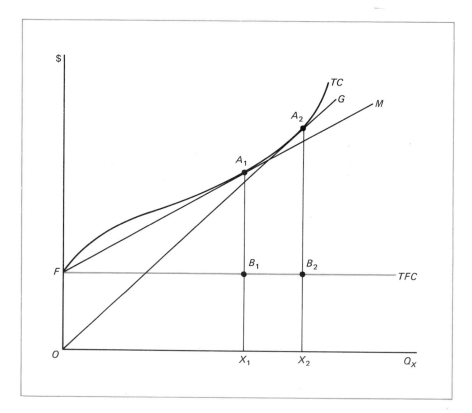

AVERAGE VARIABLE COST

The average variable cost curve expresses in monetary terms the same information that the average product curve states in physical terms. The average product of a variable input (labor) is given by the formula

$$AP_L = \frac{Q_X}{Q_L}$$

Average variable cost is defined as total variable cost divided by the number of units of output. It is given by the formula

$$AVC = \frac{TVC}{Q_X}$$

But total variable cost is equal to the number of units of the variable resource employed multiplied by the unit price of that variable input. Thus, we may rewrite the formula as

$$AVC = P_L \left(\frac{Q_L}{Q_X} \right)$$

The ratio in parentheses is the reciprocal of the formula for the average product of labor. Therefore, we may once again rewrite the formula for average variable cost, this time as

$$AVC = P_L \left(\frac{1}{AP_L} \right) = \frac{P_L}{AP_L}$$

Multiplying the reciprocal of any point on the average product (of labor) curve by the unit price of the input yields a corresponding point on the average variable cost curve. Figure 7-5 shows how the average product and average cost curves are related. The highest point, A', in chart (a) on the average product curve corresponds to the lowest point, A'', on the average variable cost curve in chart (b). Let us see why. In chart (a), when L_A units of labor are used, the average product of labor, $L_A A' = (X_A / L_A)$, is at its maximum. We now wish to determine a corresponding point on the average variable cost curve. First, let us locate the total output of X associated with the maximum average product of labor. It is the output OX_A in chart (b). The magnitude we seek is the average variable cost of producing this output. Using our formula, we multiply the reciprocal of the average product of labor by the price of the labor input; that is, $AVC = P_L(L_A / X_A)$. This particular average variable cost of producing OX_A units of X is shown as the distance $X_A A''$. Since we know from chart (a) that the ratio of X_A / L_A is the greatest value the average product of labor can assume, we know that its reciprocal, L_A / X_A, is the smallest value that the ratio of labor to output can take. Therefore, $P_L(L_A / X_A)$ must establish the minimum average

The Theory of Production: A Value Analysis

variable cost of producing any output of X, and it follows that point A'' is the minimum point on the average variable cost curve. Other points on the average variable cost curve can be found by repeating our procedure for different inputs of labor. For example, if OL_1 units of labor are used, the average product of the input is $L_1B' = X_1/L_1$ units. Again, find the output of $X(OX_1)$ associated with this particular level of labor usage. The average variable cost of producing this volume of output is $P_L(L_1/X_1) = X_1B''$ in chart (b). Point B' is, thus, another point on the average variable cost curve. As we move from B' to A' on the average product curve of chart (a), average productivity (the ratio of X to L) rises. Necessarily, then, the reciprocal of that ratio (L/X) falls. Therefore, as we move from output OX_1 to OX_A in chart (b), an ever-decreasing L/X is being multiplied by the constant P_L. Consequently, the average variable cost of producing X falls over this range of output. If more than OL_A units of labor are used to produce X, the average product of labor will fall. Chart (a) shows us that when OL_2 units of labor are used, the average productivity of labor is $L_2C = X_2/L_2$ units of X. Since $L_1B = L_2C$, the average productivity of labor is the same at OL_1 and OL_2 units of labor usage. For this reason, the average variable cost of producing OX_2 units of X must be equal to that of producing OX_1 units. Consequently, $X_2C'' = X_1B''$. By drawing a smooth curve through as many points as we wish to obtain, we can derive the average variable cost curve from the average product curve. The average variable cost curve must be very close to a mirror image of the average product curve, since the cost curve is the reciprocal of the product curve multiplied by a constant (the input price).

From this reasoning, it follows that when a firm has minimized its average variable cost, it has minimized the average product of the variable input. If the output per unit of the variable input continues to rise as more input units are

FIGURE 7-5

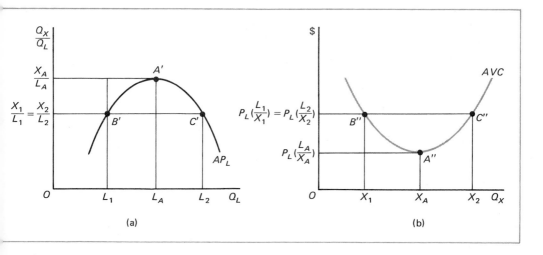

(a)   (b)

employed, it must be that each addition to output causes per unit cost to fall. The *price* of the input is assumed to be constant, but since Q_x/Q_L is rising, and thus, necessarily, Q_x/Q_L is falling, average variable cost must decline until the output per unit of input is maximized. When input usage exceeds L_A units, the ratio of Q_x/Q_L falls, and, necessarily, Q_x/Q_L rises. Therefore, when average productivity is falling, average variable cost is rising. If the firm finds that its average variable cost of operation is declining as it expands output, the efficiency of the variable input on a per unit basis must be increasing. When the firm has achieved the lowest possible per unit variable cost, the average efficiency of the variable input must be at a maximum. When output has been expanded to the extent that per unit costs begin to rise, the average efficiency of the variable input must be waning.

A graph of average *total* costs can be obtained by summing vertically the points associated with any given level of output on the average variable and average fixed cost curves. This is done in Figure 7-6. Since $ATC = AVC + AFC$, the vertical distance between the average variable and average total cost curves at any particular level of output is the average fixed cost.[2] The average total cost curve reaches its minimum point, A_2'', to the right of the minimum point, A_1'', on the average variable cost curve. This means that minimum per unit *total* costs occur at a higher output level than minimum average *variable* costs. This relationship between the minimum points on the two curves is explained by the presence of continuously falling average fixed costs. Beyond A_1'', average variable costs are rising, but average fixed costs are falling; and for a time the latter outweigh the former, forcing average *total* costs downward. Finally, the influence of the continuously falling average fixed

FIGURE 7-6

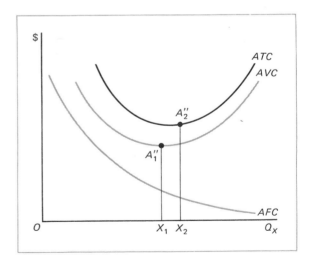

$$^2 ATC = \frac{TC}{Q_x} = \frac{TFC + TVC}{Q_x} = \frac{TFC}{Q_x} + \frac{TVC}{Q_x}$$

cost is overcome, and beyond point A_2'', the effect of the rising variable cost component causes average total costs to rise. This relationship can be seen in the cost curves of Figure 7-4. The ray *FM*, drawn from point *F*, is tangent to the total cost curve (here, viewed as the variable cost curve) at A_1. This shows that the average variable cost of production is minimized at the output OX_1. Falling average total cost does not reach its minimum, however, until output reaches OX_2 units, as is shown by the tangency of ray *OG* with the total cost curve at point A_2.

THE MARGINAL COST CURVE

Marginal costs are defined as the change in variable (or total) costs produced by a change in output. This definition is expressed in the formula

$$MC = \frac{\Delta TVC}{\Delta Q_X} = \frac{\Delta TC}{\Delta Q_X}$$

where ΔQ equals a 1-unit change. The alternative formulation is possible because fixed costs have no effect on marginal costs, as is shown in Table 7-2. The reason for this is that since fixed costs do not change, they do not contribute anything to the *change* in TC.

TABLE 7-2	Q_X	TFC	TVC	TC	MC
	0	$100	0	$100	
					$100
	1	100	$100	200	
					75
	2	100	175	275	
					100
	3	100	275	375	
					125
	4	100	400	500	
					150
	5	100	550	650	

Geometrically, marginal cost is represented by the slope of either the variable cost curve or the total cost curve. In the limit, at which ΔX approaches zero, marginal cost is defined as the slope of a straight line drawn tangent to the curve at a point corresponding to a particular level of output. In Figure 7-7, the point marginal cost for the output OX_0 is given by the slope of line *TT'* tangent to the TC curve at point *J*. Marginal cost at output OX_0, therefore, is equal to *UT'/TU*.

A marginal cost curve can be derived from the total cost curve by plotting the slope of the latter curve at various outputs. However, let us instead derive the marginal cost curve from its counterpart product curve.

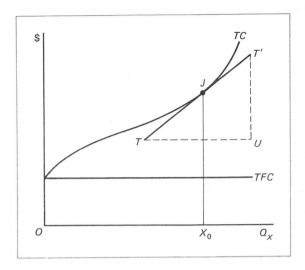

FIGURE 7-7

Marginal product is given by the formula

$$MP_L = \frac{\Delta Q_X}{\Delta Q_L}$$

Marginal cost is expressed by the formula

$$MC = \frac{\Delta TVC}{\Delta Q_X}$$

Assuming a constant unit price for the variable input, the change in variable cost associated with a given change in output is the change in the variable input multiplied by the input price, as shown in the formula

$$MC = P_L\left(\frac{\Delta L}{\Delta X}\right)$$

The expression in parentheses is the reciprocal of the formula for marginal product, so we may write the formula for marginal cost as

$$MC = P_L\left(\frac{1}{MP_L}\right) = \frac{P_L}{MP_L}$$

In other words, marginal cost is the reciprocal of marginal product except for a multiplicative constant, that constant being the price of the variable input.

Now we can compare the two marginal curves. In Figure 7-8, the marginal product curve in chart (a) reaches its maximum at point I'. This is the point of diminishing marginal returns. At this point, the ratio of $(\Delta X/\Delta L)$ is greater than at any other point on the curve. To locate point I'' on the marginal

FIGURE 7-8

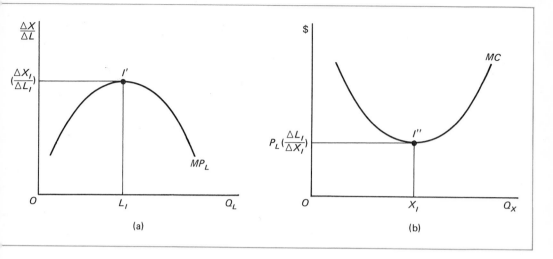

(a)

(b)

cost curve in chart (b), locate the input, L_I, at which marginal product is a maximum. Multiply the reciprocal of (maximum) marginal product by the input price. This will establish the vertical distance. Point I'' must be the lowest point on the marginal cost curve, since if the ratio $\Delta X_I/\Delta L_I$ establishes the maximum point on the marginal product curve, its reciprocal, $\Delta L_I/\Delta X_I$, must establish the minimum point on the marginal cost curve. Similarly, any point on the marginal cost curve can be located for a corresponding point on the marginal product curve.

To say that output increases at an increasing rate up to point I' in chart (a) is to say that the marginal efficiency of the variable input is increasing. Equal increments of labor bring about successively greater increments in output. The same idea expressed in cost terms is that equal incremental expenditures for labor yield ever larger increments in product. Alternatively, equal increments in output can be obtained for continually diminishing increments in outlay. Beyond point I', marginal productivity is shown to decline in chart (a), while the same phenomenon expressed in terms of rising marginal cost is shown in chart (b) in the portion of the curve lying to the right of point I''.

RELATIONSHIPS AMONG THE COST CURVES

The relationships among the cost curves are shown in Figure 7–9. They mirror the relationship of the average and marginal product curves.

As long as marginal cost is less than average variable cost, average variable cost must fall. The fact that marginal cost is rising to the right of point I'' does not change this situation. Only when marginal cost exceeds average

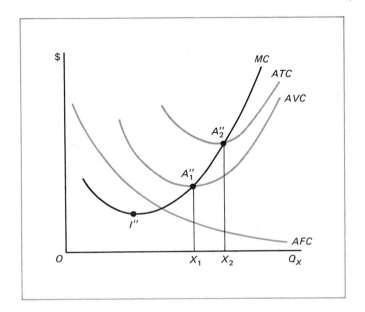

FIGURE 7-9

variable cost will the average variable cost rise. When marginal and average variable costs are equal, average variable cost is constant, so point A_1'' is the minimum point on the average variable cost curve.

For the same reason, despite the presence of fixed costs, the marginal cost curve intersects the minimum point on the average total cost curve. Up to point A_2'', the average total cost curve falls because both average variable and average fixed costs are falling. At output OX_1, average variable costs cease to fall. Thus, over the output interval X_1X_2, the only reason for the decline of the average total cost curve is falling average fixed costs. When average total cost does begin to rise, it does so because rising average variable cost overcomes the effect of the continually falling average fixed cost. As *additions* to cost become greater than the average of total cost, the average must rise, even if that average includes a continuously falling component.

LONG–RUN OPTIMIZATION: THE ISOQUANT–ISOCOST METHOD

Having described the basic concepts of cost analysis, we now consider the situation in which the firm alters all its inputs, subject only to the limitations of its budget. In this context, we shall analyze how the firm assembles a least-cost, or optimal, combination of inputs to produce a desired output. The concept of long-run optimization is ideally suited to the isoquant-isocost approach, since movements along isoquants correspond to changes in all inputs.

The Theory of Production: A Value Analysis

ISOCOST CURVES

In Figure 7-10, we assume that the firm has a given production budget of D dollars and that it spends its entire budget purchasing the inputs (labor and capital) required to produce some quantity of output X. The prices of the capital and labor inputs are P_K and P_L, respectively. These prices are parameters to the firm; that is, we assume that no matter how much the firm purchases, it cannot affect input prices. When the firm spends D dollars for inputs,

$$D = Q_K \cdot P_K + Q_L \cdot P_L = TC$$

The D dollars spent on production are equal to the number of capital units purchased multiplied by their unit price plus the number of labor units purchased multiplied by their unit price; and, of course, D dollars equal the total cost of production.

If the firm were to spend its entire budget of D dollars on the input capital, it could acquire OK^* units, as is shown in Figure 7-10, but could hire no labor. Similarly, if the firm were to spend its entire budget of D dollars on labor, it could hire a maximum of OL^* units but no capital.

What the firm could buy if it were to spend some of its budget on *each* input is shown by the straight line joining points K^* and L^*. The straight line K^*L^* is called an *isocost* curve because every point on it represents the same total outlay for factor services. Thus, the total cost of using the input combination given by point a is equal to the total cost of using the input combination given by point b.

FIGURE 7-10

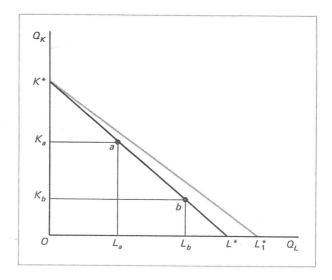

Under the assumption that varying the output level of the firm does not affect input prices, the isocost curve must be a straight line. Given the firm's budget, point K^* is fixed as the maximum amount of capital services the firm can buy at a given P_K. Thus, $OK^* = D/P_K = TC/P_K$. For example, if the production budget of the firm is $100,000, and the price of a unit of capital is $1,000, the firm can acquire a maximum of 100 units of this input. Similarly, if the price per unit of labor service is $50, the firm can hire a maximum of 2,000 labor units. In terms of units of capital, the cost of OL^* labor units is OK^* capital units forgone, or the ratio of OK^* to OL^*. But $OK^* = D/P_K$, and $OL^* = D/P_L$, and $OK^*/OL^* = D/P_K \div D/P_L = D/P_K \cdot P_L/D = P_L/P_K$. These expressions are the formulas for the slope of a line, and since the input prices are constant, the slope of the line that they express must itself be constant. Therefore, an isocost curve is a straight line joining a point on the capital axis with a point on the horizontal axis.

The slope of the isocost curve, as shown above, is determined by the input prices. Input prices and the total outlay of the firm for its inputs determine the intercepts of the isocost curve. Given the input prices, the farther the isocost curve lies from the origin, the greater is the production budget it represents.

Suppose the price of an input does change. The slope of the isocost curve must then be affected because its slope is P_L/P_K. If the price of labor falls, the firm can buy more labor, *ceteris paribus*. In Figure 7-10, the firm's budget and the initial input prices established the isocost curve K^*L^*. If the price of labor were to fall enough for the firm to be able to buy $L^*L_1^*$ more units of labor if it were to spend its entire production budget for this resource, the labor axis intercept of the new isocost curve would occur at point L_1^*. The vertical intercept will be the same as in the initial situation, since there has been no change in the price of capital and hence no change in the amount the firm could buy if it were to spend its entire budget for that input. Thus, the new isocost curve appropriate to the fall in the price of labor is the gray line $K^*L_1^*$.

If the prices of both inputs change, the shift in the position of the isocost (linear) curve will depend on the relationship between the prices. Unless the prices keep the same relation to each other after the change—say, for example, they both fall by 5 percent—the slope of the isocost curve will change. If all input prices change in the same direction and in the same proportion—a rare situation—the effect will be equivalent to a change in the firm's production budget, and the isocost curve will shift rightward or leftward (always maintaining parallelism with the previous curve) depending on whether all prices fall or all prices rise.

THE ISOCOST–ISOQUANT MAP

The iso*cost* curve is limited to the economic aspects of the input mix; that is, it shows how the firm can substitute inputs economically. The iso*quant* curve shows what the firm is able to do technologically; that is, how the firm

can substitute inputs technologically. If we put both types of curve together, they will reveal what the firm actually will do.

In Figure 7–11, the isocost curve K^*L^* is superimposed on the firm's isoquant map. Given the input prices, the firm has a large enough budget to produce any amount of output up to and including X_3. Any larger output, such as X_4, is out of the question because the firm cannot buy sufficient resources. In other words, it cannot operate at any point on any isoquant lying to the right of X_3.

From an economic standpoint, we know that the firm can buy inputs sufficient to produce an output located in the area bounded by the isocost curve and the two axes, including the two end points of the isocost curve and all points along the curve. If we assume that the isocost curve represents all the costs of producing a given output and that the production of any given amount of output requires the use of some or all the inputs, we can mark the area under the isocost curve and its end points as representing feasible points of solution.

A glance at the graph shows that the firm will choose to produce output X_3, using OL_3 and OK_3 units of labor and capital, respectively. The rational firm wants the largest output it can get for its outlay; therefore, it will not produce any output smaller than X_3, such as X_1 or X_2, although it possesses the financial ability to acquire the inputs to produce such outputs. If the firm is to produce X_3—the largest output it can afford—it can do so only by using quantity OL_3 of labor and quantity OK_3 of capital. Any other combination of labor and capital required to make X_3 is beyond the firm's budget. Production is therefore denoted graphically by T, the point of tangency between the isoquant curve X_3 and the isocost curve K^*L^*. The input combination indicated by point T—

FIGURE 7-11

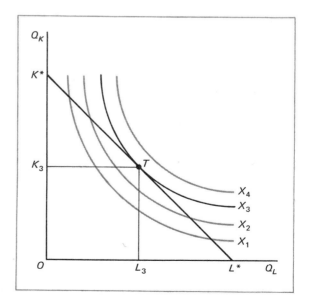

namely, $OL_3 + OK_3$—is the least-cost combination of inputs for producing the desired volume of output. Suppose the firm desires to produce the output represented by isoquant X_0 in Figure 7–12. If it uses the combination of resources given by point A, its total outlay is shown by the isocost curve $K_1^*L_1^*$. At point A, the slope of the isoquant X_0 exceeds the slope of the isocost curve $K_1^*L_1^*$. This means that the marginal rate of technical substitution of labor for capital exceeds the price ratio, or

$$(MRTS_{LK})_A = \left(\frac{\Delta Q_K}{\Delta Q_L}\right)_A > \frac{P_L}{P_K}$$

Stated another way, the rate at which the firm is substituting labor for capital in the process of manufacturing X_0 units of X exceeds the rate at which labor may be substituted for capital in the input market. The practical significance of this is that the firm can reduce its costs if it will replace capital with labor. A numerical example may help to make this clear. Suppose that at point A, $(MRTS_{LK})_A = \Delta Q_K / \Delta Q_L = 4/1$. If the price of a unit of labor is \$400 and that of a unit of capital \$200, the ratio $P_L/P_K = \$400/\$200 = 2/1$. The marginal rate of technical substitution at point A means that if the firm decides to replace capital with labor, maintaining production at the desired level X_0, it can replace 4 units of K with 1 unit of L. However, in the resource market, the economic rate of substitution of labor for capital is 2/1. To acquire 1 unit of labor, the firm must give up only 2 units of capital. At point A, although labor is the more expensive input economically, capital is the more expensive technologically; a unit of

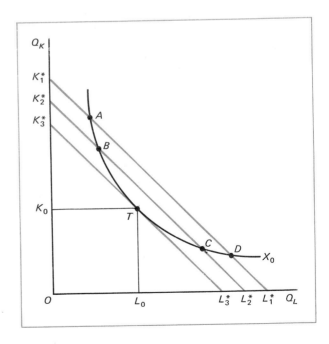

FIGURE 7-12

labor costs twice as much as a unit of capital but delivers four times the output. Under these circumstances, the firm will find that additional units of labor are a "bargain."

Under the preceding conditions, the rational firm will begin to substitute labor for capital. As it does so, it moves along isoquant X_0, meeting successively lower isocost curves. At the same time, since the slope of the isoquant decreases as the firm substitutes labor for capital, $MRTS_{LK}$ decreases also. Point B lies on the intersection of isoquant X_0 and isocost $K_2^* L_2^*$. There being no change in input prices, isocost $K_2^* L_2^*$ is parallel to $K_1^* L_1^*$. Assume that at B the slope of X_0 is 3/1. Labor is losing some of its ability to substitute for capital. At B, 1 unit of labor is capable of replacing 3 units of capital, whereas at A, 1 unit of labor was able to replace 4 units of capital. But at B, additional labor units are still a "bargain"; the unit of labor that costs twice as much as a unit of capital (the economic rate of substitution of labor for capital still being 2/1) can contribute three times as much to output. It is evident, therefore, that the rational firm will not stop at point B but will continue to substitute labor for capital, thereby moving along X_0 and continuing to strike successively lower isocost curves until it reaches $K_3^* L_3^*$. This isocost curve represents the lowest possible cost of producing output X_0. At T, isoquant X_0 and isocost $K_3^* L_3^*$ (representing the lowest production outlay) are tangent and thus have the same slope. In symbolic terms, $(MRTS_{LK})_T = (\Delta Q_K / \Delta Q_L)_T = P_L / P_K = 2/1$. The technological rate of substitution has been brought into conformity with the economic rate of substitution. At point T, 1 unit of labor can replace 2 units of capital, and output will remain at X_0. On the resource market, 1 unit of labor has the value of 2 units of capital. The rational firm will substitute no further. The input combination $OK_0 + OL_0$ is the least-cost combination of resources for producing the desired quantity of X. By substituting labor for capital until the technical rate of substitution at the margin is equal to the economic, or market, rate of substitution, the firm has decreased its necessary production outlay to a minimum.

Before we leave this example, let us note what would occur if the firm had been overly enthusiastic in its substitution of labor for capital and had slipped past point T, arriving, say, at point C. At C, the slope of isoquant X_0 is less than the slope of the intersected isocost $K_2^* L_2^*$. In production terms, $(MRTS_{LK})_C = (\Delta Q_K / \Delta Q_L)_C < P_L / P_K$. This means that the marginal technical ability of labor to substitute for capital is less than its marginal economic substitutability. The productive contribution of an additional unit of labor is not worth its economic cost. Suppose that at C, $(MRTS_{LK})_C = 1/3$. At this point on the isoquant, 3 units of labor are required to substitute for 1 unit of capital. But a unit of labor costs twice as much as a unit of capital. The rational firm would want to replace labor with capital and would do so, moving away from point C toward point T. As the firm moves along the isoquant, the marginal rate of technical substitution of labor for capital rises until, at point T, the technical ability of labor to substitute for capital is equal to the market rate of substitution.

EXPANSION PATHS

For any desired output, there is a least-cost combination of inputs. Once the firm achieves that point, it must increase its production budget if it wishes to expand its output—assuming that input prices remain constant. A curve tracing out the cost-minimizing input combinations for different outputs is called an *expansion path* and is shown in Figure 7–13 as the curve OZ. The farther any point on OZ is from the origin, the greater is output. With input prices as given, the least-cost input mix to produce the output X_2 is indicated by point T_2. The output X_2 can also be produced using the input combination denoted by point G, but because G does not lie on the expansion path, by definition that input combination does not minimize production costs.

Obviously, the expansion path is merely the locus of points of tangency between isoquant and isocost curves for various outputs and associated outlays. In Figure 7–13, the expansion path OZ is determined by drawing a smooth curve through the points of tangency (denoted by T) between the isoquant and isocost curves. The isocost curves are drawn parallel to each other since input prices are held constant.

COST PATTERNS IN THE LONG RUN

In the long run, all costs of the firm are variable, because all inputs are variable in this conceptual time period. Furthermore, the firm is free to change its inputs as to proportion, absolute amount, and basic character. For example, a firm may not only increase the ratio of calculating equipment to operators, it may change its calculating equipment from sharpened pencils and pads to

FIGURE 7-13

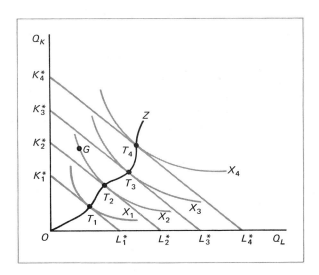

high-speed electronic computers. As the firm increases given inputs with constant prices to produce larger outputs, its total costs will rise. The per-unit, or average, change in costs may be constant, decreasing, increasing, or some combination of all three patterns. Table 7–3 illustrates the behavior of long-run total and average costs under several different hypothetical conditions.

The first pair of columns, LTC_1 and LTC_1/Q_X, illustrates a case of constant long-run average costs. Each 1-unit increment in output causes costs to rise by the same amount—in this case, $100. There are neither efficiencies nor inefficiencies in unrestricted input changes. The second pair of columns, LTC_2 and LTC_2/Q_X, corresponds to a case of ever-increasing efficiencies as all

TABLE 7–3

Q_X	Constant LTC_1	$\dfrac{LTC_1}{Q_X}$	Decreasing LTC_2	$\dfrac{LTC_2}{Q_X}$	Increasing LTC_3	$\dfrac{LTC_3}{Q_X}$	Eclectic LTC_4	$\dfrac{LTC_4}{Q_X}$
0	0	0	0	0	0	0	0	0
1	$100	$100	$100	$100	$ 100	$100	$100	$100
2	200	100	160	80	220	110	160	80
3	300	100	180	60	390	130	180	60
4	400	100	200	50	640	160	240	60
5	500	100	225	45	1000	200	400	80

inputs are varied to meet the requirements of output expansion. Long-run total costs rise with each 1-unit increment in output, but long-run average total costs fall continuously. The third pair of columns, LTC_3 and LTC_3/Q_X, show the firm encountering mounting inefficiencies as it expands output. Not only do total costs rise, but total costs per unit of output also rise. The final pair of columns, LTC_4 and LTC_4/Q_X, shows an example of what most economists believe to be a characteristic response of long-run average total costs to an expanding output. This pair of columns is headed "eclectic" because it displays all three of the previous patterns. In the eclectic case, long-run *average* total costs fall up to and including the third unit of output. This pattern discloses the existence of efficiencies inherent in larger productive combinations. From the third to the fourth units of output, long-run average total costs remain constant. Apparently, there are no efficiencies or inefficiencies realizable in a larger plant within this range. At and beyond the fifth output unit, we see average cost behavior equivalent to that shown in the third pair of columns. Long-run average total costs are rising; the firm has encountered inefficiencies in assembling a plant capable of producing 5 units of output at the lowest possible costs.

LONG–RUN COST CURVES

The curve in Figure 7–14(a) shows the behavior of costs in the long run. A long-run total cost curve has associated marginal and average curves

FIGURE 7-14

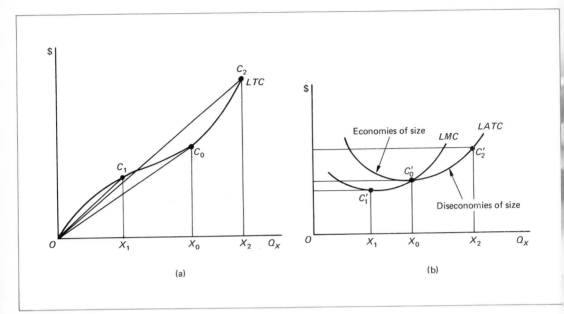

(a)

(b)

as is the case with its counterpart short-run curve. The formula for long-run marginal cost is

$$LMC = \frac{\Delta LTC}{\Delta Q_X}$$

In the limit, when $\Delta Q_X \to 0$, long-run marginal cost is equal to the slope of a straight line tangent to the long-run curve at a point corresponding to a given output. In Figure 7–14(a), C_1 is the point of inflection of the long-run total cost curve. Therefore, long-run marginal cost falls up to this point, reaches its minimum at C_1 (this is the least steep point on the curve), and increases thereafter.

Long-run average total cost may be determined graphically by drawing straight lines from the origin to points on the long-run total cost curve corresponding to given outputs. Long-run average total cost declines up to point C_0, reaches its minimum at this point, and rises thereafter. (A line drawn to any other point on the curve will lie above the line drawn to point C_0.) It is therefore obvious that the output OX_0 is unique; it is the one output at which the total per-unit costs of producing good X are minimized in the long run. It is, in this sense, an optimal volume of output. (Whether this volume of output is also optimal in terms of demand for the product cannot be determined from this

The Theory of Production: A Value Analysis

diagram, which deals only with the optimal quantity in terms of the costs of production.)

Using the graphical approach developed in the preceding chapter, we may derive the marginal and average curves associated with a particular long-run total cost curve. In Figure 7–14(b), the letters on the long-run marginal and average cost curves correspond to the points on the total cost curve in chart (a). Long-run marginal cost falls up to a point C_1' at output OX_1 and rises thereafter. Since the slope of the line OC_0 drawn from the origin in chart (a) concurrently establishes the values of both long-run marginal and average total costs at output OX_0, the marginal curve intersects the average curve at point C_0' in chart (b).

EXPLAINING THE BEHAVIOR OF COSTS IN THE LONG RUN

Why do long-run costs show the patterns exhibited in Table 7–3? Since the patterns of the first three pairs of columns in that table are combined in the fourth pair of columns and the associated U-shaped cost curve, we will use that pair of columns as an example.

ECONOMIES OF SCALE

Many economics texts attribute decreasing long-run average costs to *economies of scale*; increasing per-unit costs are attributed to *diseconomies of scale*.

Economies and diseconomies of scale are the cost theory equivalents of increasing and decreasing returns to scale, respectively. If a proportionate change in all inputs causes output to expand more than proportionately (increasing returns to scale), cost data would show the phenomenon as decreasing long-run average total costs, or economies of scale. Conversely, if increasing all inputs proportionately caused output to undergo a less-than-proportionate increase (decreasing returns to scale), cost data would show this phenomenon as increasing long-run average total costs, or diseconomies of scale. In the third and final case, constant returns to scale (neither economies nor diseconomies of scale), a proportionate change in all inputs results in a proportionate change in output.

ECONOMIES OF SIZE

In this text, we will depart from the usage of many other texts and not attribute the behavior of long-run costs to returns to scale for the simple reason that they do not reflect the ordinary cost behavior of business firms.

Firms do not necessarily, and indeed are unlikely to, change their inputs proportionately. Unless the circumstances are unusual (such circumstances

are discussed later in this chapter), a firm will follow the expansion path as it changes its input combinations to effect a change in the level of output. For any desired output, the firm seeks the least-cost combination of inputs. This practice is not often consistent with changing all inputs in the same proportion.

If the firm moves along its expansion path as it changes its output volume, the long-run total product curve must lie on the production surface vertically above the expansion path. Alternatively, the expansion path may be regarded as the map of the long-run total product curve. The long-run total cost curve is, therefore, the monetary, or value, expression of the long-run total product curve.

Since returns to scale are not involved in movements along an expansion path (inputs are not changed proportionately), we will refer to the behavior of output in regard to movements along the expansion path as *returns to size*. The monetary (value) counterpart of returns to size is *economies* or *diseconomies of size* as the case may be.

We will, therefore, regard the falling portion of the U-shaped long-run average total cost curve of Figure 7–14(b) as being caused by economies of size. Economies of size are the result of the efficiencies inherent in using more of all resources. For example, two units of labor using one unit of capital may be able to excavate more earth than one unit of labor with one unit of capital. But, given the opportunity to vary all its inputs freely, the firm may find that the most efficient (least-cost) input combination is two units of labor and three units of capital. Such an input combination may remove more earth than two units of labor with two units of capital. If average costs fall whenever the firm moves along its expansion path to a higher isoquant, we can conclude that there are efficiencies in increasing size, where an increase in size is defined as moving rightward along an expansion path.

If long-run average total costs remain constant, as at the minimum point (C_0') of the U-shaped *LATC* curve of Figure 7–14(b), when the firm moves along its expansion path, neither efficiencies nor inefficiencies occur in response to changes in the least-cost combination of inputs. If long-run average total costs rise as the firm moves rightward along its expansion path, we may conclude that it encounters inefficiencies as it increases its plant size (as all inputs are increased in least-cost combinations). This is shown by the positively sloped segment of the *LATC* curve of Figure 7–14(b).

RELATIONSHIPS BETWEEN LONG– AND SHORT–RUN COST CURVES

We assume that in the long run a firm uses only economically (and, necessarily, technically) efficient processes to produce a desired output. Consequently, any point on the long-run total cost curve must represent the minimum cost of producing an associated output. Consider Figure 7–15. The lowest possible cost of producing output OX_1 is X_1b. The distance X_1b' rep-

The Theory of Production: A Value Analysis

resents another possible cost of producing OX_1 (as does any vertical distance greater than X_1b), but any such distances represent economically inefficient ways of producing quantity OX_1. The firm cannot produce OX_1 for any amount less than X_1b, such as X_1b''. By definition, then, any point on the long-run total cost curve is the lowest cost of producing the associated volume of output.

SHORT–RUN AND LONG–RUN TOTAL COST CURVES

Each short-run cost curve is drawn to represent a specific quantity of fixed inputs; that is, given a set of fixed inputs (in illustrations, generally assumed to be capital), the curve shows how cost changes as total output changes. The change in cost occurs solely as the result of changes in the amount used of the variable input (in illustrations, generally assumed to be labor).

In Figure 7–15, the short-run total cost curve, STC_1, is tangent to the long-run total cost curve, LTC, at b. In the long run, it is possible to produce OX_1 at a cost of X_1b. It is also possible to produce OX_1 at any higher cost—say, X_1b'—using an input combination represented by the short-run total cost curve STC_2. The curve STC_2 depicts a firm having a more expensive aggregation of

FIGURE 7-15

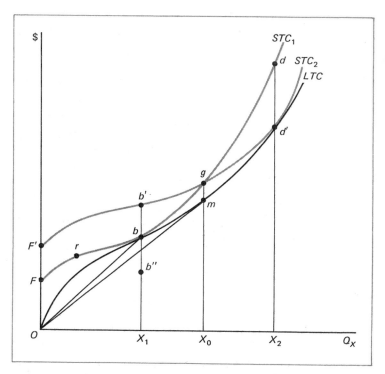

fixed resources (capital) than that represented by STC_1, since the vertical inter-cept (F') of STC_2 is higher than that (F) of STC_1. If the firm wishes to produce OX_1 at the lowest possible cost, it should employ a combination of capital inputs having a fixed cost of OF.

Suppose the firm finds it more profitable to produce OX_2 units of X. With all resources fixed except one (labor), the firm must move along STC_1. The total cost of producing OX_2 under these circumstances is X_2d. We know that this is an inefficient use of resources since the long-run total cost curve shows that OX_2 units of output can be produced at a total cost of only X_2d'. The cost reduction requires that the firm employ a larger amount of capital, the addi-tional cost of which is FF'. In the sense that STC_2 represents a greater use of capital than does STC_1, it is customary to say that the plant represented by STC_2 is "larger" than the plant depicted by STC_1. Alternatively, we may say that since plant 2 (represented by STC_2) is able to produce the larger of the two depicted outputs more efficiently than plant 1 (represented by STC_1), it is the larger of the two plants.

It may seem strange that the firm can lower its total cost of production by *increasing* the fixed component of that cost. The explanation is that with the larger aggregation of capital, represented by curve STC_2, variable cost rises less rapidly. Up to g, the cost of production in plant 2 exceeds that in plant 1, but over the range of output from zero units to the quantity OX_0, the cost in plant 1 rises more rapidly than does the cost in plant 2. At point g, the cost of operating plant 1 has risen to equal the cost of production in plant 2. This means, incidentally, that the two plants can produce the output OX_0 equally efficiently. Beyond point g, the more rapid rise in the cost of operating plant 1 causes it to be less efficient than plant 1 for all outputs exceeding OX_0.

SHORT–RUN AND LONG–RUN AVERAGE TOTAL COST CURVES

The use of average cost curves facilitates discussion of the behavior of the firm undertaken in the next several chapters, so we will now depict the information conveyed by the short- and long-run total cost curves, using the appropriate average cost curves. We know from our previous discussions that curves having the general configuration of those in Figure 7–15 (i.e., curves having a segment showing falling marginal cost) yield U-shaped average curves. This being so, our next problem is to place the average curves in the proper relation to each other. Consider the relationship between STC_1 and LTC in Figure 7–15. Except at output OX_1, short-run total cost is everywhere greater than long-run total cost. Output OX_1 is the only output plant 1 can produce at the lowest possible cost.

Since short-run average total cost is equal to short-run total cost divided by the accompanying output, and long-run average total cost is long-run total cost divided by the same output, short-run average total cost must exceed long-run average total cost at all outputs except that at which the short-run and long-run total cost curves are tangent to each other. In Figure 7–15, at

output OX_1, the short-run average total cost of operating plant 1 is equal to the long-run average total cost of producing that output since the slope of OA_1 defines the average value for both short- and long-run costs. The relationship pattern we have deduced for plant 1 is also true for plant 2. In the case of the larger plant, the short-run average total cost and the long-run average total cost of producing output OX_2 are equal, as would be shown by the slope of a straight line joining points O and b'.

The shapes of the short- and long-run total cost curves show that there is only one output at which these two kinds of cost are equal and, hence, at which the cost of producing that output is minimized. That output is indicated by the tangency of the short- and long-run cost curves. At every other output, the short-run cost of production exceeds long-run cost, showing that the firm is incurring potentially reducible costs.

Curves of the general shape of those shown in Figure 7–15 yield the U-shaped average cost curves shown in Figure 7–16. Since the potentially efficient short-run average cost curves lie above the long-run average cost curve everywhere except at the point of tangency, the long-run curve forms an *envelope curve* for the associated short-run curves. Let us assume that the long-run average cost curve of Figure 7–16 is derived from the long-run total cost curve of Figure 7–15. Similarly, we shall assume that curves $SATC_1$ and $SATC_2$ are derived from STC_1 and STC_2, respectively, in Figure 7–15.

Both Figures 7–15 and 7–16 show that long-run average cost is minimized at output OX_0, since a line drawn from the origin to point M is less steep than any line that could be drawn between the origin and a point on the $LATC$ curve. Output OX_1 is a smaller level of production than OX_0; hence, the tan-

FIGURE 7-16

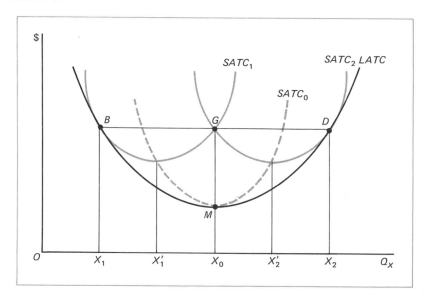

gency point, B, of $SATC_1$ lies to the left of the minimum point, M, on the long-run average cost curve. Similarly, since OX_2 is a larger output than OX_0, the tangency point, D, of $SATC_2$ lies to the right of point M.

The short-run average total cost curve for plant 1 is tangent to $LATC$ at B. This point corresponds to point b in Figure 7–15. Just as $X_1 b$ is the minimum *total* cost of producing output OX_1, $X_1 B$ is the minimum *per unit* cost of producing the same output. Similarly, $X_2 D$ represents the smallest possible per unit cost of producing output OX_2. Finally, we see that either plant can produce the output OX_0 at an average cost of $X_0 G$.

Note that the minimum points of curves $SATC_1$ and $SATC_2$ cannot be tangent to the $LATC$ curve. A simultaneous coincidence of points of minima between the $LATC$ curve and a constituent $SATC$ curve is possible only at the minimum point, M, of the $LATC$ curve in Figure 7–16. This means that there is only one plant—the unique optimal plant—(shown by the dashed line curve $SATC_0$) able to achieve the lowest per unit cost of operation. And it will do so only if it produces output OX_0. At any other output, the per-unit cost of operation will exceed the minimum of $X_0 M_0$. In this case, some other plant could offer lower average costs.

It may seem strange that the minimum point on a short-run average total cost curve can never be tangent to the long-run average total cost curve except in the case just noted. This would appear to mean that firms deliberately operate their plants inefficiently. Is this statement true, or have we a case in which geometry fails to depict economic reality? Should not efficiency require that the minimum points of each short-run average cost curve be tangent to the long-run average cost curve? Consider $SATC_1$ in Figure 7–16. It is tangent to $LATC$ at B. This means that when the firm produces any output other than OX_1, it is not minimizing the cost of production in a short-run sense. In terms of the average *product* curve, from which $SATC_1$ is derived, at output OX_1, output per unit of the variable input is not maximized. The firm has stopped short of using sufficient variable inputs to maximize its average output. From output OX_1 to OX_1', the average product of the variable factor would rise. It would appear, then, that the firm has built a plant larger than is necessary for its purposes and that it operates this plant inefficiently. Now, consider plant 2, represented by $SATC_2$. In this case, the point of operation, D, lies to the right of the point of greatest short-run efficiency at the output OX_2'. In terms of the average product curve from which $SATC_2$ is derived, the firm has pushed the employment of the variable input beyond the point of maximum average productivity. It appears that the plant is too small, and that the firm is operating it inefficiently.

LONG–RUN ECONOMIC EFFICIENCY

Behavior that is efficient in the short run may be inefficient in the long run. Consider Figure 7–17, which may be regarded as an amended version of Figure 7–16. Suppose that profit would increase if the firm were to expand

its output by XX_1' units. In the short run, the firm cannot change the amount of all its resources and must move along $SATC_1$. As it does so, the average efficiency of the variable input rises; in fact, it must be at a maximum at point H. Because of the increasing efficiency of the variable input, average total costs fall from X_1B to $X_1'H$. However, an inspection of the graph shows us that the same output can be produced at the lower per unit cost of $X_1'H'$ if the firm will acquire more of the short-run fixed inputs and assemble them into the larger plant represented by $SATC_3$. Although the firm has reduced the average total cost of producing output OX_1' to a minimum, it now operates to the left of the minimum point of a short-run average total cost curve, as it did initially.

Therefore, when *all* costs are considered, the firm is not necessarily operating inefficiently when production does not occur at the minimum point of an $SATC$ curve. By building a new plant to accommodate the increased output, X_1X_1', the firm will use the short-run variable input in an amount at which it will yield less than its maximum average output, but the greater economies of size inherent in a new combination of *all* inputs more than offset the loss of efficiency of the short-run variable input.

This same principle holds in reverse for a reduction in plant size when diseconomies of size are involved. Suppose, as is shown in Figure 7-17, that profit would increase if the firm were to reduce output from OX_2 to OX_2' units. In the short run, average costs fall from X_2D to $X_2'J$, since the average productivity of

FIGURE 7-17

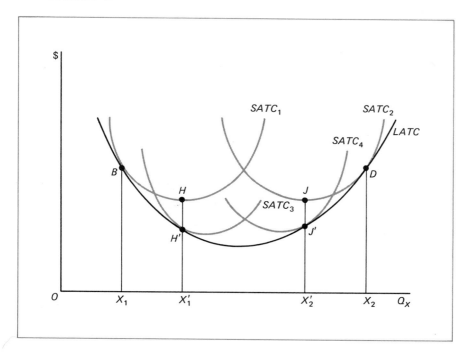

the variable input rises as its use is decreased. However, costs will fall still further if the firm can rid itself of some diseconomies of size by assembling the smaller plant represented by $SATC_4$. When this is done, costs will fall in the amount $J'J$. Although this reduction in the size of the plant will result in the overuse of the variable input, the reduction in overall costs of operation will more than offset the inefficient use of the short-run variable input at the output level OX_2'.

We can now made some generalizations about the plants that firms will tend to assemble in the long run. For those plants operating under conditions of economies of size, the firm will tend to build plants that will underutilize the variable input—that is, too little of it will be used to maximize the average product. In this sense, the size of the plant is "too large" in respect of the most efficient use of the variable factor. For those plants operating in the region of diseconomies of size, the firm will tend to build plants that will overutilize the variable input in that too much of it will be used to maximize its average productivity. In this sense, the plant is "too small" relative to the variable factor.

At the point of constant returns to size (the minimum point of the LATC curve), the firm will build that size of plant at which the average productivity of the variable input will be maximized when least-cost operation is achieved.

AVERAGE AND MARGINAL COST CURVE RELATIONSHIPS

The arrangement of the cost curves of a given set of curves is not a matter of chance; their relationships to one another, shown in Figure 7-18, are wholly logical. Previously, we showed the association between the short-run marginal and average cost curves for a particular plant. We also noted this same marginal-average pattern in the case of the long-run cost curves. Now we shall explain the relationships among the short- and long-run curves.

All short-run marginal cost curves intersect the long-run marginal cost curve at points associated with the output level at which the SATC curve is tangent to the LATC curve. At that particular output, the short-run total cost curve and the long-run total cost curve are tangent to each other. If these two curves are tangent, their slopes necessarily are equal; therefore, whenever $SATC = LATC$, it follows that $SMC = LMC$.

Figure 7-18 shows that in the region of economies of size, the intersection of the SMC and LMC curves takes place below the LATC curve. In the region of diseconomies of size, the SMC and LMC curves intersect each other above the LATC curve. At the point of constant returns to size, the intersection takes place at the minimum of the LATC curve.

Suppose the firm is operating at point r on STC_1 in Figure 7-15. As it moves toward the output OX_1, both short- and long-run costs rise. At output OX_1, they are equal; but if at any output less than OX_1 short-run total costs

FIGURE 7-18

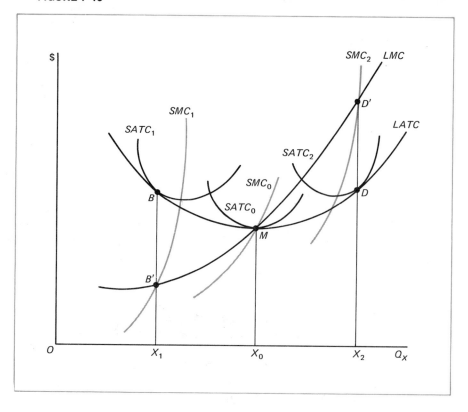

were greater than long-run total costs, for the two costs to become equal at OX_1, long-run total costs must increase faster than short-run costs. Thus, long-run marginal cost must exceed short-run marginal cost for any output less than OX_1 (for any output less than that at which tangency occurs between the *STC* and *LTC* curves). If the firm produces an output larger than OX_1, using the size of the plant represented by STC_1, both short- and long-run costs rise, but to the right of point *b*, STC_1 lies above the *LTC* curve. Short-run costs increase faster than long-run costs. Thus, at outputs greater than that associated with the tangency point, the *SMC* curve must lie above the *LMC* curve. These relationships are shown in Figure 7–18. Since the same relationships between the marginal curves apply in the region of diseconomies of size, the explanation is the same for the position of SMC_2 relative to *LMC* in Figure 7–18.

Having explained the relationships of *SMC* and *LMC* to each other, we shall now turn our attention to the relative positions of the intersections of the marginal curves and the long-run average cost curve. In Figures 7-18 and 7-15, all outputs less than OX_0 are produced under conditions of economies of size.

The equal slopes of STC_1 and LTC at b (Figure 7-15) are less than the slope of the line Ob. Therefore, at output OX_1, short- and long-run marginal costs, which are necessarily equal, are less than long-run average cost. For that reason, the intersection of SMC and LMC must occur below the $LATC$ curve, as is shown at B' in Figure 7-18.

The firm produces all outputs greater than OX_0 under conditions of diseconomies of size. At point d' (Figure 7-15), the equal slopes of STC_2 and LTC are greater than the slope of a line segment joining O and d'. Therefore, at output OX_2, short- and long-run marginal costs are greater than short- and long-run average costs; hence, the intersection of the SMC and LMC curves must take place above the LAC curve. This situation is shown at point D' in Figure 7-18 for the output OX_2.

At output OX_0, returns to size are constant. The slopes of the short- and long-run cost curves must be equal to the slope of a line joining points O and M. Thus, at OX_0 (the simultaneous minima of the short- and long-run average cost curves), $LMC = SMC$. This situation is shown in Figure 7-18 at output OX_0, where the SMC and LMC curves intersect at the minimum point, M, of the $LATC$ curve.

RESTATEMENT OF COST–MINIMIZATION IN TERMS OF ISOQUANT AND ISOCOST CURVES

The tangency of isoquant and isocost curves depicts the same conditions as does the tangency of the short-run average total cost curve and the long-run average total cost curve or, alternatively, the equality of short- and long-run marginal costs. Both types of diagram show the least-cost combination of producing a given output.

We can express this relationship in terms of simple mathematical symbols. When a firm has correctly allocated its production budget between its inputs,

$$\frac{MP_L}{P_L} = \frac{MP_K}{P_K}$$

At the margin, each dollar spent on any one input must contribute the same amount to total output as each dollar spent on any other input. Consequently, if the ratios are unequal—for example, if we know that

$$\frac{MP_L}{P_L} < \frac{MP_K}{P_K}$$

—the firm is not minimizing its costs. At the margin, on a per-dollar basis, capital is contributing more to output than is labor. The firm should reallocate some of its input expenditures from labor into capital. As it does so, the marginal productivity of labor will rise, and the marginal productivity of capital

will fall, causing the marginal productivities per dollar of each resource to move toward each other. The firm will cease input reallocation when the two ratios are equalized.

Let us take the cost-minimizing condition

$$\frac{MP_L}{P_L} = \frac{MP_K}{P_K}$$

and restate it as[3]

$$\frac{MP_L}{MP_K} = \frac{P_L}{P_K}$$

Since $MP_L = \Delta Q_X / \Delta Q_L$ and $MP_K = \Delta Q_X / \Delta Q_K$, we may write the cost-minimizing condition as

$$\frac{\dfrac{\Delta Q_X}{\Delta Q_L}}{\dfrac{\Delta Q_X}{\Delta Q_K}} = \frac{P_L}{P_K}$$

But

$$\frac{\dfrac{\Delta Q_X}{\Delta Q_L}}{\dfrac{\Delta Q_X}{\Delta Q_K}} = \frac{\Delta Q_K}{\Delta Q_L} \qquad MRTS_{LK}$$

Thus, in the least-cost equilibrium,

$$\frac{MP_L}{MP_K} = MRTS_{LK} = \frac{P_L}{P_K}$$

As the general case,

$$MC = \frac{\Delta TC}{\Delta Q_X}$$

If labor is defined as the variable input, we know from previous discussions that

$$SMC = P_L \left(\frac{\Delta Q_L}{\Delta Q_X}\right) = \frac{P_L}{MP_L}$$

[3] This is accomplished by dividing both sides of the original equation by MP_K and then multiplying both sides of the resulting equation by P_L.

In the long run, all inputs may be adjusted to obtain the cost-minimizing condition

$$\frac{MP_L}{P_L} = \frac{MP_K}{P_K}$$

from which it necessarily follows that

$$\frac{P_L}{MP_L} = \frac{P_K}{MP_K}$$

It must also be the case that

$$LMC = \frac{P_L}{MP_L} = \frac{P_K}{MP_K}$$

since in the long run the costs of using all inputs to produce a marginal increase or decrease in X must be changing at the same rate. This means that if the firm were to expand output by changing the variable input, the total cost of production would exceed the least-cost combination, or, equivalently, $SMC > LMC$. Along the expansion path OM in Figure 7-19, the marginal productivities of the inputs remain constant. Hence, at any point on OM, $SMC = LMC$. This means that it makes no difference which ratio we use—P_L/MP_L or $P_K MP_K$—to represent short-run marginal cost.

Assume that the firm is currently producing X_2 units of output using the least-cost input combination denoted by T_1 (i.e., $L_1 K_1$) and that it desires to increase output to $X_3(X_3 - X_2 = \Delta Q_X \rightarrow 0)$. At T_1, $MRTS_{LK} = P_L P_K = (MP_1/P_1 = MP_K/P_K)$; hence, $SMC = LMC$.

FIGURE 7-19

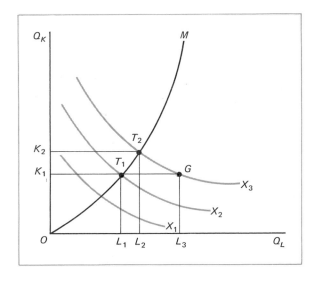

The Theory of Production: A Value Analysis

When the firm is able to vary inputs so that it can assemble the least-cost combination to produce the desired increase in output, it will follow the expansion path, arriving at point T_2. Labor will be increased by $L_1 L_2$ units and capital by $K_1 K_2$ units. Since an expansion path intersects all isoquants at points of equal slope, at T_2 the marginal productivities of the inputs will not have changed, and at T_2, $MP_L / P_L = MP_K / P_K$, just as was the case at T_1.[4] Hence, at the larger output, $SMC = LMC$.

In the short run, assuming capital to be the fixed input, the firm would have to achieve the desired increase in output by using $L_2 L_3$ more units of labor. This would place production at point G on X_3. At G, more L is used to produce X_3 than is used at T_2; therefore, the marginal productivity of labor is less at G than at T_2. Consequently, at G,

$$\frac{MP_L}{P_L} < \frac{MP_K}{P_K}$$

$$\left(\frac{P_L}{MP_L}\right)_G > \left(\frac{P_K}{MP_K}\right)_{T_2}$$

$$\left(\frac{P_L}{MP_L}\right)_G = SMC$$

but at T_2

$$\left(\frac{P_L}{MP_L}\right)_{T_2} = \left(\frac{P_K}{MP_K}\right)_{T_2}$$

and as shown previously,

$$SMC = LMC$$

Thus, at point G, $SMC > LMC$. The firm can lower the cost of producing output X_3 if it will substitute some capital for labor, since production at G requires the firm to operate on an isocost curve lying to the right of the isocost curve tangent to X_3 at T_2.

A UNIQUE PRODUCTION FUNCTION: CONSTANT RETURNS TO SCALE

In Figure 7-20, OS is a scale line, since it is a straight line out from the origin of the isoquant map. It traces the amounts of output produced by proportional changes in all inputs. The scale line OS is also an expansion path, since it passes through the points of tangency between isoquants and isocosts. Proportional changes in all inputs are economical for a firm whenever the expansion path is a scale line. Indeed, that is what the linearity of the path from

---

[4] Recall that along an expansion path, input prices remain constant.

FIGURE 7-20

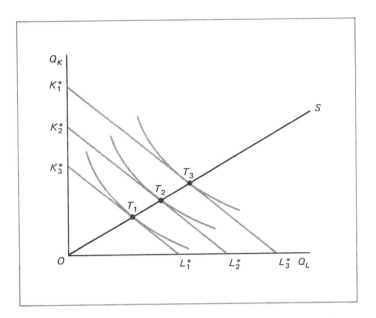

the origin means. *Along a linear expansion path,* constant returns to scale obtain. Thus, if X_2 is twice as large an output as X_1, twice as many labor and capital units are used at T_2 as are used at T_1.

For a linearly homogeneous production function, the concepts of returns to scale and returns to size coalesce. Returns to scale are the phenomena observed when the firm moves along a scale line—that is, when inputs are changed equiproportionately. Returns to size are phenomena observed when the firm moves along an expansion path—that is, when it changes output, keeping $SMC = LMC$. Since OS is both an expansion path and a scale line, any returns to size must also be identical returns to scale. In cost terms, economies or diseconomies of size and scale are the same for a linearly homogeneous production function.

On the production surface, the scale product curve and the long-run total product curve coincide vertically above OS. The product curve rises at a constant rate, reflecting the proportionate change in output in response to the proportionate change in all inputs, and therefore forms a straight line path along the production surface. With input prices held constant (as they must be for any expansion path), the long-run total cost curve is a straight line from the origin, having a positive slope equal to the long-run average total cost of production.

In the case of constant returns to size (here, also constant returns to scale), there are neither economies nor diseconomies of size (scale), since long-run average total cost is constant for all outputs, as is shown in Figure

7-21. The rate of change in long-run total cost being constant, the long-run average total cost curve and the long-run marginal cost curve are identical.

Each short-run average cost curve is tangent to the long-run average cost curve at the point where the given plant can produce the indicated output at the lowest cost. For example, at output OX_1, $SATC_1 = X_1T_1 = LATC$. But, more than this, at every point of tangency for all levels of output, $SATC = minimum$ $LATC$. Figure 7-21 shows that it is possible for any efficient plant to have the minimum point of its representative $SATC$ curve tangent to the $LATC$ curve. This means that there is no uniquely optimal size of plant. Suppose the firm is producing output OX_2 with plant 2. Whether the demand falls to OX_1 or increases to OX_2, in the long run the average cost of production is always the same. Thus, for any output, an optimal scale (size) of plant may be built.

RETURNS TO SCALE AND SIZE —A FINAL SUMMATION

The case of the linearly homogeneous production function helps to illustrate why a distinction has been made between economies of size and economies of scale. In physical production theory, returns to scale occur when the firm moves along the scale line. In cost theory, the expression "economies (diseconomies) of scale" is used to identify the same phenomenon. Thus, if increasing returns to scale obtain for a certain segment of a production function, the (long-run) average total cost of production will fall as all inputs are

FIGURE 7-21

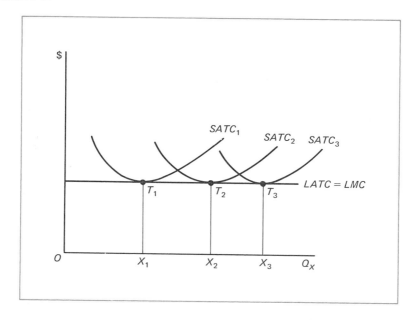

increased proportionately. We may, therefore, regard economies of scale as the cost theory counterpart of the physical production phenomenon of increasing returns to scale. As we have argued previously, increasing and decreasing returns to scale—and, therefore, economies and diseconomies of scale—are not likely to be observed in empirical data derived from the operations of business firms. Unless the expansion path is a scale line, there is no reason to expect firms to increase their inputs proportionately in the long run. A firm will follow its expansion path and, except in the case of the linearly homogeneous production function, will increase its inputs disproportionately, as it changes its output. The changes occurring in output in regard to movements along a nonlinear expansion path, then, cannot be said to be manifestations of returns to scale. It would seem, therefore, that the cost counterpart of the physical phenomena should not be called economies or diseconomies of scale. If long-run average total cost falls when the firm expands output, it would seem better to call this an example of economies of size, meaning that when all inputs are freely variable, increasing all inputs in an efficient combination to produce a larger output will bring cost reduction that is attributable to a "larger" collection of inputs. Similarly, when long-run average total cost increases as output is expanded, all inputs being freely variable, this should not be thought of as a case of diseconomies of scale if the firm is following a nonlinear expansion path. Since more inputs are being used to produce the larger output but are being increased disproportionately, we identify this behavior of long-run average total cost as being due to the diseconomies of size.

In the case of the linearly homogeneous production function, returns to scale are constant; and so are returns to size, since the expansion path is also a scale line. Because returns to scale and size are constant, neither economies nor diseconomies are encountered in any long-run adjustment of inputs.

THE CHARACTERISTICS OF AN INDUSTRY

The symmetrical, U-shaped long-run average total cost curve is a favorite of theoretical economists. For illustrative purposes, it is a highly useful curve. However, the empirical curves of business firms may not be so perfectly U-shaped. The shapes of particular long-run average total cost curves may reveal a great deal about the behavior of firms in a particular industry.

In Figure 7-22, three different possibilities for the behavior of long-run average costs are shown. Curve number 1 (the black line) shows continuously declining long-run average costs of production over a wide range of output. If economies of size can be obtained only at very high output volumes, it is not worthwhile for a firm to exist unless it can be large. For example, the technology of steel making demands that steel producers be large. "Large" usually means that there are few firms in the industry, and "few" signifies to many people the absence of effective competition. This fear for the state of competition is heightened if it is assumed that the long-run average total cost curve

The Theory of Production: A Value Analysis

FIGURE 7-22

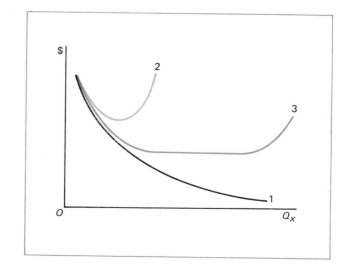

of a particular firm continues downward without a predictable limit. The ultimate result of the nonterminable downward slope is generally held to be the development of a one-firm industry—that is, a practicing monopoly. With some regularity, the financial press worries about the existence of firms that have what some writers incorrectly call "unending economies of scale." Such firms are supposed to be "cursed" with efficiency. Because their costs continue to fall as they expand output, their natural tendency is to exploit their unused economies of size, and in doing so, to drive their rivals out of business. Some financial commentators believe that the only remedy for this situation is to use antitrust procedures to break up such firms into smaller, hence less efficient, enterprises. Many supporters of this procedure concede the desired result could be a Pyrrhic victory, since the economy would lose the benefit of low per unit cost of production.

Curve number 2 (the light gray) indicates that size offers few or no advantages. Economies of size are rapidly dissipated. Firms in an industry characterized by long-run average cost curves such as this will be small. Such firms may be those in which a high degree of personal craftsmanship or personal attention is an essential requisite of manufacture.

Curve number 3 (the gray line) shows that economies of size are attained at low levels of output, but diseconomies do not set in until an extremely high output volume is reached. Economies of size are constant over a wide range of output. Apparently the good can be produced efficiently by both large and small firms. Retailing is an example of such an industry. Small specialty stores selling the same goods as are found in the large department stores of national retailing organizations do not operate at a competitive disadvantage. Probably a great number of businesses experience this type of long-run average cost pattern. There is no particularly compelling cost advantage in largeness.

For various reasons, none of the efficiencies associated with size are realized as inputs are varied in least-cost combinations. For example, beyond a certain point, specialization may offer no advantages. Indeed, it may be a disadvantage in a retailing establishment to have tasks so finely divided that one clerk sells suits, another shirts, and still another ties. It may be advantageous to both buyer and seller to have one clerk accompany the customer through one coordinated shopping experience. When such firms grow, quite possibly the impetus was something other than the lowering of the per-unit costs of operation. Diversification may be one of the other motives, or there may be a "mystique of growth" prompting businessmen to act in a less than completely rational manner.

SUMMARY

Cost theory is merely production theory restated in money, or value, terms. Costs as a manifestation of the basic economic condition of scarcity are best seen in the concept of opportunity costs. An opportunity cost is the sacrifice entailed in giving up some quantity of the next-best alternative in order to achieve a most-desired end.

The costs of the business firm are divided into two broad categories: fixed costs and variable costs. Fixed costs are those that do not change with variations in the level of output, while variable costs fluctuate directly with the level of output. Given a sufficiently long period of time, all costs are variable. Therefore, fixed costs are defined only for the short run, that period of time in which the business firm is unable to change all its inputs in any desired absolute amount.

For economic analysis, it is useful to know what it costs to produce a unit of output (average cost) and the rate at which total cost changes (marginal cost). A given plant is represented by a short-run average cost curve. Assuming this curve to be U-shaped, the firm is operating the plant efficiently if the level of output is denoted by the minimum point on the curve. At that point the firm has achieved the least-cost combination of inputs in the short run; that is, given the amount of fixed inputs, no other amount of the variable input can yield lower unit costs of production.

Reduction of the average costs of production to a minimum in the short run does not mean that further cost reductions are impossible. Costs may be further reduced if the firm has the opportunity to change all its inputs without restriction—that is, in the long run.

The geometric locus of all minimum unit costs under conditions of complete input substitutability *ceteris paribus,* is the long-run average total cost curve. Depending on the frame of reference, the shape of the long-run average total cost curve is determined by either (1) returns to scale or (2) returns to size. Returns to scale involve the behavior of costs when all inputs are changed

The Theory of Production: A Value Analysis

in the same proportion. Returns to size occur whenever all inputs are varied in whatever proportions will yield the lowest unit costs for a given output.

The least-cost combination of inputs may also be shown on an isoquant-isocost map. At the point of tangency between an isoquant representing a desired level of output and an isocost representing the firm's production budget, the costs of production are minimized, for then the marginal rate of technical substitution between the inputs is equal to the economic rate of substitution. The locus of points of tangency between isoquants and isocosts is the expansion path. The expansion path conveys in another form the data conveyed by the long-run average total cost curve—namely, the least-cost combination of inputs.

It is possible that over a wide range of outputs, long-run average total cost may be constant (constant returns to scale *and* size). This situation is shown by a horizontal segment of the long-run average total cost curve. If the production function is linearly homogeneous, the entire long-run average total cost curve will be a horizontal line. Within the output bounds indicated by the straight-line segment, it is possible to build economically optimal plants of any size.

Building on the theories of consumer behavior and the theories of production (both physical and value), we shall construct the theories of business firm behavior in the next five chapters.

8

The Theory
of Market Behavior
Under Competitive
Conditions

THE PERFECTLY COMPETITIVE MARKET

A *market* is the context (not necessarily the location) in which buyers and sellers confront each other to work out how goods and services are to be exchanged for money (indirectly, other goods and services). In this chapter, we meet the most basic and probably the most important of the various market models, that of perfect competition.

There is no denying that the perfectly competitive model is highly abstract, but in that quality lies its great elegance, refinement, and usefulness. No one supposes that this model comprehends the fantastic complexity of today's markets, or that it is the last word in theoretical statements on market structure. But the perfectly competitive model is at the core of every more complicated model. It can stand in the absence of the others; but remove it and the more complicated constructs will fall. Moreover, because it *is* highly abstract, the perfectly competitive model can strip away complexities that often hide the underlying nature of a problem. The solution of a perfectly competitive model usually will not be a final one, but it probably will be an excellent first approximation. Its use often "roughs out" a solution. A more complete answer may then be obtained by applying specialized techniques to the areas needing further refinement and clarification.

THE ASSUMPTIONS OF THE MODEL

All the conclusions of this chapter derive logically from the following assumptions:

1. *Product homogeneity.* The firms in a given market produce homogeneous, or completely standardized, outputs. No differences can be detected among the goods produced by the various firms in the market. Customers are totally indifferent to the identity of any seller. Units of output are so well standardized that they are completely gradable and may be bought and sold by specification.

2. *Large number of firms.* The greater the number of firms in a market, the less impact will the actions of any one firm have on the conditions under which exchanges take place. The competitive model requires that firms be so numerous in relation to the markets for those things they sell (outputs) and those things they buy (inputs) that no one firm acting independently is able to affect output or input prices.

3. *Ease of entry and exit.* Firms are able to enter or exit from the market in response to economic forces. In this chapter the economic, or market, force motivating the entry into or exit from a particular industry is assumed to be profit. Firms enter an industry in response to a higher-than-normal profit and exit from the industry when their profit falls below the normal rate of return; thus, by assumption, there are no legal or customary impediments to entry or exit. If an entrepreneur wishes to enter an industry, he needs no license. If he desires to exit from the industry, he does not need the permission of any regulatory agency.

PURE COMPETITION AND PERFECT COMPETITION

A market made up of firms that conform to these three postulates is said to be *purely competitive,* and each member firm is a *pure competitor.* No value judgment is implied by the word "pure"; it is a technical expression stating merely that the three postulates apply to the firms under discussion.

A market made up of pure competitors may be perfectly or imperfectly competitive. *Perfect* competition requires one additional postulate:

4. *Perfect knowledge.* Firms and customers have perfect knowledge of the market and act on that knowledge. *Perfect knowledge* is a technical term; it means merely that all economic units in a market have complete and instant knowledge of the prices being charged by any firm and that any change in price is immediately noted. Moreover, firms and customers respond quickly and

smoothly to any change in market information. The chain of communication is complete; it carries its messages speedily; and the response to the information it transmits is virtually instantaneous.

USE OF THE COMPETITIVE MODEL

The primary purpose of the competitive model is to serve as the core of the theory of the firm, but in certain respects, the model is a reasonably accurate depiction of a number of actual firm and market situations. For example, a number of firms, such as those in agriculture, produce homogeneous goods, and the action of many such firms cannot affect the prices of the goods they sell. It is not difficult to find examples of firms that fulfill the requirements imposed by the first two postulates.

What about the other two postulates? Perfect mobility does not seem to be a widespread phenomenon. In many industries, there are numerous, and high, barriers in the way of would-be entrants. For example, American Medical Association practices and state licensing requirements are rather effective in preventing an otherwise expected response to the economic profit obtainable from a medical practice. As to exit, for years many railroads lamented their enforced continuance in the passenger business, under the half-hearted insistence of the Interstate Commerce Commission. Also, some individuals seem not to respond to economic signals, preferring to live as they want and where they want, even if it means accepting a much lower return than they could earn in another occupation in a different locality. Of course, many people who would like to leave one occupation for another do not do so because they are unable to change their skills frequently enough to keep up with constant technological change. At the other extreme, there are those persons who are mobile for noneconomic reasons. These individuals throw aside a materially rewarding occupation for one that is psychically more satisfying.

Yet, in the long run, firms may be quite mobile. Firms do tend to move to those markets in which the highest rates of return exist. Capitalists who have their funds tied up, say, in an industry marked by high labor costs, will, over a period of time, liquidate their investments in low-return enterprises, and transfer their funds to enterprises yielding higher rates of return. Even some railroads, representative as they are of the most circumscribed business enterprises, have been moving into nonrail businesses.

Perfect knowledge is probably the least realizable of the postulates, yet in some segments of the economy, it does exist. In the organized commodities markets (e.g., the Chicago Board of Trade) and in the securities markets (e.g., the New York Stock Exchange), information about prices is widespread and travels fast. Price information flows by wire from the floors of the organized exchanges to brokers' offices and their customers throughout the nation in a practically continuous stream.

Our conclusion, then, is that the model does approximate a number of significant firms and markets well enough to permit us to draw conclusions

about their behavior directly from it—although its major use continues to be as a foundation for further economic analysis.

THE PRICE–TAKER FIRM

Unless otherwise noted, we will assume that the main force affecting the firm is its desire to maximize its profit. Here and in the next chapters we define total economic profit as the difference between the firm's gross receipts and its total costs. Usually, gross receipts are called the *total revenue* of the firm and are proceeds from the sales of the firm's total output over a specified time period. Generally, we assume that the firm's principal motivation is to maximize the difference between total revenue and total cost—a difference that we, here, call total economic profit.

Some firms act on the assumption that they can do nothing about the price at which they can sell their outputs. Regardless of how price is set, it is to them a parameter. These firms can be called *price-takers*. The price policy of such firms consists wholly of accepting the price established in the market. Since the price-taker firm has no control over price, it is never concerned about how the price it charges affects its competitors or its customers. Price is determined by outside forces (which we will search out at a later time), and the firm, its competitors, and its customers must live with the price.[1]

Thus, the price-taker firm may be considered the "introvert" of the economic world. Believing itself unable to affect the price at which its goods are sold, it takes no action to maximize its profit by attempting to adjust price. This does not mean that it is passive in its acceptance of a given rate of economic profit. Profit is not viewed as a parameter. The firm does act to make its total economic profit as large as possible, but it does so by trying to minimize its costs. Moreover, all such actions must be internal to the firms, for it believes that its sphere of influence is limited to its own internal economy. (Remember that it considers as given the prices it pays as well as the prices it charges.) It is, therefore, inward-turning, and to maximize its profit it is forced to consider continuously how efficient it is.

If the firm is efficient—that is, if it keeps the total cost of producing any output at the lowest possible level—what does the firm do to achieve the profit-maximizing combination of total revenue and total cost? The answer, as we shall see, is that it seeks to produce that output at which the difference between the total revenue derived from the sale of its goods exceeds the total costs of producing that output by a maximum amount. Thus, the price-taker firm is also a *quantity-adjuster.* Its search for a maximized total economic profit leads it to search for an output that will achieve its objective.

---

[1] In the next four chapters, we shall see how the decision of what price to charge may be one of the most important decisions the firm can make, and the most important consideration in the pricing policy of some firms may be the effect any price change will have on their competitors and customers. But in this chapter, the firm has no such worries.

THE TOTAL REVENUE CURVE
OF THE PRICE-TAKER FIRM

Total revenue (the gross receipts of the firm) is the arithmetic product of price multiplied by quantity of output and is expressed by the formula

$$TR = P \cdot Q$$

Table 8-1 shows hypothetical total-revenue data for a price-taker firm. The table shows that total revenue increases proportionately with quantity sold. Given the externally determined price, if the quantity is doubled, total revenue doubles, and if quantity is quadrupled, total revenue quadruples, and so on.

A graphical depiction of total revenue must show the proportional relationship between receipts and quantity sold and is, therefore, a straight line of positive slope radiating from the origin. In Figure 8-1, the curve TR is the total

TABLE 8-1

$P = AR$	Q	TR	MR
			—
$5	0	$ 0	
			$5
5	1	5	
			5
5	2	10	
			5
5	3	15	
			5
5	4	20	
			5
5	5	25	

FIGURE 8-1

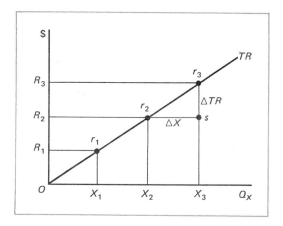

revenue curve of a price-taker firm. The distances OR_1, OR_2, and OR_3 are the total revenues associated with the sale of the outputs OX_1, OX_2, and OX_3, respectively. An increase in output is matched by a proportionate increase in total revenue. Thus, the curve described by points such as r_1, r_2, and r_3, which indicate the revenue and quantity combinations for the goods sold by a price-taker firm, must lie on a straight line. Since any increase in output is matched by a proportionate increase in total revenue, $OR_1/OX_1 = OR_2/OX_2 = OR_3/OX_3$.

THE AVERAGE REVENUE CURVE OF THE PRICE–TAKER FIRM

The slope of the total revenue curve of a price-taker firm is the given selling price. Since price is a constant, the slope of the total revenue curve is constant. The formula for price, or average revenue, is

$$P = \frac{TR}{Q} = AR$$

Thus, in Figure 8-1, $P = X_1 r_1/OX_1 = X_2 r_2/OX_2 = X_3 r_3/OX_3$, and these fractions expressing the ratio of the vertical distance to an accompanying horizontal distance conform to the formula for the slope of a straight line.

The constancy of average revenue at every level of output means that the average revenue curve is a horizontal straight line lying everywhere above the quantity axis by a distance equal to price. The average revenue curve is shown in Figure 8-2.

If we assume that Figures 8-1 and 8-2 are prepared from the same data, the following relationships must hold true: $O\bar{P} = X_1 a$ in Figure 8–2 is the same as $X_1 r_1/OX_1$ in Figure 8-1. Since total revenue is equal to price times quantity, the graphical depiction of total revenue in Figure 8-2 is the area of the rec-

FIGURE 8-2

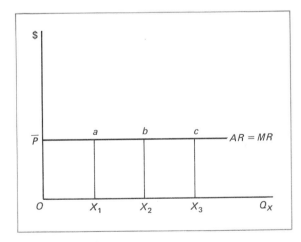

Market Behavior under Competitive Conditions

tangle inscribed under the average revenue curve at any given level of output. Thus, the total revenue derived from the sale of OX_1 units of output and shown as $OR_1 = X_1r_1$ in Figure 8–1 is represented by the rectangle $OX_1a\bar{P}$ in Figure 8–2. Similarly, if output is expanded to OX_2, total revenue is shown as the rectangle $OX_2b\bar{P}$ in Figure 8–2, whose area is equal to the vertical distance $OR_2 = X_2r_2$ in Figure 8–1.

THE MARGINAL REVENUE CURVE OF THE PRICE–TAKER FIRM

Marginal revenue is the change in total revenue that occurs in response to a change in output. In Figure 8-2, the average revenue curve is designated $AR = MR$ because, as we will see, *the average revenue curve of the price-taker firm is identical to its marginal revenue curve.* The behavior of the marginal revenue of a price-taker firm is indicated in the fourth column of Table 8-1. The table shows that if total revenue changes proportionately with output, marginal revenue is a constant and is equal to average revenue.

The formula for marginal revenue is

$$MR = \frac{\Delta TR}{\Delta Q}$$

As this formula expresses the ratio of a change in vertical distance to a change in the corresponding horizontal distance, the formula for marginal revenue is the slope of the total revenue curve. Since the slope (see Figure 8-1) of the total revenue curve of a price-taker firm is constant (and equal to average revenue), it follows that

$$\frac{sr_3}{r_2s} = MR = \frac{X_3r_3}{OX_3} = AR = P$$

Therefore, for a price-taker firm, the average and marginal revenue curves are congruent, and the marginal revenue of the firm is always equal to price. Whenever the AR curve is horizontal, $AR = MR$.

NORMAL PROFIT

The term *profit* has so many meanings that its usage can be troublesome. In accounting, profit is a residual. It is the amount remaining after all costs of operating the firm have been paid. It belongs to the owners of the firm. This definition is entirely appropriate for accounting reports, but for economic analysis, it is not useful because it does not count a portion of profit as a true cost of production.

The economists' opportunity cost concept includes all costs of production. Any compensation is considered a necessary cost if production would cease were it not paid. The owner of a business firm requires a certain return,

or he will exit from the market. Whatever sum he requires to stay in business is called *normal profit.* A normal profit is a true cost of production in that if it is not paid, the firm will cease production. Thus, economists hold that a normal profit is not a mere residual. It is just as much a cost of production as wages or interest, and it must be included in any cost curve.

Total profit can be greater than *normal* profit because the return to the firm's owners may exceed the amount required to induce them to stay in business. An amount over and above normal profit is called, variously, economic profit, abnormal profit, or excess profit. Economists do view this type of profit as a residual, or surplus, because it is what is left over after the true costs of production (including a normal profit) have been paid.

Suppose that a firm owner requires $10,000 per year to maintain his enterprise. If he does not receive this return, he will go into some other kind of remunerative activity. The $10,000 a year return is his normal profit. If the accounting profit of his firm is $12,000, then his economic profit is $2,000 per year. If his accounting profit is $10,000 per year, his economic profit is zero. And, finally, if his income statement shows an $8,000 accounting profit, economists would hold that the firm is incurring an economic loss; economic profit is, in this case, a negative $2,000.[2]

Each businessman may have his own idea of a normal profit. This idea is dependent largely on the return he could make in some other line of endeavor—that is, for doing approximately the same type of work in another firm's employ. Despite the apparently subjective nature of normal profit, a study of an industry of price-taker type firms may show whether profits are normal or not. A normal profit is the amount that in the long run is sufficient to maintain the number of firms in the industry. There is neither entry nor exit. A normal profit is not large enough to induce firms to enter a particular industry, but it is not small enough to cause firms currently in the industry to leave. Economic profits probably exist when firms enter a particular industry; if firms leave the industry, it is likely that profits are below normal. In the latter case, economists hold that the firms are encountering economic losses (negative economic profits) even if the enterprises' income statements show an accounting profit.

THE SHORT-RUN EQUILIBRIUM
OF THE PRICE-TAKER FIRM

Under our assumption that the firm's objective is to maximize its total profit, we will hold that the firm is in equilibrium when it has achieved a maximum total profit at a specified (parametric) price. If, after equilibrium has been

[2] It is important to recognize that any person can make a surplus. The concept of "surplus" is not limited to the return of capitalistic business enterprises as Marxists hold. If a dishwasher would pursue his humble calling for $2,400 per year but is actually paid $3.200, he is realizing a surplus of $800. This "extra" $800 is not a true cost of his services, because it could be reduced or eliminated and he would still wash the dishes.

Market Behavior under Competitive Conditions

achieved, price or cost conditions change, the firm will be in a state of disequilibrium and will seek a new profit-maximizing equilibrium output.

To see how a model firm behaves under the assumption of profit maximization, we will juxtapose the graphs of short-run total cost and total revenue as is done in Figure 8-3. At any output to the left of point B_1, total cost exceeds total revenue, so if the firm produces an output smaller than OX_1 it will incur a loss. If it produces the output OX_1, the firm will break even since total costs (including a normal profit) are equal to total revenue, as is shown by the intersection of the STC and TR curves at B_1, the firm's first "break even" point.

FIGURE 8-3

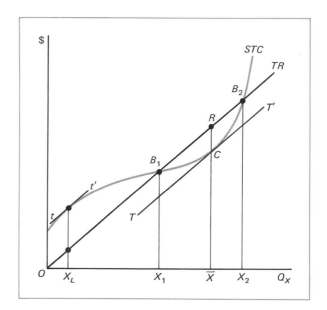

Point B_2 is the firm's second break-even point, for at that output, short-run total costs are again equal to total revenue. Between B_1 and B_2, the total revenue curve lies above the short-run total cost curve, so at any output greater than OX_1 but smaller than OX_2, the firm can realize an economic profit. The greater the distance between the two curves, the greater will be the total economic profit since

$$\pi = TR - TC$$

where π is total economic profit. If the firm produces the output $O\bar{X}$, its total profit will be maximized, since at that output, the total revenue and short-run total cost curves are separated by the greatest possible distance, CR. The total revenue derived from the sale of $O\bar{X}$ units of output is $\bar{X}R$, while the total cost of producing that output is $\bar{X}C$. The *maximized* total economic profit, π^*, is CR, since

$$\pi = \bar{X}R - \bar{X}C = CR = \pi''$$

We will now locate the distance *CR* in a way that will be useful to our understanding of the basic idea of profit maximization. Let us draw a line, *TT'*, parallel to the *TR* curve and tangent to the *STC* curve. Line *TT'* will be tangent to the *STC* curve at point *C*. If this procedure is carried out for any pair of *STC* and *TR* curves, the point of tangency between the *STC* curve and the tangent line will always establish the output (necessarily, the profit-maximizing output) at which the *STC* and *TR* curves are separated by the greatest vertical distance. In addition, since *TT'* is parallel to the total revenue curve, the slopes of both lines are equal, and since *TT'* is tangent to the short-run total cost curve at *C*, the slope of the cost curve at *C* must equal the slope of the total revenue curve. We know that the slope of the total cost curve *is* marginal cost and that the slope of the total revenue curve *is* marginal revenue. Therefore, when economic profit is maximized

$$MC = MR$$

This profit-maximizing condition can be summarized graphically using the two marginal curves shown in Figure 8-4. In Figure 8-4, the output $O\bar{X}$ is assumed to be the same output as the equilibrium output $O\bar{X}$ in Figure 8-3. In Figure 8-4, the intersection of the marginal cost and marginal revenue curves at *E* shows they are equal at the profit-maximizing output.

The reason for the equality of marginal cost and marginal revenue at the profit-maximizing output follows from the logic of the problem. As the firm expands its output from zero units to a positive amount, both total cost and total revenue increase, as is shown in Figure 8-3. Up to the output $O\bar{X}$, the slope of the total revenue curve exceeds the slope of the total cost curve; that is, $MR > MC$. The slope of a curve is the rate of change in the magnitude the curve represents. Therefore, up to $O\bar{X}$, in the region in which $MR > MC$, total revenue is increasing faster than total cost. Thus, as output is expanded the firm is adding to both cost and revenue, but revenue increases faster than cost, and as long as this condition continues, economic profit must increase. At output $O\bar{X}$, since the slopes of both curves are equal, cost and revenue are changing at the same rate, and $MR = MC$. Beyond $O\bar{X}$, total cost and total revenue continue to increase, but total cost increases faster than total revenue; that is, $MC > MR$. If the firm adds to its cost faster than it adds to its revenue, its total economic profit must shrink.

The marginal curves in Figure 8-4 are graphs of the slopes, or rates of change, of the curves in Figure 8-3. In Figure 8-3, we can read the values of marginal cost and marginal revenue directly. But, although we know that at *E* total profit is at a maximum, we do not know how much that maximized total profit is, whereas we do know the amount of total profit in Figure 8-3.

For $\pi = \pi^*$, $MC = MR$, but if $MC = MR$, it is not necessarily the case that

economic profit will be at a maximum. The equality of marginal cost and marginal revenue is a necessary but insufficient condition for profit maximization. This can be seen in both Figures 8-3 and 8-4. In Figure 8-3, at output OX_L, total costs exceed total revenue in the amount rc, which, in the region to the left of the first break-even point (B_1), is the maximum distance between the two curves. Obviously, at output OX_L, total *losses* are at a maximum. Yet, it is also obvious that at OX_L, $MC = MR$. The line tt' is tangent to the short-run total cost curve at c, and, being a constant vertical distance from curve TR, it is parallel to the revenue curve. Thus, we see that the equality of marginal cost and marginal revenue determines only an output at which either profits *or* losses are maximized. We can tell immediately which is the case, of course, by seeing whether total costs exceed total revenue or vice versa. This is clear in Figure 8-3.

An inspection of Figure 8-4 shows that here, too, there is a readily discernible difference between the two points, e and E, at which $MC = MR$. At the loss-maximizing output OX_L, $MC = MR$, but the MC curve cuts the MR curve at e from above. At the profit-maximizing output $O\bar{X}$, $MC = MR$, but the MC curve cuts the MR curve at E from below.

The marginal revenue curve of Figure 8-4 has a constant slope, which is equal to zero. At point e, the slope of the marginal cost curve is negative and is therefore less than the slope of the marginal revenue curve. At point E, the slope of the marginal cost curve is positive and thus exceeds the slope of the marginal revenue curve. Consequently, for profit to be at a maximum, not only must marginal cost be equal to marginal revenue, but the slope of the marginal cost curve must exceed the slope of the marginal revenue curve.

We know that the slope of a curve is the rate of change in the magnitude it represents. At point E, since the slope of MC exceeds the slope of MR, the rate of change in marginal cost exceeds the rate of change in marginal revenue.

FIGURE 8-4

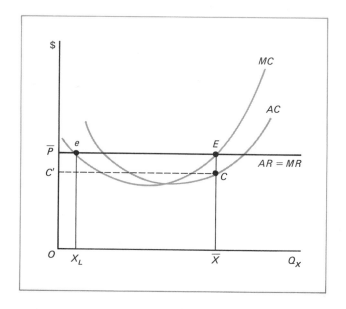

Therefore, we can state the profit-maximizing condition in still another way. For profit to be at a maximum, the rate of change in total cost (*MC*) must be equal to the rate to change in total revenue (*MR*), but the rate of change in marginal cost must exceed the rate of change in marginal revenue.[3]

[3] The profit-maximizing condition may be stated succinctly in calculus terms. Profit, the difference between total revenue and total cost, may be expressed symbolically as $\pi = R - C$. When the firm changes its output, it affects total profit by changing both total revenue and total cost. Thus,

$$d\pi = dX\left(\frac{dR}{dX}\right) - dX\left(\frac{dC}{dX}\right)$$

Dividing both sides of the equation by dX, we have

$$\frac{d\pi}{dX} = \frac{dR}{dX} - \frac{dC}{dX}$$

Profit maximization requires that

$$\frac{d\pi}{dX} = 0$$

that is, it must be impossible to change profit by changing output. From this requirement it follows that

$$\frac{dR}{dX} - \frac{dC}{dX} = 0 \quad \text{or} \quad \frac{dR}{dX} = \frac{dC}{dX}$$

Since dR/dX is marginal revenue, and dC/dX is marginal cost, profit maximization requires that marginal revenue be equal to marginal cost.

The equality of marginal cost and marginal revenue, although a necessary condition for profit maximization is not a sufficient one. The statement $d\pi/dX = 0$ is a first-order condition, since it merely establishes an extreme point (a point of zero slope) on the firm's profit function; that extreme point may indicate either a maximum profit or a maximum loss. To determine which is the case, we must employ a second-order condition. Suppose we move away from the point on the profit function established by $d\pi/dX = 0$. What will happen to profit? If it increases, the point must have been one of maximum loss; if profit falls, the point must have denoted maximum profit. To find what would happen in consequence of a small change in output, we must find the rate of change in the marginal profit, $d\pi/dX$; therefore, we take the second derivative of the profit function

$$\frac{d^2\pi}{dX^2} = \frac{d^2R}{dX^2} - \frac{d^2C}{dX^2}$$

The ratio d^2R/dX^2 is the rate of change in marginal revenue, and the ratio d^2C/dX^2 is the rate of change in marginal cost. If a movement away from the extreme point causes profit to fall, the rate of change in marginal cost must exceed the rate of change in marginal revenue; that is

$$\frac{d^2C}{dX^2} > \frac{d^2R}{dX^2} \quad \text{or} \quad \frac{d^2R}{dX^2} - \frac{d^2C}{dX^2} < 0$$

Therefore, profit maximization requires that not only must

$$\frac{d\pi}{dX} = 0 \quad \text{(the first-order condition)}$$

but also that

$$\frac{d^2\pi}{dX^2} < 0 \quad \text{(the second-order condition)}$$

THE USE OF AVERAGE COST CURVES

The superimposition of a short-run average total cost curve on Figure 8-4 enables us to read the maximized total profit implied by the intersection of MC and MR at E. In Figure 8-4, the average revenue, or price, derived from the sale of $O\bar{X}$ units of output is $\bar{X}E = O\bar{P}$. Total revenue equals price times quantity—that is, the distance $\bar{P}$ times the distance $O\bar{X}$, which is the area of the rectangle $O\bar{X}E\bar{P}$. The per unit costs of producing $O\bar{X}$ units of output are $\bar{X}C$; hence, total costs equal the area of the rectangle $O\bar{X}CC'$. The difference between average revenue and average cost is CE; this is the profit per unit of output. Total profit is equal to the area of the rectangle representing the difference between total revenue and total cost, namely $C'CE\bar{P}$. The intersection of MC and MR at E tells us that the area of rectangle $C'CE\bar{P}$ represents a maximized total profit. A rectangle representing profit at any other level of output—i.e., for some output at which $MC \neq MR$—would be smaller in area than $C'CE\bar{P}$.

Assuming Figures 8-3 and 8-4 to be drawn from the same data, a comparison between them is made in Table 8-2 for the profit-maximizing output $O\bar{X}$.

ZERO–PROFIT EQUILIBRIUM AND LOSSES

What happens to the curves in Figure 8-3, if price falls? Price is the slope of the total revenue curve, since for a price-taker firm, $\bar{P} = MR$. In Figure 8-5, curve TR_0 shows that price has declined to a level at which the entrepreneur makes only a normal profit; economic profit has been eliminated. Yet, since $MC = MR$, total economic profit is maximized. Symbolically, we can write

$$\pi = \pi^* = 0$$

The figure shows that the firm has only one break-even point, B, and at this point, the firm makes only a normal profit. The equality of total cost and total revenue is shown by the distance $\bar{X}B$.

Price can decline so as to force a loss on the firm. If losses persist, the firm must leave the industry. Curve TR_1 in Figure 8-5 illustrates a (temporary)

TABLE 8–2	Magnitude	Figure 8–3	Figure 8–4
	TR	$\bar{X}R$	$O\bar{X}E\bar{P}$
	TC	$\bar{X}C$	$O\bar{X}CC'$
	$\pi = \pi^*$	CR	$C'CE\bar{P}$
	$P = AR = MR$	$\bar{X}R/O\bar{X}$	$O\bar{P} = \bar{X}E$
	$MC = MR$	Slope of $TT' = \bar{X}R/O\bar{X}$	$\bar{X}E$
	Q	$O\bar{X}$	$O\bar{X}$

FIGURE 8-5

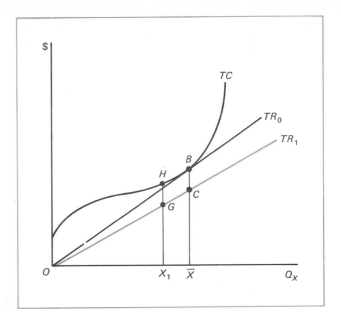

loss situation in which the firm is unable to break even at any output. Rational conduct for a firm faced with an unavoidable short-run loss dictates that the loss be minimized. As the graph shows, the total cost of producing the output $OX_1 = X_1H$, while the total revenue derived from the sale of the output is X_1G. Costs exceed revenue in the amount GH. Visual inspection shows that CB is the smallest vertical distance between the two curves. Further inspection shows that the slope of the short-run total cost curve is equal to the slope of the total revenue curve at output OX_1. Thus, if a firm facing unavoidable short-run losses follows the $MC = MR$ rule, its inevitable loss will be held to a minimum. Although the firm is incurring a loss, the output OX_1 is defined as an equilibrium output because once attained the firm will have no incentive under *existing* cost and revenue conditions (i.e., short-run conditions) to produce any other output.

THE SHORT–RUN SUPPLY CURVE OF THE PRICE–TAKER FIRM

In Figure 8-6, a short-run average variable cost curve has been added to the diagram. The firm is making a maximized economic profit, since at output $O\bar{X}_1$, $MC = MR_1$ and $AR_1 > SATC$.

If price were to fall below $O\bar{P}_1$, the firm would continue to make an economic profit until $AR = SATC$—that is, until the average revenue curve is tangent to the minimum point of the short-run average total cost curve. As price falls, the pursuit of a maximized economic profit causes the firm to reduce its output. Thus, if the price falls to the profit-eliminating price $O\bar{P}_2$, the firm

will reduce output in the amount $\bar{X}_1\bar{X}_2$. The points lying between E_1 and E_2 on the MC curve establish the quantities the firm would offer at any price between $O\bar{P}_1$ and $O\bar{P}_2$.

Now let us consider a case, such as at price $O\bar{P}_3$, in which the average total cost curve lies above the average revenue curve at all possible outputs, but the average variable cost curve does not. Average cost exceeds average revenue in the amount $\bar{P}_3E_3TT'$, and we know this is a minimized total loss, since the firm produces that output at which $MC = MR_3$. But notice that although the firm cannot cover all its costs at the price $O\bar{P}_3$, it does cover an amount greater than the variable costs of production. Unit variable costs are $\bar{X}_3V$; therefore, total variable costs are $O\bar{X}_3VV'$. Since total costs are $O\bar{X}_3TT'$, total fixed costs are $V'VTT'$. But rectangle $V'VE_3\bar{P}_3$ is common to both total costs ($O\bar{X}_3TT'$) and total revenue ($O\bar{X}_3E_3\bar{P}_3$); thus, in producing the output $O\bar{X}_3$ at price $O\bar{P}_3$, the firm not only fully covers all the total variable costs of production, but is able to cover some of its fixed costs as well.

Should the firm continue to produce even though it appears to be in difficulty? Yes, it should in the short run, because if it does not produce at all, its loss will exceed $\bar{P}_3E_3TT'$. Fixed costs continue whether the firm produces or not. The total fixed costs, as we have noted, are $V'VTT'$, and this, rather than

FIGURE 8-6

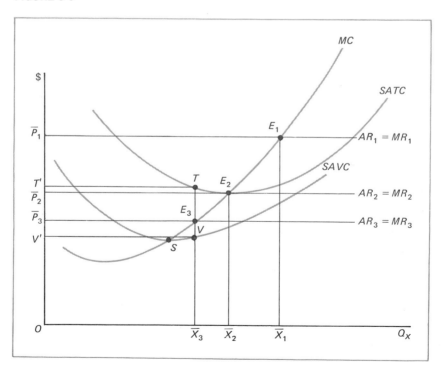

$\bar{P}_3E_3TT'$, would be the amount of the loss, if the firm did not produce at all. So if the firm has ongoing costs, such as rent, taxes, contracted salaries, interest, it should continue to produce, even at a loss, to hold its unavoidable loss to a minimum. The firm will do better economically by covering some of its fixed costs than by covering none of them.

The firm always will be able to cover fully its total variable costs and make a contribution to total fixed costs as long as price exceeds the average variable cost of production. Point S is the minimum point on the average variable cost curve; if price fell to a point at which the marginal revenue curve were tangent to S, the firm would be indifferent to operating or shutting down. Thus, the marginal cost curve above point S shows the outputs the firm would be willing to produce at a given price. A curve that relates quantities forthcoming to given prices is a supply curve; hence, for a price-taker firm, *the segment of its marginal cost curve lying above the minimum point on its short-run average variable cost curve is its short-run supply curve.*

If the firm cannot cover its variable costs of production at any level of output, it should shut down. Its existence as a firm costs more than its non-existence. Even if the firm follows the $MC = MR$ rule, it will fail to meet fully any of its costs of production. If it exits from the industry, it is true that its fixed costs will continue, but by abandoning operations, it will at least rid itself of the uncovered costs that are associated directly with the volume of production.

Figure 8-7 shows the case for continued operation despite a loss in terms of total costs and revenue. The firm is producing the loss-minimizing output $O\bar{X}$. The loss is equal to RC, but the amount of the loss is less than the total fixed costs, $\bar{X}F$. Since variable costs are equal to FC, total revenue $\bar{X}R$ clearly exceeds variable costs. The difference by which the firm covers its variable costs is $FC - \bar{X}F = FR$. Since FR is greater than RC, the firm is able to cover

FIGURE 8-7

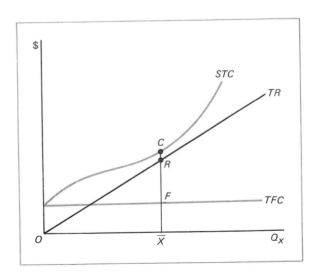

all of its variable costs and make a contribution toward covering fixed costs. It should stay in business, for if it were to cease operations, its loss would expand from RC to $\bar{X}F$.

In the long run, if the firm can incur only losses, regardless of its rate of output, it must exit from the industry, for an unsubsidized firm cannot sustain losses permanently. Eventually, it will run out of both cash and credit and be unable to hire inputs. The principle that firms should not operate if they cannot cover their variable costs is always true; and in the long run, *all* costs are variable.

SHORT–RUN MARKET EQUILIBRIUM IN A COMPETITIVE INDUSTRY

An industry is comprised of the firms producing a particular (homogeneous, in this chapter) output. For example, we speak of the soft coal industry, the anthracite industry, and so on. The total output of an industry is the sum of the outputs of the individual firms that produce the good in question. The supply curve of the industry must be simply the horizontal summation of the individual supply curves of the firms in the industry. (Recall that the short-run supply curve of each individual price-taker firm is the portion of its marginal cost curve above the minimum point of the average variable cost curve.)

Just as the individual firm's supply curves show what a single firm would produce at each specific price, given the opportunity to adjust the rate of output of a given plant, so the industry supply curve provides the same information for the aggregate case.

THE THEORY OF SHORT–RUN EQUILIBRIUM PRICE

If we now superimpose the market demand curve of Chapter 2 on the industry supply curve (as is done in Figure 8-8), we can determine the prevailing market price for the short run. At price $O\bar{P}_1$, firms are willing to operate their plants at such levels of output that $O\bar{X}$ quantity of the good will come on the market. At the same price, consumers will be willing to buy $O\bar{X}_1$ units. So if, in fact, $O\bar{X}_1$ units do appear on the market, the quantity demanded will be equal to the quantity supplied, and there will be neither upward nor downward pressure on the prevailing price. Since the price $O\bar{P}_1$ clears[4] the market, as indicated, it is the equilibrium price. As long as supply and demand conditions do not change, this price will be maintained in the market, and firms will send a flow of goods to the market equal to the demand of buyers at price $O\bar{P}_1$.

Suppose now that there is an increase in the demand for the good. The demand curve shifts rightward from D_1 to D_2. If the price were to remain at

---

[4] The market is *cleared* when quantity demanded is equal to quantity supplied.

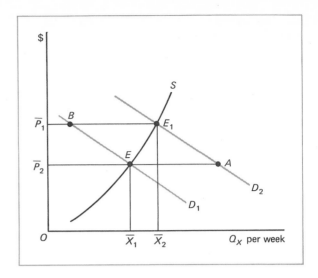

FIGURE 8-8

$O\bar{P}_1$, the quantity demanded would exceed the quantity supplied, and there would be a shortage equal to EA. Clearly, $O\bar{P}_1$ is no longer the equilibrium price. Equally clear is the likelihood that the market price will rise above $O\bar{P}_1$. The demand curve D_2 shows that there are a number of buyers willing to pay a price higher than $O\bar{P}_1$ rather than go without the good. Thus, buyers will bid against one another for the available supply. As they do so, the price will rise, and, in consequence, some intended purchase plans will be canceled, reducing the shortage to less than EA.

While the decrease in the quantity demanded of good X helps to eliminate the shortage, action by firms on the supply side of the market has the same effect. As the price is pushed up by the competitive bidding of prospective buyers, sellers find that their profits will be increased if they produce more. In the short run, each firm, by utilizing its plant and equipment more intensively, manages to expand production.

Price will continue to rise until it reaches $O\bar{P}_2$. At $O\bar{P}_2$, the supply curve indicates that firms will put $O\bar{X}_2$ on the market, and the demand curve shows that consumers will demand OX_1. The market is thus cleared with OP_2 as the new equilibrium price.

Suppose now that the good becomes unpopular; the demand curve registers this change in consumer opinion by falling back to D_1. Until firms are able to reduce their rates of output, a surplus flowing at the rate of BE_1 units per week will be coming onto the market. Profits cannot continue to be maximized by producing outputs for unintended and unwanted inventories. Attempting to maintain their profits at the highest level possible, the firms will begin to cut back on production by reducing the rates of operation of their existing plants and equipment. The action of each firm in reducing its rate of output shows up on the industry supply curve as a downward movement from

Market Behavior under Competitive Conditions

E_1 to E. As price continues to fall, the amount each firm is willing to put on the market undergoes a cutback, while the amount consumers wish to buy increases. The rate of the weekly surplus flowing onto the market diminishes but does not disappear until the price falls to OP_1, at which the quantity demanded equals the quantity supplied ($O\bar{X}_1$)

The entire burden of adjustment—the movement of output from $O\bar{X}_1$ to $O\bar{X}_2$ and then back to $O\bar{X}_1$—was accomplished by firms altering the rates at which they utilize their *existing* plant and equipment. This, then, is what is regarded in economics as a short-run adjustment; hence, we must designate the supply curve of Figure 8-8 as a *short-run* supply curve.

LONG–RUN ADJUSTMENTS OF PRICE–TAKER FIRMS

In the long run, firms are able to adjust their outputs by altering any or all of their inputs or by entering or leaving the industry.

CONSTANT–COST INDUSTRY EQUILIBRIUM

Figure 8-9(a) shows the industry supply and demand curves; Figure 8-9(b) shows the diagram for a single firm within the industry. Initially, both the firm and the industry are assumed to be in equilibrium at price $O\bar{P}_1$, with industry and firm producing $O\bar{X}_1$ and $O\bar{x}_1$ units of output, respectively. Then, an increase in demand shifts the industry demand curve rightward from D_1 to D_2. The demand curve now intersects the industry short-run supply curve at B_2,

FIGURE 8-9

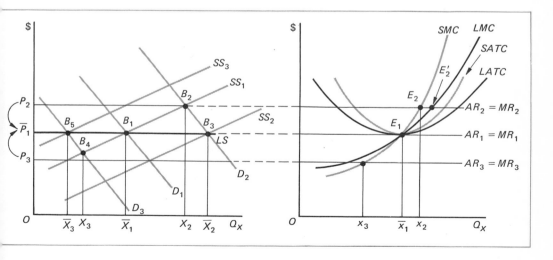

and the market price rises to OP_2. The industry will achieve a short-run equilibrium at the output OX_2.

The $AR_1 = MR_1$, curve of the firm moves upward to $AR_2 = MR_2$. At the new price, $MR_2 > SMC$. This means that if the firm expands its output, although total cost will increase, total revenue will increase faster; so total profit must rise. If $\pi^* = 0$ in the initial equilibrium, $\pi^* > 0$ in the new situation.

Responding to the opportunity to make a greater profit, the firm will expand its production by a more intensive use of its existing plant and equipment. The expansion of output ceases with the production of Ox_2 units, when short-run marginal costs are equated to the new level of marginal revenue. The firm is now making an economic profit, since E_2 on the new average revenue curve lies above the short-run average total cost curve.

We know that the action we have just described will not be the firm's final adjustment. It is a short-run adjustment, and the firm, eyeing the possibility of doing even better, will contemplate the effects of changing its plant. The graph shows $SMC = MR_2 > LMC$. This means that although the firm is maximizing profit in a short-run sense—that is, within the limitations of its existing plant and equipment—it is not maximizing its profit in the context of the long run; for that would require $SMC = MR = LMC$. Given the opportunity to alter all its inputs to put them in the most optimal relation to one another, the firm would move along the LMC curve to E_2' and produce the output appropriate to that point. Point E_2' does not, of course, lie on the existing SMC curve. Only a different SMC curve could intersect the LMC curve at E_2'. This means that the firm must build a larger scale plant, having an associated SMC curve that will intersect the LMC curve (and $AR_2 = MR_2$) at E_2'. The new short-run average total cost curve will be tangent to the long-run average total cost curve at a point vertically beneath E_2'. The firm will be operating in the region of diseconomies of size or technology, as the case may be, and moreover, will be operating the larger-than-socially-optimal scale of plant at a rate beyond its least-cost output. Nevertheless, from the standpoint of the firm, the expansion of output from the short-run profit-maximizing output is worthwhile in that revenue increases faster than costs, so that profit must, in consequence, increase.

The market, however, will rob the firm of its opportunity to maximize profit further. In the new short-run equilibrium, economic profit exists. The higher-than-normal reward is more than sufficient to keep existing firms in the industry and, indeed, will attract new entrepreneurs. Since the industry short-run supply curve is drawn for a given number of firms, a change in their number must affect the curve. Entry causes the short-run supply curve to shift rightward until it reaches SS_2. As it moves rightward along D_2, the market price falls, and economic profits are reduced. As the price falls, and, hence, as the $AR = MR$ curve of the competitive firm moves downward, the plant that could have maximized profit in the long run is no longer a feasible opportunity for the firm. With sales shrinking, it loses interest in building a new facility or, if it had enough time to build a new plant before entry began to squeeze out the economic profit, it will consider reducing its scale of plant.

Market Behavior under Competitive Conditions

When will the short-run supply curve end its rightward course? Not until the opportunity for any entrant to make an economic profit is closed; for, by definition, entry will continue as long as the possibility to make an economic profit exists. The economic profit of the subject firm is eliminated entirely when the price returns to $O\bar{P}_1$ and industry output is $O\bar{X}_2$.

The firm is now in equilibrium in both the long- and short-run senses, for at $O\bar{P}_1$, $SMC = MR_1 = LMC$. Moreover, $\pi^* = 0$; that is, maximized economic profit is zero, since $AR_1 = SATC = LATC$.

To complete the picture, let us now consider a reduction in price below the existing equilibrium level, as shown in Figure 8-9. The initial equilibrium price is $O\bar{P}_1$; the industry output is $O\bar{X}_1$; and the output of the representative firm is Ox_1. Now suppose that the demand for the good falls, with the result that the industry demand curve shifts leftward to D_3. The market price falls to OP_3, and the industry output is reduced to OX_3. This reduction in output is accomplished solely by the existing firms in the industry cutting back the rates at which they utilize their existing plant and equipment. For example, the firm in Figure 8-9 will slide down its SMC curve until an intersection is established with the new MR curve. At the new lower price, $SMC > MR$. This means that if the firm reduces its output, even though both revenue and costs will fall, total costs will fall faster than total revenue, and, in consequence, the loss the firm is forced to sustain will be minimized. Since the firm is following the equi-marginal rule, we know that Ox_3 is a loss-minimizing output.

What will the subject firm do? Without more information, we cannot be sure. If $SMC < SAVC$, the firm is not even covering the costs directly associated with the production of output OX_3 and will be forced to leave the industry. Suppose, however, that for the subject firm $SMC > SAVC$. In accord with the discussion of the previous section, the firm will find it worthwhile to continue operating at a loss in the short run.

Firms incurring persistent losses will exit from the industry in the long run. Exit will cause the short-run supply curve to shift leftward to, say, SS_3. Its leftward progress halts when the losses of all firms have been eliminated. This occurs at point B_5, at which the market price has returned to $O\bar{P}_1$. Industry output has fallen to $O\bar{X}_3$, but the subject firm has found it worthwhile to return to its initial, $O\bar{x}_1$. We conclude, therefore, that the reduction in industry output is the result of the elimination of a number of firms in the industry. The loss of the output of the departed firms more than offsets the resumption of the previous levels of output by the remaining firms.

Given sufficient time for the adjustment of plant and equipment, no matter what happens to demand and to the short-run supply curve, price always returns to $O\bar{P}_1$. We infer that this price must be unique. Our inference is correct because it is the *long-run equilibrium price of the industry*—i.e., the price that prevails in the market over the long run. In the short run, market prices may fluctuate around $O\bar{P}_1$, but the unimpeded adjustments made by the competitive firms tend always to bring price back to $O\bar{P}_1$.

Joining the several points of long-run equilibrium, B_5, B_1, and B_3, we de-

rive curve LS, the long-run supply curve of the industry. The horizontal long-run supply curve shows that in the long run, the industry will supply any desired quantity of the good at price $O\bar{P}_1$. Demand does not enter into the determination of price in the long run; it is a determinant solely of the quantity produced. The long-run supply curve—or, rather, the cost of production—is the one determinant of price in the long run.

The reason for this lies in the complete immobility of the long-run average total cost curve. No matter what happens in consequence of the shifting demand and short-run supply curves, the long-run average total cost curve stays put, and, when the period of adjustment is over, price always returns to equality with the minimum long-run average total cost of production. This immobility of the long-run average total cost curve means that entry and exit of firms cause no change in the prices of the industry's inputs. In the case of entry, the new firms do not bid up input prices, and in the case of exit, the diminution of firms does not cause input prices to fall. In other words, input supplies to these firms are infinitely elastic. Input supplies are so large relative to the firms' use of them that entry and exit of the member enterprises of the industry have no effect on input prices. The case we have been examining is thus that of a *constant-cost* industry.

In a competitive industry, the output price always tends to equal the minimum long-run average total cost of production. If, in addition, the industry is one of constant costs, price always tends toward a fixed level.

The constant-cost industry case is the oldest model of long-run industrial equilibrium, having been developed and discussed by Adam Smith in his *Wealth of Nations* in 1776. Smith did not use our techniques of analysis, but his logic was sufficiently persuasive to establish the constant-cost case as *the* classical explanation of value, or long-run price.

INCREASING COSTS

Now we will look at a case in which costs do not remain constant in the long run but vary directly with the entry and exit of firms.

The graphs of Figure 8-10 depict the attainment of long-run equilibrium in an industry of increasing costs. Initially, the industry and the subject firm are in equilibrium, total industry output being $O\bar{X}_1$ and the firm producing $O\bar{x}$ units. Price is $O\bar{P}_1$. Now, let us suppose that demand increases, so that the demand curve shifts rightward to D_2. At the new industry short-run equilibrium point, B_2, price rises to OP_2, and the total industry output increases to OX_2. The firm, attempting to maximize its profit, follows its short-run supply curve, SMC_1, and produces output Ox. The diagram shows that economic profit accrues to the firm at this new price and output combination. Economic profit encourages the entry of new firms, and, in response, the short-run supply curve begins to move rightward. Unlike the previous case of the constant-cost industry, however, the short-run supply curve will not shift as far right as was

indicated by curve SS_2. The rightward shift of the short-run supply curve is halted at point B_3 on demand curve D_2. What has precluded the equilibrium solution of the previous case? Entering the industry in their quest for economic profits, the new firms add their demand for inputs to that already existing. The demand curves for labor and capital shift rightward, but in this case, the prices of these inputs rise. The input demand curves must be moving along upward-sloping supply curves for labor and capital; the factor supply curves are finitely elastic. This indicates that as the firms expand output, they encounter, and contribute to, relative input limitations. In order to acquire more input units, the firms must bid against each other and attract inputs away from other firms. Faced with positively sloped input supply curves, the increasing demand of the firms for productive factors caused input prices to rise. Input prices are the costs of the business firm, and any changes in them must be reflected in the cost curves. So, with the increase in input prices occasioned by entry, the $LATC$ curve rises to $LATC_2$, indicating higher production costs at every level of output. Entry continues until the opportunity to make economic profits is eliminated. This occurs when the short-run supply curve reaches point B_3, on demand curve D_2. Price is once again equal to the firm's minimum average total costs of production, but costs are higher than they were before the expansion of the industry; thus, the new equilibrium price $O\bar{P}_2$ exceeds the initial price $O\bar{P}_1$.

At the new price, the industry has expanded total output to $O\bar{X}_2$, but our subject firm has returned to output Ox its initial level. This need not necessarily be the case. It has occurred here because the long-run average total cost curve has shifted vertically upward with its minimum point directly above

FIGURE 8-10

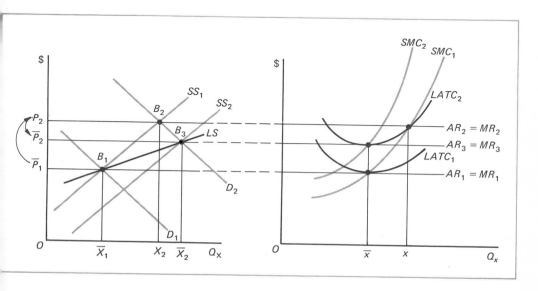

the minimum point of $LATC_1$. It is possible for the curve to shift to the left or right as it rises. Since the production surface is unaffected by changes in input prices, the horizontal shift, as well as the vertical movement, is caused purely by a change in input prices. If the curve shifts rightward, a larger output than before is required to exhaust the economies of size or technology. A short-run average total cost curve tangent to the minimum point of the new long-run average total cost curve also lies to the right of the initial short-run average total cost curve. The farther a short-run average total cost curve lies to the right, the greater is the firm's use of plant and equipment—those inputs regarded as "fixed" in the short run. A leftward shift shows that economies of size are exhausted at a lesser output than previously. The firm will cut back on the size of its plant and the quantity of capital equipment. The socially optimal size of plant is smaller. The optimal rate of operation of this smaller plant requires that it produce a smaller output than the pre-entry level. These situations are shown in Figure 8-11. In chart (a), the increase in the demand for the final good, has pushed the price up from OP_1 to OP_2. Entry has forced up input prices, causing the long-run average total cost curve to rise to $LATC_2$. Besides rising, it has shifted to the right. This means that to reduce costs to a minimum, consistent with the new higher input prices, the plant must produce a larger output. Efficient production of the larger output requires a larger plant than that used previously.

Now consider chart (b). Initially, the output is OZ_1 at price OP_1. When price rises to OP_2, resulting in economic profits for firms currently in the industry, the ensuing entry of new firms pushes up input prices and thus causes

FIGURE 8-11

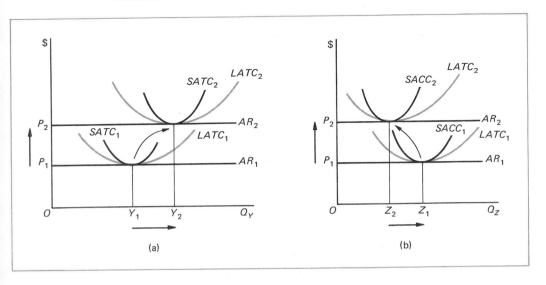

(a)

(b)

the long-run average total cost curve to move upwards. The firm now finds it advisable to spend less on plant and equipment than formerly, and a plant that will yield the lowest costs of operation is smaller than the previous plant. The *SATC* curve of such a plant must be above and to the left of the initial *SATC* curve. If the new *SATC* curve is the socially optimal scale of plant, its minimum point must be tangent to the minimum point of the new *LATC* curve. Consequently, the *LATC* curve must shift leftward as it rises.

Despite arguments to the contrary, it is not possible, in the absence of information about a specific firm and its technology, to deduce from proportional changes in input prices what a firm will do. It is just as likely that a firm will buy more of an input whose price has risen more than the prices of all other factors as that it will buy less of that input. It may be that if the price of capital rises by a greater percentage than the price of labor, the firm will still build a larger plant. If this happens, the *LATC* curve must shift rightward despite the relatively greater rise in the price of plant and equipment.

The main reason for the indeterminacy of the horizontal shift of the *LATC* curve is the fact that some productive factors are *inferior* inputs. Input inferiority was discussed in Chapter 6. The possibility of input inferiority means that the firm may purchase a relatively, or even absolutely, greater amount of the input following a rise in its price.[5]

The predictability of the horizontal shift in the *LATC* curve is a matter of little practical consequence. A firm is unlikely to leave its production technique unchanged if input prices rise in different proportions. If, as the demand for output increases, the prices of all inputs rise, but the increase in wages consistently outpaces increases in the prices of capital equipment, the firm is likely to look for an entirely new capital-intensive, laborsaving technology. For example, the farmer faced with labor costs that rise faster than the prices of hoes, shovels, rakes, and land, will not simply buy more land, hoes, rakes, and shovels, and relatively less labor; rather, he will become a potential customer for capital equipment more powerful than simple hoes and for automated picking equipment far faster than the now relatively more expensive field hands. Once he has acquired the larger plant using the new technology, he may hire more labor than he used formerly, but it will not be as much as if he had expanded output to the same degree using only *more* hoes instead of *better* ones. Rather than a horizontal shift in a long-run average total cost curve, rising input prices are much more likely to cause the introduction of a new production function, with the result that the *existing LATC* curve neither rises nor shifts. A different production function means that a *completely new LATC* curve of the appropriate configuration and in the proper position must be drawn.

Notice in Figure 8-11 how the increasing-costs case differs from that of constant costs in two respects. First, price does not return to the initial long-

---

[5] For an extended discussion of input inferiority, see Charles E. Ferguson, *The Neoclassical Theory of Production and Distribution* (Cambridge, Eng.: Cambridge University Press, 1969), pp. 187–200.

run equilibrium level. Rising input prices, caused by the entry of firms, force the price of the final good up as consumer demand increases. Second, demand, along with the conditions of long-run supply, is a determinant of long-run price. When the supply curve is positively sloped, price changes directly with changes in demand. This direct relationship is the hallmark of the increasing-cost industry.

The long-run supply curve of the increasing-cost industry is reversible. If demand was initially at D_2 and were to fall to D_1, price would fall from $O\bar{P}_2$ to $O\bar{P}_1$. This does not mean that the industry is a decreasing-cost industry, although costs (input prices) obviously fall if demand decreases. An increasing-cost industry is one in which long-run price changes are related directly to changes in demand.

DECREASING–COST INDUSTRY

The decreasing-cost industry is considered a rather unusual case. It is an industry in which increases in demand are related *inversely* to price changes. In Figure 8-12, a line drawn through the points of short-run market equilibrium produces a negatively sloped long-run market supply curve.

The downward-sloping supply curve results from the curious behavior of the long-run average total cost curve, which falls as entry occurs. This is shown in chart (b) of Figure 8–12. Initially, the industry demand and supply curves, D_1 and SS_1, respectively, intersect at B_1, and the price is $O\bar{P}_1$. The industry produces $O\bar{X}_1$ units of output, and a firm is shown to be in long-run equilibrium producing $O\bar{x}_1$ units. If the demand increases to D_2, price will

FIGURE 8-12

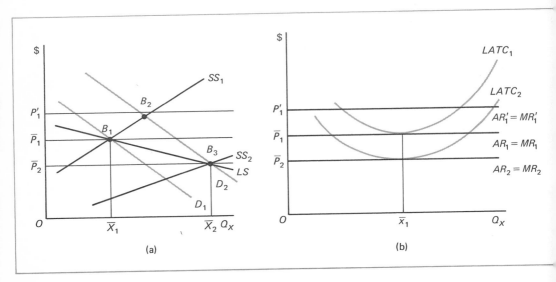

(a)   (b)

rise in the short run to OP_2, increasing economic profits in the industry. For that reason, entry ensues.

In this case, entry is accompanied by falling average revenue *and* long-run average total cost curves. The falling $AR = MR$ curve is, of course, the result of a downward shift in the industry supply curve. But why does the long-run average total cost curve fall? To put the question another way, why is entry accompanied by falling input prices? Whatever the case, decreasing costs must come from forces outside the subject industry. The explanation must lie in new efficiencies effected by input suppliers. Their *internal* economies become the *external* economies, or decreasing costs, of the subject industry. *Coincident* with entry, input prices fall. Suppose, for example, entry and a fall in the wage rate (owing to an increase in the supply of labor) occur simultaneously. If the fall in the wage rate outweighs changes in the prices of other inputs, the long-run average total cost curve will fall. In consequence, the new long-run equilibrium price must lie below the initial equilibrium level.

A COMPARISON OF ECONOMIES OF SIZE AND EXTERNAL COST CONDITIONS

Economies of size and external cost conditions are not the same thing. Let us compare these different sets of phenomena. The downward-sloping portion of the long-run average total cost curve shows that as output and *plant* size are expanded, the per unit costs of operation fall. Economies of size involve a downward movement along a *given* long-run average total cost curve. With the curve given, input prices cannot change. The reduction in costs accompanying an expansion of output is due solely to changes in productive relationships *within* the firm. On the other hand, decreasing costs come about because of reductions in costs *external* to the firm. The negatively sloped long-run supply curve is the result of continued downward shifts of the long-run average total cost curve. The cost curve shifts downward because falling input prices accompany the expansion of output. The economies of size of other firms become the decreasing costs of the subject firm. Similarly, the minimum point of the long-run average total cost curve, at which there are constant returns to size, has nothing in common with the horizontal long-run supply curve. This is true even if the long-run average total cost curve is itself a horizontal line. Again, if a firm experiences constant returns to size, it is due not to constant input prices but to the productive relationships within the firm. The existence of external economies or diseconomies has nothing to do with the firm's own production function. The same reasoning holds for the diseconomies of size region of the long-run average total cost curve and the long-run supply curve of the increasing-cost industry.

Any case of economies or diseconomies of size can be compatible with any kind of external cost condition. For example, a firm could be operating in the economies of size region of its long-run average total cost curve while, at the same time, being a part of an increasing-cost industry. Thus, as the firm

expands its output, its internal costs will be falling while its external costs will be rising. In other words, the firm is moving down the negatively sloped portion of its long-run average total cost curve while that curve is itself rising.

EQUILIBRIUM OF THE PURE COMPETITOR IN AN IMPERFECT MARKET

Suppose the firm is purely competitive—that is, it cannot affect price by itself—but it operates in an imperfect market. Because of entry barriers (imperfect mobility, imperfect knowledge), excess profit tends not to be competed away. What is the equilibrium condition for a firm so situated? Obviously, it cannot be the solution at which the minimum points on the short- and long-run average cost curves are concurrently tangent to the horizontal average revenue curve. The perfectly competitive long-run equilibrium is stated symbolically as: $AR = MR = SMC = SAC = LMC = LAC$. But such cannot be the case for the firm protected against the entry of new firms. Thus, $SMC = SAC = LMC = LAC$ is not essential for the fulfillment of a *purely* competitive equilibrium. What is? It can only be the equality of SMC and LMC with MR. Such a case is depicted in Figure 8–13. Price exceeds the average cost of production. This situation is no different from a short-run (or a long-run) disequilibrium of a perfect competitor, except here the tendency of price is to remain above the perfectly competitive long-run level.

Assume that the firm has sufficient time to adjust to price $O\bar{P}$. In the short run, it equates SMC to MR, but it cannot be in long-run equilibrium until $SMC = MR = LMC$. As long as $SMC \neq LMC$, the firm has incorrectly allocated its inputs in the sense that, at the given price, its profit is not a maximum. So

FIGURE 8-13

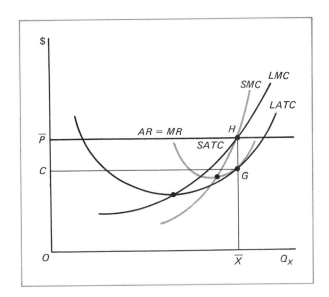

Market Behavior under Competitive Conditions

long as *LMC* is less than $MR = P$, the firm will add more to revenue than it will to cost if it expands output. If *LMC* is less than $SMC = MR$, then if the firm expands its output, it should attempt to derive a proportionately greater amount of its increased output from plant and equipment rather than from labor; that is, the firm should increase the size of its plant until $LMC = SMC = MR$. In the preceding chapter, we found that this equality could obtain only at the minimum point of the long-run average total cost curve (i.e., at the point of constant returns to size) or above the long-run average total cost curve (i.e., in the region of diseconomies of size). Since the solution *on* the long-run average total cost curve is the perfectly competitive solution, the purely competitive solution with impaired entry must occur in the region of diseconomies of size. Such is the case for the firm depicted in Figure 8–13. Total revenue exceeds the total costs of production. The maximized total profit is $CGH\bar{P}$.

In the next chapter, we will discuss a charge commonly alleged against monopoly firms: that they restrict output and build plants of less-than-optimal size, which they operate at a rate below peak efficiency. But the opposite nonoptimal case may be alleged against protected pure competitors, as Figure 8–13 shows. With price above minimum long-run average total cost, it is worthwhile for the firm to build a scale of plant larger than the social optimum and to operate it at a rate greater than its ideal volume.

SUMMARY

A purely competitive firm must accept the price set in the market by the forces of supply and demand. To such a firm, its demand (or average revenue) curve is a horizontal straight line having a height equal to the imposed selling price. Because the firm can sell any amount of its output at the going market price, the marginal and average revenue curves are identical. To maximize economic profit (the return over and above the normal profit, which is a true cost of production), the firm must sell that quantity of its output which will cause marginal cost to equal marginal revenue.

Economic profit is maximized in the short run when short-run marginal cost is equal to marginal revenue. This means that the firm is utilizing its *existing* fixed inputs to its own best advantage. When short-run marginal cost is equal to marginal revenue but not equal to long-run marginal cost, profit is not maximized in the context of the long-run. This means that the firm could improve its profit situation given a sufficient period of time in which to alter *all* its inputs without restriction.

In *perfect* competition, the maximized economic profit of firms tends toward zero. Unimpeded entry and exit cause firms to tend to build plants having the lowest possible costs of operation. Geometrically, this is shown by the tangency of the minimum point of the short-run average total cost curve of the optimal plant with the minimum point of the envelope long-run average total cost curve. The motive of profit maximization requires $SMC =$

$MR = LMC$. Unimpeded entry and exit force the equality to occur at the minima of both cost curves. Thus, in the perfectly competitive equilibrium, the total costs of production are equal to total revenue, and maximized economic profit is zero.

Depending on what happens to input prices as a result of entry or exit, the industry may be characterized as one of constant, increasing, or decreasing costs. These cost phenomena must be distinguished sharply from returns to size. Returns to size occur wholly in response to changes *within* the firm. Constant, increasing, and decreasing costs represent changes *external* to the firm. Returns to size are shown geometrically as movements *along* a *given* long-run average total cost curve, whereas external cost changes are reflected in the movement (or lack of movement) of the long-run average total cost curve *itself*.

The equilibrium price set in the competitive market may be dynamically stable or unstable depending on the actual conditions prevailing in production and in the market. Time lags in production and in the communication of market information may delay or even preclude the attainment of a stable equilibrium.

Market Behavior under Competitive Conditions

The Theory
of Market Behavior
Under Purely
Monopolistic Conditions

MONOPOLY

In a modern enterprise economy, some firms, unlike the firms of the preceding chapter, *do* have some control over the selling prices of their goods. They have *market power.* Firms having market power cannot be introverted as are the competitive firms of Chapter 8; on the contrary, they must be concerned with the world outside the firm. For them, price is not a parameter, so they cannot be concerned solely with purely internal adjustments. Rather than *adjusting* to a price, they must *search* for a price that will maximize their profits. In doing so, they must be alert to the effects price changes will have on buyers, and in many cases, they must be conscious of the reactions of rival firms.

Businesses derive their ability to influence their prices from some measure of monopoly, or market, power. In economics, monopoly power means that the quantity of output a firm sells varies inversely with the selling price. Given the demand for its goods, the firm can sell a greater quantity by reducing its price, or it can increase its price but lose some sales. Contrast this situation with that of the competitive firm, which would price itself out of the market if it were to raise its price and would do itself no good if it were to lower price.

Monopoly power is a spectrum, not a precise situation. Some firms have it in abundance; other firms may have such a modest

amount that they can be distinguished only with difficulty from competitive firms. We will begin discussing monopoly power with the simplest case—pure monopoly.

Pure monopoly exists when the firm and the industry have a single identity. Whether or not there are such firms, the theory of pure monopoly remains useful, for it reduces to the barest essentials the techniques of analyzing firms with negatively sloped demand curves. Much of this theory is applicable directly to the behavior of actual firms even if they are not pure monopolies. The rest will serve as a foundation for the more complicated behavior patterns of those firms that fall somewhere in the spectrum between the perfectly competitive and purely monopolistic cases.

Pure monopoly exists when there is only one seller of a particular good. But what is a particular good? Clearly, the Coca-Cola Company has a monopoly of the trademarked good Coke, but it has a less than monopolistic position in the good known as "cola," still less of a monopolistic position in "soft drinks," and virtually no monopoly at all in "beverages." But monopoly cannot be defined away. Even people with a very casual knowledge of the economy are aware of the real power exerted by so-called monopolies.

For operational purposes, an alternative definition of monopoly has been suggested: a monopoly is a firm that sells a good for which there are no close substitutes. But what are "close substitutes"? Several years ago, when the Aluminium Company of America (Alcoa) was the sole (American) producer of virgin aluminum, it was characteristically and confidently used in the classroom as the embodiment of the economics texts's "pure monopoly." But is virgin aluminum a good for which there are no *close* substitutes? The answer is subjective. Perhaps the reader cannot think of a single desirable substitute for the aluminum beer can, but generally, function for function, there are reasonably good substitutes for aluminum. Aluminum can conduct electricity rather well, but so can copper. Aluminum provides nonrust car bodies and cooking utensils, but so does stainless steel. Aluminum makes light air frames, but magnesium makes them lighter still. Yet, the case may be made that Alcoa was, or did come close to, the textbook model of the pure monopoly, for whenever a *combination* of attributes is wanted—lightness, resistance to corrosion, electrical conductivity, and so on—there may well be no close substitutes for aluminum.

For our purposes, definitional arguments over the nature of the monopolistic firm are unimportant; what is important is to develop a set of techniques that will help us analyze the behavior of a firm that has a great deal of market power. The most expedient way to begin this task is to *postulate* the existence of a monopolized industry (i.e., a single-firm industry) and work out the logical implications of this postulate. Much of what we learn from this procedure will be applicable to firms possessing a large amount of monopoly power even if they are not monopolies in the sense of being the only seller of a good for which there are no close substitutes. Monopoly power means the ability to exercise

discretion in the setting of price; the greater the amount of that discretion, the greater is the amount of monopoly power.

THE FOUNDATIONS OF MONOPOLY POWER

There are several bases of monopoly power. Usually, they are called collectively, *barriers to entry*. Their principal effect is to restrict, or prevent entirely, the entry of firms that would result in the elimination of economic profit. There is nothing inherent in the nature of monopoly that guarantees the existence of profit, to say nothing of economic profit. Yet, if there is an above-normal profit, entry barriers may ensure that it will not be reduced or eliminated by the inflow of competitors. While a single entry barrier may give a firm a tremendous amount of market power, many firms have their monopolistic attributes rooted in more than one source. Some of those sources, or barriers to entry, are:

1. *Raw materials.* Alcoa was mentioned as having once been a classic example of monopoly. Despite the fact that aluminum is the most widely distributed metal in the earth's crust, the only practical source of the element for electrolytic extraction is bauxite clay. Alcoa's predominant position was based on its almost exclusive ownership of that raw material.

2. *Economic power.* Some firms may possess sufficient economic power to discipline the members, or would-be members, of an industry or prevent entry altogether. The early days of industrial expansion in the United States provide a number of examples of such behavior. One of the most famous is that of John D. Rockefeller, Sr., and the Standard Oil trust. Standard Oil led many potential competitors to believe that it would be worthwhile for them to turn over their stock in independent petroleum firms to the Standard Oil trust in exchange for trust certificates. Rockefeller was able to convince them, with the later well-proved assertion, that they would all do better together under a single management than they would going it alone. For those who could not be persuaded, Standard Oil had an effective disciplinary device. The trust would enter the rival's market area and underprice him until he could not survive. Standard Oil's immense financial power made its temporary losses sustainable and well worth the future profits brought about by this coercion. Somewhat similar to the persuasive effect of financial power is physically coercive power. In the early days of the western railroads, when one major line was attempting to enter California and found it necessary to cross the existing tracks of another major railroad, the early arrival simply kept a steam locomotive moving back and forth along its tracks day after day at the projected crossing point. Later negotiations solved the impasse. Obviously, physical coercion was a method widely used by the underworld in the 1930's for gaining control of lucrative (albeit illegal) business firms.

3. *High initial capital requirements.* Some industries, such as steel and automobiles, require enormous capital investments before a single unit of a good can be produced. Today, entry into the mass-produced automobile industry would require such an amalgamation of capital that entry is extremely unlikely. Entry might occur if there were a complete change in automobile technology. If the internal combustion engine is ever entirely eliminated as a power source, perhaps some other firms, themselves already industrial giants, might become entrants.

4. *Control over distribution channels.* There is little point in manufacturing a product if it cannot be marketed. Some firm, or firms, may control the distribution channels so completely that a rival who can meet every requirement for the production of the good will be unable to gain access to the market. The history of the motion picture industry in the United States provides an excellent example. The main reason for the existence of the major motion picture studios was not to produce pictures for rental but to supply a product to the chains of theaters that owned the studios. In the heyday of the industry, a studio that was not an adjunct of a major theater chain could have a difficult time in arranging for distribution of its movies. Often the only feasible way for an independent studio to reach the market was through the offices of the chain-owned studios, who acted as releasing agents—for a substantial fee and other concessions.

5. *Limited market.* If one firm achieves maximum efficiency at a rate of output that supplies the total market demand while simultaneously maximizing its profit, the market is able to support only one firm. Economic history shows that if two or more firms attempt to exist in such a market, a number of undesirable patterns of behavior usually result. Because of the inability of firms to expand their markets and thereby achieve a maximum profit, they may attempt to lower costs by reducing standards of service. If firms see the existence of rivals as the obstacle to the attainment of a higher profit, they may engage in "cutthroat" competition, which can be severely disruptive to both sides of the market.

At one time, two major telegraph companies, Western Union and Postal Telegraph, existed simultaneously in the United States. A town did not have to be very large to boast two separate telegraph offices. Railroad stations and hotels offered their clients a choice of message carrier. That two telegraph companies were ever needed is unclear; but when long-distance telephony underwent a rapid improvement and the demand for telegraph service diminished, it became clear that the market would not support two separate firms. The receipts of both Western Union and Postal Telegraph fell until it appeared there might be no telegraph service at all. Congress recognized this economic reality when it passed legislation ordering the stronger firm, Western Union, to absorb Postal Telegraph, thus ending an untenable market situation.

A somewhat similar situation occurs when consumers are worse served by competition than by monopoly. Unnecessary duplication of fixed equipment may raise both private and social costs above what they would be were monopoly to serve the market.

Once consumer acceptance of telephones became fairly widespread in metropolitan areas, some cities had more than one local telephone company. In those days, long before technological improvements permitted a number of messages to be sent over one slender wire in a compact cable, the streets were defaced by an unsightly profusion of telephone cables suspended from the numerous crossarms of a graceless forest of telephone poles. Subscribers to one company's service could not reach the subscribers to another line, so a person who wished to reach every telephone subscriber in the city would have to rent as many telephones as there were firms. It was inevitable that this chaotic system would give way to the present governmentally regulated, integrated system.

6. *Patents and copyrights.* For a limited time, patents and copyrights may secure for their possessor some degree of monopoly power. For example, patents granted to the Polaroid Corporation gave that firm an enhanced market position in the production and sale of cameras giving rapid access to finished prints.

In some cases, owners of patents related to a basic good or process may pool their patents, making the use of them available to all the members of the pool but effectively eliminating from the market any firm that is not a member of the pool, even if that firm might itself possess a patent affecting the particular good.

Several years ago a number of light-globe manufacturers assigned their patents to a pool, the light bulbs then bearing, in addition to the name of the manufacturer, the trademark "Mazda."

7. *Government licenses and franchises.* In some cases, entrepreneurs may not operate a particular type of business without governmental permission. Often such permission is contingent on passing an examination or convincing a state body that the firm should be granted a semi-exclusive right to perform a particular function. Examples of such firms are a number of the professions (law, medicine, dentistry, teaching, barbering, dry cleaning, and embalming), communications (radio, television, postal service), and transportation (railroads, buslines, airlines). The excuse usually given for requiring the state's permission is protection of the general public (which, for example, often cannot tell a good physician from a bad one until it is too late), rather than the advancement of a particular monopoly. In some cases, as in the original construction of the transcontinental railroads, the roads simply would not have been built if the government had not agreed to confer semi-exclusive franchises for certain areas. Whatever the case, be it the protection of the public or the necessity of having a particular service, a government grant of exclusivity does

confer a measure of monopoly power as an unavoidable side-effect. Thus, the public may be protected in one sense by the requirement that only those licensed by the state may practice medicine; in another sense, they may be exploited by the exercisers of monopoly power.

The existence of monopoly power cannot be condemned a priori as "good" or "bad" without specific information and value judgments. A monopoly may exist purely to exploit consumers. On the other hand, without the degree of monopoly power conferred by copyrights, Beethoven might have chosen a different career.

THE NEGATIVELY SLOPED DEMAND CURVE

Consider a hypothetical situation in which a competitive industry consisting of numerous small firms is taken over by a single firm, the successor firm purchasing each of the competitors. The demand curve of the formerly competitive industry now becomes the demand curve of the single firm.

In Figure 9-1, the demand curve, D_F, of the monopoly firm is shown as identical to the market demand curve, D_M. Following the customary practice, we refer to the demand curve of a firm (as distinct from that of a market, or industry) also as labeled AR, for it is the average revenue curve of the firm. The curve indicates, for every relevant output level, that the average revenue the firm can derive from that output is the price per unit at which the output can be sold.

THE FIRM'S PERCEPTION
OF ITS NEGATIVELY SLOPED DEMAND CURVE

A firm knows that it has a negatively sloped demand curve if it can raise its price without pricing itself out of the market or lower its price and sell more. The impact of this discovery on the firm is that it knows it can make pricing decisions, unlike the pure competitor. Price is not a parameter to which it must conform; instead, price-seeking itself becomes a major concern of the firm. Indeed, such firms are often called price-seekers. The price they seek is generally assumed to be the one that will maximize profit.

TOTAL REVENUE, MARGINAL REVENUE, ELASTICITY, AND PRICE

THE TOTAL REVENUE CURVE
OF THE MONOPOLY FIRM

Finite elasticity. A firm facing a negatively sloped average revenue curve faces a demand curve having finite elasticity except at its end points. As we have seen in Chapter 2, the elasticity of demand controls the behavior of

FIGURE 9-1

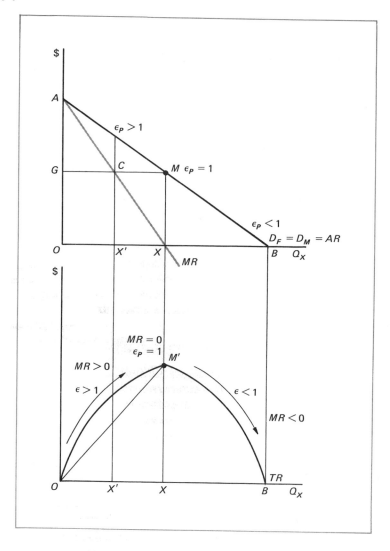

total revenue. For a negatively sloped demand curve, the elasticity of demand with respect to price is infinite at the vertical intercept, falling continuously over the length of the demand curve until it reaches zero at the horizontal intercept. In between intercepts A and B in the upper portion of Figure 9-1, the elasticity of demand is greater than 1 at all points above the midpoint, M. At M, the elasticity of demand is 1, and below the midpoint it is less than 1. From our discussion in Chapter 2, we know that total revenue increases until the midpoint of the average revenue curve is reached, at which point it is at its maxi-

mum and after which it declines. Therefore, the total revenue curve of a firm having a demand curve of finite elasticity, unlike the total revenue curve of the competitive firm does not continue upward at a constant rate without limit. Instead, the monopoly firm's total revenue curve is usually taken to increase at a decreasing rate, reaching a maximum, and then falling until it reaches zero, as is shown in the lower portion of Figure 9-1.

The maximum point on the total revenue curve must occur at the output at which the elasticity of demand is equal to 1. Therefore, the maximum point on the total revenue curve is vertically above a point on the horizontal axis midway between the origin and the quantity demanded when the price is zero. The maximum point of the total revenue curve associated with a linear average revenue curve never can be skewed to the left or right. To see why this is so, recall the formulas for elasticity. In Figure 9-1, the elasticity of demand at point M is equal to $BM/MA = BX/XO = 1$. Thus, $BX = XO$, and, therefore, the total revenue maximizing output is midway between the origin and the horizontal intercept of the average revenue curve. Since the horizontal axes of both the average and total revenue curve diagram plot the same quantity point, X lies halfway between the two points of zero total revenue.

At a price equal to OA, the quantity sold is zero, and total revenue is zero. As price is reduced, elasticity becomes a finite number approaching 1 until the midpoint is reached, where it becomes 1, and, thus, total revenue increases until elasticity is equal to 1. If price is lowered below that indicated by point M, the elasticity of demand becomes less than 1 tending toward zero until the horizontal intercept at B is reached, at which it becomes zero. Consequently, beyond output OX, total revenue falls, becoming zero at quantity OB, at which price also is zero.

MARGINAL REVENUE

As defined in the preceding chapter, marginal revenue is the change in total revenue occurring with a change in output, the relation being expressed by the formula

$$MR = \frac{\Delta TR}{\Delta Q}$$

For the competitive firm, total revenue changes proportionately with the quantity sold, and so marginal revenue is a constant equal to price. This is not true of the marginal revenue of the monopoly firm. To sell more output, it must reduce its price, and, as we can see from the shape of its total revenue curve, total revenue does not change proportionately with changes in output. When price is decreased, marginal revenue falls more rapidly than average revenue. These relationships are shown in Table 9-1 and Figure 9-1. The figure reflects the assumption of the ability of the firm to make continuous changes in price; thus, the marginal revenue curve in the upper chart is drawn as a smooth line.

This is shown in the numerical example in Table 9-1, in which ΔQ is a 1-unit change in output.

POSITIONING THE MARGINAL REVENUE CURVE

The formula for marginal revenue is the slope of the total revenue curve. In Figure 9-1, the total revenue curve is assumed to yield linear average and marginal revenue curves. The average revenue curve is a graph of the slopes of lines drawn from the origin of the total revenue curve to points on the curve corresponding to given outputs. Thus, point M has the value of the slope of $OM' = XM'/OX$.

The marginal revenue curve plots the slope, or rate of change, of the total revenue curve. At any given output, the slope of the total revenue curve is less than the slope of a line drawn from the origin of the curve to a point corresponding to a given output. Therefore, the marginal revenue curve must lie below the average revenue curve at all outputs.

We now want to find out exactly *where* it lies under the average revenue curve. At M', the maximum point on the total revenue curve, the slope of the curve is zero. Since marginal revenue *is* the slope of the total revenue curve, its value is zero, and at that output, the marginal revenue curve must intersect the horizontal axis on its graph. When total revenue is at a maximum, the elasticity of demand is unitary. Thus, the horizontal intercept of the marginal revenue curve is directly beneath the midpoint, M, of the average revenue curve. As we noted in the preceding section, the maximum point of the total revenue curve lies above a point on the horizontal axis one-half the distance from the

TABLE 9-1	P_X	Q_X	TR_X	MR_X
	$10	0	$ 0	
				$ 9
	9	1	9	7
	8	2	16	
				5
	7	3	21	
				3
	6	4	24	
				1
	5	5	25	
				−1
	4	6	24	
				−3
	3	7	21	
				−5
	2	8	16	
				−7
	1	9	9	

origin to the right-hand intercept of the total revenue curve. Since the quantity axes of the two graphs in Figure 9-1 are identical, the *MR* curve cuts the horizontal axis midway between the origin and the horizontal intercept of the average revenue curve. Our conclusion, then, is that a linear marginal revenue curve lies midway between the vertical axis and the average revenue curve. Alternatively, we may say that marginal revenue falls twice as fast as average revenue. This can be seen on the graph. Marginal revenue has reached zero at output *OX*, but an additional equal horizontal distance, *XB*, must be traversed before average revenue (and, of course, total revenue) falls to zero.

Beyond output *OX*, total revenue is still positive, but falling. The slope of the curve is negative. Thus, the marginal revenue curve falls below the horizontal axis beyond the revenue-maximizing output. Average revenue is falling, but positive, throughout its entire length, as total revenue is never less than zero.

THE SHORT–RUN EQUILIBRIUM OF THE PURE MONOPOLIST

PROFIT MAXIMIZATION IN TERMS OF TOTAL COST AND TOTAL REVENUE

If the goal of the monopolistic entrepreneur is to maximize his total profit, then, obviously, he must equate his firm's marginal cost to its marginal revenue (for the reasons given in the preceding chapter). Graphically, this condition holds at those points at which the slopes of the cost and revenue curves are equal (provided that total revenue exceeds total cost).

There is a significant difference between the nature of the adjustment of price-taker and price-seeker firms, although a casual use of the graphs of each case might lead one to believe that the adjustment processes are similar. In both cases, the firms may be thought of as moving along their respective cost and revenue curves until an output is found at which *MC* = *MR*. Strictly speaking, this is true only for the price-taker firm; for as it moves rightward along its linear total revenue curve, price remains constant, so the whole object of its adjustment is to find a point on its short-run total cost curve that has the same slope as the total revenue curve. In other words, (marginal) cost is brought into the desired relationship with an exogenously determined price. Cost is manipulated by adjusting output. For the monopolist, the adjustment process is more complicated. Although we can think of the monopolist as moving along his cost and revenue curves, price continuously changes as he moves along his nonlinear total revenue curve. Unlike the competitive case, here there is a particular (different) price for every level of output. Thus, within the limits imposed by the market demand curve, the firm must determine the selling price of its output. Such a firm not only *can* have a price policy, it *must* have one. It is the search for the profit-maximizing price that makes the theory of price-seeker firms considerably more complicated than the theory of price-taker firms.

PROFIT MAXIMIZATION IN TERMS
OF THE DEMAND CURVE APPROACH

The demand, or average revenue, curve depicted in Figure 9-2 shows that there is an infinite number of possible prices between P_0 and P_n at which the firm can sell its output. Assuming that the firm cannot practice price discrimination (to be discussed in Chapter 10), its object is to select that one price which will maximize its profit. This quest, a matter of no consequence to the firm analyzed in Chapter 8, is a problem of tremendous significance for the monopoly firm. Its pricing techniques may range from the crudest trial-and-error procedure to the use of the most sophisticated economic and marketing methods, and it may even involve extremely complex, and in some cases illegal, pricing arrangements. We will deal with some of these problems in later chapters. For present analytical purposes, we can represent the price-seeking process of the monopolistic firm as a series of movements along the firm's demand curve, keeping in mind that these movements may represent the implementation of an exceedingly complex pricing procedure.

If the firm sets its price at $\bar{P}$, consumers will buy $O\bar{X}$ units. At this price, $SMC = MR = \bar{X}G$, and total profit is, therefore, at a maximum. If profit maximization is the goal of the entrepreneur, the firm will have no reason to charge any other price; hence the sale of $O\bar{X}$ units at $\bar{P}$ is the short-run equilibrium solution for the firm. Given the present data, we are unable to determine whether it

FIGURE 9-2

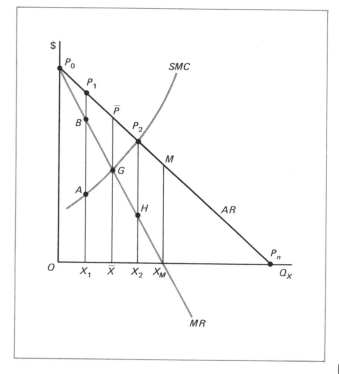

is also the long-run equilibrium solution. But in the short-run at least, given the exogenous cost and demand conditions, the firm will adhere to price $\bar{P}$.

Suppose in its quest for a profit-maximizing price, the firm had selected price P_1, at which consumers would demand OX_1 units of output. In this case, marginal revenue would be X_1B and marginal cost X_1A, the excess of marginal revenue over cost being AB. This is a clear indication that if the firm would lower its price so that the quantity demanded would increase, revenue would increase at a faster rate than cost, and total profit would, in consequence, rise. From the diagram, we can see that total revenue increases faster than cost and that the course of profit is thus upward until price is reduced to $\bar{P}$.

OUTPUT RESTRICTION

Suppose the firm attempted to follow the profit-maximizing rule of the price-taker firm and set price equal to marginal cost, as is the case at P_2. Because marginal revenue is always less than the average revenue of the monopolistic firm, marginal cost always exceeds marginal revenue at the $P = MC$ output. If the monopolist reduces price below $\bar{P}$, costs will increase faster than the increase in revenue, and total profit will fall. Clearly, the monopolist who has mistakenly set price at P_2 will raise his price to $\bar{P}$. This upward movement along the demand curve causes costs to fall faster than the reduction in revenue, so profit increases. In taking this action to increase its profit, the firm reduces output in the amount $X_2\bar{X}$. *This gives rise to the charge that monopolies are output restrictors.* The motive of profit-maximization causes the price-taker firm to set price equal to marginal cost. For the firm with a negatively sloped demand curve, the same motive causes price to be set higher than marginal cost.

Suppose a monopoly takes over a formerly competitive industry. Let us examine the implications of this conversion on the welfare of consumers. The pure monopolist's average revenue curve is the market demand curve, and the firm's marginal cost curve was the market supply curve when the good was produced by the competitive industry. Under competitive conditions, the industry produced OX_2 units at a price of P_2. If we assume that P_2 is the competitive price, it is obvious that the absorption of a formerly competitive industry into a monopoly results in a diminution of output from OX_2 to $O\bar{X}$. The self-interest of the monopolist makes it worthwhile for the firm to raise price and restrict output. As a result of this internally consistent policy, the welfare of consumers is sacrificed to the well-being of the firm. Consumers have less of the good, and they pay a higher price for it.

The conclusion of this argument depends on the behavior of the marginal cost curve following the takeover. If the marginal cost curve remains in the position occupied by the supply curve of the formerly competitive industry, the analysis is unexceptionable: monopoly does result in output restriction.

But unlike independent firms, a monopoly may be able to realize a saving in costs. For example, since a single large firm will make much larger purchases than any of its formerly independent firms, it may be able to negotiate

quantity discounts on the prices charged by some of its suppliers. Borrowing costs may be reduced because of its greater financial strength. The use of superior techniques, personnel, and large-scale, specialized equipment, unavailable to small firms, will also help to reduce costs. If costs fall, the short-run marginal cost curve will shift downward. Suppose the supply curve of the competitive industry had passed through point P_1 on the demand curve in Figure 9-2. The creation of the monopoly firm would then result in a decrease in price and an increase in output. If the competitive industry supply curve had passed through point $\bar{P}$ on the demand curve, conversion of the industry into a monopoly would not affect price and output.

It is possible, of course, for costs to rise after a takeover. For example, a large firm might be unionized and be forced to raise wages. If the marginal cost curve shifts upward after the monopolization of the industry, the welfare of consumers would deteriorate even more markedly than in our original analysis.

But suppose price does fall and output does increase following the conversion into monopoly of the formerly competitive industry. There is still an inescapable loss of consumer welfare inherent in the nature of monopoly. This problem is rooted in the fact that regardless of what happens to marginal cost in consequence of the monopolization of an industry, the nature of monopoly is such that the profit-maximizing entrepreneur will always charge a price greater than marginal cost.

Price is the measure of the marginal benefit a good confers on consumers. For any amount of the good up to $O\bar{X}$, consumers are willing to pay $\bar{P}$. Any consumer who buys the good feels that any unit of the good gives him a benefit at least equal to the price he pays for it. Since all $O\bar{X}$ units of the good can be had for the price $\bar{P}$, the market's valuation of the marginal worth of the good to the consuming public is its going price. Marginal cost measures the values of alternatives forgone; it shows how much of all other goods consumers are willing to give up in order to have another unit of the subject good. If production of the good ceases at $O\bar{X}$, the marginal benefit of the good exceeds the marginal sacrifice entailed in its production. This means that society would like to have more of the good. It desires to have the production of the subject good expanded at the expense of other less-wanted goods. As long as the marginal benefit (price) exceeds the marginal sacrifice (marginal cost), consumers want more resources allocated to the production of good X. In the estimate of consumers, resources are underallocated to the production of a good until marginal cost is equal to price. When they are equal, marginal sacrifices and benefits are equalized, and the resource allocation patterns consumers desire are realized. Figure 9-2 shows that the "ideal" allocation of resources to the production of good X would require the reduction of price to P_2, a price that would increase the quantity demanded of the good by $\bar{X}X_2$ units. But this price is inconsistent with the profit-maximizing goal of the monopolist. Thus, regardless of what one speculates about the comparative behavior of costs between a highly competitive and a monopolized industry, *given* the costs of production, the monopolistic firm, from the point of view of consumers, under-

allocates (underemploys) resources to the production of the good it sells. In this sense, a monopoly is an absolute output restrictor.

RANGE OF OPERATION

An examination of Figure 9-1 shows that a rational monopolist will always operate in the elastic segment of his demand curve. As long as the monopolistic firm has positive costs, the equality of short-run marginal cost and marginal revenue requires that average revenue exceed $X_M M$. Thus, the price charged by any firm having a negatively sloped demand curve must fall between the vertical intercept of the curve and the midpoint. If the firm's marginal costs were zero, the profit-maximizing price would be identical with the total-revenue-maximizing price XM. The only noncoercive way to induce a monopolist to produce an output greater than OX would be to grant the firm a subsidy.

DETERMINATION OF THE AMOUNT OF THE FIRM'S PROFIT

A graph such as the one in Figure 9-2 can tell us whether a given price maximizes the firm's profit. But, it does not, except in the case of the firm having zero marginal costs (because total profit = total revenue), show us the magnitude of the profit associated with a particular price. As noted in the previous chapter, we cannot even be certain from the simple intersection of the MC and MR curves—even if the MC curve cuts the MR curve from below—that there is a profit to maximize. Perhaps we are observing a loss-minimizing solution. To ascertain the magnitude of the total profit (whether positive, zero, or negative), we must add the short-run average total cost curve. This has been done in Figure 9-3.

The upper chart of Figure 9-3 shows that if the firm chooses price $O\bar{P}$, the quantity demanded of its output will be $O\bar{X}$. Since the SMC curve intersects the MR curve at I, this price will maximize profit (or minimize an inevitable loss). In this case, the firm has maximized an economic profit. The lower panel of the figure shows the same information using the total cost and revenue curves. For comparative purposes, the information supplied by the two graphs is summarized in Table 9-2.

TABLE 9-2	Price (average revenue)	$O\bar{P} = \bar{X}A$	Slope of OJ
	Total revenue	$O\bar{X}A\bar{P}$	$\bar{X}J$
	Per unit cost	$OC = \bar{X}K$	Slope of OG
	Total cost	$O\bar{X}KC$	$\bar{X}G$
	Per unit profit	$C\bar{P} = KA$	Slope of OJ − slope of OG
	Total profit ($\pi = \pi^*$)	$CKA\bar{P}$	GJ
	Marginal revenue	$\bar{X}I$	Slope of TT'
	Marginal cost	$\bar{X}I$	Slope of tt'

FIGURE 9-3

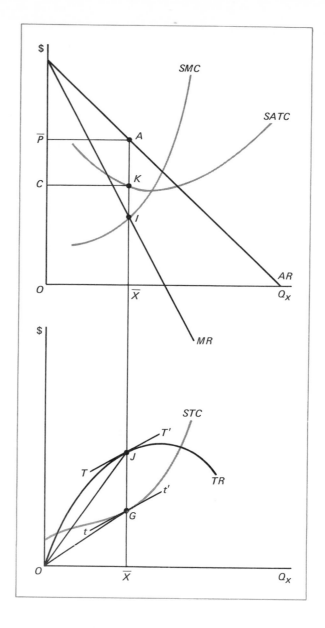

Zero-profit equilibrium of the pure monopolist. Possession of even an enormous degree of monopoly power is not infallible assurance of economic profit. The state of market demand, of costs, or of both, may force a zero, or even a negative, profit on the monopolist. Figure 9–4 shows the profit-maximizing short-run equilibrium solution for a pure monopolist when $\pi = \pi^* = 0$.

FIGURE 9-4

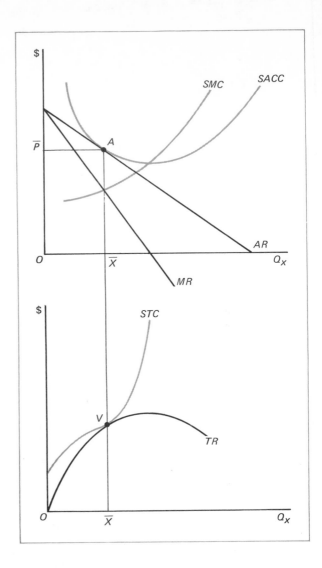

The tangency of the average revenue and short-run average total cost curves in the upper chart and the tangency of the short-run total cost and total revenue curves in the lower chart show that the maximized total economic profit is zero. Any other price would result in a lower (negative) profit; so the zero value is a maximum.

The expression *zero-profit equilibrium* does not mean that the monopolistic entrepreneur receives no return. As was discussed in Chapter 8, the cost curves contain the requisite normal profit—that profit which is a true

cost of production. Figure 9–4 depicts a monopolist-entrepreneur receiving all that he requires to continue offering his services to the economy.

A monopolistic zero-profit equilibrium has some features in common with the competitive zero-profit solution, but some important aspects of the latter cannot be duplicated in the monopoly case. In both situations, consumers pay no more than the true costs of production. No "private tax" is exacted from consumers in the form of an economic profit. However, there are two more effects accompanying the zero-profit solution in the competitive case that do not occur in the monopoly situation. First, as we have already seen, the monopolistic allocation of resources is not optimal from the standpoint of consumers because the monopolist sets his price above the marginal cost of production. Second, owing to its negative slope, the demand curve of the zero-profit monopoly firm cannot be tangent to the minimum point of the short-run average combined cost curve. This means that in a zero-profit equilibrium, the plant cannot be operated at its lowest achievable costs. The monopolist, therefore, is inherently not a minimum cost producer. Since tangency, when it does occur, must be to the left of the minimum point of the short-run average total cost curve, the inefficient operation of plants owned by monopolists takes the form of underutilization. A zero-profit monopolist does not use enough of the variable input in combination with his fixed inputs to achieve the least-cost combination of resources. Since the tangency of the average revenue and the short-run and long-run average total cost curves can occur only in the downward-sloping segment of the latter curve, the monopoly firm in long-run zero-profit equilibrium must operate in the region of economies of size. Given the opportunity to alter its scale of plant, the zero-profit monopoly firm must leave some economies of size unexploited.

The flatter the slope of a firm's demand curve, the more nearly will a zero-profit equilibrium approach the minimum point of the short-run average total cost curve, but as long as the firm faces a demand curve of finite elasticity, completely efficient operation of a plant in a zero-profit equilibrium is impossible.

A positive-profit monopolist, however, can operate his plant efficiently, as Figure 9–5 shows. Here, the profit-maximizing price, $O\bar{P}$, allows the firm to produce $O\bar{X}$ at the minimum attainable short-run unit cost of $\bar{X}K$. But efficient operation of the plant is marked by the absence of the two other results of the competitive equilibrium: resources are underallocated, since $O\bar{P}$ is greater than marginal costs of OC; and $\pi^* = CKB\bar{P} > 0$, meaning that consumers pay more for this output than its true costs.

A monopolist may have to accept losses in the short run; in the long run, he cannot accept them. The monopoly firm depicted in Figure 9–6 is forced to accept the short-run loss $\bar{P}BKC$. However, the firm has succeeded in holding its loss to a minimum by charging $O\bar{P}$ for its output. At this price, the quantity $O\bar{X}$ can be produced and sold, and $SMC = MR = \bar{X}I$. Any other price would result in a greater loss. At the loss-minimizing price, $O\bar{P}$, the firm is more than

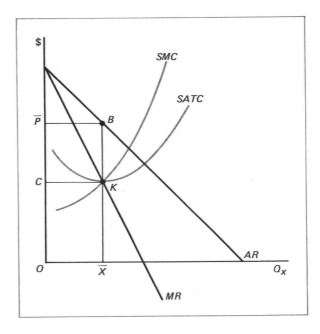

FIGURE 9-5

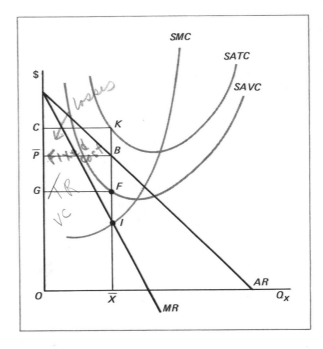

FIGURE 9-6

Market Behavior under Purely Monopolistic Conditions

covering the variable costs of production and should continue to operate. These costs are $O\bar{X}FG$. Since total revenue, $O\bar{X}B\bar{P}$, exceeds the amount of the costs directly associated with production, the firm has the amount represented by $GFB\bar{P}$ to apply toward its continuing fixed costs. Average fixed cost is the vertical distance between the short-run average variable cost and short-run average total cost curves; therefore, the total fixed cost of producing $O\bar{X}$, or any other output, is $GFKC$. If the firm were to cease production, its losses would increase to this amount. By continuing to produce in the short run, the firm can hold its losses to $\bar{P}BKC$. In the long run, the firm must close down.

If the short-run average variable cost curve were to lie entirely above the average revenue curve, the firm would be unable to cover any costs and would improve its financial position by closing down.

Table 9–3 shows three states of short-run equilibrium and demonstrates that in each of the three cases, $SMC = MR$. Assuming that at $MC = MR$, the MC curve cuts the MR curve from below, this equality indicates fulfillment of the equilibrium condition. In every case, $MR < AR$. This tells us we are dealing with a firm that must make pricing decisions; that is, it will base its actions on the knowledge that it faces a negatively sloped demand curve. In case 1, AR exceeds $SATC$. Since revenue exceeds the cost of production, the maximized economic profit is a positive amount. In case 2, $AR = SATC$, showing that revenue just covers the true cost of production, and the maximized economic profit is zero. In case 3, AR is less than $SATC$; revenue does not fully cover costs. The symbol π^* indicates that the profit figure is for a short-run equilibrium (i.e., it is either a maximized economic profit or a minimized loss). In this case, $\pi^* < 0$, showing that the firm has reduced its inescapable loss to the lowest possible amount.

TABLE 9–3   Three States of Short-Run Equilibrium

---

1. *Economic profit*
   $SMC = MR < AR > SATC$: $\pi^* > 0$

2. *Zero profit*
   $SMC = MR < AR = SATC$: $\pi^* = 0$

3. *Minimized loss*
   $SMC = MR < AR < SATC$: $\pi^* < 0$

THE LONG–RUN EQUILIBRIUM OF THE PURE MONOPOLIST

Although there are similarities in the long-run equilibrium conditions of firms in a perfectly competitive industry and a pure monopoly, the differences are more striking and more important. These differences become critical if

profit maximization is not the primary motive of the monopoly firm.[1] The viable competitive firm is forced by its very nature to be a profit-maximizer. In the long run, its only alternative to the relentless pursuit of maximum profit is an exit-inducing loss. The competitor in an imperfect market may be able to accept a less-than-maximum profit with impunity, but he is certainly in a much more vulnerable position than is the pure monopolist. With entry incompletely protected, economic profit may not be completely extinguished, but it is subject to the threat of diminution, so the prudent course for the competitive firm in an imperfect market is to remain alert for all possible sources of further profit. If the firm ignores indicated profit-increasing internal adjustments, its profit margin may become so thin as to give insufficient protection to the fulfillment of objectives other than the attainment of a maximized economic profit.

Regardless of what its motives may be, the competitive firm has only one course of action open to it. The monopolistic firm, on the other hand, not only has the route of quantity adjustment open to it but can engage in meaningful demand-creating activities. Moreover, entry being protected, it is not under as much pressure to be efficient as is the competitive firm.

If the competitive firm is forced by the perfect market to reduce its costs at every opportunity, its tendency in the short run is to operate its plant with the least-cost combination of resources. In the long run, it tends to build the most efficient scale of plant. In the perfectly competitive model, it *must* build the optimal scale of plant. In this latter case, profit maximization and individual and social efficiency are coincident goals. The monopolist, however, can separate these goals. For him profit maximization need not (and probably rarely does) involve the efficient operation of an optimal scale of plant.

In the perfectly competitive model, economic and technical efficiency converge. For the monopolist, profit maximization may preclude technical efficiency, so if maximum profit is the goal of the monopolist, technical and social efficiency would be discarded.

The monopolist depicted in Figure 9–7 is in long-run equilibrium at price $O\bar{P}$, despite the fact that unlike the perfectly competitive firm, he is operating in the region of economies of size. This firm is realizing the maximum economic profit $CKB\bar{P}$.

The hallmark of the long-run monopoly equilibrium is not zero economic profit but the equality of long-run marginal cost with short-run marginal cost, or, symbolically, $LMC = SMC$. The equality, at a particular level, of these two marginal cost schedules reveals that the firm has correctly allocated fixed and variable inputs. No further adjustment could improve the firm's situation. The diagram shows that when price is $O\bar{P}$, $MR = SMC_2 = LMC$; the firm is maximizing profit in both the short- and long-run senses.

How can there be a short-run and a long-run profit maximum? The

---

[1] A monopolistic firm might wish to maximize total sales revenue, return on capital, its own size, its market power, or its life. Goals alternative to profit maximization are considered here and in Chapter 10.

answer is that in the short run, the profit maximum is the best the firm can do with its present plant and equipment. If $SMC = MR \neq LMC$, we know that the potential long-run profit maximum is greater. Since the firm will seek a price that will allow it to reallocate its resources in the quest for this larger profit, we know that until $SMC = LMC$, regardless of either the short- or long-run *average total* costs of production, the firm is in disequilibrium. For example, the firm depicted in Figure 9–7 is in a short-run equilibrium at price OP_1. Although $SMC_1 = MR$, since SMC_1 is greater than LMC we know that the firm can reduce price and gain a larger monopoly profit if it will build a plant capable of producing the quantity demanded at price $O\bar{P}$. The diagram shows that at the present price of OP_1, LMC is less than MR. Additions to output would add to revenue at a rate exceeding the additions to cost; therefore, until output has been expanded sufficiently to bring about the equality of LMC and MR, profit will increase. Thus, the firm can increase its profit to the maximum possible amount, given the parametric conditions of demand, input prices, and

FIGURE 9-7

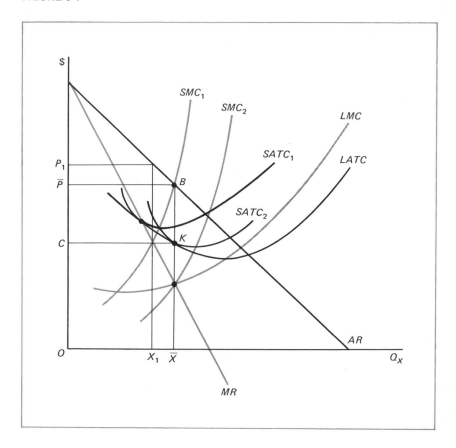

technology, by lowering price to $O\bar{P}$. Quantity demanded will increase to $O\bar{X}$. At price $O\bar{P}$ short-run average total cost is equal to long-run average total cost. In the absence of parametric changes, the firm will make no further adjustments, since it will be in long-run equilibrium.

We may summarize the situation at price $O\bar{P}$ in Figure 9-7 as follows:

$$AR \geq MR = SMC < SAC = LAC > LMC$$

The excess of average revenue over marginal revenue indicates that we are considering a firm that must make pricing decisions. The equality of marginal revenue and short-run marginal cost is evidence that the firm is maximizing its short-run profit. Short-run marginal cost is less than short-run average total cost, so we know that whatever the scale of plant, whether optimal or nonoptimal, the firm is operating it at less than peak efficiency. The equality of short-run and long-run average total cost conveys the same information as the equality of long- and short-run marginal cost—namely, that the firm has so allocated all its inputs that no further cost reduction is possible at the selected price. So far as the *firm* is concerned, it has built the economically efficient scale of plant. But so far as society is concerned, the firm has built a plant of less than optimal size. This is shown by the excess of long-run average cost over long-run marginal cost. The plant is being operated in the region of economies of size.

LONG–RUN EQUILIBRIUM WITH A LINEARLY HOMOGENEOUS PRODUCTION FUNCTION

Suppose the monopoly firm has a linearly homogeneous production function. It will encounter constant returns to size (and scale). In the long run, it will do, in part, what a competitive firm would do—that is, build the optimal size of plant and operate it efficiently. This follows from the fact that under constant returns to size, every plant is socially optimal. Assume that the firm depicted in Figure 9-8 has the size of plant represented by $SATC_1$. To maximize the profit obtainable from this plant, the firm would set price such that $SMC_1 = MR$. This price is OP_1, at which the output sold is OX_1. The maximized profit is the shaded area. As the diagram shows, LMC (a constant) exceeds $SMC_1 = MR$. This shows that the plant is too large. Given the opportunity, the firm will reduce the scale of plant until $LMC = SMC = MR$. Thus, the firm will build the scale of plant represented by $SATC_2$. To sell the profit-maximizing output, the firm will raise price to $O\bar{P}$ and reduce output to $O\bar{X}$. Profit is now $CTV\bar{P}$.

Although the monopoly will build a socially optimal scale of plant and operate it efficiently, $\pi^* > 0$ and $SMC = LMC < AR$. Consumers pay more than the true costs of production for a product that is underproduced. There is another difference from the competitive firm in the attainment of equilibrium.

FIGURE 9-8

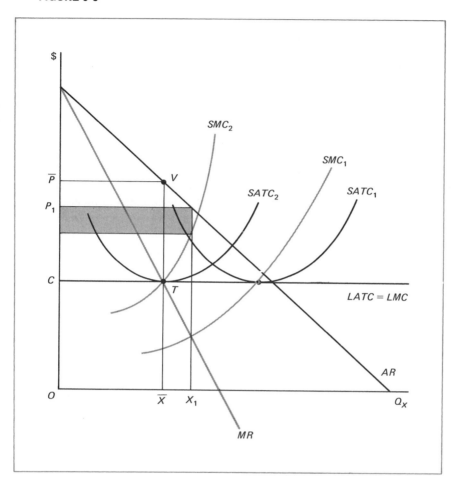

The competitive firm takes price as given. In this case, the firm believes it could increase profit if it increased price. It knows that if it does this, it must reduce its output, so its plans are made on the basis of its *LATC* curve. This calls for a reduction in plant size. Pricing decisions are the heart of the profit-maximizing monopolist's decision-making process, whereas they can be of no concern to the competitive firm.

This analysis probably has a considerable degree of applicability to the behavior of many monopolistic firms. Empirical data indicate that for many firms, long-run average total costs tend to be fairly constant over a wide range of output. If this is so, we can conclude that many monopolistic firms (those that are the most common in our economy) actually *do* tend to build plants of a socially optimal size in the long run.

BILATERAL MONOPOLY

Suppose a single firm is the sole provider of telephone service in a fairly well defined market (e.g., a nation). It, in turn, buys all its equipment from a single supplier. Thus, two firms confront one another in a situation of *bilateral monopoly*—that is, a single seller facing a single buyer. What will happen?

In Figure 9-9, curve *DD* is the demand curve of the telephone operating company for equipment. Since the firm is the sole customer of the equipment manufacturer, *DD* is also the market demand curve facing the supplier. Curves *KK* and *MM* are, respectively, the supplier's marginal cost and marginal revenue curves. The supplier's aim is to maximize its profit; this would be done if it could charge price OP_M and sell quantity OE_M to the telephone company.

However, the telephone company's goal (also profit maximization) is antithetical to the objectives of its supplier. From the telephone company's point of view, the ideal situation would be if it could employ its monopolistic buying power to force several weak suppliers to behave as if they were price-takers. It could force the input price to the minimum costs of production, and curve *KK* would become the *supply* curve of the industry composed of firms forced to behave competitively.

How much equipment would the telephone company buy, and what price would it pay if it could force competitive behavior on its suppliers? If *KK* is the supply curve of the equipment industry, it shows how much equipment will be forthcoming at each particular price; and it also shows, therefore, the *average cost* of equipment to the telephone firm. Since the telephone company is the sole buyer in the market, any change in its purchases will

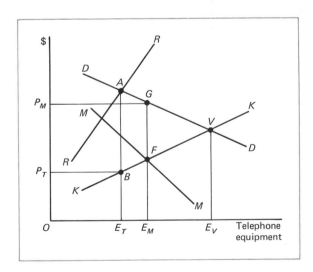

FIGURE 9-9

Market Behavior under Purely Monopolistic Conditions

affect the price of the input. Accordingly, as it increases the quantity of equipment it demands, the price of the input must rise. The rate of that increase is shown by the curve RR, which is marginal to curve KK. The telephone company would be willing to buy equipment up to the point at which the *marginal* cost of the input's acquisition is equal to the demand price. Curve RR is the curve marginal to KK; it is the marginal cost of equipment. Thus, the intersection of curve RR with the telephone company's demand curve determines how much equipment it would buy from competitive suppliers, the amount being OE_T. The price paid would be OP_T, determined at point B on the supply curve KK.

Since the telephone company faces, not competitive suppliers, but another monopolist, it cannot force the price down to OP_T. And since the supplier is not facing competitive buyers, it cannot charge the monopoly price OP_M. Thus, the actual price must be somewhere between OP_T and OP_M, and the quantity purchased will be greater than OE_T but less than OE_M. The precise outcome will depend on the bargaining strength, skill, and other stratagems of the respective firms.

Besides analyzing the nature of bilateral monopoly, Figure 9-9 shows the meaning of the concept of *indeterminacy* in economics. Indeterminacy does not mean that it is impossible to give a theoretical explanation of a particular economic phenomenon. (Indeed, the simple graph of Figure 9-9 casts considerable light on the nature of bilateral monopoly.) Neither does it mean that no price agreement will be reached. The parties will come to some kind of agreement, even if it is fairly transitory. Thus, indeterminacy means that the *final* solution is not fully predictable by economic analysis—and this is because the final outcome may not rest on economic considerations. Our simple analysis does, however, establish the boundaries of the final solution; the final price-quantity agreement must lie on, or within, the boundary $BFGA$.

Bilateral monopoly is probably most frequently encountered in trade union–employer wage negotiations. In such a case, employers organized into a monolithic group—for example, shipowners—face another monolith—the longshoremen's union. Here, the effectively sole buyers and sellers of a particular kind of labor input square off for economic (and often physical) battles.

Between firms, the final solution is likely to be the absorption of one firm by the other. Although our example was entirely hypothetical, the two largest telephone operating companies in the United States do own their own suppliers. What is the result of such an arrangement? The answer may be somewhat surprising.

If the telephone company were both the producer and user of telephone equipment, it would continue to manufacture equipment for its own use until the marginal cost of production was equal to the marginal revenue derived from the employment of the equipment. The marginal cost of production of telephone equipment is, as we know, given by KK. The marginal revenue accruing to the telephone operating company from the *use* of the equipment produced by its subsidiary must be shown by the curve DD. The reason that the telephone company demands equipment is that its use contributes to the

revenue of the firm. Each price on the demand curve for the input represents the marginal contribution of equipment to the revenue of the firm at a particular level of input use. For example, at quantity OE_M, the marginal revenue accruing to the firm from the use of that amount of equipment is E_MG = price = OP_M. The profit-maximizing telephone company will find it worthwhile to continue to add equipment until the marginal revenue derived from its use is equal to the marginal cost of its production; this occurs at point V.

The conclusion is that the combined operation will produce and use OE_V units of equipment at a per-unit cost of E_VV dollars. This arrangement appears to have potentialities for better public service than does the bilateral monopoly situation. The increase in the use of equipment, E_TE_V, means that service to the public is expanded. And, since the telephone operating company itself faces a negatively sloped demand curve for its services, the expanded service made possible by the use of a greater amount of equipment can be sold to the public only if the firm charges lower rates.

SUMMARY

A monopolist, strictly speaking, is the single seller of a good. The broad purpose of our analysis of such a firm, however, has been to simplify the analysis of monopolistic firms—that is, firms having a great deal of market power. The foundations of this power are usually control of raw materials, economic power, high initial capital requirements, control of distribution channels, a naturally limited market for the product, patents and copyrights, and government licenses and franchises.

Some degree of monopoly power, however small, is indicated by a firm's negatively sloped demand curve. The negative slope means that the seller must search for a profit-maximizing price. Given the demand for its products and the quantity demanded at a given price, the firm must reduce price in order to sell more goods. This necessity causes marginal revenue to be lower than average revenue at any given quantity sold.

Any profit-maximizing firm must equate marginal cost with marginal revenue. Since for the monopolistic firm, marginal revenue is lower than marginal cost, in the profit-maximizing equilibrium, marginal cost is less than price. The significance of this inequality is that any profit-maximizing monopolistic firm is an output restrictor. With respect to the market demand for the product, resources are underallocated to the production of goods made under monopolistic conditions.

Monopolistic long-run equilibrium is similar to competitive long-run equilibrium, but in the former case there is no necessary incentive to build plants of socially optimal size (except when the firm has a linearly homogeneous production function).

When a powerful seller faces a powerful buyer (when a single seller faces a single buyer), the market situation is one of bilateral monopoly. The

analysis of bilateral monopoly is indeterminate insofar as final price is concerned. Analysis can indicate the boundaries of the settlement, but since the final adjustments are usually determined not by economic considerations but by the bargaining skill and power of the parties, the final price can be associated only after an actual settlement. Nevertheless, economic theory can shed light on the behavior of the bilateral monopolists and the nature of possible outcomes.

10

Profit-Maximizing Practices of Monopolistic Firms

Not all firms with negatively sloped demand curves are pure monopolies. Two others discussed in several of the following chapters are monopolistic competitors and oligopolies. Although price-seeker firms are substantially different from one another, they have enough in common to permit a general treatment of some typical aspects of their behavior.

A monopolistic firm (as distinguished from a firm that is a pure monopoly) is an enterprise that has *some* degree of monopoly power; that power, generally speaking, is the ability to exercise some control over price. A firm does not have to be a pure monopoly in order to have this power. It need only have a negatively sloped demand curve. The negative slope (finite price elasticity of demand) may derive from any of a number of conditions, among them product differentiation (real or imagined),[1] location, capital requirements, government licensing. Depending on the particular

[1] Product differentiation refers to qualities, actual or fictitious, of basically similar goods that induce consumers to distinguish among them. For example, color film is a type of good, but the various brands of color film vary widely in the way they render the original colors. Depending on their tastes, many photographers prefer one brand over the others. The distinctions in this case are real, but in other cases product differentiation may be entirely in the minds of consumers—for example, when a seller convinces some buyers that one brand of USP aspirin is superior to another brand of USP aspirin when, in fact, all brands of aspirin bearing the designation "USP" (United States Pharmacopoeia) have conformed to the same set of rigid specifications. So long as the consumer acts on such distinctions, it is unimportant to economic analysis whether the distinctions are real or not.

situation, these conditions may confer only a partial monopoly, but as long as the firm need not accept price as a parameter, it will qualify for inclusion in the general category of monopolistic firms.

The possession of monopoly power allows firms a number of interesting options other than the opportunity to search for a profit-maximizing price. Monopolistic firms may find it worthwhile to charge different customers different prices, to associate with each other in cartel or price-fixing agreements, or to allow one firm within their particular industry to act as the price leader. In some instances, monopoly power may so profoundly affect the public interest that the government may regulate its exercise.

Whatever manifestation the employment of monopoly power assumes, in this chapter we will be concerned with practices that tend to unite monopolistic firms into a general group. In the next three chapters, we will consider practices that tend to separate monopolistic firms into the distinguishable groupings of pure monopolies, monopolistic competitors, and oligopolies.

THE MULTI-PLANT MONOPOLY

The majority of large (monopolistic) firms have more than one plant. How does the monopolistic multi-plant firm allocate production among its several plants?

If each plant is identical in *every* respect, not only in its internal aspects but in its distance from input and output markets as well, then in the long run each plant will be assigned an equal share of the firm's output. Usually, however, each plant will have different characteristics, so the firm's plants will have varying degrees of efficiency. These differences will be evidenced by cost variations.

To simplify our analysis, we will consider a two-plant monopolistic firm. Table 10-1 presents hypothetical cost and revenue data for such a firm.[2]

The first through the fourth columns present the conventional quantity and revenue data for a monopoly firm. The fifth column, MC_I, shows the marginal costs of production in plant I. The sixth column, MC_{II}, gives the same type of data for plant II. The last column, MC_F, shows marginal costs for the *firm.* Note that it is *not* derived by the addition of the marginal costs of both plants at a particular level of output.

Table 10-2 shows how the marginal costs of the firm *are* derived from the marginal cost data of the plants. Suppose the firm is considering producing only 1 unit of output; it will assign that output to plant I, since the marginal cost in this plant is $1.40, as compared with $1.65 in plant II. Hence, the marginal cost of production for the firm is the marginal cost in plant I. If the firm decides to produce a second unit of output, it will continue to assign the entire produc-

---

[2] It is obvious from the total revenue figures that the cost and revenue data of the monopolistic firm are hypothetical. For purposes of simplicity, they have not been inflated to more "realistic" proportions by adding a number of zeros to the left of the decimal point.

TABLE 10-1	Q	P	TR	MR	MC_I	MC_{II}	MC_F
	1	$6.00	$ 6.00	$——	$1.40	$1.65	$1.40
	2	5.90	11.80	5.80	1.60	1.85	1.60
	3	5.70	17.10	5.30	1.80	2.05	1.65
	4	5.40	21.60	4.50	2.00	2.25	1.80
	5	5.00	25.00	3.40	2.20	2.45	1.85
	6	4.50	27.00	2.00	2.40	2.65	2.00
	7	3.90	27.30	.30	2.60	2.85	2.05

TABLE 10-2	Q	Assignment	MC_F
	1	1 in I	$1.40
	2	2 in I	1.60
	3	2 in I, 1 in II	1.65
	4	3 in I, 1 in II	1.80
	5	3 in I, 2 in II	1.85
	6	4 in I, 2 in II	2.00
	7	4 in I, 3 in II	2.05

tion quota to plant I. Producing the second unit in plant I will cost an additional $1.60, which is below the $1.65 marginal cost in plant II. Once again, the firm's marginal cost is the marginal cost in plant I. The situation changes if the firm decides to raise the level of production to 3 units. Assigning the extra unit to plant I would raise total costs by $1.80, but if the extra unit were assigned to plant II, total costs would rise by only $1.65. Consequently, if the firm wishes to produce 3 units, it should produce 2 of those units in plant I and 1 unit in plant II. Increasing total output to a level of 3 units, the marginal cost for the firm is the marginal cost of 1 unit in plant II. If the firm decides to produce a fourth unit of output, the additional unit will be assigned to plant I. One more unit added to the current production of plant I would raise total costs by $1.80, whereas producing the additional unit in plant II will add $1.85 to the firm's total costs. Thus, of the four units of output, three units will be produced in plant I and the remaining unit in plant II. This is the process by which the schedule of marginal costs for the multi-plant firm is derived.

The profit-maximizing price for the firm is determined by the usual method. The marginal cost of the firm, which, of course, reflects cost conditions in its plants, is used to set the profit-maximizing price. Thus, the firm will price its output at $4.50, at which the marginal cost of $2.00 is equal to marginal revenue and will produce 6 units, directing plant I to produce 4 units and plant II to make 2 units.

Figure 10-1 is the graphical analysis of monopolistic multi-plant equilibrium. Chart (a) shows the marginal cost curves of two plants. The firm's marginal cost curve is shown in chart (b) as ΣMC. It is derived by horizontally summing the marginal cost curves of the plants. Note, that as in Table 10-1,

FIGURE 10-1

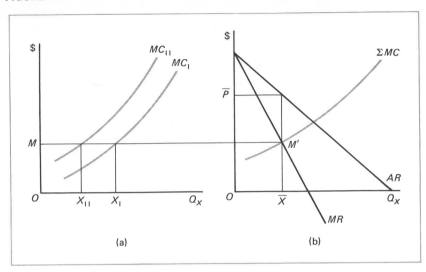

(a)   (b)

the firm's marginal cost is not the sum of the plants' marginal costs at a specific output level.

To maximize profit, the firm equates ΣMC with MR and sets price at $O\bar{P}$. The output is assigned to each plant so that $MC_I = MC_{II}$. Thus, plant I produces OX_I and plant II makes OX_{II}. The combined output $O\bar{X} = OX_I + OX_{II}$. Equated marginal cost is $\bar{X}M' = OM$.

Suppose the firm assigned output quotas to the plants so that $MC_{II} > MC_I$. The firm would not minimize its costs. The cost of producing a marginal unit in plant II exceeds the cost of production in plant I. If the firm intends to produce its current level of output, it should transfer some inputs out of plant II and into plant I. In doing so, it will reduce marginal cost in plant II and raise it in plant I. MC_{II} and MC_I will move closer together. When inputs have been allocated between the two plants so that $MC_I = MC_{II}$, no further input adjustment can lower costs.[3]

What would such a multi-plant monopoly do in the long run? Suppose

[3] In Table 10-1, the profit-maximizing output is 6 units, at which $MC_F = \$2.00 = MR$. Although the marginal cost of production of 4 units in plant I is $2.00, the marginal cost of producing 2 units in plant II is $1.85. Obviously, $MC_I \neq MC_{II}$, which seems not to agree with the above analysis of Figure 10-1. The reason for the apparent discrepancy in the table is that the data are stated in discrete units, whereas in the graph, the data are subject to continuous variation. If the data cannot be adjusted any more finely than the 1-unit increments stated in the table, the firm must make the closest approximation it can to $MC_I = MC_{II}$. For example, if the firm were producing 5 units of output, it would minimize costs, as is shown in Table 10-1, by producing 3 units in plant I and 2 units in plant II. If it now desires to maximize profit, it must sell 6 units of output at a price of $4.50. If it were to allocate to plant II resources sufficient to raise output by 1 unit, total costs would rise by $2.05. In this case, the disparity between $MC_I (= \$1.80)$ and $MC_{II} (= \$2.05)$ would be greater than if plant I produces 4 units and plant II produces 2. The more the output of the plants is subject to minute variation, the closer the firm can come to an actual equality between MC_I and MC_{II}.

its profit-maximizing output exceeds the amount at which long-run average cost is minimized. Suppose that the long-run profit-maximizing output of the firm is 180,000 units. The firm currently has two plants, and *with these plants*, cost-minimizing output is 150,000 units in one plant and 30,000 in the other. But the most efficient size of plant, say, is one that (when operated efficiently) produces 60,000 units. In the long run, the multi-plant monopolist will build three plants of optimum size to produce a total of 180,000 units of output. The firm would reduce its costs in the long run by abandoning plants I and II and using three plants of the size that can produce 60,000 units each at minimum long-run average total costs.

In the short run, further expansions of output must be met by operating the currently owned optimal-size plants at higher-than-optimal rates, but in the long run, the firm will tend to accommodate increases in output by building more plants of optimal size. *In effect*, this means that the firm has a horizontal long-run average total cost curve.[4]

If the *effective* long-run average total cost curve is horizontal, the long-run marginal cost curve must coincide with it. The firm's consequent long-run behavior is shown in Figure 10-2. The least-cost output of a plant of optimal size is $O\bar{x}$. To maximize profit, the firm will set price at $O\bar{P}$ and produce $O\bar{X}$ quantity of output. If all its plants are of optimal size, the number of them, n, may be determined from the formula

$$n = \frac{\bar{X}}{\bar{x}}$$

Thus, the total output of the firm is $\bar{X} = n\bar{x}$.

FIGURE 10-2

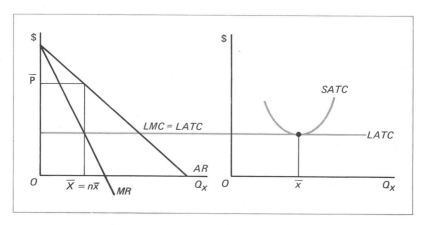

If the demand for the firm's output increases, the firm will increase the rate of operation of its hitherto optimal plants. When the demand gives evidence of becoming large enough to make the construction of another plant worthwhile, the firm will construct the new facility of optimal scale, setting price such that $MR = \overline{LMC}$ (the bar indicates that long-run marginal cost is constant).

The fact that a multi-plant monopoly tends to build plants of optimal scale does not mean that such a monopoly has achieved results equivalent to those of the perfectly competitive equilibrium. Since $P > MC$ for *any* monopoly, the operation of optimally scaled plants does not correct the monopolistic underuse of inputs. As can be seen in Figure 10-2, any monopolistic firm able to produce a profit-maximizing output with an optimal scale of plant must make an economic profit. Thus, although multi-plant monopolies tend to operate plants of optimal size, such firms persist in underallocating resources, and consumers are forced to pay a price that more than covers the true costs of production.

PRICE DISCRIMINATION

We shall now assert that the monopolistic firm depicted in Figure 10-2 is not maximizing total profit at price $O\overline{P}$, although it appears, according to the preceding analysis, that every condition requisite to this state has been met. The reason for this paradox is that we have assumed up to now that the firm must charge all its customers the same price for its goods. If that is true, then the firm *is* maximizing its profit. But, if it need not charge every customer the same price, then it is *not* maximizing its profit. Does this contention violate the $MC = MR$ rule? Before we consider this question, let us define price discrimination.

THE DISCRIMINATING MONOPOLISTIC FIRM

A firm that practices price discrimination is able to charge different customers different prices for identical units of the same good. Price discrimination has no inherent connection with forms of discrimination that pertain to race, sex, or religion. The firm does not discriminate against those customers who are charged the highest prices because it dislikes them; on the contrary, the firm is very likely to discriminate against its best customers. Price discrimination is purely economic; the firm's only motive is to realize all the profit potentials that exist in the market.

CONDITIONS FOR SUCCESSFUL
PRICE DISCRIMINATION

It is obvious that only firms with some degree of monopoly power can be price discriminators, since price discrimination is an aspect of pricing decisions. A purely competitive firm that attempted to charge a group of custo-

mers a price higher than that set in the market would lose the patronage of that group.

The potential for the practice of price discrimination lies in the negatively sloped demand curve, which shows that some consumers are willing to pay a higher price than others rather than go without the good. But there is an additional requirement. Suppose that a firm having a negatively sloped demand curve attempted to charge one set of customers $2 for a unit of its output and another set of customers $1 for the identical product. It would be worthwhile for the more favored consumers to buy all they could at the $1 price and attempt to undercut the discriminator. Competition among the re-sellers would tend to drive the price back down to $1, so there would be no incentive for the monopolist to discriminate in the first place. The good that the discriminating monopolist sells must be one that cannot be resold in this way—for example, electricity, transportation, personal services.

Even if the good cannot be stored for resale, a monopolist may not be able to discriminate unless he can separate those customers who can be charged a higher price from those who cannot. A few years ago, the major airlines had difficulty with this problem. Attempting to turn empty seats into revenue, they offered students below the age of twenty-two flight space at less than the price charged other patrons. Persons who could pass themselves off as students were able to avail themselves of student rates—a situation very different from what the airlines had intended. If the carriers had been able to identify and separate students from nonstudents, the price discrimination scheme might have been more successful. It is certain that if the firm cannot separate its clientele, it cannot practice price discrimination.

If customers *can* be segregated by age, sex, income level, and the like, what criterion should a firm use? The answer lies in the differing attitudes consumers have toward the same product. As we have said, some people are willing to pay more for a unit of a good than others. In economics, differences in willingness to pay for the same quantity of a good are expressed by the price elasticity of demand. The most inelastic demand will be that of consumers who think that they must have the good, while those whose demand is very elastic are not very concerned whether they get any of the good or not. Thus, a firm desiring to discriminate must separate its customers, not on the basis of an outward characteristic such as race or sex, but on differences in elasticity of demand, charging the highest prices to those with the most inelastic demand and reducing price as elasticity increases. In other words, sex, age, race, or income are useful only as possible means of identifying and separating consumers with different demand elasticities.

Take, for example, "Ladies' Day" at the ballgame. Undoubtedly, both male and female customers have differing price elasticities of demand for baseball games, but short of mind reading or personally interviewing each customer, ball clubs cannot ascertain the state of mind of each fan. Therefore, they operate under the assumption that in general the male demand for admission to ballparks is less elastic than the female demand. If all seats of

identical grade in the ball park could be sold at the highest price for each grade, no price concessions would be made to anyone. But when seats, representing largely fixed costs, go unsold, the management will consider reducing the price of some tickets. One way is to lower the price of tickets to women.

The requirements for successful price discrimination, then, are:

1. The possession of some amount of monopoly power.
2. Customers who have differing elasticities of demand for the same good.
3. A market in which those buyers having differing elasticities of demand can be separated.
4. A good that cannot be purchased and then offered for resale.

FIRST–DEGREE (PERFECT) PRICE DISCRIMINATION

From the standpoint of sellers, the ideal form of price discrimination is one in which a seller can force each buyer to pay the highest price he is willing to pay rather than go without the good. Such a pricing policy is called *first-degree*, or *perfect*, price discrimination. In general, most firms are unable to discriminate this finely, since they do not know each consumer well enough to know how high a price they can charge him before he will drop out of the market. About the best that firms such as airlines, ballparks, and theaters can do is to divide their customers into groups on the basis of a presumed demand elasticity for each group as a unit. Obviously, some persons in each group will be charged a price below what they would pay rather than go without.

There are some firms, however, that have sufficient information to estimate rather closely what each of their clients will pay rather than forego consumption of the good. Such firms usually deal in services in which they meet with their clients on an individual basis. The more confidential the relationship, the more accurately the discriminating firm can estimate what the client will pay, and clients are less likely to discuss with one another what the firm charges them. The best examples of such firms are physicians, lawyers, hairstylists, and tailors.

The following model is rather abstract, but it is realistic enough to show how firms dealing with consumers about whom they have detailed information tend to set their prices. Assume that Figure 10-3 depicts the demand curve for a physician's services. The output is an identifiable medical or surgical procedure. The demand curve shows how many units of this service the physician can sell at various prices. If the physician did not discriminate, his profit-maximizing price would be P_3, at which he would sell 3 units of the service. (It is important to note that in the absence of discrimination, all of his patients would be charged price P_3.)

To analyze the effects of discrimination, we will alter our customary model slightly. The units on the horizontal axis now represent sales to idividual patients, each of whom will consume 1 unit of the particular medical

service in the specified time period if he can get it for the indicated price. Thus, patient number 1 is willing to pay price P_1 rather than go without the service. If the physician charges price P_1, he will sell just 1 unit of this service to one patient. If the physician lowers the price to P_2, he will have two patients, both of whom, in the absence of discrimination, will pay price P_2. It appears, then, that patient 1 will be getting something of a bargain. He is willing to pay price P_1 for the service rather than do without, but the physician offers this service to him at price P_2. In this, the nondiscriminatory case, a reduction of price to obtain patient 2 causes a gross loss of total revenue because price is also lowered for patient 1. Of course, total revenue rises as long as the gross loss is less than the gross gain. Whenever the same price is charged to all customers, the monopolistic marginal revenue curve lies below the demand curve.

However, if the physician knows that patient 1 will still pay price P_1 even if patient 2 is charged a lower price, he can increase his profit above the non-discriminatory maximum. Why is this so? If the physician can practice first-degree price discrimination, he can keep the entire total revenue of P_1 derived from patient 1, as well as the full amount patient 2 pays him—a gain of AP_1 (in Figure 10-3) over the nondiscriminatory situation. In this case, marginal reve-nue is not less than price; it is equal to price. The change in total revenue resulting from selling one more unit of output is P_2. The same analysis applies as the physician decreases his price to each additional patient on an indi-vidual basis. It follows that the demand curve of the perfect price discriminator is also his marginal revenue curve. This being the case, the profit-maximizing rule of $MC = MR$ is not abandoned; the perfect price discriminator reduces

FIGURE 10-3

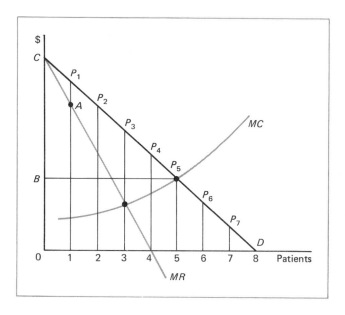

price until $P = MR = MC$. The physician described in Figure 10-3 will provide 5 units of the specified service to five different patients, charging each one a different price, ranging from a high of P_1 to a low of P_5.

In the case of the price discriminator, the identity between the demand and average revenue curves is broken. Curve D in Figure 10-4 remains the perfect price discriminator's demand curve, but since it has become his marginal revenue curve, it is no longer his average revenue curve. The average revenue curve lies to the right of the present $D = MR$ curve.[5]

The conditions for perfect price discrimination help to explain the public stance on pricing policy taken by a number of professional groups, particularly the representatives of organized medicine. Typically, physicians' professional associations and individual medical practitioners are opposed to "socialized medicine." Doubtless they are inimical to government operation of health services, but "socialized medicine" is often a euphemism for alternative schemes of *private* health care, including group practice and the practice of medicine by corporations. Physicians practicing in groups often publish objective price lists and it seems reasonable to suppose that corporations, if they could practice medicine, would do the same. Published price lists would largely end the opportunity to practice perfect price discrimination because everyone would know what everyone else was paying. The loss of the profitable possibility to practice price discrimination is probably more of a threat to the health professions than the dangers of socialized medicine.

SECOND–DEGREE PRICE DISCRIMINATION

A firm that cannot practice perfect price discrimination may nevertheless be able to use a less perfect kind. Consider the case of a public utility that does not have intimate knowledge of each customer's demand schedule and even if it did, could not deal with its patrons on an individual basis. But if it is unable to price small quantities of electricity or gas separately, the utility is able to charge discriminatory prices for large blocks of service. Usually, such price discrimination takes the form of price concessions in return for the purchase of a large quantity of the service.

In the type of discrimination being examined here, the firm establishes different prices for particular blocks of the same service. Figure 10-4 shows that if the utility were to set its rate at OR_1, it would sell OH_1 kilowatt hours of electricity. If the rate were lowered to OR_2, consumers would increase their consumption of electric power by H_1H_2 kilowatt hours. Although a general rate reduction might increase the firm's total revenue, the firm's position would be better if it could charge OR_1 for the first block (OH_1) of electric power and OR_2 for the second block (H_1H_2). If the firm priced electric current at OR_1, its total revenue would be OH_1AR_1. If there were a general rate reduction to OR_2,

[5] The object of the perfect price discriminator is to increase his profit above the nondiscriminatory maximum by expropriating the consumer's surplus of each of his clients (see Chapter 5). This surplus is represented in Figure 10-3 by the triangle P_5BC.

Profit-Maximizing Practices of Monopolistic Firms

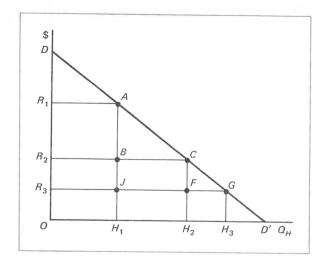

FIGURE 10-4

the firm's total revenue would become OH_2CR_2. The firm would have a gross loss of R_2BAR_1 and a gross gain of H_1H_2CB. How this affects total revenue depends on the relative sizes of the gross loss and gross gain, and this in turn depends on the elasticity of demand in the relevant region of the demand curve —that is, between points A and C. Regardless of the effect on total revenue, if the firm could price on a discriminatory basis, it would not have to undergo a gross loss of revenue. Therefore, the utility will find it worthwhile to extend a "quantity discount" to those customers who use more than a specified minimum of electricity. Using two prices, the firm sells OH_1 units of power for OH_1AR_1 dollars and H_1H_2 more units for H_1H_2CB dollars.[6] Thus, the firm incurs no gross loss. Its gross gain in revenue is also its net gain. The diagram shows that if the firm were to make a further rate reduction, H_2H_3 more units of power would be sold, and the increase in its total revenue would be H_2H_3GF, there being no gross loss involved in the sale of the other two blocks.[7]

---

[6] Note that the *addition* to the firm's revenue is not OH_2CR_2 because the firm does not sell OH_2 kilowatt hours at OR_2 dollars. It sells only H_1H_2 kilowatt hours at OR_2 dollars.

[7] Because the second-degree price discriminator cannot continuously "ride down" the consumer's demand curve, he is able to extract only a portion of the consumer's surplus from each customer. Suppose that Figure 10–4 represents an individual consumer's demand for electric power rather than the demand curve facing the firm (reduce the kilowatt hour values on the horizontal axis accordingly). The consumer is willing to pay OR_1 for up to OH_1 kilowatt hours. If his rate is reduced, he will buy more. Price discrimination would approach the perfect case if the power company could charge the customer a different price for every kilowatt hour, lowering the rate as the consumer uses more power. This is impracticable by the nature of the buyer-seller relationship. Thus, the utility announces that it will sell the householder any power in excess of OH_1 units at rate OR_3. The consumer will buy a total of OH_3 units, OH_1 at rate OR_1 and the remaining H_1H_3 units at rate OR_3. Under second-degree price discrimination, the seller can expropriate some of the consumer's surplus but not all. For example, if the one rate charged to the consumer were OR_3, he would buy OH_3 as he is doing now. His total expenditure would be OH_3GR_3, and his consumer's surplus would be R_3GD. But he does not get all OH_3 units at OR_3; he has to pay OR_1 for OH_1 units. Thus, "removed" from the area of the consumer's surplus is R_3JAR_1. Instead of the surplus being R_3GD, it is $R_3GD - R_3JAR_1 = R_1AD + JGA$.

As is the case with the perfect price discriminator, the firm's demand curve has become its marginal revenue curve. Thus, concern about pricing in the inelastic region of the demand curve has no bearing here. Suppose that in the relevant range, the firm's marginal costs are constant at R_3G; the firm will be maximizing its profit by producing OH_3 kilowatt hours of electric current *if* it is allowed to follow a discriminatory pricing policy.[8]

THIRD-DEGREE PRICE DISCRIMINATION

Third-degree price discrimination is the most common of all discriminatory pricing policies. In this type, the firm discriminates among *classes* of consumers rather than among individual clients as is the case in first-degree price discrimination. And the firm charges each member of a class the same price for as many units of the service as he or she may wish to buy unlike the case of second-degree price discrimination in which the same consumer buys different units of the same good at various prices. Obviously, the conditions for perfect price discrimination are not widespread, and the conditions for second-degree discrimination are available to relatively few sellers. However, a monopolistic firm is fairly likely to find that various groups of customers have distinguishably different elasticities of demand for its product. For example, the demands of business executives and salesmen for airline transportation will be about the same, but both will be considerably more inelastic than the demand of students for the same service. And the elasticity of demand of vacationers may vary according to the time of year. When a monopolist is faced with different *groups* of buyers, each having a characteristic elasticity of demand, the firm is effectively selling the same product in *different markets*. If it can differentiate the markets, it can discriminate in price among them.

Figure 10-5 depicts the demand of women and men for admission to baseball games played in a stadium having a fixed seating capacity. The diagrams have been placed back to back and have a common origin at O. The demand curve of women is D_w, that of men D_m. On the women's diagram, an increase in quantity demanded is shown by a movement leftward from the origin. The basic assumption of the diagram is that men have a much stronger desire to attend baseball games than do women; hence, their demand is less elastic than that of women.

To avoid complicating the diagram, we will make a simplifying assumption (which may not be very far from reality) that fixed costs are so great a proportion of the total costs of a single baseball game, that variable costs may be neglected. The stadium is there, the players are under contract; therefore,

---

[8] Typically, electric power companies and most other utilities are regulated monopolies and hence are not able to set prices independently of the limitations imposed by a public regulatory agency. Even so, economically and legally approved rate management practice encourages a multiple price schedule for different quantities of the utilities' services on the grounds that discrimination promotes better use of fixed equipment. Government regulation of monopolies will be covered shortly.

Profit-Maximizing Practices of Monopolistic Firms

the incremental cost associated with a marginal admission should be slight. If variable costs may be neglected, then marginal costs are zero.

Suppose the total seating capacity of the stadium is shown by line $SC = OA_m + OA_w$. Since the great bulk of costs are fixed, and since the seats are already there, the ball club would like to fill the stadium. Accordingly, it will price tickets to men at P_m, at which it will sell OA_m admissions. Women will receive a price concession, being charged P_w for a ticket. Women's admissions will account for the remaining $ST = OA_w$ seats.

How does the firm arrive at these prices? If it has a fixed seating capacity, it will attempt to allocate admissions among customers in its various markets so that the marginal revenue in all markets (men and women) is equalized. Prices P_m in the men's market and P_w in the women's market bring the marginal revenues in the two markets into equivalence ($MR = A_wS = A_mC = MR_m$).

It is obvious that the firm could sell all SC seats to men. Moreover, the diagram shows that if the women's admissions were sold to men, $OA_w = (A_mA'_m)$, the price need be lowered only to P'_m, which is considerably higher than the women's price. Why not, then, sell all the tickets to men? Suppose with the seats initially allocated on the discriminatory basis shown in the figure that the firm did take one seat away from the women's market and sell it in the men's market. The marginal revenue in the women's market would

FIGURE 10-5

FIGURE 10-5

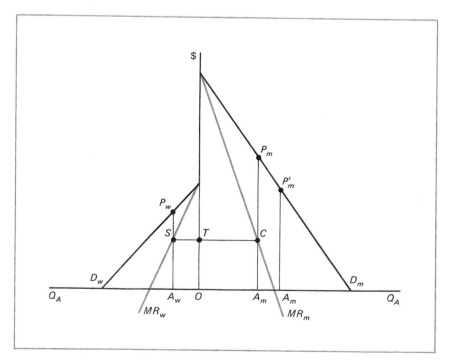

rise, and that in the men's market would fall. Then $MR_w > MR_m$. This would mean an overallocation of seats to the men's market. As long as $MR_w > MR_m$, the addition to the firm's revenues would be greater if it took seats out of the men's market and sold them to women even if the selling price of women's tickets is less than that of men's admissions.

This example has omitted consideration of variable costs in order to keep the explanation of third-degree price discrimination simple. Although most firms experience increasing variable costs as they expand output, the idea demonstrated here remains applicable: to maximize profit, the third-degree price discriminator equates marginal revenue in each of its separable markets.

Assuming that the markets can be separated, the crucial factor in price discrimination is the differing elasticities of demand in each market. This means that it can be profitable to charge a lower price in a market having a more elastic demand for the good even if, in all other markets, there remains the unsatisfied demand of customers who would be willing to pay a higher price.

In the analysis accompanying Figure 10-5, $P_m > P_w$, and even though $P'_m > P_w$, the firm would not reduce the price of men's admissions to this amount. Assume that ϵ_w and ϵ_m are the elasticities of demand in the women's and men's markets, respectively, for baseball games and that $\epsilon_w > \epsilon_m$. In the appendix to this chapter, we will prove that

$$MR = \left(P - \frac{1}{\epsilon} \right)$$

For profit maximization, it is required that

$$MR_w = P_w \left(1 - \frac{1}{\epsilon_w} \right) = MR_m = P_m \left(1 - \frac{1}{\epsilon_m} \right)$$

If $\epsilon_m > \epsilon_w$, the only way in which the marginal revenues in both markets can be equalized is for the firm to set prices so that $P_w < P_m$. The exact amount of the price differential depends on the precise difference between ϵ_m and ϵ_w.

GOVERNMENT REGULATION OF MONOPOLIES

REGULATION OF GENERAL BUSINESS ENTERPRISES

Without attempting to participate directly in the management of monopolies, government can alter business behavior through price control or tax policy. We will now analyze the effects on firms of some governmental economic controls.

Ceiling price. If government imposes a ceiling price on a competitive industry, the result will be a reduction of output. This is not the case for a monopolistic firm, as is shown in Figure 10-6. In the absence of regulation,

Profit-Maximizing Practices of Monopolistic Firms

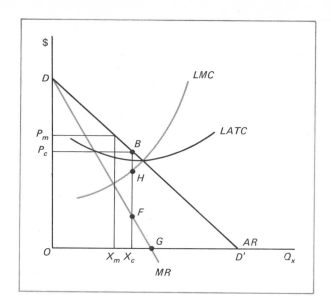

FIGURE 10-6

the firm will charge the profit-maximizing price OP_m. Suppose the government now imposes on the firm the maximum price OP_c. The demand curve facing the firm is no longer DD', but now is P_cBD', since the price can be no higher than OP_c but may be lower. For the same reason, the proper marginal revenue curve now becomes P_cBFG. Strictly speaking, the marginal revenue curve is discontinuous, the discontinuity occurring between points B and F. For any outputs between X_m and X_c, the marginal revenue is equal to price OP_c. The imposition of the ceiling price forces the monopoly to become a price-taker unless it is willing to set a still lower price. The marginal cost curve passes through the discontinuity FB at H. Accordingly, the firm will make the largest profit possible under the circumstances by expanding output to OX_c units. No longer able to act as a price-seeker, the firm has become a quantity-adjuster. Since price (OP_c) is greater than the new average total costs of production, the firm is still able to make an economic profit, but because of the enforced price reduction, it must be less than the former unconstrained maximum.

The price ceiling has improved the allocation of resources as well as lowering the price to consumers and reducing the portion of price absorbed by the firm in the form of an economic profit. A monopolistic firm is an output restrictor. Forcing such a firm to produce more goods is a move in the direction of consumer choice. Presumably a government can continue to lower price until all the economic profit has been eliminated, thereby further improving the resource allocation.

Lump-sum taxation. When a government requires a firm to be licensed, ostensibly for the protection of the public, it frequently confers valuable monopoly power on the licensee. Suppose Figure 10-7 represents a licensed professional

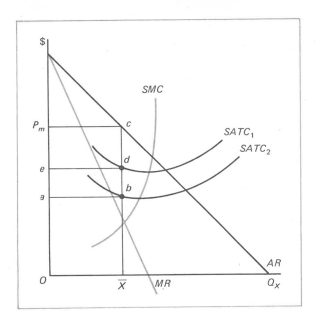

FIGURE 10-7

man, who, if he could fully exploit his monopoly power, would charge price OP_m. The untaxed economic profit is $abcP_m$. Suppose that a lump-sum tax is imposed as part, or all, of the license fee.[9] The tax is $abde$. Since this is a fixed cost to the firm, it shifts the short-run average total cost curve vertically upward from $SATC_1$ to $SATC_2$. Distance db is the *addition* to average fixed cost at an output of $O\bar{X}$ units. The $SATC$ curve slides along the given SMC curve, since marginal costs are independent of changes in fixed costs. Thus, the profit-maximizing price and output remain unchanged. The tax cannot be shifted onto consumers because any increase in price above the present level, OP_m, would reduce profit still further, owing to the consequent reduction in the quantity demanded. (Remember, the equality of MC and MR is not disturbed by a change in total fixed costs.) Under these conditions, the firm's economic profit is reduced to the amount $edCP_m$, and part ($abde$) has been recaptured by the government.

Excise tax. If the government imposes a tax on each unit of output, the *variable* costs of the firm are increased, and some of the tax will be borne by consumers. Since the total amount of the tax varies directly with output, the tax is a variable cost to the firm and affects the marginal cost curve as well as the short-run average total cost curve. In Figure 10-8, the cost curves have shifted upward by a distance equal to the amount of the tax. With the upward shift in the SMC curve, the firm raises price and cuts output. Prior to the tax,

[9] A "lump-sum" tax is a tax fixed in amount—e.g., $100—and levied without regard to the output or earnings of the taxpayer. For those firms that must pay it, it is a fixed cost.

Profit-Maximizing Practices of Monopolistic Firms

the monopolist's profit was $abcP_1$. After the imposition of the tax, the monopolist makes the smaller (maximum) profit $defP_t$. The tax on each unit of output is $he = gd$; the total amount of the tax is $ghed$. Although consumers are worse off in that there is a smaller quantity to buy at a higher price, the monopolist is unable to pass the full amount of the tax onto his customers. The rise in the price, P_1P_t, is less than the per unit increase, gd, in the tax. Thus the monopolistic firm pays part of the tax and its customers the remainder. Since the portion of the tax passed on to the consumers is P_1ifP_t, the monopolist's share of the tax is $ghed$ (the total tax) less the amount his customers pay.

Why does government impose this type of tax that reduces the welfare of consumers, to say nothing of the welfare of the firm? Possibly, the government has in mind some kind of welfare other than economic. Its intent may be to reduce the production and consumption of a particular commodity. If the intent of government regulation is to restrict the use of a particular good, the excise tax is suitable, and for this reason excise taxes are applied typically to liquor, tobacco, and playing cards. Alternatively, the government may be desperately in need of money.

FIGURE 10-8

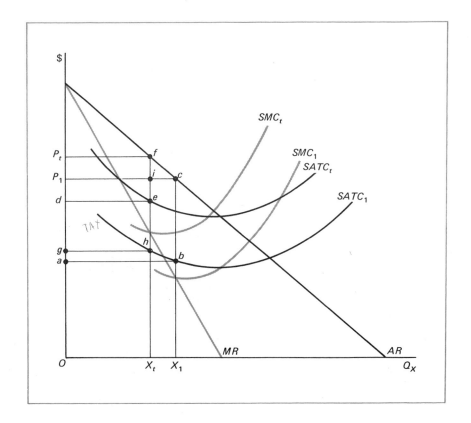

THE REGULATION OF PUBLIC UTILITIES

It may appear that a firm that is able to serve its market adequately by operating a plant of optimal size efficiently might be the most desirable sort of monopolistic enterprise. Consider firms in the electric power, telephone, broadcasting, and urban transit industries. At one time, two separate transit companies operated streetcars on San Francisco's Market Street, each using its own trackage. Despite the clangorous presence of many trolleys making their way up and down the famous "Slot," service was not good. Breakdowns were frequent, and the equipment was antiquated. As a matter of fact, there were too many trolley cars for the available patronage. Because the two firms had to split the market, both companies experienced continual financial difficulty. Revenues were too low and costs too high for both firms to survive, to say nothing of providing acceptable standards of service. Inevitably, one of the firms finally abandoned the streets of San Francisco.

When several firms attempt to operate in a market that could be efficiently served by one firm, the costs of operation for each firm are likely to be rather high as many opportunities for economies of large size must remain unexploited. The firms, realizing that the existence of rivals is the principal obstacle to higher profits, are likely to seek additional customers, and their ultimate objective may be the elimination of every rival, at least within a certain geographical area.

The fight for market supremacy may or may not be carried on in the economic arena. American economic history is filled with examples of so-called cutthroat competition, ranging from below-cost pricing to physical coercion and intimidation. Typically, the triumphant firm was in a position to exploit the possibilities for monopolistic gain.

In circumstances in which a great segment of consumers feel themselves to be exploited by monopolistic sellers, they may demand that government intervene to protect them. The demand for government intervention and regulation has been heaviest, and this demand has been met, in the case of public utilities—those businesses said to be "affected with a public interest." A business is often held to be affected with a public interest if (1) it is a *natural monopoly* and (2) a continuous flow of its services is vital to the public welfare. If the firm is not a natural monopoly, there may be sufficient competition in the market to preclude a demand for regulation. A natural monopoly is usually defined as a firm that can achieve its most efficient operation if it is the only firm in the market. This means that if the firm operates under conditions of decreasing long-run average costs (economies of size), the output of two smaller firms will cost more to produce than if the same quantity of output were produced by a pure monopolist. The long-held, popularly accepted belief is that where the difference in cost is substantial, the public interest is best served if one firm is given a monopoly of the market and that firm is regulated by the government "in the public interest."

In Figure 10-9, the firm has continuously declining long-run average costs of production over the range covered by the demand curve (*DD'*). If price is set equal to marginal cost (*OP₁*), the firm will be forced to operate at a loss. Unless the government is willing to subsidize the production of *OX₁* units with a grant of at least *AB* dollars per unit, marginal-cost pricing is an unavailable option.

The United States Supreme Court has held repeatedly that to force a firm to sell its output at less than its true cost of production amounts to taking its property in violation of the "due process" clause of the Constitution. Since normal profit *is* a true cost of production, it is the responsibility of any regulatory agency—federal, state, or local—to ensure at least that profit to the regulated concern.

How the regulatory agency determines the proper profit for a natural monopoly has been a subject of endless controversy in economics and law. Statutes usually refer to the normal profit as a "fair" rate of return on invested capital. Thus, any regulatory commission is charged with the responsibility of determining the proper basis for valuing the firm's assets and then determining the "fair" rate of return on that valuation. The regulatory agency must not simply allow the firm the rate of return that will just induce the enterprise to remain in business, but must provide that the firm is sufficiently profitable to be able to attract new capital funds when necessary, to undertake research and development programs, and to conduct a public relations program that includes the ability to lobby the regulatory agency itself and the legislature with the intent of demonstrating that the rate of return the agency has allowed it is too low.

Given the determination of the regulatory agency, the fair rate of return

FIGURE 10-9

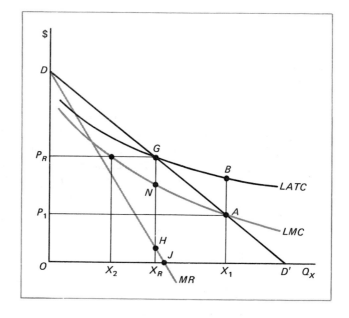

must be capitalized (included as a cost of production), and, thus, incorporated into the long-run average total cost curve. The price that will allow the firm of Figure 10-9 a fair rate of return (a normal profit) is, therefore, OP_R. The demand curve to the firm now becomes P_RGD', and the accompanying marginal revenue curve is P_RGHJ (the curve is discontinuous through the distance HG). The firm will not produce the output OX_2, at which $LMC = MR$, since at any output level between X_2 and X_R, $MR > LMC$. If the firm produces an output greater than OX_R, it must reduce price below the amount allowed it by the regulatory agency, and it would produce at a loss. Consequently, it will produce the amount OX_R, indicated by point N, the intersection of the LMC curve with the discontinuity in the MR curve.

SUMMARY

If a firm has a negatively sloped demand curve, it has some degree of monopoly power, though it is not necessarily a pure monopoly. There are marked differences among firms having monopoly power, and there are many similarities; this chapter has dealt with several of the similarities. The possession of monopoly power opens up a number of options to a firm. These are summarized below.

A multi-plant, profit-maximizing monopolistic firm equates the *firm's* marginal revenue with the marginal costs of its various *plants*. In the long run, multi-plant monopolistic firms tend to build plants of optimal size, irrespective of the nature of their production functions. But the competitive situation is not reproduced; price is always higher than marginal cost.

Price discrimination occurs whenever a firm charges customers different prices for identical units of the same good or service. Price discrimination has no necessary connection with racial or sex discrimination; its chief motive is to improve the profit position of the firm. The requirements for price discrimination are: (1) some degree of monopoly power, (2) generally a non-storable good or service, (3) differing price elasticities of demand among the firm's customers, (4) the ability to separate these customers into groups on the basis of their respective price elasticities of demand.

There are three principal degrees of price discrimination. In first-degree (perfect) price discrimination, each customer is a group unto himself. The firm attempts to charge each customer the maximum amount he is willing to pay for a unit of the good or service. In second-degree price discrimination, consumers are charged different prices for different blocks of the same good. In third-degree price discrimination, consumers are assigned to markets on the basis of their respective elasticities of demand. The price established for each group results in the equalization of marginal revenue in all markets.

When conditions are such that individual members of the public are at a severe economic disadvantage in dealing with a monopolistic firm, the government may undertake to regulate the enterprise. Among possible forms of regu-

lation are the imposition of ceiling prices (price controls) and taxes, either lump-sum or variable. In each of the three cases, the imposition of these controls causes the firm to modify its behavior if it desires to maximize profit.

The ultimate objective of regulation is to emulate the competitive equilibrium solution, but this goal is unattainable because of the negative slope of the firm's demand curve. If the regulatory agency does an effective job, the utility will be unable to maximize profit; however, the Supreme Court has held repeatedly that regulated firms must receive a "fair return" on "fair value." The precise meaning of these expressions is never definitely known until a court has made a determination, but regulatory agencies do operate under broad guidelines indicating how the utilities' properties are to be valued and what should be the rate of return on whatever value is set.

APPENDIX

ELASTICITY, MARGINAL REVENUE, AND AVERAGE REVENUE

Figure 10-10 depicts a linear average revenue curve and its associated (linear) marginal revenue curve. Assuming that price is OP, the coefficient of price elasticity, ϵ_p, is OP/PA. Distance $XB = OP$ by construction, and $ZB = PA$, since triangles PIA and BIZ are congruent as proved in the preceding section. Therefore, $\epsilon_p = OP/PA = XB/BZ$. At an average revenue of XB, marginal revenue is XZ, and $XZ = XB - ZB$. If $\epsilon_p = XB/ZB$, then $ZB = XB/\epsilon_p$, and $XZ =$

FIGURE 10-10

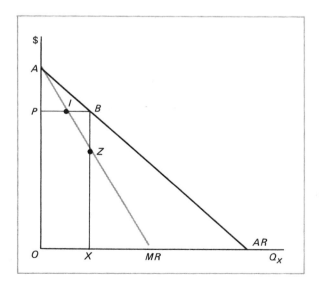

$XB - XB/\epsilon_p$. The distance XZ, as we have noted, is marginal revenue at the given price (average revenue) of XB; thus, we may write the general formula

$$MR = P - \frac{P}{\epsilon_p} \quad \text{which simplifies to} \quad MR = P\left(1 - \frac{1}{\epsilon_p}\right)$$

The formula shows that there is, indeed, a precise relationship between elasticity and marginal revenue. For example, suppose the elasticity of demand is infinite, as is the case for the price-taker firm. Then,

$$MR = P\left(1 - \frac{1}{\infty}\right)$$

One divided by an infinitely large number approaches zero, as a limit, and $MR = P(1 - 0) = P$. Thus, for the price-taker firm, marginal revenue is equal to price. When $\epsilon_p = 1$, as it does when total revenue is maximized,

$$MR = P\left(1 - \frac{1}{1}\right) = P(1 - 1) = 0$$

In addition to showing that the marginal revenue curve cuts the horizontal axis under the midpoint of the linear average revenue curve, the formula also shows that for a demand curve on which the elasticity of demand is everywhere equal to 1 (a rectangular hyperbola), the marginal revenue curve is congruent with the horizontal axis.

Profit-Maximizing Practices of Monopolistic Firms

The Theory of
Market Behavior Under
Monopolistically Competitive
Conditions

THE HISTORICAL SETTING OF THE THEORY
OF MONOPOLISTIC COMPETITION

Until the late 1930's, the standard models of firm theory were built at the opposite poles of the competitive spectrum: perfect competition at one end and pure monopoly at the other. Most neoclassical theorists were neither so blind nor so obtuse that they believed that all firms actually conformed to these two models. Indeed, Alfred Marshall stressed that there were many firms whose behavior fell somewhere between the competitive and monopolistic norms. But, in general, it was not until the late twenties that some economists began to feel uneasy about the bipolar economics of the firm. They were disturbed that there was no theory to explain the behavior of firms that probably always had comprised the majority of the business population and that were certainly growing more numerous if not more important in the advanced industrial nations of the world.

Indeed, there are a few contemporary economists who hold that the models of competition and pure monopoly remain the best bases for explaining the economic behavior of all business firms. They are convinced that it is extremely difficult to develop models having any worthwhile predictive capacities of imperfectly competitive firms. For one thing, while it is quite easy to define pure monopoly and the conditions of pure and perfect competition, it is

difficult to specify how a firm is imperfectly competitive. These economists argue that theories now commonly used to explain the behavior of imperfectly competitive firms—theories of monopolistic and imperfect competition, games, linear programming, and so on—do not offer very profound insights into the functioning of the most numerous class of firms. They assert that it is most useful to think about a problem within the framework of the two most definite neoclassical models and when refinements are needed, to supply them as elements of special theory or admit that the observed behavior is not fully explicable on the basis of any presently known theories. Of the models in this chapter they might say, in Dorothy Parker's words, "There is less to them than meets the eye."

Most economists, however, are not persuaded by the "science plus art" viewpoint. They reject this attitude as Procrustean and believe that it is possible to help understand the behavior of the very great number of firms that are neither pure competitors nor pure monopolists. This now-prevalent point of view began to develop in the late 1920's as ground-breaking work showed the "emptiness in economic boxes"—that is, in the purely classificatory schemes that served as a substitute for models based on empirical observation—and urged that patched-up competition theory was not the proper path for the advancement of economic science. A number of notable tentative steps had been made in the development of a theory of imperfectly competitive firms, when two major theoretical breakthroughs were announced almost simultaneously. The year 1933 saw the publication in England of Joan Robinson's *Economics of Imperfect Competition*[1] and of Edward Hastings Chamberlin's *Theory of Monopolistic Competition* in the United States.[2] The material in this chapter is based principally on the latter work.

CHARACTERISTICS OF MONOPOLISTICALLY COMPETITIVE FIRMS

What is monopolistic competition? One of the best answers to this question was given by the chief protagonist of the theory, Professor Chamberlin, when he defined it as a blend of monopoly and competition. Accordingly, in his theory we find a blend of the theoretical elements of the two polar models.

Monopolistically competitive firms are more numerous than any other type of firm, so examples abound. Typical are dealer-owned gasoline stations, restaurants, department stores, bookstores, motion picture theaters, repair services of all kinds, and most professional services. Small businesses are generally monopolistic competitors. Consider a service station that sells Texaco products. There are many substitutes for Texaco gasoline, yet the

---

[1] Joan Robinson, *Economics of Imperfect Competition* (London: Macmillan, 1933).
[2] Edward Hastings Chamberlin, *Theory of Monopolistic Competition* (Cambridge, Mass.: Harvard University Press, 1933).

dealer will find that he has some choice in pricing—there is no single market price which, if exceeded by his filling station, will cause it to lose all its customers. This means that his demand curve has finite elasticity; it has a negative slope. He operates in a price-seekers' market. His negatively sloped demand curve is, of course, a distinguishing characteristic of the monopoly firm. Since a monopolistic competitor must make pricing decisions, he must have some monopolistic control over his product. What is it? Not only does the Texaco dealer not have a monopoly of the gasoline market; he does not have a monopoly of gasolines marketed by the Texas Company. What, then, is the source of his monopolistic power? First, Texaco gasoline is somewhat unlike all other gasolines. Second, the Texaco gasoline in the pumps of a particular dealer is unlike that in the pumps of any other Texaco dealer. How can this be, when it has long been argued that there are no real differences among the gasolines of various refiners? The fact is that the *customer* plays a large role in endowing particular products or brands with differences. For the purposes of monopolistic competition theory, it makes no difference whether the attributed characteristics are objectively demonstrable or the purest fantasy. As long as customers impute differences to products, there effectively *are* differences. *Product differentiation* is thus the hallmark of monopolistic competition.

Product differences can be quite subtle but nevertheless very significant. They need not be imagined, yet they do not have to be intrinsic to the product itself. For example, having a Texaco credit card and not having a Shell card differentiates the two brands for a motorist who may not know gasoline from turpentine. Chemically, the same brand of gasoline in the tanks of two different dealers may show no differences, and probably most motorists assume this, but the good sold by two dealers franchised by the same refiner may be quite distinguishable. The distinguishing characteristics may be hours of operation, location, ease of entrance into the station, or simply the personalities of the pump attendants. The differences—real or imagined, subtle or obvious—that customers perceive in the output of each seller help to give some market power to the seller and thus impart a negative slope to his demand curve. So we can expect of the monopolistic competitor some of the same behavior observed in pure monopolists.

The theory of monopolistic competition assumes that the products sellers offer are not homogeneous, but at the same time, it holds that the output of each seller is not unique. Gasoline is fundamentally gasoline. But under the constructs of monopolistic competition theory, there can be neither gasoline, nor dental, nor accounting *industries,* for example, because the product of *each* seller of gasoline, dental work, and accounting is distinguishable, if not unique. Chamberlin attempted to deal with this problem by creating the common-sense concept of the *group,* which he defined as consisting of those firms producing (or selling) obviously similar, but obviously nonhomogeneous, goods. The *group* in the theory of monopolistic competition is the equivalent of the industry in the competitive and pure monopoly models. Thus, for ex-

ample, within the framework of monopolistic competition theory we encounter gasoline, laundry, restaurant, and medical groups.

How many firms are there in each product group? Certainly, there must be more than one. To help answer the question, we can make some observations on the probable consequences of the number of firms in a group. If there are only two firms—or, perhaps, four or five firms—the group will take on the condition of *fewness* that is the hallmark of oligopoly. (The word *oligopoly* means few sellers.) There are said to be few firms in an industry or group when one firm must consider the effects its actions will have on its rivals. When feedback effects are of no interest to the firm, we can hold that fewness does not exist in the industry or group.

Chamberlin developed small- and large-group cases in his theory of monopolistic competition. In the *small-group case* a high degree of interdependence exists. Many economists believe that the small-group case is properly a part of oligopoly theory and reserve the theory of monopolistic competition for the large-group case. Chamberlin, himself, strongly asserted the generality of monopolistic competition theory, always stressing that it was "roomy" enough to accommodate and explain the behavior of the whole spectrum of firms lying between the polar extremes of competition and pure monopoly. The *large-group case* is made up of firms who *believe* that they are such an insignificant part of the market that any action they take will go unnoticed by other firms in the group; that is, they see themselves in the situation of pure competitors. They feel a (perhaps unwarranted) safety in numbers.

Chapter 11 will deal only with the large-group case. The various theories applicable under conditions of perceived interdependency are explained in Chapters 12 and 13.

THE BASIC EQUILIBRIUM CONDITION OF THE MONOPOLISTIC COMPETITOR

We will assume that the monopolistic competitor is in equilibrium when profit is maximized.

In Figure 11-1, a monopolistically competitive firm is shown in long-run equilibrium. The firm's maximized economic profit is zero. If this firm were a monopoly, its profit might tend to persist in the long run; but since this firm is a monopolistic competitor, the profit will tend to be reduced to zero.

What forces act to eliminate economic profit under conditions of monopolistic competition? This is the main question to be considered throughout this chapter, but the theory can be presented briefly here.

Product differentiation gives each firm a negatively sloped demand curve. The (actual or imagined) distinctions perceived by consumers among the goods of different firms contribute an element of monopoly power to the sellers. The goods or services of one producer are only imperfect substitutes for the goods or services of other producers in the same product group. Within rather narrow

limits, sellers can take advantage of this situation, affecting the quantity of goods they sell by manipulating price. The ability of monopolistically competitive firms to manipulate the price-quantity combination indicates that the demand for the products of such firms is finitely elastic; thus, the average revenue curve of each monopolistic competitor must be negatively sloped.

The small size and great number of rival firms within a product group lead monopolistic competitors to be unconcerned with the actions of other firms in the group. A monopolistic competitor makes few, if any, strategic decisions involving the impact of its policies on other firms. Any decision of a monopolistic competitor is likely to be the result of only two prime considerations: its own internal economy and the economics of its customers (not its rivals). For example, if the firm's internal cost conditions and its conception of its demand curve convince it that a reduction in price would increase its profit, it is highly likely to reduce its price to the profit-maximizing level regardless of what other firms in the product group may do.

As in the competitive case, economic profits in a group will attract entry, and entry will continue until all economic profits are extinguished. A zero-profit equilibrium requires the tangency of the firm's average revenue and average combined cost curves at a vertical distance equal to the price of the good. The process of entry causes this tangency of the cost and revenue curves. As new firms enter the group, older firms in the group find that their share of the total market is shrinking. The reduction in the number of potential customers causes the average revenue curve of each of the firms to shift downward. This downward drift is accompanied by a diminution of eco-

FIGURE 11-1

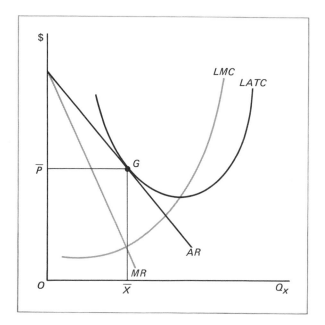

nomic profit. Since entry continues until all economic profits have been eliminated, the average revenue curves will stop falling only when tangency has been achieved with the average combined cost curve. Thus, in (zero-profit) equilibrium, as will be explained shortly in more detail, each firm operates at a point on its average combined cost curve at which the slope of that curve is equal to the slope of the group demand curve for the total group (industry) output.

The simple diagram of Figure 11-1 does not in itself show that a monopolistic competitor is different from an ordinary monopoly; it could be a depiction of the long-run equilibrium of a pure monopoly. Although the long-run equilibrium is one of zero profit, as in the competitive case, tangency does not occur at the minimum point of the average cost curve; tangency must occur to the left of that point. This means that the monopolistic competitor uses a plant of less than optimal size and that he operates it below its ideal capacity. The proliferation of gasoline stations, liquor stores, and professional offices in many localities is an example of what this analysis discloses. Cost would be reduced if a single and larger service station were built to replace the four that are often found at one intersection. Four stations within a few yards of one another tend to be underutilized. The space they occupy and the personnel they employ are, to a great extent, wasted. One single station, occupying perhaps more space than any one of the four existing stations but less space than the total of the four, and employing more attendants than any one station but fewer than all four, could fill the tanks of as many cars (possibly more cars because of returns to size) in a given time period at a cost below that of the four existing stations. The same principle holds true for liquor stores and professional offices. Many liquor stores, because of their small size, offer their customers a poor selection, about which the clerks are poorly informed. In order to make a normal profit, they must operate at odd hours, leaving themselves more susceptible to robbery, which of course, adds to the costs of operation. In the case of health services, a clinic, combining the office staffs, laboratory facilities, air conditioning, piped-in music, and specialized skills of several physicians, would be able, in many cases, to deliver the same (or better) health care to patients at lower cost. Underutilization of plant and equipment, in the case of monopolistic competition, tends to do neither seller nor buyer any good. Profits tend to be lower and prices higher than they would be if the plant were larger. Determining which side of the market would tend to be helped by more economical methods of production requires further analysis. These matters are considered in more detail later in the chapter. The more strongly the competitive elements assert themselves in the blend, the less steep will be the slope of the average revenue curve, and the more nearly will the point of tangency approach the minimum point of the long-run average total cost curve. But if the case is one of *monopolistic* competition, the average revenue curve must exhibit finite elasticity; therefore, tangency at the minimum point of the long-run average cost curve is precluded. On the assumption that the costs of a monopolistic competitor are the same as they would be for a pure com-

petitor, consumers must absorb higher production costs even if they need pay no tribute in the form of economic profit. However, under monopolistically competitive conditions, consumers may get what they pay for to the extent that product differentiation is the salient characteristic of monopolistic competition.

THE BASIC CHAMBERLIN THEORY OF MONOPOLISTIC COMPETITION

We have discussed the long-run equilibrium solution of the Chamberlin large-group case. Using Chamberlin's model, we shall now consider the attainment of that solution.

THE ASSUMPTION OF SYMMETRY

Chamberlin utilized what he called the "*heroic*" *assumption of symmetry* —that all firms in a product group face the same demand and cost conditions.[3] The analytical impact of this assumption is that *all* firms within the group have identical demand and cost curves. As a result, the model depicts all firms within the group having zero economic profits in the long-run equilibrium solution.

Whether the assumption of symmetry is actually heroic or not depends on the facts for particular firms in particular groups. It does seem likely that firms within a given group will face the same input prices, especially if the group is defined for a limited geographical area. Operating in the same markets for inputs and lacking sufficient economic power to obtain price concessions, monopolistic competitors can reasonably be assumed to pay the same prices for their inputs.

That all firms within a product group face the same internal cost (production) conditions is more conjectural. Are the inputs that monopolistic competitors buy—even at identical prices—of identical quality? Quite possibly, but then some inputs might be unique. Are all monopolistic competitors within the given group equally efficient? Can nonhomogeneous but highly substitutable goods be produced at the same costs per unit? Although these questions can be answered only by empirical investigation, an affirmative answer to each of them does not seem to be too far-fetched. Small firms are not nearly as likely to possess unique cost conditions as are large-scale oligopolistic firms. In other words, it seems reasonable to argue that despite product differentiation within the group, monopolistic competitors themselves are likely to be rather homogeneous.

The same line of argument may be applied, perhaps less convincingly, to the demand situation. Since the products of each firm within the group are heterogeneous, it would seem that the demand conditions facing each firm

[3] Chamberlin, *Theory of Monopolistic Competition*, p. 82.

ought to be different. However, the goods are also highly substitutable. The argument can be advanced that consumers are not particularly loyal, flitting from one seller to the next in their search for variety, thus distributing themselves rather evenly across the group. One reason that consumers might be expected to distribute themselves evenly among sellers is their quest for variety. The very attribute of variety is assumed to be a desirable quality of the goods sold under conditions of monopolistic competition—a quality that consumers value as much as the intrinsic qualities of the goods of a particular firm. If consumers do not tend to distribute themselves fairly continuously over a large numbers of sellers, they would fail to realize the benefits of variety. Moreover, if one firm could sufficiently differentiate its product on a once-and-for-all basis, and thereby bias the redistributive flow of customers in its favor, the group would tend away from a monopolistically competitive market to one of fewer sellers. Of course, it must be remembered that since monopolistically competitive firms are supposed to bridge the gap between the poles of monopoly and competition there should be a wide divergence between groups of monopolistic competitors, some approaching pure monopoly and others pure competition. Thus, Chamberlin's heroic assumption may be fairly valid for the middle of the spectrum but become less valid as the firms move away from the center.

One final assumption that Chamberlin makes about the cost functions of firms is that the members of the group, taken together, operate under conditions of constant cost. The entry and exit of firms do not affect the position of the long-run average total cost curve of any firm in the group.[4]

CHAMBERLINIAN GEOMETRY AND THE CONDITION OF STABLE EQUILIBRIUM

Although conventional diagrams can be used to show the attainment of the equilibrium solution by monopolistic competitors, Chamberlin's original geometry—an informative exercise in itself—facilitates the explanation of his model.[5]

Curve DD' in Figure 11-2 is the objective (i.e., actual) demand curve facing a monopolistically competitive seller of good X. In monopolistic competition theory, good X must be a member of a general class of highly substitutable but nonhomogeneous goods. The curve $LATC$ is the usual long-run average total cost curve.

Our analysis commences at point B, at which OX_0 units of the good are sold at price OP_0. Since price exceeds the unit costs of production, X_0A, the firm makes an economic profit of $CABP_0$.

The curve dd' is the essential feature of Chamberlin's analysis. It shows the sales the subject firm would gain by lowering price if it were the only seller

---

[4] See Chapter 8 for an explanation of conditions of constant cost.

[5] Note that in Figures 11-2 and 11-3 (adapted from the Chamberlin originals) the marginal revenue curve does not appear.

FIGURE 11-2

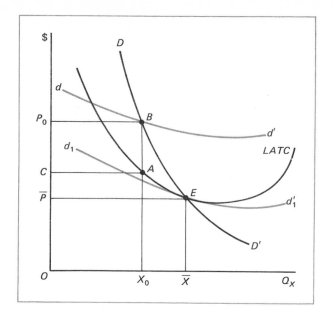

in the group to do so. Curve dd' is more elastic than DD' (which shows changes in sales if other firms match the subject firm's price changes). For any given price reduction, moving along dd' would expand the firm's sales volume by a much greater amount than if it were to follow DD'.

What is the significance of dd'? It is the seller's subjective demand curve. It shows how a firm *believes* its sales would change if it were to adjust its prices. The explanation for this subjective demand curve is based on the number of firms comprising the group. The group is sufficiently large for each member to feel a certain anonymity. The monopolistically competitive firm feels itself to be such an insignificant part of the group that it can lower its prices without fear of retaliation from rivalrous competitors. Accordingly, the monopolistic competitor with a pure profit, believing that it can attract enough new sales to raise its profit, lowers its price below OP_0. But its anticipations will be frustrated. Why?

Each firm is such a small part of the total number of firms in the group that it correctly feels it can reduce its prices without being noticed by any other member of the group. Under this tenable assumption, the subject firm attempts to lower its price, confident of moving along dd'. However, independent of our firms, all other firms also find it profitable to reduce their prices, so our firm moves, not along dd' as it anticipated, but along DD', and as a result, its profit, rather than increasing, falls. The reason for this and the source of the firm's frustration lie in Chamberlin's assumption of symmetry. Since every firm within the group faces identical cost and demand functions, what is true of the subject firm of Figure 11-2 is also true of every other firm in the group. Each firm believes that it can move down along its own dd' curve and increase its profit.

Because all firms act on this belief, none of them moves along its own subjective *dd'* curve; instead, each firm moves along its *DD'* curve, the curve that obtains for matching price behavior. The *dd'* curve does not disappear; it slides downward along *DD'*. At any moment in time, each member of the group believes the *dd'* curve depicts an anticipated pattern of price-quantity behavior. Each continues to believe that if it could reduce its price it would improve its profit. Be sure to note that the firms are not wrong in their commonly held belief that a price reduction will cause no retaliation; other firms reduce their prices because *all firms are in the same situation.*

Each firm is frustrated in its attempt to gain more profit because sales do not increase as expected in response to the price reduction. The simultaneous price cuts do not allow any one firm to acquire customers from its rivals. What additonal sales there are occur in resonse to the law of demand; lower prices bring new buyers into the group's market. More sales are made by all members of the group but not at the expense of any one member.

The price cuts cease when the economic profit of each firm has been eliminated. This occurs at point *E*, at which the subjective demand curve, having slid down along *DD'* to the position denoted by d_1d_1', is tangent to the *LATC* curve. The price $O\bar{P}$ and the quantity $O\bar{X}$ represent the equilibrium solution for the subject monopolistic competitor. Because of symmetry, this particular solution is also the solution of every firm within the group; hence, with the attainment of point *E* by the subject firm, the industry or group is in long-run stable equilibrium.

THE FORCES LEADING TO TANGENCY

Why does curve *dd'* become tangent to the *LATC* curve at the latter's point of intersection with the *DD'* curve? What forces operate to give the subjective demand curve the slope that makes tangency possible? Accepting the proposition that the *dd'* curve slides down *DD'*, why could it not simply pass through point *E* rather than being tangent to it?

The answer lies in the entry and exit of firms. Nontangency means either economic profit or economic loss. For example, consider Figure 11-3, and imagine a demand curve d_3d_3' lying entirely beneath the *LATC* curve. In this situation, all price-quantity combinations yield losses. The costs of production are everywhere greater than the associated revenue. Now, consider demand curve d_1d_1', which does have a segment lying entirely above the *LATC* curve. The profit-maximizing entrepreneur will not operate at point *A* or at any point on d_1d_1' to the left of *A*. He will begin making an economic profit as he moves rightward from *A*. If he moves too far to the right, however, his profit will fall, becoming zero at the right-hand point of intersection *J*, and negative to the right of this point. Only at a point of tangency between a *dd'* curve and the *LATC* curve can there be neither economic profits nor losses.

Let us assume an initial state of economic profits for the members of the group. For analytical purposes, assume that new firms attracted by the profit

FIGURE 11-3

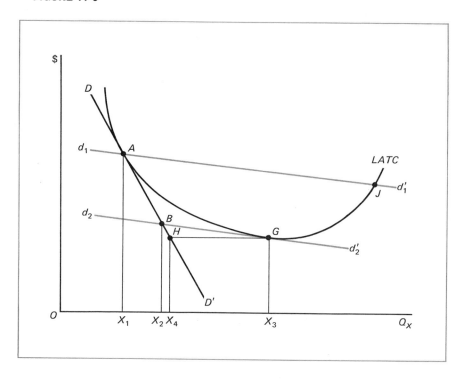

potential of the group enter before the original member firms are able to reduce their prices. Entry will cause the DD' curve of each firm to move because, *ceteris paribus,* each firm will now serve fewer customers.[6] It will continue its leftward (downward) drift until economic profit has been eliminated—as at point A in Figure 11-3, where the DD' curve has attained tangency with the $LATC$ curve. Seemingly, the requirements for equilibrium are met; economic profit has been eliminated; entry must cease.

But consideration of the d_1d_1' curve shows that the equilibrium attained at A cannot be stable. Each firm will attempt to cut price. As it does so, the d_1d_1' curve will begin to slide down DD', but any movement to a point below A will cause an economic loss. From the unstable equilibrium at A, the group must move into a state of disequilibrium that can be resolved only by the exit of firms. Suppose that price reductions move the dd' curve to d_2d_2'; at the price X_2B, the firm will experience a loss that it will estimate could be eliminated if it could cut price still further to X_3G. At price X_3G, tangency has been established between the dd' and $LATC$ curves at point G. This may seem to be a zero-profit equilibrium solution, but it cannot be, owing to the condition of

---

[6] Alternatively, each firm, in order to maintain quantity sold at the pre-entry level, would have to reduce price. Thus, for any given quantity (per firm) there must be a price reduction. This is shown by a downward shift in the demand curve.

symmetry. Every firm seeing the changing of price to X_3G as the solution to its own loss problem will attempt to reduce price to that level from X_2B. As all the firms in the group take this action, each firm slides down DD'. No customers are gained from rival members of the group. At a price equal to X_3G, the only addition to the sales of each firm is X_2X_4 units rather than X_2X_3. Point H, instead of point G, is realized, and the economic losses in the group continue.

It is obvious that no manipulation of price can solve the problem in which the members of the group find themselves. Any single firm attempting to raise price would likely eliminate itself from the market. If all the members of the group were to raise their prices, they would approach an unstable equilibrium. If price is lowered below X_3G, losses will increase. The only possible solution is the exit of some of the less tenacious firms. As they leave, the DD' curve of each remaining firm must move rightward. It will continue to move until losses are eliminated, at price X_3G. When this occurs, the DD' curve will intersect the point of tangency between the dd' and $LATC$ curves. Thus, the precise condition of slope, tangency and intersection essential to the stable equilibrium solution are produced by a combination of price reductions and entry and exit. There are, then, as Chamberlin points out, two conditions necessary for a stable equilibrium in the monopolistically competitive group: (1) the dd' curve must be tangent to the $LATC$ curve, (2) and the DD' curve must intersect the dd' and $LATC$ curves at their point of tangency.[7]

PRODUCT DIFFERENTIATION

A principal characteristic of monopolistic competition is that the products of the firms in a specific group, although highly substitutable, are not homogeneous; they are distinguishable. This attribute opens to each firm the possibility of competing on some basis other than price. Possessing some degree of control over the character of its product, its appearance, or the way it is sold, a firm may decide to use some variable other than price as a vehicle for obtaining a higher profit. This means that firms within the same group may try to gain larger market shares in a number of ways; for example, through price competition or by redesigning their products.

Suppose that the firm depicted in Figure 11-4 is a hotel. The product group consists of the hotels in a large city. The quantity measured on the horizontal axis is the number of guests per day. The hotel could increase the number of its daily registrations by lowering its rates or by doing some remodeling and redecorating.

To simplify, let us assume that the hotels in the product group confine their competition to differentiation. Initially, the subject hotel is operating on the long-run average total cost curve $LATC_1$, and the current room rate is OR, at which OG_1 guests are in occupancy each day. The total revenue of the firm

---

[7] Chamberlin, *Theory of Monopolistic Competition*, p. 93.

Market Behavior: Monopolistically Competitive Conditions

is OG_1NR; total costs are OG_1SF, and total economic profit is *FSNR*. Under the assumptions of symmetry, if one firm has an economic profit, so do the other firms in the group. Thus, with free entry, the group cannot be in equilibrium. Entry will occur and continue until economic profits are eliminated. For the subject hotel, this will occur when the number of guests per day falls to OG_2.

An individual hotel firm in the situation depicted by point *W* will strive to improve its profit position. Let us assume that instead of attempting to increase its share of the market by lowering price, it decides to hold price constant and differentiate its product further by refurbishing its rooms. The cost of this increased product differentiation is shown by the upward movement of the long-run average cost curve. The limit of the shift must be $LATC_2$, since with room rates held steady at *OR*, any higher increase in costs would cause the hotel to incur a loss.

But as in the case of price reductions, every hotel can attempt additional product variation. Unless there are exogenous factors, such as a convention, to augment the demand for hotel rooms, there is a limit to which the number of guests can be increased for the entire group by product improvement. The members of the hotel group will refurbish their rooms only to the extent that each hotel can increase the number of its daily guests above the amount OG_2. As long as any economic profit accrues from this process, entry will occur. We can assume, therefore, that costs will rise until they consume all the added revenue. Say each hotel is able to build up its clientele to pre-entry levels. The cost curve will shift to the position indicated by the curve *BB'*. With price remaining unchanged at *OR*, point *N* denotes the equilibrium solution.

The end result of these adjustments has not benefited the hotels. Each

FIGURE 11-4

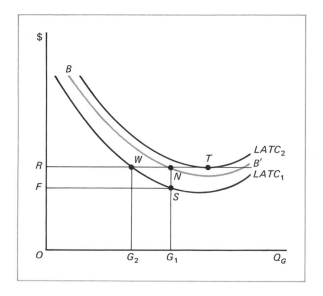

hotel, by attempting to gain more business, has raised the costs of operation, making the maximized profits zero.

Although the maximized economic profits are zero, the *goal* of profit maximization leads to this result. As a monopolistic competitor, the entrepreneur has no choice other than the modernization of his hotel. If he did not refurbish his building when other hotel owners were doing so, he would be forced into an economic loss as paying guests deserted him for the redecorated establishments of his competitors.

NONPRICE COMPETITION

The preceding analysis assumed, for simplicity's sake, that price is fixed at *OR*—that is, that price competition played no role in the adjustment process. And, indeed, such situations are far from unusual. Among the possible reasons are custom, ethics, or some pecuniary goal other than profit maximization. For example, firms may aim merely for "satisfactory" rather than maximum profit. Perhaps they seek to maximize total revenue rather than profit. Although it is less common in the United States, nonprice competition is a highly regarded form of business behavior in Europe. A traditional social code has led entrepreneurs to regard as highly unethical any attempt to take a competitor's clientele away from him by cutting price. On the other hand, striving to improve one's own sales by building a better crafted product or giving one's customers more value at the same price does not violate the code of gentlemen-entrepreneurs. Perhaps this helps to explain why many Americans look to European products as the embodiment of fine craftsmanship.

Such "European" competitive behavior is common also in some sectors of the American economy. Many independent professionals are good examples of monopolistic competitors. Certainly, the canons of most professional associations rule out overt price competition. As we saw in Chapter 8, many professionals are ideally situated to practice perfect price discrimination; open price competition not only is forbidden but, as we concluded, would seriously impair the professional's ability to practice price discrimination.

Moreover, despite the high fees enjoyed by many professionals, the general tendency in many fields may be toward the elimination of economic profit, and much of the economic activity of professional associations is simply an effort to stop, or at least retard, this tendency. When the economic profits have been eliminated, the principal economic concern of professional associations is likely to be the maintenance of "orderly" (that is, nonprice competitive) conditions within the profession. Under these circumstances, the number of professionals in a given field may increase rather markedly without any price benefits accruing to the general public. This is especially unwelcome news to those who assume that the cost of medical services would decrease if only more students could be graduated from medical school. To analyze this problem further, let us return to Figure 11-3.

The existence of an economic profit is a powerful attraction for those out-

side a field to enter it. Despite the public's romantic illusions about the motivation of the members of some professions, the lure of an extraordinary reward is certainly as effective an input allocator as is the lure of a cause or an art. As new firms (individuals) enter a profession, the DD' curve of each of the existing members of the group moves leftward, threatening the elimination of economic profit. If the profession is made up of intelligent, informed, and well-disciplined members, it can, and will, take action to forestall the leftward movement of the DD' curves of its members. The methods used are evident: supervision over the admissions policies of training schools, examining boards, licensing, and so on. Any and all of these devices are used frequently for controlling entry.

There is an even more socially appealing device to stave off (or, better, reverse) the leftward movement of the DD' curve. This is to promote the demand for the service. Obviously, it is difficult, if not downright wrongheaded, to point out to a health-conscious public that more publically financed health plans, more private health insurance, and a greater concern over one's bodily pains will, regardless of any possible health benefits, cause the DD' curve of each firm to move rightward as surely as the advertising policy of any crassly materialistic firm.

Occasionally, the prices of those professional services the public regards as essential become so high that there is widespread discontent. Although the public probably will never be much interested in interfering with the market for architectural talent, it has shown signs of becoming increasingly annoyed with the restrictive practices of the various health professions. Thus, from time to time, representatives of the public devise measures to bring down the cost of medical services. Usually, the core of such plans is an increase in the number of medical schools or an increase in the size of existing ones, so that the greater number of physicians eventually flowing onto the market will depress the general price level for medical services.

Figure 11-3 shows why this plan may well be frustrated. Suppose enough new physicians are produced to eliminate the economic profits in the medical profession (the monopolistically competitive group). As we have noted before, there are strong motivations not to engage in price competition in many professions. With no incentive to cut the existing price, the leftward movement of the DD' curve, reflecting the entry of new firms, will not be accompanied by a fall in price. Should the economic profit be eliminated, the equilibrium will occur at a point of tangency between the DD' and the LATC curves such as A in Figure 11-3. The analysis accompanying this figure asserted that point A cannot represent a state of stable equilibrium because price-cutting would ensue. In the present situation, we are assuming that price competition is ruled out by the nature and organization of the group. Should the economic profits of the group be eliminated, the clientele will not pay an amount above the true costs of production for the services they receive, but they will be obtaining these services from high-cost producers. Their higher-than-necessary costs represent largely the inefficient delivery of the subject service.

The offices are too small (in the sense that they operate in the region of economies of size) and are located in high-rent buildings; the clerical staff is too large; there is considerable overlapping and duplication because of the large number of independent practitioners. In short, there is no way of benefiting from the economies inherent in a larger, unified firm. Moveover, as a result of entry and its threat to economic profits, costs are likely to rise, so the long-run average cost curve will shift upward. Although price competition is regarded as unethical, nonprice competition may be admired, albeit grudgingly. In an attempt to attract more, or more affluent, clients, better addresses will be sought; more and newer equipment will be purchased; formerly functional offices will be invaded by interior decorators; and the office staff will proliferate. Entry into a *nonprice* competitive group may actually raise the price of the group's output even if maximized economic profit is reduced to, or approaches, zero.

This analysis suggests that some change much more fundamental than an increase in the supply of certain professionals is necessary to reduce their prices. What seems to be called for in the case of the health professions is a radical transformation in the way their services are packaged and delivered. One possibility is more and larger group practices—what one economist has called "department stores of medicine." The advantages of group practice are those associated in this book with economies of size. Office staffs, nurses, laboratories, equipment, parking lots, magazines, and other ancillary services could be combined into one single, and more efficient, plant. One could also suggest the elimination of the ban on competitive pricing. This could be facilitated, as was suggested in Chapter 8, by the publication of objective price lists.

Many remedial measures are likely to meet stronger opposition from clientele than from practitioners. For example, a public, long accustomed to thinking sentimentally about the relation between doctor and patient might find the unadorned impersonality of a department store of medicine so distasteful that it would convince itself it would rather pay higher medical fees and preserve its illusions. In the following section, we consider the desire of customers to pay for nonintrinsic product characteristics.

EXCESS CAPACITY AND WASTE

Excess capacity is the unutilized ability of firms within an industry or group to lower their average costs of production by expanding output.

THE EXCESS CAPACITY OF A GIVEN PLANT

When a monopolistically competitive firm is in zero-profit equilibrium, any and all of its plants must have excess capacity. Because of the negative slope of the firm's average revenue curve, tangency must occur to the left of

FIGURE 11-5

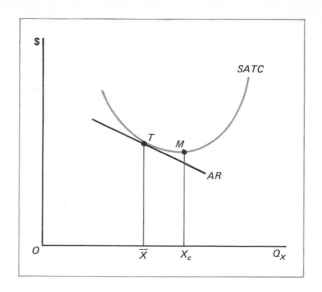

the minimum point of the given short-run average combined cost curve. The zero-profit equilibrium of a purely competitive firm would occur at point *M* in Figure 11-5. The fragment of the average revenue curve of this competitor shows tangency at point *T*. The monopolistic divergence between private and social gain motivates the firm to underutilize its present plant. If the firm were to employ enough units of the variable input to reduce the unit costs of production to the lowest possible level, it would incur a loss. The output OX_c—the competitive output—would be the output of the most efficient operation of the plant, but the nature of the market prevents this outcome and dictates that the profit-maximizing output must be less than the ideal output; hence, the plant has a capacity for production in excess of the profit-maximizing rate. That excess capacity is shown by the (potential) output $\bar{X}X_c$. This is the cost that the economy incurs in exchange for product differentiation. Monopolistic output restriction means consumers must pay higher costs. Price, which would be X_cM in a competitive market, is $\bar{X}T$ in monopolistic competition. Since monopolistic competitors operate under conditions of increasing returns to size (economies of size), merging their plants (in the example, combining separate medical offices into clinics) would provide the public with the same total output at a lower real cost.

THE EXCESS CAPACITY OF THE FIRM AND INDUSTRY

In an *existing* plant, excess capacity occurs as a result of the discrepancy between the profit-maximizing and ideal outputs. The capacity is there, but it is unused. The other aspect of Chamberlin's excess capacity theorem—that of the firm and industry—may seem to be of less consequence because

excess capacity does not occur; nevertheless, it is the more serious of the cases.

In Figure 11-6, three possible states of zero-profit equilibria are depicted. Point M shows the zero-profit equilibrium solution of the pure competitor. Point A shows the solution for a monopolistic competitor when price competition is present, and point H shows the equilibrium condition for the monopolistically competitive firm in the absence of price competition. In the case of output OX_c, the firm has built the most efficient plant and operates it at the optimal rate. The firm producing output OX_p has built a plant smaller than the social optimum. From the preceding section, we know that it must be operating such a plant at less than its optimal rate and that excess capacity clearly exists. Assume the optimal rate of operation would yield the output OX_p'. Excess capacity in the previously defined terms is X_pX_p'.

What about $X_p'X_c$? Chamberlin defines this, too, as excess capacity, although no plant exists capable of producing this additional output at a unit cost of X_cM. Thus, there are two components of excess capacity. One element, represented by the distance X_pX_p', occurs because a given plant is operated at less than its ideal capacity. The remaining component, shown as $X_p'X_c$,

FIGURE 11-6

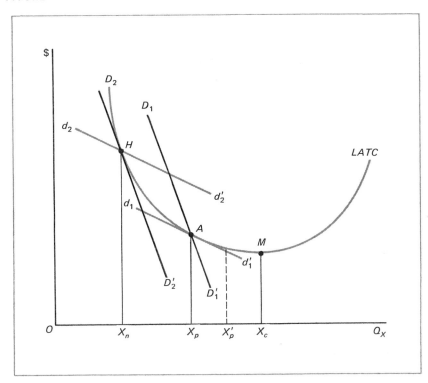

Market Behavior: Monopolistically Competitive Conditions

is the additional capacity lost because it is not worthwhile for the firm to build a socially optimal plant. Although this excess capacity does not exist technically, it does exist as economically, or socially, unused capacity.

Together, the two components are usually termed excess capacity. Figure 11-6 shows that there is a considerable difference in excess capacity when there is price competition and when there is not. In the absence of price competition, excess capacity increases from $X_p X_c$ to $X_n X_p$. The difference between OX_c and OX_n is often called a *waste of competition.* We must be careful about what this means. The expression itself is misleading; for, as Chamberlin points out, excess capacity is not really a waste of competition since it occurs only when a *non*competitive (i.e., monopolistic) element is introduced; excess capacity could not possibly occur in the zero-profit equilibrium of the pure competitor.[8] Moreover, Chamberlin does not feel that every case of excess capacity can be adjudged a waste. He distinguishes sharply between the solutions at A and at H. He observes that product differentiation can be a valuable component of a good. To escape from dreary sameness, to have a choice among highly substitutable goods, to be able to display and satisfy one's tastes —these are qualities for which consumers are willing to pay a premium. It is product differentiation that has given rise to the excess capacity $X_p X_c$ in Figure 11-6. If excess capacity were eliminated and the good were priced at $X_c M$, every unit of the good from every producer would be the same. The difference between the prices $X_c M$ and $X_p A$, then, can be regarded as the amount consumers are willing to pay to have variety in the general class of X goods. The existence of price competition brings the price of the goods to the lowest possible level consistent with the desired degree of product differentiation. When price competition exists, Chamberlin objects to defining $X_p X_c$ as excess capacity and would deny that it represents a waste of (non)competition.

However, Chamberlin holds that the case is different when price competition is not present. The absence of price competition precludes price from being reduced from $X_n H$ to $X_p A$. The difference between the two prices does not compensate consumers with a desired degree of product differentiation; indeed the differentiation may be regarded as being carried to an undesired excess. For example, the difference between the two prices might be represented by the seller giving his customers trading stamps or free pottery when they would rather have a price reduction. Lower prices are the equivalent of higher real wages. The individual consumer can apply the savings he receives to the purchase of anything he wants—even to more of the same product. Premiums and prizes, on the other hand, are a sort of enforced consumption. Trading stamps, while probably more acceptable than a milk jug or a framed picture of Old Faithful in action, generally confine individual choice to items in stock at the redemption center. Lower prices leave it up to the individual to determine the precise form his "premium" will take.

Since $X_p X_c$ has been defined as not representing excess capacity, only

8 *Ibid.,* p. 109.

the distance X_nX_p should be regarded as excess capacity in the nonprice competitive case. This case of excess capacity properly may be termed waste, but if it is, then it must be seen as a waste resulting from *non*competition, not as a waste of a competitive economic order. The elimination of this "waste" lies in measures to break down the ability of the group to maintain price levels in the face of entry.

The argument of this section is *not* that the output of X necessarily should be increased. Given full employment, we cannot assume that more X is unequivocally a good thing. For example, in Figure 11-6, assume that the total output of the group is $100(OX_n)$; that is, there are 100 firms, each producing OX_n units of X. Total group output of $100(OX_n)$ may be sufficient in that consumers do not wish to have more resources devoted to the production of X. Suppose $OX_p = 2(OX_n)$. Then our argument holds merely that each firm should produce OX_p. Since it follows that $50(OX_p) = 100(OX_n)$, the firms within the product group should be consolidated so as to replace 100 smaller firms with 50 larger enterprises, each firm being twice as large as the antecedent firms. Chamberlin's reasoning concludes that in the case of monopolistic competition, any given *total* output such as $100(OX_n) = 50(OX_p)$, *if* it is produced by 100 plants, should be manufactured in fewer and larger plants.

THE ECONOMICS OF ADVERTISING—SELLING COSTS

Since the hallmark of monopolistic competition is product differentiation, it is natural to expect that monopolistic competitors will attempt to call attention to their distinguishable, though highly similar, wares. Such promotional activities can be placed under the general classification of advertising. Advertising practices may range from the sponsorship of a Boy Scout troop to the solemn televised assurance that the little hammers in one's brain that cause headaches will be stopped by imbibing some kind of fizzy drink. Whatever the case, the firm that advertises incurs promotional costs over and above production costs. This class of expenses may be called *selling costs*. As Chamberlin defines the terms, production costs include all expenses necessary to bring the good into existence and put it in the hands of its ultimate consumers; selling costs are outlays made to move or alter the shape of the demand curve.[9]

Advertising activities are a subject of much popular concern. Increasingly, they are deplored for intentionally creating dissatisfaction, denounced for creating wants that would not otherwise exist. The assumption, of course, is that some wants never should be deliberately and externally inspired. Advertising is condemned for using up resources that could go into the production of goods and services. It is criticized for subsidizing media—for example, television and magazines—which the public would not demand if it *knowingly* had to pay the full costs of their production. On the other side, proponents

[9] *Ibid.,* pp. 117, 123.

of advertising assert that sales promotion creates jobs, that it informs consumers about products they may have been searching for, and that if it does create new wants, it makes people feel better for having discovered a new source of enjoyment.

Many of these arguments are wholly or partly noneconomic, so analysis can shed no light on them. However, we can analyze the purely economic aspects of advertising, one of which is the increase in costs attributable to promotional activity.

An argument favorable to promotion is shown in Figure 11-7. The *LPC* curve (long-run *production* cost curve) shows all long-run average total costs of production *exclusive* of selling costs. In the absence of sales promotion, the sales of the firm are currently OX_0, at which its total unit costs are OC_0. Suppose the firm decides to advertise, hoping thereby to increase the demand for its products. This decision will raise its costs. The curve depicting average selling costs is assumed to be U-shaped. The U shape means that over some range, returns to advertising are increasing. As the advertising audience increases, the cost per member of that audience may fall. Another likely source of economies is the more effective use that can be made of a combination of media as the promotional budget is increased. People can be reached in different ways; media that are ineffective with some persons will have an impact on others. The benefits of specialization also may contribute to economies. A larger promotional program allows the use of specialized talent in art, copy,

FIGURE 11-7

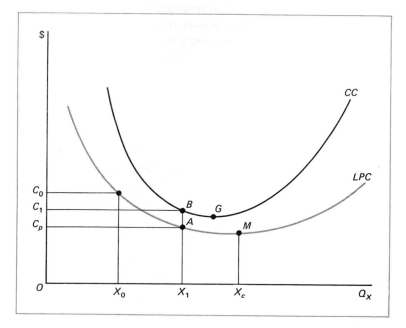

and sales. Diseconomies, beyond some point, also seem possible. The cease-less repetition that initially gains many new customers eventually loses its effect, perhaps even driving some of the audience away from the product. Another potential cause of diseconomies is that the receptive people will react quickly, while further expenditures on advertising may never lure some re-sistant persons into the market.

The curve of average selling costs is not shown in Figure 11-7. The up-per curve, CC, shows the combined cost of production and selling. The verti-cal distance between the two depicted curves is the selling cost associated with a particular output level. For example, at output OX_1, the average cost of production is X_1A; the average combined cost of producing *and* selling this output is X_1B; and, therefore, the average selling cost of inducing people to buy OX_1 units is AB.

The minimum point on the CC curve bears no predictable relation to the minimum point on the LPC curve. *Under Chamberlin's definition of selling costs,* there is no relation between the production costs of a good and what it costs to attempt to move the demand curve for that good rightward. Sharply increasing diseconomies of advertising can cause the minimum point on the CC curve to occur at an output below the point of minimum per unit production costs, as is shown in Figure 11-7.

REDUCTION OF COSTS THROUGH ADVERTISING

Suppose the firm initially is producing the output OX_0. If it has no selling expenses, the average cost of production will be OC_0. Now assume the firm decides to advertise its product. If the advertising outlays cause the sales vol-ume to rise to OX_1, then, despite the addition of sales expenses to the firm's costs, the average combined cost, OC_1, of producing *and* selling the larger out-put is less than the average cost of producing the smaller output. The firm's total advertising budget has expanded from O to the amount shown by rectan-gle C_PABC_1, but the economies of size inherent in the firm's production function (shown by the downward sloping segment of LPC) have caused the unit costs of producing the larger output to fall so low that they more than offset the cost of the advertising program.

ADVERTISING AND PROFIT MAXIMIZATION

For an explanation of the equilibrium solution of the firm and industry when advertising is used to increase demand, we must turn to Figure 11-8. Our analysis will begin with the assumption that the nature of the product and its selling price already have been determined.

Suppose the firm initially is producing the output OX_0 at price OP (the horizontal line PP' is not the firm's demand curve; it is used merely to indicate the constancy of price OP at various outputs). If the combined unit cost of pro-duction and selling is given by curve CC_1, the firm, although it more than cov-

ers all the costs associated with this level of output, cannot be maximizing its profit. By utilizing the curve MCC, which is marginal to CC_1, we are able to determine that if the firm were to produce OX_1, it would maximize its economic profit. This superior situation will be achieved if the firm increases its advertising expenditures per unit of output from AB to CF. Since price is constant at OP, marginal revenue is $OP = X_1E_1$. At output OX_1, marginal cost is also X_1E_1; therefore the conditions for a profit maximum are met.

As was the case with product variation, in monopolistic competition the anticipated results from the advertising campaign will not accrue to any firm. The members of the group will frustrate one another's plans. Any firm initially producing output OX_0 will aspire to sales of OX_1 and a maximized profit of GFE_1P. That is the point; every firm in the group has the indicated profit as its target. The desired output can be achieved only by one firm if that one firm is allowed to increase its advertising while the remaining members of the group do nothing. This will not happen, since each of the firms in the group will attempt to increase its sales by expanding its advertising budget to a total of

FIGURE 11-8

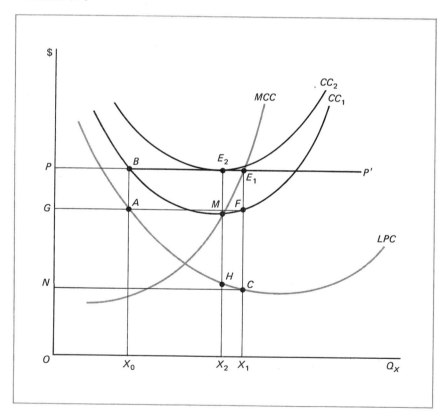

NCFG dollars. And in the competition for the attention of customers, advertising by all firms tends to cancel out the benefits of advertising by any one firm. So there is a treadmill effect. Any firm attempting to hold its average advertising expenditures to *CF* will find its sales do not advance, and it will spend even more; then every other firm must also spend more merely to maintain its place. With all firms attempting to increase sales through advertising, *CF* dollars per unit of output is an insufficient amount to stimulate any firm's sales to OX_1 units. More must be spent to offset the effects of each rival's advertising. How much more? Since expenditures must exceed *CF* dollars per unit to achieve the objective of each firm, the selling cost must rise. This is reflected by an upward shift in the combined production and selling cost curve. Only when the economic profit attributable to advertising has been eliminated will the curve cease its upward course. In Figure 11-8, this is represented by the tangency of CC_2 and the price line *PP'* at E_2. The combined cost of production and promotion now being equal to total revenue at an output level of OX_2 units (an amount less than the original goal), each firm will maintain its advertising expenditures at the equilibrium amount HE_2 dollars per unit of output.

SUMMARY

Monopolistic competition theory is a blend of the theories of monopoly and competition. The hallmark of monopolistic competition is product differentiation. This attribute gives each firm at least enough monopoly power over its output that it must search for the profit-maximizing price. Like all noncompetitive sellers, monopolistic competitors price above marginal cost. The competitive element in this type of market structure is manifested in a long-run zero economic profit equilibrium. Such a solution follows from the presence of a rather large number of firms in the product group and conditions of fairly easy entry and exit.

In monopolistic competition, all firms tend to follow the same strategies of pricing, product differentiation, and sales promotion. There need be no collusion, and no firm takes action in retaliation for what another firm does. The firms are correct in assuming that they are sufficiently small in relation to the market that their independent actions will tend to be unnoticed. The reason for the unanimity of their actions is that every firm in the group sees the same potential advantages, and the end that each strives to attain is the goal of all.

Some economists identify the difference between the perfectly and monopolistically competitive outputs as excess capacity, meaning that under perfectly competitive conditions, plants of socially optimal size would be operated at optimal rates, while monopolistic firms tend to build plants of less than optimal size and operate them at sub-optimal rates. Some writers have decried this situation as a waste of competition, but as Edward Hastings

Chamberlin correctly pointed out, a less than optimal output can only be a waste of *non*competition—if, indeed, the expression has any significance. Chamberlin refused to recognize the long-run monopolistically competitive equilibrium as indicative of waste as long as price competition is present. In such a case, he argued, the reduction in output below the competitive level is merely the cost of product variation. Only when price competition is absent would Chamberlin agree that waste occurs.

Although monopolistic competition theory does not, in itself, support or refute any particular stand on advertising, *given* advertising and promotional costs, the model will show whether prices are increased or decreased as a result of promotional activities.

More complicated models can show the combined effects of a number of typical monopolistically competitive selling techniques—for example, product variation, non-price competition, and sales promotion. Among the results predicted by monopolistic competition theory is the sobering possibility that simply increasing the number of health service personnel, without taking any other actions, may do little to reduce the cost or improve the quality of health care in the United States.

The Theory of Market Behavior Under Oligopolistic Conditions, I: Basic Oligopoly Models

OLIGOPOLY: THE STATE OF FEWNESS

The word *oligopoly* expresses succinctly the popular conception of the American economy—a system dominated by giant business firms, a world of great corporations, a world with few, and powerful, inhabitants. And, indeed, most large corporations are oligopolists (when firms are extremely large, few enterprises are required to serve a given market). But oligopolists do not have to be industrial giants, or even corporations; what they must be is *few* in number. *Fewness* is the essence of oligopoly; the literal meaning of the word being "few sellers."

Precisely, what is fewness? How many firms are "a few firms"? How can one recognize an oligopolistic industry? Expressions such as "Big Three," "Top Four," or, simply, "Big Business" are a practical guide to the identification of oligopolies. Using these commonplace expressions as guidelines, we would expect oligopolistic firms to be found in such industries as automobiles, steel, nonferrous metals, light globes, fountain pens, television and radio broadcasting, tobacco, distilled beverages, drugs, paper, airlines, computer hardware, agricultural implements, heavy chemicals, cameras, phonograph records, trucks, glass, and elevators. This list is not exhaustive, but it does suggest the characteristics of industries comprised of oligopolistic firms.

In oligopolistic industries, a relatively small number of firms accounts for a large percentage of the total sales of the industry. For example, in the domestic automobile industry, General Motors sells 51.6 percent of the total output; General Motors and Ford account for 80.4 percent; General Motors, Ford, and Chrysler account for 96.6 percent; and if American Motors is added to the group, four firms are responsible for virtually all domestic passenger car production.[1] This general pattern displayed by the automobile industry is representative of that found in other oligopolistic industries.

The question we must still answer is: How few is few? Economic theory holds that the state of fewness exists whenever one firm must be concerned with the impact that any of its actions will have on other firms in the industry. Thus, we are now encountering the "extroverts" of the business world. Oligopolists, of necessity, must be outward turning; their interests cannot be confined to their internal cost structures; they must be concerned with every action—with every *future* action—of the other (rival) firms in their particular industry. In other words, an oligopolist must be concerned with what his rivals think he is thinking. If this sounds to you more like a description of the mental state of poker players than an introduction to a segment of the theory of the firm, then you already have a good insight into the basic nature of the problems of oligopoly theory.

INTERDEPENDENCE: THE CONSEQUENCE OF FEWNESS

Interdependence is the natural consequence of fewness. Monopolists, pure and perfect competitors, and monopolistic competitors (at least in the Chamberlin large-group case) are unconcerned with what other firms in their own industry or group do or are contemplating doing. For oligopolists, however, profit maximization and, indeed, survival depend on their reacting to every move each other firm in the industry makes. Furthermore, successful performance depends on anticipating the moves of each other firm in the industry. For this reason, oligopolists do not have simple competitors; they have *rivalrous* competitors, which are defined as firms that must be profoundly concerned with the plans and actions of other firms. The more rivalrous the state of competition, the more firms need to be concerned with what their competitors do.

Oligopolists, as we have just said, must anticipate the actions and reactions of their rivals; in other words, oligopolists must make *strategic* decisions. This necessity makes the study of oligopoly the most interesting, as well as the most frustrating, part of the theory of the firm. The decision-context of oligopolists is wholly unlike that of any other form of market organization, but it resembles closely the worlds of military, political, and poker-playing strategists. For this reason, many of the theories of these rivalrous endeavors are interchangeable.

[1] *New York Times,* Dec. 2, 1972.

A SIMPLE STATEMENT OF THE OLIGOPOLISTIC FIRM: THE KINKED DEMAND CURVE

We shall begin our discussion of oligopoly theory with one of the more classic—and frequently disputed—analyses in the literature: Paul Sweezy's kinked oligopoly demand curve.[2] Suppose the oligopolistic firm depicted in Figure 12-1 is selling good X in the quantity and at the price indicated by point P. Assume that the firm believes the price-quantity combination indicated by P does not maximize its profit. The firm will be strongly motivated to move away from point P. But the very nature of its oligopolistic industry—the quality of fewness—will inhibit such a move. The oligopolistic firm cannot hide in the anonymity offered by large numbers; any move the firm makes will be noticed by its rivalrous competitors. The firm can thus be expected to act (or, better, fail to act) on the assumption that any move it makes will invite the retaliation of its rivals. The threat of retaliatory action is so inhibiting to the firm that it does nothing, and the price-quantity combination remains that indicated by P. Let us see why.

Suppose the firm believes it would be advantageous to raise price. Such a decision would be a sound one if all the other firms in the industry would raise their prices as well. But they have a definite incentive *not* to go along. If they maintain the original price, the price-raiser will price himself out of the market, leaving his rivals heir to his market share. Since, in oligopoly, unlike

FIGURE 12-1

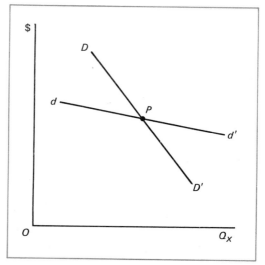

[2] Paul M. Sweezy, "Demand under Conditions of Oligopoly," AEA *Readings in Price Theory*, George J. Stigler and Kenneth E. Boulding, eds. (Homewood, Ill.: Richard D. Irwin, 1952), pp. 404–09.

the other market structures, a few split the total market among themselves, the departure of the price-raiser would mean a substantial increase in the market shares of each of the remaining firms.

Since a purely competitive firm cannot raise price without pricing itself out of the market, there must be a resemblance between the demand curves faced by the pure competitor and the oligopolist. This is so, as Figure 12-1 shows. The oligopolist, knowing that his rivals are highly unlikely to follow him in a price increase, perceives his demand curve as dd', a curve showing great elasticity. So he dismisses as unfeasible the thought of raising price above P, since an appreciable price rise will drive many customers to patronize his standpat rivals.

What about a price decrease? Following curve dd' would indicate that a small price reduction would gain many new sales. But in the case of a price reduction, rivalrous competitors will not stand firm. Unwilling to see the initiator of a price reduction take a great share (if not all) of the market away from them, they will retaliate by lowering their prices. In fact, the members of an oligopolistic industry may justifiably fear that the ultimate outcome of a price reduction by a single firm would be a devastating price war. The extreme likelihood of competitive price reductions leads an oligopolist to conclude that he will gain very few new sales as a result of a price reduction. He may gain some patronage from new customers drawn into the market by lower prices (all oligopolists in the industry would have a similar experience), but the universality of the competitive price reductions would leave the firms with roughly their previous percentage distribution of customers. What is more, it would result in a decrease in revenue, even though sales volume would be the same or slightly higher.

The predicted response to an initial price decrease indicates that oligopolists must be thinking about a demand curve other than dd' when price reductions are under consideration. The demand curve must be highly inelastic and resemble DD' in Figure 12-1. Along DD', price reductions will yield proportionately smaller increases in sales.

This analysis seems to suggest that the oligopolist has, not one, but two demand curves; one, dd', is for price increases, and the other, DD', is for price reductions. This observation is correct if it is specified that the base price referred to in both cases is P. Therefore, the Pd' portion of curve dd' and the DP segment of DD' are inoperative and hereafter can be eliminated. Instead of holding that the firm has two demand curves, it is conventional to say that the oligopolistic firm of the model depicted in Figure 12-1 faces the single *kinked* demand curve dPD', the sharp kink occurring at point P.

THE KINKED DEMAND CURVE AND PROFIT MAXIMIZATION

Oligopoly confers no immunity on *input* price changes. If input prices change, the firm's marginal cost curves will shift. So far, our analysis has

Market Behavior: Basic Oligopolistic Conditions

suggested that oligopolistic firms are unlikely to initiate price changes. But suppose there is a substantial decrease in input prices, so that the marginal cost curve shifts downward markedly. In previous analyses, we have seen that unless the firm reduces price so as to decrease marginal revenue, $MR > MC$, and profit will no longer be maximized. Must either the attribute of price rigidity or the goal of profit maximization be abandoned? If the $MC = MR$ rule is to be followed, are we to conclude that oligopolists will change price if their input prices are changed? Or, since price rigidity is a pervasive aspect of the oligopolistic market structure, must we hold that oligopolists over-whelmingly prefer industrial price stability to profit maximization?

According to the Sweezy model, neither the oligopolistic attribute of price rigidity nor the widely accepted goal of profit maximization need be abandoned. They are compatible with each other as an examination of Figure 12-2 will show. The very sharp kink in the firm's average revenue curve at P causes a vertical gap in the marginal revenue curve between points G and G'. The marginal revenue curve, then, consists of the discontinuous segments MG and $G'R$. The segment MG is the marginal revenue curve appropriate to the AP portion of the firm's average revenue curve, while segment $G'R$ is the marginal revenue curve proper to the average revenue curve segment PB. Thus, below point P, over the vertical distance $G'G$, no marginal revenue curve exists. The marginal cost curve can shift throug out the gap between G and G' without inducing the firm to change price. At point G, $MC = MR$, and, thus, P is the profit-maximizing price; but the same is true at point G' (i.e., $MC = MR$), and P remains the profit-maximizing price. We conclude, therefore, that for any position of the marginal cost curve between G and G', P is always

FIGURE 12-2

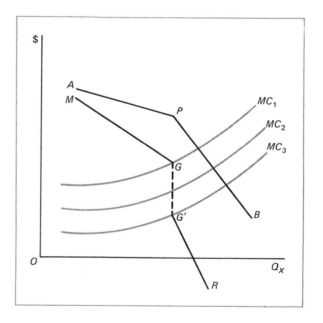

the profit-maximizing price. Changes in costs that cause shifts in the marginal cost curve confined to these limits will not result in price changes.

What if the shifts in the marginal cost curve exceed the limits of the gap? According to this model, we would then expect the firm to change price. The firm would be unwilling to accept cost increases raising the *MC* curve above point *G* without passing on some of the increase to its customers. If a decline in input prices were to lower the *MC* curve below point *G'*, the advantages to be derived from a price reduction would be so pressing that the firm would make the cut.

Behind this reasoning lies the assumption that cost changes powerful enough to move the *MC* curve in either direction beyond the confines of the gap will be sufficiently widespread to affect all members of the industry. Price changes, then, will not be a matter merely of the strategic decision of one firm, but will reflect a fundamental change in the underlying cost conditions of the industry. In such a situation, rival firms are unlikely to regard a price change by any one firm as a strategic move requiring retaliation; in fact, all of the firms in the industry will be considering similar price changes. Therefore, upon adjustment, no competitive advantages or disadvantages will result.

A CRITIQUE OF THE SWEEZY MODEL

Although it is an almost universal feature of oligopoly theory, the Sweezy model has been subjected to heavy criticism. Comments have had two bases, one theoretical, the other empirical.

Theoretical criticism. The supposed theoretical deficiencies of the model center on a single question. How is the point *P* (the point of the kink) determined? What forces have established price *P*? It is one thing to say that demand abruptly becomes elastic above point *P* and inelastic below point *P*, thereby creating a kink in the (composite) demand curve; but it is another thing to explain the location of the kink.

This model, unlike others in the theory of the firm, starts with price as a parameter to which all the reasoning of the model must conform. Thus, the Sweezy model is charged with being improperly placed in the body of price theory; obviously, it does not explain *how* oligopolists set their prices.

What, then, does the Sweezy model accomplish? It *assumes* a price (at the kink), and once the price is given, the Sweezy model is an admirably simple model of price rigidity. Given the price and the observation that oligopolistic prices *are* rigid, the kinked demand curve represents an attempt to explain why oligopolists would find it prudent to follow the observed policy of stable prices. The explanation centers on observed interdependence. Rivals will not match an initiating firm's increase in price because it is to their advantage to allow the initiator to price itself out of the market. In the case of an initial price reduction, all members of the industry will follow because they are unwilling to lose their customers to the price cutter. Therefore, the Sweezy

model explains the *existence* of a kink in an oligopolist's demand curve, but it does not explain the *location* of the bend. Appraised as an explanation of rigidity at a *given* price, the Sweezy model does not seem to deserve the rather considerable amount of negative comment it has received.

Empirical criticism. A more damaging criticism of the Sweezy model has been made at the empirical level. If it could be shown that oligopolistic prices are not rigid, or at least are no more rigid than the prices of nonoligopolists, then the Sweezy thesis would be an explanation of a non-event. This would certainly disqualify it for inclusion in the body of price theory.

The charge of nonrelevancy has been made against the Sweezy thesis by economist George J. Stigler.[3] After studying a ten-year record of price fluctuations of about one hundred firms comprising twenty-one well-known oligopolistic industries, Stigler concluded that price changes were so frequent as to negate any factual basis for the existence of a kink in the demand curves of oligopolistic firms. Stigler's statistical evidence does tend to support the view that the more oligopolistic the industry (the greater the state of fewness), the less frequent are price changes. Even so, he found that there were price changes in duopolistic industries (the most extreme form of oligopoly).

Stigler believes that the kinked demand curve theory is at variance with the generally accepted goal of profit maximization. He characterizes the kink as a barrier to the price flexibility necessary to meet this goal. If a kink exists, business executives must be responsible for it; but why, asks Stigler, would they set up barriers to the attainment of their most important goal? One possible answer to this argument is that in those oligopolies that do exhibit some price rigidity, the firms have goals other then profit maximization—for example, the maintainance of orderly (i.e., live-and-let-live) conditions in the industry. Regardless of this possibility, the Stigler article is based on a sufficiently large number of typical oligopolistic industries to cast definite doubt on the assertion that the prices of oligopolies are rigid. And if oligopolistic prices are not rigid, there are *no* kinks in the demand curves of oligopolistic firms.

THE SEARCH FOR A THEORY OF PRICE DETERMINATION: FOUR HISTORICALLY SIGNIFICANT OLIGOPOLY MODELS

Oligopoly theory long has been the most intractable component of the theory of the firm; possibly it has offered more problems than any other segment of the entire body of microeconomic theory. Oligopoly theory is not new; it predates the theory of monopolistic competition; and some of the earliest developments in the field predate Alfred Marshall's *Principles*. The history of oligopoly theory is connected intimately with the earliest develop-

---

[3] George J. Stigler, "The Kinky Oligopoly Demand Curve and Rigid Prices," *The Journal of Political Economy,* LV (1947), pp. 432–49.

ments in mathematical microeconomics. Despite its long history and the enthusiasm and sense of anticipation that have greeted the sporadic discoveries in the field, it remains one of the least perfected areas of economics. The principal reason is the multitude of ways in which the oligopoly game can be played. There is a Japanese game of strategy called *go*, in which the possible moves and responses are even greater than those of chess, making a theoretical explanation of the game, as of chess, extremely difficult. The explanation of oligopolistic behavior is of about the same order of difficulty.

The purpose of this introduction is not to scoff at oligopoly theory. We are at a stage in the development of oligopoly theory at which we are grateful for the least gleam of light. In pursuit of a better understanding of the nature of ogliipoly, we shall explore some of the landmark contributions. Although they are worth studying for their historical value, they accomplish quite well at least three other important goals. First, they show clearly the nature of the oligopoly problem—namely, the meaning of rivalrous competition, the reactions of firms to any move initiated by another firm. Second, their several inadequacies clearly show the gaps that a satisfactory theory of oligopoly must fill; they mark out the path for future theorists. Finally, the rather heroic simplifications forced on the theorists of oligopoly show how very difficult this segment of economics is. If in studying these theories, one can empathize with their creators, one may develop a real feeling for the intrinsic nature of the oligopoly problem.

THE COURNOT MODEL

The Cournot model, the oldest and most famous of the oligopoly theories, was introduced by the French economist and mathematician Augustin A. Cournot in 1838.[4] Strictly a duopoly theory (an oligopoly of two firms), it provides valuable insight into the nature of oligopolistic interdependence. It is an admittedly crude, but pathbreaking, theory.

The Cournot process. Cournot's theory is one of the earliest attempts to deal rigorously with the theory of *strategic* decisions. In this, it is a precursor of game theory.[5] Out of his theory have come at least two important concepts used in present-day oligopoly theory: the analytical tool known as reaction curves and the idea of the conjectural variation. However, its chief virtue, is as a good introduction to the difficulties of constructing even a limited, to say nothing of a general, theory of oligopoly.

To focus on the essential problem in oligopoly—that of interdependence —Cournot simplified his theory by assuming costless production. Assume that each duopolist owns a mineral spring whose waters have marvelous

---

[4] *Recherches sur les principes mathématiques de la théorie des richesses.* A translation in English by Nathaniel T. Bacon and Irving Fischer is entitled *Researches into the Mathematical Principles of Wealth* (New York: Macmillan, 1897 and 1927).
[5] Game theory is discussed in Chapter 13.

restorative properties. Customers, bringing their own containers, pay for permission to fill their jars with the miraculous waters bubbling forth from the natural springs.

Figure 12-3 shows the market demand curve, PW, for the health-giving waters purveyed by the duopolists. The demand curve shows that no one would pay a price greater than OP for the waters, and that if access to the springs were free, no more than OW would be consumed in a given time period. For additional simplicity, the demand function is assumed to be linear. To facilitate the analysis, numbers will be supplied along with the letters denoting the price-quantity schedule. Thus, we assume that no water is demanded at a price above $10.00, and that 10 units of spring water would be demanded if the good were free. To begin our analysis, let us suppose that A discovers his spring first. Until B locates water of similar qualities on his property, A is a monopolist, and the market demand curve is his average revenue curve.

Following the rule of profit maximization, the monopolist sets his price at $OP_1 = 1/2 \, (OP)$, or $5.00, at which he will sell $OW_1 = 1/2 \, (OW)$, or 5 units of water, as is shown in Figure 12-3. Since his marginal cost is zero, the $MC = MR$ rule is fulfilled when $MR = 0$. The costless production of water means that the condition of total revenue maximization—that is, setting price so that $\epsilon = 1$—simultaneously fulfills the profit-maximizing condition; thus $TR^* = \pi^* = OW_1 MP_1 = \$25.00$. At this point, A is acting as a pure monopolist, and there are no reasons for this monopoly equilibrium solution to change.

A substantial change will occur, however, when the monopoly of firm A becomes a duopoly of firms A and B with the entrance of entrepreneur B into the miraculous-water industry. Entrepreneur B, finding that there is a market for the water flowing from the natural spring on *his* property, decides to intrude upon the exclusive province of A. After assessing the market and finding that the competitive output would be 10 units (where $P = MC$, and $MC = 0$), and that

FIGURE 12-3

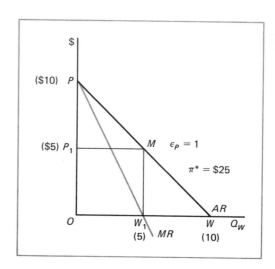

the monopoly output is one-half of this, *B* concludes that the presently unful-filled demand of 5 units is left to him to exploit. In other words, *A* is presently supplying one-half of the total demand for the water, so there is an unfulfilled demand. More units would be sold if the price 1/2 (*OP*) = $5.00 were reduced.

Since *B* knows that his added presence will make a fundamental differ-ence in the market for miraculous water, he must make a prediction about what *A*'s reaction will be to his entry. Here, for the first time in our theory of the firm, we see an entrepreneur faced with the necessity of making a strategic decision. *B*'s problem is not merely to set a price that will maximize profit; he must set his price both in the light of the demand for the water *and* in considera-tion of what *A*'s reaction will do to the market. In the language of economic theory, this prediction is called the *conjectural variation*.

In his treatment of the duopoly problem, Cournot assumed that the con-jectural variation of each seller is zero. For Cournot, this meant that each firm assumes that its rival will continue to sell the quantity being sold at the time the conjectural variation is framed. Probably, it is this assumed conjectural varia-tion of zero with regard to quantity sold that has brought down intense and excessive criticism on the Cournot model. The criticism is extremely easy to make. It holds that Cournot's duopolists *never* learn from experience. Without fail, each of Cournot's duopolists assumes that his rival will take no action in response to any action he may take, despite the fact that there is *always* a reaction to the move of one's rival. Admittedly, this is rather irrational entre-preneurial behavior. But in Cournot's defense, at least two points may be made. First, this questionable learning pattern does set the duopoly system in motion. Second, economic theory has been criticized for leaning heavily on the presumed rationality of the decision-makers of its models. If, then, the critics believe that economic theory should include some models comprehend-ing irrational behavior, here is one!

Entrepreneur *B*, in assessing his segment of the market, sets his price and sells the quantity depicted in Figure 12-4. Profit-maximizing behavior and zero marginal cost cause *B* to set his price at $2.50, at which he sells 2 1/2 units of water to the cash-and-carry customers. His maximized profit is $6.25. *B* must sell his water at a price of less than $5.00 to exploit the segment of con-sumer demand untouched by *A*; therefore, the vertical intercept of *B*'s demand curve is at 1/2 *OP* = $5.00.

With *B*'s entry into the industry, the oligopolistic game begins. Industry output is now 1/2 *OW* + 1/4 *OW* = 7 1/2 units, and the industry price is now $2.50. Since *A* has been forced to cut his price in half to meet *B*'s competition, he is no longer maximizing his profit. He must reassess his price policy. Basing his assessment on a conjectural variation of zero, *A* assumes that *B* will continue to supply one-fourth of the market's competitive output, or 2 1/2 units of water. This assumption leaves *A* with three-fourths of the market; that is, if he reduced the price of the water to zero, he would dispense 7 1/2 units. Figure 12-5 shows *A*'s pricing decision after he has reappraised his position.

With only three-fourths of the market (i.e., maximum possible sales of 7 1/2 units open to him), *A* now plans to maximize his profit by setting price at

FIGURE 12-4

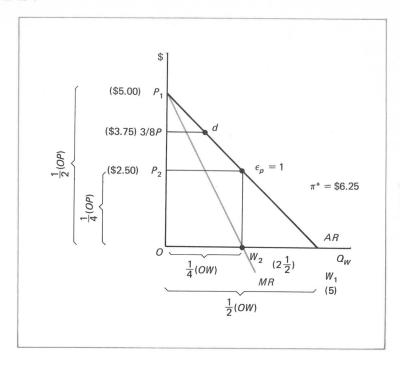

3/8 (OP) = $3.75. At this price, he will sell 3 3/4 units. A's total maximized profit (total revenue) will be $14.06. His profit has fallen from its former maximized level of $25.00, but now, in the face of competition, this is the best he can do.

   Now it is B's turn to have his plans spoiled. The unanticipated action of A has raised the going price of the water to $3.75. No longer must B sell his 2 1/2 units of water at a price of $2.50; because of A's reappraisal, he, too, can sell water at a price of $3.75. Formerly, if he had priced at this figure, he would have cut his sales back to below 2 1/2 units. In Figure 12-4 this action is shown as a movement from the midpoint of B's demand curve to point d. Of course, at point d, MR > MC, and profit is not maximized. B will take further action.

   To show how A and B work to a limit, we shall break from our step-by-step method and examine the logic of Cournot's model. It is obvious that the model produces fluctuations in the price-quantity combinations but that the fluctuations become smaller as the adjustment process continues.

   Consider the pattern of A's adjustments. As a monopolist, the entrepreneur began by selling one-half of the competitive output. Then B entered the market, making the industry a duopoly and selling an output of one-half of the remaining portion of the competitive output. The motive of profit maximization then forced A to reconsider his output plans. At that point, A was supplying one-half of the competitive output and B one-quarter of it. Therefore,

FIGURE 12-5

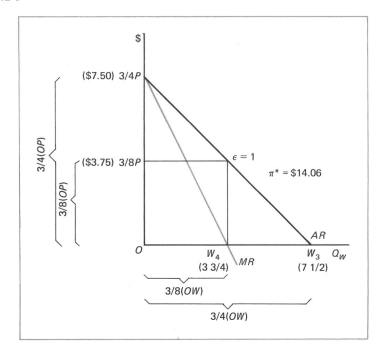

the duopolistic industry was selling three-fourths of the competitive output. *A* now sees three-fourths of the competitive market as available for his exploitation; that is, the one-half he now occupies plus the remaining one-fourth that is unsold. To maximize profit under these conditions, *A* determines to sell one-half of this three-fourths, or three-eighths, of that output. This is a reduction by one-eighth of his previous output. By continuing this process, we see that *A* will make the adjustments shown in Table 12-1.

A begins with one-half of the competitive output, and, then, at each adjustment, diminishes his output by the fraction shown. The progression is the sum of a series of (negative) fractions to infinity, but the sum of the numbers is nonetheless finite and is 1/3. The series begins to choke off rapidly, and by the third adjustment, *A* has reduced his sales to eleven thirty-seconds of the competitive output, which is very nearly one-third.

B proceeds in the opposite direction, adding to his sales. On entering the industry, *B* plans to supply one-fourth of the competitive output. *A*'s adjustment to *B*'s entry necessitates a reaction on *B*'s part. *A*'s first adjustment

TABLE 12-1	*Adjustments*	*1st*	*2nd*	*3rd*	*4th*	*Remaining*	*Total*
	A	1/2 − 1/8	− 1/32	− 1/128 −	⋯	= 1/3
	B	1/4 + 1/16	+ 1/64	+ 1/256 +	⋯	= 1/3

is to reduce his output by one-eighth of the competitive amount, and B sees a greater amount of the market open to him. In addition to the one-fourth of the competitive output already in hand, B can exploit the one-eighth abandoned by A. The possible sales now available to B constitute three-eighths of the competitive output. To maximize profit, B will make one-half of his potential sales, or three-sixteenths of the competitive output. This output is larger than B's entry output by one-sixteenth of the competitive total. Thus, the process of duopolistic adjustments leads B to increase his sales according to the pattern shown in Table 12-1. This, too, is the sum of an infinite series, but the sum of the series is finite and is 1/3.

The conclusion of the Cournot duopoly theorem is that at the final adjustment, each duopolist will sell one-third of the competitive output. Duopolistic industry output is two-thirds of what a competitive industry would supply. It is unnecessary to write out even a part of the series of either firm to determine the industry output. The formula for the equilibrium solution of the industry is

$$\bar{X}_I = \bar{X}_C \left(\frac{2}{2+1} \right)$$

where $\bar{X}_I$ is the equilibrium output for the industry and X_C is the competitive output. Substituting in the formula for the competitive output $\bar{X}_C = 10$

$$X_I = 10 \left(\frac{2}{2+1} \right) = 6\frac{2}{3}$$

Each firm will sell one-half of this amount, or 3 1/3 units of miraculous spring water.

Continuing to utilize Cournot's assumption about the nature of the conjectural variation, the formula may be generalized for any number of firms by substituting n for the number 2. Thus,

$$\bar{X}_I = \bar{X}_C \left(\frac{n}{n+1} \right)$$

The formula shows that duopoly imposes a loss of one-third of the competitive output on the economy, but that as the number of firms increases (as n grows larger), the industry output ever more nearly approaches the competitive output.[6]

Reaction curves. A reaction curve shows how one firm will react to the actions of other firms in an industry characterized by fewness. The event to which any one firm reacts can involve a rival's output, price, product quality, advertising, and so on, or some combination of these.

---

[6] The limit of $(n/n+1)$ is 1.

In Figure 12-6, $R_A R'_A$ is the reaction curve of firm A. The variable here is output. Assuming duopoly, A's sole rival is B, so the horizontal axis measures A's output, and the vertical axis shows B's output. The reaction curve $R_A R'_A$, therefore, shows how A will react to any output decision made by B.

If firm B is excluded from the market, A will produce the monopolistic output of 5 units, equal to one-half the competitive output. Similarly, $R_B R'_B$ shows B's reaction to any output decision of A. For example, suppose A chooses to produce 5 units of X. This establishes point 1 on B's reaction curve. But if B sells the output indicated by point 1, A will move to point 2 on his reaction curve. The move to point 2 by A calls for a move by B to point 3 on $R_B R'_B$, and so on. As the adjustments continue to be made, the firms approach the point of intersection at E.

Point E describes a *consensus* situation. The point lies on both reaction curves. Thus, E is that point at which A will produce $1/3\ X_C$ if B produces $1/3\ X_C$ units, and B will produce $1/3\ X_C$ units of X if A will produce $1/3\ X_C$ units. As there is a coincidence of plans and fulfillments, the duopoly has achieved an equilibrium of output at point E. Until an exogenous factor (such as a change in consumer demand or a change in input prices) alters the conditions under which the equilibrium is maintained, we would expect no further adjustments in the industry.

We have now examined a pioneering effort to solve the oligopoly (duopoly) problem. Despite the extreme unreality of its assumptions, the Cournot

FIGURE 12-6

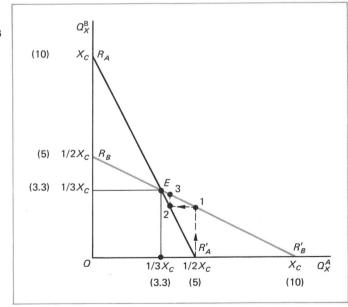

Market Behavior: Basic Oligopolistic Conditions

analysis does depict the nature of strategic moves and provides a solution to a given set of circumstances in a duopolistic situation.

THE BERTRAND SOLUTION

In 1883, Joseph Bertrand, a French economist, criticized Cournot's duopoly model for the obvious problems inherent in assuming a zero conjectural variation with regard to quantity. Thus, this obvious criticism is almost as old as the Cournot model itself. Bertrand did more than object to an important assumption of the Cournot theory; he suggested what he believed to be a superior assumption—namely, that an oligopolistic entrepreneur assumes his rivals will maintain a constant price in the face of his adjustments. Bertrand's so-called improvement, therefore, is to trade a conjectural variation of zero on quantity for the same assumption about price! There seems to be little justification for debating the merits of either assumption; both theories feature remarkably obtuse entrepreneurs. Nevertheless, the Bertrand theory does shed some light on oligopolistic behavior as well as on the problems of oligopoly theory.

The Bertrand theory is much simpler than the Cournot model; it is based on the assumption that each entrepreneur shades price in order to monopolize the entire market. The reaction curves of Figure 12-7 show the pattern of

FIGURE 12-7

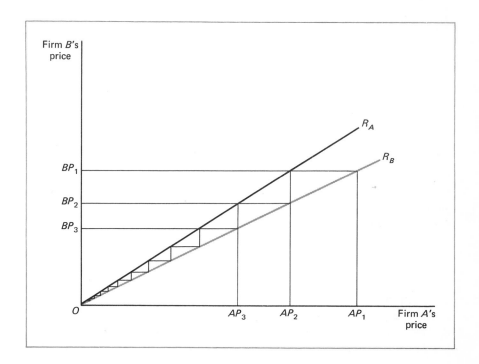

adjustment under the assumptions of the Bertrand model. The prices of firms A and B are measured on the horizontal and vertical axes, respectively. Curves OR_A and OR_B are the reaction curves of firms A and B, respectively. Curve OR_A shows how firm A will react to any price set by B, while curve OR_B shows how firm B will react to any price set by A. Assume that when A has the market to itself, it sets the monopoly price AP_1. Upon entering, firm B, in an attempt to supplant A as the monopolist, sets a lower price than AP_1—namely, BP_1. Firm B sets this price on the scarcely tenable assumption that firm A will not reduce its price below the monopoly level. Of course, firm A does reduce price, to AP_2, all the while thinking that firm B will hold its price constant at the entry level of BP_2. Firm B's unexpected retaliation takes the form of a price reduction to BP_2. The process continues on and on in the pattern shown by the reaction curves. The obvious culmination of the descending stairstep pattern occurs at the origin. At point O, the industry price has been reduced to the competitive level. The zero price depicts a stable equilibrium, for, once reached, either rival would price itself out of the market if it attempted to raise price.

There seems to be no reason why one firm should not price itself out of the market, since the reward for remaining in the market has no tangible *economic* value. But it should be remembered that the model, like that of Cournot, does not consider costs. The addition to the model of positive costs of production would indicate that pricing oneself out of the market would be as irrational in a duopolistic situation as it would be in pure competition.

If the firms have positive costs, their reaction curves will not radiate from the origin but will begin at some positive distance along the proper axis of a graph, as shown in Figure 12-8. Suppose A enters the market charging price AP_0. Then Firm B enters. The arrows show the path of adjustment culminating at point E. In equilibrium, both firms charge a positive price (i.e., greater than zero) since the duopolists are assumed to have positive costs.

It is obvious that Bertrand's analysis offers no advance over Cournot's theory, although it is as valid formally as its predecessor. Both models suffer from the same defect; a serious analysis of oligopoly cannot assume such a severe case of entrepreneurial myopia. Certainly, two economically motivated owners of a valuable resource will not allow themselves to be pushed into a zero-price equilibrium. This would be a determinism more severe than anything found in Karl Marx or the Greek tragedies! At this point, it seems reasonable to contend that long before competition reduced the industry price to the competitive level, some method would be evolved to permit a more agreeable exploitation of the market's possibilities.

THE EDGEWORTH MODIFICATION OF THE BERTRAND MODEL

In 1897, the Irish economist Francis Ysidro Edgeworth suggested a modification of the Bertrand model. The basic situation of the Edgeworth version is that depicted in the Cournot model: two entrepreneurs, A and B, sell water from their respective mineral springs at no cost of production to themselves.

FIGURE 12-8

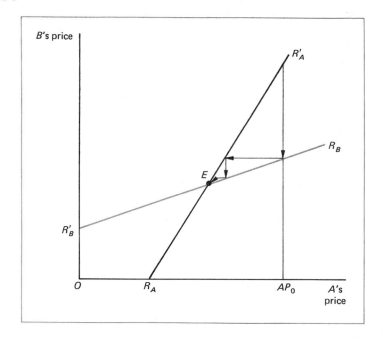

Since each firm faces the same market and produces its output under the same conditions, the demand curves facing each firm are identical and are shown back to back in Figure 12-9. The demand curve of A is in the conventional position; that for B has been reversed. The quantities depicted on the horizontal axis are all positive and increase with the distance from the origin.

FIGURE 12-9

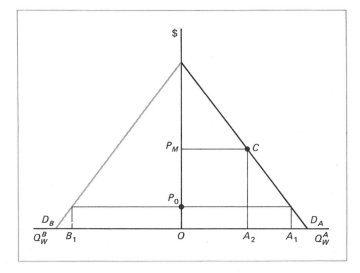

An important assumption of the Edgeworth analysis is that neither firm can supply its entire market for the product. Therefore, the duopoly cannot produce enough water to satisfy the entire market demand. Presumably (Edgeworth was never clear about this), some physical limitation—possibly a maximum rate of flow from the springs—causes the output limitation. In consequence of the naturally limited output, the price of the good must always be positive. This apparently slight change in the assumptions of the original Bertrand model precludes the attainment of a stable equilibrium in which the water would be a free good. In conformity with Edgeworth's assumption, we shall specify that the maximum daily output of A is OA_1 units of water and that the maximum daily production of B is OB_1 units.

Let us suppose that A is the first entrepreneur to enter the market. Since he is currently a monopolist, he charges the profit-maximizing price OP_M and sells OA_2 units of water from his spring (A_2A_1 units are unsold). A's maximized total profit (total revenue) is OA_2CP_M.

When B surveys the market for miraculous water, he sees that potential sales are OB_1 units (his entire output) plus the A_2A_1 units that A is not selling because A is currently a monopolist. With this sales potential awaiting exploitation, B decides to enter the market. In order to gain a foothold, B decides to price his spring water slightly below the monopoly price. Edgeworth assumed that B's conjectural variation is zero in regard to A's pricing policy.

At a price below OP_M, B successfully captures a great part—perhaps all—of the miraculous water market. At any price lower than OP_M, B will gain all of A's present customers and so will sell an amount equal to OA_2 units, plus an additional amount to consumers who are willing to buy some water at a price lower than OP_M. Suppose that B has set his price so that he sells his entire daily output of OB_1 units. (Note that his price can exceed OP_0 because he is undercutting the former monopolist's position.)

Contrary to B's conjectural variation of zero, A will not maintain the monopoly price of OP_M, at which he now sells no water. To regain the market, A slightly undercuts B's present price. A's conjectural variation with regard to B's price is zero. Temporarily, A's move accomplishes his intended purpose as customers desert B for A. If B was selling his capacity output, OB_1, at his entry price, then we may be sure that at A's new price, he is selling his entire output, OA_1. Now, it is B's turn to reassess the situation. The outcome of his reflection is for him to reduce price below the level of A's current price. And so the pattern of move and countermove continues until inevitably the price each firm charges falls to OP_0, at which each firm is able to sell its capacity output; that is, the total daily output of the duopoly is OA_1 (A's output) plus OB_1 (B's output), or B_1A_1 units.

At this point, the Edgeworth model breaks sharply with Cournot's theory, showing that the results of conjectural variations of identical numerical value (here, zero) are not the same when applied to different variables. In the Cournot solution, the pattern of adjustment and readjustment ceases when each firm captures an equal share (one-third) of the market. In the present case, each

firm has an equal market share, but a stable equilibrium will not occur. Why not?

We can rule out the possibility of either further competitive price reductions or price stability. Suppose A is the first entrepreneur to take stock of the situation. He knows there is no point in a further price reduction because he has no more output to sell at a price lower than OP_0. Curiously, despite his blindness about B's affairs, he knows that B is in an identical situation, so he need fear no further competitive price reductions. If A believes that B will not change price from the present level, why should he not raise price—indeed, why not raise it to the monopoly profit-maximizing level of OP_M? A does this, and his sales now decrease by A_2A_1 units, but his profit increases as marginal revenue (negative at OP_0) is brought into equality with marginal cost (zero).[7]

A's move is protected by B's inability to make any further meaningful price reductions. Since B is now at a severe profit disadvantage and A is charging OP_M price, the motive of profit maximization will lead B to raise his price too, but to some amount less than OP_M. The duopoly is now back where it was at the point of B's original entry. Obviously, the duopoly is doomed to repeat the described process without limit.

Evaluation. By now, the perceptive reader probably has noted so many implausible assumptions in the Bertrand-Edgeworth model (among them the conjectural variation of zero and the absolute fixity of supply) that he is ready to dismiss the theory as being wholly without merit. But Edgeworth's work does lead to some insights. Rather than showing the price rigidity supposedly characteristic of oligopoly, the Bertrand-Edgeworth model depicts an oligopolistic industry beset by severe price instability. And, as we noted previously, in connection with the kinked demand curve, Stigler's study indicated that price inflexibility was not the rule in oligopolistic industries. But we need not use the Stigler investigation to support the behavior displayed in the Bertrand-Edgeworth model. Even if oligopolistic firms *do* have inflexible prices, the inflexibility stems from the unwillingness of any single member of the industry *to initiate* a price change. Once the change is initiated, it is characteristic of the other members of the oligopolistic industry to react very quickly and vigorously. One change by one rival firm can set off an uncontrollable and undesirable round of price adjustments that may culminate in the destruction of the entire industry. If we drop the highly implausible assumption of zero conjectural variation, the Bertrand-Edgeworth model, itself, may explain the inflexibility of oligopolistic prices: precisely because oligopolistic industries are highly unstable with regard to price, each member feels strongly constrained not to spoil any existing industry price arrangement.

The entry of a new firm into an oligopolistic industry will surely cause major reactions. In the absence of collusion, it seems likely that price would

---

[7] Note that the customers A has lost are only those unwilling to pay the higher price. A has lost no customers to B since B is already selling as much of his output as he can.

be a major element in the reactions. Although the type of response to an initial price change depicted in the Bertrand-Edgeworth model may be theoretically sound, what about the prediction that changes in price that follow the entry of the second firm will be *perpetual?* Should there not be a stable equilibrium at some point? The answer is that a stable equilibrium may be *imposed* but, according to the model, does not inhere in the nature of the industry. Rather than endure the effects of continual price changes, the members of an oligopoly may resort to some form of collusion to bring an imposed stability on the industry. Some of these stabilizing devices—such as price leadership and cartelization—are discussed later in this chapter.

An argument in support of a model should not go too far. Since a theory is an incomplete rendering of reality, it cannot provide us with a perfectly clear insight into the essence of our observations. But, taken with proper precautions, the Bertrand-Edgeworth model does illuminate the situation in which an oligopolistic firm would make a price change (when its economic situation is severely threatened, as in the case of entry) and indicates why an inherently unstable industry may seek relief in a collusive arrangement.

THE CHAMBERLIN DUOPOLY MODEL

E. H. Chamberlin's remarkably simple solution of the duopoly problem is a logical extension of the Bertrand-Edgeworth model. The Chamberlin solution begins with the same circumstances as those of the original Cournot problem: two duopolists sell water from their respective mineral springs at zero cost of production.

Figure 12-10 shows the demand curve for the industry. The competitive output is OW_C. As long as A is the sole member of the industry, the monopoly price will be OP_M, at which OW_M units of spring water will be sold.

Now suppose entreprenuer B decides to sell the water from his spring. He sees that the portion of the market left open to him is the one-half of total industry output remaining unserved by A and, therefore, that his demand curve is $P_M W_M$. B makes the initial judgment ascribed to him by Cournot: to maximize his profit he should set price at one-half the monopoly price, at which he will sell one-half of the monopoly output (one-fourth of the competitive output). If no adjustments were made upon B's entry, the two firms would be providing three-quarters of the competitive output. This situation is identical with the first stage of the original Cournot analysis. It differs from the Bertrand-Edgeworth model in that B is not attempting to invade the monopolized industry by offering water at a price slightly below OP_M. B takes OP_M as the zero sales price for himself because he views his province as the market for $OW_M = W_M W_C$ units.[8]

If B charges one-half the monopoly price for his spring water, he will cause severe repercussions in the industry. A must take action. In the Cournot

---

[8] Note that B's demand curve could be represented as the segment MD of the industry demand curve as well as by $P_M W_M$.

FIGURE 12-10

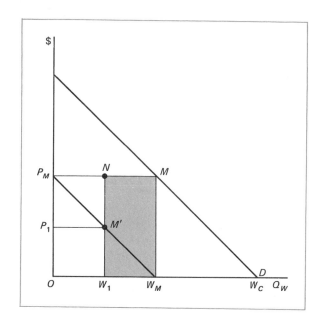

solution, it is at this point that *A* adjusts his price, assuming that *B* will continue to charge one-half the monopoly price. In the Chamberlin model, the involved session of readjustment that culminates with each firm selling one-third of the competitive output never begins. The reason is that Chamberlin abandons the assumption of a conjectural variation of zero with regard to price. *B* knows that his entry will upset the industry. When all the members of an oligopolistic market know that any move on the part of one of them will cause an appropriate response by all the others, what would be the sensible thing to do? Collusion is one possible answer, but if all firms are of equal size and face similar market and cost conditions, as the duopolists in this example, collusion is unnecessary. With or without collusion, the result will be the same. Each firm must accept the other's presence in the industry. The intelligent thing for them to do is to split the market between them. *B* therefore holds its output constant at the contemplated level, $1/2 \ (OW_M)$, and *A* reduces his output to the level of *B*. Between the two of them, they supply the previous monopoly output OW_M. Since, they now produce the monopoly output together, they should charge the monopoly price. Although the industry is duopolized, the two firms are operating in unison, so they charge the full monopoly price OP_M. Industry profit is the same as the previous monopoly profit, namely $OW_M M P_M$. This amount is split evenly between the members of the duopolized industry and is equal to the shaded rectangle. *A*'s profit is reduced by 50 percent from the monopoly amount, while *B*'s profit is increased by 100 percent over that contemplated at entry.[9]

[9] To make sure that you understand the Chamberlin analysis, you might try to analyze the adjustments that would occur upon entry of a third firm.

Let us make some observations about this solution. We see that, given the initial monopoly, consumers have not been harmed. There is no change in either output or price, and there is no greater amount of economic profit to be imposed as an implicit tax on consumers. On the other hand, the equilibrium solution is less satisfactory to consumers than that shown in the Cournot version, in which output is greater and price lower. Here, there is no benefit to consumers at all in the conversion of the industry from monopoly to duopoly. There are no benefits of competition. Further, A's position is worsened; the former monopolist's profit has been cut in half. The sole beneficiary of B's entry is entrepreneur B himself. Unless it can be shown that B's gain exceeds A's loss, there seems to be no economic value to B's entry. This is a matter we will consider in Chapter 16.

The Chamberlin solution is commendable on at least two points. First, the conclusion of the model is consistent with much reported oligopolistic behavior and with some other theoretical models of oligopoly. Second, each duopolist of this model appears to make a much more realistic assessment of his rival's probable reaction than is the case in the three preceding models.

Even if the model can be criticized for its extreme simplicity, its conclusion is compatible with the actual market-sharing practices of oligopolistic firms. It shows that the consumer is not necessarily intentionally victimized by the illegal collusive acts of oligopolistic industrialists. Here, the oligopolists have acted as if they were in a formal cartel (illegal in the United States except under certain specified conditions), yet without any collusion, a collusive result is obtained—namely, the firms have set price at the monopoly level to yield a maximized *joint* profit, which they split evenly. Should the demand for their product increase, both firms will set a new and higher price. This may appear to the public to be a collusive act, but it is not. The two firms are acting quite independently to maintain orderly market conditions. The Sherman Antitrust Act and similar antimonopoly legislation do not apply here. Moreover, in cases such as this, it is wise to undertake a thorough economic analysis before commencing legal action. Otherwise, an antitrust action would waste time, legal talent, and taxpayers' money since collusion could not be proved. Even the threat of legal action could lead to an uneconomic result. The firms, fearful of impending action, might begin a pattern of behavior that would bring about considerable market instability, leading, if not to the demise of one of the firms, certainly to higher costs of production; so the result of an action supposedly taken in the public interest would be less output at higher prices. One of the most important lessons of the Chamberlin model is, then, that things are sometimes not what common sense would lead one to believe they are.

With the Chamberlin model, the history of oligopoly has made a notable advance. At the outset of this chapter, we noted that an essential element of an industry characterized by the state of fewness is interdependence. In all three duopoly models, the fact of interdependence is clear, but in the first two models, it never becomes clear to the members of the industry. The interdependence is unperceived. Chamberlin eliminates this peculiar economic

myopia from his model. The equilibrium solution occurs precisely because the duopolists recognize their interdependence. Thus, the Chamberlin theory is our first encounter with a model incorporating *perceived* interdependence into its structure. However, for all its admirable qualities, the Chamberlin model shows the oligopolistic industry as strangely quiescent. We will now explore a somewhat more complicated model that will make clearer the ramifications of perceived interdependence.

COLLUSIVE OLIGOPOLY: THE CARTEL

The cartel is probably the most famous form of collusive business organization. A true cartel is an association of business firms based on a written agreement or contract. Where cartels are illegal, the contract exists only in verbal form and is called a "gentlemen's agreement." The main purpose of a cartel is to increase its members' profits. It usually accomplishes this by eliminating the costs of oligopolistic uncertainty, banning price and trade wars, erecting barriers to competition, discouraging or eliminating competition by nonmembers, assigning marketing quotas and areas, setting standard prices, pooling patents, and enforcing certain standards of conduct among its members.

Cartels are a typically European form of industrial organization. Not only have they been tolerated and encouraged by a number of European countries, they have been promoted by various governments. One reason for this is that cartels are well suited to the pursuit of mercantilistic (i.e., state-building) goals. No wonder, then, that the two most notable sponsors of cartelization in modern times were Nazi Germany and Facist Italy.

Cartels are not in conformity with the American business ethos, a fact made clear in the Sherman Antitrust Act and other legislation. Despite the prohibitions in this long-standing legislation, American firms have, at times, participated in cartels. Usually such participation is short lived for two basic reasons. First, it is illegal, so participating firms and their executives are liable to prosecution. Second, cartels appear to be antithetical to the competitive spirit of American business, so firms are likely to break their gentlemen's agreements, sacrificing the interest of the illegal group to the welfare of a particular business firm.

Such cartels or cartellike organizations as do exist in the United States are the creatures of government. The NRA of the 1930's was the most extreme instance of cartelization in this country.[10] The present has its own examples of government-business cartelization. The most common are fostered by so-called fair-trade laws, which allow manufacturers to set and maintain *retail* prices. Other examples include the production controls and import quotas

---

[10] National Recovery Administration. The two famous symbols of this organization were the Blue Eagle and the motto "We do our part," a rather obscure, but succinct, expression of the place of an economic unit in the corporate state.

permitted domestic petroleum firms.[11]   Under the aegis of government, many ordinary businesses and professions exhibit numerous characteristics of cartels.   They are usually allowed—even encouraged—to engage in this noncompetitive behavior (generally to the detriment of their customers) in the name of "business ethics."

THE ECONOMIC ANALYSIS OF CARTELS

If a hitherto unorganized industry is formed into a cartel, the resulting arrangement is, effectively, a monopoly. The cartel than follows typical monopolistic pricing and output procedure. When the agreement is signed, the industry demand curve becomes the cartel demand curve. As an organic entity, the cartel has its own marginal revenue curve. If one of the goals of the cartel is the maximization of cartel profit, the selection of the proper price can be accomplished if cartel marginal cost is known. The marginal cost to the cartel is simply the horizontal summation of the marginal ᴗosts of the member firms. Accordingly, in Figure 12-11, the curve ΣMC is simply the horizontal summation of the marginal cost curves of the constituent firms. Using the curve ΣMC as the marginal cost curve for the cartel, the cartel's managers follow the $MC = MR$ rule to determine the monopoly price, $O\bar{P}$. At price $O\bar{P}$, the now cartelized industry produces a total output of $O\bar{X}$ units. The number of units each member firm produces and the allocation of the cartel's economic profits among member firms are determined in accordance with the cartel document.

FIGURE 12-11

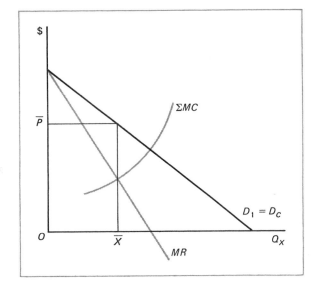

---

[11] These laws help to maintain the price of petroleum products at an artifically high level by restricting both the production of domestic crude oil and the importation of foreign oil.

A CARTEL FROM A MEMBER'S VIEWPOINT

Let us see what it is like to be a member of a cartel. In Figure 12-12, the curve AR_1 is the firm's average revenue curve before cartelization. The firm, although possessing some monopoly power, is making only a normal profit, selling quantity OX_0 at price OP_0. Attracted to the cartel in the hope of improving its profit situation, the firm finds its anticipations realized when the price is raised, in accordance with the cartel document, to $O\bar{P}$.

The firm, no longer having the option to vary its price, perceives its demand curve as the perfectly elastic $AR_2 = MR_2$. Allowed to pursue its profit-maximizing inclinations, the firm would elect to produce output OX_1. Obviously, the cartel would expire soon after its birth if the member firms were allowed to equate their new marginal revenue schedule with marginal cost. To raise price, the cartel must restrict total output, and this means that each member firm, on the average, must restrict its own output. If each member firm were allowed to maximize its own *independent* profit, there would be an increase in industry supply, and, as a result, the higher cartel price and the cartel itself would be impossible to sustain.

To maintain the cartel, it is essential that each member firm accept an output quota. Suppose the firm depicted in Figure 12-12 has been assigned a

FIGURE 12-12

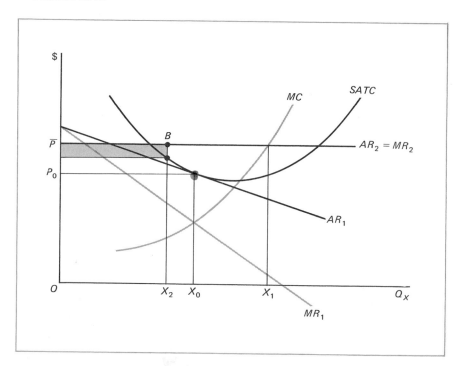

quota of OX_2 units. At the imposed price of $O\bar{P}$, the firm realizes an economic profit equal to the area of the shaded rectangle. Since the firm now has a positive nonmaximized economic profit whereas before its maximized economic profit was zero, its membership in the cartel has proved to be worthwhile.

Even if all firms experience an improvement following their affiliation with the cartel, they may not all be content with the arrangement. All of them will be acutely aware of the inequality of marginal cost and marginal revenue, and all will be strongly tempted to try to increase their profits.

One way for a firm to realize a profit greater than that offered by the cartel is not to join the organization in the first place! Of course, this works only if all or nearly all the other firms in the industry do join. Suppose the firm of Figure 12-12 had managed to remain outside the cartel while the rest of the firms join together. If the subject firm were small in relation to the total market, it could raise its price from OP_0 to $O\bar{P}$ and produce the profit-maximizing output OX_1.

Our analysis shows one of several reasons why cartels are difficult to organize and maintain. Each firm has an incentive to remain outside the cartel or, if in, to get out. From the point of view of an individual firm, especially if it is small in relation to the market, the optimal situation is for every firm in the industry *except itself* to be in the cartel. The outside firm then gets a "free ride." It can charge the higher cartel price and also produce the profit-maximizing output. Thus, to attract and hold members, a cartel must be able to exercise some kind of persuasive force—which perhaps explains why the most successful cartels tend to be those with government sponsorship.

If a firm is large in relation to the market, it may be unable to dispose of an output greater than its quota without affecting the market price of the good. For example, if the firm depicted in Figure 12-12 accounts for a large percentage of the cartel output, it may be unable to sell a quantity much over its quota of OX_2 units without depressing the price below $O\bar{P}$. Therefore its demand curve, as long as it remains in the cartel, may consist of segment $\bar{P}B$ of $AR_2 = MR_2$ and become negatively sloped to the right of point B. Taking advantage of this situation, the firm may offer secret price concessions to a number of its customers in an effort to increase its profit beyond the amount allowed by the cartel document. If a number of firms are attempting to do the same thing, and it seems reasonable to suppose that they would, the cartel will fall apart. Therefore, unless there is either government or social coercion, cartels are not likely to last very long. Since both pressures are absent in the United States, cartels have been an ephemeral form of business organization in this country.

OUTPUT QUOTA ASSIGNMENTS WITHIN CARTELS

Figure 12-13 (c) depicts the profit-maximizing solution for a cartel. Charts (a) and (b) show two member firms within the cartel. The two firms differ in

their productive efficiencies. For any given output, marginal cost is higher for the firm shown in chart (a). If the cartel wishes to minimize the cost of producing output $O\bar{X}$, it should equalize the marginal costs of production in all member firms. It can accomplish this goal if its managers assign the inefficient firm of chart (a) the quota OX_I and the efficient firm of chart (b), the quota OX_E. Once the marginal costs of all firms have been brought into equality with cartel marginal cost (ΣMC) and, therefore, into equality with each other, no other distribution of output among the members can yield lower costs to the cartel.

The reward accruing to the individual member firms from such an arrangement is that each firm is assured of making at least as much profit as it would outside the cartel and, in all likelihood, a greater profit.

There are two reasons for the better profit situation. First, the formation of the cartel permits the imposition of a presumably higher (monopoly) price. Second, once the cartel is operative and the new price is in effect, production can be allocated among the member firms on a rational basis. The efficient firms can now be assigned outputs greater than those they produced as independent firms, and the high-cost producers will have smaller quotas imposed on them than those they produced as independent units. As the marginal costs of the inefficient firms are reduced and those of the efficient firms are increased until the marginal costs of all firms are equal, the total costs of the cartel will fall, thus increasing total profit. A larger pool of profits means that after redistribution each firm may be made better off than it would be if it were operating independently. There is always the danger, of course, that the most efficient firms will feel severely put upon and be faced with a temptation to desert. To reduce possible disloyalty, the cartel agreement may provide for somewhat better treatment of the efficient members.

FIGURE 12-13

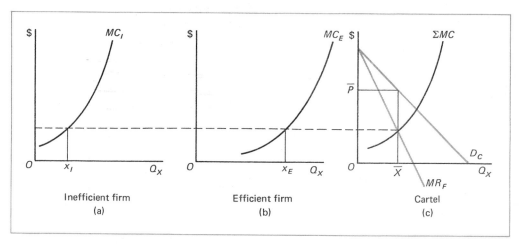

Inefficient firm
(a)

Efficient firm
(b)

Cartel
(c)

MERGERS

The preceding reasoning can also be applied to mergers. Instead of forming a cartel, a number of independent firms may merge to form a single corporation. After the merger, the new firm can act as a cartel does to reallocate output among the formerly independent units. In the United States, the difference between merger and cartel may be one of legality versus criminality. Mergers are legal unless the government can show that they tend to restrain trade, a fact that must be proved in court. Why mergers are routinely allowed and cartels generally prohibited probably rests on the philosophy and psychology of Americans. The Anglo-American common law always has been hostile to conspiracies, and perhaps the agreement of the cartel, as opposed to the transfer of ownership involved in the merger, seems to be the difference between a dark conspiracy and an ordinary business transaction.

PRICE LEADERSHIP

Almost anyone who glances at the financial press has seen the following sequence of events. First, a firm—typically a prominent member of an oligopolistic industry—announces a price change; then, over the next few days, the remaining members of the oligopoly bring their price schedules into conformity with the list announced by the first firm. Such behavior is so common that if it did not occur, most financial observers would be flabbergasted. This behavior pattern is generally called *price leadership.*

Price leadership is a noncollusive alternative to oligopolistic uncertainty. If there is no collusion (better, if collusion cannot be proved), there is no legal impediment to any firm within an industry changing its prices to match those of any rival.

The price leader of an industry is the firm that initiates a price change.[12] In noncollusive oligopoly, the leader is selected informally. Very often the dominant firm in the industry assumes the leadership role simply as a consequence of its economic power. If an oligopoly includes a firm such as General Motors or U. S. Steel, the effect of any price change made by so strong a firm is

---

[12] That firm need not be the largest firm in the industry. In 1958, a new wage contract substantially increased costs throughout the steel industry. It was widely expected that U. S. Steel, the assumed dominant firm, would announce a price increase that would be followed immediately by the remaining firms in the industry. Instead, U. S. Steel announced no price changes, and the industry took no action until about one month later, when Armco Steel, a relatively small firm, announced a schedule of higher prices. The industry then immediately followed this unanticipated price leader.

Actually, this case conforms closely to the results predicted in economic theory. Oligopolistic prices *will* change if there are industrywide reasons for changing them. Economic theory holds that some way of raising price will be found if the costs of all firms are increased. The present illustration shows that in the case of the dominant firm's inaction, some other firm will act spontaneously as the price leader, and prices will change.

bound to be a persuasive argument for a similar change by the smaller oligopolists.

DOMINANT FIRM LEADERSHIP

Figure 12-14 shows price leadership by the dominant firm. The dominant firm merely follows the $MC = MR$ rule, maximizing its profit, and allows the other firms to do the best they can with the price it imposes. Curve D_I is the oligopolistic industry demand curve. It shows industry sales for any given price. For example, if the price were $O\bar{P}$, the total sales for the oligopoly would be $O\bar{X}_I$. The curve ΣMC is the horizontal summation of the marginal cost curves of all firms in the industry other than the dominant firm itself. Since price is a parameter to all the follower firms, curve ΣMC may be regarded as the aggregate follower supply curve. If, for example, the price is $O\bar{P}$, the follower firms will supply the quantity $O\bar{X}_F$. Since the total quantity supplied by the industry at this price is $O\bar{X}_I$, the dominant firm must be supplying $O\bar{X}_I - O\bar{X}_F = O\bar{X}_D$ units. This shows how the demand curve of the dominant firm is derived. Suppose the dominant firm sets the price at OP_1. By this action, it would price itself out of the market, since the follower firms' output of P_1N would constitute the entire industry production. Accordingly, point P_1 on the price axis must be the vertical intercept of the dominant firm's demand curve. Suppose the dominant firm sets the price at $O\bar{P}_2$. Industry demand would be P_2K units. The follower firms would supply P_2H units. The remaining amount of the industry demand, HK units, would constitute the demand for the dominant firm's output. Subtracting the follower's output, P_2H, from industry demand, P_2K, leaves P_2J units; therefore, point J must lie on the dominant firm's demand curve. We have already determined that point L lies on the dominant firm's demand curve. The linear industry demand and ΣMC curves allow us to postu-

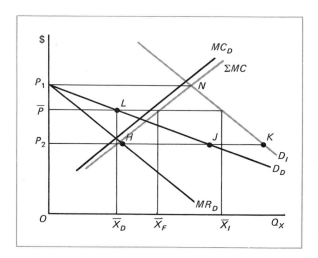

FIGURE 12-14

late that the dominant firm's demand curve is a straight line passing through points P_1, L, and J. Curve MR_D is the marginal revenue curve proper to the dominant firm's demand curve. Given MC_D, the dominant firm's marginal cost curve, the firm maximizes profit at price $O\bar{P}$, at which it sells $O\bar{X}_D$ units. The follower firms, accepting $O\bar{P}$ as an imposed price, together produce $O\bar{X}_F$ units. The combined outputs of the dominant and the follower firms are identical with the industry output ($O\bar{X}_D + O\bar{X}_F = O\bar{X}_I$).

EFFICIENT FIRM LEADERSHIP

Sometimes a price leader emerges without being the dominant firm and without formal recognition. Assume that Figure 12-15 depicts a situation of homogeneous duopoly. Both firms produce identical products, such as aluminum ingots or sheet steel. The curve D_I depicts industry demand. For simplicity, we will assume that the curve D_F is the demand curve of either firm. The marginal cost curves, MC_H and MC_L, show that the firms vary in efficiency. Left to itself, the high-cost producer (represented by the curve MC_H) would prefer the price OP_H, since at this price, it would maximize profit. At OP_H price,

FIGURE 12-15

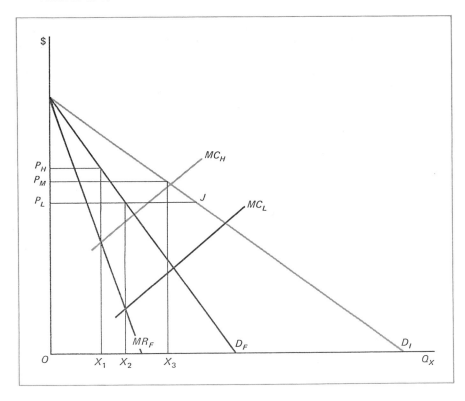

Market Behavior: Basic Oligopolistic Conditions

its output would be OX_1. Clearly, the low-cost producer, with the marginal cost curve MC_L, will not choose this price; for at OP_H, its marginal revenue exceeds the marginal cost of production. The efficient firm will push for an expansion of output to OX_2, which can be sold at price OP_L. The low-cost firm has the advantage. In the case of homogeneous oligopoly the inefficient producer has no way of convincing his customers that his product is worth the differential $P_L P_H$. The inefficient producer must bow to the firm with the lower cost curves and accept a situation in which its marginal cost exceeds its marginal revenue.

The stage is now set for further action. The high-cost firm probably will not acquiesce to this type of leadership. Much of what happens depends on the location of the high-cost firm's average total cost curve. Suppose the minimum point of the curve lies above the line $P_L J$. In this case, the inefficient firm would incur an economic loss and would be forced to exit from the industry. Such an action would convert the duopoly into a monopoly. In the glory days of the trusts, the low-cost firm likely would have ardently desired this outcome. Today, owing to antitrust legislation and a changed public attitude, the efficient producer may prefer to make less than a maximum profit in order to avoid becoming a monopolist and thereby run the risk of antitrust prosecution and the hostility of the public.

Surprisingly, the survival of an efficient oligopolist may depend on the survival of rival firms. The necessity of ensuring the viability of competitors thus modifies the goal of profit maximization. The low-cost producer may be able to make an above-normal profit, but the necessity of allowing his rivals the chance at least to break even may preclude the low-cost price leader firm from maximizing its profit. In such a case, the low-cost firm depicted in Figure 12-15 would have to permit price to rise sufficiently above OP_L to allow the inefficient producer at least a normal profit.

Maintaining competition may be costly to the economy. The full benefits of low-cost operation are unrealized. But what would happen if the inefficient producer were allowed to expire? The industry demand curve, D_I, would become the demand curve of the surviving firm. Since the previously defined firm demand curve, D_F, lies midway between the vertical axis and D_I, it becomes the marginal revenue curve of the new monopoly firm. To maximize profit, the surviving firm would charge the monopoly price OP_M and produce the output OX_3. The solution, however, may be no less economic than the attempt to preserve the oligopolistic nature of the industry. Price OP_M is lower than what the high-cost firm would impose as price leader, and OX_3 is greater than $2(OX_1)$. Moreover, OP_M may be no higher—perhaps lower—than the support price the low-cost firm would have to allow in order to maintain the inefficient firm.

The principal simplification in this model has been the assumption of equal market shares. Probably, the lower cost firm will eventually acquire a larger market share. It can use its greater profit to innovate and expand. Nevertheless, the problem pointed out in this illustration remains: if the industry is to be unmonopolized, it may be necessary for the more efficient firm

to subsidize the higher-cost firms by setting price above its own profit-maximizing level.

SUMMARY

Oligopoly is the state of fewness in an industry. Firms are few in number when any one firm must anticipate the response of other firms to its actions. The necessity of anticipation forces oligopolistic firms to make strategic decisions—that is, decisions made in the light of what rivals will do.

Uncertainty and interdependence are the facts of life in an oligopolistic industry. Although a firm must consider what its rivals may do, it never knows what they will do. These conditions force so many different patterns of conduct on an oligopolistic industry that thus far it has been impossible to develop a general theory of oligopoly. At present, the body of theory consists of a large number of separate models designed to illuminate particular facets of oligopolistic behavior.

Some observers of the oligopoly scene believe that they perceive price rigidity as an important characteristic of this type of market structure. The so-called kinked demand curve is a theoretical explanation of the inflexibility of a given price. Other observers see no greater price rigidity in oligopoly than in any other market structure. Accordingly, they dismiss the kinked demand curve model as an explanation of a non-event.

Oligopoly theory is one of the oldest areas of microeconomics. Over the years, a number of landmark models have been developed that, if they do nothing else, show the extreme difficulty of constructing even a limited model of oligopoly.

The earliest of the great historical models, that of Cournot, assumed that oligopolists (in this model, duopolists) believe that a rival firm will not change output in regard to the action of any competitor—that is, they have a conjectural variation of zero with regard to the quantity offered on the market. In the final stable equilibrium, each duopolist has an equal share of the market, and together the duopolists produce two-thirds of the output of a competitive industry.

The Bertrand model replaces the peculiar assumption of the Cournot model with the equally peculiar assumption that the duopolists have a conjectural variation of zero in regard to price. The Edgeworth modification of the Bertrand model adheres to this conjectural variation, but, by adding the assumption that the duopolistic industry cannot supply the total market demand, depicts a situation of never-ending price changes. Although seemingly at variance with empirical evidence of oligopolistic price rigidity, the Bertrand-Edgeworth model may, in fact, suggest an explanation of that very rigidity. If rigidity does exist in oligopolistic industries, it may be *imposed* by the firms to avoid the extreme instability pictured in the model.

The Chamberlin model takes up where the Edgeworth-Bertrand model

leaves off and assumes that the duopolists do come to an agreement (formal or informal) and split the maket so as to yield a maximized joint (monopoly) profit in a stable equilibrium situation. The Chamberlin model, although extremely simple, is a major advance over the preceding oligopoly models, for, in place of the short-sighted entrepreneurs of earlier theory, it features enterprisers who clearly perceive their interdependence and determine to do something about it.

To escape from the costs of uncertainty, oligopolists may collude. One of the best-known methods of collusion is the cartel. A cartel is a written agreement to share the market, assign output quotas, fix prices, and apportion profits. Unless businessmen are temperamentally well disposed toward life in a cartel, the agreement is likely to be violated so frequently that eventually the cartel will fail.

In the United States, cartels are unpopular with business and are illegal as well, so a more usual way of escaping uncertainty is the use of price leadership. Price leadership may or may not be collusive. (Collusive leadership is illegal in the United States.) The price leader of a particular industry is often the dominant firm, although leadership may be given to the most efficient firm. Price leadership usually results in most of the *firms* in the industry realizing less than maximum profits, but, the *industry's* nonmaximized profits under leadership are likely to be greater than maximized profits without leadership.

Despite the many uncertainties of oligopoly theory, then, it does reveal the reasons for, and the methods to avoid, that prevailing uncertainty which is the bane of an oligopolistic firm's existence.

The Theory of Market Behavior Under Oligopolistic Conditions, II: Further Topics in Oligopoly Theory

ALTERNATIVES TO PROFIT MAXIMIZATION MODELS

Imperfectly competitive firms *need not* maximize their profits if doing so would preclude the attainment of a higher ranked goal. In previous sections, we have mentioned other ends to which profit-maximization may be subordinated, such as industrywide stability or the survival of competitors. Among other possible goals that may modify the profit-maximization motive are power maximization, maximum salary and perquisites for executives, satisfactory or stable (as opposed to maximum) profits,[1] employee welfare, public service, innovation, avoidance of public scrutiny, sales maximization, and the like. The business firm that attempts to fulfill any of these motives does not wholly dispense with profit-making as a goal. Despite ardent argument by some that profit-making is not, or should not be, a goal of business firms, the ethos of our present

[1] John M. Blair, *Economic Concentration: Structure, Behavior and Public Policy* (New York, Harcourt Brace Jovanovich, 1972), argues that many major corporations set prices and output levels so as to achieve the same return year after year, rather than the maximum return possible in any given year.

system, not to mention its economic realities, maintains profit-making as a highly important goal for privately owned enterprises. At the least, profit gives firms a measure of staying power.

Most firms probably seek a maximum profit *subject* to the attainment of other ends. In other words, regardless of their principal motivation, they maximize profit subject to the constraints imposed in fulfilling some other target, the joint end being only partially fulfilled. This situation is demonstrated in the following model

THE BAUMOL REVENUE MAXIMIZATION HYPOTHESIS

William J. Baumol has developed a model of a firm that seeks to maximize the value of its total sales rather than the amount of its total profit.[2]

In Figure 13-1, the curves depict the total revenue, total cost, and total profit functions for an oligopolistic firm. To maximize profit, the firm must produce output OX_p. If the firm desires to maximize total revenue, it must increase its output to OX_m units. This output would permit the firm the non-maximized profit $O\pi_1$.

Suppose the firm desires to maximize total revenue subject to some *satisfactory* level of profit. For example, if the firm is satisfied with a profit equal to $O\pi_2$, it must restrict output to OX_2 units, thereby reducing total revenue to X_2R_2 but increasing its profit over what it would be at the revenue-maximizing level. If $O\pi_2$ is not a sufficiently high profit level, but $O\pi_3$ is acceptable, the firm must restrict total revenue to X_3R_3 and output to OX_3 units.

The graph shows that the profit $O\pi_2$ can be achieved at either of the output levels OX_0 or OX_2. The Baumol hypothesis asserts that the firm will attain the desired profit level by producing that output which yields the greatest total revenue. Therefore, the firm will produce output OX_2. This outcome follows from the assumption that the firm is sales oriented—subject, of course, to the condition that it achieves an acceptable level of profit.

The total revenue maximization model is a hypothesis about the motivation of large business firms. Small firms often do not make large enough profits to allow them any goal other than maximized profits. They may well incur losses unless every effort is made to produce a profit. Even if smaller business firms are in a position to choose among multiple goals, the power of their owners may be sufficient to subordinate the interests of other members of the enterprise—sales staff, engineers, and so on—to the owners' interest in a maximized profit. In the modern large corporation, however, the power of the owners—the stockholders—is a small deterrent to the goals of the professional managerial class, which now firmly controls the great oligopolistic enterprises. Total revenue is a widely appreciated, if not fully understood, measure of business performance. In many instances, companies are ranked

---

[2] William J. Baumol, *Business Behavior, Value and Growth,* revised edition (New York: Harcourt Brace Jovanovich, 1967), pp. 43–55.

by the size of their total sales. They may be ranked by other criteria, too, but profit has so many definitions in business literature (although not in economic theory) and the value of a firm's assets has often so little to do with performance (e.g., the railroads) that sales figures may be the most persuasive evidence of the relative status of business firms. Frequently the compensation of business executives is tied directly to sales, while bonuses seldom fluctuate with changes in asset value. Since their corporations, and hence their own effectiveness, are likely to be rated on the basis of sales, and since their personal incomes are often tied to sales performance, the managers of corporations have a power-ful incentive to adopt sales revenue as their chief goal.

Many large corporations—automobile and television manufacturers are examples—sell to the public through networks of semi-independent dealers. To a great extent the success of such corporations depends on the loyalty and morale of their dealer organizations. Large and growing sales and the oppor-tunity to make large sales are an important factor in maintaining dealer satis-faction. Suppose, for example, that a manufacturer is operating at an output greater than OX_p in Figure 13-1. Let us assume that the firm undergoes a change of objective and decides to maximize profit. To do so, it must cut sales back to OX_p. How would such news be accepted by rivals, dealers, the sales staff, stockholders, customers, and the general public? Probably, they would not understand it. Many people, even if they are reasonably knowledgeable,

FIGURE 13-1

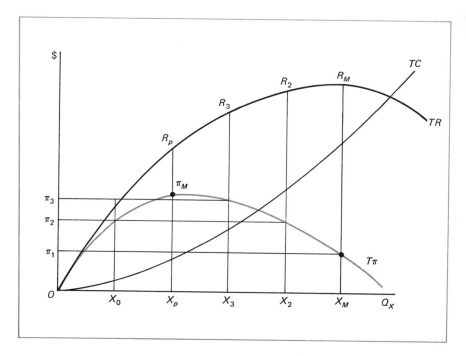

will refuse to concede that a cut in sales can promote a greater profit. Even if it is understood as a pro-profit move, many people will not like it and may respond in a way harmful to the corporation.

However, regardless of the strength of sales-oriented persons in the firm, the necessity of realizing a profit does impose a constraint on the desire to maximize sales revenue. Stockholders, despite their present state of docility, could rise to "throw the rascals out" if dividends remained below some critical amount. Also, dividends must be kept at a certain level if the firm is to retain access to the financial capital markets.

Baumol's model holds that once a profit level has been determined that will allow management an area of free choice—a level that will satisfy the non-managerial power groups associated with the firm—the firm's managers will choose to make total revenue as large as possible.

Since the Baumol model first appeared in 1959, it has been subjected to considerable empirical testing, both formal and informal. The evidence is generally favorable to the hypothesis. This should not be surprising since, to an ever increasing extent, the scions of the founding families who once dominated the major corporations have been replaced by the M.B.A. alumni of graduate schools of business. These people tend to form a professional managerial class. Thus, the goals of many important business firms reflect the goals of this class, and since the members of this class are, in fact, employees, their goals may be closer to those of labor than they are to those of ownership.[3]

A UTILITY MODEL OF BUSINESS BEHAVIOR

Using the ordinal utility theory of Chapter 3, we can analyze the behavior of a two-goal firm employing a model developed by Martin Shubik.[4] This model is interesting in that it combines two business goals considered in this chapter —profit maximization and achievement of a desired share of the market. In addition, the Shubik model shows that techniques associated primarily with consumer behavior can be applied in the theory of the firm.

In Figure 13-2, the I curves are the indifference curves of the firm's chief manager(s) showing the marginal rate of substitution of profit and market share. The curve $AMEB$ depicts the actual opportunities open to the firm in the trade-off between profit and market share. The curve shows that the firm does not have the option of becoming a pure monopolist—that is, the point where the market share is 100 percent lies beyond $AMEB$. It also shows that the firm must achieve a market share at least equal to OS_1 percent before any positive

[3] Besides showing how the goal of a firm may be constrained sales revenue maximization, the Baumol model shows how marginal analysis may be applied to various maximands other than profit maximization. Recently a number of managerial models of the firm have appeared in which alternatives to profit maximization are considered. Among these other maximands are efficiency of resource utilization, the viability of the firm, freedom from managerial work and worry, maximization of the firm's growth rate, and the maximization of managerial perquisites.

[4] Martin Shubik, "Objective Functions and Models of Corporate Organization," *Quarterly Journal of Economics,* LXXV (August 1961), p. 367.

FIGURE 13-2

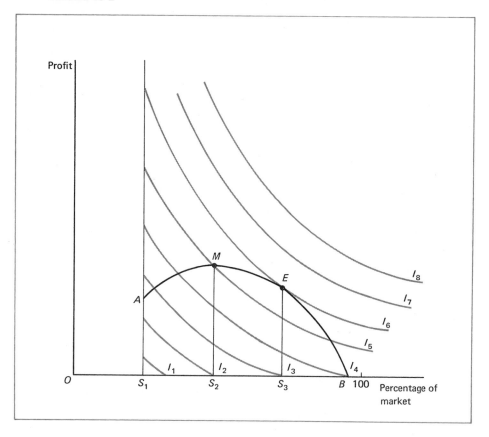

profit is possible. If the firm wishes to maximize profit it must confine itself to OS_2 percent of the market. This decision would place it (its managers) on in-difference curve I_5. But a higher indifference curve is attainable if the firm will increase its share of the market to OS_3 percent. At point E, profit is not maxi-mized, but the reduction in net income is compensated by the addition of S_2S_3 percent to the firm's share of the market. At point M, the marginal rate of substitution of market shares for profit exceeds the rate at which the objective market situation allows the firm to make the substitution. Therefore, the firm should, in its own interests, continue to sacrifice profit to a greater market share until the objective possibility is equal to the subjective rate. This is accom-plished at point E.

It is important to note that multiple goals call for compromises, not the complete abandonment of one or more of the goals. Profit maximization may still be a desired goal, but for some reason, the firm depicted by the diagram regards a greater share of the market as more important than maximizing profit —at least for the present. Its goals may change. Perhaps profit maximization

is a long-run goal, while increased market share is not. Curve *AMEB* is drawn to reflect the presence of rivals in the market; its shape may change if the added percentage, S_2S_3, eventually results in their demise. The managers themselves may change, and with new managers may come new goals.

Suppose we now apply indifference curve analysis to the usual assumption of profit maximization. What would the indifference curves of the profit-maximizing firm look like? They must reflect the firm's uncompromising insistence on maximizing profit as opposed to all other alternatives. For such a firm, the marginal rate of substitution of all other goals for profit would be zero, and the indifference curves of such a firm would be parallel to the horizontal axis. This situation would lead to an optimal solution (from the point of view of the firm) involving tangency between point *M* on the opportunity curve and an indifference curve.

CONSIDERATION OF "REALISTIC" PRICING PRACTICES —MARKUP PRICING

A common, and one hopes by now discredited, viewpoint is that economic models do not confirm to the behavior of business firms and their executives. Like Molière's *bourgeois gentilhomme,* who was astounded to find that he had been speaking in prose all his life, a profit-maximizing entrepreneur need not know economics and calculus in order to equate marginal revenue to marginal cost.

Supposedly, many merchants price their goods by some rule of thumb. As a common practice, they determine the retail price of their inventory by adding some suitable percentage—say, 20 or 25 percent—of the wholesale price to the cost of the goods they want to sell. Economic theorists are frequently challenged to show how this "realistic" observation can be reconciled with the $MC = MR$ rule. There are several possible answers. One is that the markup pricing practices of certain retailers may not conform to the $MC = MR$ rule; the firm may have objectives other than the maximization of profit—one of which, perhaps, is to use a simple pricing procedure! Alternatively, it is possible that the entrepreneur is so inept that he has no idea how to price to obtain a maximum profit even though he desires such a result. The whimsies of entrepreneurs do not disprove the theories of economists; they merely challenge the latter's ingenuity.

We are entitled to be skeptical about assertions that smaller firms, in particular, do not aim for maximized profits. The exigencies of business life are such that firms seeking other goals, and particularly those which do not know how to maximize profit, are likely to be short-lived. This observation re-reflects no discredit on the practice of markup pricing; on the contrary, the use of markups can be completely consistent with the $MC = MR$ rule.

For the profit-maximizing entrepreneur, the markup is not an immutable figure. Different product lines often have different markups, and the same

product line has different markups at different times of the year. Christmas cards have a markup on December 27 rather different from the one they bore one month earlier. Changing markups reflect the attempt of the seller to improve his profit situation.

How does a profit-maximizing retailer employ markup pricing? First of all, the goods he buys for resale are likely to have a constant wholesale price per unit. Since the wholesale cost of goods sold is by far the most important component of total retailing costs, a large part of the marginal cost is constant. To the cost of goods sold the retailer must add a markup sufficient to cover salaries, advertising, store overhead, and his profit. Many of these costs are constant over a wide range, since store maintenance and salary expenses can be regarded as fixed costs. The markup is simply the difference between the cost of goods sold and the amount the entrepreneur wishes to realize on sales. If we wish to relate this markup to the $MC = MR$ rule, we must show how the *size* of that markup is determined.

The profit-maximizing, markup-using entrepreneur generally determines the proper markup from experience. Whether he is conscious of it or not, experience provides him with evidence of the shape and position of his demand curve. More particularly, it gives him an idea of the *elasticity* of the demand for his goods. For example, sellers of toys, clothing, and travel are keenly aware of changes in the elasticity of demand for their goods and services at different periods of the year. The fact that they change their markups (selling prices) at various times is eloquent evidence of their basic desire to maximize profit and their ability to do so, given some knowledge of the price elasticity of demand. The closer sellers can come to the exact value of the coefficient of price elasticity, the more nearly will they be able to maximize their profits.

From previous experience (see Chapter 10), we know that

$$MR = P\left(1 - \frac{1}{\epsilon}\right)$$

and that for profit maximization

$$MC = P\left(1 - \frac{1}{\epsilon}\right) = MR$$

from which it follows that the profit maximizing price is

$$P = MC\left(\frac{\epsilon}{\epsilon - 1}\right)$$

In retailing, particularly in the case of smaller stores, long-run average costs are likely to be fairly constant over a wide range of output (see Chapter 7); that is, in situations of constant returns to size, $LATC = LMC$. Thus, as an

approximation, we may substitute long-run average cost for marginal cost and write

$$P = LATC\left(\frac{\epsilon}{\epsilon - 1}\right)$$

Assume that at the profit maximizing price, $\epsilon = 6$, then

$$P = LATC\left(\frac{6}{6 - 1}\right) = LATC\left(\frac{6}{5}\right)$$

Since the cost (the wholesale price) of the good is 100 percent, or 5/5 of itself, we may write

$$P = LATC\left(\frac{5}{5}\right) + LATC\left(\frac{1}{5}\right)$$

$$P = LATC + \frac{1}{5}(LATC)$$

Thus, to maximize profit on the sale of a good for which the selling price is equal to its wholesale price plus a markup of 20 percent, the retailer must be able to determine the elasticity of demand for the good at the proposed price.

Rule-of-thumb markup pricing will maximize profit only in the happenstance event that the selling price of the good and, hence, the markup percentage are appropriate to the elasticity of demand for the good at the contemplated price. Suppose that the wholesale price of the good is $10. If the retailer uses a rule-of-thumb markup of 20 percent, the selling price of $12 will maximize profit only if at $P = \$12$, $\epsilon = 6$. Suppose that the elasticity of demand for the good changes to 5; a 20 percent rule-of-thumb markup will no longer maximize profit. What markup should the profit-maximizing entrepreneur now employ? From the formula, we see that

$$P = LATC\left(\frac{5}{5 - 1}\right) = LATC\left(\frac{5}{4}\right) = LATC\left(\frac{4}{4}\right) + LATC\left(\frac{1}{4}\right)$$

The entrepreneur should increase his markup to 25 percent. Under the new market conditions, the good that has a wholesale price of $10 should be priced to retail customers at $12.50

Markup pricing *can* be consistent with profit maximization *if* the seller alters his markup to conform to changes in the elasticity of demand. Observations of merchants who practice markup pricing will tend to indicate that markups are often influenced by the elasticities of demand of the goods in question. Goods having many substitutes and many alternative sellers (groceries, soft drinks, magazines, and so on) typically have low markups. Since consumers have a wide range of products and sellers from which to choose, the price elasticity of demand for the highly substitutable items is high. Our

markup pricing formula indicates the profit-maximizing markup must be low. At the other extreme, goods for which buyers believe there are few substitutes and which have few outlets (high fashion items, prestige automobiles, handmade rugs, and so on) will have high markups reflecting a low price elasticity of demand. When the profit-maximizing businessman prices with markups, he is, in effect, estimating the elasticity of demand. He may not know the numerical value of the coefficient of price elasticity, and, indeed, he may not know of the term *elasticity,* but he does know that to attain the profit he desires, he must estimate the sensitivity of his customers to his price changes, and that is, of course, what the elasticity of demand is all about.[5]

THE STACKELBERG OLIGOPOLY MODEL

In 1934, the German economist Heinrich von Stackelberg published his theoretical analysis of oligopoly, in which the oligopolists clearly perceive the interdependence that exists among them.[6]

ISO-PROFIT CURVES

The graphical analysis of the Stackelberg model utilizes the iso-profit contours shown in Figure 13-3. Prices charged by firms A and B are measured on the horizontal and vertical axes, respectively. The iso-profit contours are those of A. At any point on a given contour, A makes the same profit. Thus, on A_1, A's profit is the same at points g, d, e, and f. Therefore, given the profit A_1, A is indifferent to charging AP_1, AP_2, or AP_3. The iso-profit contour is, thus, a type of indifference curve. The farther these curves lie from the A-price axis, the higher is the profit. Therefore, given the price AP_2, A would prefer to be at h on A_2 rather than at e on A_1.

What determines the iso-profit contour on which A operates? Since the firms are interdependent, whatever firm B does will have a great deal to do with A's conduct, and vice versa. The iso-profit curves of Figure 13-3 show how A can react to B's pricing decisions. Suppose for the moment that B is the price leader of the duopoly; he sets the price, and A reacts to it. Say B sets the price at BP_1. A line parallel to the horizontal axis extended from BP_1 intersects the iso-profit curve A_1 at points d and f. This shows that given the price B sets for itself, A will realize the profit represented by A_1 if it charges either of the two prices denoted by points d and f. Point e shows the same profit, but not for

[5] As a practical test of the sophistication of some ordinary markup pricers, you might note how the price of gasoline changes a day or so before a three-day holiday weekend.

[6] *Marktform und Gleichgewicht* (Berlin: Verlag Von Julius Springer, 1934). This highly original work has not yet been translated into English. However, Stackelberg's ideas have been made available in Alan Peacock's English translation of Stackelberg's *Grundlagen der Theoretischen Volkswirtschaftslehre,* the English rendering of which is *The Theory of the Market Economy* (Fairlawn, N.J.: Oxford University Press, 1952), and also in William Fellner's *Competition Among the Few* (New York: Knopf, 1949).

FIGURE 13-3

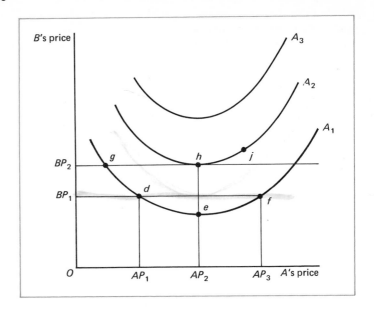

the price BP_1. B would have to set a lower price for e to become a feasible point. What will A do in the light of B's choice of price BP_1? Will he choose the price associated with point d or the higher, but equally profitable, price associated with point f? The answer is that he will choose neither price. Like all indifference curves, the iso-profit curves are everywhere dense, and, therefore, there is an iso-profit curve higher than A_1, but lower than A_2, that will indicate the highest profit A can make given B's price. It's lowest point will be tangent to the horizontal line extending from BP_1.

For any given price that B may set, there will be a unique profit-maximizing price for A. It will be established at the lowest point on the highest attainable iso-profit curve. For example, assume that B sets his price at BP_2 and that A commences his reaction from the initial point g on A_1. As A moves along the horizontal line projecting from BP_2, he will strike successively higher iso-profit curves until he reaches point h on A_2, the lowest point on the highest attainable iso-profit curve. A point such as j would yield an equal profit to A but would become a possible point only if B were to set some price higher than BP_2.

The iso-profit curves can be used to show the rivalrous behavior of oligopolistic firms when output is the variable. In Figure 13-4, A's iso-profit curves are drawn to show how any change in B's output will be reflected by a change in A's output. When output is the relevant variable, the iso-profit curves are *concave* with respect to the proper axis, and the curves *nearer* the axis represent higher profit levels. Thus, curve A_3 denotes a profit greater than curve A_2, which, in turn, represents a profit greater than that depicted by A_1.

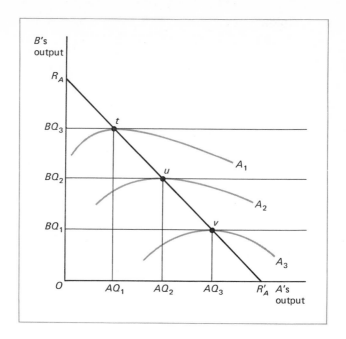

FIGURE 13-4

For the moment, assume that B is the output leader. Suppose B chooses to produce BQ_3. The highest profit A can make, given B's output decision, is that denoted by A_1, and he can make that profit *only* if he decides to produce AQ_1. Accordingly, A will operate at point t on A_1. Suppose B *reduces* his output to BQ_2. A can now make a greater profit by *increasing* his output, since in a duopoly, the goods are substitutes for each other, and B having abandoned part of the market, leaves it open for A's exploitation. Given B's choice, the highest profit A can attain is A_2. This is possible only if he moves from t to u, expanding his output to AQ_2 units. Similarly, should B decide to restrict his output to BQ_1 units, A will respond by moving from u to v, producing AQ_3 units.

A smooth curve drawn through points t, u, and v shows the path of A's reactions to B's various output moves. Therefore, the line $R_A R'_A$ is A's *reaction curve.* It is the locus of all points of profit maxima associated with those outputs A will produce in response to any given output decision made by B.

PRICE–LEADERSHIP, FOLLOWERSHIP MODELS

Using Figure 13-5, we will analyze the interactions between oligopolistic (strictly, duopolistic) firms. Both firms are depicted as manipulating price to gain a particular profit position. An advantage of the Stackelberg analysis is that the variable need not be price. The axes could be relabeled to show output as the variable. It is possible also to show one firm manipulating price and the other adjusting quantity. Curve $R_A R'_A$ is firm A's reaction curve, and curve $R_B R'_B$ is the reaction curve appropriate to firm B.

FIGURE 13-5

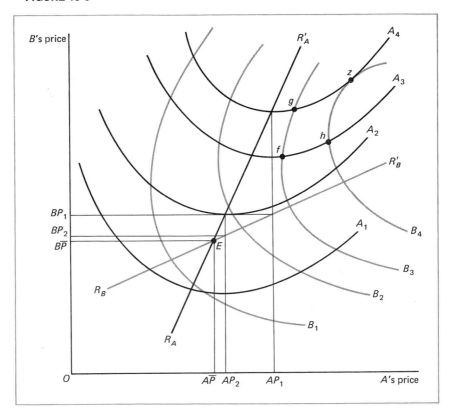

Unperceived interdependence. We start with a situation in which the oligopolists are unaware of their interdependence. We shall assume that A, as the first entrant, has set the monopoly price AP_1, yielding the profit A_4. When B enters the market, his reaction curve shows that he will set price at BP_1. This action will cause A to reconsider and to reduce his price to AP_2. In an attempt to remain in the market, B reduces price to BP_2. Move and countermove continue until both firms arrive at point E—the intersection of the reaction curves. Their prices are now $A\bar{P}$ and $B\bar{P}$ for A and B, respectively. These prices represent the attainment of a stable equilibrium. There is no motivation for either firm to change the prices denoted by point E. Here, the Stackelberg analysis has depicted the Bertrand solution of the preceding chapter, but price has not been competed down to zero owing to the existence of positive costs. The solution at E is the expected outcome, as long as member firms never perceive the interdependence that is the hallmark of oligopoly.

Perceived interdependence. The Stackelberg analysis is an advance over the Cournot and Bertrand (and Bertrand-Edgeworth) cases. Let us as-

Market Behavior: Further Oligopolistic Conditions

sume that having arrived at point E, the entrepreneurs do recognize their interdependence. They will conclude that if they cooperate, they can escape the tyranny of their reaction curves and become better off. For example, they could decide to proceed to point f at which both firms would make higher profits. From point f, they could proceed to g, at which B's position would remain unchanged and A would be made better off. If they were to proceed from point f to point h, the situation would be reversed; A's profit would remain unchanged while that of B would increase. A superior solution would seem to be that at point z. By proceeding from f to z, *both* firms are made better off, instead of limiting the effect of the change to the improvement in the profit situation of only one firm. Points f, g, and h are unstable points; for at any of them, at least one firm can press the case that an improvement in its position would do no one in the industry any harm.

An argument for operating at a point such as z is reminiscent of a customary practice in European oligopolized industries. Many of the large firms in Europe are oligopolies, and they have developed under a somewhat different business ethos than that which prevails in the United States. As long as the interest of any one firm is not severely compromised, European businessmen are likely to accede to a request by a rival that he be permitted to improve his position. Such would be the case if the firms depicted in Figure 13-5 were at, say, point g; A would not be likely to stand in the way of B's suggestion that both of them change their prices so that the industry could move to point z. American firms, with their more intensely competitive spirit, might be unwilling to grant anything to a rival, even if the concession were a costless one.

Now can we say any more about point z? No further changes can be made without a fight. It is impossible to move from point z without one firm having to suffer for the other's gain; therefore, point z must represent a type of equilibrium. Once attained, no firm will be willing to allow its rivals to move from it. Thus, point z must lie on a *contact curve*. It is a point that may be reached by mutual consent, but one that can never be left if (unanimous) free consent is required for its abandonment.

Figure 13-6 focuses on a pattern of points forming a contract curve. As with indifference curves, the contract curve is the locus of points of tangency between the iso-profit curves of the rival duopolists. From any point off the contract curve, it is always possible to reach *one* point on that curve representing a new set of prices that will improve the profit position of at least one firm without harming the profits of any of the other firms. This new contract curve point must either lie on, or be bordered by, the initial iso-profit contours of the respective firms. For example, suppose the firms are initially at point s, firm A making the profit indicated by A_2 and firm B realizing the profit indicated by B_2. The profit position of *at least one* of the firms will be improved if the industry moves to any point on CC' lying on or between the segment defined by the iso-profit curves A_2 and B_2. *Both* firms will be better off if an agreement can be struck that will place them at point s', for then both firms would be on higher iso-profit curves. As to the desirability of a particular point within the defined segment of CC', A would prefer a point as near to t as possible, while

FIGURE 13-6

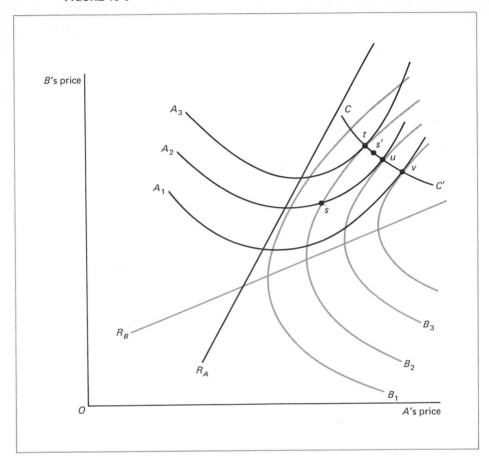

B would prefer a point as near to *u* as possible. If the firms were to move from *s* to *v*, *B*'s position would improve, but *A* would suffer. Even so, this does not violate our observation that from a position off the contract curve, it is always possible to move to *one* point on the curve at which at least one firm is benefited, no other firms being harmed. If mutual consent is required for a movement to the contract curve, a move from *s* to *v* is ruled out since *A* would never agree to it.

Once one of the points lying between *t* and *u*, and including *t* and *u*, has been selected, the unanimity principle precludes further price changes. Here is another argument for price stability in oligopoly. If the maintenance of orderly conditions is an objective of the members of the oligopoly, the firms will be unwilling to leave a point on the contract curve once it has been attained. To leave a contract curve point would indicate that at least one firm is able to

Market Behavior: Further Oligopolistic Conditions

coerce the others. If the firms are of approximately equal size, coercion is impossible unless a group of firms organizes an alliance against the others. Under antitrust laws, such an alliance may be neither legal nor possible. In such a case, firms of unequal size may live amicably together.[7]

In an oligopolistic situation, why would price changes occur? The answer is that given previously in connection with the kinked demand curve. Something must happen to alter the position of the contract curve, making the attained point no longer satisfactory to the firms. The contract curve would shift in response to changes in the positions of the iso-profit curves. These curves, in turn, would be shifted by changes in demand or cost conditions or both. Again, we see that oligopolistic prices *can* change but that such changes are not likely to be initiated by an individual firm *if* the particular industry is one that values serenity. This is probably all that oligopolistic price rigidity means.

Once a contract curve is abandoned, there may be considerable maneuvering before a position is attained on the new contract curve. For example, suppose that point s was on the former contract curve. Subsequently, a shift in the iso-profit curves moved the contract curve to CC'. It seems likely that a battery of strategic techniques will be employed as each firm strives to obtain the most advantageous position on the curve. Firm A would prefer a position as near to t as possible, and firm B would like to get as close to point u as it can. The techniques open to the firm are threats, bluffing, advertising, sophisticated negotiation, the use of economic power, and so forth. Although one firm might attempt to press a moment of industry disequilibrium to its advantage and move to a point lying outside the segment defined by points t and u, we are assuming here that the desire to preserve a spirit of amity within the industry requires that, at the least, the position of no firm is worsened. Assuming this, we can then assume that the new price arrangements will be denoted by a point lying on CC' between points t and u, the precise location of which will be determined by bargaining or strategic moves between the member firms.

Perceived interdependence—price leadership. Suppose the industry pricing arrangements tend to be unstable to the detriment of the member firms. Perhaps the firms are uncooperative or highly rivalrous. The resulting uncertainty could be costly to the firms or simply make life somewhat more difficult than managements would like. In either case, the firms may decide, either through collusion or tacit agreement, that some measure of discipline should be brought to the industry—even if that discipline reduces the likelihood of any firm making a maximized economic profit. Price leadership is one technique the industry could employ. One firm becomes the price leader; the other firms simply follow. The price leader may be selected formally (illegal in the United States); or the price leadership of the industry may fall to a firm through

---

[7] Plentiful examples of this situation can be found, among them steel, automobile, and soap firms.

the tacit agreement of member firms. No vote is ever taken; no document is ever signed. What emerges is that one firm is always the first to announce its own price changes, which are duplicated soon after by the other firms in the industry. Since there is no overt action and no conspiracy involved, this type of price leadership is legal in the United States. In the case of a tacit agreement, the position of price leader usually falls to the firm with the greatest economic power.[8]

A requirement of successful price leadership is that the member firms *accept* the decisions of the leader firm. If they do not, dissolution of the arrangement and possible demoralization of the sellers can result. The necessity for acceptance stems from the fact of oligopolistic interdependence. Even though one firm is the leader, its actions must be conditioned by what the other firms will accept. The followers will follow the leader, but what the leader will do is contingent upon what the followers will let him do. Interdependence is a condition for oligopolists regardless of interindustry arrangements.

Firm *A* as price leader. The willingness to accept price leadership is shown by the reaction curves of the member firms of Figure 13-7. The reaction curves provide the evidence of acceptability. When *A* chooses a particular price to yield a certain profit, that price and the profit must be consistent with *B*'s acceptance. Suppose, for example, that when the price leadership arrangement is initiated, *A* sets his price at AP_0. Whatever profit that price will yield is contingent upon *B*'s reaction. Price AP_0 is associated with point *f'* on iso-profit curve A_2. However, only curve A_1 has any significance, for *B*'s reaction curve passes through point *f*, the point directly above AP_0 on A_1. Owing to the limitations that *B*'s reaction imposes on *A*, the highest profit *A* can make setting price at AP_0 is A_1. For any price selected by the leader, the profitability to the leader of that price depends, then, on *B*'s reaction—that is, his acceptance of *A*'s action.

Once the price leadership arrangement has been established, experimentation, market research, or consultation among the rivals will lead *A* to expect that he can increase his price to make a higher profit. For example, he can proceed to point *g* on *B*'s reaction curve, raising his profit to A_2. *A*'s price now becomes AP_1, and *B* raises his price to BP_1 and joins *A* in making a higher profit.

Profit A_2 is not the best that *A* can do. *B*'s reaction curve shows that it is possible for *A* to set still higher prices and improve his profit position. The greatest profit that *A*'s rival(s) will permit him to make is A_3. By raising price to $A\bar{P}$, *A* will move along $R_B R_B'$, to point *t* at which *B*'s reaction curve is tangent to the iso-profit curve A_3. *B* will respond by raising price to $B\bar{P}$ and will increase his profit. The profit denoted by curve A_3 is the highest level of profit *A* can attain as price leader. Presumably, he would prefer to be at point *u* on A_4, but the reaction of his rival(s) precludes the attainment of that point and limits *A* to the profit A_3.

---

[8] The steel and automobile industries are leading examples of this last solution.

FIGURE 13-7

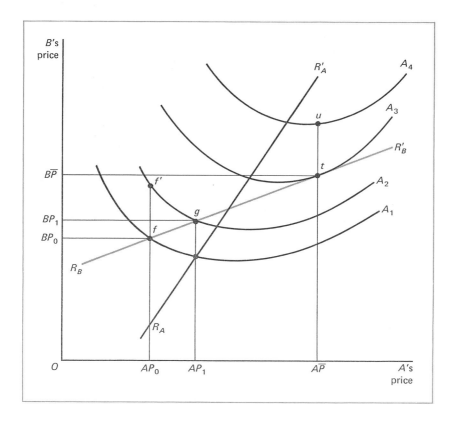

That A's rivals will allow him to set prices higher than $A\bar{P}$ is shown by the reaction curve $R_B R_B'$. If he does so, however, his profit level will recede from A_3. Thus, the profit level A_3 is A's maximum, consistent with the constraints imposed on him by the reaction of his follower(s). This solution to the case of price leadership is stable. As long as the members of the industry are willing to respond to A's leadership, the maintenance of discipline and order in the oligopoly is assured.

Firm B as the price leader. Figure 13-8 shows the iso-profit curves of both firms and depicts the solution when B is the leader. Now B will attempt to find the price that will allow him the highest profit consistent with the reaction of the follower(s). If B sets his price at $B\bar{P}$, A, following his reaction curve $R_A R_A'$, will move to point T, the point at which B_5 is tangent to A's reaction curve. A's response will be to set his price at $A\bar{P}$. Constrained by A's response, B can realize no greater profit than B_5.

Again, we have a stable equilibrium. *Who* is the leader does not matter as long as the members of the oligopoly are willing to accept leadership.

FIGURE 13-8

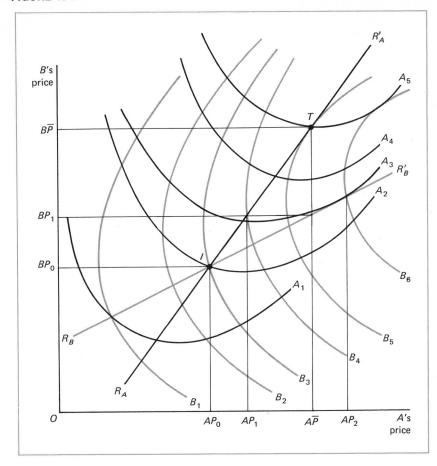

Every firm a follower. Suppose no firm in the oligopoly desires to be a leader but each is willing to be a follower. The result must be the same as unperceived interdependence; that is, the solution is the same as in the Bertrand case. For example, suppose B, as the first firm in the market, sets his initial price at $B\bar{P}$ as shown in Figure 13-8. A will respond with price $A\bar{P}$. B, not wishing to be a price leader, but preferring to follow another firm (here, A) will not maintain price $B\bar{P}$ but will lower his price to BP_1. This readjustment leaves A in the role of price leader, a position he refuses to accept. A, therefore, responds with price AP_1. B, in turn, is then cast in the role of price leader, which he, too, refuses to accept. To avoid the unwanted mantle of price leader, B must reduce his price in an attempt to follow A's lead. The process must culminate at point I, the point of intersection of the reaction curves of both firms. When point I is attained, firms A and B will charge prices AP_0 and BP_0, respec-

tively. Since this is the Bertrand solution (Cournot solution if the variable here had been quantity), the attainment of point *I* represents a stable equilibrium solution.

Every firm a price leader. Suppose that no firm in the industry is satisfied with being a follower; each insists on being a price leader. Will the outcome be chaotic or stable? Analysis will show that the outcome approaches the case of the intra-industry agreement and cooperation discussed in connection with Figures 13-5 and 13-6.

Assume that *A* is the first firm to attempt price leadership. In Figure 13-9, it is shown as setting its price at $A\bar{P}$, since this price maximizes its profit contingent on *B*'s expected response of price *BP'*. Firm *B*, however, refuses to accept *A*'s leadership. Attempting to act as the oligopoly price leader, firm *B* sets price at $B\bar{P}$. If *A* were to follow *B*'s expectation, *A* would respond with price *AP'*. The price $B\bar{P}$ *would* maximize *B*'s profit, *if* *A* were willing to follow *B*'s lead. However, *A* is no more willing to play follower than was *B*. Accordingly, neither firm responds as its rival predicted it would. The reaction curves have not been followed. They are not meaningless, however, because they were instrumental in determining the opening prices set by each firm.

What is the result of the actions of these obstinate firms? Firm *A* maintains its opening price of $A\bar{P}$, but cannot be at the expected point *k*, since *B* did not respond with price *BP'*. Firm *B* has established price $B\bar{P}$ but cannot be at point *j*, since *A* refuses to budge from $A\bar{P}$. Given the stubborn determination of each firm to play the role of price leader, the members of the duopoly have brought themselves to point *I*.

FIGURE 13-9

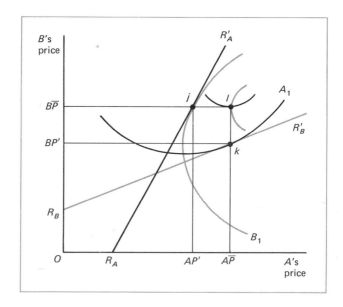

What are the properties of point I as a possible solution? It must be more attractive to both firms than the initial solution either of them had in mind, for I lies on higher iso-profit curves for each firm. Point I lies within an area bounded by iso-profit curves A_1 and B_1; therefore, it is preferable to the solutions originally contemplated by the firms.

Point I may or may not be a point of stable equilibrium. If it lies on the contract curve (a point of tangency between the iso-profit curves of the rival firms) it will represent a stable solution. If it does not lie on the contract curve (that is, if it lies on a point of *intersection* between the respective iso-profit curves of the respective firms rather than a point of tangency), further attempts at price leadership on the part of both firms or some type of agreement (formal or informal) can be expected to bring the firms to a contract curve solution. The important conclusion of this analysis is that contested price leadership works toward a stable equilibrium solution. The market does not become chaotic because the efforts of each firm to become the price leader advance the interests of every firm within the oligopoly.

SOME CONCLUSIONS FROM STACKELBERG

Unless stabilizing arrangements can be negotiated and maintained, oligopolistic industries appear to tend, under certain conditions, to unstable equilibrium solutions. This is a unique conclusion. Much of neoclassical economics suggests, at the least, the attainment of stable equilibria in most cases, if not the attainment of an optimal solution for at least one party. Whether an equilibrium or an optimum or both are attained, few models in orthodox microeconomic theory suggest demoralization. Marxian economic theory, of course, predicts that the free market economy (in Marx's lexicon "capitalism") will collapse because of its inherent instability. But Stackelberg was no Marxist. He believed that state intervention would be necessary to save *privately* owned firms from becoming the victims of their own intrinsic characteristics. Considering the time and conditions under which Stackelberg worked, it is not surprising to find that the precise form of government intervention he recommended was that provided by the corporate state (e.g., Fascist Italy).

Whatever the reasons for Stackelberg's policy conclusions, however, his belief in the necessity of the intrusion of a totalitarian state into the affairs of the market economy seems rather strained. A number of other solutions can mitigate or preclude conditions approaching industrial anarchy. Two obvious methods for promoting order are implicit in the Stackelberg model itself— namely, price leadership and collusion. As noted before, noncollusive price leadership is both possible and legal in the United States; in fact, it is quite common. In Europe, cartels and cartellike organizations—often with government encouragement—serve to maintain orderly market conditions, particularly with regard to output quotas and marketing areas. For the very short period before the National Industrial Recovery Act was declared unconstitu-

Market Behavior: Further Oligopolistic Conditions

tional, this country fostered intra-industry cooperation to promote stable conditions.[9]

The most significant criticism of Stackelberg's policy judgments (as distinct from his economic theories) is that he presupposed instability to be an undesirable situation. Actually, it may be healthy for an economy for its firms to be kept alert through the necessity of anticipating the actions of their rivals. Moreover, price and quantity decisions are obviously not the only variables firms can use in their competitive battles with one another. Realizing that price warfare may injure all firms in the industry, oligopolists usually choose to compete on bases other than price and market quotas. Typically, their competitive behavior features product innovation and modification. Whether such competitive activity is beneficial or not to consumers is an argument with partisans on both sides. It is not within the purview of a book on economic theory to debate this question, but one may observe that American oligopolistic firms, along with those of Europe and Japan, do not display any marked tendencies, in the moderately long run at least, to destroy their own industries.

THE THEORY OF GAMES

Table 13-1 summarizes some of the results of the preceding section in which price was the relevant variable. These four outcomes are also summarized below.

1. *A Leader–B Follower.* When an agreement provides that A shall be the leader and B shall be the follower, the outcome is that A's profit is maximized subject to B's willingness to follow A's lead. In the table, this outcome is written $\pi_A^* = f(R_B)$.

2. *B Leader–A Follower.* Under this arrangement, B's profit is maximized subject to A's willingness to accept B's leadership. The table shows this outcome as $\pi_B^* = f(R_A)$.

3. *Contested Price Leadership.* When A attempts to lead in the belief that B will follow, but B does not and vice versa, the outcome is the attainment of a contract curve position.

4. *Unanimous Followership.* When all firms try to be price followers, the outcome is the Bertrand solution.

TABLE 13-1

	B Leader	B Follower
A Leader	Contract curve	$\pi_A^* = f(R_B)$
A Follower	$\pi_B^* = f(R_A)$	Bertrand

[9] The main purposes of the NIRA were to help end the Great Depression and to promote employment. The advocates of the act apparently believed that cooperation among firms within various industries would serve these purposes.

THE IDEA OF A GAME

Although Table 13-1 is merely a convenient summary of some of the conclusions of the Stackelberg oligopoly theory, it reveals the gamelike nature of oligopolistic, or rivalrous, competition. Rivalrous competition, in which each firm must anticipate what any rival will do in reaction to his own actions, is remarkably similar to the state of mind of players in any game involving strategy, such as chess, checkers, or poker. In these games, each player must calculate the response of his opponents to any move he may make. For example, if A and B could collude, they might decide jointly on a course that would allow each of them to make the greatest possible profit contingent on the continued presence of each in the market. In such a case, they would probably proceed deliberately to the contract curve solution. In the absence of collusion, each firm must take its chances. If A enters the market, he must try to anticipate B's reaction. A may attempt to be a price follower. If he tries this, B can respond by assuming leadership or try also to be a follower.

Some preliminary definitions. We may regard the courses open to any firm as *strategies*. A strategy is one firm's plan of action adopted in the light of its belief about the reactions of its rivals. Thus, the left column in Table 13-1 shows A's two possible strategies: either assume price leadership or try to be a price follower. The row at the top of the table shows B's alternative strategies.

The *game* itself is defined by the table or *matrix* shown in Table 13-1. The game here is an aspect of the Stackelberg theory in which price is the relevant variable. The *players* in the game may be thought of as the firms (or their managers) comprising the oligopolistic industry. The players make their *moves* when they actually decide on the strategy to be employed. Thus, when A decides to be a follower, that is his move. The *play* of a firm consists of a detailed description of the firm's activities in carrying out its move. Thus, if A and B were to decide to move to a contract curve, their play would be a description of how they have made their decision to collude, how they propose to carry it out, and so forth. The *outcome*, or *payoff*, of the game is the result of the players' moves. In the Stackelberg game of Table 13-1, if A's move is to be leader and B's response is to be a follower, the outcome is that A's profit will be maximized consistent with B's willingness to respond to A's leadership.

In the late 1920's, the French mathematician Emil Borel wrote a series of articles to show how games, war, and economic behavior were similar activities in that they all involve the necessity of making strategic decisions. Borel's work eventually gained the attention of a number of economists and mathematicians who believed that if a full-fledged theory of games could be developed, it might provide a much better understanding of oligopolistic behavior than that offered by orthodox economic theory. In later developments, game theory was advanced by the work of a number of scholars; the most significant

achievement was the publication in 1944 of John von Neumann and Oskar Morgenstern's monumental *Theory of Games and Economic Behavior.*[10]

A TWO–PERSON, CONSTANT–SUM GAME

Oligopolistic firms have many strategies available to them, including product line variation, model variation within product lines, pricing, service, advertising, output quotas, store location, warranty policies, community relations. These are only a few possibilities, of course, and no firm has to choose one strategy to the exclusion of all others. But we can imagine firm R deciding to introduce a new product, with the response of rival firm C being to intensify the advertising of its existing products.

Table 13-2 is a hypothetical game matrix for a duopoly consisting of firms C and R, which are competing for market shares. Firm C's strategies are arranged in *columns* and are labeled C_1, C_2, C_3, and C_4. The strategies of firm R are arranged in *rows* and are denoted R_1, R_2, and R_3. The payoffs, or outcomes, are stated in terms of R's percentage of the market. For example, if R were to pursue strategy R_1 and C were to respond with strategy C_1, the payoff to R would be 99 percent of the market; C would, of course, receive a 1 percent share of the market as his payoff.

The type of game depicted here is formally referred to as a two-person, constant- (zero-) sum, strictly adversary, strictly determined game. It is a *two-*

TABLE 13-2

C's Strategies

		C_1	C_2	C_3	C_4	Row Minimum
	R_1	99	2	50	40	2
R's Strategies	R_2	60	75	55	90	55
	R_3	30	35	33	10	10
Column Maximum		99	75	55	90	55

◯ = row minimum   △ = column maximum

▢ = minimax (maximin)

[10] John von Neumann and Oskar Morgenstern, *Theory of Games and Economic Behavior* (Princeton, N.J.: Princeton University Press, 1953). Originally published in 1944. Other landmarks in this area of economic theory are: R. Duncan Luce and Howard Raiffa, *Games and Decisions* (New York: Wiley, 1954); Martin Shubik, *Strategy and Market Structure* (New York: Wiley, 1959); and, especially for the interested, but nontechnical, reader, J. D. Williams, *The Compleat Strategyst* (New York: McGraw-Hill, 1954).

person game because only two players (firms *R* and *C*) are involved, which simplifies the construction of the matrix. It is a *constant-sum* game because the sum of the shares of the two players is always constant. Here, the game is for market shares; the constant sum is 100 percent, since if *R* has 30 percent of the market, *C* must have 70 percent. (Games of this type are usually called *zero*-sum games. This game may be considered a constant-sum game in which the particular constant sum is zero since the algebraic sum of what one firm gains and the other loses is always zero; for example, if *C* *adds* 30 percent to his share, *R* must necessarily *lose* 30 percent.) The game is *strictly adversary* because in the simple game depicted here, each firm employs a *pure*—that is, unmixed—strategy. This means, for example, that if firm *R* chooses strategy R_2 (which represents, say, the introduction of a new model), firm *C* responds with strategy C_4 (which we shall assume to be an increase in its advertising budget). In more complicated games, firms may employ mixtures of various strategies. Finally, the game is *strictly determined* because there is, as we shall find, a unique stable equilibrium solution.

Assuming that firm *R* has available to it the strategies shown in the rows of Table 13-2 and firm *C* can counter with the strategies represented in the columns of the same table, what should firm *R* do? If *R* could be sure that *C* would respond with C_1, R_1 would be the optimal strategy for *R* since it would get 99 percent of the market for itself. Strategy R_1, given *C*'s response of C_1, yields the largest payoff in the matrix from *R*'s standpoint, and the worst from *C*'s viewpoint, so *R* can be virtually certain that *C* will never respond to R_1 with C_1. Will *C* respond with C_2, C_3, or C_4? For safety's sake *R* has to assume that *C*'s response will be C_2, which would leave *R* with only 2 percent of the market. By assuming the worst possible response, *R* predicts the outcome for his use of the strategies in row 1 will be the minimum payoff—that is, a 2 percent share of the market. We indicate that 2 is the row minimum by enclosing it in a circle.

It would appear reasonable for *R* to reject strategy R_1 as too risky. As he views it, the strategy offers him an almost all or nothing gamble. If *C* responds with C_1, *R* will win nearly all of the market, but if *C* responds with C_2, *R* will lose nearly all of the market. Thus, *R* is very likely to prefer another strategy. What about R_2? R_2 offers the potentially large reward of 90 percent of the market if *C* can be counted on to respond with strategy C_4. But *R*, playing it safe, will assume that *C* will not be so guileless and that he is very likely to employ strategy C_3, which would allow *R* 55 percent of the market. This is the least possible market share for *R* if he uses strategy R_2; accordingly, the 55 percent figure is circled to show it is the minimum of all the outcomes of row 2. In row 3, a 10 percent market share for *R* is the worst possible payoff, so the number 10 is circled.

After assessing all the possibilities, what will *R* do? In considering every strategy, he has noted the least attractive outcome in every case. *C* may not employ a strategy that would reduce *R*'s market share to the lowest possible percentage, but, playing a cautious game, *R* assumes that this is what *C* will do to him. It would appear reasonable, then, for *R* to make the best of three

gloomy outcomes—that is, to pick the greatest of the least. Doing this, he will choose to employ strategy R_2, which gives him, at worst, 55 percent of the market. This is the maximum of all the possible minima, and, in game theory language, R is said to be using a *maximin* strategy.

We have now seen what R will do. He will select strategy R_2, expecting C to respond with C_3. If C does respond this way, the oligopoly problem has a solution; R gets 55 percent of the market, and C gets 45 percent. Will C respond as R anticipates? To answer this, let us look at the game from C's point of view. Suppose C considers the possibility of using strategy C_1. This strategy offers R the possibility of gaining 99 percent of the market if he adopts a new strategy of R_1, as opposed to outcomes for R_2 and R_3 of 60 and 30 percent, respectively. Like R, C has to assume that his opponent will use the strategy most favorable to himself and, by definition, least favorable to C. So C assumes that if he uses C_1, A's response will be the use of R_1. Accordingly, the number 99 has been enclosed in a triangle to show that it is the largest number in column 1—the worst from C's viewpoint. Appraising the possibilities of C_2, the worst thing that can happen to C is for R to respond with R_2, gaining 75 percent of the market and leaving only 25 percent for C. A triangle encloses the number 75 since it is the column maximum. For strategy C_3, C, again assuming the most adverse outcome, will anticipate that R's answer will be R_2. The enclosing triangle indicates that the number 55 is the column maximum. In column C_4, the number 90 is the column maximum as shown by the triangle. This implies that C fears that R will respond with R_2 if he uses C_4.

Firm C has now picked out the highest possible outcomes in terms of R's payoffs. For strategies C_1, C_2, C_3, and C_4, they are 99, 75, 55, and 90 percent, respectively. To obtain the most for himself, C will choose a strategy that will hold R to the lowest of the greatest possible outcomes. Accordingly, C will choose to employ strategy C_3, which allows R 55 percent of the market. Confining R to the least of the greatest, C is said to be employing a *minimax* strategy, choosing the minimum of the column maxima.

We conclude, then, that this game has a unique equilibrium solution. The number 55 is both the row minimum and the column maximum. It is the only number in the matrix to be enclosed by both a circle and a triangle. If R chooses R_2, C will respond with C_3; and if C decides on C_3, R will reply with R_2. This is the meaning of a strictly determined game. In the technical language of game theory, the number 55 is said to be the *saddle point* of the game (so-called because the three-dimensional graphical solution of a strictly determined game yields a saddle-shaped configuration). Games with saddle points have unique stable equilibrium solutions.

If the game is strictly determined, Stackelberg's fears of market disintegration appear to be groundless. The firms of this example will work to a stable equilibrium solution. Until they arrive at the saddle point, it will always be possible for at least one firm to better itself by changing its strategy. When no firm can improve its position by switching to a new strategy, the firms have arrived at the saddle point of the game. In a strictly determined game, all that

is necessary for a stable equilibrium solution is for at least one firm to employ consistently a minimax strategy. As long as all firms act rationally, a stable equilibrium solution will be achieved.

NONSTRICTLY DETERMINED GAMES

The salient feature of the preceding game is its property of being strictly determined; in other words, it has a saddle point. The maximum of the row minima is also the minimum of the column maxima. This is an unusual event, having perhaps a frequency of occurrence equal to that of a total lunar eclipse. What if the game is not strictly determined? This seems a more likely situation. If it obtains, must Stackelberg's prediction of a chaotic industry be fulfilled?

Consider Table 13-3. It depicts a simple 2 x 2 game (it allows only two strategies per player), but it has the disconcerting attribute of having no saddle point. As in the previous game, the row minima are circled, and the column maxima are enclosed with triangles. In no case is a single number enclosed by both shapes. We continue to assume that this game has a constant (zero) sum as in the preceding game.

TABLE 13-3

2 x 2 GAME
Nonstrictly Determined

C's Strategies

		C_1	C_2	Row Minimum
R's Strategies	R_1	③	④	3
	R_2	⑤	①	1
Column Maximum		5	4	

In this game, neither participant will be motivated to use the minimax strategy. Suppose R has to learn this from experience and strives to pursue the maximin strategy. He chooses R_1, expecting a payoff of 3. When C learns about R's decision, he counters with C_1, restricting his loss to 3 units rather than the 4-unit loss the selection of C_2 would entail. But now R learns an expensive lesson: *if C is going to play C_1, R should select R_2 for a gain of 5.* Suppose, R, having seen his mistake, now decides to shift to R_2. It is obvious that C will respond with C_2, holding R's gain to 1 rather than 5. Once again, R sees he has made a poor choice. *If C is going to play C_2, R should counter with R_1,* a strategy that would allow him a gain of 4 instead of only 1. But, of course, if R does play R_1, C will not play C_2; rather C will play C_1. Thus, there can be no equilibrium point. A move by one firm induces a countermove by the rival, which, in turn, forces the initiator to move again—and so on, apparently endlessly. Instability, in itself, is not necessarily bad unless it produces un-

damped oscillations (oscillations that continue ceaselessly) that can cause an industry to fly apart.

Even if the industry will not be destroyed and the continual readjustments are not harmful to the economy, we can nevertheless predict that typical entrepreneurs would like to free themselves from the costs of making continuous adjustments and the annoying aspect of seeing one's best plans repeatedly frustrated. Is there any escape from the tyranny of the nonstrictly determined game?

The business life of firms is ongoing, not a once-and-for-all situation. The game must be played not once but many times. As the adversaries meet repeatedly in rivalrous competition, they will come to question the wisdom of pursuing *pure* strategies in every encounter. They will discover that it is worthwhile to use *mixed* strategies—that is, to employ one strategy part of the time and the other strategy the rest of the time. A game in which mixed strategies are employed is called a *nonstrictly* adversary game.

How should rivalrous competitors select their mixed strategies? The question really is: How *often* should they use each of their respective strategies? Whatever they do, neither should allow the other to discover its strategy use schedule. If, for example, C knows that R plans to use strategy R_1 every other time, C will be ready with a response that will ruin R's plans every single time. The best procedure for the firms is to randomize the use of their strategies. This way, the rival firm could never know what the subject firm was planning to do since no firm would know the course of its own actions until it had utilized its random choice-maker.

Assume that firm R decides to employ strategy R_1 with a probability of P, then, necessarily, the probability of using R_2 must be $(1 - P)$; and if firm C decides to use its strategy C_1 with probability Q, then, necessarily the probability of using C_2 is $(1 - Q)$.[11]

If R and C play a long series of games (so that the law of probability is applicable), the average gain of R (necessarily the average loss of C) will be the mathematical expectation

$$E = 3(P)(Q) + 4(P)(1 - Q) + 5(1 - P)(Q) + 1(1 - P)(1 - Q)\text{ [12]}$$

Suppose that for R the probability (P) of R_1 is 4/5 and the probability

[11] Suppose a gumball machine has been loaded with 100 gumballs, some black and some red. If there are 75 black balls in the glass bowl, and the balls have been thoroughly mixed to prevent a biased delivery, the chances of getting a black ball for your penny are 75 out of 100, or 3/4. Since the probability of getting *either* a black ball *or* a red ball is 100 percent, the probability of finding a red ball in the chute is $(1 - 3/4) = 1/4$.

[12] A word about *compound* probabilities: What is the likelihood of strategies R_1 and C_1 being used at the same time? Suppose that the probability (P) of R choosing R_1 is 1/2 and that the probability (Q) of C using C_1 is 2/5. The probability of R_1 and C_1 coinciding is thus $(P)(Q) = (1/2)(2/5) = 1/5$. In other words, the likelihood of an event occurring 1/2 of the time happening concurrently with an event having a probability of occurrence of 2/5 is 1/5. If the game is played a sufficient number of times, R_1 and C_1 will coincide 20 out of each 100 plays.

$(1 - P)$ of R_2 is thus 1/5. For C, assume that the probability (Q) of C_1 is 3/5, and, therefore, the probability $(1 - Q)$ of C_2 is 2/5. The mathematical expectation of the game from R's point of view (remember that R's gain is C's loss) is

$$E = 3(4/5)(3/5) + 4(4/5)(2/5) + 5(1/5)(3/5) + 1(1/5)(2/5) = 3\,2/5$$

The expected value of the game to R is 3 2/5. This means that in a long series of games, R will gain, on the average, at least 3 2/5 per game, and C will lose no more than 3 2/5. So the use of mixed strategies improves the situation for both firms. The matrix of Table 13-3 shows that using pure strategies, R could gain as little as 1 per game and C could lose as much as 5.

But the mathematical expectations of the firms depend not only on the values of the payoffs but also on the probabilities assigned by each firm to the use of its strategies. What would happen if Q remained unchanged but R used a different set of probabilities—say, $P = 1/8$ and $1 - P = 7/8$? The new mathematical expectation would be

$$E' = 3(1/8)(1/3) + 4(1/8)(2/3) + 5(7/8)(1/3) + 1(7/8)(2/3) = 2\,1/2.$$

Under these circumstances, the mathematical expectation of the game (E') is 2 1/2. This means that in a long series of games, R could expect to gain, on the average, at least 2 1/2 per game, while C could expect an average loss of no more than 2 1/2 per game. This is not as good as the mathematical expectation of E (i.e., 3 2/5), which resulted when strategies R_1 and R_2 were employed with probabilities 4/5 and 1/5, respectively.

Obviously, the probabilities assigned to the strategies affect the mathematical expectation. Since $E = 3\,2/5$ and $E' = 2\,1/2$, there must be a unique set of probabilities that will maximize the mathematical expectation. We can be certain that the set yielding E' is not the optimal set, since we have discovered E, which has a greater value than E'. Since R wishes to maximize his mathematical expectation, his search must be for that set of probabilities—call them P^* and $(1 - P^*)$—that will satisfy his goal.

One way of determining the optimal set of probabilities is through the time-consuming and tedious process of trial and error. The better way is to use the mathematics of game theory, which (probably to the relief of many readers) is beyond the scope of this book.[13] We can, however, illustrate the logic of R's quest. Suppose R were to choose the probabilities 1/4 and 3/4 for use with R_1 and R_2, respectively. If C were to employ strategy C_1, the mathematical expectation of R would be

$$E_{R_1} = 3(1/4) + 5(3/4) = 4\,1/2$$

If C were to use strategy C_2, R's mathematical expectation would be

[13] For an excellent survey of game theory, see William J. Baumol, *Economic Theory and Operations Analysis*, 2nd edition (Englewood Cliffs, N.J.: Prentice-Hall, 1965), pp. 529–49.

Market Behavior: Further Oligopolistic Conditions

$$E_{R_2} = 4(1/4) + 1(3/4) = 1\ 3/4$$

But $E_{R_1} \neq E_{R_2}$. The inequality indicates that the probabilities 1/4 and 3/4 are not optimal. R is still vulnerable to C's countermoves. C can select a strategy that will affect R's mathematical expectation. Now suppose that R employs the probabilities 4/5 and 1/5. If C chooses strategy C_1, R's mathematical expectation is

$$E_{R_3} = 3(4/5) + 5(1/5) = 3\ 2/5$$

If C uses strategy C_2, R's mathematical expectation is

$$E_{R_4} = 4(4/5) + 1(1/5) = 3\ 2/5$$

The probabilities 4/5 and 1/5 apparently fulfill the requirements of an optimal set, for R has now put himself beyond the reach of C's strategic decisions. Over a series of repeated games, it makes no difference to R which strategy C uses. R's mathematical expectation remains an imperturable 3 2/5.

SOME REMARKS ABOUT GAME THEORY

The theory of games has been hailed by some as an exciting new wave in economic theory and dismissed by others as being no advance over more conventional theories of the firm. One of the strengths of game theory is that it emphasizes the strategic decisions characteristic of the conduct of business under oligopolistic conditions. Rivalrous competitors will strive to keep one another guessing. Firm R does not know whether firm C will meet a price cut or respond in some other way. An attempt to assign odds to the possible responses of a rival is likely to be an exercise in futility, as experience will quickly reveal. How, then, short of collusion, can rivalrous competitors avoid total chaos? Possibly, they can do nothing against a hectic business life, but game theory suggests that there is a way of transforming unacceptable chaos into reasonable disorder. That way is the solution of generals on the battlefield and card players at the poker table; in a word, it is *strategy*. One puts oneself in the place of one's rivals and asks, "What would I do in response to my own strategy *if I were my own rival?*" Firm R, knowing what it would like to do, attempts to determine firm C's response to its own conduct and then plans a defense against firm C's response. In the business world, as in game theory, the subject firm's defensive strategy is predicated on the rival firm's intelligent response to any action the subject firm may take. This is strategy, and this is the lesson of game theory.

Game theory, in the simple form presented here, probably will not enable the reader to outthink the more established oligopolies. Whether the more advanced forms of game theory offer practical guidance for the practicing oligopolistic strategist is, at this time, conjectural. One hears many con-

flicting reports. But if game theory today does not provide the desired answers, perhaps it will tomorrow when we have better theories, better computers, and better gamesters. In the meantime, and for most of us, game theory offers interesting insights into the types of problem besetting rivalrous competitors and the general outlines of possible solutions to those problems.

THE MEASUREMENT OF COMPETITIVE IMPURITY

The market structure of an economy is a spectrum with subtle variations in the degree of competitiveness of firms. Can the monopolistic power of firms be compared? Particularly, can it be compared quantitatively?

THE LERNER INDEX

Abba P. Lerner suggested that an index of monopoly power, or competitive impurity, can be constructed, using as its criterion the divergence between price and marginal cost.[14]

The average and marginal revenue curves of the pure competitor are identical, and, therefore, in the profit-maximizing equilibrium, $P = MC$. Imperfectly competitive firms have demand curves of finite elasticity with a downward-sloping demand (average revenue) curve. $AR > MR$, so in the profit-maximizing equilibrium $P > MC$, and $MC = MR$. Lerner has constructed his index on the assumption that the greater the divergence between price and marginal cost, the greater is the degree of competitive impurity or monopoly power.

Let us denote the Lerner index as I_L and establish as the limiting values $I_L = 0$ in the purely competitive case (the complete absence of monopoly power) and $I_L = 1$ for costless monopoly.[15] Thus, the more nearly the value of the index approaches zero, the greater the competitiveness of a given firm.

The Lerner index is based on the idea that if price is used as a base, the discrepancy between price and marginal cost for various firms can be made comparable, that is,

$$I_L = \frac{P - MC}{P}$$

Since in equilibrium $MC = MR$, and

$$MR = P\left(1 - \frac{1}{\epsilon}\right)$$

[14] Abba P. Lerner, "The Concept of Monopoly and the Measurement of Monopoly Power," *Review of Economic Studies* (June 1934), pp. 157–75.

[15] For a costless monopoly, at the profit (total revenue) maximizing output, $\epsilon = 1$. (See Chapter 9 and the Cournot theory of Chapter 12 if you do not recall why.)

we may write

$$I_L = \frac{P - P\left(1 - \frac{1}{\epsilon}\right)}{P}$$

which simplifies to the convenient

$$I_L = \frac{1}{\epsilon}$$

The Lerner index shows the intuitively acceptable idea that the impurity of competition varies inversely with the firm's coefficient of price elasticity, for if $\epsilon = \infty$, then $I_L = 0$. And if $\epsilon = 1$, then $I_L = 1$. Note that whatever ϵ may be for the industry demand curve, we may expect ϵ for the firm to rise as the number of firms in the industry increases.

THE ROTHSCHILD INDEX

The Chamberlin theory of monopolistic competition employs two demand curves, *DD'* and *dd'*, as shown in Figure 13-10. The curve *DD'* is the firm's objective demand curve and shows the price-quantity combination when all firms within the industry or group make matching price changes. Curve *dd'* is the firm's subjective demand curve—the curve it believes it can follow because it assumes that its pricing policy does not affect other firms.

In the figure, a line perpendicular to the vertical axis has been drawn between points $\bar{P}$ and *E*. This line forms angle *x* with respect to the *dd'* curve and

FIGURE 13-10

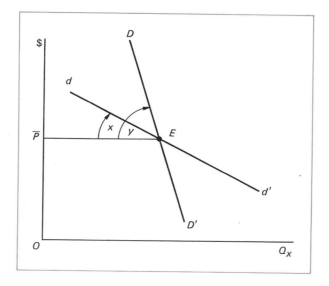

angle *y* with respect to the *DD'* curve. The more nearly curve *dd'* approaches horizontal, the more the firm will behave as a pure competitor. In the limiting case, angle *x* will disappear. The fewer competitors the firm has—the more it recognizes the existence of rivals—the more nearly will curve *dd'* approach *DD'*. In the limiting case, angle *x* = angle *y*. From these observations, K. W. Rothschild [16] has constructed an index of monopoly power that utilizes the ratio of angle *x* to angle *y*. The index is written

$$I_R = \frac{x}{y}$$

The maximum value of the ratio is 1, for the fewer the rivals, the more nearly will angle *x* approach angle *y*. When the firm recognizes that *DD'* is its own demand curve, angle *x* = angle *y*. The minimum value of the index is zero, since in the purely competitive case angle *x* = 0. We conclude, then, that the smaller the value of I_R, the less the monopoly power of a given firm.

Notice that the angle (*x*) that *dd'* makes with respect to the horizontal line $\bar{P}E$ is insufficient to determine the degree of the impurity of competition except in the limiting case in which angle *x* = 0. This follows from the fact that the degree of market power of the firm exists in relation to the rival firms in the industry. The discrepancy between angles *x* and *y* shows the degree to which the firm feels itself to be free of the necessity of considering the reactions of rivals. The more nearly the angles approach each other in value, the fewer are the number of rivals, and the more will interdependence be recognized.

OLIGOPOLY AND ECONOMIC DEVELOPMENT

There has been considerable discussion of whether or not the apparent social costs of oligopoly—higher prices, output restriction, heavy advertising, forced obsolescence, and so on—are offset by attributes such as innovation, product quality, and variety. First, attempting an answer by indirection, it seems that highly competitive industries—those industries that most nearly approach the competitive model—have not been notably progressive. Indeed, a number of them—coal mining and textiles—are usually used as examples of "sick" industries. Their lack of vitality may not be due necessarily to the state of competition, since highly oligopolistic industries—aircraft, steel—may also be considered sick. However, highly competitive firms may not have much economic staying power, since the tendency of economic profits to zero leaves them with scant financial resources to maintain themselves when they encounter economic adversity. Similarly, their slim finances do not permit innovation, nor would the forces that make an industry highly competitive be likely to afford any would-be innovator a return on his effort.

[16] K. W. Rothschild, "The Degree of Monopoly," *Economica* (1942), p. 24.

In certain instances, firms in highly competitive industries may appear to be progressive; note, for example, the prodigious increase in the productivity of American agriculture. But this increase in productivity did not originate *within* the industry. It is attributable to new hybrid crops, pesticides, agricultural implements, and fertilizers developed in agricultural colleges and in the laboratories mainly of oligopolistic business firms.

Having concluded that highly competitive firms do not in themselves show marked progressive tendencies, the question remains whether oligopolistic firms are responsible for the significant economic advances of the industrialized world. There seems to be some readily observable evidence in favor of oligopolies in that such firms are characteristic of the economies of Western Europe, the United States, and Japan.

Oligopolistic firms are usually the sources, at least from the standpoint of consumers, of sophisticated products such as television, aircraft, automobiles, computers, and so on. Yet a number of commentators assert that such firms are not the principal originators of new ideas, do not market new products unless they are severely pushed, and, indeed, often impede the flow of new and better products to the market. For example, transistor radios, ballpoint pens, longer lasting razor blades, rotary internal combustion engines, commercial television sets, copying machines, and photo-finishing cameras were pioneered by small firms, with considerable time elapsing before the most familiar names in a particular industry were willing to market the new items. At this point, much of the argument becomes confused because the distinction between *bigness* and *fewness* is clouded. As pointed out at the beginning of this chapter, oligopoly is not a matter of bigness; its essential quality is *fewness*. It seems that big firms may or may not be progressive; one cannot generalize but must consider specific cases. To some extent, it is probably the lure of achieving the supposed rewards of bigness that drives small entrepreneurs to accept the often great financial and personal costs associated with innovation. Once the innovation has been accomplished, the widespread dissemination of a new product usually requires the resources typical of the large-scale oligopolistic enterprise.

Perhaps the best assurance of a highly productive economy is open channels of upward mobility. If access to input and output markets is always a possibility, innovators will be encouraged to undertake their risky tasks, and the older established firms will have to remain alert or submit to the ultimate consequences of the most severe form of competition, the battle for survival itself.

SUMMARY

Many imperfectly competitive firms have goals other than a maximized profit. One notable model assumes that some firms attempt to maximize total sales revenue subject to the attainment of a satisfactory level of profit. Profits

are satisfactory if they allow the managerial group in control of the corporation to retain its position. Since executive performance and, hence, compensation frequently are tied to sales, sales maximization would appear to be a reasonable goal of many firms.

Although markup pricing may appear to be mechanical, and thus inconsistent with profit maximization, the successful practitioner of this form of pricing, whether he is conscious of it or not, is attempting to estimate the price elasticity of demand for his output. As marginal revenue and elasticity are alternative expressions of the same basic fact, if the seller knows the price elasticity of demand for his goods, he knows the marginal revenue schedule. By adding a suitable markup to a largely fixed wholesale price, he is attempting, in effect, to equate marginal cost and marginal revenue.

The Stackelberg oligopoly models are noteworthy for their forthright handling of perceived interdependence. These models can depict entrepreneurial behavior using either price or quantity or both as the relevant variables. The models considered in this chapter deal with the effects of interdependence both with and without collusion. Among the collusive arrangements analyzed are price and output leadership and contests between firms both to gain the price leader's position and to avoid it.

Game theory stresses the role of strategic decision-making when one firm does not know how his rivals will react to his decision. The plans of one firm may be frustrated if they become known by a rival. If a firm alternates among various strategies (uses mixed strategies) on an optimal basis, it can reduce the likelihood of less desired outcomes occurring.

Indices to measure the degree of the monopoly power of firms have been developed by Lerner and by Rothschild. The Lerner index is based on the divergence between price and marginal cost. The index, I_L, ranges between zero and one. The closer its value approaches one, the greater the monopoly power of a given firm. The Rothschild index relies on the angle of divergence between an imperfectly competitive firm's subjective and objective demand curves (as defined in the Chamberlin theory of monopolistic competition). The value of the index, I_R, ranges between one and zero. The more nearly the index approaches one, the greater the monopoly power of the subject firm.

14

The Theory
of the Competitive
Input Market

IDENTIFYING
THE PRODUCTIVE CONTRIBUTION OF INPUTS

One of the oldest problems in economic thought is the determination of a just recompense for those who participate in the productive process. Discussions of this matter can be found in Aristotle, in the Bible—both Old and New Testaments—and in the works of Saint Thomas Aquinas. Theoretical analysis had no part in early economic thought. The prescriptions for just rewards were based solely on value judgments. The problem of distributive justice remained at this level until the development of economic analysis.

Some of the earlier classical economists—those following Adam Smith—took a rather fatalistic view of earned rewards, contending that because of the tendency of the population (and hence of the labor supply) to expand as far as the supply of necessities permits, the inevitable tendency of wages is toward a subsistence level and the course of economic profit is toward extinction. On the other hand, they believed that the rental income of landlords would continue to grow until the economy reached the conclusive equilibrium of a predicted *stationary state*. Justice became a moot issue in such a context.

Karl Marx, reacting fiercely to the economic system he identified as *capitalism*, attempted to prove that human labor is the source

of all economic value and thus should not be compelled to share the social product with any other economic class.

In great part reacting to Marx's (socially necessary) labor theory of value, members of the early Marginalist school of economics attempted to isolate the productive contributions of all inputs. They felt that if they could show that factors other than labor contributed to the value of output, it would have to follow that labor is not necessarily exploited if other economic classes share in the social product. One of the most famous Marginalists, the American economist John Bates Clark, stated at the outset of his monumental work, *The Distribution of Wealth,* that the main force motivating him to develop a theory of factoral productive contribution was his desire to find an objective basis for justice in the distribution of income.[1] He reasoned that if the productive contribution of each input could be identified and if the recompense of the input owner were equal to the monetary value of the productive contribution of his input units, the factor owner would have a just reward.

Suppose that the daily output of a firm is 1,000 units of good X. For simplicity, assume that all the workers have the same productivity. Now suppose that one worker is withdrawn from the labor force. In response, output falls to 996 units. We may conclude that when 100 workers are employed, the marginal contribution of labor to output is 4 units of X. Output will rise or fall by 4 units as a marginal laborer is added or subtracted. The marginalists argued that the marginal product of an input is its contribution to output. Some marginalists, such as Clark, were prepared to go on to argue that if the input owner received the value of the marginal product of his input units he had received a just income distribution. In our example, the marginal product of labor is 4 units of X per day. If the value of a unit of X is $5, the value of the marginal product of labor would be $20. Clark would have argued that $20 per day would be a just wage.

THE EFFICIENT EMPLOYMENT OF INPUTS

In Chapter 6 (on production theory), we found that a firm employs its inputs in the proper relationship to each other when

$$\frac{MP_L}{P_L} = \frac{MP_K}{P_K} = \cdots = \frac{MP_n}{P_n}$$

If an inequality obtains among the ratios, the firm should allocate more of its production budget to that input with the highest marginal productivity per dollar and reduce its outlay for the input having the lowest marginal productivity per dollar. When each input yields the same marginal product per dollar, the given

---

[1] John Bates Clark, *The Distribution of Wealth* (New York: Macmillan, 1927), pp. 1–7.

output is being produced at the lowest possible costs. Another way of putting this is to say that for a given budget, no other input combination will yield so large an output.

THE POINT OF PRODUCTION
ON THE MARGINAL PRODUCTIVITY CURVE

In Chapter 6, the marginal product curve usually was given the shape an inverted U. In this chapter, we will eliminate the positively sloped segment of the curve because a rational firm operates only on the negatively sloped segment of a marginal product curve. This means that the firm hires inputs only when their marginal products are positive but falling. Why is this?

In the upward-rising segment of the marginal product curve, total output is increasing at an increasing rate. Suppose that the price of a unit of labor is $10 and that in the least-cost combination the value of $MP_L/P_L = 5/1$. The marginal product curve of Figure 14-1 shows that this condition obtains at points A and C, at which OL_1 and OL_3 units of labor, respectively, are used. It might seem reasonable for the firm to choose to operate at point A, since there it achieves the desired ratio using less labor than at C and would, therefore, have a lower total wage bill. But suppose the firm experiments and acquires further labor inputs—say, L_1L_2; this action would put it at point B on the MP_1 curve, at which the marginal product of labor is 60 units of X. With a wage rate of $10, the marginal output of labor is now 6 units of X per dollar instead of the former 5 units per dollar. Clearly, producing at point B is more of a "bargain" than producing at point A, even though the correct ratio of the marginal product of labor to the wage rate is 5 to 1. As long as the firm gets more output per

FIGURE 14-1

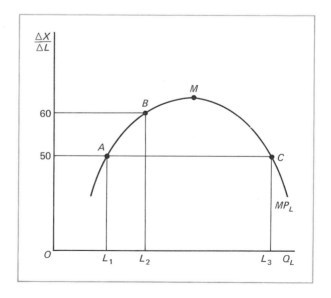

dollar for every additional dollar it spends on the labor input, it should keep using more labor. This will be its experience until it has hired sufficient labor to arrive at point M. Since labor becomes an increasingly better bargain up to point M, the rational firm will never operate in the positively sloped segment of the marginal product curve of any input. Therefore, from now on we will disregard that segment of the marginal product curve and the corresponding segment of any curve derived from it. At point M, we know that the ratio of the marginal product of labor to the input price exceeds 5 to 1, so the firm must continue to hire labor until the principle of diminishing marginal productivity (the law of diminishing marginal returns) reduces the marginal product of labor to 50 units of X. This will occur when the firm reaches point C, at which it uses OL_3 units of labor.

HIRING THE RIGHT ABSOLUTE AMOUNT OF AN INPUT

Assume now that, as in the preceding section, the firm has equalized the ratios of the marginal products of all inputs to their respective prices. For a two-input model, this means

$$\frac{MP_L}{P_L} = \frac{5}{1} = \frac{MP_K}{P_K}$$

and this in turn means that for the reciprocals,

$$\frac{P_L}{MP_L} = \frac{1}{5} = \frac{P_K}{MP_K}$$

In the preceding example, the ratio 5 to 1 (or 1 to 5 in the case of the reciprocals) was given, and the firm was depicted as adjusting to this parametric ratio. The equality of the ratios, by itself, indicates only the correct input *proportions*—for example, that the firm should use 7 units of labor with 5 units of capital. The question of how many (what absolute amount of) input units should be hired is as yet unanswered. We do not know whether the firm should hire, say, 14 units of labor and 10 units of capital or 49 units of labor and 35 units of capital. We know only that the 7 to 5 ratio between labor and capital must be maintained in the least-cost combination of inputs.

We must now determine how the *firm* establishes the correct ratio. We know that for profit maximization it is required that $MC = MR$, and, from Chapter 7 (on cost theory), we know that[2]

$$\frac{P_L}{MP_L} = \frac{P_K}{MP_K} = SMC_X$$

[2] Recall that $SMC_X = \frac{\Delta TC}{\Delta X} = P_L\left(\frac{\Delta L}{\Delta X}\right)$, but $\left(\frac{\Delta L}{\Delta X}\right) = \frac{1}{MP_L}$.

The Theory of the Competitive Input Market

Therefore, for profit maximization, the firm must hire inputs in quantities at which

$$\frac{P_L}{MP_L} = \frac{P_K}{MP_K} = MR_X$$

In the case of the purely competitive firm, $MR = P$, so the proper absolute amount of each input can be fixed by the expression

$$\frac{P_L}{MP_L} = \frac{P_K}{MP_K} = P_X$$

When this equation is fulfilled, the purely competitive firm is producing the profit-maximizing quantity of output at the lowest possible total cost.

Now we know now only the least-cost input proportions but the absolute amounts of inputs that the firm should hire in order to maximize profit. The equality of the ratios of input prices to the marginal productivities of their respective inputs indicates only the proper input proportions for the minimum-cost production of a given output. When, in addition, the ratios are also equal to the price at which the firm's output is sold, we know that the proportion *and* amount in which the firm has hired its inputs will yield a profit maximum.

THE DEMAND OF THE FIRM FOR ONE VARIABLE INPUT

Let us assume a short-run situation in which the firm can change the quantity of only one input. Under conditions of profit maximization, what will be the firm's demand for that input? Suppose labor is the variable input. We know from the preceding section that the firm is in equilibrium in regard to its use of labor when

$$\frac{P_L}{MP_L} = P_X$$

This equation can be rewritten

$$P_L = P_X(MP_L)$$

The right-hand side of this equation is the value of the marginal product of labor, so let us rewrite it as

$$P_L = VMP_L$$

The value of the marginal product of a variable input is precisely what the expression implies; it is the market value, or price, of the marginal physical

product of the variable input. Because in competition, price is equal to marginal revenue, it is also the additional revenue contributed to the firm from the sale of the marginal product of labor. For example, suppose the price of X is $4 and the marginal product of labor is 10 units of X. The value of the marginal product of labor is $40. If the marginal product of labor were 3 units of X, the value of the factor's marginal product would be $12. The relationship among the price of the good, the marginal physical product of the variable input, and the value of the marginal product of the input is shown in Table 14-1. Remember that the selling price of good X is invariant with respect to the quantity sold since the firm is defined as a pure competitor. The table begins at a positive level of input use (10L), since we have determined that the rational firm operates only in the downward-sloping portion of the marginal product curve.

TABLE 14-1	Labor	MP_L	P_X	VMP_L
	10	10	$4	$40
	11	8	4	32
	12	5	4	20
	13	1	4	4

Suppose the price of labor (the wage rate) is $20 per day. According to Table 14-1, the firm will hire 12 units of labor. Hiring fewer units would not be reasonable, since at any level of employment less than 12 units, the value of the marginal product of labor is greater than the cost of hiring additional labor units; at the margin, further hiring would add more to the revenue of the firm than it would to cost. Similarly, the firm would not hire 13 labor units, for at that level of employment, the cost of hiring additional labor exceeds the return it would bring to the firm. It must be, then, that the VMP_L schedule constitutes the firm's demand for labor.

THE FIRM'S DEMAND CURVE FOR A VARIABLE INPUT

Each point on a VMP curve is the arithmetical product of the selling price of the good and the marginal physical productivity of the given input; therefore, the VMP curve of an input is a *derived* demand curve for that input; it is derived from the value of the good the input helps to make and the productive capabilities of the input. Only the negatively sloped portion of a VMP curve has significance as the demand curve of an input, the explanation being the same as that given for the relevance of the negatively sloped segment of the marginal (physical) product curve.

Figure 14-2 depicts a hypothetical VMP curve for labor. If OL_1 units of labor are employed, the value of the marginal product is L_1A dollars. Increasing the input of labor by $L_1\bar{L}$ units causes the value of the marginal product to fall to $\bar{L}E$ dollars. Since P_X is held constant for a given VMP curve, the fall in

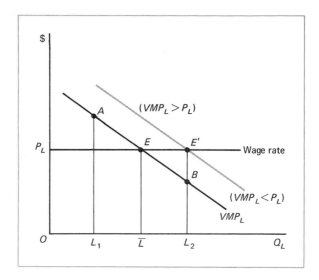

FIGURE 14-2

the value of the marginal product is explained entirely by a decrease in the marginal productivity of labor as more labor units are employed. At an employment level of OL_2 units, the value of the marginal product is L_2B dollars.

Consider point B. The firm is employing OL_2 units of labor. Suppose the price of good X increases: the VMP_L curve must shift upward, since for every level of input use, the marginal product of that input becomes more valuable. Assume that the increase in the price of X is sufficient to shift the VMP_L curve into the position shown by the gray line. The value of labor's marginal product would rise from L_2B to L_2E' dollars. At an employment level of OL_2 labor units, the value of the marginal product of labor would rise to the value formerly obtaining if only $O\bar{L}$ units had been employed ($L_2E' = \bar{L}E$).

Assuming a particular VMP_L schedule, when the price of labor (the wage rate) is given, the quantity of labor demanded is known. Suppose the firm's demand curve for labor is VMP_L and the wage rate is OP_L. Under these circumstances, the quantity of labor demanded is $O\bar{L}$ units. At an employment level below this, the value of labor's marginal product exceeds the wage rate, and it would be worthwhile to employ more labor. At a level of employment exceeding $O\bar{L}$ units, the value of labor's marginal product is less than the wage rate, and thus the firm is using too much labor relative to the other (fixed) inputs.

THE DEMAND OF THE FIRM FOR AN INPUT IN THE LONG RUN

The long-run analysis of the firm's demand for a single input is rather tedious, but if one keeps in mind the essential nature of the long run, the prin-

ciple is easy to grasp. At first, it might seem reasonable to assume that when the price of an input changes, the firm moves along the *VMP* curve of that input, whether the other inputs are variable or not. In Figure 14-3, assume that initially the firm is operating on VMP_0, hiring OL_0 units of labor at a wage rate of OP_0. Assume that the wage rate then falls to OP_1. Our short-run analysis held that the firm moves down VMP_0 from A to B', increasing the amount of labor used by L_0L_1 units. This is true as long as the firm is precluded from making adjustments in any other input.

Even though the firm cannot change the quantity of capital in the short run, let us consider what is happening to the state of that (other) input. Figure 14-4 shows two total product curves for capital. (Remember that a total product curve for a given input is drawn for a specified amount of all other inputs.) The curve TP_0 is drawn on the assumption that the firm employs L_0 units of labor. If the firm employs any other input of labor, its point of operation in regard to capital lies on a different total product curve. Initially, we assumed that the firm was using L_0 units of labor. Suppose that it was also using K_0 units of capital. Graphically, this state is shown at point A in Figure 14-3 and at point J in Figure 14-4.

When the price of labor fell to OP_1, the firm moved along VMP_0 to point B', and increased its employment of labor by L_0L_1 units. Because we have assumed the short run in our discussion, the firm could do nothing about the employment of capital, which had to remain fixed at K_0 units. Yet, when the employment of labor was increased to L_1 units, the appropriate total product curve for capital became the TP_1 curve of Figure 14-4. The firm now operates at point J', and the same amount of capital combined with a greater amount of labor produces a greater amount of X.

FIGURE 14-3

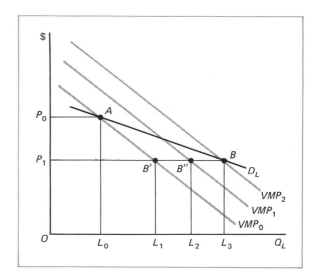

The Theory of the Competitive Input Market

FIGURE 14-4

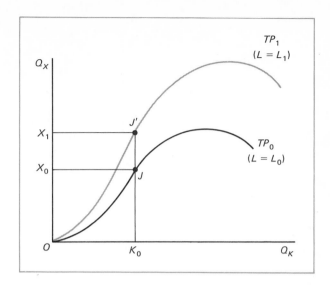

What does the upward shift of the total product curve of capital do to the marginal product curve of the input? Recall that the area under the marginal product curve is total output. It is obvious that when a greater amount of X is produced using a fixed amount of capital, the marginal product curve of capital also must shift upward. This is shown in Figure 14-5. Although the amount of capital used has remained constant, its marginal productivity has risen from $K_0 j$ to $K_0 j'$. This follows since capital, having become scarcer relative to labor, has become more productive at the margin. The equilibrium condition of the

FIGURE 14-5

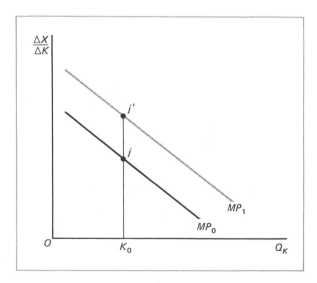

FIGURE 14-6

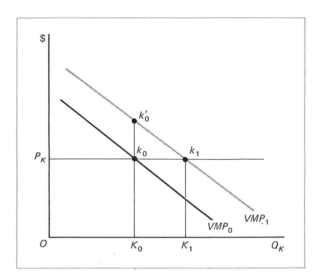

firm is altered, and this ensures that the long-run combination of labor and capital will *not* be L_1 and K_0 units, respectively.

Since the marginal product curve of capital has shifted upward, so must the value of the marginal product curve ($VMP_K = MP_K \cdot P_X$, where P_X is a constant), and, consequently, the value of the marginal product of capital increases. In equilibrium, $P_K = VMP_K$, but with the rise in the value of the marginal product of the input, the inequality $P_K < VMP_K$ holds. Given the opportunity (the long run), the firm will increase its input of capital to establish equality between the price of the input and the value of its marginal product. As it increases its input of capital, the firm moves along curve MP_1 in Figure 14-5, and thus along a *VMP* curve that lies above the initial curve. This is shown in Figure 14-6. With the employment of OK_1 units of capital, the firm has equalized the value of the marginal product of capital with its price ($VMP_K = K_1k_1 = OP_K$).

But, the situation we have now described—summarized in the input package $L_1 + K_1$—cannot be the final equilibrium employment of either input. Just as each total product curve for capital in Figure 14-4 is drawn for a specific level of labor, so each total product curve for labor is drawn for a specific amount of capital. As a result of the greater input of capital, the total product curve for labor will shift upward, and the marginal product and the value of the marginal product curves of the input will shift upward also. Therefore, the firm must increase the use of labor beyond the level OL_1 shown in Figure 14-3, but moving to the right of B' on VMP_0 would result in the disequilibrium condition $P_L > VMP_L$. We conclude, therefore, that *in the long run,* the *VMP* curve cannot be the firm's demand curve for an input.

Suppose the VMP_L curve appropriate to the use of K_1 units of capital is VMP_1 in Figure 14-3. Temporarily, we may assume that the firm would operate

at point B'', employing OL_2 units of labor, but this cannot be a long-run solution either, since there is another total product curve for capital, call it TP_2, appropriate to the use of OL_2 units of labor. Once again, the VMP curve for capital shifts upward. The firm, then, employs more capital—and, in consequence, employs still more labor, since the VMP curve for labor, in accord with our preceding analysis, shifts upward once again. Where will it all end?

It may seem a case of perpetual motion, the upward movement of the VMP curve for capital inducing an upward movement in the VMP curve for labor, which in turn induces another upward movement in the VMP curve for capital, and so on, apparently without limit. But, of course, there must be a limit, and that limit is imposed by the goal of the firm to maximize its profit. This goal is achieved in the long run when $SMC = P_X = LMC$. After the initial fall in the wage rate, the short- and long-run marginal cost curves shift downward, and the firm must begin its effort to fulfill the profit-maximizing condition. The analytical steps we have just gone through show the nature of the firm's quest. It may be thought of as an effort to bring SMC and LMC into equality with each other, with P_X as the desired value of that equality. Thus, the firm starts the adjustment process with the gap between SMC and LMC relatively wide, but the gap is successively narrowed as the corrections in input use are made. We may regard the process as one of feedback and correction with a built-in limit. As the firm makes its corrections in the use of all its inputs, the ratios P_L/MP_L and P_K/MP_K come closer together, and the shifts in the VMP curves of the various inputs approach a limit, that limit being achieved when

$$\frac{P_L}{MP_L} = \frac{P_K}{MP_K} = P_X$$

or, in the alternative expression, when

$$\frac{VMP_L}{P_L} = \frac{VMP_K}{P_K}$$

Let us assume that profit maximization is achieved when the VMP curve for labor has reached VMP_2 in Figure 14-3. In the long run, at a wage rate of OP_1, the firm operates at point B on VMP_2 and demands OL_3 units of labor. The line drawn through points A and B is the locus of points showing the quantity of labor demanded at various wage rates when the firm can adjust all other inputs. Accordingly, we may regard it as the firm's long-run demand curve for labor.

In the long run, the firm's demand for an input is more elastic with respect to price than it is in the short run. In the short run, the firm increases its demand for labor by only L_0L_1 units in response to a wage reduction of P_0P_1 dollars. However, in the long run, the same price reduction causes the quantity demanded to increase by L_0L_3 units. The reason for this is that with all in-

puts variable, the marginal productivity of labor rises as more capital is employed, so it becomes profitable for the firm to hire more of it at any given price than would be true in the short run.

An isoquant analysis. An aspect of input theory not shared with utility theory is demonstrated in Figure 14-7. Initially, suppose that the firm is producing the most profitable output X_0 using the input combination indicated by point T_0. Now, let us assume that the wage rate falls, so that the isocost curve becomes AB'. This new budget line is tangent to the isoquant representing the larger output X_1. The least-cost combination required to produce X_1 is $L_1 + K_1$. This means that if the firm were to retain the budget that is represented by the isocost AB', the firm could produce the maximum output X_1. But will the firm produce X_1? The answer is no, because X_1 is not the profit-maximizing output. The firm will not retain the budget represented by isocosts AB and AB' but will make a larger production expenditure. The profit-maximizing budget will not be AB' but will be an isocost parallel to and lying to the right of (above) AB'. In other words, the new profit-maximizing output is larger than X_1, but isoquant analysis, in itself, does not permit us to determine what it is.

The simplified graph of Figure 14-8 shows why an isoquant solution is indeterminate. Initially, assume that the firm maximizes profit by producing the output OX_0. The output is determined by the intersection of the $AR = MR$ curve with SMC_0. The latter curve has been drawn under an assumption common to all cost curves—that input prices are constant. If the wage rate falls, the marginal cost curve must shift downward, showing that at every level of output the costs of production have decreased. If the fall in the wage rate shifts the marginal cost curve from SMC_0 to SMC_1, the firm will find that the

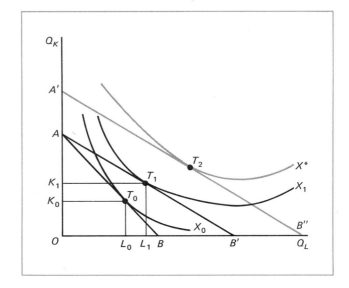

FIGURE 14-7

FIGURE 14-8

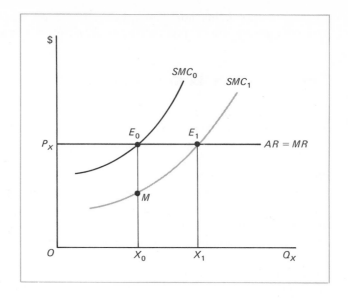

marginal cost of producing output OX_0 has fallen from X_0E_0 to X_0M. The output OX_0 can no longer be a profit-maximizing output, for, if $SMC = X_0M$, then $SMC < P_X$; this is the signal that output must be expanded. The firm, then, expands output until marginal cost is equal to X_1E_1, at which it once again is equal to P_X. To do this, the firm must increase its outlays. In the long run, we know that the firm must equate short- and long-run marginal costs. To keep the diagram simple, the appropriate long-run marginal cost curves are not shown, but assume that the long-run equilibrium conditions are fulfilled at E_0 and E_1. Assume that the firm's costs of producing the output OX_0 were $OX_0E_0P_X$ and that, after the long-run adjustment, the total costs have become $OX_1E_1P_X$. To maximize its profit, the firm has been forced to spend $X_0X_1E_1E_0$ more dollars. Thus, in Figure 14-7, we know that the isocost must shift rightward until it attains a value $X_0X_1E_1E_0$ dollars greater than isocost AB'. This new isocost can be determined by dividing the addition to total cost by the price of capital and adding the result to the distance OA. This new point, A', on the vertical axis is the vertical intercept of the desired isocost. The location of the firm's new isocost curve is now determined, since the curve is parallel to AB'. The profit-maximizing output X^* will be represented by the one isoquant tangent to $A'B''$. The least-cost combination of inputs to produce this profit-maximizing output will be that indicated by the point of tangency.

The "extra step" required to determine the profit-maximizing output of the firm may seem strange to readers who recall the analogous situation of consumer utility maximization, in which the tangency of an indifference curve and the budget line established the consumer's optimal basket. The difference between the consumer and firm equilibrium cases results from the fact that the consumer's expenditure is fixed by his income, while the firm's equilibrium

is not. The firm gains more money by selling more product, and it will continue to spend more (move its budget curve rightward) as long as its profit increases.

THE MARKET DEMAND FOR AN INPUT

Owing to the presence of feedback and correction effects, the derivation of the market demand curve for an input is more complicated than the simple summation of the individual demand curves of firms for the particular factor. The market demand curve for an input does show the summation of the quantities demanded at various prices by the firms in the market, but these quantities are aggregated from *different* demand curves within each firm. In the consumer goods markets, summing individual quantities demanded at particular prices does not cause repercussions on individual consumers that cause them to correct the initial quantity demanded. But in the case of firms buying productive factors, a change in their demand for inputs will be reflected in a change in the quantity of goods these purchasing firms produce, and, in consequence, the market supply curve of the good they produce must shift. A shift in supply, *ceteris paribus,* will cause a change in the price of the good. Since the price of a good is a determinant of the demand for its inputs, any change in the output price must result in a change in the demand for an input.

Figure 14-9(a) shows the demand curve D_1 of an individual firm for labor. Chart (b) of the figure shows the market demand curve D_N for the same input. The demand curve of the firm is that derived in the preceding section; it is not the VMP_L curve. Initially, suppose the wage rate is OP_0. The firm is at point a on its demand curve and employs OL_0 units of labor. Point A on the market demand curve is obtained by summing all the quantities demanded at price P_0 by all the firms in this particular input market. At the current wage rate, the aggregate quantity demanded is ON_0.

Assume now that the wage rate falls to OP_1. In the case of an individual's demand curve for a good, the consumer would ride down demand curve D_1 to point b'. Summing a number of such points on the demand curves of individuals would yield point B' on the right-hand graph. Thus, although for a consumer's good, points A and B' lie on the same demand curve, this is not the case for an input. The procedure used to obtain the market demand curve for a consumer good overstates the quantity demanded of an input.

The difference between the demand for a consumer's good and the demand for an input is, as we have said, that the factor demand curve is affected by the feedback from the consumer's good market. The demand curve for an input is a derived demand curve (that is, the demand for the input depends on— is derived from—the demand for the good it is used to produce). When the wage rate falls, the firms in the particular labor market tend to demand more of the input. A greater use of an input leads to a greater output of the good into which the factor is transformed. As all firms in a particular industry adjust their production schedules to produce greater quantities of the good, the mar-

The Theory of the Competitive Input Market

FIGURE 14-9

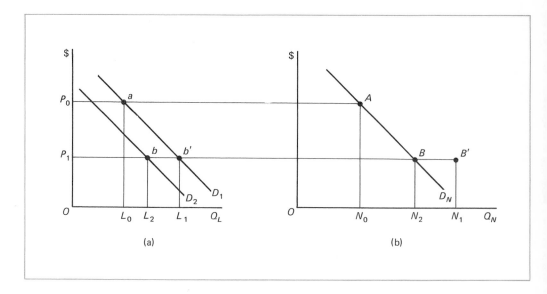

(a)   (b)

ket supply curve for the good moves downward, and with this movement the price of the good falls. The fall in the price of the good reduces the value of the marginal product of the input at every level of input use. The VMP curves must move downward. For example, the hypothetical VMP_L curve that we may imagine passing through point b' on D_L must move downward. This causes the demand curve for labor to shift downward—say, to D_2. Thus, when the wage rate falls to OP_1, the firm demands OL_2 units of labor rather than OL_1. Point B on the market demand curve, D_N, is, in turn, obtained by the horizontal summation of all the b points on the labor demand curves of all the firms in the industry.

THE SUPPLY OF A FIXED INPUT

Up to this point, we have been concerned solely with the demand side of the input market. A complete theory of input pricing requires that we consider the supply side. The simplest case of supply is that of an input fixed in amount. The most usual examples of fixed input supplies involve natural resources: oil pools, lakes, forests, mineral deposits, and so on. The reason for the prominence of natural resources in these examples is obvious: nature is utterly unmindful of the pricing mechanism; the total supply of a natural resource is wholly unresponsive to economic stimuli.

Figure 14-10 shows that price cannot affect the total amount of the good supplied. Regardless of the price, the quantity supplied is $O\bar{Z}$. This does not

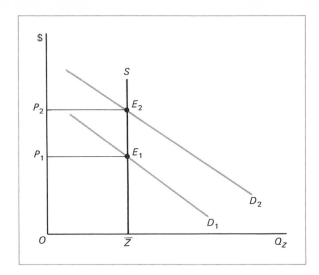

FIGURE 14-10

mean that the supply of good Z is immutable. An example may make this clearer. Suppose that Z is water flowing from a spring; the amount $O\bar{Z}$ can stand for some rate of flow—so many gallons per hour. The number of gallons cannot be influenced by economic signals. The flow may very well fluctuate—profuse in spring, a trickle in late summer—but insofar as price is concerned, the quantity supplied is invariant. Accordingly, the supply curve shows perfect supply inelasticity at quantity $O\bar{Z}$.

When an input is fixed in supply, demand is the sole determinant of price. Suppose that Z is a parcel of real estate situated in Anaheim, California. Two hundred years ago when that parcel was probably worth almost nothing, the King of Spain used to reward his colonizers with enormous grants of the then little-valued California land. Less than one hundred years ago, Anaheim was found to be ideally suited to the raising of oranges, and we can imagine that the resulting land boom raised the demand curve to D_1. No longer was the land a free good; it could command a price of OP_1. A few years ago, the orange trees began to disappear at a rapid rate as the arrival of Disneyland raised the demand curve sufficiently to price the orange growers out of the land input market. We shall assume that today the price of the same unit of land is now OP_2.

Why is the land valuable? Solely because there are competing claims for its use. Price fulfills an allocative, but not an incentive, function. The land is there at any price, but the price ensures that the land supplied by nature is used to support Mickey Mouse and his friends instead of orange trees.

Suppose the illustrative parcel of land were owned by the descendants of a fictional California don who received the land originally from the Spanish king. If there were no demand for the land, the family would receive nothing for their patrimony. If the demand were D_1, they would realize $O\bar{Z}E_1P_1$; and if

The Theory of the Competitive Input Market

it were D_2, they would receive $O\bar{Z}E_2P_2$. Suppose a property tax were imposed equal to $P_1E_1E_2P_2$. There would be no loss in the quantity of the factor, just as there would be no diminution if the tax were to consume all the total revenue.

When the amount of revenue received from a productive factor has no bearing on the quantity of it that is supplied, that revenue is called *rent*. Thus, if there is no demand for Z, its rent is zero, but if demand is D_1 or D_2, the rent is $O\bar{Z}E_1P_1$ or $O\bar{Z}E_2P_2$, respectively.

In economics, *rent* is often used synonymously with *surplus*. A surplus is an amount that need not be paid to bring an input into existence (see footnote 2, p. 210). Obviously, if the supply of something is not dependent on economic forces, anything its owners receive is a surplus. They are not being rewarded for *producing* the input; they are being paid *to allow* its use. The legal institution of private property permits owners to derive incomes from the resources they own. Some resources must be coaxed into existence by incentive payments. For those inputs fixed in supply, no incentive payment is necessary. We have seen that if partial (or entire) confiscation takes place through the imposition of taxes, the quantity of a fixed resource is unaffected. In the case of a variable resource, the imposition of a tax can have pronounced effects on the available quantity.

Although rent is usually associated with fixed inputs, it is proper to use the term to describe any portion of income that is unnecessary to the supply of the input. For example, a television personality may command $200,000 per year. If, as an experiment, we could impose a finely adjusted income tax on him, we could discover how much of his *wage* is actually rent. Suppose that if he netted at least $10,000 annually, his appearances turned out to be as frequent as before the tax. We could then conclude that of his total wage, $190,000 is rent, or surplus, since there is no need to pay this amount in order to induce him to offer his services.

Rent has considerable economic significance as an *allocational* device. Consider once again Figure 14-10. If a tax equal to $P_1E_1E_2P_2$ were imposed on the owners' receipts from Disneyland and agricultural land were tax exempt, the owners would be indifferent as to whether their land was occupied by an orange grove or an amusement park. If the decision were made in favor of the orange grove, in the judgment of the economy the land would be misallocated. Society has chosen to have the land provide entertainment rather than oranges, and this enables the proprietors of Disneyland to outbid orange growers for the services of the land. Rent helps to ensure that an input is used in its highest yielding occupation. To the extent that the yield reflects a rational social judgment, rent allocates a fixed input to its most desired social usage.

SHORT–RUN FIXED INPUTS: THE CASE OF QUASI RENTS

Quasi rent, unlike true rent, disappears in the long run. In Figure 14-11, the purely competitive firm is able to produce $O\bar{X}$ at a pure profit equal to the

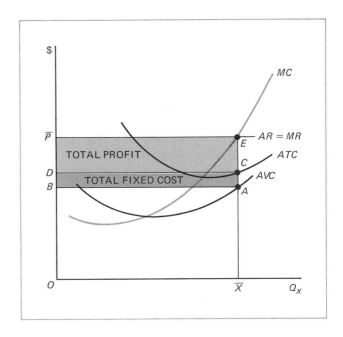

FIGURE 14-11

area of the lighter shaded rectangle $DCE\bar{P}$. The total costs of production are $O\bar{X}CD$ dollars. Of this amount, the total variable costs, $O\bar{X}AB$, are the only costs directly associated with output. Total fixed costs are equal to the darker shaded area of $BACD$, but they have nothing to do with the level of output. We may, therefore, regard the amount represented by the entire shaded rectangle $BAE\bar{P}$ as a return over and above the costs directly associated with production. If the variable input is paid the total sum $O\bar{X}AB$, the rectangle $BAE\bar{P}$ must show the income attributable to the fixed factor. Should the price of X rise, the profit-maximizing firm would expand output and would necessarily have to hire more of the variable factor. Total variable costs and total revenue would increase, but total fixed costs would not. The greater difference between the costs associated directly with production and total revenue is attributable to the fixed factor. In the short run, the income share of the fixed input has nothing to do with the *provision* of the factor; it is merely a short-run surplus over and above the costs associated directly with production. It is, then, in the nature of a rent, and owing to its short-run existence, the difference between total variable cost and total revenue, shown as the entire shaded rectangle $BAE\bar{P}$, is designated quasi rent. In the short run, the fixed input cannot be increased or reallocated in response to profit-maximizing opportunities; its income share is price determined. The cost of previously acquired fixed inputs having no influence on short-run marginal cost, their costs cannot, in the short run, be a determinant of the price of good X.

Quasi rent and profit must not be confused. Quasi rent is the excess over the total *variable* costs of production; economic profit is the excess over all

(total variable *and* fixed) costs of production. For example, suppose you, as the owner of a hotel (capital), have 1,000 rooms to rent. Those rooms are there whether the town is dead or a major political convention is in your city. In the short run, your supply of rooms is fixed, and as a profit-maximizing entrepreneur, you will vary your rates with the demand for them. If it is not the tourist season, you may charge only enough to cover variable costs, but if the American Medical Association is in town, you may charge rates which, if maintained, would pay off the cost of the hotel in one year. Because the supply of rooms is fixed in the short run, whatever return you do make in that period resembles the rent of a resource permanently fixed in supply; hence, the reward to the owner of a short-run fixed input is called a *quasi rent*.

Why does quasi rent disappear in the long run? Because, given sufficient time, the supply of the resource *is* responsive to price. As long as the quasi rent persists, more resources will flow into the market, the inflow ceasing only when the increased amount of the input has reduced the quasi rent to zero.

THE SUPPLY OF A VARIABLE INPUT: THE CASE OF LABOR

When an input is variable—when its use varies with output—its reward serves not only to allocate the resource but to call forth its supply. Our analysis turns now to the situation in which an input is fully variable; if its owners do not receive an incentive payment, no input services will be forthcoming.

In Figure 14-12, the individual worker's daily pay is plotted on the vertical axis, and the hours of work he supplies each day are measured on the horizontal axis. The maximum number of hours he is willing (able) to supply per day is OH^*. The number of hours he will supply between zero and OH^* depends on his remuneration.

Each indifference curve shows the rate at which the individual is willing to substitute hours of *non*work for pay. The indifference curves are positively sloped because we assume remunerated effort to be irksome to the supplier. The positive slope simply indicates that we are not dealing with *two* goods. Labor has negative utility; more pay must accompany more work to offset the disutility of extra labor. Thus, labor is not a substitute for remuneration. The convexity of the curves (with respect to the horizontal axis) shows that each additional hour of labor requires successively greater amounts of remuneration to maintain a given utility index.[3]

The higher the indifference curve, the greater the worker's utility. For example, at points *A* and *E*, the individual supplies OH_1 hours of work, but he

---

[3] If the indifference curves were convex to the origin, the individual would be willing to substitute work for income. He would pay for the privilege of working. Such conduct could be completely rational. The activity involved would be some kind of hobby or charitable activity—for example, the home workshop enthusiast who pays to do what the professional cabinet maker must be paid to do or the volunteer church organist who plays the organ and pays for the church's music program. But this type of situation is not representative of the labor market.

FIGURE 14-12

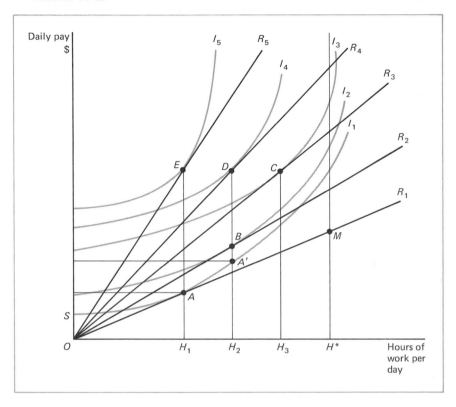

judges himself to be better off at *E* than at *A* because at point *E* he receives *AE* more dollars for the same quantity of work. Note that the system of indifference curves does not begin at the origin. The individual is unwilling to supply any labor for a remuneration of less than *OS* dollars per day.

Each of the *OR* rays is a locus of points showing the total wage payment corresponding to the number of hours worked at a given wage rate. Suppose that at a certain wage rate the individual would be paid H_1A dollars for working OH_1 hours and H^*M dollars for OH^* hours of work. Since the wage rate is constant ($H_1A/OH_1 = H^*M/OH^*$), points *A* and *M* lie on the same linear path. The slope of that linear path is the wage rate, and the steeper the slope, the higher the wage rate.

Despite some similarities, the rays are not isocosts. By definition, an isocost has the same money value along its entire length. For the rays of Figure 14-12, this is not the case. The money value of ray OR_1 at point *M* is greater than the money value at point *A*. The one constant along a given ray is the wage *rate*.

Suppose the individual is offered a daily wage of H_1A dollars. His indifference map shows that he would be willing to furnish up to OH_1 hours of work per

day. At this total daily income, he would, of course, be glad to supply less labor. This would, in effect, raise the wage rate and put him on a higher indifference curve. However, we shall assume that competition in the labor market forces him to provide OH_1 hours at the specified remuneration.

How can the worker be induced to provide more work? Suppose the employer must have OH_2 hours. The worker is indifferent between points A and A'. However, the difference between H_1A and H_2A' dollars is insufficient to compensate him for H_1H_2 more hours. It appears, then, that the worker would have to be paid H_2B dollars per day, rather than H_2A' dollars, if he is to offer OH_2 hours to his employer. Since A' lies on the same indifference curve as A, why is the payment of $A'B$ dollars necessary?

At point A', the slope of indifference curve I_1 exceeds the slope of OR_1. This means that the rate at which the worker is willing to substitute income for the loss of leisure time (i.e., nonworking time) exceeds the rate at which the economy will compensate him. At the margin, nonwork is more valuable to him than the compensation. If he is to be induced to furnish more than OH_1 hours, the wage rate must be raised to the level represented by OR_2. At point B, the rate at which the economy is willing to compensate the worker for his labor is equal to the rate at which he is willing to combine income and work.

OVERTIME PAY

Let us look at this another way. Suppose an employer would like a worker to furnish OH_2 hours of labor, as shown in Figure 14-13. If the worker is to furnish more hours than OH_1, the financial incentive must be sufficient to make the worker feel better off than he does at G. Thus, if he is to furnish more work, he must be able to move to a higher indifference curve.

Point T on indifference curve I_2 corresponds to OH_2 hours. The associated total income is H_2T dollars per day. The wage rate that would permit the worker to receive this daily income is shown as the slope of OR_2. But OR_2 is not tangent to indifference curve I_2 at point T; rather it passes *through* that point. At point T, the slope of indifference curve I_2 is steeper than the slope of OR_2. At the margin, an hour of the employee's time is worth more to him than it is to his employer; therefore, he will not provide H_1H_2 more hours of work at the given rate of remuneration. A further incentive is required if the worker is to furnish more hours. For example, should the wage rate be raised to the amount shown by the slope of OR_3, the worker would reach point V on indifference curve I_4. In exchange for the total daily income of H_2V dollars, the worker would supply the desired H_1H_2 more hours for a total of OH_2 hours per day.

But the employer has a less costly alternative. Instead of paying the employee a total of H_2V dollars for OH_2 hours of work, he can get the same amount of labor by paying $H_1G = H_2G'$ dollars for the first OH_1 hours of work and $G'T$ dollars for the remaining H_1H_2 hours. Thus, the employer obtains OH_2 hours of work for a total expenditure of H_2T rather than H_2V dollars, a saving of TV dollars per day.

FIGURE 14-13

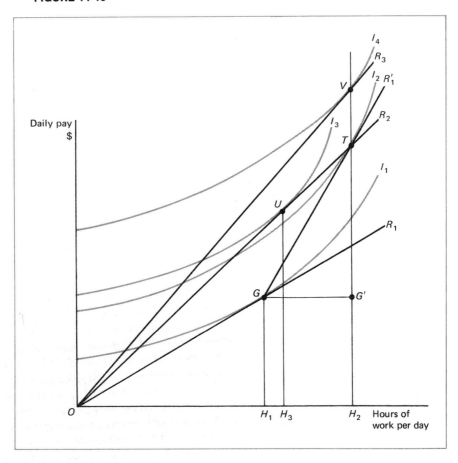

The employer accomplishes the saving by utilizing overtime rates. Rather than hiring workers at the uniform hourly rate shown by the slope of OR_3, the employer pays for the first OH_1 hours at the rate shown by the slope of OR_1. The remaining H_1H_2 hours are compensated at the higher rate shown by the slope of the line segment GR_1'. This rate exceeds that shown by the slope of OR_3 but, when used in combination with the rate of OR_1, results in a lower total daily wage bill than would be the case if a uniform rate were used to obtain OH_2 hours.

Figure 14-13 shows why employers often prefer extremely steep over-time rates (sometimes called *penalty rates* in labor contracts) to a more moderate uniform daily rate. The worker, however, would prefer a lower rate that would yield a higher total daily income, but he will accept premium overtime rates because he makes his decision to supply extra work at the margin. Suppose, for example, that the basic wage rate is $5 per hour and that the length of the working day is eight hours (assume that these data are shown by the

The Theory of the Competitive Input Market

slope of OR_1 and the distance OH_1, respectively). Under these conditions, the worker would receive a total daily compensation of $40. Suppose that his employer can induce the worker to furnish four more hours (represented by the distance H_1H_2) by increasing the total daily wage to $80 (shown in the diagram as H_2T). But if the employer offers $80 pay for twelve hours at the hourly wage of $6.66 (shown by OR_2), the worker will voluntarily supply only OH_3 hours of work for the total daily income of H_3U dollars. Offering the worker a chance to make $80 for a twelve-hour day paid at the rate of $6.66 per hour will not accomplish the employer's objective; the worker will not put in the time desired.

Suppose, now, the employer changes the basis on which $80 for a twelve-hour day is offered to the worker. The first eight hours (OH_1) are to be compensated at the rate of $5 per hour (shown by the slope of the line segment OG), and the remaining four hours are to be remunerated at double time—that is, $10 per hour (shown by the slope of line segment GR_1'). How can an alternative way of offering an $80 daily income to the worker make so great a difference?

Beyond point U, the worker subjectively values an hour of leisure time at more than $6.66. But as long as he considers his extra hour of leisure time to be worth less than $10 per hour, he will continue to supply more work. Since the worker's estimate of the value of one more hour of leisure time does not equal $10 until he reaches point T on indifference curve I_2, he will supply OH_2 hours of work for a total daily wage of $80. Offered the chance to make $80 per day at the rate of $6.66 per hour, the worker will voluntarily supply only OH_3 hours, but if he is compensated for OH_1 hours at the rate of $5 per hour and all hours in excess of OH_1 are paid for at the rate of $10 per hour, he will voluntarily work OH_2 hours. Thus, it is the marginal remuneration that is important to the worker, not the total compensation. This emphasis on marginal remuneration may seem irrational, but it is easily explained. At $5 an hour, the worker earns $40 for a normal eight-hour day; at $6.66 an hour, he would earn in excess of $53 for a normal day's work. Clearly, an additional (marginal) dollar of income will be worth more to him if his pay is $40 than if it is $53.

Figure 14-13 portrays one cause of labor-management conflicts. Because of its lower total cost, management will favor the use of overtime rates. In addition, overtime probably allows the firm greater flexibility in the use of the labor input, since management can schedule extra hours when they are needed. The worker would be better off if the high overtime rates were replaced by a higher normal wage rate. A union is likely to push for a uniform hourly wage rate that will provide a total daily income of H_2V dollars if OH_2 hours are worked.

THE BACKWARD–BENDING SUPPLY CURVE

An inspection of Figure 14-12, shows that as the wage rate is raised a greater amount of hours of effort is supplied until the wage reaches the level depicted by OR_3. When the wage rate reaches the level shown by OR_4, the worker supplies only OH_2 hours—the same amount he supplied when his income was only H_2B dollars and the wage rate was OR_2. If the wage rate is

raised still further—say, to OR_5—the hours supplied drop back to OH_1. Figure 14-12 indicates that wages can have a disincentive effect.

The pattern of response to the increasing wage rates shown in Figure 14-12 will produce a backward-bending supply curve of the type shown in Figure 14-14. At least up to wage OW_3, increases in wage rates perform their incentive function. However, at some rate between OW_3 and OW_4, the ability of wages to bring forth extra effort reaches a maximum and then exerts a negative effect. A wage rate of OW_4 calls forth less effort than the lower wage OW_3. The reason for this behavior is the worker's attitude toward income and leisure. As the wage rate rises, the worker's income rises. Leisure becomes more attractive as a greater income enhances the ability of the worker to pursue its uses. Therefore, beyond a certain level of total income, further increases in income are valued less highly than the opportunity to use one's income on leisure activities. By the time the wage rate has reached OW_4, wage increases have lost their incentive function, and more labor would be elicited if the wage rate were cut.

The backward-bending supply curve of labor does seem to depict the attitude of an increasing number of individuals as the general level of affluence increases. Formerly, such behavior was confined largely to high-income persons. The high incomes of many surgeons, lawyers, and entertainment personalities could open a world of pleasure only if these individuals could take time to enjoy themselves. For many less well-compensated people, however, the pleasures to be bought from the proceeds of working were greater than the pleasures of more leisure time at a reduced income.

FIGURE 14-14

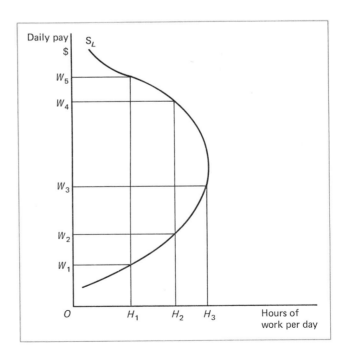

The Theory of the Competitive Input Market

Perhaps now the backward bending supply curve of labor is coming to be typical of the market behavior of more members of the labor force. As the general standard of living increases, more people find themselves able to afford those accessories they believe are essential to the proper use of leisure time. If they do not get the time to enjoy the material accoutrements of leisure, they see little point in working the hours necessary to acquire the income to buy those accoutrements. Thus, as incomes expand beyond the point at which workers are able to maintain their families securely and comfortably, greater demands are made in labor negotiations for more holidays, longer vacations, shorter work weeks, and fewer hours per working day.

To some extent, the income incentive is its own undoing. Adding to the general disincentive aspect of higher wages is the questioning of consumption goals themselves. When fur coats, cars, and trips cease to be sought-after goals, when people seek ends that cannot be bought with the proceeds of ever higher rates of remuneration, purely economic signals, such as rising wage rates, become less effective in their intended incentive function.

THE OPTIMAL SOLUTION

How likely is it that optimal solutions such as those depicted by the tangency points in Figure 14-12 will be attained? Most workers do not have precise control over the length of time they spend at their work. For most people, the workday is fixed by social convention or the exigencies of a specific vocation. It would be pure happenstance for an eight-hour day to be the optimal solution for an individual worker. Consequently, most of us must remain on indifference curves below the one we could attain if we were free to adjust our subjective marginal rates of substitution of leisure for income to conform with the rates imposed by the market.

Inability to attain a point of equilibrium means that labor is not allocated optimally from the standpoint of its suppliers. Experience indicates that adjustments in wages and working conditions are easier to come by than adjustments in the hours of work. Perhaps some of the feelings of vague discontent that many workers associate with their jobs can be traced to the relative inflexibility of the length of their workday.

THE SHARES OF INPUT OWNERS: PRODUCT EXHAUSTION THEOREMS

This chapter opened by noting that to a great extent the pioneers of the marginal productivity theory of distribution constructed the theory in an attempt to define a just income distribution. Some historians of economic thought attribute the marginalists' efforts to their desire to combat that essential principle of Marxian economics which holds that workers are exploited if they do not receive the full use value of their labor services.

To see the problem in its historical setting, suppose that a bakery pro-

duces 100,000 loaves of bread per day. If the bread is sold for 50¢ a loaf, the total daily income of the productive enterprise of labor and capital is $50,000. On what basis *should* this income be shared? Notice that this question is not one of economics but of ethics. A *theoretical* question would ask: "On what basis *is* this income shared?" Early classical theory argued that the wage payment tended toward a subsistence level and that the share of the property owners was a residual. Whether or not the system was seen as ethically satisfactory depended on the personal orientation of the particular theorist. Karl Marx attempted to demonstrate that the members of the working class (the proletariat) are deprived of their rightful share of income if they do not receive all the proceeds from the sale of the output of a productive enterprise. Under Marxian doctrine, the income share of the bakers in our hypothetical example should be $50,000 per day. Since workers, as a class, do not receive all the revenue from the sale of output, Marx concluded that they were exploited, this exploitation being an inescapable feature of the capitalistic (Marx's term) system. Others argued against the Marxian doctrine, but the question of the legitimacy of the income share of the owners of each productive input remained. The early marginal theorists addressed themselves to this problem.

As was noted before, John Bates Clark and several other early marginal productivity theorists saw as their first project the *identification* of the share of each input owner in the total revenue of a productive enterprise. The basic quantum of this productive contribution was defined as the marginal product of a given input. The contribution of an input owner was taken to be the marginal product of the class of inputs he owns multiplied by the number of units he furnishes to the enterprise.[4] For example, if the marginal productivity of the bakers in our example is 50 loaves of bread per day, and the bakers furnish 1,000 units of labor input per day, the contribution of labor to the daily product of the bakery is 50,000 loaves.

Accepting the Aristotelian proposition that justice is what is due a man, the early marginal productivity theorists believed that input owners would be treated justly if their reward was equal to their contribution. According to this doctrine, the workers in our example should receive the proceeds from the sale of 50,000 loaves of bread, which would be, of course, the total value

[4] Ownership, being a social and legal, rather than an economic, concept, is not explained by economic theory. Therefore, our discussion of input supply does not consider conditions of ownership such as inheritance (of both property and money) and inborn physical, mental, and biological characteristics, predation, tradition, and so on. One's total income depends, in part, on how many units of an input one owns. The ethics of income distribution, then, cannot be settled simply by identifying the productive contribution of those inputs; it must also take into account the legitimacy of the size of one's stock of inputs or the conditions under which those input units were acquired. Assuming that the marginal productivity theory does identify one's productive contribution, does it follow that one is entitled to neither more nor less than the monetary value of his contribution? These questions show why the early marginalists could not find an ethic of distribution in the theory of marginal productivity. If the marginal productivity theory is to be relevant to the ethics of income distribution, then not only must a distributive ethic call for the sharing of the social product on the basis of one's contribution to that product, but the distribution of inputs among persons must be *morally justified*. The ambiguity of the expression *morally justified* is the essence of the problem.

The Theory of the Competitive Input Market

of their marginal products. If the price of a loaf of bread is 50¢, the workers' share of total daily revenue would be $25,000. If there are 1,000 bakers employed in the bakery, their average daily wage would be $25.[5]

If the bakers are paid $25,000, then an equal amount is left for the owners of the other inputs. Is this amount merely a residual, or is it, too, the total value of the contribution of the owners (of ovens, delivery trucks, and so on)? Capital has a marginal productivity, and if its marginal product is multiplied by the number of units of capital in use, will the monetary value of the product be equal to $25,000? If it is less than $25,000, this would suggest that payment of such an amount is unjustified, as the owners of capital have not contributed that amount of value to the output of the firm. Suppose the productive contribution of capital as measured by marginal productivity theory were found to exceed $25,000. Then, the owners of capital would be rewarded insufficiently; it would even be possible to allege that *they* are "exploited." Notice that in all these cases of "exploitation," it is impossible to identify who is the "exploiter" or how he gets his "unjustified" income share.

Put another way, the question we are considering may be stated by asking: "Do the sums of the values of the marginal products of labor and capital exactly exhaust the value of the total output of the firm?" In our example, this would mean: Does $\Sigma VMP_L + \Sigma VMP_K = \$50,000$? If so, it is possible to pay each input owner in accordance with his contribution to production. If $\Sigma VMP_L + \Sigma VMP_K > \$50,000$, some input owners cannot be rewarded commensurately with their marginal productivity. If $\Sigma VMP_L + \Sigma VMP_K < \$50,000$, it is, of course, possible to pay the input owners in accord with their respective marginal productivities, but what is to be done with the residual?[6]

The early marginal theorists originally held, largely on faith, that the sums of the values of the marginal products of the respective inputs did exactly exhaust the total product of the firm. J. B. Clark and some of his contemporaries, forced as they were to rely entirely on intuition aided by geometrical techniques of analysis, apparently satisfied themselves and many other economists that the product was exhausted by payment to all factor owners on the basis of the marginal productivities of their inputs.

In our treatment of the product exhaustion theorem (see Figure 14-15), it makes no difference which input is variable and which is fixed. In Figure 14-15 the roles of the inputs are interchanged in the two graphs. In graph (a), labor is treated as the variable input. The number of labor units multiplied by the *average* product of the input yields the total output of the firm; this is shown as the area of rectangle *OLAB*. If *OLAB* represents total product and

---

[5] Review Chapter 5 if you think that bakers 1, 2, 3, and so on, are exploited because they do not receive more than the marginal product of baker 1,000.

[6] Notice that this problem cannot be solved by considering any excess over the sums of the values of the marginal products of all inputs as "profit." In a two-input model, either the function entrepreneurship is assumed away or it is subsumed under the two input headings. In a multi-input model in which entrepreneurship is explicitly identified as an input, it, too, has its own marginal product. On the other hand, if the residual is assumed to be economic profit, then the question remains. What is to be done with the economic profit?

FIGURE 14-15

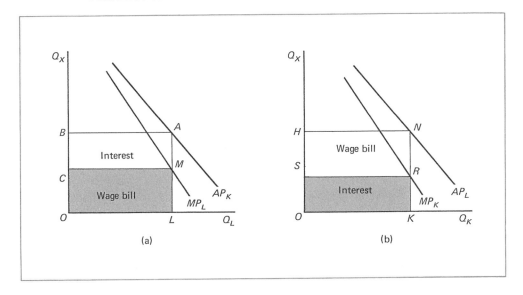

(a) (b)

OLMC represents the real contribution of labor, the remaining portion of total product, *CMAB*, must be attributed to the fixed input capital. This amount is shown as a residual. If these amounts multiplied by the sale price of the output are paid to the owners of the labor and capital inputs, we may regard the monetized values of rectangles *OLMC* and *CMAB* as the total wage and interest bills, respectively.

The nature of the problem of product exhaustion becomes clear when the input formerly assigned the residual is now defined as the variable input. This has been done in Figure 14-15(b), in which the units of capital are measured along the horizontal axis. The marginal product of capital when *OK* units are used is *KR*; thus, the total productive contribution of capital in real terms is shown by the area of rectangle *OKRS*. This time, the contribution of labor, *SRNH*, is shown as a residual.

To show that payment in accord with marginal productivity to the factor owners exactly exhausts total product, it is necessary to show that the area of rectangle *OLMC* is equal to the area of rectangle *SRNH*. In other words, the total productivity of one input calculated with the margin must be equal to its total productivity calculated as a residual.

We will now take a simple arithmetical example that does not prove the product exhaustion theorem but does show how it operates. The simple production function introduced in Chapter 5 was

$$X = \sqrt{L \cdot K}$$

Suppose the firm is currently using 400 units of labor with 2,500 units of capi-

404   The Theory of the Competitive Input Market

tal. According to our production function, total output will be

$$X = \sqrt{400 \cdot 2500} = \sqrt{1,000,000} = 1,000 \text{ units}$$

To find the marginal product of labor, let us increase the input of labor by 1 unit, holding all other inputs constant. Then,

$$X = \sqrt{401 \cdot 2500} = \sqrt{1,002,500} = 1,001.249 \text{ units of } X$$

$$MP_L = 1.249X$$

Repeating the process for capital,

$$X = \sqrt{400 \cdot 2501} = \sqrt{1,000,400} = 1,000.20 \text{ units of } X$$

$$MP_K = 0.2X$$

Let us now multiply the marginal products of the inputs by the number of input units used in the initial specific production function. This will show whether the sums of the marginal products of each input when added together exactly exhaust the total output of the firm. Symbolically,

$$L(MP_L) + K(MP_K) = X$$

Substituting,

$$400(1.249) + 2500(.2)$$
$$= 499.6 + 500$$
$$= 999.6$$

This so closely approximates the desired figure of 1,000 units of X that we may conclude that the combined sums of the marginal products of the inputs are equal to the total product of the firm, and that, therefore, it is possible to apportion to each productive agent the full market value of its contribution to production.[7]

[7] Some readers may wonder if there is any significance to the difference between the amount of total product indicated by the production function and the value of the combined sums of the marginal products of the inputs. (The discrepancy is an extremely small percentage of the desired figure.) The sole reason for the difference between the desired and actual figures is the use of relatively large changes in the inputs. For example, the marginal product of labor was calculated on a base of 400. Increasing the figure to 4,000 would reduce the ratio of the 1-unit change to the base figure and would improve the approximation of the marginal product of labor and also the solution of the "adding-up" problem. If the base figure were increased to 4,000,000, the result would be still better, and using 40,000,000,000, it would be better yet. In other words, the more negligible the incremental change becomes in relation to its base, the closer will our result be to the desired figure. In the limit, when ΔL and ΔK approach zero, there would be no discrepancy. This is shown in the following section, in which calculus is used.

Before we conclude too much from this example, we should note the nature of our simple production function. It is linearly homogeneous and therefore yields constant returns to scale. (See Chapter 6, in which the properties of this function are demonstrated.) Trial calculations confirm that any linearly homogeneous production function would yield results consistent with the product exhaustion theorem. If production functions are not linearly homogeneous, then the theorem does not hold.

In the following section, the basic idea of the product exhaustion theorem is discussed with the aid of some calculus. (Those readers whose mathematical background does not include calculus may skip the next section since it is merely a more precise statement of the arithmetic approximations of this section.)

THE EULER THEOREM

In a linearly homogeneous function, where $X = f(L, K)$, for any uniform increase, n, in the variables L and K

$$nX = f(nL, nK)$$

The mathematician Leonhard Euler proved that for such a function

$$X = \frac{\delta X}{\delta L} \cdot L + \frac{\delta X}{\delta K} \cdot K$$

The first partial derivative of the function with respect to L, $\delta X/\delta L$, is the marginal product of labor, and the first partial derivative of the function with respect to K, $\delta X/\delta K$, is the marginal product of capital. When the marginal products of all the inputs are multiplied by the respective number of input units used, the total will equal the amount of total output. Hence, if the production function is linearly homogeneous, payment of input owners in accord with marginal productivity will exactly exhaust the value of the total product (total revenue) of the firm. There is no residual to be paid as an unearned share of income; neither is any input owner less than fully compensated for his contribution to production.

For example, using our customary illustrative production function

$$X = \sqrt{L \cdot K} = L^{1/2}K^{1/2}$$

The partial derivatives of thus function are

$$\frac{\delta X}{\delta L} = \frac{1}{2}L^{-1/2}K^{1/2} = \frac{1}{2\sqrt{L}}\sqrt{K} = \frac{\sqrt{K}}{2\sqrt{L}}$$

$$\frac{\delta X}{\delta K} = \frac{1}{2}K^{-1/2}L^{1/2} = \frac{1}{2\sqrt{K}}\sqrt{L} = \frac{\sqrt{L}}{2\sqrt{K}}$$

Substituting, we obtain

$$X = \frac{\sqrt{K}}{2\sqrt{L}} L + \frac{\sqrt{L}}{2\sqrt{K}} K$$

$$= \frac{\sqrt{K}\sqrt{L}}{2} + \frac{\sqrt{L}\sqrt{K}}{2} = \sqrt{K}\sqrt{L}$$

Suppose the values of L and K are 4 and 16, respectively. Then, for the production function,

$$X = \sqrt{4 \cdot 16} = \sqrt{64} = 8$$

Substituting into the formulation for Euler's theorem

$$X = \sqrt{16}\sqrt{4} = 4 \cdot 2 = 8$$

The Euler theorem demonstrates product exhaustion when the production function is linearly homogeneous—that is, when the production function yields constant returns to scale over its entire range. This is what Clark desired to show in his general model.

In 1894, economist Philip Wicksteed unsuccessfuly attempted the proof of the product exhaustion theorem. Wicksteed's failure, however, was no loss, for in a review of Wicksteed's book, A. W. Flux conclusively proved the theorem for linearly homogeneous production functions. Finally, Leon Walras, the great general-equilibrium theorist, proved the product exhaustion theorem for the general competitive case. Walras' proof means that regardless of the production function, payment to all input owners in accord with the marginal productivity of their factor units will exactly exhaust total product in the long-run competitive equilibrium. The proof will not be shown here, but its essential nature is easy to grasp.

Since the Euler theorem is an identity, it hoids for all values of the variables under all circumstances. But the assumption of a linearly homogeneous production function is quite restrictive. It can be shown in the case of production functions yielding decreasing returns to scale that paying all input owners in accord with marginal productivity will not exhaust total product (revenue). A residual will remain. Conversely, in the case of production functions yielding increasing returns to scale, it can be demonstrated that payment of all input owners in accord with marginal productivity would more than exhaust total product (revenue). There would not be enough to go around. As was noted in Chapter 7, returns to scale are not empirically significant since, unless the production function is in fact linearly homogeneous, the expansion path of the firm will not describe a path showing returns to scale. Thus, it may seem that the product exhaustion theorem does not have applicability in cases of nonlinear production functions, in particular, in cases defined in Chapter 7 as economies of size. However, in those cases in which the long-run average

total cost curve is U-shaped, *at the minimum point* constant returns to scale prevail (Chapter 7 explains why this is so). This was precisely Walras' point. In the long-run competitive equilibrium, the firm does operate at the minimum point of its long-run average total cost curve, and, therefore, the requirements of the Euler theorem are met. Although the Walras proof holds only for the long-run equilibrium solution of the competitive firm, it is more significant than the Euler theorem, since product exhaustion need not be thought of as a phenomenon of only a special class (linearly homogeneous) of production functions. Moreover, Walras' proof establishes Clark's case. Clark, an equilibrium economist in the classical sense, assumed the long run in his analyses. If his assumptions are taken as given, he was correct in holding that the payment of income shares to input owners in accord with the marginal productivities of their input units will exactly exhaust total product (revenue).

SUMMARY

Underlying the theory of the input market is the principle of marginal productivity. Under competitive conditions in both the output and input markets, the firm will hire inputs so that the ratios of the prices of all inputs to their respective marginal productivities are equal to the selling price of the firm's output.

In the short run, the demand of the competitive firm for a single variable input is shown as the schedule of the value of the marginal product of the variable factor. The *VMP* curve is a *derived* demand curve. It is derived from the market demand curve for the firm's product and the marginal (physical) productivity curve of the subject input. The profit-maximizing firm will hire units of the input so that the value of the marginal product will equal the market price of the input.

In the long run, the *VMP* curve is not the demand curve of the firm for an input, since alterations in the level of input use shifts the output supply curve of each firm and, thus, the market supply curve of the industry. The shifting supply curve, in turn, causes the price of the output to vary. Since a *VMP* curve is drawn for a given output price, a change in that price must shift the entire *VMP* schedule. The long-run demand curve of the firm for an input is, therefore, the locus of points of equilibrium on each of a family of *VMP* curves.

When the supply of an input is invariant with respect to price, as shown by a perfectly inelastic supply curve, any remuneration received by the owner of the input may be regarded as a rent. Rent is defined in economic theory as a nonincentive payment. It is useful in helping to allocate a fixed input to its highest paying use, but it does not affect the quantity supplied of that input.

Since some inputs are fixed in supply in the short run, the payments made for their use are in the nature of rents and are therefore called quasi rents. A quasi rent differs from profit in that the former is in excess of the variable costs

of operation, whereas the latter is an excess over and above the total true costs of production. In the long run, quasi rents disappear.

In general, most inputs have positively sloped supply curves. The supply curve of individual workers, however, may bend backwards. Up to a certain level of wages, the supply curve is positively sloped, but once a critical wage level is reached, the curve may bend backward—that is, become negatively sloped. The reason for this is that above a certain wage rate, the worker's income becomes sufficiently large that, rather than earn additional income, he would prefer some leisure time to enjoy the income he is presently earning.

Early writers on marginal productivity theory were unsure whether or not the total payments to factor owners exactly exhausted the sum of the values of their respective marginal productivities of their input units. The Euler theorem proved that they did in the case of a linearly homogeneous production function of the first degree. The Walras-Flux product exhaustion theorem proved the same proposition for the general long-run equilibrium of the competitive firm.

15

The Theory of the Imperfectly Competitive Input Market

In the preceding chapter, the buyers and sellers of inputs met in a competitive market. What would happen under noncompetitive conditions? For example, would it make any difference if a firm buying inputs competitively sold its products under imperfectly competitive conditions? What would be the effect of imperfect competition in the input market? What are the effects of wage and hour agreements between a union and an employer? Must the imposition of a minimum wage always reduce employment as supply and demand analysis seems to suggest? These, and similar questions, are considered in this chapter. They are important questions because imperfectly competitive conditions are pervasive in both product and input markets.

THE MONOPOLISTIC FIRM IN THE COMPETITIVE INPUT MARKET

MARGINAL REVENUE PRODUCT

We will first assume that a monopolistic firm—a firm with a negatively sloped demand curve—buys its inputs under competitive conditions. In order for any firm to produce more output, it must buy more units of the variable input. To sell a greater amount of an output, the monopolistic firm must reduce the price of its product. This fact causes marginal revenue to be less than average revenue

at all positive levels of output. Under this circumstance, whenever the use of a variable input is increased, the marginal contribution it makes to the total revenue of the firm must fall for two reasons: first, because of the diminishing marginal physical productivity of the input and, second, because of the falling marginal revenue of the firm.

Under imperfectly competitive conditions *in the product market*, a variable input cannot add the full market worth of its marginal product to the total revenue of the firm because each additional unit of output made possible by increasing the use of the variable input adds less to the revenue of the firm than the amount at which it is sold—that is, $MR < AR = P$. In order to understand this, we must identify two monetary measures of input productivity. The first, the *value of the marginal product,* was defined in the preceding chapter as the value (price) of the marginal *physical* product of the variable input in the product market. The second, called the *marginal revenue product,* is the contribution that the marginal product of a variable input makes to the total *revenue* of the firm.

At any given level of input use, the marginal revenue product of the variable input is less than the value of its marginal product. Let us see why. Although the marginal product of the variable input is sold at the same price as the other units of the product, its full value is not added to the revenue of the firm. The nondiscriminating monopolistic firm must lower the price on all units of its output, not just the marginal output, in order to increase its sales (that is, in order to sell the marginal product). Consequently, marginal revenue falls below average revenue (price), and, therefore, the marginal revenue product of the variable input also falls below price. A numerical example will make this clearer. Consider Table 15-1. Labor is the variable input. At an input level of 4 units of labor, the firm produces 65 units of X and sells each unit for $19, resulting in total revenue of $1,235. If the firm increases its input level to 5 units of labor, it produces 75 units of output, which it can sell only if it reduces the price of all units to $18. The marginal product of 10 units is sold for $180, but the amount this sale adds to the revenue of the firm is not $180 but $115 ($1,350 − $1,235). The marginal revenue product ($11.50) is thus less than the value of the marginal product ($18), which is the same as average revenue and price. The graphical relationship between the value of the marginal product and the marginal revenue product is shown in Figure 15-1.[1]

TABLE 15-1	Q_L	Q_X	MP_L	P_X	TR_X	MR_X	VMP_L	MRP_L
	3	50	—	$20	$1000	—	—	—
	4	65	15	19	1235	$16*	$285	$235
	5	75	10	18	1350	12	180	115
	6	80	5	17	1360	2	85	10
	7	82	2	16	1312	−24	32	−48

* *MR* figures are rounded to the nearest dollar.

[1] In accordance with the analysis of Chapter 4, only the relevant (negatively sloped) segments of the two curves are shown.

The Theory of the Imperfectly Competitive Input Market

FIGURE 15-1

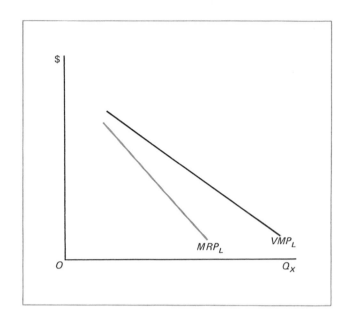

When there is no discrepancy between price and marginal revenue, the values of the marginal product and the marginal revenue product are identical. When marginal revenue is less than price, the marginal revenue product must be less than the value of the marginal product, since for a firm with a negatively sloped demand curve $P > MR$; hence $VMP_L = P_X MP_L > MRP_L = MR_X MP_L$.

The relationships among the various product and revenue concepts are shown in Table 15-1. Some items in the table require explanation. The marginal product figures do not correspond to "infinitesimal" changes in output level (i.e., they are not first derivatives). The marginal product figure corresponding to n input units is obtained by subtracting the total product at $n - 1$ input units from that produced using n units of the variable input. The marginal revenue figures can be obtained by a similar process of subtraction or directly from the marginal revenue product figures. Marginal revenue product has been defined as $MRP_L = MR_X MP_L$. And by definition we know that

$$MR_X = \frac{\Delta TR_X}{\Delta X} \quad \text{and} \quad MP_L = \frac{\Delta X}{\Delta L}$$

Therefore,

$$MRP_L = \frac{\Delta TR_X}{\Delta X} \cdot \frac{\Delta X}{\Delta L} = \frac{\Delta TR_X}{\Delta L}$$

The marginal revenue figures of the table have been computed as the change in total revenue produced by a change in labor when the change in labor is defined as 1 unit. Since the changes in the total output of good X are not unit

The Monopolistic Firm in the Competitive Input Market   **413**

changes, marginal revenue is obtained by dividing the marginal revenue product of labor by the input's marginal product, or

$$MR_x = \frac{MRP_L}{MP_L} = \frac{\Delta TR_x}{\Delta L} \div \frac{\Delta X}{\Delta L}$$

The table shows that both the values of the marginal product and the marginal revenue product of the variable input decline as more units of the input are used; but, unlike the *VMP* figures of the preceding chapter, the present figures do not fall solely because of the principle of diminishing marginal productivity. To sell more units of output, as we have said, the noncompetitive firm must reduce its price. As the marginal productivity of the input falls, the marginal revenue derived from selling the output also falls. In the imperfectly competitive case, the marginal physical product of labor falls as output increases, and that product simultaneously becomes less valuable. In contrast, in the competitive case, the marginal productivity of the input declines in conjunction with increased output, but the price at which the marginal product is sold remains constant.

Thus, if there were two comparable firms, one competitive and the other monopolistic, the VMP_L curve of the latter would fall faster than that of the former. The monopolistic firm therefore should be expected to use less labor (and produce a smaller amount of output) than would a similarly situated competitive firm. For any given quantity of output, the value of the marginal product of labor would be lower in the monopolistic firm. Consequently, at any given wage rate, it will not be worthwhile for the monopolistic firm to hire as much labor as the competitive firm. Assuming identical production functions, the firm using the smaller amount of labor will produce a lesser output. This conclusion is consistent with the hypothesis of Chapter 9 that monopolistic firms are output restrictors.

THE DEMAND CURVE OF THE MONOPOLISTIC FIRM FOR A VARIABLE INPUT

Now that we have set the stage, we can consider the actual behavior of a monopolistic seller that buys its inputs under competitive conditions.

In the short run, the firm's adjustments are constrained by the presence of fixed inputs; consequently, as we saw in Chapter 14, the firm's derived demand curve for the variable input (labor) cannot be affected by repercussions from other (fixed) input markets. The demand curve of the competitive firm for a variable input is the input's *VMP* curve. This cannot be the case for a monopolistic firm. Consider the data of Table 15-2, in which the Q_L, VMP_L, and MRP_L columns are taken from Table 15-1. The price of labor (the wage rate) is constant throughout the schedule, since in a competitive input market, the demand of any one firm for a productive factor cannot affect the factor's price.

The Theory of the Imperfectly Competitive Input Market

As we now know, a firm will continue to buy input units as long as the marginal unit adds more to the revenue of the firm than it does to cost. If the firm employs 4 units of labor, the marginal input cost (i.e., the price) of 1 unit

TABLE 15-2	P_L	Q_L	VMP_L	MRP_L
	$10	4	$285	$235
	10	5	180	115
	10	6	85	10
	10	7	32	−48

of labor is $10. At this level of input use, a unit of labor adds $235 to the firm's revenue. Clearly, the firm should continue to buy more labor services. If it expands the employment of the variable factor to 5 units at a marginal input cost of $10, the contribution of labor to the revenue of the firm is $115. With the employment of 6 units of labor, the cost of the marginal unit is equal to the amount that labor adds to the revenue of the firm. The profit-maximizing firm, then, will hire up to 6 units of the variable resource. With 7 units of labor employed, the marginal cost of the input is greater than the marginal contribution (−$48) of labor to the total revenue of the firm.[2] From this reasoning, we conclude that whether the firm is competitive or monopolistic, the marginal revenue product curve of the variable input is the firm's demand curve for the input in the short run. In the competitive case, the marginal revenue product and the value of the marginal product curves are identical, since $MR = P$. When the curves diverge, as they do in the imperfectly competitive case—when $MR < P$—the concern of the firm in input hiring is, not the amount for which the marginal product of the input can be sold, but the change in total revenue effected by that sale. Figure 15-2 shows this reasoning graphically.

To a firm in a competitive input market, the factor supply curve will appear as a horizontal straight line. The firm can acquire all the labor units it wants at the parametric price of $O\overline{W}$. Given this wage and the MRP_L curve, the firm demands $O\overline{L}$ units of labor. If it hires fewer units—say, OL_1 units—labor is adding more to the revenue of the firm than to its costs. Increasing the input of labor will cause total profit to rise. Should the firm move down the MRP_L curve to the right of point E until—say, to OL_2 units of labor—the resource would add to the costs of operation at a rate exceeding its contribution to total revenue. Accordingly, the firm will achieve equilibrium in regard to the labor market at point E, at which labor's additions to cost and revenue occur at the same rate. Any subsequent movement away from point E will reduce the firm's total profit. The marginal revenue product curve is, then, the demand curve of the firm for a single variable input.

[2] For a marginal unit of labor not to be worth hiring, that unit's marginal contribution to revenue need not be negative, as it is here; it need only be smaller than the unit's marginal cost (in this case, $10).

FIGURE 15-2

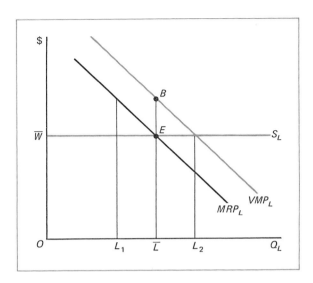

The VMP_L curve has been added to Figure 15-2 to show that the amount at which the marginal product of the variable input is sold is of no consequence in an imperfectly competitive firm's employment decisions. At $O\bar{L}$ units of labor, the value of the marginal product of labor exceeds the marginal revenue product of the input in the amount EB. Nevertheless, the firm will hire no more labor, although at the margin the amount at which the product of one additional unit of labor would sell exceeds the cost of labor. The value of labor's marginal product will exceed the cost of additional units of the input (the marginal input cost) until OL_2 units are employed. But at any level of input use between $\bar{L}$ and L_2, the marginal revenue product of labor is less than its marginal cost. Additional units of labor cost the firm more than they contribute in revenue, even if the product of those additional units sells for an amount greater than, or equal to, the additional cost their use imposes on the firm. As we have concluded previously, the value of the marginal product of a single input plays no role in the short-run employment decision of an imperfectly competitive firm.

THE DEMAND CURVE OF THE FIRM FOR A SINGLE INPUT IN THE LONG RUN

The analysis of the long-run demand curve of the imperfectly competitive firm for a single input is essentially the same as the case of a competitive firm explained in the preceding chapter. The sole difference between the two cases is that the imperfectly competitive situation utilizes the marginal revenue product curves of the subject input and not the value of the marginal product curves.

Consider Figure 15-3. Initially, assume that the marginal revenue product curve of labor is MRP_1 and that the wage rate is OW_0. The firm hires OL_0 units of labor. Now suppose that the wage rate falls to OW_1. As we saw in the pre-

ceding section, in the short run, the firm will move down MRP_1 from A to B, increasing its employment of the variable input by L_0L_1' units.

In the long run, labor is no longer the sole variable input, since there are no limitations on the firm's ability to change the quantity of *any* input. After the short-run adjustment, the ratio MRP_L/P_L appropriate to point B will be less than the ratio MRP_K/P_K. This is so because the increase in labor relative to capital *raises* the marginal physical productivity of capital, each present unit of capital now having more labor with which to work (capital has become scarce relative to labor). The increase in the marginal *physical* productivity of capital is reflected in an increase in the marginal *revenue* productivity of capital. Consequently, the firm cannot be maximizing profit in the long-run context, since now the marginal revenue productivity of capital exceeds its price. Given the opportunity, it will purchase more capital, thereby reducing the marginal revenue productivity of capital per dollar. But a greater quantity of capital will *increase* the marginal revenue productivity of labor, since each unit of labor will now have more capital with which to work. Consequently, the MRP curve for labor will shift rightward, showing that at any given wage rate the firm will demand more labor than curve MRP_1 indicates.

If the firm buys more labor, the marginal revenue productivity of capital will increase, causing the firm to buy more plant and equipment. Again, the increase in capital causes the MRP curve of labor to move farther to the right.

The initial fall in the price of labor causes the firm's long-run marginal cost curve to shift downward. A new and larger optimal output is indicated. We may expect that the firm will seek a larger production budget with which to buy more labor and capital, and that this effect will move the MRP curves of all inputs farther to the right than if the production budget were to remain fixed.

As we saw in the previous chapter, the rightward movement of the MRP

FIGURE 15-3

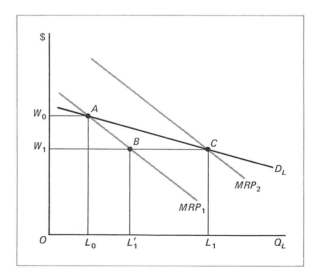

curves of all inputs will be terminated by the profit-maximizing goal of the firm. The demand for the good and the positive input prices impose precise limits on the amount of each input the firm can use in the profit-maximizing solution, and this is the force that eventually limits the rightward shift of the MRP curves of all inputs.

Assuming that the limit of the rightward shift of the MRP_L curve is MRP_2 in Figure 15-3, the firm will hire OL_1 units of labor at the wage rate OW_1. Thus, in the long run, a fall in the wage rate from OW_0 to OW_1 induces the firm to increase its usage of labor by L_0L_1 units rather than $L_0L'_1$ units. Joining the points of intersection between the ordinates of various wage rates and the shifting marginal revenue product curves (A and C, here), we obtain the curve D_L, which shows the quantity of labor the firm will demand at various wage rates when all inputs are variable. Accordingly, we may regard D_L as the firm's demand curve for labor in the long run. In the long run, we know that the firm has attained the profit-maximizing equilibrium solution when

$$\frac{MP_L}{P_L} = \frac{MP_K}{P_K} = \frac{1}{MR_X}$$

Multiplying the above terms by the marginal revenue of the firm, we can write the profit-maximizing condition in terms of the marginal revenue product

$$\frac{MRP_L}{P_L} = \frac{MRP_K}{P_K} = 1$$

When the ratio of the marginal revenue products of all inputs to their prices is 1 (and, therefore, all are necessarily equal), the firm is maximizing profit. Any changes in input price or the demand for the good will lead the firm away from the profit maximum and necessitate a chain of adjustments.

THE MARKET DEMAND CURVE FOR AN INPUT

The input market demand curves of monopolistic sellers must be explained with reference to the specific circumstances of each case. If the firm is a pure monopolist and the sole user of an input (as was the case with the use of bauxite clay by Alcoa until after the Second World War), the market demand curve is simply the long-run demand curve of the firm.

If several monopolies, each an industry unto itself, comprise the entire buyer's side of an input market, the market demand curve is derived as simply as a market demand curve for a consumer's good. Since adjustments in the sales of one firm will have no repercussions on the price and output decisions of any other firm, the market demand curve for an input, under such circumstances, is simply the horizontal summation of the individual input demand curves of all the various monopolists buying the specified factor.

The Theory of the Imperfectly Competitive Input Market

The situation with respect to monopolistic competitors and oligopolists in some ways resembles the case of purely competitive firms.[3] The reason for the similarity is the interdependence of the demands and outputs of such firms.

If the price of an input used by a monopolistic competitor falls, the firm will undertake to make the adjustments previously described. But each member of the product group will be affected identically and will attempt the same adjustments. A lower input price will lead each firm in the group to expand output, but the groupwide expansion of the output of highly substitutable goods will cause the prices of such goods to decline. As a result, the firms of the monopolistically competitive group must undertake further adjustments.

In Figure 15-4, the initial wage rate is shown as OW_0. Chart (a) shows a particular monopolistic competitor demanding OI_0 units of labor while the product group (shown in chart b) demands OL_0 units. (For simplicity, OL_0 may be regarded as $n(OI_0)$, where n is the number of firms in the group.) Assume that the wage rate falls to OW_1. At first, the individual firm may believe that the most profitable course is to move down D_L to point b and increase the input of labor by I_0I_1 units; but every firm will plan to do this. Moreover, the fall in input price creates entry-inducing excess profits. As the firms act to buy more inputs and new firms enter the group, output will increase, causing the price of the good to fall. Consequently, the marginal revenue of the good also must

FIGURE 15-4

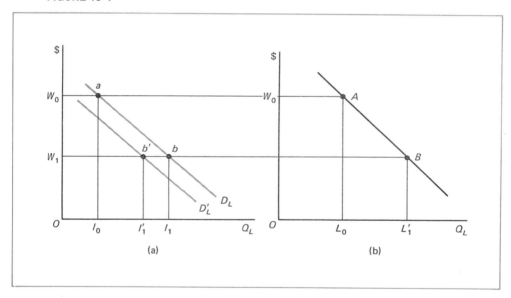

(a)   (b)

[3] Allowance must be made for the additional complications of oligopolistic uncertainty and the resulting strategic decision-making process.

fall. The increased use of labor causes the marginal product of the input to fall, and since, $MRP_L = MP_L \cdot MR_X$, the marginal revenue product of labor at every level of labor use must fall. The MRP_L curves of each firm must shift downward (leftward), in turn causing each firm's demand curve for labor to shift downward also. Assume that the downward shift in the labor demand curve of a firm is shown by D'_L. With the fall in the wage rate to OW_1, the firm proceeds, not to b on D_L, but to b' on D'_L, and it demands, not Ol_1 quantity of labor, but Ol'_1 units. Thus, the group demand for labor is shown in Figure 15-4 (b) as OL'_1 units of labor, where $OL'_1 = n(Ol'_1) < n(Ol_1)$.

MONOPSONY IN THE INPUT MARKET

THE NATURE OF MONOPSONY

Just as there may be a single seller of a good, so there may be a single buyer of some product. The case of the sole purchaser is called monopsony. In the vast majority of cases, monopsony exists in input markets rather than in product markets. It is difficult to think of any household that is the sole buyer of the output of a particular industry. In the case of inputs, however, examples of monopsony, or at least monopsonistic competition, are not unusual. The New England town dominated by one large firm for which everyone worked is disappearing, but it is a frequently encountered aspect of American economic history and fiction. And, today, examples rather closely approximating the old New England relationship can be found readily. The Boeing Company and the city of Seattle come to mind. Other instances might be the Anaconda Copper Mining Company and Butte, Montana; the Hershey Chocolate Company and Hershey, Pennsylvania; the Santa Fe Railway and Barstow, California. One evidence of monopsony in the labor market is when the economic fortunes of a geographical area rise or fall with the change in the business activities of one firm. Such behavior is readily observable in the changing fortunes of Seattle and the aircraft orders of the Boeing Company.

Other examples may involve single firms rather than geographic areas. It is not unusual to find a large retailing chain buying the entire output of a manufacturing concern or a large automobile manufacturer buying the entire output of a smaller firm, the smaller firm being a virtual subsidiary of the larger. (The form of independent ownership is preserved, but not the reality.)

MARGINAL INPUT COST

When a firm is the sole buyer in an input market, it cannot take factor price as given. It normally cannot buy various quantities of input at the same price. Since it is the sole buyer in the market, the market supply curve of the input is the supply curve to the firm. Here, we shall assume that in the relevant range (a range of feasible wage rates) the supply curve of labor is positively

The Theory of the Imperfectly Competitive Input Market

sloped. In such a situation, the firm can obtain more units of input only by raising the rate of remuneration. But if the rate of remuneration rises with every addition to input use, the *rate* of increase in factor cost must exceed the actual increase in the factor reward. These relationships are shown in Figure 15-5, in which the curve depicting the marginal input cost (*MIC*) lies above the supply curve of labor. Each increase in labor costs the firm an amount greater than the (higher) wage rate necessary to obtain the desired amount of labor (because, of course, the firm must pay the higher rate for all its labor, not just for the additional amount). The cost pattern depicted graphically in Figure 15-5 is described numerically in Table 15-3.

TABLE 15-3	Q_L	Wage Rate	Total Wages	MIC
	10	$10	$100	$—
	11	11	121	21
	12	13	156	35
	13	16	208	52
	14	20	280	72

Marginal input cost is expressed by the formula

$$MIC = \frac{\Delta TW}{\Delta L}$$

It is the change in total wages (*TW*) produced by a change in the variable input (here, labor), when the change in the input is defined as 1 unit.

We have said that the firm must increase the wages paid to *all* its employ-

FIGURE 15-5

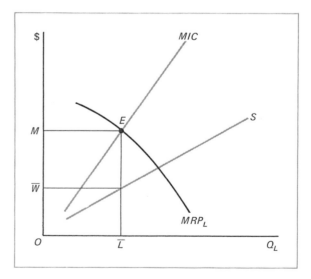

ees whenever it increases its use of labor on the assumption that the employees have full knowledge of the going wage rate and that their work would be adversely affected by discriminatory rates. But if the firm *could* discriminate against its employees—much as a seller can practice price discrimination against its customers—the marginal input cost curve would coincide with the input supply curve. Doubtless, some firms do tend to discriminate against their employees. This is one reason why employers often insist that all their wage arrangements with individual employees be kept confidential. Newcomers to the firm may be hired at rates exceeding those at which older employees were hired or even those at which they may be working currently. The more an employer is able to hold down the wages of senior employees in the face of the firm's rising demand for labor, the less the marginal input cost will diverge from the wage rate. Obviously, employers cannot discriminate in wages very well if wage rates are matters of public record, as they are likely to be in public employments or under union contracts. Consequently, most cases of discrimination in wages concern the salaried and white-collar employees of private employers. The large aerospace firm with an apparently insatiable demand for engineering and technical talent (when it has a governmental contract) may be able to attract more personnel by increasingly attractive offers to newcomers without raising its marginal input cost if salary talks among professional personnel are regarded by the firm as the greatest possible breech of good faith between the firm and its employees. On the other hand, if there is active competition for professional personnel among firms within a given labor market, the clarity of the economic signals may easily be heard despite the secretive wage policies of a particular firm.

THE EMPLOYMENT OF A SINGLE VARIABLE INPUT

Figure 15-5 depicts the employment situation for a monopsonistic employer hiring under conditions of one-input variability. A monoposonistic firm will hire a variable input up to the point at which its marginal input cost is equal to its marginal revenue product. In the diagram, this occurs at point E, at which $MIC = OM = MRP_L$. The employer hires $O\bar{L}$ units of labor at a wage rate of $O\bar{W}$. If the employer were to hire fewer than $O\bar{L}$ labor units, the marginal revenue product of labor would exceed the marginal input cost of the factor. The firm could increase its profit by hiring more factor units, since enlarging the labor force would add more to revenue than it would to costs. The firm should hire more labor, although by doing so it causes the wage rate to rise. When the wage rate has reached $O\bar{W}$, the firm will have hired the short-run profit-maximizing quantity of the variable input.

If the firm were to operate in the segment of the MRP_L curve lying to the right of point E, the marginal revenue product of the variable input would be less than its marginal input cost. The firm could increase its profit by cutting back on the use of labor. A reduction in the labor force would cause a reduction in marginal input cost and an increase in the marginal revenue productivity of labor; hence, profit would rise.

The Theory of the Imperfectly Competitive Input Market

THE EMPLOYMENT DECISION
WHEN ALL INPUTS ARE VARIABLE

When all input quantities are variable, the firm must hire resources not only so that the marginal input cost of each particular resource is equal to its marginal revenue productivity but also so that all inputs are hired in the proper relation to each other. For any firm, some inputs may be hired monopsonistically while some may be hired under competitive conditions. For example, consider a firm whose hiring of labor makes a significant impact on the employment level in a particular locality. It may hire labor monopsonistically, but its employment of capital may have no repercussions on equipment prices.

Previously, we have seen that a firm selling a good under monopolistic conditions and buying its inputs competitively is in equilibrium when

$$\frac{MP_L}{P_L} = \frac{MP_K}{P_K} = \frac{1}{MR_X} \quad \text{or} \quad \frac{MRP_L}{P_L} = \frac{MRP_K}{P_K} = 1$$

Under monopsonistic conditions in the labor market, the firm hires up to the point at which $MRP_L = MIC_L$ and, in equilibrium,

$$MRP_L = MIC_L > P_L$$

The firm hiring monopsonistically tends to use less inputs than if it were to hire competitively, just as a firm selling its output under monopolistic conditions tends to restrict production to a level below the competitive norm. The reduction of output owing to monopolistic conditions in the selling market leads the monopolistic firm to use fewer inputs than would a competitive firm similarly situated. If monopsony in the input market is added to monopoly in the product market, still further input and output reduction must result. Suppose improvements in transportation were to open a resource market so that competitive conditions were fostered. Then, P_L would become equal to MIC_L, and the formerly monopsonistic firm would expand its use of labor, expand output, and, if it is an imperfect competitor, it would lower the price of its output.

Under conditions of monopsony in both input markets, the firm would maximize profit when

$$\frac{MP_L}{MIC_L} = \frac{MP_K}{MIC_K} = \frac{1}{MR_X} \quad \text{or} \quad \frac{MRP_L}{MIC_L} = \frac{MRP_K}{MIC_K} = 1$$

Under conditions of monopsony in the labor market and competition in the capital market, we may write the equilibrium condition as

$$\frac{MRP_L}{MIC_L} = \frac{MRP_K}{P_K} = 1$$

MONOPOLISTIC AND MONOPSONISTIC EXPLOITATION

Exploitation, a concept we encountered in the preceding chapter, has from time to time served as a stimulus to the formulation of distribution theories. For the moment, disregard the supply curve of labor in Figure 15-6 and assume as a standard of comparison that the wage rate in the competitive labor market is OW. The purely competitive firm will hire OL_1 labor units at the given competitive wage rate. If each unit of labor is paid the prevailing rate, each will receive the value of its marginal product ($OW = L_1 A_1$).

Monopolistic exploitation. Now assume that the firm sells its output in an imperfectly competitive product market. Under this condition, the marginal revenue product curve of labor lies beneath the value of the marginal product curve. As we have seen, whatever the competitive case, the marginal revenue product curve constitutes the firm's demand curve for a single variable input; therefore, the monopolistic firm will employ only OL_2 units of labor. The reduction in the employment of the variable resource raises the value of its marginal product while the marginal revenue product remains equated to the prevailing wage rate. It is obvious that under conditions of imperfection in the product market, the value of the variable input's marginal product, $L_2 B$, must exceed its rate of remuneration, $OW = L_2 A_2$.

Several years ago, a few economists defined a situation in which a resource is paid less than the value of its marginal product as the monopolistic exploitation of the factor, since the factor, then, receives less than the market value of its product. However, the word *exploitation* suggests that someone is being deprived of something rightfully his, and this is not the case in what has been called monopolistic exploitation. The revenue that each unit of an

FIGURE 15-6

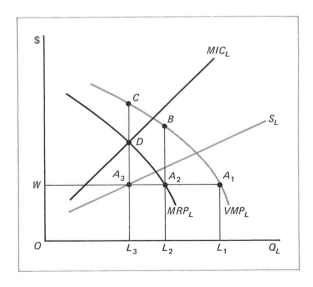

The Theory of the Imperfectly Competitive Input Market

input contributes to the firm is its marginal revenue product. Neither the firm, nor anyone connected with the firm, pockets the difference between the marginal revenue product and the value of the marginal product. Attempting to pay each owner of one class of inputs the value of the marginal product of his input units would deprive the owners of other classes of inputs of even the marginal revenue product of their factor units. There is no culpable exploitative act involved in so-called monopolistic exploitation, and, in consequence, the vast majority of contemporary economists reject the concept as virtually empty.

Monopsonistic exploitation. Now let us assume that Figure 15-6 represents a monopolistic firm buying inputs monopsonistically. The market supply curve of the input, S_L, is the supply curve to the firm. Since, at all levels of employment, the marginal cost of the input exceeds the wage rate, the firm hires OL_3 units of labor at wage OW. The value of the marginal product of the input is L_3C. The marginal revenue product is L_3D. Under conditions of monopsony, the input owner receives neither as much as the value of the marginal product nor as much as the marginal revenue product of its input units. Some economists have referred to the discrepancy between the wage rate and the marginal revenue product (A_3D) as the monopsonistic exploitation of the input. Under conditions of monopsony, the input receives less than the contribution it makes to the revenue of the firm. Since OL_3 units of labor can be hired at a wage rate of OW, the profit-maximizing firm will not *willingly* pay more for labor. Might it unwillingly pay more for the input?

INTERFERENCE WITH THE RATE OF FACTOR REWARD

Minimum-wage regulations have become increasingly widespread in recent decades. Many earnest observers of the economy decry attempts to raise the rates of remuneration of inputs above those set in the free market, or by particular employers, on the grounds that some unemployment inevitably must follow. Actually, even if unemployment were to follow, it might be desirable to interfere with the usual methods of setting input prices. Let us consider some alternatives.

Monopolistic conditions. Suppose Figure 15-7 depicts a monopolistic firm hiring labor competitively. Such a firm might be a winery growing its own grapes and bottling a differentiated product. If the labor involved in raising the grapes consists of fieldworkers, the winery will hire OL_1 units of labor at a wage rate of OW_1. Next, let us suppose that the minimum wage for field hands rises to OW_2. Since the input market has been defined as competitive, unless there is an exit of workers from this particular labor market, some extra-market force must be responsible for the increase in the wage rates. Two of the most likely causes for the increase (W_1W_2) could be the legal imposition of a uniform minimum wage or the negotiation of a uniform wage and hour contract by a labor union. In either case, the wage to the employer becomes OW_2. The firm can hire all the labor it can use at this new wage rate; therefore, the supply curve

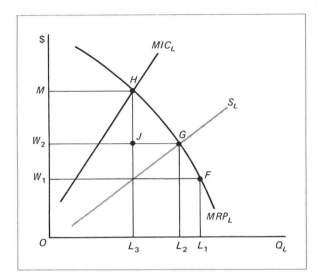

FIGURE 15-7

of labor to the firm appears to be infinitely elastic at the wage OW_2. (The up-ward-sloping supply curve of labor, S_L, plays no role in the present analysis and should be disregarded.)

Clearly, the prediction of those who assert that *ceteris paribus,* some workers must be discharged or have their hours reduced is correct. With the increase in the wage rate, the marginal revenue productivity of labor is too low to make the OL_1 level of employment profitable to the firm. In direct conse-quence of the forced wage increase, the firm must reduce the employment level to OL_2, and L_2L_1 laborers must lose their jobs. Partially offsetting this apparently unpleasant event is the fact that those workers who *do* retain their jobs now have higher wages and may improve their living standards.

Up to this point, our analysis has been descriptive of the practices of some American trade unions. When the union's objective of wage increases is fulfilled, a number of union members lose their jobs. What kind of sense does this make? It makes a great deal of sense if you are a union president. The membership demands higher wages; much else in union activity is rather peripheral. A union president cannot expect a long tenure if he does not ob-tain tangible economic benefits for his members. Rising wages help to get votes. It might seem that the accompanying rising unemployment would cost votes, but only dues-paying members vote. Dues are collected out of pay-checks, and only employed union members are on the payroll.

It is possible also to advance a social argument in favor of the unemploy-ment that must accompany wage increases in a competitive labor market. Per-haps OW_1 is too low a wage to permit OL_1 persons to live decently on their incomes. At this wage, those working may require considerable public assis-tance to be able to survive. A wage rate of OW_2, however, may allow those re-maining employed to be self-sufficient, even though those unemployed can meet none of their expenses now that they have lost their incomes. The dif-

The Theory of the Imperfectly Competitive Input Market

ference between these two situations is that at the wage OW_1, the public is, in effect, subsidizing the employer. If his workers must receive public assistance in addition to their wages in order to furnish the labor services desired by the employer, then the firm is placing some of its production costs on taxpayers, and, since all its true costs are not privately met, it may tend to overproduce. Raising wages to OW_2 may force a firm to bear the full costs of the use of the input. Those unemployed then become a readily identifiable group, and their greater visibility may help to get them equipped with the skills they need to become fully self-supporting.

In other words, it may be desirable in some cases for some workers to lose their jobs and remain unemployed for a considerable period in order that they and the employed workers may all be better off. Suppose that Figure 15-7 depicts the situation of a monopolistic employer in a competitive labor market who is employing OL_1 workers at a wage rate of OW_1. Suppose OW_1 is $6 per day, and OL_1 is equal to 5,000 workers, one-fifth of whom are below the age of eighteen and are members of families whose principal employment is with the same employer. Perhaps some of these younger people work for less than the prevailing $6 per day rate. Now let us suppose that a state minimum wage law or a union contract fixes the wage rate at OW_2, which we shall assume to be $8 per day. The employer will then discharge L_2L_1 workers. Suppose L_2L_1 is equal to 1,000 workers, or one-fifth of the labor force. Probably those fired will be the workers under eighteen. Will the families suffer a loss of income if all those capable of working are forced out of work? They will not if the demand for labor is inelastic. Let us assume that the MRP_1 curve, which is the firm's demand curve for labor is inelastic, in the region from F to G. At $8 per day, the 4,000 remaining workers must receive more total income than 5,000 workers did at a wage rate of $6 per day. The new total income is $32,000. On the average, each family will be slightly better off; at least they will have lost no income as a result of their children losing their jobs. It may now be possible for the members of the under-eighteen group to attend school full time without depriving their families of income necessary for survival.

The inelasticity of demand for labor is crucial in determining whether a wage increase will be beneficial to all the workers.[4] If demand is elastic, a wage increase will cause the total income of workers to fall. However, those released from the labor force in the short run may now have the opportunity to acquire new skills that will lead them to more rewarding positions. These examples are intended to show that even in a competitive labor market, wage increases, although causing unemployment, may have results beneficial for labor as a whole, and that simple-minded, if well-meaning, economic analysis often yields incorrect conclusions.

[4] In the short run of many industries, particularly agriculture, the demand for labor is likely to be inelastic, especially at harvest and planting times, because there is insufficient time to substitute capital equipment for labor. The history of American agriculture shows that, in the very long run, technology has provided extremely effective substitutes for human labor applied to the land. Thus, wage gains may be only a temporary benefit for migrant workers, for in the long run, the demand for their services will tend to become elastic, and further wage increases will be met with a sizable reduction in employment opportunities.

Monopsonistic conditions. Under conditions of monopsony, higher wages may lead to an *increase* in employment. Suppose the imperfectly competitive firm depicted in Figure 15-7 hires labor under monopsonistic conditions. The upward-sloping supply curve of labor, S_L, now becomes relevant. As we have seen, the monopsonistic employer will hire OL_3 units of labor at the wage rate OW_1. Each unit of labor will be monopsonistically exploited in the amount W_1M, the amount by which the wage falls short of the marginal revenue product of the input.

Suppose a minimum wage law or a union agreement raises the wage to OW_2. The firm can hire all the labor it wants at this imposed rate. The supply curve of labor then becomes W_2GS_L. In the relevant range, the marginal input cost curve is W_2G. Under the imposed wage, curves S_L and MIC_L have no significance as long as the given MRP_L curve remains applicable. With the effective MIC_L curve now being W_2G, the firm will hire OL_2 units of labor. The monopsonistic exploitation of the input is eliminated, since the marginal revenue product of labor, L_2G, is equal to the wage rate, OW_2. Thus, under monopsonistic conditions, a wage increase can be accompanied by an increase in the quantity demanded of labor.

Why should a firm use more labor when the wage rate is increased? When the wage rate is imposed by law or by an agreement, marginal input cost becomes a constant equal to the constant wage rate. The firm does not need to raise wages to hire more labor as long as the market supplies workers at wage rates equal to, or less than, that imposed. Therefore, the marginal input cost does not rise as employment is increased. Since it is profitable for the firm to hire labor until the marginal revenue product of the input has been brought into equality with the constant marginal input cost, the firm will hire more labor with an imposed wage of OW_2 than it will if the relevant labor supply curve is S_L and the indicated wage rate is OW_1. The imposed wage rate reduces the marginal input cost in the amount JH. Accordingly, the profit-maximizing firm will hire more labor until the marginal revenue product of the input has been reduced an equal amount.

The employment level OL_2 represents the maximum employment the union or a minimum wage law can secure in defeating monopsonistic exploitation. Every wage level lying between OW_1 and OW_2 will expand employment beyond OL_3 but will not fully eliminate monopsonistic exploitation. Therefore, if the union desires to obtain the maximum possible level of employment for its members, it should attempt to secure the wage rate OW_2, which will result in a higher wage rate as well as greater employment for the union members.

Suppose the policy objective of the union is to secure the highest possible wage for the number of employees hired under purely monopsonistic conditions. The union may raise the wage as high as OM without causing the employer to rid himself of the now higher-paid labor inputs. If the wage rate is raised to OM, the supply curve of labor becomes MH up to the firm's MRP_L curve. Over this relevant range, the marginal input cost curve proper to the

new labor supply curve is the horizontal line segment *MH*. To equate the marginal revenue product of labor with the marginal input cost, the firm will maintain the level of employment at OL_3. Since the wage *OM* is equal to the marginal input cost, the new wage agreement not only provides the same labor force with a higher income but abolishes the monopsonistic exploitation of labor. It is possible for the union to obtain still higher wages without monopsonistic exploitation, but at any wage level above *OM*, employment must fall below OL_3. The protection of employment offered by the monopsonistic arrangement is extinguished at wage rates higher than *OM*.

Since any factor may be the object of monopsonistic exploitation, one may wonder if some pro-labor bias tends to haunt supposedly neutral economic analysis. In some cases, particularly in earlier times in which the concepts of monopolistic and monopsonistic exploitation originated, this may have been true. There is some reason for believing that labor is somewhat more vulnerable to monopsonistic exploitation than is capital. The worker in the one-firm small town is probably not nearly as mobile as is the capital input. The market for capital funds is likely to be far wider than the market for labor. Moreover, capital does not need to be retrained or find a congenial neighborhood in which to live. Since businesses must compete for capital funds in wide markets in which funds may be quickly advanced and withdrawn and in which rates of return are readily known and easily compared, the suppliers of capital are less likely to be the objects of monopsonistic exploitation than are the owners of labor inputs. It is not often that a single private firm can, by itself, force upward the price of capital. In the absence of an upward-sloping supply curve, monopsonistic exploitation is impossible.

SUMMARY

Imperfect competition in resource markets has two principal aspects: (1) a firm selling its output under monopolistic conditions and hiring inputs under competitive conditions; and (2) the same type of firm hiring its inputs under imperfectly competitive, or monopsonistic, conditions.

A monopolistic seller hiring inputs in a competitive factor market will maximize profit by hiring the quantity of the input that will equate the price of the input with its marginal revenue product. Although this is the same rule followed by a competitive firm hiring inputs in a competitive input market, the situations are not identical since the marginal revenue product of an input hired by a noncompetitive seller is less than the value of its marginal product, whereas under conditions of competition in the product market they are the same. Accordingly, in the short run, under the conditions described, the marginal revenue product curve of an input is the firm's demand curve for that input.

In the long run, general equilibrium effects must be considered in determining the demand curve of a single input. For example, hiring more labor

causes the marginal revenue productivity of capital to rise. Consequently, the firm will hire more capital, but this, in turn, causes the marginal revenue productivity of labor to increase, and the firm will then hire still more labor. The goal of the firm to maximize its profit puts a limit on these movements, and once capital and labor are hired in the profit-maximizing proportions and absolute amounts, the input demand curves will cease to shift.

Also, owing to general equilibrium effects, the market demand curve for a particular input is not the simple horizontal summation of the appropriate marginal revenue product curves. Changes in input prices will affect the output plans of firms, but changes in output affect the marginal revenue productivities of the inputs. Consequently, changes in the conditions of input supply necessarily affect the demand for the input. Shifts in the *MRP* curves of the inputs in the affected firms are terminated when the profit-maximizing condition is fulfilled.

A firm is said to be a monopsonistic resource buyer if its hiring affects the price of an input. Under conditions of monopsony, the marginal cost of the input (marginal input cost) exceeds the price of the input. Since a profit-maximizing (or cost-minimizing) firm makes its calculations at the margin, it will seek to equate marginal input cost with the marginal revenue product of the input.

The equality of marginal input cost and marginal revenue product under conditions of monopsony produces a situation known in economic theory as monopsonistic resource exploitation. Because marginal input cost exceeds the price of the input, the input's marginal revenue product exceeds its price; that is, the input adds more to the revenue of the firm than it receives as its share of income.

Monopsonistic exploitation can be eliminated without necessarily reducing the employment of the input if the input seller can attain some measure of monopoly power. In the labor market, for example, the element of monopoly power typically comes from a union contract or a minimum wage law. The imposition of a uniform wage above the market determined price of labor causes the marginal input cost of the input to become a constant to the employer. Since the employer can now, within a certain range at least, hire labor without affecting its price, the marginal input cost is equal to the price of the input. Thus, the employer will pay every input owner the marginal revenue product of each of his input units. An adroit use of monopoly power on the part of resource owners can preclude monopsonistic exploitation and, at the same time, expand employment. However, there are limits to this process. Pushed above a certain level, a monopolistic rate of factor reward can lead to unemployment just as in a competitive labor market. Too much should not be read into techniques to ameliorate monopsonistic exploitation; like any other use of monopoly power, what is good for a particular group of persons may not be socially optimal. A detailed consideration of the effects of divergencies in private and social optima will be given in Chapter 17.

The Theory of the Imperfectly Competitive Input Market

16

The Theory of
the General Equilibrium

THE ECONOMY AS A SYSTEM

"The economy," says the typical first-year economics text, "is a system for economizing." We know that economizing is the act of making a rational choice under conditions of scarcity, but how does the system concept apply? *System* implies a unified whole made up of interrelated components. For example, a stereo sound system is not simply a turntable, an amplifier, and several speakers. Even if each component taken separately performs properly, when they are combined in a system, they may not function as desired; perhaps they will not operate at all *as a system.*

IS THE ECONOMY A SYSTEM?

Is the economy really a system, or is it simply a mixture of component parts? In previous chapters, we identified the parts and developed theories in an attempt to explain the functioning of each one. The simplest components of the economy are households and business firms. Between them, economic activity flows as if in a circle. Households are the ultimate consumers of the resources they themselves supply. To convert their resources into the goods they want, the members of individual households sell such input as they own to business firms. The function of the firms is to transform these inputs into goods, some of which are themselves inputs, and

some of which are the goods that furnish utility directly to the individuals within each household.

To this point, we have described the *real* flows within the economy. Corresponding to the real flows are *monetary* flows. In exchange for the services of productive inputs, the business firms return the households a money payment. Thus, the expenditures of firms become the money incomes of the households. Out of their money incomes, households buy the goods and services (their real incomes) produced for them in the business sector. The living expenses of households become the firm's total receipts, which they once again pay the households for the hire of their inputs. Clearly, the economy is comprised of two types of circular flow revolving in opposite directions; one type is real, the other monetary.[1]

But a circular flow by itself is not a system. When we look within the circular flow of a predominately market economy, we see individual economic units behaving in ways that have confounded many thoughtful persons both before and after the time of Adam Smith. Throughout the system, millions of economic units—consumers, resource suppliers, and firms—are making millions upon millions of self-interested (not necessarily selfish) decisions. Except within broad limits no one, not even fairly meddlesome governments, attempts to direct these decisions or even tries to keep any record of them. The question this spectacle raises is even more fundamental than the one that Smith tried to answer in his *Wealth of Nations:* How can all of these individualistic decisions and acts lead to a socially beneficial result? The more basic question is: Why doesn't the whole economy fly apart?

Throughout history, some people have believed that an economy requires conscious direction if it is to be maintained. The philosophies of mercantilism, authoritarian (centralized) socialism, and to some extent, liberal (noncentralized) socialism reflect this viewpoint. Proponents of the market economy, usually just as innocent of economic theory as their centrist antagonists, have for nearly three hundred years vigorously proclaimed the dogma of the coherent market economy.

We have now identified two main viewpoints on the viability of the market economy. One holds that an economy must be directed at a consciously determined end; the other holds that an essentially free-market economy is ideally suited to forming the countless independent actions of millions of self-interested economic units into an equilibrium of the whole. The latter point of view stresses the existence of a *general equilibrium*—that is, a situation in which all market and all economic units can *move toward* a solution that, if attained, would find all of them in simultaneous equilibrium. Whether this general equilibrium can exist is obviously an important question, for the fate of a major ideology hangs on the theoretical answer to it. It would be unhappy

---

[1] We shall exclude the government from this discussion, since in its *governmental* function, it does not enter directly into the circular flow of economic activity but rather, to varying extents, *regulates* that flow. As a participant in the circular flow, the government behaves much as the other two components, offering goods and services for sale and consuming quantities of finished goods. The fiscal and monetary roles of the government are exogenous to the circular flow.

The Theory of the General Equilibrium

news for those who believe in economic liberalism to find that the tendency of a free economy is to fly apart. At the same time, a proof of the existence of a general equilibrium in a competitive economy would not, in itself, be bad news for the advocates of centralized direction; for the existence of a general equilibrium would show clearly that all economic units are interrelated, and if these interrelationships could be discovered, control of the economy would be facilitated.

Many first-year economics texts are fond of assuring their readers that equilibrium is neither good nor bad but that it *just is*. While this advice may reassure readers that it is unnecessary for each of them to go out and work as hard as they can to help to achieve equilibrium solutions, obviously a general equilibrium solution *is* good. It *is* desirable for an economic system to move toward the solutions of the various economic problems of its constituent units rather than away from them. That predominately market economies have survived and prospered tends to indicate that they do not move away from the solutions to economic problems. The balance of this chapter is devoted to showing how a model economy moves toward the solution of the economic problems of its constituent decision-makers—that is, toward a general equilibrium—under the conditions of competition in all markets.

THE CONCEPT OF THE GENERAL EQUILIBRIUM

GENERAL EQUILIBRIUM AND THE ECONOMY

Adam Smith, David Ricardo, and most of the classical economists wrote of the economy as a system without being sure it was one. Their work was carried on generally within the framework of *partial* equilibrium analysis, as is indeed most of contemporary microeconomics, including all of this book except this chapter and the next. The idea of the partial equilibrium technique is summed up in the phrase so familiar to all economists—*ceteris paribus* ("other things being equal")—and should, by now, be equally familiar to the reader.

Generally, partial equilibrium analysis is a very sound practice. The impact of one consumer's actions, for example, on the entire economy is approximately nil. To be concerned with the impact of a small (but not isolated) event often would be as pointless as trying to ascertain the change in the level of the ocean if a new bay is dredged.

Yet, as ecologists have shown us, apparently insignificant individual acts, if there are enough of them, can have wide-ranging effects on the whole environment. What if all consumers attempt to demand more of good X? Will the price stay the same, so that every individual consumer will carry out his original intention and buy the additional units of X? And, if there is a disturbance in the economy, such as an increase in the demand for good X, will the economy move toward an equilibrium solution, or will it simply move aimlessly to no purposive end?

ELEMENTS OF A GENERAL EQUILIBRIUM

What should we look for in a general equilibrium? In a particular, or partial, equilibrium, such as the supply and demand model, we observe that the market for a given good is said to be in a state of equilibrium when the quantity of the good consumers wish to buy at a particular price is equal to the amount producers wish to sell at the same price. The unique price that clears the market is the equilibrium price.

That the market for good X is in equilibrium does not necessarily indicate that the market for good Y is in equilibrium or that the market for input Z is in equilibrium. In other words, the attainment of a partial equilibrium (an equilibrium in one market) does not assure that all markets are in equilibrium.

A *general* equilibrium exists when all markets are cleared. In addition, *within* each market, the price of the subject good, under conditions of general equilibrium, assures the fulfillment of several conditions. For example, in the consumer's goods market, equilibrium prices ensure that:

1. The quantities of goods that producers put on the market in their quest for maximized profits are exactly the quantities that consumers take off the market in their search for maximized utility.

2. The total revenues generated by the sale of all goods will generate sufficient income to allow producers to hire the inputs necessary to produce the equilibrium outputs.

3. The payments made to the input owners will be sufficient to enable them to purchase all the final goods produced with their inputs.

THE WALRASIAN SYSTEM

Can a market economy satisfy the conditions of general equilibrium? Economists were not sure until Leon Walras, using a system of simultaneous equations, showed the possibility of a general equilibrium.[2] Walras argued that *all* prices and quantities in all markets are determined simultaneously through their interaction with one another. He attempted to prove that there is no circular reasoning involved in the circular flow; like a matrix of equations, it is a system of *mutual determination.*

Walras' argument has important implications for both sides of the ideological spectrum. For advocates of laissez-faire, the Walrasian system shows that a free market can indeed function as if guided by the Smithian "invisible hand." Through interconnections of initial stimuli, feedback, and response, countless individual actions can cause the system to move to a general equilibrium. For the proponents of socialism (both centralized and decentralized), the Walrasian analysis holds forth the possibility of running a planned economy.

[2] Leon Walras, *Elements of Pure Economics,* translated by William Jaffe (London: George Allen and Unwin, 1954). Originally published in French in 1874.

All that is necessary is to solve Walras' system of equations. Actually, the phrase "all that is necessary" conceals a great deal. The socialists would have a far more difficult time using the Walrasian system than would their ideologic opponents. This is so because the socialists must *solve* the equations, and they must solve them in "real time."[3] In a laissez-faire system, the economy itself, acting as a giant computer, solves the equations in real time. In a market system, all economic units pose problems that, through interaction in the markets, they also help to solve.

To prove the existence of a general equilibrium, it is necessary first to describe the economy by means of a system of equations, the initial task being to determine how many equations are required to complete the system. Usually (there are exceptions), each unknown in a set of related variables requires an equation for its determination. For example, consider an individual member of an economy. He has two roles; he is a consumer of goods and a supplier of inputs. Thus, the individual has two distinct sets of unknowns; one set concerns the quantities of the goods he would buy, and the other set shows the quantities of inputs he would supply. Suppose the individual consumes goods X, Y, and Z and supplies the inputs L and K. Then, under the assumption that there must be one equation for each unknown, this individual has three demand and two input supply equations—a total of five equations.

What about the producing sector? Suppose, for example, that 30 firms comprise the producing sector, of which 10 make X, 10 produce Y, and 10 manufacture Z. There are, then, 10 commodity supply equations for each good, giving a total of 30 equations. Each firm uses the inputs L and K; therefore, there are six input demand equations.

How are input and output prices determined? Assuming competition, prices are determined by the forces of supply and demand. There is, then, a market-clearing equation ($Q_S = Q_D$) for each item.

But, how are the prices to be expressed? Money has not been explicitly incorporated into this system. We shall designate one of the goods—say, Z— as the *numeraire,* or unit of account (one of the functions of money). This designation provides that the prices of all the other goods shall be stated in terms of the price of good Z, where necessarily, $P_Z = 1$. Thus, for example, if X is twice as expensive as Z, and Y is four times as expensive as Z, we may say that $P_X = 2Z$, and $P_Y = 4Z$.[4] One result of designating Z as the numeraire is that in a five-commodity economy we now have only four, rather than five, prices to determine, since we know $P_Z = 1$.

---

[3] The concept of *real time* is borrowed from computer technology. It means that a solution must be obtained while it is still significant. There would be little point in solving demand and supply equations for Christmas trees if the task could not be done in less than a year.

[4] The *numeraire* here is simply the unit of account. It is the unit in which the values of all other goods are stated. Its price in terms of itself must be unity—i.e., one unit of Z is worth one unit of itself. If 600 units of X may be traded for 10 units of Z, the price of X in terms of Z (the numeraire) is 60; i.e., 1 unit of Z will buy 60 units of X. One of the most common commodities that used to serve as a numeraire was gold. Money and the numeraire are not necessarily the same thing; but frequently, as in the case of the dollar, the medium of exchange is also the unit of account.

For our simple economy, we have 540 equations.

Equations of individuals	500
Equations of firms	36
Market clearing equations	4
	540

It might be possible for a centrally planned economy to solve a system of so few equations; but for even a fairly small real economy, the likelihood of obtaining a solution in real time borders on the completely hopeless, even with the use of the most advanced computers. Various socialist theorists have suggested ways around this problem, but these will not concern us here.

A complete exposition of the Walrasian system is lengthy and difficult, so we will attempt to gain an intuitive grasp of the adjustment into a state of general equilibrium, using a graphical analysis.

A GRAPHICAL DEMONSTRATION OF THE PATH TO GENERAL EQUILIBRIUM

Let us assume a perfectly competitive economy producing the goods X and Y with the inputs L and K. The initial state of equilibrium is disturbed when, owing to some exogenous change in consumers' tastes (for example, a seasonal change), the demand for X increases. In Figure 16-1(a), the demand curve for X shifts rightward from D_0 to D_1, causing the price to rise from P_{X_0} to P_{X_1} and the quantity exchanged to increase by $X_0 X_1$ units. If this were an illustration of partial equilibrium, we might well stop here, for now we have seen what happens when the demand for X increases: given supply, the price and the quantity exchanged increase.

But now we are interested in finding out what happens in the rest of the economy in response to an increase in the demand for X. We look first at what occurs in the market for Y. We know that the price of good X is a determinant of the demand for good Y, so if P_X changes, we would expect a change to occur in the demand for good Y. Assuming that the commodities are substitutes for each other, we would expect the increase in the demand for good X to be accompanied by a decrease in the demand for good Y. Thus, in Figure 16-1(b), the demand curve for good Y shifts leftward, while the price drops by $P_{Y_1} P_{Y_0}$ dollars, and the quantity of Y exchanged decreases by $Y_1 Y_0$ units.

Consider the production possibilities curve PP' in Figure 16-1(c).[5] If more X is demanded, resources must be diverted from the production of Y. This

---

[5] The production possibilities curve is the locus of all technically efficient outputs for an economy, given the resource base and technology. At any point on the curve, all resources are fully employed in least-cost combinations. Any point inside the curve involves technical inefficiencies within the economy, and any point to the right of the curve is unattainable unless additional resources or a new technology or both are found. A more complete account of the derivation of the production possibilities curve is found in Chapter 17.

FIGURE 16-1

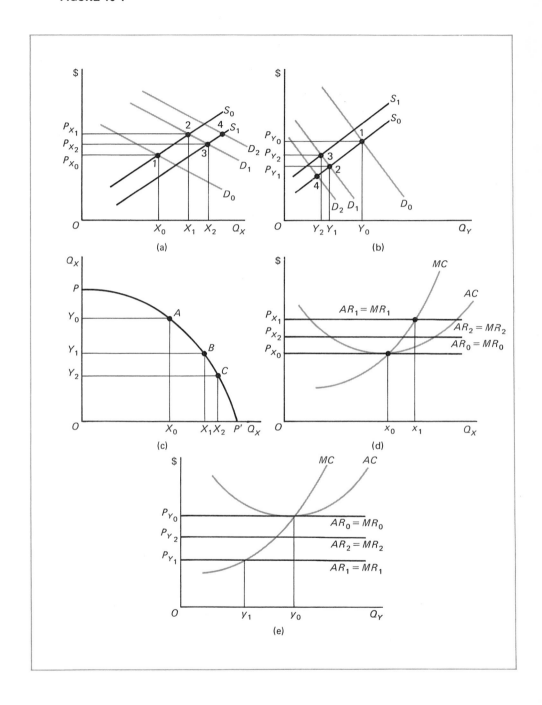

FIGURE 16-1 (con't)

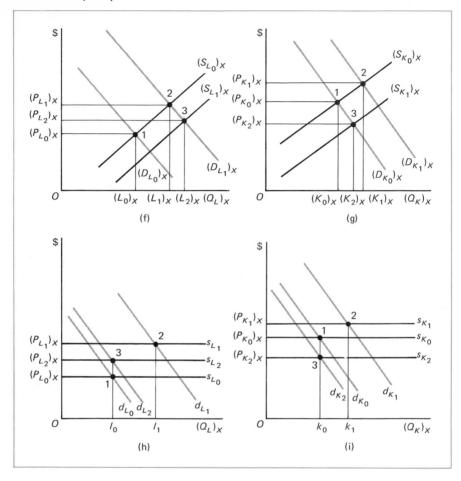

necessarily causes the production of Y to fall. Thus, the economy moves from point A to point B. This is a physical necessity; but why does the *demand* curve for Y shift leftward? Why don't consumers attempt to demand *more X* and the *same* amount of Y? Unless the production possibilities curve shifts outward, it is impossible to achieve a "larger" GNP in the sense of *being able* to produce a given amount of one good and a greater quantity of the other. Thus, given the economy's physical limitations, there can be no increase in the demand for X without a corresponding decrease in the demand for Y.

What must be the effects of the consumers' decisions on the producing sector? Let us consider the effects on one manufacturer of good X. The increase in price raises the firm's marginal revenue, and, as shown in Figure 16-1(d), the firm must increase its output of X to maximize profit. Since every

FIGURE 16-1 (con't)

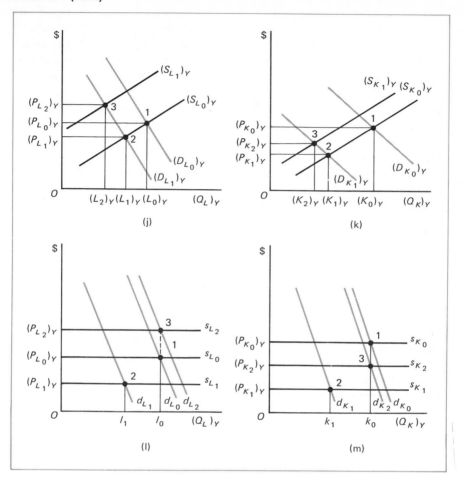

firm in the X industry is similarly affected, the output of each firm increases. It is the total of these independent actions that is responsible for the increase in the amount supplied of X, shown in chart (a) by the movement from point 1 to point 2 along S_0. The increase in the output of the industry, shown in the same chart, is equal to $X_0 X_1$ units.

In industry Y, the opposite occurs. The price of Y falls, and since $P_Y = MR_Y$ is now below the initial level, each firm, in attempting to maximize profit, will reduce its output of Y as shown in chart (e). The reduction in the output of Y by each firm is responsible for the decrease in the quantity of Y supplied to the market, as shown by the movement from 1 to 2 in chart (b).

From our discussion in Chapter 8, we know that in the short run firms can adjust their outputs by varying the intensity of plant use. In the long run,

entrepreneurs can enter or leave the industry or change the size of their plants. The representative firm in chart (d) is making an economic profit. If entrepreneurs now outside industry X believe that they too could make economic profits if they were to begin producing X, they will seek to enter the industry. As they enter, they must hire inputs in competition with firms already in the industry and with each other. Charts (f) and (g) show the labor and capital markets for the X industry. The initial prices of labor and capital in the industry are $(P_{L_0})_X$ and $(P_{K_0})_X$, respectively. Charts (h) and (i) show the demand and supply situations of one firm within the industry for the inputs labor and capital, respectively. An individual firm hiring inputs in perfectly competitive input markets can hire any amount of factors at the market price. With new firms entering the industry, and the older firms expanding, the market demand curves for labor and capital shift upward and the prices of both inputs increase. This is shown in chart (f) as the rightward shift of the market demand curve for labor from $(D_{L_0})_X$ to $(D_{L_1})_X$. In consequence of this shift, the price of labor rises from $O(P_{L_0})_X$ to $O(P_{L_1})_X$. In the capital market, the price of capital rises by $(P_{K_0})_X(P_{K_1})_X$ in consequence of the rightward shift of the market capital demand curve. Within the subject firm, the level of labor employment has risen by $l_0 l_1$ units and the level of capital use has increased to Ok_1 units.

Note that suppliers of capital and labor to the X industry appear to have incomes larger than the suppliers of inputs to the Y industry. Income is a determinant of the demand for final goods; therefore, it would be reasonable to assume that the demand curves for X and Y in charts (a) and (b), respectively, will shift rightward. However, *for the time being,* we cannot be sure what will happen to the demand curves for consumers' goods until we consider the influence on demand of the changed situation in the Y industry. The case of the Y industry is the reverse of that in the X industry. Existing firms within the former will reduce the level of input use as they seek to reduce their output of Y. Those firms faced with long-run losses will exit from the industry, further reducing the use of L and K employed in the manufacture of Y. The situation for the input markets in Y industry is shown in charts (j) and (k). The case of one Y firm is depicted in charts (l) and (m). As the demands for inputs decrease in the Y industry, the prices of L and K fall.

If, as we assumed, the input markets were in equilibrium at the outset of this demonstration, then they cannot be in equilibrium now; for the prices of L and K have risen in the X industry input market, while in the Y industry the prices of the two inputs have fallen. In perfectly competitive input markets, the disequilibrium will be self-correcting, since resources are mobile, and they will flow to markets in which the rates of reward are the highest. Thus, the owners of labor and capital will withdraw their input units from the firms of the Y industry and seek to have them employed by the firms of the X industry.

In the Y industry, the input supply curves shift upward as resources leave for employment in the X industry—see charts (j) and (k). Charts (f) and (g) show the expected results in the X industry as the supply curves of the inputs shift downward.

What will be the final levels of the rates of factor reward? Will the shifts in the input demand and supply curves be such that the initial rates will prevail once again as soon as the general equilibrium is reestablished? The shifted curves in charts (f), (g), (j), and (k) show that this is not the case. The price of labor is higher than it was initially, and the price of capital is lower. How can this be? If the price of labor has increased as a result of the demand for it increasing in the X industry, and the price of capital has fallen despite a similarly increased demand for it in the X industry, there must be a different intensity of resource use in the two industries. The X industry must be labor intensive relative to the Y industry. As the demand for Y falls off, some resources of both sorts gravitate toward the X industry, where they are absorbed, owing to the increase in the demand for both inputs. But the demand of the X industry firms for labor is stronger than their demand for capital. Not all the labor inputs the X firms want will flow out of the Y firms unless the wage rate rises above its initial level. In other words, the number of laborers that would be released by the firms of the Y industry in consequence of the decreased demand for Y is insufficient to increase the production of X to the desired level. Therefore, the relatively stronger demand of the X firms for labor causes the wage rate to rise in X employment, so that the economically motivated laborers will move out of the Y industry and into the X industry. As they move out of Y, the price of labor tends to rise in Y, and as they move into X, the price of labor tends to fall in X. The movement of labor between industries will cease when the X firms have the inputs sufficient for them to maximize their profits, and the Y firms have disposed of sufficient (superfluous) input units to maximize their profits. At this point, the price of labor necessarily must be equal in both industries.[6]

The fall in the price of capital is explained in a similar way. It is true that more capital is needed in the X industry, and this situation, taken by itself, would cause the price of capital to rise in X industry in order to pull capital inputs out of the Y firms. Yet, when all the adjustments are made, the price of capital must fall below the initial level. Again, the differing intensities of resource use is the explanation. The increased demand of the X firms for more capital fails to raise the price of capital because the X firms do not need to increase their use of capital at a rate as great as that by which they increase their employment of labor. As the Y firms release resources, capital tends to become redundant at the old price. If the price of capital did not fall, some capital would become unemployed. Perfect competition assures that the price of capital will fall until all units are voluntarily fully employed; this is shown in charts (j) and (k).

As the price of labor rises and the price of capital falls in the input mar-

---

[6] To avoid complicating a discussion that is fairly involved already, we shall abstract from the case of equalizing differences. If the conditions of employment were different in the industries—say, that the work in the Y firms was considerably more onerous than the work in X firms—the price of labor would rise in all industries (as it has in our model), but wages would not be equalized in dollar amount. Wages could be higher in the Y firms, despite the fact that there has been a decline in employment in the Y-producing sector. This difference would reflect the less attractive nature of labor performed in the Y firms and should be regarded simply as a premium on the basic wage rate that must be paid to attract the labor necessary to produce profit-maximizing quantities of Y.

kets for both industries, another adjustment is made within the firms of each industry. In X industry, the subject firm is shown as moving from point 2 to point 3 in both (h) and (i). In Y industry, the representative firm also proceeds from point 2 to point 3 in both (l) and (m).

We must now return to the first two graphs to see what has happened in the sector where all these changes were begun. The expansion of the X industry causes the market supply curve of X in chart (a) to shift downward to S_1. The industry thus moves from point 2 to point 3. The long-run price is lower than the short-run price denoted by point 2 but higher than the initial price denoted by point 1. The X firms of our model must be in an industry of increasing costs. A long-run supply curve drawn through points 1 and 3 would have a positive slope. In chart (b), the market supply curve of Y moves upward. The market moves from point 2 to point 3. For the same reasons given in the case of the market for X, the firms of Y industry comprise an industry of increasing costs.

We must return now to the producing sector to take account of the adjustments within the firms of each industry. Consider charts (d) and (e). We know that in the long run, the firms make neither economic profits nor losses. The long-run price of X is above the initial price but below the short-run price. The long-run equilibrium point, therefore, lies along AR_2. If we assume that the subject firm's long-run average total cost curve shifts vertically upward (see Chapter 8), the firm will return to its initial volume of production, the greater output of X being supplied to the market by the new entrant firms. The same case in reverse is true of the firms within the Y industry.

Now, after this rather lengthy process, have the adjustments ended? We could say that they have to save ourselves a lot of trouble, but such is probably not the case. We started by assuming an *exogenous* change in the consumers' goods market. Will there now be any *induced* changes in that market similar to those we encountered in the other sectors of the economy? We will consider only one of many possibilities. For example, what has happened to the income of the input owners? There has been an increase in the incomes of the owners of the labor inputs and a decrease in the incomes of the owners of capital. Income is a determinant of demand. How will the change in the distribution of income affect the consumers' goods markets? We cannot tell without further information on the nature of the consumers in the affected markets. Possibly the income changes will spread evenly through all markets, the increase in the demand of the group with the higher income being canceled by the decrease in the demand of the group with the reduced income. Suppose that laborers tend to have a higher marginal propensity to consume than owners of capital have.[7] Then, we may expect a further increase in the demand for X as the increase in the laborers' demand for X more than offsets the decrease in the capital owners' demand for X. This is shown in chart (a) by the

---

[7] The *marginal propensity to consume,* a concept from macroeconomics, states how much consumption changes for a given change in income.

The Theory of the General Equilibrium

rightward movement of the demand curve for X from D_1 to D_2. The X market is now at point 4. In the Y market, the demand curve for good Y shifts leftward from D_1 to D_2 as the decrease in the demand for Y on the part of capital owners more than offsets the increase in the demand for Y of the laborers. The market for Y is now at point 4 in chart (b). On the production possibilities curve of chart (c), the economy has moved from point B to point C. The economy is now producing OX_2 units of X and OY_2 units of Y.

It must now be apparent that as a result of the latest changes in the prices of X and Y, the model economy must undergo a further adjustment. Once again, the X industry will tend to expand and the Y industry will tend to contract. We will not go on with this demonstration, since our sole aim was to explain the *nature* of the general equilibrium solution.

The proof of the general equilibrium system is difficult, but we can sense it intuitively from our knowledge of perfect competition theory.[8] The demand and supply curves in the various markets and firms do not shift willy-nilly. Their movements are purposive and precisely interrelated. The curves must move as long as disequilibria in the various markets persist. We know from the theory of perfect competition that forces exist in perfectly competitive markets to produce a partial equilibrium. When an equilibrium exists simultaneously in all markets and within all economic units within the markets, a general equilibrium exists throughout the entire economy, and the movement of the curves ceases until the system is disturbed by another exogenous force. Since, in an actual economy, countless disturbances constantly occur, the system is continuously in a state of disequilibrium, but—and this is the important point—*at any moment* in time, the system automatically seeks and moves toward a position of general equilibrium. This is the practical significance of the proof.

SUMMARY

More important than the mathematics of the general equilibrium solution itself is grasping the idea that the economy is a system. If that system is perfectly competitive, it will have an inescapable tendency toward a general equilibrium solution. If that system is not perfectly competitive, the possibility of moving to a state of stable general equilibrium cannot be assured. The economic signals will be transmitted, but their impact is likely to be attenuated. For example, suppose that there is monopoly in the X industry. There will be some expansion in the output of X in response to an increase in consumer demand, but since monopolistic firms produce so that $P > MC$, resources will tend to be underemployed in the X industry, and a rise in wages may be accom-

---

[8] Leon Walras, the great pioneer of the general equilibrium system, was never able to prove the *existence* of the general equilibrium. The proof was not forthcoming until the 1930's, about forty years after Walras, when the mathematical economist Abraham Wald, proved the existence of a path to a general equilibrium in Walras' work.

panied by disequilibrium in the input markets leading to disequilibrium elsewhere in the economy.

General equilibrium is much more than an analytical concept or a particular state of an economic system. It is important in assessing both the efficiency and the normative (i.e., welfare) attributes of a given economic system. In the next chapter, we will be concerned with whether the ability of an economy to tend to a general equilibrium solution has any significance for economic welfare.

17

The Theory
of Economic Welfare

THE MEANING OF ECONOMIC WELFARE

Welfare economics is a name that at once identifies and conceals the nature of a segment of microeconomic theory. Most people, on hearing the expression, are likely to conclude that the associated subject matter must be social welfare legislation, social insurance, workmen's compensation, antipoverty, and, perhaps, antipollution programs. In a sense, these people are correct—but not in the way that they imagine. *Welfare* means *well-being,* and that is precisely what welfare economics is about. The task of theoretical welfare economics and the subject matter of this chapter is to define, study, and compare alternative states of the well-being of individuals, groups, communities, nations, and, indeed, the world.

But how can a purported science deal with the comparison of alternative states of well-being among different people or groups of people? Is not the stuff of such an inquiry interpersonal comparisons and value judgments—both of which are highly subjective and unknowable to an economist-observer-prescriber? How, for example, can we possibly claim to *know* that the welfare of the community will be improved if we tax Charlie $100 and use it to subsidize Linus? Even more, on what objective grounds can we proclaim that Linus deserves to receive Charlie's $100? We must support our proposal to prescribe the transfer by an appeal to ethics (the morality of the income redistribution) and interpersonal comparisons

(somehow the welfare of the community will be advanced if Linus gains the $100 expropriated from Charlie).

Without in the least denying the existence of (absolute or relative) ethical standards and the possibility of making valid interpersonal comparisons, we ask if such inquiries should take place in economics. Are not these matters more properly left to theology, philosophy, *political* economy, and the "softer" social sciences?

Early welfare economists plunged bravely into the business of issuing welfare prescriptions, not because they were sublimely convinced of the rectitude of their own ethics and their ability to compare the states of deservingness of various individuals, but precisely because they believed that economic analysis contained within it an objective guide to social welfare. Repeatedly, these protagonists of a scientific welfare economics were beaten down when a skeptic showed them that their supposedly positive economic analysis contained an unconsciously supplied ethic or an unsupportable interpersonal comparison or both. Usually, the welfare economists would meet their critics' objections and spring back with a new "objective" welfare theory, only to have it, too, founder under similar attacks.

The battles are now over; the outcome is clear. Two substantial aspects of making people or groups better off *are* ethical criteria and interpersonal comparisons, and these matters clearly are not the subject matter of science, despite their valid standing in other areas of study. This conclusion, however, has not killed welfare economics. Humbler than it was originally intended to be, welfare economics has become the cornerstone of the study of states of welfare and how to improve them.

The one area in which economists can speak with clear authority is *efficiency,* and this has come to be the province of theoretical welfare economics. Today, efficiency has a bad name in some quarters as being a cold, calculating business, bereft of regard for "human problems." But efficiency is not the enemy of humane considerations; indeed, it can be an aid in their fulfillment. To the extent that human welfare depends on scarce goods and services (as it surely continues to do for most of the world's people), efficiency is *the* vital means to an improved level of social welfare. Good intentions alone will never deliver the goods that can effect an increase in human welfare. Goodwill may be plentiful, but resources are not. Better, then, to be efficient than inefficient in our use of resources; for if the desire to do good motivates us, the efficient management of the natural endowment will enable us to do more good for more people. Thus, even with ethics and interpersonal comparisons removed from its domain, welfare economics is far broader than social insurance, aid to dependent children, economic inequality, poverty, and the misuse of the environment.

AN HISTORICAL SKETCH OF WELFARE ECONOMICS

Suppose that the totality of welfare in a community is W, but given the present state of resources and the knowledge of how to use them, that totality could be larger—say, W^*. The tasks of welfare economics are, first, to show that in the present state, $W < W^*$, and, second, to suggest how it is possible to raise W to W^*.

THE OLD WELFARE ECONOMICS

Adam Smith's major purpose in the *Wealth of Nations* was to show how to move toward a state in which $W = W^*$, where W^* is the maximized level of welfare. By *wealth,* Smith meant our concept of the gross national product, and GNP was his, admittedly rough, index of W. Smith advocated increasing the wealth of nations because he believed that a rising GNP must contribute to an increasing level of welfare. What was his rationale? He was not a materialist, but he contended that, given the living conditions at the time, the great majority of Englishmen would have to benefit from the effects of any increase in production. He believed that economic growth—a rising secular trend in the GNP—meant, among other things, more jobs, more food, better housing, and lower prices for those whose welfare depended on those items. To Smith, economic growth meant bringing W closer to W^*.

As the Industrial Revolution moved forward and the science of economics developed, a number of economists sought more refined methods of studying and improving economic welfare. The search for a welfare economics was aided by the widening sway of English utilitarian philosophy. Two of its most notable proponents were Jeremy Bentham and John Stuart Mill, who were also political economists.

Most people associate Bentham with his famous maxim "the greatest good for the greatest number." Implicit in the maxim is the idea that the totality of welfare in a community is simply the numerical sum of the utilities of the individuals in the community. To illustrate Bentham's rule, we will postulate that the *economic* utility of any one person is a function of the goods and services that he consumes. For the three-person community of Pooh, Eeyore, and Christopher Robin, who consume goods X, Y, and Z, we may write the utility functions

$$U_P = U_P(X_P, Y_P, Z_P)$$
$$U_E = U_E(X_E, Y_E, Z_E)$$
$$U_C = U_C(X_C, Y_C, Z_C)$$

where $X = X_P + X_E + X_C$, and so on. If the welfare of the community is simply the total of the individual utilities of its members, we may write

$$W = U_P + U_E + U_C$$

Suppose that the initial state of welfare, W_0, is less than the possible maximum, W^*. (For the moment, we shall not be concerned with how it is possible to determine that the present state of welfare is less than a maximum.) *If* welfare is simply the total of the utility levels of the members of the community, some action increasing their utilities must cause the general level of welfare to increase. But suppose the change causing welfare to increase is rather ambiguous, in the sense that $\Delta U_E > 0$, $\Delta U_C > 0$, and $\Delta U_P < 0$, and that $(\Delta U_E + \Delta U_C) > |\Delta U_P|$.[1] In other words, two members of the community benefit while one, Pooh, is harmed, but the sum of their increases in utility exceeds the loss in utility of the remaining member.

Conceivably, the result suggested by the injunction to provide for "the greatest good for the greatest number" could be accomplished by shooting Pooh and dividing his goods between the surviving members of the community. Obviously, our ethical systems are in profound conflict with this interpretation of the Benthamite maxim, and such hedonistic utilitarianism could hardly serve as the foundation of an acceptable welfare economics.

Moreover, in applying Benthamite ethics to economics, how are we to balance "the greatest good" against "the greatest number"? The greatest possible *total* good need not be spread very well over the greatest number of people. Suppose, for example, that Pooh's utility is 100, while Eeyore's is 2 and Christopher Robin's is 3. Is this better or worse than a situation in which $U_P = 50$, $U_E = 25$, and $U_C = 25$? The first case yields "the greatest good" (105 as against 100), but almost all of it accrues to just one individual; in the second instance, the total is less, but it is spread more evenly across "the greatest number."

The preceding example shows the pitfalls of attempting to incorporate a particular ethical system into a purported general body of analysis. Now, let us look at the difficulties of attempting to prescribe the route to greater welfare, relying principally on the extension of an analytical tool.

With the development of the concept of diminishing marginal utility, a number of economists became convinced of the possibility of making objective policy recommendations. Suppose the monthly income of Pooh and Eeyore is $200 each and that of Christopher Robin is $400. Since Christopher Robin's greater income allows him to purchase a larger basket of goods than can either Pooh or Eeyore, his total utility is greater than either of theirs. But, although Christopher Robin can have a basket of goods double the value of

[1] The vertical bars indicate that we are concerned only with the *absolute* value (i.e., the value with minus signs removed) of Pooh's change in utility.

that obtainable by Pooh or Eeyore, the law of diminishing marginal utility appears to hold that his total utility must be less than double the total utility experienced by either of his fellows, since his *marginal* utility of money income is less than either of theirs. Accordingly, in this particular community, some cardinal welfare theorists (so named because they use cardinal indexes of welfare) would hold that $W < W^*$. To bring W closer to W^*, the community should redistribute income from Christopher Robin to Pooh and Eeyore. As the utility of an extra dollar to Pooh or Eeyore is greater than the corresponding decrease in utility to Christopher Robin, the total welfare of the community should rise.

The logical conclusion of this procedure is an equal distribution of income to all members of the community. To maximize welfare, money should be redistributed from those who have more to those who have less, the loss of utility of the transferrers being less than the gain in utility of the transferees.

The fatal flaw in this analysis is that it contains implicit interpersonal comparisons. It assumes that all members of the community are identical in their attitudes toward money income and, therefore, have identical total (or marginal) utility of money income functions. There is no way of establishing the accuracy of this proposition without knowing each person's total utility schedule. An egalitarian policy of income redistribution could reduce total welfare. For all we know, Pooh and Eeyore may not care much for the things money can buy; on the other hand, Christopher Robin may have a most advanced case of materialism, and the loss of a dollar to him may cause a decided fall in his total utility. In other words, Christopher Robin's total utility curve of money income may lie well above those of Pooh and Eeyore. His marginal utility of money income may be greater than theirs even though his income is greater. Christopher Robin's loss of a dollar could hurt him more than it would help Pooh and Eeyore.

Increasing awareness of flaws such as this led to the eventual destruction of the welfare economics based on introspective cardinalistic assumptions. Critics pointed out also that the welfare effects of an equal distribution of income cannot be considered in isolation from those of resource allocation and incentives. That is, an equal distribution of income may not allocate resources to the most valuable uses. Without the allocational guidance and the incentive functions of differential rates of reward, production may fall off, so that there is less to distribute on an equal basis. In such a case, income redistribution may accomplish nothing more than a wider dissemination of a reduced level of welfare.

A NEW WELFARE ECONOMICS

A major theme in the development of economic theory has been the battle for a purely *positive* economics—an economics devoid of value judgments, expressed or implied. In the 1930's, a number of young and soon-to-be-influ-

ential economists became determined to drive every vestige of ethical judgments, assumptions of measurable and additive utility, and interpersonal comparisons out of economic theory and to develop once-and-for-all a purely *positive* discipline.

But there were some who thought the victory of the positivists would be pyrrhic. If economists were denied the luxuries of making value judgments, assuming cardinally measurable and additive utilities, and comparing states of welfare among individuals, could they make any recommendations at all? Permitting economists to explain something but not to *advocate* a particular course of action, the skeptics argued, would be akin to allowing doctors to diagnose but not to treat. You may judge for yourself the force of this argument as we now turn to the *New Welfare Economics.*

THE NEW WELFARE ECONOMICS

A study of welfare economics is a good way to conclude a book on microeconomic theory, for it is a combination of the theories of production, distribution, and consumption, considered together with the ruling value system of a society. We begin our description of the new welfare economics with the basic physical facts of production.[2]

In this section, we will construct a model of a two-person, two-input, two-good, two-firm economy. The associated literal symbols are as follows:

The individuals	A and B
The inputs	L and K
The goods	X and Y
The firms	F and G

OPTIMALITY IN EXCHANGE

In Figure 17-1, an *Edgeworth box* has been constructed by superimposing the indifference maps of the individuals A and B. A's map is in the customary position, but B's map has been inverted (its origin is at O_B).

Suppose point d denotes the initial distribution of goods between the individuals. A has OX_1 units of X and OY_1 units of Y. Since A and B comprise the community, B must have whatever is left over; therefore, his stock of X is X_1X^* units, and his collection of Y is Y_1Y^* units. Point d places A on his indifference curve A_2, while B is on curve B_2.

---

[2] The now classic introduction to theoretical welfare economics is Francis M. Bator's "The Simple Analytics of Welfare Maximization," *American Economic Review*, XLVII (March 1957), pp. 22–59. This author is convinced that no superior presentation of the subject is available, and so the treatment of this section is indebted to Professor Bator's beautifully simple and elegant essay. If the reader is interested in pursuing welfare economics, he can get no better start than by reading Bator's article.

Figure 17-1 tells us that the distribution of goods between individuals *A* and *B* is nonoptimal. This being the case, social welfare cannot be at a maximum. From point *d* it is possible to move to another point at which at least one person is better off and no one else (here, the other individual) is any worse off. For example, suppose *A* and *B* begin to exchange *X* and *Y* between themselves so as to move along A_2 from *d* to *e*. *A*'s level of utility would remain unchanged, but *B*'s utility would increase, for as this exchange proceeds, *B* is moving to ever higher indifference curves, while *A* stays on A_2. It follows, then, that the welfare of the community increases as the parties move along A_2 from *d* to *e*. At *e*, *B* is on indifference curve B_3, which represents the highest level of utility he can attain without adversely affecting *A*.

If *A* and *B* were to exchange *X* and *Y* so that they moved along A_2 from *e* to *h*, the welfare of the community would fall below the level indicated by point *e*, for now *B*'s utility would decrease as he encountered lower indifference curves. We conclude, therefore, that, subject to *A*'s utility being maintained at the level denoted by A_2, the welfare of the community will be maximized at point *e*. This increase in welfare has been accomplished by a redistribution of the economy's stock of goods between *A* and *B*. *A* has given X_2X_1 units of *X* to *B* in exchange for Y_1Y_2 units of *Y*.

Similarly, the welfare of the community would increase if *A* and *B*, starting from *d*, were to move along B_2 from *d* to *f*. *B*'s utility would remain constant,

FIGURE 17-1

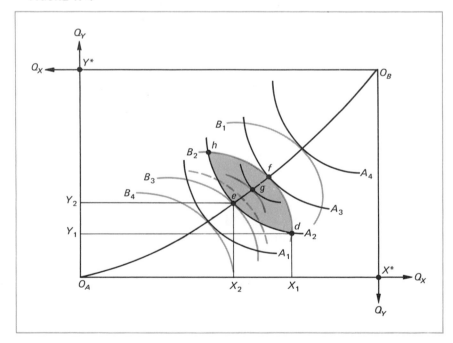

while A's utility would increase. At f, the welfare of the community would be at a maximum subject to the requirement that B must not be hurt.

Suppose A and B were to move from point d into the shaded area bounded by A_2 and B_2. The utility level of both individuals would rise, for both of them would encounter higher indifference curves. Once inside the shaded area, they could continue to increase their respective utility levels until they reached point g, the point that denotes the highest indifference curve one individual can reach while the other person also moves to higher indifference curves.

Figure 17-1 indicates that for any distribution of goods to be optimal, the indifference curves of the individuals must be tangent; for at any point of non-tangency, it is always possible to move to another point at which the utility of at least one person can be increased without the other suffering a decrease in utility.

At the point of tangency between a pair of indifference curves, the slopes of the curves are equal. Since the slope of an indifference curve is the consumer's marginal rate of substitution, at any point of tangency, the marginal rates of substitution of X for Y between the individuals are equal. We conclude, therefore, that optimality in the distribution of goods between the members of the community requires that $(MRS_{XY})_A = (MRS_{XY})_B$. When this condition obtains, any redistribution of goods between A and B must decrease social welfare.

A curve drawn through the points of tangency of the indifference curves, such as $O_A O_B$ in Figure 17-1 is the locus of all optimal distributions of X and Y between individuals A and B. Such a curve is usually called a *contract curve* because the final outcome of unimpeded trading between individuals must be represented by a point lying on this curve. The contract curve is sometimes referred to as the *conflict curve* because once the parties have established a point on it, it is impossible to move away from it or along it without one party benefiting at the expense of the other. Thus, while it is clear that moving from d to e, f, or g will increase social welfare, it is not clear whether moving from e to f will increase welfare, since A's gain in utility is accompanied by B's loss.

Having concluded that optimality in the distribution of goods requires that all parties be at a point on the contract curve—the condition expressed symbolically as $(MRS_{XY})_A = (MRS_{XY})_B$—we may now state the first marginal condition of social welfare.[3]

1. *The optimal allocation of goods among consumers.* Goods are not allocated optimally if it is possible to effect a reallocation that will benefit at least one person without harming anyone else.[4]

---

[3] The marginal conditions of welfare often are called "Pareto" or "Paretian" conditions in honor of the great Italian economist-sociologist Vilfredo Pareto (1848–1923), an outstanding pioneer in the type of welfare economics discussed in this section. Thus, a point on a contract curve is sometimes said to be "Pareto optimal."

[4] In utility terms, this condition may be written $(MU_X/MU_Y)_A = (MU_X/MU_Y)_B$.

OPTIMALITY IN PRODUCTION

Figure 17-2 is an Edgeworth box containing the isoquant maps for an economy producing goods X and Y with the inputs L and K. The isoquant map for good Y has been inverted and has its origin at O_Y. The dimensions of the box are fixed by the economy's resource endowment and its technology.

An efficient economy must operate at some point on the *production contract curve* $O_X O_Y$. To see why this is so, suppose that the economy is currently operating at point q. From q it is possible to proceed to another point at which the production of Y is greater and the production of X is no less than at q. For example, if the economy were to move along isoquant X_3 from q to r, it would move to the higher Y-isoquant Y_2. Therefore, at q, Y production can be increased without any diminution of X production. The increase in Y production is caused solely by an improved resource allocation between the firms producing X and Y. Some units of L are transferred from X production into Y production, and some units of K are transferred out of Y into X. It must be that L is relatively more efficient than K in the production of Y, and, of course, K is relatively more efficient than L in the production of X.

An inspection of Figure 17-2 shows that from any point of nontangency, it is always possible to move to a point on $O_X O_Y$, such as r, at which the pro-

FIGURE 17-2

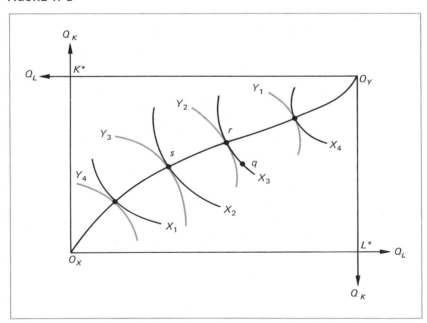

duction of at least one good may be increased without reducing the output of the other good. At r, the slopes of isoquants X_3 and Y_2 are equal. Since the slope of an isoquant is the marginal rate of technical substitution between inputs, we know that at r,

$$(MRTS_{LK})_X = (MRTS_{LK})_Y$$

From this observation, we may state the second marginal condition of social welfare.

    2. *The optimal allocation of inputs.* Inputs are allocated nonoptimally whenever it is possible to increase the production of at least one good without decreasing the production of any other good.[5]

    The production possibilities curve. The production possibilities curve was introduced in the preceding chapter. It was defined as depicting the locus of points of maximum output of one good, given any quantity of the other.

    The production possibilities curve of Figure 17-3 may be derived from an Edgeworth box isoquant map. For example, the isoquant map of Figure 17-2 shows that if the economy produces X_2 units of X, the greatest amount of Y it can produce is Y_3 units. Plotting this information as point s' in Figure 17-3, corresponding to point s in Figure 17-2, gives us a point on the economy's production possibilities curve. From point r in Figure 17-2 we may obtain point r' in Figure 17-3, at which the maximum production of Y is Y_2 units, given the output of X at X_3 units. By continuing this process of transferring points from the Edgeworth box isoquant map, we can obtain as many points as we wish in Figure 17-3. Joining these points together with a smooth curve yields the economy's concave-to-the-origin production possibilities curve Y^*X^*.

    The concavity of the production possibilities curve shows the operation of the law of increasing costs. Increasing the output of X by X_2X_3 units requires a greater sacrifice of Y (Y_2Y_3 units) than does increasing the output of X from zero to OX_2 units (the cost in terms of Y is only Y_3Y^* units). This phenomenon is the result of imperfect resource substitutability. Suppose X manufacture is capital intensive relative to Y production. Y must then be labor intensive relative to X. When inputs are transferred out of Y production and into X— say, in moving from s' to r' in Figure 17-2—the ratio of the labor units to capital units being transferred must exceed that currently existing in X production. The transfer thus causes the labor to capital ratio to increase in the X factories. But labor is not as effective in the production of X as it is in the production of Y. Therefore, equal increments in X require successively greater input transfers into X and out of Y production. Consequently, as the output of X is increased

---

[5] The condition expressed symbolically as $(MRTS_{LK})_X = (MRTS_{LK})_Y$ may be expressed in productivity terms as $(MP_L/MP_K)_X = (MP_L/MP_K)_Y$.

FIGURE 17-3

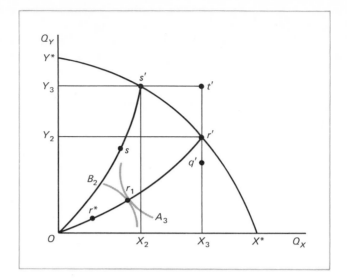

in equal increments, the decrease in Y production becomes ever greater. The cost of every increment of X increases in terms of the Y that must be given up. Thus, it is the increasing cost of X in terms of Y (or Y in terms of X) that causes the production possibilities curve to be concave with respect to the origin.

Suppose the economy does not follow the production contract curve of Figure 17-2 as it moves away from point s; suppose that instead it moves from s to q. Since we know that q represents a nonoptimal allocation of resources, the corresponding point, q', in Figure 17-3 cannot be on the production possibilities curve but must lie inside it; for given the level of X production at OX_3, the output of Y is not at a maximum.

Point t' lies outside the production possibilities curve. It represents a currently unattainable output combination. A corresponding point, t, does not exist within the Edgeworth box of Figure 17-2. The isoquant map shows that the maximum amount of Y the economy can produce with X_3 units of X is Y_2. Accordingly given the amount of X, X_3 (OX_3), only point r', not t', is currently attainable. The production possibilities curve can be made to pass through t' only if there are additional resources, a qualitative improvement in existing resources, or better use of resources—or, of course, any combination of these routes to increased productivity.

OPTIMALITY IN THE PRODUCTION AND DISTRIBUTION OF GOODS

We have now seen how an economy can optimize (1) the distribution of a given stock of goods and (2) the allocation of resources. We will now consider how the composition of output may be optimized.

The utility possibilities frontier. In Figure 17-4, we have constructed a graph on which the *ordinal* utility levels of A and B are shown. A's ordinal utility index is shown on the horizontal axis, B's on the vertical axis. Since we are using ordinal indexes, there is no way of comparing the intensity of utility felt by A or B at any point on their respective axes. Similarly, there is no way of comparing the utility levels of A and B. All we know is that the farther any point on the horizontal axis lies from the origin, the better A likes it, while the farther any point on the vertical axis lies from the origin, the more B likes it.[6] We will call the space defined by these axes *utility* space.

Consider now the Edgeworth box having the contract curve Or' inscribed beneath the production possibilities curve of Figure 17-3. Suppose A has the level of utility denoted by indifference curve A_3. The maximum possible utility level for B, given A's level, must be that shown by indifference curve B_2 attainable by B only at point r_1. If we now plot a point, r_1'', corresponding to point r_1, in the utility space of Figure 17-4, we will have obtained a point that shows the maximum amount of B's utility when A's utility level is A_3, shown as OU_{A_3} in Figure 17-4. We may regard the point r_1'' as lying on a *utility possibilities curve* for the economy. By plotting many other similar points as derived from the contract curve Or' of Figure 17-3 on the utility space of Figure 17-4, we can draw the utility possibilities curve RR'. Point r''^* is a point derived from another point—say, point r^* in Figure 17-3, at which A's utility level is OU_{A_2}, and B's level is OU_{B_3}. Since point r''^* corresponds to the contract curve point r^*, we know that r''^* lies on the same utility possibilities curve as does r''.

The utility possibilities curve RR' is drawn only for point r' on the production possibilities curve of Figure 17-3. Therefore, RR' shows maximum utility possibilities only when the economy produces the aggregate total output OX_3 and OY_2. Since there are an infinite number of points on the production possibilities curve, there must be an infinite number of utility possibilities curves—one such curve for each point on the production possibilities curve. For example, suppose the economy produces the output $OX_2 + OY_3$. This is represented by point s' in Figure 17-3. Finding a point—say, s—on the contract curve Os' permits us to locate point s'' in the utility space of Figure 17-4. This point lies on the utility possibilities curve SS'.

We have now obtained two utility possibilities curves, each corresponding to a different output mix. Is there anything we can say about the optimality of a particular output mix and the distribution of that mix?

Consider once more the production possibilities curve of Figure 17-3. The slope of curve Y^*X^* is the marginal rate of transformation between the subject goods. For example, assume that the slope of Y^*X^* at point s' is 3/1. Then, MRT_{XY}—the marginal rate of transformation of Y into X—is 3 to 1, meaning that in order to produce one more unit of X, resources capable of producing 3 units of Y must be transferred out of Y and into X production. In other words,

---

[6] Remember that one of the strictures of the new welfare economics is that it does not assume cardinal utility.

FIGURE 17-4

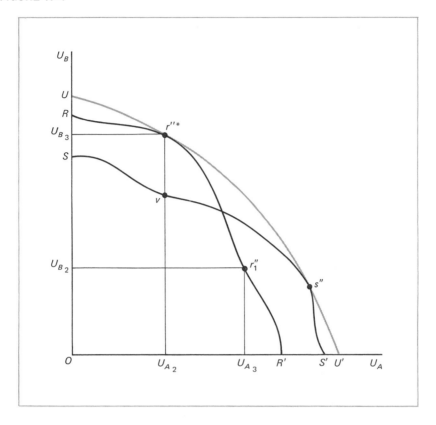

at point s', the economy is capable of transforming 3 units of Y into 1 unit of X. At point r', the slope of the production possibilities curve is steeper than at s'. The marginal rate of transformation of Y into X is greater than it was at s'. Assume that it is now 5 to 1. Increasing X production by one more unit will now require the loss of 5 units of Y.

At any point on the contract curve Or', the marginal rates of substitution of consumers A and B are equal. Suppose, however, that these equated marginal rates of substitution are unequal to the marginal rate of transformation. For example, assume that $(MRS_{XY})_A = (MRS_{XY})_B$ at point r_1 is less than the marginal rate of transformation at point r'; that is, the slope of the indifference curve pair A_3 and B_2 at r is less than the slope of the production possibilities curve at r'. What does this mean? It means that consumers A and B prefer a different output mix than the one denoted by point r'. Specifically, they would prefer to have fewer units of X and more Y. How do we know this? Assume that the equated marginal rates of substitution are 4 to 1. Both parties are willing to give up 4 units of Y to gain one more unit of X, but if the marginal rate of transformation is, say, 5 to 1, the producing sector is making 1 unit of

X at a marginal cost of 5 units of Y when consumers are willing to sacrifice only *four* units of Y to get one more unit of X. Clearly, the producing sector is making X at a rate in excess of that desired by consumers. Thus, in consumers' eyes there is a relative overproduction of X, and welfare cannot be at a maximum. *If* the individuals were at point r_1, welfare would be increased by reducing the production of X and increasing the production of Y until MRT_{XY} is brought into equality with the consumers' equated marginal rates of substitution.[7]

Now assume that the consumers have established themselves at point r^*, at which the slopes of their indifference curves are 5 to 1. Then they will desire that the marginal rate of transformation be 5 to 1 also, and, if this *is* the rate at r', we know that consumers prefer the output mix OX_3 units of X and OY_2 units of Y to any other. This output mix will be distributed as indicated by point r^*.

Returning to Figure 17-4, let us recall that point r''^* is the point corresponding to r^* in Figure 17-3, whereas point r_1'' corresponds to point r_1. Since point r''^* represents a situation in which it is impossible to make anyone better off without making someone else worse off by changing the output mix, it is a unique point on RR'. By contrast, point r_1'', which corresponds to point r_1 in Figure 17-3 does represent a situation in which the output mix can be changed to increase the utility of at least one person without harming anyone else.

To conclude this portion of our analysis, let us assume that s'' on SS' in Figure 17-4 represents a similar situation when the output mix is that defined by point s' in Figure 17-3. That is, it is a point at which the output mix cannot be changed without harming at least one person.

There is one such optimal point for each utility possibilities curve. If we draw a smooth curve through all such optimal points on each of the utility possibilities curves, we obtain the economy's *grand utility possibilities frontier.* Such a curve is represented by UU' in Figure 17-4. Any point on UU' denotes a distribution of welfare between A and B in which the marginal rate of transformation is equal to the equated marginal rates of substitution of the consumers. Therefore, a given point on UU' represents a particular output mix, a particular allocation of resources, and a particular distribution of goods. From a point within the area bounded by UU', such as v on SS', it is possible to move to a point, such as r''^*, at which the utility level of at least one person is increased without anyone else being harmed.

---

[7] Assume the economy does move leftward along the production possibilities curve from point r', reducing the output of X by 1 unit and necessarily increasing the output of Y by 5 units. Suppose A is the individual whose real income is reduced by the 1-unit reduction in X. More than enough Y has been produced to compensate him for his 1-unit loss of X. If 4 of the 5 units of Y are given to A to replace his loss of X, his utility level will not change. Unaffected by the change in production, B will experience no change in his well-being. Now, if the 1 remaining unit of Y is given to either A or B or is divided between them, the utility level of one or both of the individuals will rise and thereby increase the level of social welfare.

The Theory of Economic Welfare

Our reasoning about the grand utility possibilities frontier now leads us to the third marginal condition of social welfare.

3. *The optimal direction of production.* The output mix of an economy is nonoptimal if it is possible to increase the utility level of one person without harming anyone else by reallocating resources among existing productive employments so that the composition of the aggregate output is changed. Symbolically, we may write this marginal condition as [8]

$$(MRS_{XY})_A = (MRS_{XY})_B = MRT_{XY}$$

CONDITION FULFILLMENT AND WELFARE

We have now stated three of the most important marginal conditions of social welfare. There are at least four other generally recognized marginal conditions, but they are essentially corollaries of the three we have discussed, and so we will leave them to specialized texts on welfare economics. All that need be said here is that welfare cannot be at a maximum (in the sense that it is possible to make at least one person better off without harming anyone else) unless all the marginal conditions are fulfilled. But does fulfillment of all of them mean that welfare is, by that fact alone, maximized? And what if not all of them can be fulfilled? Should an economy strive to fulfill whatever marginal conditions it can? Does welfare increase with the number of marginal conditions satisfied? These are questions we will discuss in the following sections.

SECOND–BEST CRITERION

If fulfillment of all the conditions discussed in the preceding section results in a Pareto-optimal situation, what about the case of partial fulfillment? Should an economy strive to satisfy as many of the marginal conditions as it

---

[8] In utility and production terms, the third marginal condition may be written

$$(MU_X/MU_Y)_A = (MU_X/MU_Y)_B = (MP_R)_X/(MP_L)_X = (MP_R)_Y/(MP_L)_Y$$

Since the marginal cost of producing one more unit of a good is the sacrifice of units of the other, this condition can also be written in cost terms. As we move along a given production possibilities curve, total costs do not change. Yet, as the output mix is changed, the *marginal* costs of producing each of the goods do change. For example, as an economy moves down its production possibilities curve the marginal cost of producing good X increases, and the marginal cost of Y decreases. Since the total cost of producing any amounts of X and Y does not change, the increase in the marginal cost of X production must be matched exactly by the decrease in the marginal cost of producing Y. We know that $MC_X = \Delta TC/\Delta X$ and that $MC_Y = \Delta TC/\Delta Y$. Therefore, the ratio $MC_X/MC_Y =$ the slope of the production possibilities curve $= MRT_{XY}$. Thus, we can write the third marginal condition as

$$(MU_X/MU_Y)_A = (MC_X/MC_Y)_F = (MU_X/MU_Y)_B$$

where F is one firm in the economy producing X and Y. Competition assures that the ratio of marginal costs of production must be the same in the other firm, G.

can? A perfectly competitive economy assures the simultaneous fulfillment of the marginal conditions in the long run.[9] However, as we know, no existing economy is perfectly competitive. Suppose, in an imperfectly competitive economy, that application of appropriate policies could achieve the fulfillment of *some,* but not all, of the marginal conditions? Should such policies be followed? The common-sense answer would be, "Yes, fulfill as many conditions as possible, even if some are unrealizable." And, indeed, a number of policy recommendations (e.g., the antitrust laws) have been implemented in attempts to do just this. The trouble with the common-sense answer is that economic theory has shown it to be wrong.

A situation in which as many as possible of the marginal conditions are satisfied is known as a *second-best solution.* In "The General Theory of the Second-Best," Kelvin Lancaster and R. G. Lipsey showed that *anything less* than the simultaneous fulfillment of all the marginal conditions might not improve welfare and, indeed, could reduce the general level of welfare to less than what it would be if none of the conditions were fulfilled.[10] Thus, for example, a government policy eliminating monopolistic conditions in the producing sector but leaving the same conditions unhampered in the labor market sector could conceivably make matters worse than they would be if the government did nothing at all.

The rigorous proof of the theory of the second-best is difficult, but a simple illustration can be developed to show the essential problem involved. Suppose there are two firms in the economy, one producing good X and the other producing good Y. Assuming that both are monopolistic, in their respective profit-maximizing equilibria, $P_X > MC_X$ and $P_Y > MC_Y$. As is the case with imperfectly competitive enterprises, the firms price above marginal cost. Now suppose that it is possible for the government to cause good X to be produced under competitive conditions, possibly by using antitrust legislation to break the X monopoly firm into numerous smaller firms. At the same time, we will assume that the government cannot do anything about the state of competition in the Y producing sector. The government, believing that it is a desirable policy to fulfill as many of the marginal conditions as possible then proceeds with the reform of the X producing sector, leaving the Y sector as before. The result is that now $P_X = MC_X$ and $P_Y > MC_Y$. A step toward fulfilling the marginal conditions has been accomplished, but has welfare been increased? We must investigate the matter.

We know from the reasoning developed in connection with the fourth marginal condition (the optimal state of specialization) that

---

[9] If this is not apparent to you, review the restatements of the marginal conditions in utility, productivity, and cost terms in the footnotes to each of the marginal conditions, and then review the material on the long-run competitive equilibrium in Chapter 8. You may also wish to review the material on consumer equilibrium in Chapter 3.

[10] Kelvin Lancaster and R. G. Lipsey, "The General Theory of the Second-Best," *Review of Economic Studies,* XXIV (I) (1957), pp. 11–32.

$$MRT_{XY} = \frac{MC_X}{MC_Y}$$

Fulfillment of the third marginal condition (the optimal direction of production) requires that

$$MRT_{XY} = \frac{P_X}{P_Y}$$

This means that consumers have established the precise point on the *transformation curve* that denotes their preferred output mix.[11] But, if under governmental policy, $P_X = MC_X$ and $P_Y > MC_Y$, then

$$\frac{MC_X}{MC_Y} > \frac{P_X}{P_Y}$$

and, therefore,

$$MRT_{XY} > \frac{P_X}{P_Y}$$

This situation is depicted graphically in Figure 17-5. At the given rate of transformation, the economy is at point A. But consumers would prefer the product mix denoted by point B, at which we assume P_X/P_Y equals the equated marginal rates of substitution of all consumers. The inequality $MRT_{XY} > P_X/P_Y$ indicates that more X is being produced than consumers want at the expense of too many units of Y. Assuming full employment, whenever one producing sector of an economy is perfectly competitive and the other producing sectors are not, the competitive sector will tend to overuse resources relative to the imperfectly competitive sector. This being the case, a governmental policy of forcing fulfillment of a marginal condition while it is unable to achieve complete fulfillment has unknowingly, but deliberately, caused a distortion to be introduced into the economy. Consumers have been deprived of their sovereignty. The economy is economically inefficient (consumers would prefer to change the existing resource allocation to obtain more Y and less X). Relative to the position (point A) established by the government's intervention, consumers would prefer to move leftward (toward point B).

[11] A production possibilities curve is a special form of the transformation curve. Both curves show the rate at which the economy can transform one good into another. The difference lies in the assumption that the production possibilities curve allows for no inefficiencies (monopolistic or technical) in production, whereas a transformation curve reflects the use of resources under inefficient conditions. If monopolistic conditions are included as part of the economy's techniques of production, the transformation curve referred to here could be considered as being the economy's production possibilities curve. Therefore, *given* monopolistic output restriction, an otherwise efficient economy could be said to be operating on its production possibilities curve.

meaningful way? Can the efficient economy be just and offer its members an improved quality of life as well? The fulfillment of all the economic criteria so far discussed need not result in equity, for the conditions themselves have no ethical content; they are rules of *efficiency,* not of *equity.* The simultaneous fulfillment of all the marginal conditions assures merely the attainment of the Pareto optimum—that situation in which it is impossible to make anyone better off without making someone else worse off.

However, attainment of the Pareto optimum is not to be deprecated. After all, one would be hard put to defend the general proposition that an individual should not be helped if helping him would hurt no one else. Given the output of an economy, the Pareto criterion shows how to distribute it efficiently. For example, if the MRS_{XY} of Adam is 3/1 and that for Eve is 1/1, Adam should transfer units of Y to Eve in exchange for units of X, the transfer continuing until their respective marginal rates of substitution are equal—say, 2/1. But the Pareto criterion says nothing about the initial apportionment of X and Y between Adam and Eve; in fact, as far as the Pareto rule is concerned, it is of no consequence. Suppose we know that Adam has 24X and 12Y, while Eve has 24,000X and 120,000Y, and that Adam is suffering from malnutrition and other forms of privation whereas Eve has a severe case of obesity. The Pareto rule can do nothing with this information. All it can comprehend are the marginal rates at which each individual is willing to substitute one good for another. In other words, the initial resource endowments and preference patterns are parameters in Paretian welfare economics.

Is it possible for economists to construct a welfare economics in which ethical norms supplied by some moral authority—the majority of an electorate, a legislature, a king, a priest, a prophet, or a philosopher—can be used in conjunction with the rule of the Pareto optimum?

Using a theoretical model, let us see how such a welfare economics would work. The curve UU' in Figure 17-6 is the utility possibilities frontier for the two-person community of Punch and Judy. Its shape and position are defined by objective economic data. Any point on UU' represents the fulfillment of the Pareto optimum. Asked to comment on the situations present in Figure 17-6, economists can make two positive (nonnormative) statements: (1) any point lying beneath UU' is Pareto-inferior to any point that lies northeast of that point (e.g., A is Pareto-inferior to A' or any other point lying within the quadrant formed by the two rays radiating out of A); (2) any point lying beyond UU' is simply unattainable given the present productive capabilities of the economy. What economists cannot tell is whether one point on the curve is better than any other. For example, at point C, Punch is better off than he would be at D, but Judy is better off at D than she would be at C. Both points are optimal in the sense of fulfilling the Pareto criterion; what we now want to know is whether we can find a point on UU' that defines an *optimum-optimorum* —an optimum of all possible optima. We have now gone as far as positive economics will take us. Without an ethical judgment about how welfare *ought*

The Theory of Economic Welfare

FIGURE 17-6

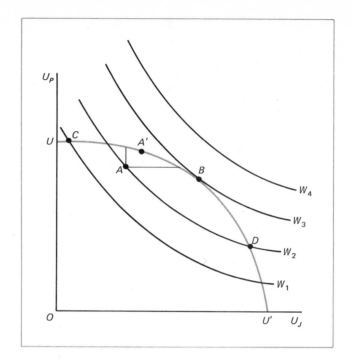

to be distributed among the members of the community, economists can make no comparisons among the infinitude of points lying on UU'. The only way to establish an optimum-optimorum is to be given normative information on what the community holds to be an equitable, or just, distribution of welfare.

It is the accepted convention in economic theory to refer to the given economic ethic supplied by the economy's decision-makers as a *social welfare function*. As economists, we will be unconcerned with how the social welfare function is determined.

Let us assume that the social welfare function of the two-person community of Punch and Judy can be represented by a family of social indifference curves such as those labeled W_1, W_2, W_3, and W_4 in Figure 17-6. The welfare contours are interpreted in a manner analogous to the treatment of the indifference curves of an individual. The farther a contour lies from the origin, the higher the index of welfare of the community. Thus, any point on W_4 would be preferred *by the community* (i.e., communally, though perhaps not individually) to any point on a contour lying nearer the origin.

The convex shape of the contours represents the attitude of the community toward the distribution of a given amount of welfare. A movement *along* a given contour shows that even though one member of the community is gaining utility at the expense of some other member, the level of total welfare in the community remains constant. But the convexity of the curve also

shows that the higher any individual's utility index, the less willing is the community to allow that individual to receive any advancement in welfare at the expense of the other members of the community.[12]

Given the utility possibilities frontier and the social welfare function, we must now determine the optimal distribution of welfare for the Punch and Judy community. Of the visible welfare contours, the community would prefer to be on W_4, but that particular level of well-being is not presently available to it; the current state of resources and technology preclude its attainment. Points C, A, A', B, and D are all attainable. However, as economists, we may rule out A and urge the economy, in the interest of efficiency, to find a Pareto-superior point on the utility possibilities frontier. Obviously, point B locates the optimum-optimorum. Like points C and D, it is Pareto-efficient, but unlike the other two points it lies on the highest attainable welfare contour. It has become customary in economic theory to refer to the point of tangency between the utility possibilities frontier and the highest attainable welfare contour as the *point of constrained bliss*. It is a bliss point because on a curve depicting all possible optima, it is the one point that satisfies the community's ethical norms; but the bliss is constrained, since the realities of production confine the location of the bliss point to a position on UU'.

Any movement away from point B along UU' will increase the utility of some individual member of the community but will lower the totality of community welfare. If the guiding norm of the economy prescribes that welfare should be at a constrained maximum, any move to point B will be endorsed and any movement away from it proscribed.

Point B represents the fusion of efficiency and equity. It shows that Pareto optimality is a necessary, but insufficient, condition for the attainment of a constrained bliss point. It seems reasonable to argue that if the economy can be equitable, it ought to be efficient as well. The rationale of the new welfare economics is to point the way to efficiency so that equity will be available at the highest attainable level of satisfaction.

In a contest between equity and efficiency, equity is the likely victor. Obviously, point C satisfies the Pareto criterion, and point A does not. Yet, moving from A to C would reduce welfare although it would improve efficiency. What could produce a situation in which an economy must choose between points C and A? Perfect competition assures the fulfillment of the Pareto criterion. Thus, point C might be attained if the economy were perfectly competitive and, hence, perfectly efficient. But suppose that the members of the economy prefer some variety in the goods they consume, requiring that there be some monopolistic imperfections in the economy and, thus, precluding the attainment of economic efficiency. In such a case, the members of the economy would prefer to be inefficient at A rather than efficient at C.

Without the social welfare function, economists can say nothing about a movement from one point to another on the utility possibilities frontier. For

---

[12] Not all social welfare functions would *necessarily* yield convex contours.

example, if the economy is initially at point C, the Pareto criterion would rule out any attempt to bring the community to point B, since that would help Judy at Punch's expense. Knowledge of the social welfare function, however, shows that if the community is at point C, the ruling ethic holds that Punch has too much of a good thing and that Judy deserves a better break even if Punch's well-being must be reduced to give it to her.

RETRACING: FROM ETHICS TO PRODUCTION AND DISTRIBUTION

To show how the normative judgment of the community establishes the objective facts of production and distribution, we shall now retrace the steps we have just taken and return to our starting point. The utility possibilities frontier demarcates the constraints on the community. Economists are able to say to the community, "*If* you want efficiency, you must choose a distribution of welfare denoted by a point on UU'." Economists cannot say to the community, "You *must* or you *ought* to operate at a point on the frontier." The economy may prefer to be inefficient, but at least it is possible for economists to point out the costs. Suppose the economy decides to be efficient and desires to maximize social welfare; then it will operate at point B in Figure 17-6. This decision will cause the economy to conform to the implications of the constrained optimum. Let us consider how this comes about.

Point B, besides being the point of tangency between the highest attainable welfare contour (W_3) and the utility possibilities frontier (UU') also lies on a particular utility possibilities *curve* for which UU' is the envelope. Each underlying utility possibilities curve represents a specific point on the production possibilities curve of the economy.[13] Each utility possibilities curve is associated with a particular composition of total output. The output mix denoted by point b on the production possibilities curve Y^*X^* in Figure 17-7 establishes the total production of X and Y that the community desires; here, the GNP is OX_0 units of X and OY_0 units of Y. Having determined the aggregate totals of the output of each good, we have now to determine the allocation of inputs between X and Y production. The process of resource allocation is shown in Figure 17-8. The matter is resolved quite simply. If OX_0 units of X are desired, the maximum possible amount of Y producible is necessarily OY_0. These quantities are denoted in the Edgeworth box of Figure 17-8 as the isoquants X_0 and Y_0. The tangency of the two isoquants at point b' on the production contract curve $O_L O_K$ (the locus of all points of efficient production for the associated production possibilities curve) corresponds to point b on the production possibilities curve Y^*X^* in Figure 17-7. The tangency, at point b', of isoquants X_0 and Y_0 establishes the allocation of resources to the production of each good. The production of good X requires $O\bar{L}$ units of labor leaving $\bar{L}L$ units to be used in

---

[13] This is the same as saying that all points on a particular utility possibilities curve are associated with a *single* point on the production possibilities curve.

FIGURE 17-7

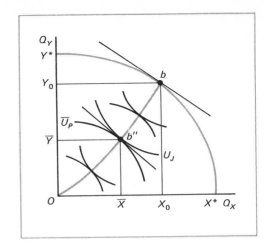

Y production. The capital allocation to X production is $O\bar{K}$ units; the remaining $\bar{K}K$ units of capital are allocated to the manufacture of Y.

The final distributional problem is the allocation of goods X and Y between Punch and Judy. The real incomes of Punch and Judy are determined from the Edgeworth box inscribed in the production possibilities curve of Figure 17-7. From the utility possibilities curve of Figure 17-6, we know that the constrained optimum called for the distribution of welfare to show an index of $\bar{U}_J$ on Judy's scale and for one of $\bar{U}_p$ on Punch's. In Figure 17-7, these indexes are represented by the indifference curves $\bar{U}_J$ (Judy) and $\bar{U}_p$ (Punch), respectively. They are tangent at b'', at which $(MRS_{XY})_J = (MRS_{XY})_P = MRT_{XY}$; that is, the equated slope of the indifference curves at b'' is equal to the slope of the production possibilities curve at b. This indicates the conclusion of our analysis. The underlying physical realities of the resource base and technology plus the

FIGURE 17-8

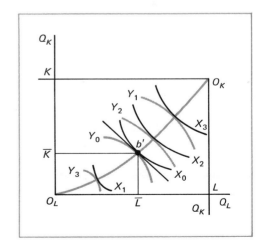

distributional norm of society as expressed in its social welfare function have together determined that Judy's real income will be $O\bar{X}$ units of X and $O\bar{Y}$ units of Y and that Punch's real income will be $\bar{X}X^*$ units of X and $\bar{Y}Y^*$ units of Y. This, then, is an efficient distribution of efficiently produced goods that at the same time maximizes the welfare of the community subject to the real constraints of production.

EXTERNALITIES

THE DIVERGENCE BETWEEN PRIVATE AND SOCIAL MEASURES

As we know, one of the requirements of a private optimum is that $P = MC$.[14] This equality expresses so-called marginal cost pricing and is a succinct statement of Adam Smith's concept of the "invisible hand." Briefly, the equation says that resource allocation is optimal when marginal benefits are equal to marginal sacrifice.[15] In a multi-good economy, the private optimum described here obtains when

$$\frac{P_X}{MC_X} = \frac{P_Y}{MC_Y} = \cdots = \frac{P_N}{MC_N} = 1$$

Since the time of Adam Smith, many economists have made much of the optimality of marginal cost pricing, often asserting that the optimality reaches beyond private transactions and into the social sphere. Is this true? It may be, but can we conclude that *every* privately optimal solution is also publicly, or socially, optimal?

Suppose good X is ethyl alcohol U.S.P. and, therefore, a homogeneous product qualifying for production under purely competitive conditions. If $P_A = MC_A$, we know that alcohol producers and consumers are participating in a privately optimal solution involving resource allocation and consumer satisfaction. But though an alcohol consumer may have achieved optimality as a consumer, has he achieved optimality as a member of the community? Suppose some of the buyers of the alsohol use it as a potable; if they drink too much, they can create problems of drunkenness, perhaps even alcoholism, that often are costly. Generally, these costs are not borne solely by the overindulgent consumers of alcohol or the producers of intoxicating beverages. The costs of accidents, deaths, and rehabilitation centers are not among the private costs of alcohol producers or of alcohol consumers. They are borne by the community as a whole; they are *social* costs. Because they do not enter into the economic calculations of the producers and consumers of alcohol, we may regard them as *external* costs involved in the production and consumption of

---

[14] This section simplifies the preceding material of the present chapter in order to give as clear a view as possible of the fundamental nature of external economies and diseconomies.

[15] For a complete review of why this is so, see Chapter 8.

alcohol. Generally, they are simply referred to as examples of detrimental *externalities.*

Suppose that for a truer insight into the total economic impact of the production and consumption of alcohol we add to the private marginal cost of production the marginal external cost of production and consumption and call their sum *marginal social cost;* that is, $MSC = MC + MEC$, where MC is the familiar marginal private cost and MEC is the marginal external cost. Thus, even though the private optimum requirement, $P_A = MC_A$, is fulfilled,

$$P_A < MSC_A$$

which indicates that the allocation of resources to the production of alcohol is not socially optimal. The inequality tells us that some costs directly attributable to the use of alcohol are borne socially and, hence, are not absorbed by consumers of alcohol *as consumers.* Therefore, in terms of the costs that society would knowingly bear, the output of alcohol is excessive. More resources than are socially optimal are being devoted to its production.

It it were possible to ascertain accurately the magnitude of the external costs attributable to the production of certain goods *and to impose them on individual firms,* then, the marginal social cost of production would enter into each firm's calculations, and they would reduce output until

$$P_A = MSC_A$$

This analysis is shown graphically in Figure 17-9. At every output level, the marginal social cost of the production of alcohol exceeds the marginal

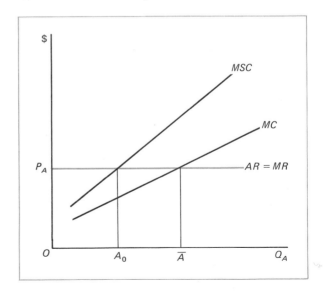

FIGURE 17-9

The Theory of Economic Welfare

private cost of production. The vertical distance between the two cost curves is the amount of the external costs incurred in the production and consumption of alcohol. If these costs can be imposed on the firm so that it will treat them as it would its own internal costs, it will reduce its output of alcohol from $O\bar{A}$ units (the privately optimal output level) to OA_0 units (the socially optimal output level).

If price *is* equal to marginal social cost, does this ensure the fulfillment of the social optimum? Not necessarily. Suppose that you are concerned with air pollution and that you would like to do your part to help abate it. You may decide, therefore, to purchase only unleaded gasoline. Assuming that unleaded gasoline does help to reduce air pollution, is the social optimum achieved when $P_G = MC_G$?[16] By using unleaded gasoline, you confer a benefit, not only on yourself, but on the countless people who enjoy somewhat cleaner air at your expense. You are not compensated for their benefit; the public does not pay for any of the gasoline you use. The price that you pay at the pump measures only your own benefit; it does not measure the external benefit to the community. Suppose we add to the price of the gasoline the value of the marginal external benefit and call the resulting sum the *marginal social benefit*. We would now know the economic value that *society* places on the use of lead-free gasoline. Then if $P_G = MC_G$, $MSB_G > MC_G$, meaning that the marginal social benefit of lead-free gasoline here exceeds its marginal cost of production.

Of course, for a total social optimum to prevail, it would be necessary to include the external costs of lead-free gasoline production in the social calculation. When all social benefits and costs are included, the social optimum will be achieved when

$$MSB_G = MSC_G$$

In a multi-good economy, the socially optimal allocation of resources must take all externalities into account, and, therefore, the allocation of resources will be socially optimal when

$$\frac{MSB_X}{MSC_X} = \frac{MSB_Y}{MSC_Y} = \cdots \frac{MSB_N}{MSC_N}$$

AN ECONOMIC THEORY OF POLLUTION

Adam Smith pointed out that even the most ideally free market does not operate in a legal vacuum. The several theories of market structure, from perfect competition to pure monopoly, presuppose the existence of property rights, the exercise of which is critical to the outcome of an economic situation.

[16] For the purposes of this illustration, the obviously monopolistic features of the petroleum industry are ignored.

For example, suppose there exists a stream whose waters have many uses—drinking, swimming, boating, viewing, and disposing. In the last capacity, it offers a cheap solution to the waste disposal problems of several plants. Suppose, initially, that the ownership of the stream is vested in no one; it is regarded as a public good; it may be used by anyone in any manner he sees fit. Assume now that some plants located on the banks of the stream begin to discharge their wastes into it. The maximum amount of effluence flowing into the stream every day is shown in Figure 17-10 as OW^*. The resulting pollution of the stream is harmful to the nonindustrial users. The plants have appropriated a great part of the benefits of the stream to themselves. These benefits are valuable and should therefore have a price. The other users of the stream could have in mind a schedule of payments they would be willing to make to clean up the stream, graphically represented by the linear curve OB. This curve is a *marginal* valuation curve, showing at a particular point how much the nonindustrial users would be willing to pay to get rid of an *additional* unit of pollution (e.g., so many pounds of waste per 1,000 gallons of water per day). Thus, if the stream could be maintained in its pre-pollution state, the nonindustrial users would be willing to pay a total sum of OW^*B dollars to the firms to eliminate the entire OW^* units of waste. The amount W^*B is the value of the removal of the marginal unit of waste when the stream has very nearly the full amount of pollution removed from it.

But, the stream is valuable as a waste disposer and, therefore, the firms can calculate what they would have to be paid to reduce, or to cease altogether, the pollution of the stream. The payments the firms would require are shown by the marginal valuation curve AW^*. Obviously, if the payment is zero, the plants will continue to pour the maximum amount of waste into the stream every day. To restore the stream to the pre-pollution condition, the firms would re-

FIGURE 17-10

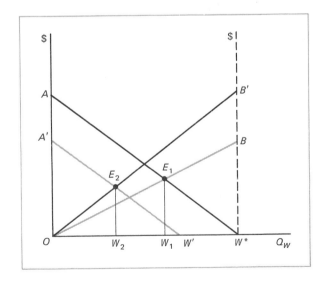

The Theory of Economic Welfare

quire a total payment of OW^*A dollars. Since area OW^*A exceeds area OW^*B in size, we see that the nonindustrial users are either unwilling or unable to pay the firms a sum large enough to eliminate all waste disposal.

That all waste disposal will not be ended does not mean that it is economically unfeasible to reduce the level of pollution. The two marginal valuation curves AW^* and OB, intersect at E_1. At that point, the nonindustrial users' marginal valuation of the worth of pollution removal is equal to the firms' marginal valuation of what they must be paid to remove the quantity W_1W^* units of waste from the stream each day. On payment of the minimum sum of $W_1W^*E_1$ dollars per day, the plants will reduce the outflow of daily waste to OW_1 units.[17] We have now one market solution to the problem of pollution, but it is not the only one.[18] At this point, a word of caution: before you conclude that we have found an easy economic solution to environmentally destructive conduct, be sure to read the section entitled "Transaction Costs."

Suppose the ownership of the stream is vested in the nonindustrial users; they could end all pollution of the stream. But, noxious as the operations of the plants may be, they produce a valuable product, and, therefore, it may be worthwhile for the owners of the plants to pay the owners of the stream some amount for being allowed to use the stream as a waste disposer. The curve $A'W'$ shows the firms' marginal valuation of the right of being allowed to use the stream for waste disposal purposes. The curve $A'W'$ lies to the left of AW^* since the former curve reflects the evaluations of the firms when they have an unqualified right to use the stream in any way. If the title to the stream is vested in the nonindustrial users, the firms must pay for the privilege of being allowed to pollute the water, and they are willing to pay less for any given amount of pollution than the sum they would charge not to pollute an asset to which they have equal rights of access along with others. For example, the maximum amount the firms would be willing to pay for the right of using the stream is $OW'A'$, in exchange for which they would be allowed to pour the quantity OW' of waste into the water.

If the stream were the sole property of the nonindustrial users, they would not have to tolerate any pollution. Consequently, their marginal valuation of conferring rights to pollute on the firms exceeds their evaluation of what they

---

[17] Note that the nonindustrial users are willing to pay as much as $W_1W^*BE_1$ to have W_1W^* units of waste removed from the water. If the nonindustrial users need pay only $W_1W^*E_1$ dollars, they realize a gain in their welfare measured by E_1W^*B dollars. If the situation were reversed, with the firms collecting the maximum amount the nonfirm users are willing to pay, the entire gain in welfare would accrue to the firms' owners. Actually, the welfare gain is likely to be divided according to bargaining arrangements that reasonably would precede any settlement. In the following section, the size of the welfare gain is an important issue.

[18] The analysis here is somewhat simplified in that it abstracts from the welfare changes that would occur as the position of the nonindustrial users or the firms or both changed. An increase in welfare would shift the marginal valuation curves upward somewhat, the extent of the shift being determined by the benefit received. For a discussion of this phenomenon and an extended review of the recent literature of externalities, see E. J. Mishan's excellent article, "The Postwar Literature on Externalities: An Interpretive Essay," *Journal of Economic Literature,* IX (March 1971), pp. 1–28. This section utilizes some ideas from Mishan's paper.

would pay the firms to reduce the effluent flow. The new marginal valuation curve is OB' and lies above OB. It shows that if the firms were allowed to pour the maximum daily amount of waste into the stream, the owners of the stream would require a payment of OW^*B' dollars. However, the marginal valuation curves of the stream owners and the firms show equality of marginal valuation at E_2. Therefore, the firms will pay the stream owners as much as OW_2E_2A' dollars in return for which they will be allowed to pump OW_2 quantity of effluent into the stream. The stream owners would be willing to accept as little as OW_2E_2 dollars to allow the plants to pollute the stream with OW_2 units of waste. If they could be induced to accept this amount, the welfare gain to the firms would be OE_2A' dollars. This would be the gain to the stream owners if the firms were to pay the maximum amount. As in the preceding case, bargaining is likely to result in a division of the welfare gain.

The lessons of economics. What does this analysis show? First, that the free market can yield a solution in the absence of government regulation and control. Government regulation might be satisfactory, but the government, in the absence of economic signals, may be unable to discover enough information on which to base sound decisions. Opening the problem to the market generates price information about the uses of the stream. This concrete information is helpful in making allocative decisions.

Second, we observe that government-established property rights do affect the free market solution. Property rights can bias the ultimate outcome. When the stream is open to public use, the amount of agreed upon pollution is greater than if the ownership of the stream were vested in the nonindustrial users. Therefore, if the government wishes to move in the direction of reducing pollution in a given area, or by some given industry, but is willing to allow the parties directly concerned to make their own agreements, the conferring of property rights to the polluted resource on those aggrieved by the pollution will accomplish this end.

The third lesson is that of compromise. Solutions in economic situations are less often "either-or" than "a little bit of everything." This outcome may offend those who believe that streams, forests, and air should not be polluted, but most people are willing to tolerate considerable amounts of pollution for whatever they consider to be additional "good causes," these good causes being the things they would rather have—such as jobs, transportation, flood control, paper, steel, and even sewage removal—than a crystal clear stream. The fact that plant owners are willing and able to pay some amount of money to be allowed to pour a certain quantity of waste into the stream indicates they produce an output some group of persons consider valuable. The total elimination of pollution might require the cessation of production. The world may not, and probably does not, regard a pure stream as worth the price. Perhaps the pollution level can be reduced to a level at which the stream is once more attractive, does not smell, and is safe for swimming and boating. It may not be fit for drinking, but the compensation paid by the firms may en-

able the householders to install plumbing or to subscribe to a bottled water service. Whatever the case, the market solution generally allows many competing voices to be heard and ends in a settlement not perfectly acceptable to any one person but not grossly unsatisfactory to a large majority of concerned individuals.

TRANSACTIONS COSTS

Each of us has ineffable ideas for reform, and it seems to most of us that reforms are seldom made and that when they are, they are seldom thorough enough. In many cases, the desired degree of change does not come because, to express the idea with an old maxim, "the game is not worth the candle."

Let us consider a situation in which automobile traffic creates noise pollution for people living near a freeway. A proposal is made that tolls be collected from freeway users and the proceeds turned over to the aggrieved householders.

Figure 17-11 shows that the maximum racket on the freeway is ON^* units of noise. The curve OR shows the householders' marginal valuation of the worth of being free of the noise nuisance. For example, they would continue to endure the existing cacophony if they were to receive the total payment ON^*R. Curve ZN^* shows the amount of tolls motorists would pay to be allowed the use of the freeway. For example, they would pay OZN^* if they could use the freeway without restriction. The marginal evaluations of motorists and householders intersect at point E, indicating that the market solution is a reduction in traffic that causes the maximum din emanating from the freeway to drop to ON_1 units.

The size of the total welfare gain is OEZ dollars. Presumably, this gain

FIGURE 17-11

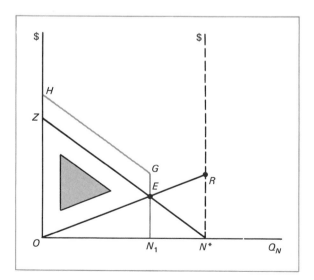

can be split among the freeway users and the householders. But now we must ask: Does such a gain come free? How do we discover where the marginal valuation curves lie? How do we manage to get householders and freeway users together so that an agreement can be reached? How do we make sure that the noise level is kept as low as ON_1 units, and how do we ensure that the freeway users get their money's worth—that, in fact, they are allowed to produce a maximum noise level of ON_1 units?

The information needed to make the noise reduction program a success is, like most other services, obtainable if the costs of getting it are met. The costs of such information are called *transactions costs* and fall into three categories:

1. *Information costs.* These are the costs of obtaining the information necessary to begin the program. In the present illustration, we must find the existing noise level, the number of households affected, the number of automobiles involved, how to collect the tolls, how to distribute the proceeds, how much money it is feasible to collect, the basis for assessing different classes of freeway users, whether the fee should be uniform throughout the day or whether a fee schedule for different hours is preferable, and so on. In short, it would appear that a thoroughgoing research program would be necessary before toll collection could begin.

2. *Contractual costs.* These are the costs of actually getting all of the parties to come to an agreement. For example, the writing of the contract itself will involve a fee.

3. *Policing costs.* Once made, the agreement must be enforced. It is necessary to make sure that the noise level does not rise above the agreed upon maximum. Freeway users must be assessed and the home owners reimbursed according to the provisions of the contract.

These costs, when totaled, will be a specific sum that can be compared with the welfare gain. Suppose the transactions costs equal the area of the shaded triangle in Figure 17-11. Here, the gain exceeds the transactions costs of pursuing the policy of freeway noise reduction, so such a program would appear to be worthwhile. But suppose the transactions costs were equal to the area of a figure coterminous with *OEZ*—that is, the costs of the program equaled the benefits. It would then seem to be a matter of indifference whether the program is carried out. Finally, what if the transactions costs were equal to the area of *OEZ* plus the area of the strip *ZEGH*? The costs of the program would exceed its benefits. Under these circumstances, it is difficult to justify the antipollution program. Even if the program is begun, it would be likely to break down or not be approved by the entire community. Since the program would not be self-supporting, it would have to be operated under subsidy, and the unaffected householders in the community might well not be interested in helping to bear the cost of eliminating a situation that is of no concern to them. The excess of transactions costs over benefits would seem to indicate

that the proposed "cure is more expensive than the disease" and that some other less costly method of reducing the noise level should be found.

The concept of transactions costs is sobering. It shows what is true of any market—namely, that markets exist only at a cost. No market will survive if its operation costs more than the benefits it yields to those who use it. Similarly, the use of a market solution to pollution problems is helpful in determining whether an abatement or reduction program costs more than it is worth. If it does, the conclusion is not necessarily that polluters should continue to go on uncontrolled, but only that a less costly approach to the problem should be found.

SUMMARY

Welfare economics seeks to appraise states of well-being. Recognizing that individuals disagree on ethical standards and on interpersonal comparisons, the new welfare economics has attempted to build a value-free body of analysis. At its core is the Pareto criterion, which holds that a given situation is not optimal if it is possible to effect changes that will enable one person to become better off (in his own subjective estimate) without harming anyone else.

The general rule of the Pareto optimum has been incorporated into a number of so-called marginal conditions of social welfare, seven of which have been examined in this chapter. Fulfillment of any one, or all, of the seven marginal conditions does not ensure that the welfare of a community is at a maximum, but *nonfulfillment* of any one does indicate that welfare is not being maximized, since a change in the existing situation can benefit at least one person without harming the position of any other individual.

Since the simultaneous fulfillment of the seven marginal conditions appears to be unlikely in an economy marked by even the slightest trace of imperfect competition, it seems reasonable to suppose that a rational society would attempt to fulfill as many of the marginal conditions as it could, on the assumption that the more conditions it fulfilled, the higher would be its level of welfare. But the theory of the second-best has shown this common-sense notion to be fallacious. If, for example, two of the marginal conditions presently are fulfilled, accomplishment of a third *may* decrease rather than increase welfare. The theory of the second-best has important implications for public policy, as it explains how governmental actions apparently moving toward greater welfare may actually be moving away from it.

The social welfare function approach to welfare economics is an attempt to integrate the community's ethical criteria with economic analysis. While the nonfulfillment of any of the seven marginal conditions does indicate that welfare can be increased, their simultaneous fulfillment does not guarantee that the best of all possible optima (i.e., an absolute welfare maximum in the *normative* and *positive* senses of the expression) has been achieved.

It is, for example, possible for a starving person to be made better off under the rule of the Pareto criterion and still to starve—in an improved situation. The social welfare function—simply the ruling (economic) ethic—supplies the criterion necessary for determining the optimum-optimorum—the best of all possible optima. The social welfare function is not generated in economic analysis but is applied to it. There has been widespread controversy over whether it is possible to use the social welfare function approach in a going economy. One important difficulty lies, not in economic analysis, but in discovering an overriding social ethic in a pluralistic society.

The divergences between private and social gains and private and social costs have important implications in environmental economics and in the use of public goods. Transactions that are optimal privately may be nonoptimal socially. If external costs and benefits can be determined and applied to their private counterparts, social and private optima may be made to converge.

Militating against efforts to force private and social optima to coincide are the so-called transactions costs—the costs of determining the economic magnitude of external costs and benefits, of undertaking measures to incorporate them into economic transactions, and of maintaining the remedial measures. These transactions costs may be too high to make a completely optimal solution feasible. This is one of the main lessons of economics—namely, that there are few, if any, pure solutions, nearly every solution being, necessarily, a compromise.

The Theory of Economic Welfare

Index

	3
B	4
C	5
D	6
E	7
F	8
G	9
H	0
I	1
J	2